T0330109

This is a landmark reference volume for the field, offering scholars and practitioners:

- Comprehensive, but accessible, coverage of classic and recent developments
- Chapters by established international experts
- Case analyses illustrating practical consequences of theories
- Guide to new research directions and theory

Paul C. Nutt is Professor Emeritus of Management Sciences in Fisher College of Business at The Ohio State University and Professor of Management at University of Strathclyde's College of Business. His research interests include organizational decision-making, strategic management, and radical change. Current research topics include averting decision debacles, decision style, formulation and implementation, ethics, learning, organizational transformation and de-development, vision, and leadership. He has written over 150 articles and seven books on these topics. He has received numerous awards for his research and teaching from the Decision Sciences Institute, the Academy of Management, Institute for Operation Research and Management Sciences (INFORMS), and others. He is a Fellow in the Decision Sciences Institute and a charter member of the Academy of Management's Hall of Fame.

David C. Wilson is Professor of Strategy and Organization in the University of Warwick where he is also Deputy Dean of the Business School. He is the author of eight books and over seventy journal articles. He was Chairman of the British Academy of Management (1994–1997) where he served for over ten years as an Executive member. He is a Fellow of the Academy, elected in 1994. He was Chairman of the scholarly society, the European Group for Organizational Studies (EGOS) from 2002 to 2006. He has had a long association with the Journal *Organization Studies*, becoming Co-Editor (1992-1996), Deputy Editor (1996-1999) and finally Editor-in-Chief (1999–2003). He is currently Chair of the Editorial Advisory Board for *Organization Studies*. He has been a member of EGOS for over twenty years and has served on the Board for the last eight years.

HANDBOOK OF DECISION MAKING

Edited by

PAUL C. NUTT AND DAVID C. WILSON

A John Wiley and Sons, Ltd., Publication

This edition first published 2010
© 2010   John Wiley & Sons, Ltd

Registered office
John Wiley & Sons Ltd, The Atrium, Southern Gate, Chichester, West Sussex, PO19 8SQ,
United Kingdom

For details of our global editorial offices, for customer services and for information about how to apply
for permission to reuse the copyright material in this book please see our website at www.wiley.com.

Library of Congress Cataloging-in-Publication Data

Handbook of decision making / editors, Paul Nutt, David Wilson.
     p. cm.
  ISBN 978-1-4051-6135-0
  1. Decision making.   I. Nutt, Paul C.   II. Wilson, David C. (David Charles), 1951–
  HD30.23.H354 2010
  658.4′03–dc22

                                                              2009052103

A catalogue record for this book is available from the British Library.

Typeset in 10/12pt Baskerville by Aptara Inc., New Delhi, India

Printed in the UK

Paul
To Nancy Davis Nutt

David
For Jo, Alex and Amy Wilson

Contents

Notes on the Contributors

Fran Ackermann

Dr Fran Ackermann is a Professor of Management Science at the Strathclyde Business School and an adjunct professor at the University of Western Australia's Business School. Her research interests range from the management of messy and complex problems, to strategy making. She has particular interests in negotiation and group decision support, project risk, and disruption and delay analysis. She has strong links with industry and not-for-profit organizations, having worked with senior and middle management teams of over 100 organizations in Europe and North America. She has published widely including three books and over 100 refereed journal articles. She serves on a number of journal editorial boards and her work is focused on practice-based research.

Claudia N. Avellaneda

Claudia N. Avellaneda is an assistant professor of political science at the University of North Carolina at Charlotte. Her research interests include comparative politics, public management, and government performance with a regional focus on Latin America. Specifically, she studies the impact of managerial quality on local governmental performance in terms of service delivery, public finance, and education quality.

Michael Barrett

Michael Barrett is Director of Programmes and Reader in IT and Innovation at Judge Business School, University of Cambridge. He is co-lead on NIHR grant in Collaborations for Leadership in Applied Health Research and Care. His research interests include service innovation, open innovation, cross cultural teams, and knowledge translation. He has studied the insurance sector, electronic trading in global financial markets, global software outsourcing, and service delivery within healthcare. His work is of an interdisciplinary nature, with publications in a wide range of journals including. *Academy of Management Journal, Information Systems Research, Accounting Organisations and Society.* He has recently co-edited a book on IT in the service economy.

Patrick Barwise

Patrick Barwise is Emeritus Professor of Management and Marketing at London Business School. He joined the School in 1976, having spent his early career with IBM. He has published widely on management, marketing, and media. Together with Vassilis Papadakis, he co-edited *Strategic Decisions* (Kluwer, 1998). His book *Simply Better* (HBS Press), co-authored with Seán Meehan (IMD, Lausanne), won the American Marketing Association's 2005 Berry-AMA Prize for the best book in marketing.

Kimberly B. Boal

Kimberly B. Boal (PhD, University of Wisconsin) is the Rawls Professor of Management at the Rawls College of Business, Texas Tech University. Kim was co-editor-in-chief of the Journal of Management Inquiry from 1997–2006. He served on the Board of Governors of the Academy of Management from 2001–2004, and as President of the Western Academy of Management in 1999–2000. His work appears in: *Academy of Management Executive, Academy of Management Review, Administrative Science Quarterly, Journal of Management, Leadership Quarterly, OBHP, Strategic Management Journal,* as well as other journals and numerous book chapters.

Philip Bromiley

Philip Bromiley (PhD, Carnegie-Mellon University) is a Dean's Professor in Strategic Management at the Merage School of University of California, Irvine. Previously he held the Curtis L. Carlson Chair in Strategic Management and chaired the Department of Strategic Management & Organization at the University of Minnesota. He has published widely on organizational decision making and strategic risk-taking. He currently serves on the boards of *Strategic Management Journal, Journal of Management Studies,* and *Journal of Strategy and Management.* Previously, he served on the editorial boards of *Academy of Management Journal, Organization Science, Strategic Organization,* and the *Journal of Management* and as associate editor for *Management Science.* His current research examines strategic decision making, the behavioral foundations of strategic management research, and corporate risk-taking. He has published over 60 journal articles and book chapters as well as two books. His most recent book, *Behavioral Foundations for Strategic Management,* argues for a behavioral basis for scholarly theory in strategic management.

Steven Cheng, PhD

Steven Cheng is a Senior Research Associate in the Knight Cancer Institute at the Oregon Health & Science University. His research interests are in process modeling/simulation, supply chain networks, and decision making within healthcare operations. His current research focus investigates the barriers to the development and conduct of oncology clinical trials. He received his undergraduate and graduate degrees at Vanderbilt University.

John Child

John Child MA, PhD, ScD, FBA, is Professor Emeritus at the University of Birmingham and a Professor at FUMEC University, Brazil. He is a Fellow of the Academy of Management, the Academy of International Business, and the British Academy of Management. In 2006, he was elected a Fellow of the British Academy (FBA). His current interests include the internationalization of SMEs and alternative forms of organization. He has published 19 books and over 140 articles. Recent books include *Cooperative Strategy* (with David Faulkner and Stephen Tallman, Oxford University Press, 2005), *Organization* (Blackwell, 2005), and *Corporate Co-evolution* (with Suzana Rodrigues, Wiley, 2008). This last book won the prestigious Academy of Management Terry award in 2009. Professor Child is a past editor-in-chief of *Organization Studies* and is currently Senior Editor for *Management and Organization Review*.

André L. Delbecq

André L. Delbecq holds the McCarthy University Chair, Santa Clara University. His scholarship focuses on executive decision making, organization design, managing innovation, and leadership spirituality. He was Eighth Dean of Fellows and prior President of the Midwest and Western Academy of Management and former Executive Director of the Organization Behavior Teaching Society.

David Dilts

David Dilts, PhD, MBA, is Professor of Healthcare Management in the Division of Management at the Oregon Health & Science University (OHSU) and Director of Clinical Research for the Knight Cancer Institute at OHSU. His research interests are in decision making, process modeling, and dynamic supply network structures, particularly those that exist in healthcare. Additional interests include strategic decision making in the context of highly complex healthcare networks, and the integration of systems engineering and complex systems theories within healthcare. His work has been supported by grants from the National Cancer Institute and the Navy, among others.

Colin Eden

Dr Colin Eden is a Professor of Management Science and Strategic Management at the Strathclyde Business School in Glasgow, Scotland. He is an operational researcher by background but has been preoccupied with 'soft-OR' for the last 30 years. His recent research activities and publications have been focused on managerial and organizational cognition, the nature of action research, project management, and strategy making. His strategy research has been concerned with understanding the practical implications of the resource-based view and competence-based management, alongside the significance of stakeholder management theories. He has published nine books and over 180 articles in the fields of management science, management, and project management.

Said Elbanna

Dr Said Elbanna, BCom Hons, MBA, PhD (Birmingham Business School), is an Assistant Professor at UAE University in UAE. His main research interests are in strategic decision making, strategic planning, and internationalization of SMEs. Dr Elbanna has published in journals such as *Strategic Management Journal, Journal of Product Innovation Management, Journal of Management Studies,* and *International Journal of Management Reviews.* He has, in addition, built up a valuable competence in executive training and consultancy. Dr Elbanna has received some awards including the JMS Best Paper Award for 2007, and the CBE (UAE University) Outstanding Junior Research Award for 2008.

Samantha Fairclough

Samantha Fairclough (DPhil, University of Oxford) is the Deloitte & Touche Post Doctoral Research Fellow in the Department of Strategic Management and Organization at the University of Alberta's School of Business, and an Associate Post Doctoral Fellow of the Saïd Business School at the University of Oxford. A former environmental lawyer, her research interests include institutional theory, the creation and reproduction of categories, business and the natural environment, and the management of professional service firms.

Lori B. Ferranti

Lori B. Ferranti, PhD, MBA, MSN, is the Director of the Office of Policy, Planning, and Assessment for the Tennessee Department of Health. Her research interests are in usage of medical registries in decision making in public and private arenas, and linking multiple data sets to develop and assess outcomes of public health policies and initiatives. Additional interests include the application of business principles of efficiencies and quality improvement in various healthcare operational settings, and the influence of education discipline on the selection of decision-making rules.

She received her undergraduate degree at Virginia Commonwealth University and graduate degrees at Vanderbilt University.

Lori S. Franz

Lori S. Franz, (PhD Nebraska, 1980) is Professor of Management in the Trulaske College of Business at the University of Missouri. Her current research interests include decision-making processes, analysis of decision characteristics as predictors of decision outcomes, and the application of modeling for improved decision making. Professor Franz's research appears in numerous journals including *Operations Research, Decision Sciences, Computers and Operations Research, European Journal of Operational Research,* and the *International Journal of Production Research.*

Dennis A. Gioia

Dennis A. (Denny) Gioia is Professor of Organizational Behavior and Chair of the Department of Management and Organization, Smeal College of Business at the Pennsylvania State University. He holds degrees in both Engineering Science and Management from Florida State University and previously worked for Boeing Aerospace at Cape Kennedy during the Apollo lunar program and for Ford Motor Company as corporate recall coordinator. He is a longstanding member of the MBA, Executive MBA, and PhD faculties and has engaged in organizational research for many years. Current research and writing interests focus on the ways in which identity, image, learning, and knowledge are involved in sensemaking, sensegiving, and organizational change.

Royston Greenwood

Royston Greenwood is the TELUS Professor of Strategic Management in the Department of Strategic Management and Organization, School of Business, the University of Alberta, and Visiting Professor at the Saïd Business School, University of Oxford. He received his PhD from the University of Birmingham, United Kingdom. His research focuses upon the dynamics of institutional change, especially at the field level of analysis. His favoured empirical settings involve professional service firms. Recently, his research has explored how and why large professional service firms developed new organizational forms with particular reference to how they are 'theorized' and thus legitimated. One paper from this research stream won the *Academy of Management Journal*'s 2006 Best Paper Award. His work has appeared in *Administrative Science Quarterly, Academy of Management Journal, Academy of Management Review, Organization Science, Organization Studies,* and the *Strategic Management Journal.* He is a founding co-editor of *Strategic Organization,* and is a co-editor of the *SAGE Handbook of Organizational Institutionalism.* He is the Chair-designate for the OMT Division of the Academy of Management.

Terri L. Griffith

Terri L. Griffith (PhD, Carnegie Mellon) is a Professor of Management and Breetwor Fellow in Santa Clara University's Leavey School of Business. She focuses on the use of new technologies and organizational practices – especially around virtual work and knowledge transfer. She also blogs on these topics at TerriGriffith.com/blog.

Aimee L. Hamilton

Aimee Hamilton is a doctoral candidate in the Management and Organization Department of Penn State's Smeal College of Business. Her research interests include innovation, organizational identity, image and reputation, and sustainability. She holds an AB magna cum laude from Harvard University and an MBA from the Yale School of Management.

Michael W. Kramer

Michael W. Kramer (PhD, Texas, 1991) is professor and chair of the Department of Communication at the University of Missouri. His organizational research focuses on employee transitions such as newcomers, exit processes, and corporate mergers. His group research focused on decision making and membership in voluntary groups. He has made theoretical contributions in the theory of managing uncertainty, group dialectical theory, and a theory of language convergence/meaning divergence. His research methods range from multivariate analysis to ethnography. His research appears in journals such as *Communication Monographs, Human Communication Research, Small Group Research,* and *Academy of Management Journal.*

Tammy L. Madsen

Tammy L. Madsen (PhD, UCLA) is Associate Professor of Strategy and Chair of the Management Department at the Leavey School of Business, Santa Clara University. Tammy's research interests are at the intersection of strategy, innovation, competitive dynamics, and organizational evolution. Her most recent work explores how innovation contributes to sustained differences in superior profits among rivals. Her work has received various awards from the Business Policy & Strategy (BPS) Division of the Academy of Management and appears in a variety of journals including *Strategic Management Journal, Organization Science, Industrial and Corporate Change, Journal of Knowledge Management,* and *International Marketing Review.* She serves on the editorial review boards of SMJ, SEJ, and AMR and is 2010 Chair-elect for the BPS Division of the Academy of Management. Tammy teaches strategy in the MBA and Executive MBA programs at SCU.

Mark Meckler

Mark Meckler, PhD is an associate professor of management in the Robert B. Pamplin School of Business Administration at The University of Portland in Portland, Oregon. His research focuses on the relationships between events, theories, truth, and knowledge. His work is published in such quality journals as *Organization Studies, Journal of Business Ethics,* and *Journal of Management Inquiry.* Dr Meckler teaches graduate and undergraduate courses in leadership, strategic management, and management of technology and innovation. He has served the US Government as a Fulbright Professor in Eastern Europe, and is a former professional chef. He received his PhD from Florida Atlantic University in 2001, his MBA in hospitality management from Michigan State University in 1990, and his undergraduate BA in philosophy from Brandeis University in 1985.

Susan Miller

Susan Miller is Professor of Organizational Behaviour at the Business School, University of Hull in the UK. She has research interests in the fields of strategic decision making and strategy implementation and has published widely in these areas. She is also interested in issues to do with management education and has written about the nature of business and management knowledge and education.

Henry Mintzberg

Henry Mintzberg is Cleghorn Professor of Management Studies in the Desautels Faculty of Management at McGill University in Montreal. His research has dealt with issues of general management and organizations, focusing on the nature of managerial work, forms of organizing, and the strategy formation process. Currently, he is completing a book about *Managing* (which explores 29 days in the lives of managers), a book on *Organizing* (a revision of *Structure in Fives*), and an electronic pamphlet entitled *Getting Past Smith and Marx ... Towards a Balanced Society*. He is also promoting the development of a family of masters programs for practicing managers in the private and health sectors. His own teaching activities focus on ad hoc seminars for managers and work with doctoral students.

Professor Mintzberg earned his doctorate and Master of Science degrees at the M.I.T. Sloan School of Management and his mechanical engineering degree at McGill, working in between in operational research for the Canadian National Railways. He has been named an Officer of the Order of Canada and of l'Ordre Nationale du Québec and holds honorary degrees from 13 universities in eight countries. He also served as President of the Strategic Management Society from 1988–1991, and is an elected Fellow of the Royal Society of Canada (the first from a management faculty), the Academy of Management, and the International Academy of Management. He was named Distinguished Scholar for the year 2000 by the Academy of Management.

Tim Morris

Tim Morris is Professor of Management Studies at Saïd Business School, Oxford University. His research interests in professional service firms concern the ways in which they organize to innovate and processes of decision and change.

Eivor Oborn

Eivor Oborn is a Lecturer in Public Management and Organisations at Royal Holloway University of London. She is an honorary research associate in the Medical Faculty at Imperial College London and a Fellow at Judge Business School, Cambridge University. Her research interests include healthcare, organisational change, knowledge translation, multidisciplinary collaboration, and service innovation. She has published work related to multidisciplinary knowledge work in a number of peer reviewed journals including *Human Relations*, *Public Administration*, and *British Journal of Management*.

David Obstfeld

David Obstfeld is a Visiting Professor of Management and Organizations at New York University's Stern School of Business. Professor Obstfeld's research examines how the knowledge-intensive, network-based social processes, which result in organizational change and innovation, unfold at the local and firm levels. Currently, his interests focus on how the interaction of social network-based linking activity, knowledge articulation, and creative projects influence entrepreneurship, innovation, and firm strategy.

Vassilis M. Papadakis

Vassilis M. Papadakis is a Professor and Chairman of the Department of Business Administration at the Athens University of Economics and Business. With a PhD from the London Business School, his main research interests are in the areas of strategic decision making and mergers and acquisitions. He has published articles in *Strategic Management Journal*, *Organisation Science*, *British Journal of Management*, and others. Two of his papers have been published in the best papers proceedings of the US Academy of Management, in 1996 and 2003. He is a reviewer for international academic journals, including *Academy of Management Review*, *Management Science*, *Journal of Management Studies*, and *British Journal of Management*.

Marshall Scott Poole

Marshall Scott Poole (PhD, University of Wisconsin-Madison) is a professor in the Department of Communication, Senior Research Scientist at the National Center for Supercomputing Applications, and Director of the Institute for Computing in the Humanities, Arts, and Social Sciences at the University of Illinois Urbana-Champaign. He is the author or editor of ten books and over 130 articles and book chapters. Recent books include *Theories of Small Groups: Interdisciplinary Perspectives* and *Organizational Change and Innovation Processes: Theory and Methods for Research.* His research interests include group and organizational communication, organizational change, and information technology, particularly its implementation and impacts.

Hal G. Rainey

Hal G. Rainey is Alumni Foundation Distinguished Professor in the School of Public and International Affairs at the University of Georgia. His book, *Understanding and Managing Public Organizations*, was recently published in its fourth edition. In 2009, he received the Dwight Waldo Award for career scholarly contributions from the American Society for Public Administration. Rainey serves as a Fellow of the National Academy of Public Administration.

Devaki Rau

Devaki Rau earned her PhD in management at the University of Minnesota and is currently a faculty member in the Department of Management at Northern Illinois University. Her research focuses on the recognition and utilization of expertise in teams and individuals, managerial decision making, and top management teams. She has published her research in journals such as the *Journal of Applied Psychology*, *Small Group Research*, and *Journal of Business Research*. She worked as a business development executive in CMC Ltd, a software development and maintenance firm in Bangalore, India, prior to obtaining her PhD.

Suzana Rodrigues

Suzana B Rodrigues MSc, PhD holds the Chair of International Business at the Rotterdam School of Management, Erasmus University. She is also a Professor at FUMEC University in Brazil. Her current interests include the relevance of inter-organizational arrangements in SME internationalization, and the internationalization of R&D facilities and mechanisms of knowledge development in MNCs. She has published in *Human Relations, Journal of International Management, Journal of Management Studies, Management and Organization Review, Management International Review* and *Organization Studies*. The book she co-authored with John Child, *Corporate Co-evolution: A Political Perspective*, received the Terry Book Award at the 2009 Academy of Management Meeting.

John C. Ronquillo

John C. Ronquillo is a doctoral candidate in the School of Public and International Affairs at the University of Georgia. His primary research interests are in public and nonprofit management, innovation and organizational change, and social entrepreneurship. Prior to entering academia he worked in the areas of social impact assessment, intergovernmental relations, and public policy analysis.

Kathleen M. Sutcliffe

Kathleen M. Sutcliffe (PhD) is Associate Dean for Faculty Development and Research and the Gilbert and Ruth Whitaker Professor of Management and Organizations at the University of Michigan Ross School of Business. Her research program has been devoted to investigating how organizations and their members perceive and cope with uncertainty and how organizational designs influence reliability and resilience. In particular, Professor Sutcliffe has studied the antecedents of untoward organizational events such as errors and crises as well as ways in which organizations, their units, and their members can anticipate untoward events or cope with them after they are manifest.

Ioannis C. Thanos

Ioannis C. Thanos holds an MSc in Marketing and Strategy from Warwick Business School (UK) and is a doctoral candidate and a research assistant at the Athens University of Economics and Business in Greece. His research interests are in the area of strategic decision making and mergers and acquisitions. His research has appeared in the *British Journal of Management* and has been presented in conferences including the Academy of Management, the British Academy of Management, and the European Academy of Management.

Haridimos Tsoukas

Haridimos Tsoukas is the George D. Mavros Research Professor of Organization and Management at the Athens Laboratory of Business Administration (ALBA), Greece and a Professor of Organization Studies at Warwick Business School, University of Warwick, UK. He obtained his PhD at the Manchester Business School (MBS), University of Manchester, and has worked at MBS, the University of Warwick, the University of Cyprus, the University of Essex, and the University of Strathclyde. He has published widely in several leading academic journals, including the *Academy of Management Review, Strategic Management Journal, Organization Studies, Organization Science, Journal of Management Studies*, and *Human Relations*. He was the editor-in-chief of *Organization Studies* (2003–2008) and serves on the editorial board of several journals. His research interests include: knowledge-based perspectives on organizations; the management of organizational change and social reforms; the epistemology of practice; and epistemological issues in organization theory. He is the editor (with Christian Knudsen) of *The Oxford Handbook of Organization Theory: Meta-theoretical Perspectives* (Oxford University Press, 2003). He has also edited *Organizations as Knowledge Systems* (Palgrave Macmillan, 2004, with N. Mylonopoulos) and *Managing the Future: Foresight in the Knowledge Economy* (Blackwell, 2004, with J. Shepherd). His book *Complex Knowledge: Studies in Organizational Epistemology* was published by Oxford University Press in 2005. He is also the author of the book *If Aristotle were a CEO* (in Greek, Kastaniotis, 2004).

Andrew H. Van de Ven

Andrew H. Van de Ven is Vernon H. Heath Professor of Organizational Innovation and Change in the Carlson School of the University of Minnesota. His books and journal articles over the years have dealt with the Nominal Group Technique, organization theory, innovation and change. His most recent book is *Engaged Scholarship* (Oxford University Press, 2007).

Karl E. Weick

Karl E. Weick is the Rensis Likert Distinguished University Professor of Organizational Behavior and Psychology, and Professor of Psychology at the University of Michigan. His PhD is from Ohio State University in Social and Organizational Psychology. He is a former editor of the journal Administrative Science Quarterly (1977–1985) and former Associate editor of the journal Organizational Behavior and Human Performance (1971–1977). Dr. Weick's research interests include collective sensemaking under pressure, handoffs and transitions in dynamic events, high reliability performance, improvisation, and impermanent systems.

Frances Westley

Frances Westley holds as the JW McConnell Chair in Social Innovation at the University of Waterloo, Ontario. Dr. Westley is a renowned scholar and consultant in the areas of social innovation, strategies for sustainable development, middle management and strategic change, visionary leadership and inter-organizational collaboration. Her most recent book, *Getting to Maybe* (2006) focuses on the dynamics of social innovation, and institutional entrepreneurship in complex adaptive systems. Before joining the University of Waterloo, Frances Westley held the position of Director, Nelson Institute for Environmental Studies (2005–2007) at the University of Wisconsin-Madison. Other positions she has previously held include the James McGill Professor of Strategy at McGill University's Faculty of Management.

Frances Westley serves on the editorial board of several journals, including *Journal of Applied Behavioral Science* and *Ecology and Society*. She is the recipient of several awards including the Ulysses S. Seal award for innovation in conservation, and the Corporate Knights Award.

Jennifer L. Woolley

Jennifer L. Woolley MBA, PhD, is an Assistant Professor of Management at the Leavey School of Business, Santa Clara University. Her teaching focuses on international business, strategy, and entrepreneurship. Jennifer's research examines the emergence of technology, firms, and industries. Prior to joining Santa Clara University, Jennifer worked in international finance.

About the Editors

Paul C. Nutt

Paul C. Nutt is Professor Emeritus of Management Sciences at the Fisher College of Business at The Ohio State University and Professor of Management at University of Strathclyde's College of Business. He received his PhD degree from the University of Wisconsin – Madison and a BS and MS from the University of Michigan, all in Industrial Engineering. He has written 150 articles and eight books on subjects that include organizational decision making, strategic management, planning, and radical change. His books include *Why Decisions Fail* for Berrett-Koehler and *The Strategic Management of Public and Third Sector Organization* and *Making Tough Decisions* for Jossey-Bass. He is a fellow of the Decision Sciences Institute and is a charter member of the Academy of Management's hall of fame. His work has appeared in many academic journals as well as *Fortune*, the *Wall Street Journal*, *Fast Company Magazine*, and NPR/PRI's *Marketplace*. He serves on numerous editorial review boards and regularly consults for public, private, and non-profit organizations.

David C. Wilson

David Wilson is Professor of Strategy and Organization in the University of Warwick where he is also Deputy Dean of the Business School. He is the author of eight books and over 70 journal articles. He was Chairman of the British Academy of Management (1994–1997) where he served for over 10 years as an Executive member. He is a Fellow of the Academy, elected in 1994. He is listed in *Who's Who in Social Science* a list of leading international scholars in their field, published by Edward Elgar (2000). He was Chairman of the scholarly society, the European Group for Organisation Studies (EGOS) from 2002 to 2006. He has had a long association with the journal *Organization Studies*, beginning as Editorial Assistant (1981–1996), becoming Co-Editor (1992–1996), Deputy Editor (1996–1999), and finally Editor-in-Chief (1999–2003). He is currently Chair of the Editorial Advisory Board for *Organization Studies*. He has been a member of EGOS for over 20 years and has served on the Board for the last eight years.

Part I

INTRODUCTION

1

Crucial Trends and Issues in Strategic Decision Making

PAUL C. NUTT AND DAVID C. WILSON

INTRODUCTION[1]

Studies of strategic decision making are central to organization theory. March and Simon (1958) suggested that managing organizations and decision making are virtually synonymous. The dynamics of organizing require a deep understanding of decision making. As organizations grow and become more complex, decision making becomes a central activity. Managers are expected to make choices among alternatives that are often uncertain and to choose wisely in order to benefit both the organization and its key stakeholders. This has prompted researchers to study decision processes to find ways in which decisions can be improved.

The study of decision making has spanned a number of levels of analysis, which range from individual cognition to the cultural characteristics of nation states. Many disciplines inform our knowledge from mathematics to behavioural theories of social science. The term *strategic* decision making is often used to indicate important or key decisions made in organizations of all types. The term *organization* includes any collective social, economic or political activity involving a plurality of human effort. Strategic decisions emphasize the social practice of decision making as it is carried out among and between individuals in the organization. When studying decision making, both the organizing of decision activity as a collective phenomena and the cognitive processes of individual decision makers take centre stage.

Strategic decision making is more than computation carried out to make judgements and choices. Various branches of mathematics can inform us about risk, options, game theory and choice. All have their utility in understanding choice processes, but are less useful when considering how people in organizations make decisions. As an example, consider the most well known variant of game theory (decisions between two players), the prisoners' dilemma. Two criminals in separate cells have to decide whether to betray each other, having agreed not to betray one

Handbook of Decision Making. Edited by Paul C. Nutt and David C. Wilson
© 2010 John Wiley & Sons, Ltd

another in advance of the game. The greatest pay-off results when both prisoners stick to their agreement, but most betray each other and experience a significantly reduced pay-off. Computational mathematics help the players maximize their returns, but this is just part of the strategic decision-making story.

Why consider *strategic* decisions? As we will discuss later in this chapter, the term strategic has become more confusing than enlightening. Popularized by Mintzberg *et al.* (1976), strategic decisions are seen as large, expensive, and precedent setting producing ambiguity about how to find a solution and uncertainty in the solution's outcomes. Once implemented, a strategic decision stipulates premises that guide operational decisions that follow. A strategic decision is often difficult to reverse once human and financial resources have been committed to their cause. Furthermore, strategic decisions have the following characteristics:

- They are elusive problems that are difficult to define precisely.
- They require an understanding of the problem to find a viable solution.
- They rarely have one best solution, but often a series of possible solutions.
- Questions about trade-offs and priorities appear in the solutions.
- Solution benefits are difficult to assess as to their effectiveness, in part because they lack a clear final end point against which effectiveness can be judged.
- Other problems in the organization are connected to solutions for a focal problem.
- High levels of ambiguity and uncertainty are associated with solutions.
- Realizing hoped for benefits has considerable risk.
- Strategic decisions have competing interests that prompt key players to use political pressure to ensure that a choice aligns with their preferences.

Strategic decision making is often treated as an instantaneous choice between two or more known alternatives. However, this 'point of decision' approach is unable to capture the richness and complexity of the processes that unfolded to the point of decision including how problems were uncovered, the way in which search was conducted, what was done to ensure decision adoption and the steps taken to assess benefits. Decision making from a point of decision perspective also assumes that managers have complete control over decisions. It is more likely that the decision maker has limited discretion in selecting among courses of action. This occurs, for example, when strategic decisions are constrained by interventionist government policies, such as privatization or deregulation, requiring all strategic actions to be framed and shaped by this wider context. Nevertheless, managers still have some degree of strategic choice even if the wider context (e.g. privatization) is firmly set in place. This includes strategic decisions involving topics such as organizational design, choice of suppliers, choice and sophistication of information systems and general product or service portfolios.

Theorists such as Drucker (1974) and Weick (1995) show how decision-making processes in organizations are as much about defining the question as they are about providing an answer. To understand a strategic decision one must decide whether there is a need for a decision and, if so, what that decision is about. Weick likens this process to those of boards of inquiry following a disastrous event. Such a board has a number of roles. The board acts like a historian – reconstructing the past to make sense of what happened and to prevent future disasters happening again should similar events occur. The 'historian' takes an outcome and interprets it as the result of a series of decisions, which are seldom seen by those involved as discrete choices made to resolve a problematic situation. Much of strategic decision-making research requires this kind of social reconstruction.

There are many other views of strategic decision making. Mintzberg (1987) provided a useful way to categorize decisions with his five Ps classification. We summarize it here because it raises some key questions about the nature and definition of a strategic decision. Strategic decisions can be viewed as a *Plan*: the decision is an intended course of action carried out in advance with a clear purpose. Alternatively, strategic decisions can be seen as a *Ploy*. Here, decisions take shape as a set of actions designed to outwit the competition, which may not be the 'obvious' content of the decision. For example, a decision to build a new building in order to expand may not be the overt strategy, but is more concerned with increasing barriers to entry for potential competitors. There are connections here with the military roots of strategic decision making. The plans of campaigns may have similar characteristics to those of a ploy to outwit the 'enemy'. Thirdly, strategic decisions can be seen as a *Pattern*: decisions are not necessarily taken with a clear planned purpose and decision makers do not always have access to the range of knowledge required to create a plan of action. However, decisions taken over time form a pattern. It is this pattern of resulting (emergent) behaviour that we call the strategy of the firm. Strategy is therefore characterized as a pattern that emerges from a stream of decisions and may not be an attribute or descriptor of a single decision.

Strategic decision making can be seen as achieving a *Position*. A decision is less about the dynamics of planning or gamesmanship and more about trying to realize a match between the organization and its environment. This position can be one of alignment, so that the organization matches its environment, such as designing highly decentralized structures to cope with a turbulent and unpredictable environment, or one of trying to secure competitive advantage, where the organization solidifies a unique position in the market.

Finally, strategic decision making can be viewed as a *Perspective*. Here decisions are characterized as a reflection of how strategists in an organization perceive the world and their organization. To illustrate, the strategic perspective of Nokia is one of continuous and sometimes radical change (Nokia began as a paper and pulp company); IBM favours a dominant marketing perspective; and Hewlett-Packard favours an engineering excellence perspective. Such a perspective, if pervasive enough, can influence the kinds of decisions taken, in respect of their content and their processes. We can see the effects of this embedded view of decision making by observing that organizations in similar industries often choose similar strategic decisions and become second movers. From this perspective universities tend to follow broadly similar strategies, as do large retailers and service organizations.

These decision types divide into strategic and organizational. Organizational decisions tend to result in plans or ploys. However important or costly such individual decisions may be, the *strategic* element of them is apparent only when a number of decisions are examined together and the patterns and themes in them are uncovered. Using the term strategic for individual (or single) decisions that are plans or ploys seems poor practice. Strategic decisions are more apt to be a pattern, a position, or a perspective. Interestingly, researchers often examine plans and ploys using a process perspective whereas patterns, positions, and perspective receive very little attention by researchers to uncover their generative nature. We return to this debate surrounding the application of the term strategic to decision making later in this chapter.

Over the last 50 years, there have been radical changes in how strategic decision making is researched. For example, in the 1950s and 1960s research emphasized a planning approach to decision making. Such tools included industry structure analyses and portfolio matrices, for example, the matrices offered by Ansoff and the Boston Consulting Group. In this era, strategic decision making was mostly about planning. The 1970s onwards saw a different emphasis. Decisions began to emphasize the pay-offs to organizations should different strategic directions (options) be pursued. Typical options were diversification decisions, but this was also the era of innovation (R&D), acquisition, joint venture, and internationalization decisions.

The 1980s saw a move away from examining the content of strategic decisions – what they were about – to examining them more as processes. The question became whether we could map the progress of a strategic decision and make inferences about why such processes might occur. David Hickson and his colleagues (1986) characterized such processes as sporadic (discontinuous), fluid (continuous and smooth), or constricted (restricted to a small group of stakeholders and highly political). This work also underscored the importance of such processes since they underpinned the recognition among managers of the need for strategic change. The 1990s onwards have seen a continuing interest in unfolding the characteristics of decision processes, but the emphasis has changed to focus on whether or not there are any links between decision making and results. For example, did the decision succeed or fail (e.g. Nutt, 1999, 2002; Hickson *et al.*, 2003)? Do a number of failed strategic decisions lead to organizational failure as Landis Gabel and Sinclair-Desagne (2008), for example, suggest?

Finally, some recent approaches to strategic decision making have concentrated upon the more micro aspects of how managers think, act, and interpret strategic decisions. Such an approach has been termed the *strategy as practice* perspective (Whittington, 1996) or as activity-based (Heracleous, 2003; Jarzabkowski, 2005). Here, the thrust is to dig into what managers actually 'do' when they 'strategize', a term that seems to have emerged alongside the emerging popularity of this perspective. As Jarzabkowski and Wilson (2006) note, much of 'traditional' strategic decision-making theory has been criticized because it is not actionable in practice, so researchers should concentrate on what managers do when they engage in strategic activities. However, it is by no means easy to tell when strategic activity is taking place and when it is not; nor is it easy to identify an appropriate level (or levels) of analysis to examine such activities. For example, should we examine the cognitive and psychological aspects of individuals when they engage in strategic activities, or should we look at their physical activities and try to describe the processes in which they engage (such as decision making), or all three? There are no concrete answers to the above questions. All would be legitimate ways of drilling deep into what managers do when they engage in decision making.

Jarzabkowski (2005) provides a useful perspective to the practice approach by concentrating on what she terms an 'activity-based' view. By this, she means that managers themselves define what is, and is not, strategic by their actions. These discussions and decisions constitute an important part of understanding decision making. One of the key contributions made by Jarzabkowski's (2005) study is that decision making is a 'situated' activity. Although there are many arguments about what is meant by the term 'situated', it identifies the relational nature of managers as actors with situations being the contexts in which they operate. Any particular action by managers must be seen and understood in the context of the situation in which that action occurs. Managers are both recipients and creators of the situational context in which they carry out the activities that go into decision making.

Why is such a micro focus useful? The main answer is that the strategy as practice perspective highlights differences in strategic decision making that might otherwise be missed. From a more macro perspective, organizations can look fundamentally similar. They face similar social, political, and economic contexts in which they are embedded. However, this similarity can be deceptive. Jarzabkowski (2005) shows how three Universities, all facing the same often mutually contradictory tensions of increasing revenue from research and from commercial activities, craft and implement very different decisions to try and resolve these tensions and increase revenue streams. Only a micro focus can reveal these key differences between organizations in the ways in which their managers handle decision making.

The practice perspective shows how face-to-face interactions between managers are imbued with the context of administrative and organizational procedures, all of which can influence decision making over time. There is no sharp distinction between decision formulation and implementation from this perspective. Decision making is a blend of individual interactions and the organizational context over time and is not necessarily a step by step or a logical sequence.

Heracleous (2003) also argues for a situated and micro perspective on decision making. He views decision making as a performative art, represented both by what managers do (practice) and what and how they communicate (discourse). Decision making can be best understood by looking at the language managers' use and the activities in which they engage.

As a field of study, strategic decision making has experienced many attacks on its theoretical and empirical foundations. It has not only survived these attacks, but has prospered in recent years. Many established authors are returning to some of the original key ideas in decision making and applying them to other areas of organization theory. Two recent examples provide illustrations. One recent theme can be seen with March's emphasis on the importance of knowledge and what he terms 'organizational intelligence' in decision making (March, 1999). Another can be found in Karl Weick and others who focus on specific decisions needed to prepare organizations for extreme or highly uncertain events, such as a disaster or a terrorist attack (Weick and Sutcliffe, 2007; Starbuck and Farjoun, 2005; Sullivan-Taylor and Wilson, 2009).

Following the organizational intelligence theme, March examines the characteristics of decisions that allow decision makers to follow courses of action to ensure that the organization continues to benefit in the face of scarce resources and heightened competition. March categorizes these as intelligent decisions that merge desires, actions, and outcomes in a positive way (i.e. outcomes fulfil desires as far as possible). March shows how intelligence (information, experience, and aspirations) can lead to poor decision making. Accelerating errors found in decisions initially thought to be clever can lead to poor performance. The trick according to March is to assemble intelligence in decision making in ways that facilitate successful performance.

Following an 'extreme event' theme, authors such as Weick and Sutcliffe focus on decision making in which levels of uncertainty and ambiguity are very high. They suggest that decision making needs to create and sustain what they term 'high reliability organizations' that are not only capable of withstanding extreme events better than other organizations, but are also highly resilient – they can recover quickly after disasters strike.

In the above two broad themes we can see how relatively modern concerns of organization, competing on knowledge and being prepared for extremes, are being addressed by reference to decision-making theories. Such extensions of decision-making research to other aspects of organization theory have a considerable history. For example, the notion of *incrementalism* or the piecemeal attention to small steps in any process came from Lindblom's (1959) research into how decisions are made. The notion of *problemistic search* (managers seek only information when they have to or when there is a pressing problem) came out of work by Cyert and March (1963). The concept of *enacted environments* (managers only see and interpret the bit of the operating environment that they focus upon) came out of research by Weick (1979). All of these concepts were developed within the field of strategic decision making and to become more generically applied to organizational processes. Strategic decision making has proved a rich ground for the emergence of such concepts.

The work of James G. March identifies many of the key features and debates in strategic decision making. His approach can be illustrated in Figure 1.1. The major contribution of this simple flow diagram is twofold. The processes it identifies underpin most key organizational processes, revealing the centrality of decision making in organization theory generally. Secondly, its very simplicity can be misleading. The cycle shown in the figure can be broken or can malfunction at each stage of the process and between stages. March taught us to beware assumptions of rationality both in individuals and in organizations. Actions can be taken for a variety of reasons that correspond to the ways in which organizations are structured (each specialized function developing its own view on what should happen). This entered the vocabulary of organizational decision making in the form of 'local rationality' (Cyert and March, 1963).

March (1994) was later to refine this concept by emphasizing local preferences, rather than rationality. He argued that the main thing in organizational decision making was forming *interpretations,* not making choices. Interpretations cover a wide

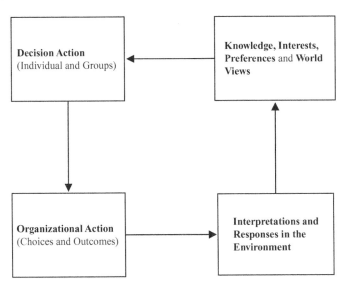

FIGURE 1.1 Strategic decision-making processes.
Adapted from March (1994)

arena when examining organizational decision making. In particular, March set out to show the differences between decisions that are choice-based and those that are rule-based. The main distinction was whether decision makers pursue logic when making choices among alternatives and evaluating their consequences in terms of prior preferences, or whether they pursue a logic of appropriateness, fulfilling identities or roles by recognizing situations and following rules, which match appropriate behaviours to the situations they encounter. In this respect, organizations provide the context in which such interpretations are formed and sustained, and sometimes changed.

March (1994) also pointed out that organizations could engender two very different types of decision behaviour. One can be characterized by clarity and consistency and the other by ambiguity, inconsistency, and chaos. In the former, organization is all about coherence and reducing uncertainty to avoid equivocality. In the latter, organization is anarchic and acts as a background for decisions that may not be linear in process and may not be logical in a consistent sense and where solutions may precede outcomes. Here organizations, by their very nature, are collections of solutions already made – waiting for new decision opportunities to apply each solution.

Finally, March (1994) argued that decision outcomes can be seen as primarily attributable to the actions of autonomous actors in organizations, or can be the result of the systemic properties of organizations as an interacting ecology. This makes the links between organization and decision explicit. Is it possible to describe decisions as emanating from the intentions, identities, and interests of independent actors? Alternatively, is it necessary to emphasize the ways in which individual actors, organizations, and societies fit together?

There is no doubt that decision making is both complex to study and replete with conceptual and empirical dilemmas. We explore these in the next sections of this chapter.

Issues Confronting Decision-making Research

Decision-making research has offered many insightful studies that have illuminated an interesting and complex field. A vast number of empirical investigations, descriptions, prescriptions, structuring techniques, as well as mathematical models that offer analytical tools have been produced. Despite all these notable efforts, few have made headway in integrating this body of knowledge into coherent theory. We will offer our view of some of the reasons for this state of affairs, identifying key issues that must be addressed to construct such a theory. In brief, these issues are unit and level of analysis, purpose, dilemmas in conceptualizing decision making, and the influence of contingency, frameworks, and methodology.

Unit of analysis

Decision-making researchers selected both decisions and choice opportunities (sorting alternatives) as their unit of analysis (Mintzberg *et al.*, 1990, Bell *et al.*, 1998). In our view, the decision is the preferred unit of analysis. Such a focus considers the full range of issues that can arise during decision making. Choice considers only the comparison of alternatives, an overly narrow interpretation of what is required to make a decision. The level of analysis is another crucial consideration, which poses considerations that differ from those posed by the unit of analysis. In past efforts, the unit of analysis has often been confounded with level of analysis. Confounding arises in several ways. Some studies have attempted to deal with decisions that span a number of managerial levels (Bell *et al.*, 1998) or consider the choices or the decisions made by CEOs, top management teams, middle managers, and department heads (Nutt, 2001c). Choices or decisions must be separated by level or type of decision maker in such studies. Confounding also results when there is a mixing of several related decisions or choices to capture an organizational project, such as in disaster management (Weick, 2001) or a large-scale initiative (Cameron and Lavine, 2006). Decisions (or choices) are confounded with organizations when multiple cases are drawn from several organizations, without accounting for the nesting of decisions within each organization. Although Hickson *et al.*, (1986) found these nesting effects to be minimal, they should not be overlooked in future research efforts.

To deal with confounding, factors that denote who is involved, the type of decision maker (e.g. CEOs), the link of decisions to major projects, and the organization in which each decision (or choice) takes place must be identified for analysis. We contend that researchers must carefully make these distinctions and include factors for each in their research. Action theory depends upon generalizing about decisions as well as comparing prescriptions across organizational levels, etc.

Purpose

Purpose poses a formidable challenge to integration. Investigators have examined decision making with many purposes in mind ranging from developing decision-making techniques, to prescription, to descriptions of what decision makers do. This has led to a vast outpouring of projects that consider facets of decision making, with only a few addressing the entire decision episode. Attempts to integrate have been frustrated by framing dilemmas, the difficulties of amalgamating description with prescription, and arguably misguided attempts to deal with process.

Framing dilemmas. A variety of frames can be found in decision-making research. Eisenhardt and Zbaracki (1992) contend that bounded rationality, power and politics, and chance provide the more useful frames. Bounded rationality draws on Dewey's (1910) notions of logical inquiry in which he calls inquiry a process. Qualifications and elaborations have followed, exemplified by the work of March and Simon (1958). Still further extensions made decision rules explicit, modified process steps, and incorporated uncertainty (e.g. Thompson, 1967; Perrow, 1976; Allison, 1971). Research in this tradition has found process steps to unfold in a variety of ways that are subject to cycling and interrupts (Mintzberg *et al.*, 1976). Others define what are believed to be essential steps, such as intelligence gathering, direction setting, option search, option selection, and implementation (e.g., Nutt, 1989; Daft, 1995; Hickson *et al.*, 2003; Miller *et al.*, 2004). Behavioural research finds that decision makers often ignore recommendations derived from these findings (Nutt, 1984; 2002) and simplify their decision-making processes when faced with conflict or novel situations (e.g. MacCrimmon and Taylor, 1976; Janis, 1989).

Power/politics and chance have been suggested to overcome the limitations found in framing with bounded rationality. Both chance and power/politics are thought to have face validity. The exercise of power and the emergence of happenstance fit one's everyday experiences with decision making. Those advocating a power or a politics frame contend that whereas individuals can be rational, a collective, made up of these same people, is not (Pfeffer, 1992), and that the collective must be managed should conflict arise (Langley, 1995). Emphasis is placed on resolving differences using tactics such as coalitions, cooptation, information control, and influence (Pettigrew, 1973). Studies find that managers also turn to politics when thwarted; and when there is a power vacuum. The value of turning to politics can be questioned. Empirical studies find that politics prompts animosity, which slows down decisions and leads to poor results (Eisenhardt and Bourgeois, 1989). Dean and Sharfman (1996) find the pervasiveness of politics to be exaggerated.

The chance frame treats decision making as the accidental connection of a choice opportunity (the call for a decision) with a fortuitous solution. In what has become know as the 'garbage can' (Cohen *et al.*, 1972) choice situations, ideas that zealots and others believe to be useful, concerns, and people looking for action meet due to chance. To be adopted, a solution must be conspicuous and have the support of the right people (Cyert and March, 1963). The chance frame contends that decision makers, distracted by many concurrent demands, connect a solution with a problem to appease stakeholders (Carley, 1986; Masuch and LaPotin, 1989). Timing and luck are the operant ingredients. However, a chance explanation lacks both prescriptive and explanatory power.

To complicate things further, the frames appear to be self-fulfilling. Look at a decision as a process with unfolding steps and one sees a process with steps. Look for politics or chance and they appear (Harrison and Phillips, 1991). This suggests that each frame offers a particular view and that no single view is best. One way to cope is to merge frames, as suggested by Eisenhardt and Zbaracki (1992). For example, a merger of the more powerful frames, politics and bounded rationality, in the study of decision making seems feasible. This calls for studies that account for both a rational perspective, which uncovers cognitions, and a political perspective, which reveals the social context.

Prescription/description conflicts. Some investigators stress description and offer a rich commentary on the events, motivations, and circumstances surrounding a decision. Others concentrate on prescription and offer guidelines for taking action. Both draw upon the other to justify many of the key positions and conclusions provided. Surprisingly, few advocates of either position attempt to measure success. Many of the descriptions and the prescriptions in the literature fail to include empirical investigations that demonstrate effectiveness or generalizability. Even prescriptions that embody mathematical tools (which are not considered in this volume) seldom go beyond a case that illustrates how the tool works to studies that offer empirical evidence, such as comparing one tool to another. As a result, description and prescription have become disconnected, which has kept the conflicting claims made in support of each from being reconciled.

As with many management topics, decision-making research *can be* focused either descriptively or prescriptively. Many contemporary researchers have become strident proponents of one and implicitly, sometimes explicitly, opponents of the other. Contemporary researchers prefer to deal with decision making from a single perspective. In addition, there has been a not so subtle shift in what journals prefer to publish to what is (and is not) acceptable. These trends have led to description dominating research efforts and creating a near mandate for this type of research, which has pushed out prescriptive work. As a result, much of the effort in the prescriptive arena has been shunted to consultants that rarely share their approaches and insights. The descriptive domination of research has also influenced methodology. An explanatory focus has led to a set of methodologies that are far less useful for prescriptive research, which we will discuss in more detail later.

This shift has become troublesome, because description and prescription represent two sides of the 'same coin' (Nutt, 2004a). On the one hand, there is action theory and normative science. On the other, there are behavioural/explanatory explanations of what the researcher observes. Prescription calls for the researcher to identify frameworks, tactics, and the like to test them to see if they produce something of value in real world applications. Description deals with use. How many people act in a certain way, how many subordinates get involved, what is the skill level of key players? One informs the other. Theory that denies or invalidates one or the other is incomplete. Linking the actions taken to success provides a key piece of the action-theory puzzle. Noting whether a prescription is followed, and how, also informs practice. One of the intents of this volume is to call for a more balanced approach to decision-making research. To provide this balance, we will discuss some of the benefits and the pitfalls that follow the research focus found in both approaches.

Misrepresenting process.   Management research was founded with case studies. Before empirical studies were initiated by Ford Foundation funding, the case study offered the primary insight from which people in the field wrote books and taught their classes. Cases, often with little or no generalizability, are still dominant in fields such as strategic management. Decision-making research also has its roots in the case study approach. Its origins can be traced to the Cyert and March (1963) seminal case study of decision making in organizations. Many such studies followed (e.g. Bower, 1970). The description offered by a well-constructed case provided powerful imagery that indicated what was done and sought to uncover why. There have been many useful findings from this kind of work. Perhaps the most important was the deep understanding that a rich case provides, with its focus on the specifics of what happened and its attempts to tease out why this happened. Cases have been particularly useful in reaching out to practitioners, where there is a decided preference for explicit discussion of application. Unfortunately, this has led to discounting action science (also called action theory), like that found in medicine and engineering, which has produced many breakthroughs in both arenas.

Action theory offers an if-then approach to taking action in which an approach is crafted to deal with issues of interest to managers, much like the book of signs and symptoms used by Internists that connect signs and symptoms with possible therapies. Action theory calls for a shift in emphasis from the *is* to the *ought,* which is context dependent. An 'is emphasis' captures what was done and ignores possibilities. An 'ought' approach identifies what can be used to improve the results of action taking and offers tests of what works and what benefits can be expected as a contingency. Prescription offers tools, techniques, and procedures as well as best practices by expert practitioners, fitting each to a process to deal with issues that arise during decision making.

Action theory could have been incorporated into past efforts, but case study researchers invariably ignore *how* the decision was crafted – the steps taken to produce it. Thus, the core for constructing an action theory is missing from the case. This skips over what organizational theorists call process, which has led to process being neglected in most of the research being reported in management journals. This is due in part to the descriptive tradition, noted above with its implicit focus on what is, and its ostensible preference to ignore how things got this way. We will discuss the needs to consider process and its role in formulating an action theory for decision making throughout the book.

This challenge is daunting. Such processes often take place over time, posing problems of observation and codification. The process itself has been seen by some to be somewhat structured and by others as chaotic. Many researchers have also changed their conceptual position over time. For instance, Mintzberg has shifted his view of process from structured (Mintzberg *et al.*, 1976) to messy (Mintzberg and Westley, 2001). Initially, he appeared to argue that decision making was more like planned activity with periods of formulation followed by periods of implementation, with some internal cycling to deal with each. His more recent position seems to argue that decision-making processes are a messy mixture of formulation and implementation that do not necessarily precede one another in temporal sequence (as case studies portray more often than not). Instead, they should be conceptualized as inextricably interlinked. It makes no sense, under this view, to try to separate them out as distinct 'phases' of a process. Still another view is that decision making is rarely planned and mostly emergent, with people reconstructing a story of what happened afterwards. This means that decision making is more about making sense of what has happened (such as reconstructing a pattern in the process of decision making) and less about planning in advance (e.g. Weick, 1979; 1995). Both the chaotic and the sensemaking view pose many conceptual problems to codify and understand process.

Conceptualizing decision making

The framing noted above gives decision-making research efforts their direction. The frame points a researcher down a particular path and suggests how key factors are to be imaged. This has led to many very different conceptualizations. When different frames are used, it complicates attempts to integrate the action taking undertaken by a decision maker (what decision makers do). First, the frame imposes a perspective that influences how the procedures followed by a decision maker are conceptualized. Different actions would be sought (and then measured) if the investigator sets out to uncover steps suggested by bounded rationality, observe how a decision maker reacts to chance events, or follow a negotiation. In each case, the frame suggests a conceptualization that dictates what kind of action-taking steps will be recognized. In addition, approaching a decision-making study as a description leads the researcher away from codifying procedure and toward describing the action taken. Finally, investigations seldom look for a frame that allows both emergent and chaotic features of a process to emerge.

Second, researchers have approached the conceptualization of action very differently. Some draw on philosophy of science (e.g. Dewey, 1910) to gain insight into how decisions should be made. This has led to prescribing procedures (e.g. Simon, 1977; Perrow, 1967; Thompson, 1967; Nutt, 1989; and Daft, 1995). There have been many of these efforts, which has prompted some to seek hybrid processes that integrate procedural elements, seeking an underlying process, and others to suggest processes for particular applications, such as decision making (e.g. Havelock, 1973; Nutt, 2004a). Another kind of effort has investigated what decision makers do, looking for underlying logic (e.g. Witte, 1970; Soelberg, 1967; Mintzberg et al., 1976). Such studies have examined decision-maker action by means of on-site observations, interviews, and surveys to uncover the procedures that are used in practice (e.g. Nutt, 1984; Fredrickson, 1985; Hickson et al., 1986, 2001, 2003; Dean and Sharfman, 1996; Miller et al., 2004).

In many of these efforts, the aim is to document 'process'. Such studies attempt to identify the steps followed to make a decision (Bell et al., 1998). Other researchers go further, looking for steps that seem essential (Nutt, 1984). Related research combines prescriptive and behavioural perspectives to uncover what decision makers do and how this deviates from recommendations (Nutt, 1999). Finally, some add cognition and measure process features (Rajagopalan *et al.*, 1998; Nutt, 2002). This asserts that cognition determines the kind of process selected. All this has led investigators to conceptualize process very differently. As a result, research efforts seldom specify action elements in a way that allows for integration. These research efforts have identified some features of a process, or its motivation, but not how the decision was made. For example, Dean and Sharfman (1993) classify a process by procedural features such as rationality (systematic collection and interpretation of information), political behaviour (using power), and flexibility (adaptability). Hickson *et al.* (1986) use process descriptors such as sporadic (with delays and negotiation), fluid (formalized process), or constricted (restricted to a very small number of senior executives). Fredrickson (1985) classified process by its comprehensiveness. Bell *et al.* (1998) identifies rational, comprehensive, political action, and subunit involvement processes. Others treat process as coalition formation or social process control and focus on measuring decision-maker attributes such as tolerance for ambiguity, uncertainty, or risk aversion (Poole and Van de Ven, 2004). Although interesting, such research says little about how decisions are and should be made. Classifications, such as comprehensive, analytical, or political, fail to explain how a decision maker acts comprehensively, conducts analyses, or engages politically. They characterize the process not the actions that take place within it.

We call for studies that treat decision-maker action taking as a process with several steps that embrace intelligence gathering and implementation, in addition to choice, and allow for emergent ideas and messy recycling among key ideas such as formulation and search.

Contingency theory

Contingency approaches have dominated management thinking for decades. According to this view, a research hypothesis must include situational factors that can influence a main effect under study, such as action taking steps. Justifications stem from assertions by methodologists, who call for studies to account for plausible outside influences (Hitt *et al.*, 2009) and by the many contingency models found in organizational behaviour textbooks in the past two decades. This gives the appearance that contingency models have considerable empirical support. Surprisingly, few contingency models have been subjected to empirical testing and many journals resist publishing this kind of research, arguing that the models are old or that widespread use provides sufficient justification. Nevertheless, a comprehensive research effort will have considerable difficulty being published without including a number of widely accepted contextual factors, such as importance and urgency.

In all such models, contingencies lay out boundary conditions that identify *when* a particular kind of action is preferred. The boundary conditions are often suggested situational factors. Environmental stability, time pressure, novelty, complexity, and resource dependency may identify when a given decision approach (a set of action taking steps) works best. Researchers empirically test such assertions by including both the action taking steps and the contingency as factors in a study that assesses each independently, and as a statistical interaction (Nutt, 2008). This allows the researcher to determine if one kind of action taking works best under a particular set of conditions.

Two kinds of contingencies are recommended for such studies: content and context.

Content. Content identifies the decision type. A variety of decision types has been studied. Some focus on the crucial but infrequent decisions made by top managers that select core businesses offering competitive advantage (e.g. Hitt *et al.*, 1997). This limits the purview to core business choices made by top management teams. As noted above, Mintzberg *et al.* (1976) in their seminal work call strategic decisions important choices that have long-term consequences due to the resources required and precedents set. The Mintzberg position takes a much more inclusive view that sweeps in a greater variety of somewhat smaller scale decisions, which have both top and middle manager involvement. This opens the door to a wide scope of decisions. The Bradford studies (Hickson *et al.*, 1986, and Nutt 2002) have adopted this view, as have many others. All this suggests that researchers claim to study 'strategic decisions', but define strategic quite differently. Some focus on the decisions made to select a core business, which may involve patterns, position, or perspectives. The study of such is a sadly neglected topic. As a result, we know little about strategic decisions defined in this way. More work in this area is needed.

Calling a decision 'strategic' to suggest importance and significance has become poor practice. We call for strategic decisions to be accounted for and characterized much more precisely in future work. This can be done in at least two ways. One approach is to classify decision by the degree to which it has strategic implications. There is no doubt that different decisions in organizations will vary in terms of their importance to the organization, the degrees of risk and novelty involved, and the amount of resources that need to be committed. The Bradford studies revealed that organizations have between five and seven such decisions being processed at any one time. Such decisions can be ranked in terms of their 'strategicness'. Many of the less-strategic decisions in organizations are not strategic at all – they are merely costly, for example, and have no connection to a strategic action in the sense understood by writers in the field of strategic management. To illustrate, decisions made about positioning, a core business selection, or about securing competitive advantage are called 'strategic' in strategic management. Each is essentially a one-off decision. Organizational level decisions that follow, however resource hungry or risky, would be viewed using this perspective as operational. Effectively, they capture some of the many actions that put a strategy into practice. What is defined as strategic depends upon your frame of reference.

An alternative approach is to account for the distinction between the strategic and organizational decisions in empirical analyses. Strategic decisions would be classified as those that deal with a new line of business. Organizational decisions would be defined as strategic decisions that have been defined: important, precedent-setting, high-resource, and large-commitment decisions. Furthermore, an organizational decision can be either subjective or objective. Subjective choices involve agenda setting, selecting topics for future decisions (Bell *et al.*,1998), and ethical considerations, value positions to be taken when making a decision (Nutt,

2002). Hickson *et al.* (1986) looked at decisions 'objectively', stressing action, and identified several types: products/services, financing, personnel policy, marketing, buildings, technologies, and reorganizations. Nutt (2001b) found internal operations/control systems to be a separate type.

Content is believed to influence the choices made, the benefits realized, and the processes applied (Butler, 1998). Clarity about the kind of decisions being addressed is essential. In addition, decision scope, as indicated by the level of the managers involved, can be confounded with type and should be included as a study factor. Top executives are more apt to be involved with strategic matters and others with control systems, inputs, etc. Thus, we call for studies that consider the decision type differentiating the strategic from the organizational as well as maintaining the subjective and objective distinction and specifying the span of the study (the number of decision types included). Together, conclusions about such factors should provide a test of the generalizability of the study findings.

Context.   Context identifies the environment in which a decision is made, providing a second set of boundary conditions. Both internal and external environmental factors are believed to influence what is decided as well as how a decision is made (e.g. Thompson, 1967; Perrow, 1967; Bell *et al.*, 1998). Internal factors include surprise, confusion, and threat (March and Simon, 1958); organizational features, such as approaches to communication and control and resistance to change (e.g. Nutt, 2002), as well as decision importance (Bell *et al.*, 1998), complexity (Nutt, 1998), and uncertainty (Thompson, 1967). Decision-maker attributes such as the propensity to take risks, tolerance for ambiguity, creativity, decision style, intelligence, need for control, power, experience, education, and values have been suggested (Bell *et al.*, 1998). External factors include organizational differences, such as public or private (Hickson *et al.*, 1986; Nutt, 2004b), as well as prevailing economic conditions (Bell *et al.*, 1998).

Context, like content, is believed to influence choices, benefits realized, and processes applied (Nutt, 1998a; Bell *et al.*, 1998). Thus, clarity about the situation in which a decision was rendered is required as well. As with content, certain kinds of managers may be involved when certain conditions arise. Top executives are more apt to be involved with high stakes efforts or costly ones. We call for studies that consider the managerial level, identifying both level and contextual factors, since these are needed to deal with the influence of situation (or context). A test of this contingency argument determines whether context influences how a choice is made, and its outcome. Such studies also provide greater generalizability to finding out about process and other matters of concern to decision-making research.

Decision outcomes

Identifying decision outcomes has been a particularly difficult challenge for decision researchers. Decision outcomes are frequently multifaceted and often difficult to fully grasp and quantitatively measure. For example, a resort may measure occupancy, sales by cost center, and commissions. It is often difficult to codify the effects of outstanding customer service or to create a metric that translates increases in occupancy, due to discounts and other factors that influence room revenues, to profits.

Relevant measures identify decision benefits and whether the benefits can be justified given the cost, disruptions, and distractions required by a decision. Determining benefits requires documenting outcomes and measuring their effects (Hickson *et al.*, 1986; Nutt, 1986; Bell *et al.*, 1998; Papadakis and Barwise, 1998; Hickson *et al.*, 2003; Miller *et al.*, 2004). These effects can take many forms. Bower (1970) argues that training is important. Others call for determining changes in people's behaviour and interpretations (Bryson *et al.*, 1990), measuring process outcomes (timeliness, commitment, and learning), documenting features of action taking, such as disruption and scope of negotiations (Hickson *et al.*, 1986), or developing indicators of success (Nutt, 2002; Hickson *et al.*, 2003). The Bradford Studies and Nutt (1998c) specifically examined the relationships between implementation and outcomes. Using the extent to which stated objectives had been achieved (as a surrogate for performance), these studies revealed the importance of not only the structural and cultural aspects of organization, (such as, do structures impede or facilitate outcomes?), but also the knowledge base of the organization (can managers accurately specify and assess both information and resources?). These studies also indicated that outcomes were directly associated with the above factors and were also influenced by intervening variables, namely how acceptable a decision is to key stakeholders and to what extent the decision was made a priority in the organization. These measures are surely only the tip of the iceberg in terms of identifying factors that influence outcomes. Researchers must push their measures further toward documenting actual benefits.

Relationships explored

Astute investigators call for studies that examine decision making within an organization in which managers, facing an important concern or difficulty, take action to make choices that produce outcomes with immediate and downstream effects. How a decision maker takes action appears to influence the choices made and their benefits (Nutt, 1984; Dean and Sharfman, 1996; Hickson *et al.*, 2003). Context and content are also believed to influence both the choices made and their benefits (Hickson *et al.*, 1986; Nutt, 1998a; Bell *et al.*, 1998).

To do this research, a relationship must be posited between process (action taking steps), context (importance, urgency, etc.), content (e.g. strategic and non-strategic; the eight Hickson types), and the costs and benefits of a decision. Several relationships have been suggested in which process is causal, mediating, or an outcome. For example, Butler (1998) identifies relationships among what he calls problem (content), solution (outcome), and choice (process) in which each can be a cause, an effect, or an interaction; linking them to computation, expertise, negotiation, and inspirational kinds of decisions (context is not considered). In expertise decisions, outcomes dictate content and process with process and content interacting. Negotiation calls for process to be causal with content and outcome interacting. Bell *et al.* (1998) posits a relationship in which context is causal, first influencing process and content, and then outcomes. Downstream effects are acknowledged, contending that a choice influences the host of tangential interpretations (Bryson *et al.*, 1990) and that benefits can be delayed (Nutt, 2002). Rajagopalan *et al.* (1998) contend that context (made up of environmental and organizational factors) and content jointly influence decision-maker cognitions and the process that is embraced, with the outcome stemming from process as well as being influenced by context and content. Drawing on such relationships, researchers speculate about how outcomes are influenced by process, the situation, the type of decision, or by combinations of these factors.

Methodology

How data are collected in decision-making studies is important as well. The conclusions drawn from decision-making studies can be incompatible due to the wide variety of methods that are applied. Research approaches in such studies have varied from qualitative to quantitative, simulation to case study, interviews to surveys. The result has created something of a hodge-podge of investigations with little insight into amalgamating the findings to help build a coherent theory. In this way, decision making is similar to many areas of social science investigation with different paradigms, different mother disciplines, different data collection methods, and analytical coding schemes being the norm rather than the exception, which has created two major difficulties for the field of decision making as well as social science. The first concerns rigour and the second, relevance.

Rigour measures the quality of the research effort, asking how good the research is. This is often presumed synonymous with how 'scientific' the research is. A great deal of decision-making research is qualitative. Qualitative research is often criticized as lacking rigour. Once termed 'unscientific', the findings from such studies become suspect because, at least in many Western countries, the highest form of knowing has demonstrated scientific rigour. Decision-making researchers, who use qualitative research methods, tend to reject formal quantitative methods because they associate formal modelling with positivism or, worse still, with over-quantifying. An emphasis on quantification coaxes the researcher to exclude things that are difficult to measure. Often these exclusions matter – factors difficult to measure can have an overriding importance. Nevertheless, qualitative research is subject to interpretive biases that reduce objectivity, lessening rigor. In addition, qualitative efforts often produce a limited number of cases. This can lead to limited generalizability of the findings. Researchers may see what they want to see in the analysis, and little else. Critics contend that qualitative research is often little more than an assembly of anecdotal and personal impressions, both subject to observer biases. This can make qualitative research nonreproducible. It is unlikely another researcher would come to a similar set of conclusions.

However, qualitative and quantitative research approaches have many striking similarities. Claims that they are fundamentally different have been successfully challenged. For example, May and Pope (1995) and Dingwall (1992) argue that looking for the distinctions in qualitative and quantitative approaches create methodological fallacies. They believe that research is about a state of mind and the particular conditions that allow such an attitude to be expressed. As May and

Pope (1995) argue, quantitative analysis allows the generation of numerical representations of research that give the impression of solidity and a factual base, but in essence they are highly dependent on the skills and judgement of the researcher (as well as to what extent the measures used were appropriate to the issues studied). This chimes with the view that qualitative research is also dependent upon skill, judgement, and the interpretive frame of reference of the researcher or researchers.

Britten and Fisher (1993) argue that quantitative methods are more apt to be seen as reliable but not valid and that qualitative methods are viewed as valid but not reliable. Such positions are often expressed when assessing decision-making research. Those who have advocated mixing quantitative and qualitative methods (Nutt, 1999, 2008; Hickson *et al.*, 1986, 2003; Jick, 1979; Brannen, 1992) must justify sacrificing reliability to improve validity. Critics implicitly favour one or the other. Researchers are forced to collect additional data to comply instead of dealing with the many difficulties inherent in combining the two approaches.

Finally, it should be noted that there are cultural differences in what is considered rigorous science, particularly between Europe and the United States. An in–depth case study or series of comparative case studies can be hailed as 'insightful, rigorously researched, and sophisticated' by European scholars, while the same piece of work can be dismissed as 'sloppy science' by scholars from the United States. This can be seen in the anonymous statements from European and American reviewers, offered in a peer review of the same paper.

In our view, decision-making research must balance rigor and relevance. Decision making is arguably *the* key activity of a senior manager and poor decisions can lead to the demise of an organization. Relevance stems from confronting the phenomena of interest, a decision, and not some artificial simulation with naïve participants. Dealing with a decision and not an abstraction makes it more likely that the research finding will be useful in practice.

Like much of Social Science, decision-making research suffers from questionable relevance (Jarzabkowski and Wilson, 2006). The lack of relevance arises in several ways. First, conditions change. Today managers face globalization, the advent of new technologies, as well as deregulation and re-regulation, recession, and competition in what has become a knowledge-based economy. Decision-making theory and empirical research say little about these factors. When much of the extant decision-making research was carried out, different technologies were foremost in people's minds. Data that were collected from noncomparable sectors of the economy under different conditions can not be generalized to current conditions. Furthermore, what constitutes organizational performance in a global knowledge driven economy must be rethought.

Still another complication arises from managers who make decisions by drawing decision-making research findings without considering the theories underpinning the research (see Baldridge *et al.*, 2004; Jarzabkowski and Wilson, 2006). This creates a fundamental problem for the relevance of much research. The creation and design of a study, from the researcher's perspective, also constructs the interpretation and implications of the data. If a practitioner just applies the findings as if they were objective and generalizable, it disconnects context from findings making the applicability of the findings questionable and possibly irrelevant.

OUR APPROACH

The Wiley Handbook series has gained considerable recognition as a primer for research in management-related fields. When we were contacted to write a Handbook for decision making, it was agreed that we would follow this well-established tradition. To do so we first ruminated about what was out there and what was needed, much the way one would put together a seminar series. After some reflection, we selected some topics and set out to recruit people in the field who, in our judgement, could make novel and cutting-edge contributions in the discussion of each topic as well as addressing the issues that we identify in the previous section. Our authors were invited to confront these topics but to do so by expressing their own ideas. We made no effort to edit what was submitted for content, only offering suggestions regarding extensions and elaborations to the arguments made that seemed needed to clarify and justify. In this way, each author was offered the freedom to approach his or her topic, as each believed was appropriate, including taking positions that we may not support. We leave it up to the reader to sort this out as differing framing, approaches, and world-views are inherent in decision making, as in any field of study.

We are pleased with the result. Our authors represent a cross-section of the scholars interested in decision making on both sides of the Atlantic. We believe that each has provided insight into the issues that we raised They include many who have written important summative or integrative discussions of decision making as well as those who have been leaders in reporting a stream of original research. We believe our contributors offer many original ideas and new directions for decision-making research that will guide research effort for some time. This should make the Handbook a valuable adjunct to faculty and students interested in the study of decision making. We see the Handbook as providing a useful compendium for PhD programmes in business schools around the world with an interest in decision making. We believe that the decision-making researcher will find the ideas for research projects that offer a jumping off point for their inquiries into this most interesting and challenging field of study. It should offer a reference point for new ideas and topics of interest for years to come. In addition, managers will find many of the processes offered in the Handbook to have immediate application. We believe that the forward-looking leaders in public and private organizations will find many ideas in the Handbook on how to improve the practice of decision making in their organizations.

The Handbook is organized by sections that present what we believe are the key issues facing decision makers and researchers. In Part I, we offer two chapters that introduce the volume. We identify trends and issues in decision making in Chapter 1. We discuss some of the dilemmas and conundra that have plagued the field. From these we identify what we believe must be attended to if the field of decision making is to move forward. Here we also consider the normative and prescriptive approaches taken to decision making that have, regrettably, become mutually exclusive. We show how this has become counterproductive and pose issues that must be resolved to formulate a viable theory of decision making. In Chapter 2, Vassilis Papadakis, Ioannis Thanos, and Patrick Barwise offer a summary of research that has been undertaken in the decade following their taking stock of the field (Papadakis and Barwise, 1998). Previously, Papadakis and Barwise argued for empirical work with more emphasis on outcomes, inclusions of context, conceptualizing decision making broadly to include more of the intellectual effort required, focus on the actions of top managers, and finally including implementation and related topics. Their assessment of the field from these perspectives provides an appraisal of empirical efforts, limitations of these efforts, and suggests some of what remains to be done.

Part II provides some key theoretical perspectives that lie behind much of the past work in decision making. In Chapter 3, Henry Mintzberg and Frances Westley discuss decision-making approaches found in their classic see-first, do-first, think-first typology. These distinctions have become a trilogy that now make up how many writing with a prescriptive intent have framed their action theory of decision making. Interestingly, Mintzberg has come full circle on this, beginning with a process-like structured action theory (Mintzberg et al., 1976) followed by a shift to calling decision making idea-driven (Mintzberg and Waters, 1982) and then moving to a more chaotic view (Mintzberg and Westley, 2001). In this piece, the trilogy is fitted to a kind of contingency representation, along with improvising. In Chapter 4, Karl E. Weick, Kathleen M. Sutcliffe, and David Obstfeld offer sensemaking as an explanation for how decision makers act in practice. This recent rendition of Weick's work discusses a theory-like conceptualization of decision making (sensemaking) that has captured the attention of many researchers. As a result, sensemaking has become one of the key foundations of action theory based on improvising. Many embrace such an approach. In subsequent chapters we will identify these and other ways that decision making has been conceptualized, such as chance (e.g. Cohen et al., 1972), and present theoretical and empirical arguments that support each. In Chapter 5, John Child, Said Elbanna, and Suzana Rodrigues discuss the political aspects of decision making. This chapter reminds us of the centrality of power and interests and the key parts they play in influencing both the processes and the outcomes of decision making. In Chapter 6, Dennis Gioia and Aimee Hamilton consider organizational identity. These authors highlight the importance of central concepts, such as who we are and what the organization really is. Because these drive both normative assessments of what decisions should be made (or are considered right to be made in a moral sense), they strongly influence what happens in decision-making processes.

Part III offers several of the many unique conceptualizations of decision making that must be appreciated to see how the field has been developed and the task ahead to find a way to integrate it. In Chapter 7, Paul C. Nutt offers the beginnings of a process-based action theory. He summarizes 30 years of empirical work that collected and then analysed decisions made by top managers. Drawing on analyses of more than 400 decisions, he formulates an action theory that identifies the key steps taken in successful and unsuccessful processes used by top managers. He illustrates traps and how to avoid them, drawing on four cases taken from his database. In Chapter 8 Andre Delbecq, Terri L. Griffith, Tammy L. Madsen, and Jennifer L. Woolley provide an approach that facilitates innovation, showing key steps and illustrating each with cases and demonstrations. In Chapter 9, Colin Eden and Fran Ackerman illustrate how group decision making draws on similar principles and faces similar difficulties as those identified in Chapter 7, by using causal mapping and group decision support.

In Part IV, we take up a series of special topics with importance in studying and understanding decision making. Tim Morris, Royston Greenwood, and Samantha Fairclough in Chapter 10 provide a discussion of strategic decision making in professional firms. Their arguments are that both the structural forms and the strong value bases of individuals within professional service firms provide a context in which both decisions and decision making are distinctly different from other types of organization. Phillip Bromiley and Devaki Rau, in Chapter 11 discuss risk as viewed through the lenses of prospect theory, information processing, and similar approaches favoured by psychologists. They examine treatments of risk by three key decision-making approaches: the behavioural theory of the firm, behavioural decision theory, and agency theory. They conclude with a discussion of the implications of this research for managers, and identify some future areas of study in risk in decision making. In Chapter 12 Kim Boal and Mark Meckler discuss what they call errors of the fourth, fifth, and sixth kind to complement classic type one and type two errors, which arise when interpreting evidence to determine problem causes, and a type three error, which arises when a false problem is addressed. Action errors of the fourth and fifth kind arise when deciding whether and when to act. A compound error of the sixth kind can arise from combinations of the other errors that produce interactions with unforeseen consequences. These errors call attention to looking at actions beyond those surrounding a choice. In Chapter 13, Hal Rainey, John Ronquillo, and Claudia Avellaneda consider a key feature in the context of decision making, offering a discussion of how public sector decisions provides special challenges and difficulties. In Chapter 14, Hari Tsoukas discusses strategic decision making and knowledge, emphasizing the key roles played by knowledge as both a form of rationality in decision making as well as a basis for making sense of, and helping reduce, uncertainty and encouraging learning. In Chapter 15, Michael Barrett and Eivor Oborn discuss using information technology (IT) to support knowledge sharing in decision making. Using empirical data from a multi-disciplinary healthcare team these authors reveal the complex role of IT in supporting knowledge sharing between different professional groups during the decision-making process.

Part V offers some recent empirical findings that support theories and views presented thus far. In Chapter 16 Sue Miller presents an overview of the Bradford Studies. Summarizing 20 years studying decisions and drawing on the evidence of nearly 200 decisions, she locates the Bradford process studies both in the context of decision-making research and organizational approaches to understanding decisions. The chapter outlines the earlier work of the Bradford group that concentrated on the decision process up to the point of authorization. Miller then examines recent work by the team on the implementation and performance of strategic decisions. The work finds strong linkages between how decisions are implemented and their success, a combination of organizational context and managerial action. Miller shows that implementation and formulation are inter-connected in distinct ways, lending support to the view that, although difficult to separate completely, deciding and implementing are two distinct phases of decision making. Next, in Chapter 17, Paul C. Nutt provides an empirical look at four decision-making processes used by top managers, drawing on analyses of more than 400 case studies. He distinguishes between successful and unsuccessful processes, and then identifies how particular steps in each process, carried out by tactics, influence the success of each process. This study considers context and content as well and differentiates between the process and tactics, using the success produced by the decisions to determine best practice. Several key practice-based recommendations emerge from the study. Lori Ferranti, Steven Cheng, and David Dilts, in Chapter 18, offer an interesting study of medical decision making that departs from traditional topics. They consider decision-making issues with respect to numeracy and focus on how this influences informed consent, patient knowledge, and healthcare provider communication. In Chapter 19, Lori Franz and Michael Kramer provide a new methodology to study decision content. They offer a comprehensive approach that can be extended to real decisions and real decision makers. This provides another way to treat decision content that complements the approaches offered by Nutt (2002) and the Bradford Studies (e.g. Hickson *et al.*, 1986).

Part VI offers methodologies for the study of decision making. In Chapter 20 Scott Poole and Andrew Van de Ven provide a comprehensive summary of approaches that have been applied to or recommended for the study of change, which they adapt to decision making. Poole and Van de Ven contrast variance theory with process theory, examining how each can be productively applied to the study of decision making. They also consider several other issues that include levels of analysis, the impact of perspective, and the treatment of time. In Chapter 21, Paul C. Nutt offers several new approaches to the study of process, applied to decision making. Nutt contrasts process with structure and shows how research into both is required before an action theory of decision making can be formulated. The focus of the chapter is on investigating process, which has been neglected in the past. Discussion links process research in decision making to several emergent theories found in other fields that consider process. Standards for process research are identified and compared with the traditional standards offered for structural studies. A new research paradigm is proposed that treats process and structure (the decision) as two sides of the same coin. Finally, in Chapter 22 David Wilson discusses the research approach followed in the Bradford Studies. These studies used a plurality of methods ranging from participant observation through intensive case studies to quantitative, multi-variant characterizations of process. Wilson assesses both the strengths and limitations of these approaches and discusses how future research in decision making might benefit from these observations.

The book concludes with Part VII, which provides directions and perspectives in Chapter 23. We sum up what we have learned to date and where research must go from here to begin to formulate a viable action theory for decision making.

CHALLENGES FACING RESEARCHERS

In this final section of our chapter, we outline what we believe to be the crucial challenges facing researchers. Challenges arise because, after almost four decades of research, the concept of a 'decision' remains ambiguous and ill defined. After all this effort, there is no consensus about basic questions, such as whether decisions can be planned or must emerge. Additionally, ambiguity surrounds whether decisions contribute to organizational strategy, and if so, how. The approaches used to study decision making range from the study of individual choice drawing on cognitive or psychoanalytic insights, through decisions as processes with identifiable characteristics, to the practice of decision making that considers implementation, action taking, and performance. A researcher searching for a research topic might view all this as overly complex and look elsewhere. Yet, there is something seductive and intuitively interesting about studying how decisions are made, who makes them, and what happens as a result. Human activity of all kinds is derived from common-sense notions of decision making such as what to do today, what to buy, whom to invite, whom to exclude. Decisions have passed into common parlance – we know a decision when we see one. When one speaks of a decision there is little uncertainty about meaning. Nevertheless, many challenges arise when attempting to conduct a scientific study of decisions. We address a few of the more important ones.

Decision-making research has become 'de-humanized' over the past few decades. We know more about the characterization of decision processes, such as fast/slow, continuous/nonlinear, comprehensive/simple, and the like, than we do about the behaviours of individuals carrying out the decision-making process. To explain what people do and how they behave during decision making poses a significant challenge.

We would argue that much of the early work on decision making began by attempting to study behaviours but, instead, characterized decision processes (e.g. Cyert and March, 1963; Mintzberg *et al.*, 1976; Nutt, 1984; and Hickson *et al.*, 1986). Such an assertion creates debates that our authors address in their various ways. In this chapter, we emphasize the need for what we call action research to uncover and identify both the behaviour and the process. Such research would give us insight into what decision makers do when they engage in decision activities, but also would enable more fundamental and more closely aligned relationships to performance. As a result, decision research could begin to address the more normative aspects of decision making, such as what managers should do when facing a particular kind of decision situated in a particular way. Such an 'ought' perspective has not been popular or indeed considered proper science for some time. Currently, the preference of organization theorists is to describe what 'is' and then account for what they find using variables found in well known organizational contingencies, such as urgency and risk. Certainly, the relatively recent development in the field that has become known as 'strategy as practice', described earlier in this chapter, has made substantial moves towards rich behavioural description and has made more tentative moves toward more normative approaches. Situating a decision in the actions taken enables the researcher to comment on practice and its relationship to outcomes, such as measures of performance.

The study of decision making as action becomes the study of the localized exercise of judgement within the organization (Tsoukas and Cummings, 1997). As Jarzabkowski and Wilson (2006) note, this involves viewing decision makers as getting things done within situational demands. Decision makers become reflexive actors, situating activities in the context of past actions, current organizational context, and future aspirations. They can also become innovative decision makers, changing these situated activities to suit their needs both now and in the future (Garud *et al.*, 2002). In both cases, simply characterizing the decision process will not reveal how decision makers make do, improvise, and adapt their actions and behaviours in what de Certeau (1984: xviii) has termed 'artisan-like inventiveness'.

We realize there are always counter arguments. One often cited argument asserts that context matters more than individual action. This leads proponents to claim that an understanding of context (and history) will yield a greater understanding of decision making than efforts spent drilling deep into managerial action and behaviour. Micro foci have their limits too. Wilson presents these micro/macro arguments in Chapter 22 and we capture these debates and the various contributions in Chapter 23 that spell out in detail directions and approaches for future decision-making research.

NOTES

1. Parts of this introduction are based upon Wilson (2007).

REFERENCES

Allison, G.T. (1971) Conceptual models and the Cuban Missile Crisis, *American Political Science Review*, 63, 689–718.

Baldridge, D., Floyd, S., and L. Markoczy (2004) Are managers from Mars and academicians from Venus? *Strategic Management Journal*, 25, 1063–1074.

Bell, G., Bromley, P., and Bryson, J. (1998) 'Spinning a Complex Web: Links Between Strategic Decision Making Context, Content, Process, and Outcome', in V. Papadakis and P. Barwise (eds) *Strategic Decisions*. Boston, MA: Kluwer.

Bower, J.L. (1970) *Managing the Resource Allocation Process: A Study of Corporate Planning and Investment*. Homewood, IL: Irwin.

Brannen J. (1992) 'Combining Qualitative and Quantitative Approaches: An Overview', in *Mixing methods: qualitative and quantitative research*. Aldershot: Avebury, 3–37.

Britten, N, and Fisher, B. (1993) Qualitative research and general practice [editorial]. *British Journal of General Practice*, 43, 270–271.

Bryson, J.M., Bromiley, P., and Jung, V.S. (1990) The influences of context and process on project planning success, *Journal of Planning Education*, 9 (3), 183–195.

Butler, R. (1998) 'Strategic Decision Making: A Contingency Framework and Beyond', in V. Papadakis and P. Barwise (eds) *Strategic Decisions*. Boston, MA: Kluwer.

Cameron, K., and Lavine, M. (2006) *Making the Impossible Possible: Leading Extraordinary Performance – the Rocky Flats Story*. San Francisco, CA: Barrett-Koehler.

Carley, K. (1986) 'Measuring Efficiency in a Garbage can Hierarchy', in J. March and R. Weissinger-Baylor (eds) *Ambiguity and Command*, Marshfield: Pitman, 165–194.

Cohen, M.D., March, J.P., and Olsen, J.P. (1972) A garbage can model of organizational choice, *Administrative Science Quarterly*, 17, 1–25.

Cyert, R.M., and March, J.G. (1963) *A Behavioral Theory of the Firm.* Englewood Cliff, NJ: Prentice-Hall.

Daft, R. (1995) *Organization Theory and Decision*, St. Paul, MN: West Publishing Co.

Dean, J. and Sharfman M. (1993) Procedural rationality in the strategic decision making Process, *Journal of Management Studies*, 30, 607–630.

Dean, J., and Sharfman, M. (1996) Does decision making matter? A study of strategic decision making effectiveness, *Academy of Management Journal*, 39 (2), 368–396.

Dewey, J. (1910) *How We Think.* New York: Heath.

De Certeau, M. (1984) *The Practice of Everyday Life.* Berkeley: University of California Press.

Dingwall R. (1992) "'Don't mind him—he's from Barcelona': qualitative methods in health studies', in J. Daly, I. MacDonald, and E. Willis (eds) *Researching Health Care: Designs, Dilemmas, Disciplines.* London: Tavistock/Routledge, 161–175.

Drucker P. (1974) *Management: Tasks, Responsibilities and Practices.* New York: Harper & Row.

Eisenhardt, K., and Bourgeois, J. (1989) 'Charting Strategic Decisions in the Micro Computer Industry: Profile of an Industry Starr', in M. Van Glenow and S. Moherman (eds) *Managing Complexity in High Technology Organizations, Systems, and People.* New York: Oxford University Press, 74–89.

Eisenhardt, K., and Zbaracki, M. (1992) Strategic decision making, *Strategic Management Journal*, 13, 17–37.

Fredrickson, J.W. (1985) Effects of decision motive and organizational performance on strategic decision processes, *Academy of Management Journal*, 28, 821–843.

Garud, R., Jain, S., and Kumaraswamy, A. (2002) Institutional entrepreneurship in the sponsorship of common technological standards: The case of Sun Microsystems and Java, *Academy of Management Journal*, 45 (1), 196–214.

Harrison, M., and Phillips, B. (1991) Strategic decision making: An integrative explanation, *Research in the Sociology of Organizations*, JAI Press vol. 9, 319–358.

Havelock, R.G. (1973) *Planning for Innovation.* Ann Arbor, Michigan: CRUSK, The Center for Utilization of Scientific Knowledge, fourth printing.

Heracleous, L. (2003) *Strategy and Organization: Realizing Strategic Management.* Cambridge: Cambridge University Press.

Hickson, D., Butler, R., Cray, D., Mallory, G., and Wilson, D. (1986) *Top Decisions: Strategic Decision Making in Organizations.* San Francisco, CA: Jossey-Bass.

Hickson, D., Butler, R., and Wilson, D. (2001) *The Bradford Studies of Decision Making: Classic Research in Management.* London: Ashgate.

Hickson, D.J., Miller, S., and D.C. Wilson (2003) Planned or prioritized? *Journal of Management Studies*, 40 (7), 1803–1836.

Hitt, M., Beamish, P., Jackson, S., and Mathieu, J. (2009) Building theoretical and empirical bridges across levels: Multilevel research in management, *Academy of Management Journal*, 50 (6) 1385–1400.

Hitt, M., Ireland, D., and Hoskisson, R. (1997) *Strategic Management.* St Paul, MN: West.

Janis, I.J. (1989) *Crucial Decisions.* New York: Free Press.

Jarzabkowski, P. (2005) *Strategy as Practice: An Activity-Based Approach.* Sage: London.

Jarzabkowski, P., and Wilson, D.C. (2006) Actionable strategy knowledge: A practice perspective, *European Management Journal*, 24 (5), 348–367.

Jick, T. (1979) Mixing qualitative and quantitative methods: Triangulation in action, *Administrative Science Quarterly*, 24, 602–611.

Landis Gabel, H., and Sinclair-Desgagne, B. (2008) From market failure to organizational failure, *Business Strategy and the Environment*, 3 (2), 50–58.

Lindblom C. (1959) The science of muddling through, *Public Administration Review*, XIX (2), 79–88.

MacCrimmon, K.R., and Taylor, R.N. (1976) 'Decision Making and Problem Solving', in M. Dunnette (ed.) *Handbook of Industrial and Organizational Psychology*. Chicago: Rand-McNally.

March, J. (1994) *A Primer on Decision Making: How Decisions Happen*. New York: Free Press.

March J. (1999) *The Pursuit of Organizational Intelligence*. Oxford: Blackwell.

March, J.G., and Olsen, J.P. (1986) 'Garbage Cans of Decision making in Organizations', in J.G. March and R. Weissinger-Baylon (eds), *Ambiguity and Command*. Marshfield, MA: Putman.

March, J.G., and Simon, H.A. (1958) *Organizations*. New York: McGraw-Hill.

Masuch, M., and LaPotin, P. (1989) Beyond garbage can: An AI model of organizational choice, *Administrative Science Quarterly*, 34, 38–67.

May, N., and Pope, C. (1995) Qualitative research: Reaching the parts other methods cannot reach: An introduction to qualitative methods in health services research, *British Medical Journal*, 311, 42–45, July.

Miller, S., Wilson, D.C., and Hickson, D.J. (2004) Beyond planning: strategies for successfully implementing strategic decisions, *Long Range Planning* 37 (3), 201–218.

Mintzberg, H. (1987) The Strategy Concept I: Five Ps for strategy, *California Management Review*, Fall, 11–24.

Mintzberg, H., and Waters, J. (1982) Tracking strategy in an entrepreneurial firm, *Academy of Management Journal*, 25 (3), 465–499.

Mintzberg, H., Waters, J., Pettigrew, A., and Butler, R. (1990) Studying deciding: An exchange between Mintzberg and Waters, Pettigrew and Butler, *Organization Studies*, 11 (1), 1–16.

Mintzberg, H., Raisinghani, D., and Theoret, A. (1976) The structure of unstructured decisions, *Administrative Science Quarterly*, 21 (2), 246–275.

Mintzberg, H., and Westley, F. (2001) Decision making: Its not what you think, *MIT Sloan Management Review*, 42 (3), 89–93.

Nutt, P.C. (1984) Types of organizational decision processes, *Administrative Science Quarterly*, 29 (3), 414–450.

Nutt, P.C. (1986) The tactics of implementation, *Academy of Management Journal*, 29 (2), 230–261.

Nutt, P.C. (1987) Identifying and appraising how managers install strategic changes, *Strategic Management Journal*, 8 (1), 1–14.

Nutt, P.C. (1989) *Making Tough Decisions*, San Francisco, CA: Jossey-Bass.

Nutt, P.C. (1998a) Framing strategic decisions, *Organizational Science*, 9 (2), 195–206.

Nutt, P.C. (1998b) Leverage, resistance, and the success of implementation approaches, *Journal of Management Studies*, 35 (2), 213–240.

Nutt, P.C. (1998c) Evaluating complex strategic choices, *Management Science*, 44 (8), 1148–1166.

Nutt,, P.C. (1999) Surprising but true: Half of organizational decisions fail, *Academy of Management Executive*, 13 (4), 75–90.

Nutt, P.C. (2000) Context, tactics, and the examination of alternatives during strategic decision making, *The European Journal of Operational Research*, 124 (1), 159–186.

Nutt, P.C. (2001b) A taxonomy of strategic decisions and tactics for uncovering alternatives, *The European Journal of Operational Research*, 132 (3), 505–527.

Nutt, P.C. (2001c) 'Strategic Decision-Making', in M. Hitt, R. Freeman, and J. Harrison (eds) *The Blackwell Handbook of Strategic Management*. Oxford, United Kingdom: Blackwell Publishers Limited.

Nutt, P.C. (2002) *Why Decisions Fail: Avoiding the Blunders and Traps that Lead to Debacles*. San Francisco, CA: Barrett-Koehler.

Nutt, P.C. (2004a) On doing process research, *International Journal of Management Concepts and Philosophy*, 1 (1), 3–26.

Nutt, P.C. (2004b) Expanding search during strategic decision making, *Academy of Management Executive*, 18 (4), 13–28.

Nutt, P.C. (2008) Investigating decision making processes, *Journal of Management Studies*, 45 (2), 425–455.

Papadakis, V., and Barwise, P. (1998) *Strategic Decisions*. Dordrecht, Netherlands: Kluwer Academic Publishers.

Perrow, C. (1967) A framework for the comparative analysis of organizations, *American Sociological Review*, 32 (4), 194–208.

Pettigrew, A. (1973) *Politics of Organizational Decision Making*. London: Tavistock.

Pfeffer, J. (1992) *Managing with Power: Politics and Influence in Organizations*. Boston, MA: Harvard University Press.

Rajagopalan, N., Rasheed, A., Datta, D., and Spreitzer, G. (1998) 'A Multi-theoretic Model of Strategic Decision Making Processes', in V. Papadakis and P. Barwise (eds) *Strategic Decisions*. Boston, MA: Kluwer Academic Publishers.

Simon, H.A. (1977) *The New Science of Management Decision*. Englewood Cliffs, NJ: Prentice Hall (revised edition).

Soelberg, P. (1970) Unprogrammed decision making, *Industrial Management Review*, Spring, 19–29.

Starbuck, W.H., and Farjoun, M. (eds) (2005) *Organizations at the Limit: Lessons from the Columbia Disaster*. Oxford: Blackwell.

Sullivan-Taylor, B., and Wilson, D.C. (2009) Managing the threat of terrorism in British travel and leisure organizations, *Organization Studies*, 30 (2/3), 115–140.

Thompson, J.D. (1967) *Organizations in Action*. New York: McGraw Hill.

Tsoukas, H., and Cummings, S. (1997) Marginalization and recovery: The emergence of Aristotelian themes in organization studies, *Organization Studies*, 18 (4), 655–674.

Weick, K. (1995) *Sensemaking in Organizations*. London: Sage.

Weick, K., and Sutcliffe, K. (2007) *Managing the Unexpected: Resilient Performance in an Age of Uncertainty*. San Francisco, CA: Jossey-Bass.

Weick, K.E. (1979) *The Social Psychology of Organizing*. Reading, MA: Addison-Wesley, 2nd edition.

Weick, K.E. (2001) *Making Sense of the Organization*. Oxford, England: Blackwell.

Whittington, R. (1996) Strategy as practice, *Long Range Planning*, 29 (5), 731–735.

Wilson, D.C. (2007) 'Strategic Decision Making', in G. Ritzer (ed.) *The Blackwell Encyclopedia of Sociology*. Oxford: Blackwell.

Witte, E. (1972) Field research on complex decision making process – The Phase Theory, *International Studies of Management and Organization*, 56, 156–182.

2

Research on Strategic Decisions: Taking Stock and Looking Ahead

VASSILIS PAPADAKIS, IOANNIS THANOS, AND PATRICK BARWISE

INTRODUCTION

Twelve years ago, Papadakis and Barwise (1997) gave a personal view of the way forward for research on strategic decisions (SDs), drawing on a wide range of authors and on three review papers from the early 1990s (Schwenk, 1995; Rajagopalan, Rasheed and Datta, 1993; Eisenhardt and Zbaracki, 1992). Their substantive proposals were grouped under five headings:

- Increase the focus on *outcomes* (both financial performance and other outcomes such as learning, innovation, and commitment) in order to increase managerial relevance
- Explore the influence of the broader *context* on strategic decision-making (SDM) processes and outcomes, e.g. the organization, the specifics of the decision, planning systems, national culture, and corporate governance.
- More integrative research, especially research bridging the gap between strategy process and *strategy content.*
- Bringing the *CEO and top management team* into SD research.
- Three emergent themes: *learning, implementation,* and *information systems.*

In addition, the authors made a number of suggestions on *methodology* in future SD research.

This chapter aims to take stock of research on SDs since the publication of these suggestions by Papadakis and Barwise (1997), and broadly under the same headings. It is organized as follows. We first outline the method we used to identify the relevant literature. We then propose an integrative model that takes into account context, process, content, and outcomes. Next, we discuss the evolution of SD research under each of the above headings, including methodology. We conclude with a tentative revised wish-list of priorities.

Handbook of Decision Making.   Edited by Paul C. Nutt and David C. Wilson
© 2010 John Wiley & Sons, Ltd

METHOD

To review the recent literature on SDs we conducted a content analysis of papers appearing in top-tier academic and practitioner journals during the years 1998–2008. Our starting point was the list of journals selected by Hutzschenreuter and Kleindienst (2006) which can be 'considered validated knowledge and are likely to have the highest impact in the field' (Hutzschenreuter and Kleindienst, 2006: 674). We added to this list a number of other journals from both Europe (e.g. *Organization Studies, British Journal of Management, Scandinavian Journal of Management, Management Decision, Technology Analysis and Strategic Management, European Journal of Operations Research, Business Strategy Series*) and the USA (*Journal of Behavioral Decision Making, Journal of Business Research, Omega, Decision Support Systems*) because in the past 11 years they have published some influential papers on SDs.

We conducted an online search of these journals using keywords that reflected the substantive priorities: *SD outcomes* (learning, innovation, satisfaction, effectiveness, commitment, etc.), *SD process characteristics* (rationality/comprehensiveness, politicization, centralization, implementation, etc.), and *strategy content and context* (uncertainty, hostility, culture, organization size, decision magnitude of impact, decision uncertainty, etc.).

The search returned around 700 hits from 123 papers. We studied the abstract of each of these 123 papers and selected those which, in our judgment: (a) were empirical papers relevant to the aims of the current study, (b) explicitly or implicitly addressed one or more of the substantive priorities, and (c) expanded the field of SDM.

We further enriched our bibliography with information from other recent reviews and books on decision making (e.g. Nutt, 2002; Wilson, 2003; Elbanna, 2006) strategy process issues (e.g. Chakravarthy and White, 2002; Szulanski, Porac, and Doz, 2005; Hutzschenreuter and Kleindienst, 2006) and the role of top management teams (Carpenter, Geletkanycz, and Sanders, 2004; Lohrke, Bedeian, and Palmer, 2004).

This procedure gave us a core list of 46 empirical papers. Of course we do not claim that this list is exhaustive but we believe that it gives a good representation of how SD research has evolved since the publication of Papadakis and Barwise (1997). Our next step was to create an integrative framework that would map the 'terrain' of SD research during this period. Please note that our review focuses only on the issues raised by Papadakis and Barwise (1997) which do not include all the possible linkages.

FRAMEWORK DEVELOPMENT

Traditionally, research on strategic management has been separated into two distinct categories: 'content research' and 'process research' (Huff and Reger, 1987; Blair and Boal, 1991; Elbanna, 2006). Content research deals with the 'what' of strategy while process research deals with the 'how' of strategy (Pettigrew, 2003).

Some researchers (e.g. Huff and Reger, 1987; Ketchen, Thomas, and McDaniel, 1996; Maritan and Schendel, 1997; Elbanna, 2006) have questioned this dichotomy, urging future researchers to explore the relationship between process and content. Others have argued that we cannot understand process unless we (a) understand the context in which it takes place (Papadakis, Lioukas, and Chambers, 1998; De Wit and Meyer, 2005; Hutzschenreuter and Kleindienst, 2006) and (b) study both formulation and implementation (Huff and Reger, 1987; Blair and Boal, 1991; Pettigrew, 2003). In the words of De Wit and Meyer (2005: 5), 'Strategy process, strategy content and strategy context are the three dimensions of strategy that can be recognized in every real-life strategic problem situation.' In a similar vein, Pettigrew and Whip (1991) argued that process, content and context all have a central role in explaining organizational performance.

In response to these concerns, we developed an integrative framework that encompasses the broader context, the process, the content, and their effects on outcomes (Figure 2.1).

For the description of the broader *context* we followed past research (Rajagopalan, Rasheed, and Datta, 1993; Rajagopalan, Rasheed, Datta, and Speitzer, 1997; Papadakis *et al.*, 1998; Elbanna and Child, 2007a) which states that managerial processes can be explained from a multiplicity of factors relating to the external environment (environmental determinism perspective), the internal organization environment (firm characteristics perspective), the characteristics of the members of the top management team (strategic choice perspective), and decision-specific characteristics (decision perspective). As far as *process* is concerned, we distinguish between formulation and implementation (Pettigrew, 2003). By strategy *content* we mean the method of developing competitive advantage. Finally the last section of the model refers to both *decision process outcomes* (e.g. effectiveness, quality, and commitment) and *organizational outcomes* (ROA, ROS, organizational effectiveness).

Table 2.1 summarizes the 46 core studies: author(s), sample, data collection method(s), analysis method(s), the linkage(s) that they represent in the model, and major findings.

We now review the literature with respect to the four substantive priorities.

LITERATURE REVIEW ON SUBSTANTIVE PRIORITIES

1 Increase focus on outcomes in order to increase relevance (Linkages 5A, 5B, 7A, 7B, 9)

Twelve years ago, Bower (1997) argued that there had been little work on the relationship between process characteristics (e.g. rationality, decentralization, politicization, etc.) and performance. This was echoed by Papadakis and Barwise (1997) who stated further that strategy process researchers had devoted less effort than strategy content researchers to performance issues and also largely ignored the influence of processes on nonfinancial outcomes such as commitment, satisfaction, learning, and innovation.

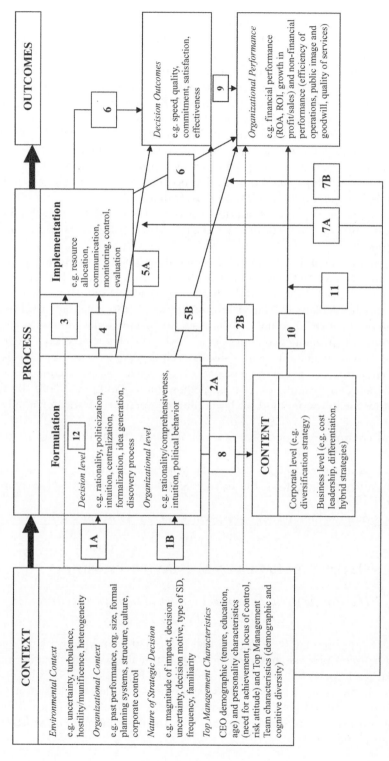

FIGURE 2.1 An integrative framework for studying strategic decisions.

TABLE 2.1 Studies appearing in the SD literature during 1998–2008

Author(s)	Sample	Design/Sources of Information	Analyses	Linkage(s)	Main Findings
Atuahene-Gima and Li (2004)	373 Chinese firms involved in technological ventures	Survey research, cross-sectional, multiple TMT responses	CFA and Hierarchical Regression	5A, 2A, 7A	The relationship between strategic decision comprehensiveness and new product performance was negatively moderated by technology uncertainty but positively moderated by demand uncertainty.
Atuahene-Gima and Murray (2004)	149 US manufacturing firms	Survey research	CFA and Hierarchical Regression	1A, 5A, 2A, 7A	Marketing strategy comprehensiveness is influenced by organizational and environmental factors. The relationship between marketing strategy comprehensiveness and product performance is positively moderated by implementation speed and technology uncertainty and negatively by market uncertainty.

(Continued)

TABLE 2.1 (Continued)

Author(s)	Sample	Design/Sources of Information	Analyses	Linkage(s)	Main Findings
Baum and Wally (2003)	318 CEOs of US firms	Survey research, Cross-sectional, multiple respondents, subjective measures of performance	SEM	2A, 9, 2B	Strategic decision speed is influenced by a multiplicity of organizational and environmental factors and moderates the relationship between dynamism, munificence centralization, formalization, and firm performance.
Brouthers et al. (1998)	90 Dutch Firms	Survey research, cross-sectional	Descriptive Statistics	1B	Executives of small firms tend to rely more on intuition.
Brouthers et al. (2000)	42 Dutch financial institutions	Field study, cross-sectional, survey research	Multiple Regression	1B	Strategic aggressiveness is shaped by environmental and management factors
Brenes et al. (2008)	81 firms operating in Latin America	Survey research, cross-sectional	Descriptive Statistics	4, 3,6	Strategy formulation process, CEO leadership, systematic execution, and strategy control and follow-up influence the successful implementation of business strategy.
Carr (2005)	28 UK, 35 German, 14 US and 13 Japanese vehicle component firms	Interviews, longitudinal	Content Analysis	1B	Institutional and cultural factors have a profound effect on the decision-making style.

Chou and Dyson (1998)	80 Strategic Investment Decisions from Taiwanese firms	Survey research, cross-sectional	PCA and Correlations	2A, 1A	IT intensity in the investment project is negatively related to the effectiveness of SDs and to several proces characteristics (duration, interaction, involvement).
Collier *et al.* (2004)	6394 managers attending an executive course in a UK university	Survey research, cross-sectional	Correlations	4, 6	There is a positive relationship between involvement in strategy-making and rationality and a negative one between involvement and politics.
Covin *et al.* (2001)	96 manufacturing firms in Southwestern Pennsylvania	Field Study, cross-sectional, multiple sources, performance is measured with archival data	Multiple Regression	5B, 2B, 7B	The relationship between decision-making style and organizational performance is moderated by environmental and technological sophistication.
Elbanna and Child (2007a)	169 Strategic Decisions from Egyptian manufacturing firms, employing more than 100 employees	Field Study, cross-sectional, both qualitative and quantitative approaches	Hierarchical Regression and PCA	1A	Rationality is shaped by decision, environmental and firm characteristics.

(*Continued*)

TABLE 2.1 (Continued)

Author(s)	Sample	Design/Sources of Information	Analyses	Linkage(s)	Main Findings
Elbanna and Child (2007b)	As that of Elbanna and Child (2007a)	As that of Elbanna and Child (2007a)	Hierarchical Regression and correlations	5A, 2A, 7A	Rationality and political behavior influence strategic decision effectiveness more than intuition. This relationship is shaped by decision, environmental, and firm characteristics variables.
Elbanna and Younies (2008)	As that of Elbanna and Child (2007a).	As that of Elbanna and Child (2007a)	PCA	12	Decision makers can be simultaneously rational, political, and/or intuitive.
Forbes (2005)	98 Internet start ups from the 'Silicon Alley' Community	Field Study, cross-sectional	T-tests and OLS regression	2A, 5A	Firms managed by older and experienced managers make faster strategic decisions.
Goll and Sambharya (1998)	92 large US manufacturing firms	Survey research, Cross-sectional, performance is measured with archival data	Multiple Regression	5B, 8	Diversification strategy acts as a mediator in the relationship between rational decision making and firm performance.

Goll and Rasheed (2005)	159 manufacturing firms operating in the USA	Rational decision making was measured based on a survey, while all the other variables are archival, multiple TMT responses	Multiple Regression	1B, 2B, 5B, 7B	Top Management Team demographic characteristics (age, tenure) influence the degree of rational decision making. Environmental munificence moderates the relationship between rational decision making and firm performance.
Gottschalk (1999)	190 Norwegian firms	Survey research, cross-sectional	Multiple Regression	4	There is a positive relationship between planning and implementation.
Hickson et al. (2003)	55 UK firms	Case study design, longitudinal	PCA and Multiple Regression	2A, 4, 6	Planned and prioritized options influence the success of strategic decisions.
Hough and White (2003)	400 decisions	Simulation	ANOVA, correlations and logistics regression	5A, 2A, 7A	Environmental dynamism moderates the relationship between rational decision making and decision quality.
Hough and Ogilvie (2005)	749 Executives	Simulation	SEM	5A, 7A	Cognitive style influences decision outcomes.

(Continued)

TABLE 2.1 (*Continued*)

Author(s)	Sample	Design/Sources of Information	Analyses	Linkage(s)	Main Findings
Khatri and Ng (2000)	221 US companies drawn from three sectors (computers, banks and utilities)	Survey research, cross-sectional, subjective measure of performance	ANOVA and Regression Analyses	5B, 2B, 7B	A positive relationship exists between intuition and firm performance in an unstable environment and a negative in a stable one.
Kim and Mauborgne (1998)	Interviews with 48 senior executives from 8 firms (round 1).	Qualitative deign	Content analysis	4, 5A	A sense of procedural justice among the team enhances the right execution of strategic decisions.
Martinsons and Davison (2007)	133 Americans, 82 Japanese and 88 Chinese top managers.	Multi-method (questionnaires and interviews), cross-sectional	Pairwise t-tests	1B	Executives from the three countries have distinct decision-making styles.
Miller (2008)	79 US firms from various industries	Survey research, cross-sectional, multiple respondents, performance is measured with archival data	Multiple Regression	5B, 2B	In nonturbulent environments comprehensiveness and performance exhibit an inverted U-shaped relationship, while in turbulent environments there is appositive relationship that is concave downward based on diminishing effects.
Miller et al. (2004)	As that of Hickson et al. (2003)	As that of Hickson et al. (2003)	PCA and Correlations	2A, 4, 6	Managerial experience and organizational context (structure, culture) influence the successful implementation of strategic decisions.

Study	Sample	Research design	Analysis		Findings
Miller *et al.* (1998)	Study 1: 38 CEOs of USA firms operating in various industries. Study 2: 108 CEOs from hospitals in Texas. Study 3: TMT responses for 71 companies operating in various industries in the USA	Survey research, cross-sectional	Multiple Regression	1B, 5B	Comprehensiveness and extensiveness of strategic planning are negatively related to Top Management Team cognitive diversity. Firm performance is positively related to both comprehensiveness and strategic planning. Also, an indirect relationship exists between executive diversity and firm performance.
Mueller *et al.* (2007)	42 undiversified US manufacturing firms	Survey research, cross-sectional, multiple respondents	Hierarchical Regression	5B, 2B, 7B	The elements of rationality are related to firm performance (ROA). Environmental dynamism moderates this relationship.
Nutt (1998a)	376 Strategic Decisions in US and Canadian firms	Field study, longitudinal, multi-method, multiple respondents	Duncan Test, Chi-Square	6	4 distinct implementation approaches (i.e. intervention, participation, persuasion and edict). The first two seem to lead to more successful decisions than the last two.

(Continued)

TABLE 2.1 (*Continued*)

Author(s)	Sample	Design/Sources of Information	Analyses	Linkage(s)	Main Findings
Nutt (1998b)	317 Strategic Decisions in US and Canadian firms	Field study, longitudinal, multi-method, multiple respondents	ANOVA, Duncan Test	5A	Political tactics although rarely used are quite effective. Judgmental tactics (intuitive) have the poorest success record. Analytical tactics are most widely used and successful in most of the cases.
Nutt (2000a)	376 Strategic Decisions in US and Canadian firms	Field study, longitudinal, multi-method, multiple respondents	ANOVA, Duncan Test	1A	Public, private and third sector organizations follow different tactics to uncover alternatives.
Nutt (2000b)	As that of Nutt (1998b)	As that of Nutt (1998b)	Multiple Regression and Duncan Test	5A, 2A	Decision makers use nine tactics (e.g. bargaining, judgment, analysis) to uncover alternatives.
Nutt (2005)	As that of Nutt (2000a)	As that of Nutt (2000a)	ANOVA, MANOVA	5A	A rational, goal-oriented search is more apt to produce more successful outcomes.
Nutt (2007)	As that of Nutt (2000a)	As that of Nutt (2000a)	ANOVA	5A	Performance Gapping and Premising influence the search approach that managers use to uncover alternatives.

Nutt (2008)	202 Strategic Decisions in US and Canadian firms	Field study, longitudinal, multi-method, multiple respondents	ANOVA, MANOVA	5A, 7A	Controlling for context and content (type of decision), discovery processes lead to more successful strategic decisions than idea imposition, redevelopment, and emergent opportunity processes.
Nooraie (2008)	44 firms operating in Malaysia	Survey research, cross-sectional	Hierarchical Regression	5A, 1A	Rationality mediates the relationship between decision magnitude of impact and decision satisfaction. There is a positive relationship between decision magnitude of impact and rationality.
Olson, Bao, and Parayitam (2007)	252 Chinese managers	Survey research, multiple TMT responses	Hierarchical Regression	2A, 5A	Cognitive diversity has a negative relationship with decision commitment and quality. This relationship is moderated by affect-based and cognition-based trust.
Olson, Parayitam, and Yongjian (2007)	85 Top Management Teams from US hospitals	Survey research	CFA and SEM	2A, 5A	Cognitive diversity has a positive relationship with task conflict. Task conflict mediates the relationship between cognitive diversity and decision outcomes.

(Continued)

TABLE 2.1 (*Continued*)

Author(s)	Sample	Design/Sources of Information	Analyses	Linkage(s)	Main Findings
Papadakis (2006)	107 Strategic Decisions from 59 manufacturing firms operating in Greece	Field study, cross-sectional, multiple sources	Hierarchical Regression	1A	Broader context is more influential than the characteristics of the CEO. CEO's demographic characteristics appear to influence some process characteristics, while personality characteristics exert no influence.
Papadakis and Barwise (2002)	As that of Papadakis *et al.* (1998)	As that of Papadakis *et al.* (1998)	Hierarchical Regression	1A	TMT and CEO influence the strategic decision-making processes, but the former has more influence.
Papadakis *et al.* (1999)	A Greek chemical firm	Qualitative, longitudinal	Content analysis	1A	The categorization of an issue (i.e. crisis, opportunity) influences the processes followed.
Papadakis *et al.* (1998)	70 Strategic Decisions from 38 manufacturing firms operating in Greece	Field study, cross-sectional, multiple sources	Multiple Regression and PCA	1A	Decision processes are shaped by multiple factors, though decision-specific characteristics have the most important influence.

Study	Sample	Methodology	Analysis	Hypotheses	Findings
Papadakis (1998)	As that of Papadakis et al. (1998)	As that of Papadakis et al. (1998), both objective and subjective measures of performance	Correlations	1A	Long-term performance is related more to 'structural' characteristics of SD processes (rationality, financial reporting) while short-term performance is related to more 'behavioral' characteristics of SDs.
Sadler-Smith (2004)	141 firms operating in the UK	Survey research, cross-sectional, performance is measured with archival data	Correlations, Hierarchical Regression	5B, 2B, 7B	Intuition is positively related to firm performance. Environmental instability does not moderate this relationship.
Simons et al. (1999)	57 Top Management Teams from 57 electronic components manufacturing US firms	Survey research, multiple TMT responses	Hierarchical Regression	5B	Comprehensiveness mediates the interactive effects of diversity and debate on firm performance.
Walter et al. (2008)	106 strategic alliances from high-technology US firms	Survey research, cross-sectional	CFA for scales and Multiple Regression	5A, 2A, 7A	The relationship between alliance performance and processes (rationality, openness, recursiveness) is moderated by micro political context.

(*Continued*)

TABLE 2.1 (Continued)

Author(s)	Sample	Design/Sources of Information	Analyses	Linkage(s)	Main Findings
Walters and Bhuian (2004)	89 acute-care hospitals operating in the USA	Survey research, cross-sectional, objective and subjective measures of performance	SEM	10, 11, 2B, 5B, 7B	Environmental dynamism positively moderates the relationship between comprehensiveness and performance and hybrid strategy and performance.

Note: Explanation of the linkage(s)

Linkage 1A: Context influences on the process of making strategic decisions (decision level)
Linkage 1B: Context influences on the process of making strategic decisions (organizational level)
Linkage 2A: Context influences on the success of strategic decisions (decision level)
Linkage 2B: Context influences on organizational performance (organizational level)
Linkage 3: Context influences on implementation
Linkage 4: The relationship between formulation and implementation
Linkage 5A: Process influences on the success of strategic decisions (decision level)
Linkage 5B: Process influences on organizational performance (organizational level)
Linkage 6: Implementation influences on outcomes (organizational and decision level)
Linkage 7A: Moderating effects of context variables on the relationship between process and decision success
Linkage 7B: Moderating effects of context variables on the relationship between process and organizational performance
Linkage 8: The relationship between process and content
Linkage 9: The relationship between decision process outcomes and organizational performance
Linkage 10: Content influences on organizational performance
Linkage 11: Moderating effects of context variables on the relationship between content and outcomes (organizational and decision level)
Linkage 12: The relationship between the characteristics of the strategy process

This situation has changed dramatically. More than half of the studies we reviewed (24 out of the 46) have included either economic or process outcomes as a dependent variable. Research on SD outcomes can be classified into two sub-streams.

In the first sub-stream, researchers use the whole organization as their unit of analysis (e.g. Khatri and Ng, 2000; Goll and Rasheed, 2005; Mueller, Mone, and Barker, 2007; Miller, 2008) and examine whether there is a relationship between average SDM processes and firm performance. There is now convincing evidence that this relationship exists when organizations employ either rational (Goll and Sambharya, 1998; Goll and Rasheed, 2005; Mueller *et al.*, 2007) or intuitive processes (Khatri and Ng, 2000). In broad terms, more rational processes lead to more favorable outcomes, but this relationship is moderated by environmental variables.

For instance, Goll and Rasheed (2005) in their study of 159 US manufacturing firms found that the positive association between rational decision making and firm performance was stronger in more munificent (high growth industries in initial stages of industry evolution) environments. Mueller *et al.* (2007) and Miller (2008) have argued along similar lines regarding the moderating effects of other environmental variables, such as dynamism and instability respectively, on the relationship between rational decision making and firm performance. Similar moderating effects have been found in organizations that employ more intuitive SDM processes. In particular, Khatri and Ng (2000) found that intuition was positively related to organizational performance in an unstable environment and negatively in a stable one. In the same vein, the degree of environmental technological sophistication and the organization structure have been found to have an impact on the relationship between managers' decision-making styles (technocratic or intuitive) and firm performance (Covin, Slevin, and Heeley, 2001; Sadler-Smith, 2004).

In the second sub-stream of this research, we encounter studies using individual decisions as their unit of analysis (e.g. Olson, Bao, and Parayitam, 2007; Olson, Parayitam, and Yongjian, 2007; Elbanna and Child, 2007b; Nooraie, 2008). This sub-stream has grown at a torrid pace since 1997. Previously, only a few studies had measured the effects of processes on outcomes (Judge and Miller, 1991; Wally and Baum, 1994; Amason, 1996; Dean and Sharfman, 1996). This increase may have been encouraged by the recommendations of past reviews (Rajagopalan *et al.*, 1993; Papadakis and Barwise, 1997) and by the fact that, even within the same organization, the process may differ from one decision to another (Papadakis and Lioukas, 1996; Elbanna, 2006). Hence, it may be more valid to focus on individual decisions. Studies within this sub-stream assume that: (a) different processes lead to different choices and (b) different choices lead to different outcomes (Dean and Sharfman, 1996: 369).

The majority of these studies confirm that the processes followed during a specific SD do affect outcomes such as decision quality (Hough and White, 2003; Olson, Bao, and Yogjian, 2007; Olson, Parayitam, and Yongjian, 2007), decision effectiveness and efficiency (Elbanna and Child, 2007b; Nutt, 2008), decision pace (Baum and Wally, 2003; Daniel, 2005), decision commitment (Olson Bao, and Yogjian, 2007; Hough and White, 2003; Olson, Parayitam, and Yongjian, 2007), new product performance (Atuahene-Gima and Li, 2004), satisfaction with the decision (Nooraie, 2008), timeliness, value, (Nutt, 1998b, 2000b, 2005), and that environmental context acts as a moderator on these relationships.

For example, Nutt (2005) in a sample of 376 strategic, nonroutine decisions attempted to discover the search approaches that managers use to uncover solutions ideas and link them with indicators of success. Results indicated that a rational, goal-oriented search approach tends to lead to more successful outcomes. Two years later, Nutt (2007) expanded this research and tried to uncover a number of intelligence gathering techniques, with results showing that 'performance gapping' and 'premising' are activities that influence the search approach that managers use to uncover alternatives. Hough and White (2003) in a simulated environment found a positive relationship between rationality and decision quality and that this relationship was contingent upon environmental dynamism. Similarly, Atuahene-Gima and Li (2004) examined 373 Chinese firms involved in technological ventures and found that the relationship between strategic decision comprehensiveness and new product performance was moderated negatively by technology uncertainty and positively by demand uncertainty. In a recent Malaysian study, Nooraie (2008) found that rationality mediated the relationship between decision magnitude of impact and decision quality.

The role of the broader context as a moderator in the relationship between decision processes and outcomes is further shown in a sophisticated study by (Elbanna and Child, 2007b) of 169 SDs in Egyptian manufacturing firms. Elbanna and Child adopted an integrative framework to explore the effects of decision process characteristics on decision effectiveness. Their model comprised three SDM process variables (procedural rationality, political behavior, intuition), seven moderating variables covering the environment (uncertainty, hostility), organization (size, past performance), decision characteristics (importance, uncertainty, and motive), and with SD effectiveness as a performance variable. Results suggest that rational and political processes had more influence on outcomes than intuition and that SD effectiveness was both context- and process-specific. To this study, we should add the results of another more recent and very ambitious research (Nutt, 2008), which has adopted an integrative framework taking into account the relationship between process characteristics (idea imposition, discovery, redevelopment, and emergent opportunity), context (importance, urgency, etc.), decision content (type of decision, the eight Hickson types), and decision outcomes (effectiveness, efficiency). According to the author (p. 425): 'Discovery process is more successful than the other three processes no matter what the urgency, importance, resource level, initial support, decision maker level, support or type of decision.' To the best of our knowledge these are the only two studies at the decision level examining the moderating effects of several layers of context on the relationship between multiple process characteristics and outcomes.

Only one of the 46 studies, Baum and Wally (2003), examined the relationship between the two sub-streams of this research, i.e. at both firm and individual decision levels. Baum and Wally's (2003) study of 318 US firms found that decision-making speed mediates the relationship between several context variables (e.g. normalization, centralization, dynamism, and munificence) and organizational performance.

2 Explore the influence of the broader context on SDM processes (Linkages 1A, 1B)

The second substantive priority proposed by Papadakis and Barwise (1997) was the impact of the broader context on SDM processes:

> (i) there has been little research on the influence of broader context on SDM, (ii) most of the studies focus on a limited number of antecedents and ignore other important sources of influence on SDM ... (iii) most of the studies focus on just one characteristic of the process, ... despite the fact that SDM is multidimensional, and (iv) much of the evidence is contradictory and far from establishing a coherent theory. (p. 291)

Several of the studies in Table 2.1 address these concerns by exploring the relationships between context variables and SDM processes. Most adopt a specific context perspective such as the decision-making perspective (Nooraie, 2008), the strategic or management choice perspective (Miller, Burke, and Glick, 1998; Papadakis and Barwise, 2002; Goll and Rasheed, 2005; Papadakis, 2006), the environmental determinism perspective (e.g. Atuahene-Gima and Murray, 2004), or the firm characteristics perspective (Brouthers, Andriessen, and Nicolaes, 1998; Nutt, 2000a). We now have consistent evidence of a positive relationship between rationality and both decision magnitude of impact (Papadakis *et al.*, 1998; Elbanna and Child, 2007a; Nooraie, 2008) and past performance (Papadakis, 1998; Elbanna and Child, 2007a). These represent the decision-making and firm characteristics perspectives respectively. For the environmental determinism perspective, however, the results to date have been contradictory (Elbanna and Child, 2007a; Papadakis *et al.*, 1998).

In contrast to these studies, which adopt a single perspective on context, others have used more integrative models (Elbanna and Child, 2007a; Brouthers *et al.*, 2000; 1998; Papadakis *et al.*, 1998). Papadakis *et al.* (1998) studied 70 SDs in 38 manufacturing firms and showed that process characteristics (comprehensiveness, financial reporting, decentralization, politicization, formalization, lateral communication, and problem-solving dimensions) were shaped by a multiplicity of external, internal, top management, and – especially – decision-specific variables. Brouthers *et al.* (2000), in a study of 42 Dutch financial institutions, found that environmental factors (turbulence, entrepreneurial style, organization structure), managerial characteristics (age, educational level, work experience), and their interactions accounted for much of the variation in SDM processes. Finally, Elbanna and Child (2007a) found that decision, environmental, and firm characteristics all influenced the degree of procedural rationality.

National culture. 'Most research on SDs ... comes from the USA. In an era of increasing globalization, it is important managerially as well as scientifically to investigate how closely these results apply to SDs in other country settings' (Papadakis and Barwise, 1997: 292). The same criticism was made by Schwenk (1995) and Bower (1997). With few exceptions (Hickson, Butler, Cray, Mallory, and Wilson, 1986;

Axeisson, Cray, Mallory, and Wilson, 1991; Carr, 1997; Lu, 1997) virtually all research on SDs had used US data.

This, too, has changed dramatically as SD researchers have become more sensitive to potential national cultural influences on SDM (Elbanna and Child, 2007a). Indeed, 27 out of our 46 core papers include non US data, from both developed countries (Netherlands, Japan, Germany, and Norway) and emerging economies (China, Egypt, Greece, Taiwan, and Malaysia). In one cross-national study, Carr (2005) compared SDM styles in British, US, German, and Japanese manufacturers in the vehicle component industry. SDM styles in the German and Japanese firms differed from those in the USA and Britain. Similarly, Martinsons and Davison (2007) observed contrasting SDM styles among US, Japanese, and Chinese business leaders: the Japanese leaders were more 'behavioral', exhibiting limited interest in data processing and focusing more on intuitive procedures, the Chinese were more 'directive', showing less interest in large-scale data analysis and focusing more on the use of power, while the Americans were more analytical, relying mostly on careful analysis of large volumes of codified data.

Overall, the results to-date from non-US studies suggest that some of the US findings generalize to other cultures while others do not. It may be too soon to find a high-level pattern in these similarities and differences, but the amount of available evidence has already increased greatly over the last 12 years.

Corporate governance structure. Another neglected influence on SDM highlighted by Papadakis and Barwise (1997: 292–293) was the role of corporate governance structure. For instance, there might be many reasons why the type of ownership (public versus private) or control (local versus multinational) might influence SDM processes. This remains a little-researched topic directly addressed by only two of the 46 papers in Table 2.1. Both suggest that ownership and control do indeed influence SDM processes, in line with the much earlier conclusions of Mallory *et al.* (1983) who found systematic differences between the SDM processes of local British firms versus the British subsidiaries of non UK multinationals. In the first of the more recent papers, Papadakis *et al.* (1998) found that locally owned Greek firms used less rational SDM processes than did subsidiaries of multinationals. In the other paper, Nutt (2000a) found that public, private, and third sector organizations used different tactics to uncover alternatives.

3 Bridging the gap between strategy process and strategy content (Linkage 8)

As noted in the framework development section, research on strategic management has been divided into content research and process research. Many scholars have criticized this split and urged researchers to consider content and process as complementary perspectives and not as alternatives (Elbanna, 2006) because the process can significantly influence the content (Ketchen *et al.*, 1996) and vice versa (Miller, 1989).

Unfortunately, our review of the evidence suggests that this dichotomy continues to dominate the field. Only two of our 46 core studies were concerned with strategy content as well as process. In the first, Walters and Bhuian (2004) explored the influence of process (comprehensiveness) and content (hybrid strategies) on organizational performance taking into account two context variables (environmental dynamism and organization structure) in the acute-care hospital industry. Results showed that comprehensiveness and hybrid strategies were related to performance with dynamism moderating this relationship. However, structure was found to moderate the process-performance and the content-performance relationships only when performance was measured subjectively. Even this study did not directly examine the relationship between process and content (linkage 8).

The second study dealing with strategy process and content (at the corporate level only) is that of Goll and Sambharya (1998), who used data from 92 large US manufacturers. In their words (p. 488) '[T]he more top management emphasizes rational decision making, the more the firm diversifies, particularly into unrelated industries.'

4 Bringing the CEO and top management team into SD research (Linkages 1A and 1B)

Since the publication of Hambrick and Mason's (1984) seminal paper on 'upper echelons' the characteristics of top management teams (TMTs) have received a central role in management research (refer to Hodgkinson and Sparrow, 2002; Carpenter *et al.*, 2004; Lohrke *et al.*, 2004, for analytical reviews on Top Management Teams). Nevertheless, by the late 1990s, there had been little empirical work on the link between top management characteristics and SDM processes (Rajagopalan *et al.*, 1993; Bower, 1997; Papadakis and Barwise, 1997). Several theoretical questions remained unexplored. Does this relationship exist in reality? How much do the CEO and the TMT matter in SDM, relative to each other and to the broader context?

Fortunately, within the past 12 years several studies have dealt with these questions (e.g. Miller *et al.*, 1998; Brouthers, Brouthers, and Werner, 2000; Papadakis and Barwise, 2002; Goll and Rasheed, 2005; Papadakis, 2006). Miller *et al.* (1998) concluded that cognitive diversity within the TMT exerts a negative influence on the degree of comprehensiveness and the extensiveness of strategic planning. Papadakis and Barwise (2002) explored the influence of both CEO and TMT characteristics on the SDM process. The results suggested that (a) the characteristics of both the CEO and the TMT mattered, but the CEO had more influence and (b) the broader context of SDs is more influential than either the CEO or the TMT.

In an extension of this study, Papadakis (2006) investigated whether the personality and demographic characteristics of the CEO have more impact than the broader context in shaping the SDM process. Again, results showed that the broader context was more influential than the CEO's characteristics. Demographic characteristics (tenure, education) did influence several process variables (e.g. rationality, politicization) but personality characteristics (need for achievement, risk propensity, locus of control) had no measurable effect. These results differ from those of Brouthers *et al.* (2000), who found that SD processes were influenced less by environmental factors than by decision makers' characteristics. These contradictory results show that more research is needed with respect to the impact of TMT characteristics on SDM processes.

5 Three emergent themes: learning, implementation, and information systems

Adaptiveness and organizational learning.   Papadakis and Barwise (1997) also noted three emergent themes. The first was the role of improvisation in SDM. Eisenhardt (1997) argued that the fundamental paradigms of SDM research (rationality, power and politics, and the garbage can model) had greatly increased our understanding of decision making but each had its own limitations. She recommended that researchers move towards other paradigms, incorporating notions such as insight, intuition, and emotion. She then went a step further, likening a firm to a jazz band where members sometimes need to improvise in order to improve performance. Although the recent literature has considered intuition, emotion, and insight, the concept of improvisation – and more generally, organizational learning – remains largely unexplored.

Implementation (linkages 3, 4, 6).   The second emergent theme identified by Papadakis and Barwise (1997) was implementation. Researchers have long recognized that strategy process research ought to be concerned with both the formulation and implementation of a decision. In an early review of strategy process research, Huff and Reger (1987) grouped process studies into nine topics. The first four referred to formulation issues, the next four to implementation issues, while the ninth referred to integrative research which simultaneously explores both formulation and implementation. Later reviews echoed Huff and Reger's recommendation for such integrative research incorporating implementation (see for example Blair and Boal, 1991; Schwenk, 1995; Hutzschenreuter and Kleindienst, 2006).

However, despite these and other calls for research on implementation (e.g. Nutt, 1999; Pettigrew, 2003; Wilson, 2003), researchers have continued to be mainly preoccupied with formulation issues. Of the 46 papers in this review, only six address implementation issues. These studies test three linkages of our model. The first of these linkages concerns the relationship between formulation and implementation (linkage 4). Four studies have dealt with this relationship, providing tentative evidence of an association between formulation and implementation. Gottschalk (1999), using Norwegian data, found that prior planning tended to facilitate implementation. However, other evidence suggests that managerial planning does not ensure implementation success, as shown in a longitudinal study of 55 decisions in UK firms (Hickson, Miller, and Wilson, 2003; Miller, Wilson, and Hickson, 2004). Furthermore, Collier, Fischwick, and Floyd (2004) in a large research of 6394 middle managers, found that involvement in strategy making was positively correlated with rationality and negatively with political behavior.

The second linkage tested is that of the relationship between the implementation process and the outcomes (linkage 6). Nutt (1998a) identified four distinct implementation approaches (i.e. intervention, participation, persuasion, and edict). The first two were found to lead to more successful decisions than the last two. Similarly, Hickson *et al.* (2003) identified two distinct approaches to implementation management, namely the *Experience-based approach* and the *Readiness-based approach.* The authors argued that, while following either of these approaches can improve performance, the approach most likely to be successful was a dual strategy which combined the two.

Finally, Brenes *et al.* (2008) used an integrative framework to explore three linkages in our model (linkages 3, 4, 6). Results suggested that the successful implementation of business strategy was dependent on multiple factors referring to both process (e.g. strategy formulation, systematic execution) and context (CEO leadership and corporate governance).

Information systems (linkages 1A, 2A). The last emergent theme identified by Papadakis and Barwise (1997) was the impact of information systems on SDM. In one of the few studies, Molloy and Schwenk (1995) studied eight strategic decisions involving the use of information technology (IT), concluding that IT can improve both the efficiency and the effectiveness of the SDM process. However, other evidence appears to contradict this conclusion. Chou and Dyson (1998), using a sample of 80 SDs by Taiwanese enterprises, explored the relationship between the degree of IT intensity, process characteristics (e.g. duration, interaction, involvement), and outcomes (effectiveness). Results indicated that IT intensity was *negatively* associated with the effectiveness of SDs and with interaction and involvement. These contradictory results indicate that further research is required with respect to the impact of IT on SDs.

RESEARCH METHODS

As well as discussing the substantive issues in research on SDs, Papadakis and Barwise (1997) also recommended a number of methodological developments under the following headings:

- ◆ Large-sample field research with rigorous testing
- ◆ Longitudinal research
- ◆ Laboratory research
- ◆ Common terminology
- ◆ Careful operationalization and measurement of constructs
- ◆ Validation of retrospective data.

In the following paragraphs we review the literature with respect to each of these methodological issues.

1. Need for large-sample field research with rigorous testing. The first methodological priority suggested was that future research on SDs should include the building and sharing of some *large-sample databases.* A tactic of this kind could give researchers the benefit of both rigor (through larger samples) and substance (through wider, multivariate description, including outcomes) and allow the development and testing of more integrated theory. In this way, future researchers could use the already existing large databases (e.g. those collected by Nutt, Dean, or the Bradford studies) and extend them. For instance, a doctoral candidate could use an existing research database that includes context and SDM process variables and conduct further research on some of the same companies by collecting further data on implementation and outcomes. A successful example in the literature is that of Susan Miller who cooperated with two members from the initial Bradford research team (Hickson and Wilson), conducted further research in 55 of the 150 companies from the original Bradford study (Hickson *et al.*, 1986), and measured implementation characteristics and the success of strategic decisions (Miller *et al.*, 2004). Such efforts are extremely demanding but offer a powerful way of addressing the complexity of SDM with a relatively large sample and, therefore, statistically significant conclusions.

2. Longitudinal research. Papadakis and Barwise (1997) noted that most of SDM research was cross-sectional, limiting our ability to draw causal inferences or explore how SD processes change and develop over time. This continues to be the case. Eighty per cent of the studies listed in Table 2.1 (36 out of 46) use cross-sectional data. But to understand the intertwined relationships between context, decision-making processes, implementation, content, and outcomes we need *longitudinal research designs* (Van De Ven, 1992; Elbanna, 2006). We share Pettigrew's (2003: 302, 309) view that to understand how decision processes unfold over time someone should look in the same way as a historian and study the connections between past, present, and future. Therefore, we believe that longitudinal studies represent a fruitful area of research.

3. Laboratory research. Because of the difficulty of collecting longitudinal data on SDM with a significant sample size, as well as the near impossibility of experimentally controlling any of the variables with real-world SDs, some researchers in the past 11 years have turned to *laboratory research* (e.g. Hough and White, 2003; Hough and Ogilivie, 2005). This also avoids a number of measurement problems associated with survey methods, provides the opportunity to examine a large number of issues, allows for the controlled manipulation of the variables, and may be used for variables which cannot be easily accessed in the field such as the characteristics of the decision process (Hough and Ogilivie, 2005; Papadakis and Barwise, 1997; Schwenk, 1995). However, as Table 2.1 indicates, laboratory research continues to be rare within the SD field.

4. Adoption of a common terminology. It has been argued that SDM research is in need of a common terminology (Papadakis and Barwise, 1997; Bower, 1997). An example within the SD research is that of the conflict literature, where prominent researchers have used alternative terms to describe the same construct:

- Cognitive versus affective conflict (Amason and Sapienza, 1997)
- Positive versus negative conflict (Schwenk, 1997)

◆ Substantive versus interpersonal conflict (Eisenhardt *et al.*, 1997)
◆ Functional versus dysfunctional conflict (Amason, 1996).

Until today, we are not aware if a common terminology has emerged in this specific area. With the exception of one study (Olson, Parayitam, and Yongjian, 2007) dealing with conflict issues in the past 11 years, research has not focused on its potential role in strategic decision making. Therefore, we cannot argue if the lack of common terminology is a smaller or a bigger issue today.

5. Careful operationalization and measurement of constructs.   Another issue raised by Papadakis and Barwise (1997) is that research on SDs suffered from a plethora of definitions and operationalizations. Unfortunately, this still holds true. The most notable example is that of rationality, which is widely used in the SD literature but defined and measured in numerous ways (Table 2.2). Fredrickson and his colleagues (e.g. Fredrickson, 1984; Fredrickson and Mitchell, 1984; Fredrickson and Iaquinto, 1989) and Miller (2008; Miller *et al.*, 1998) conceptualize rationality as comprehensiveness. Langley (1989) and Mueller *et al.* (2007) operationalize it as formal analysis. Miller and Friesen (1983) and Priem *et al.* (1995) operationalize it as scanning, analysis, and planning. These different operationalizations of rationality may explain some of the contradictory results on the impact of rationality on firm performance (Mueller *et al.*, 2007; Elbanna, 2006; Priem *et al.*, 1995).

A somewhat different methodological issue suggested by the two authors in their previous review is that of construct validity and reliability. They also stressed the importance of reporting the necessary reliability and validity tests. We are of the opinion that SD research has made some progress with respect to reliability and validity issues.

A common technique for evaluating construct validity in the SD literature has been exploratory factor analysis (Elbanna and Child, 2007a, 2007b; Hickson *et al.*, 2003; Chou and Dyson, 1998; Papadakis *et al.*, 1998). We argue that exploratory factor analysis (EFA) techniques such as principal component and factor analysis are of great value in testing validity issues. However, confirmatory factor analysis (CFA) (e.g. Spanos and Lioukas, 2001: 930) has the advantage of allowing hypothesis testing regarding the construct validity of a set of measures, leading to a stricter and more objective interpretation of validity than does EFA. Therefore, we encourage researchers to proceed to confirmatory factor analysis for testing their measurement scales. Lately, some studies (Baum and Wally, 2003; Walters and Bhuian, 2004; Olson, Parayitam, and Yongjian, 2007; Walter, Lechner, and Kellermanns, 2008) within the SD literature have conducted CFA analysis.

6. Validation of retrospective data and minimization of common method bias.   Two final methodology issues were the validation of retrospective data and the minimization of common method bias.

Most of the studies in Table 2.1 rely on managers' recall of past events. However, studies based on participant recall are known to suffer from various limitations (Kumar, Stern, and Anderson, 1993). Several tactics are available to reduce these

TABLE 2.2 Constructs, conceptualizations, and studies of rationality

Scale developed by:	Construct of rationality	Conceptualization	Examples of studies using this scale
Dean and Sharfman	Procedural rationality	The extent to which the decision process involves the collection of information relevant to the decision and the reliance upon analysis of this information in making the choice	Dean and Sharfman (1993); Dean and Sharfman (1996); Sharfman and Dean (1997); Elbanna and Child (2007a, 2007b) Walker et al. (2007); Elbanna and Younies (2008)
Fredrickson	Comprehensiveness	The extent to which organizations attempt to be exhaustive or inclusive in making and integrating strategic decisions	Fredrickson (1984, 1985); Fredrickson and Mitchell (1984) Fredrickson and Iaquinto (1989) Miller et al. (1998, 2008); Papadakis et al. (1998); Papadakis (1998, 2006); Papadakis and Barwise (2002); Atuahene-Gima and Li (2004); Atuahene-Gima and Murray (2004)
Goll and colleagues	Rational decision making	The extent to which the company explicitly emphasizes rational decision making	Goll and Sambharya (1998); Goll and Rasheed (2005)

Hough and colleagues	Rational-comprehensive decision making, captured by availability and pervasiveness	Availability captures the degree to which the available cues were known by the team when they made their decision. Pervasiveness assesses to what extent all team members were informed of the available information	Hough and Ogilvie (2005); Hough and White (2003)
Kukalls	Planning comprehensiveness	The completeness of the strategic planning process and the number of areas in which strategic planning is often applied	Kukalls (1991)
Langley	Formal analysis	Written documents reporting the results of some systematic study of a specific use	Langley (1989); Mueller *et al.* (2007)
Miller	Strategy making rationality	Perception's of the firms existing scanning, analysis, and planning processes	Miller and Friesen, (1983); Priem *et al.* (1995); Walters and Bhuiar (2004)

Note: Ideas for the creation of this table were taken from Elbanna (2006). The table is updated with more recent information and adapted to the needs of the current study.

limitations, such as the study of archival records documenting the process, the selection of recent decisions, interviewing only the managers who were most involved with the decision, and cross-checking the data against others managers' recollections. (Huber and Power, 1985; Kumar *et al.*, 1993).

Another major challenge is to minimize common method bias. Several procedures have been suggested to control for this type of bias (refer to Podsakoff, MacKenzie, Lee, and Podsakoff, 2003, for an overview). First, where possible, researchers should aim to collect data on different variables – especially independent and dependent variables – from different sources. For instance, a researcher interested in the relationship between process and performance might obtain the measures of processes through a questionnaire and the measures of performance through archival information. Goll and Rasheed (2005) and Covin *et al.* (2001) have used this method. Second, the items used in the analysis need to be distributed throughout a lengthy questionnaire and scale anchors should be reversed in several places so as to reduce and compensate for the development of response patterns. Third, a statistical test known as Harman's one factor test can be employed (Podsakoff *et al.*, 2003). Finally, it has often been argued that relying on a single respondent per firm can be problematic as his or her responses may be subject to individual bias. Therefore, whenever possible, the use of multiple respondents is recommended (Miller, 2008; Mueller *et al.*, 2007; Atuahene-Gima and Li, 2004).

THE WAY FORWARD

The above review shows that over the last 12 years researchers have accumulated significant knowledge with respect to several substantive aspects of strategic decisions. However, it has also identified several areas that remain unexplored – results to date are either very limited or contradictory. In the following paragraphs, we propose a set of substantive priorities to be addressed over the next few years. We then propose a similar set of priorities for the development of research methods, reflecting the comments on methodology in the final sections of the earlier review by Papadakis and Barwise (1997).

Substantive priorities

1. Tradeoffs between process characteristics and the effects of all aspects of context on the relationship between processes and outcomes. Several studies since 1997 have explored the links between process characteristics and outcomes, at either the decision or the organizational level. Within this stream of research we identify three major opportunities.

The first lies in the *examination of process from the perspective of multiple criteria*. The vast majority of the studies have examined the effects on outcomes of a single characteristic of processes such as rationality (e.g. Miller, 2008; Goll and Rasheed, 2005) or intuition (e.g. Khatri and Ng, 2000). Given that we now have ample evidence that process is multidimensional (Dean and Sharfman, 1993; Elbanna and

Younies, 2008), we feel that future researchers need to move away from these one-dimensional perspectives which provide a very partial understanding of a complex process (Chakravarthy and White, 2002). A related issue is the likely complementarity of rationality and intuition (Elbanna and Child, 2007b). Simon (1987) and Pondy (1987) noted that effective organizations need a combination of both rational and intuitive decision-making processes. Therefore, a question remains as to whether, or under which conditions, the combination of intuitive synthesis and rational analysis is better than using either rational analysis or intuitive synthesis alone (Khatri and Ng, 2000: 79). This combination deserves further empirical investigation as Elbanna and Child (2007b: 450) stress.

The second opportunity within the process-outcome relationship is that of the possible *moderating effects of the various aspects of context*. Several researchers have recently started to explore the moderating effects of context but, with only two exceptions (Covin *et al.*, 2001; Elbanna and Child, 2007b), they all focus on specific aspects of the external market environment such as *munificence* (Goll and Rasheed, 2005), *instability* (Sadler-Smith, 2004; Khatri and Ng, 2000), *dynamism* (Hough and White, 2003; Walters and Bhuian, 2004), and *uncertainty* (Atuahene-Gima and Li, 2004). It may be that the internal organizational environment or the characteristics of top management are equally important moderators. More research is needed.

Finally, the third research opportunity within the process-outcome stream refers to the *relationship between decision outcomes and organizational performance* (linkage 9 in the model). Previously, we referred to one study (Baum and Wally, 2003) which touched on aspects of this relationship. Forbes (2007) calls for future researchers to study the relationship between decision quality and firm performance. He also warns (p. 366) that 'the link between decision quality and firm performance is likely to be subject to moderating effects that do not necessarily apply to the link between comprehensiveness and decision quality.' Such variables could be industry structure or government regulation. We agree.

2. *The overall as well as the individual impact of context variables on SDM processes.*   In our review we referred to various papers which examine context influences on the SDM process and three which have adopted more integrative models (Elbanna and Child, 2007a; Brouthers *et al.*, 2000; Papadakis *et al.*, 1998). In the first, Elbanna and Child (2007a) examined the overall impact of decision, environment, and firm characteristics on the rationality of SDM. In the second, Brouthers *et al.* (2000) tested the effect of environmental factors and managers' characteristics as well as their interaction on strategic aggressiveness, while in the third, Papadakis *et al.* (1998) explored the individual effects of variables coming from four layers of context on several characteristics of the decision process. What is still missing in the literature is a study examining *both the individual and the overall impact of different perspectives (as well as their interaction) on multiple process characteristics* such as rationality, intuition, and political behavior.

A second research opportunity is related to *the influence of context on intuitive decision making*. While many authors argue that executives rely on intuition when making decisions (Burke and Miller, 1999; Khatri and Ng, 2000; Miller and

Ireland, 2005), there exists no research examining the effect of context variables on intuition.

3. The limitations of demography research ('black box' criticism).   Our review identified three studies dealing with the impact of top management team demographic diversity on SDM processes within the past 12 years (Brouthers *et al.*, 2000; Papadakis and Barwise, 2002; Goll and Rasheed, 2005). Lately, TMT demography research has received huge criticism (see for example Pettigrew, 1992; Lawrence, 1997; Priem, Lyon, and Dess, 1999). The most serious critique, known as the 'black box' criticism, is that it hypothesizes that demographic diversity is a proxy of cognitive diversity and that it has an indirect effect on process or outcomes through cognitive diversity. Kilduff, Angelmar, and Mehra (2000) showed that this assumption may be invalid. Using a simulated environment with 35 teams, they found no relationship between demographic and cognitive diversity. Future research should therefore take the 'black box' criticism into account. It would be particularly interesting to see in a single study which aspect of top management diversity – demographic, cognitive, or experiential – has most influence on SDM.

4. National context.   Previously, we recognized in our review that although the earlier literature on SDs came overwhelmingly from the USA, many studies from the last 12 years use data from both developed and developing countries. In a globalizing world economy, this is a welcome trend. What has not yet emerged is any cross-cultural research on possible *systematic patterns in the similarities and differences of SDM in different countries*, i.e. what seems to be universal and what is more culture-specific and, for the latter, how these differences might relate to other, more general, research on cultural differences.

5. Service organizations.   Another potential contextual factor begging for attention is that of organization type, notably the need for *more research on service organizations*. In the developed economies, services now account for a majority of businesses and virtually all public and nonprofit organizations yet Table 2.1 shows that, with only a few exceptions (Brouthers *et al.*, 2000; Walters and Bhuian, 2004), research on SDs is still largely about manufacturing firms. The same holds for other strategy process studies as noted by Hutzschenreuter and Kleindienst (2006). Are the findings of these studies also applicable to service organizations? Brouthers *et al.* (1998: 135), in the only study directly addressing this issue, argue that small services and manufacturing firms in Netherlands appear to be equally rational and follow similar strategies. What about other process characteristics and outcomes? What about implementation characteristics, given the huge challenge of reliable service delivery? What about public services and nonprofit organizations, which account for a significant proportion of economic activity and employment around the world? We believe that future studies should provide answers to such questions.

6. The synergistic effects of context, process, and content on outcomes.   One of Papadakis and Barwise's (1997) substantive priorities was the *bridging of content and process research*. Our literature review highlighted that this is still under-explored. Process and content streams of research continue to develop independently of one another, despite several researchers having emphasized that they are complementary (Pettigrew and Whip, 1991; Maritan and Schendel, 1997; Elbanna, 2006). As Chakravarthy and White (2002: 182) accurately put it 'Unfortunately, in their preoccupation with the journey, process researchers too often lose track of the destination, the strategy outcome.'

Ketchen *et al.* (1996) provide empirical support to the argument that the distinction between strategy process and strategy content has limited the ability of strategic management research to explain the determinants of organizational performance.

7. Putting implementation at the centre of SD research.   Our literature review confirms that *research on implementation* still tends to be seen as inferior to research on formulation (Hutzschenreuter and Kleindienst, 2006). The relatively small number of papers on implementation characteristics makes it hard to draw robust conclusions with respect to several linkages in the model. Several theoretical questions remain unanswered. For instance, what is the relationship between decision-making processes and implementation process characteristics (linkage 4)? How does the broader context affect implementation characteristics (linkage 3)? How do implementation characteristics influence outcomes, both at the decision and the organizational level (linkage 6)? Dholakia and his colleagues (Dholakia and Bagozzi, 2002; Dholakia, Bagozzi, and Gopinath, 2007) have sought answers to these questions in a consumer research setting. We feel that their research approach could be extended to the SD setting.

In sum, given that half of the decisions in organizations fail (Nutt, 1997) and that the mistakes take place mainly during the implementation phase (Nutt, 1999), studying implementation is not a simple academic recommendation. It is an imperative.

Research methods

1. Need for large-sample field research with rigorous testing and for small-sample inductive studies.   Previously we referred to the need for large-sample field research studies with rigorous testing and discussed a study (Miller *et al.*, 2004) which attempted to conduct further research in a sub-sample of 55 firms of the original Bradford study. We also mentioned that such efforts are welcomed as they can generate significant findings. However, there is a potential limitation with this methodology. This is that managers find it hard to appreciate the importance of these studies for their everyday life. If we assume that one of the ultimate goals of SD research is to provide knowledge of practical value, then future efforts may have to turn to small-sample inductive studies. A study in progress at London Business School examining which type of academic research managers find useful seems to verify the argument that practitioners on average consider small-sample inductive studies as more likely to yield managerially relevant results than large-sample hypothetic-deductive studies published in the same journals. A question remains as to whether these two types of research can be combined in the future.

2. Longitudinal research. Our review of the evidence suggests that the majority of the studies continue to adopt a cross-sectional design. It may be that researchers have largely avoided conducting longitudinal studies due to the serious limitations associated with this type of research (costs in time and resources). We argue that if we want to progress as a field, understand the multiple and intertwined relationships between context, process, content, and outcomes and establish valid causal relationships, we need to turn to longitudinal research.

3. Laboratory research. We argue that future researchers should not abandon this method as we believe that laboratory studies have a role in suggesting and testing possible relationships, and their strengths and weaknesses are complementary to those of other methods. Of course, we should bear in mind some of the limitations associated with this method. The most important limitation of laboratory research is obviously the difficulty of establishing a proper level of external ecological validity (Bryman and Bell, 2003: 44) since the setting is so different from the real-world situation. Additionally, the results need to be interpreted cautiously, especially if the participants are students rather than managers (Schwenk, 1995).

4. Careful operationalization and measurement of constructs. Our review indicated that SD research still suffers from a plethora of definitions and operationalizations. This variety may have kept back our knowledge on SDs. We argue that future studies should exercise particular caution in the operationalization and measurement of their constructs. Additionally, we still stress the need for proper reliability and validity tests. Future studies should continue employing Confirmatory Factor Analysis techniques.

5. Validation of retrospective data and minimization of common method bias. Two issues that continue to be of importance are the validation of retrospective data and the minimization of common method bias. As far as the first is concerned, future researchers should consider tactics such as the study of only recent decisions, the use of archival information documenting the process, and the interviewing of 'key' people with a high degree of involvement with the decision (Huber and Power, 1985; Kumar *et al.*, 1993).

As far as common method bias is concerned, researchers should collect data from different sources (Podsakoff *et al.*, 2003), distribute items through a lengthy questionnaire and use multiple respondents.

6. Consistency between unit of analysis and outcome measures. Another issue is that of the consistency between the unit of analysis and the outcome measure employed (Bell, Bromiley, and Bryson, 1997; Elbanna, 2006). If the focus of the study is on the average organizational decision-making processes (linkage 5B), the researcher should measure organizational outcomes such as ROA, ROS, and organizational effectiveness. If the study is about the success of individual SDs (linkage 5A), then decision outcomes such as effectiveness, quality, and commitment should be employed.

7. Need for more advanced statistical techniques and examination of more complex relationships.   Finally, Table 2.1 shows that the SD literature is still dominated by studies using relatively simple statistical techniques such as correlations, ANOVA, and multiple linear regressions. This is not to suggest that they are of no value, but if we want to progress as a field and examine integrative frameworks that take into account the multiple relationships among context, process, content, and outcomes we need to employ more advanced statistical techniques such as structural equation modeling. SEM allows for a simultaneous analysis of multiple dependent variables and strategic management researchers are starting to use it (Shook *et al.*, 2004).

A related recommendation is the examination of more complex relationships. Traditionally, SD literature has searched for linear relationships between single process characteristics (e.g. comprehensiveness, politicization, centralization) and firm performance. Miller (2008) argues that these relationships may be nonlinear. In his research of 79 US firms, he found an inverted U-shaped relationship between comprehensiveness and performance in non-turbulent environments, while in turbulent environments the relationship was positive but concave because of diminishing returns. Then, the author tries to interpret his findings based on economic theories of information. We argue that similar curvilinear relationships may exist between other process characteristics such as intuition, politicization, and decentralization and believe that more research efforts are needed.

CONCLUSIONS

Twelve years ago, Papadakis and Barwise (1997) argued for integrative research that takes into account context, process, content, and outcomes. We still believe that this typology is required. Our revised wish-list of substantive and methodological priorities for future research on SDs is as follows:

Substantive priorities

1. Consider the tradeoffs between process characteristics and the effects of all layers of context on the relationship between processes and outcomes.
2. Consider the overall as well as the individual impact of context variables on decision-making processes.
3. Consider the limitations of demography research ('black box' criticism).
4. National culture.
5. Research on services firms.
6. Examine the synergistic effects of context, process, and content on outcomes.
7. Put implementation at the centre of SD research.

Methodological priorities

1. Need for large-sample field research with rigorous testing and for small-sample inductive studies.
2. Longitudinal research.
3. Laboratory research.

4. Careful operationalization and measurement of constructs.
5. Validation of retrospective data and minimization of common method bias.
6. Consistency between unit of analysis and outcome measures.
7. Need for more advanced statistical techniques and examination of more complex relationships.

References

Amason, A.C. (1996) Distinguishing the effects of functional and dysfunctional conflict on strategic decision making: Resolving a paradox for top management teams, *Academy of Management Journal*, 39 (1), 123–148.

Amason, A.C., and Sapienza, H.J. (1997) The effects of top management team size and interaction norms on cognitive and affective conflict, *Journal of Management*, 23 (4), 495–516.

Atuahene-Gima, K., and Li, H. (2004) Strategic decision comprehensiveness and new product development outcomes in new technology ventures, *Academy of Management Journal*, 47 (4) 583–597.

Atuahene-Gima, K., and Murray, J.Y. (2004) Antecedents and outcomes of marketing strategy comprehensiveness, *Journal of Marketing*, 68 (4), 33–46.

Axeisson, R., Cray, D., Mallory, G.R., and Wilson, D.C. (1991) Decision style in British and Swedish organizations: A comparative examination of strategic decision making, *British Journal of Management*, 2 (2), 67–79.

Baum, J.R., and Wally, S. (2003) Strategic decision speed and firm performance, *Strategic Management Journal*, 24 (11), 1107–1129.

Bell, G., Bromiley, P., and Bryson, J. (1997) 'Spinning a Complex Web: Links Between Strategic Decision Making Context, Process and Outcome,' in V. Papadakis and P. Barwise (eds) *Strategic Decisions*. Boston: Kluwer Academic Publishers, 163–178.

Blair, J.D., and Boal, K.B. (1991) Strategy formation processes in health care organizations: A context-specific examination of context-free strategy issues, *Journal of Management*, 17 (2), 305–344.

Bower, J.L. (1997) 'Process Research on Strategic Decisions: A Personal Perspective' in V. Papadakis and P. Barwise (eds) *Strategic Decisions*. Boston: Kluwer Academic Publishers, 17–33.

Brenes, E.R., Mena, M., and Molina, G.E. (2008) Key success factors for strategy implementation in Latin America, *Journal of Business Research*, 61, 590–598.

Brouthers, K.D., Andriessen, F., and Nicolaes, I. (1998) Driving blind: Strategic decisionmaking in small companies, *Long Range Planning*, 31 (1), 130–138.

Brouthers, K. D., Brouthers, L. E., and Werner, S. (2000) Influences on strategic decision-making in the Dutch financial services industry, *Journal of Management*, 26 (5), 863–883.

Bryman, A., and Bell, E. (2003) *Business Research Methods*. Oxford: Oxford University Press.

Burke, L.A., and Miller, M.K. (1999) Taking the mystery out of intuitive decision making, *Academy of Management Executive*, 13 (4), 91–99.

Carpenter, M.A., Geletkanycz, M.A., and Sanders, W.G. (2004) Upper echelons research revisited: antecedents, elements, and consequences of top management team composition, *Journal of Management*, 30 (6), 749–778.

Carr, C. (1997) 'Strategic Investment Decisions and Short-Termism: Germany Versus Britain,' in V. Papadakis and P. Barwise (eds), *Strategic Decisions*. Boston: Kluwer Academic Publishers, 107–125.

Carr, C. (2005) Are German, Japanese and Anglo-Saxon strategic decision styles still divergent in the context of globalization?* *Journal of Management Studies*, 42, 1155–1188.

Chakravarthy, B.S., and White, R.E. (2002) 'Strategy Process: Forming, Implementing and Changing Strategies,' in A. Pettigrew, H. Thomas, and R. Whittington (eds) *Handbook of Strategy & Management*. London: Sage Publications, 182–205.

Chou, T.-C., and Dyson, R.G. (1998) An empirical study of the impact of information technology intensity in strategic investment, *Technology Analysis & Strategic Management*, 10 (3), 325.

Collier, N., Fishwick, F., and Floyd, S.W. (2004) Managerial involvement and perceptions of strategy process, *Long Range Planning*, 37 (1), 67–83.

Covin, J.G., Slevin, D.P., and Heeley, M.B. (2001) Strategic decision making in an intuitive vs. technocratic mode: structural and environmental considerations, *Journal of Business Research*, 52 (1), 51–67.

Daniel, P.F. (2005) Managerial determinants of decision speed in new ventures, *Strategic Management Journal*, 26 (4), 355–366.

De Wit, B., and Meyer, R. (2005) *Strategy Synthesis: Resolving Strategy Paradoxes to Create Competitive Advantage*. London: Thomson Learning.

Dean, J.W., and Sharfman, M.P. (1993) The relationship between procedural rationality and political behavior in strategic decision making, *Decision Sciences*, 24 (6), 1069–1083.

Dean, J.W., and Sharfman, M.P. (1996) Does decision process matter? A study of strategic decision-making effectiveness, *Academy of Management Journal*, 39 (2), 368.

Dholakia, U.M., and Bagozzi, R.R. (2002) Mustering motivation to enact decisions: how decision process characteristics influence goal realization, *Journal of Behavioral Decision Making*, 15 (3), 167–188.

Dholakia, U.M., Bagozzi, R.P., and Gopinath, M. (2007) How formulating implementation plans and remembering past actions facilitate the enactment of effortful decisions, *Journal of Behavioral Decision Making*, 20 (4), 343–364.

Eisenhardt, K. (1997) 'Strategic Decision Making as Improvisation,' in Papadakis V. and P. Barwise (eds) *Strategic Decisions*. Boston: Kluwer Academic Publishers, 251–257.

Eisenhardt, K.M., and Zbaracki, M.J. (1992) Strategic decision making, *Strategic Management Journal*, 13, 17–37.

Elbanna, S. (2006) Strategic decision-making: Process perspectives, *International Journal of Management Reviews*, 8 (1), 1–20.

Elbanna, S., and Child, J. (2007a) The influence of decision, environmental and firm characteristics on the rationality of strategic decision-making,* *Journal of Management Studies*, 44 (4), 561–591.

Elbanna, S., and Child, J. (2007b) Influences on strategic decision effectiveness: Development and test of an integrative model, *Strategic Management Journal*, 28 (4), 431–453.

Elbanna, S., and Younies, H. (2008) The relationships between the characteristics of the strategy process: evidence from Egypt, *Management Decision*, 46 (4), 626–639.

Forbes, D.P. (2007) Reconsidering the strategic implications of decision comprehensiveness, *Academy of Management Review*, 32, 361–376.

Fredrickson, J.W. (1984) The comprehensiveness of strategic decision processes: extension, observations, future directions, *Academy of Management Journal*, 27 (3), 445–466.

Fredrickson, J.W. (1985). Effects of decision motive and organizational performance level on strategic decision processes, *Academy of Management Journal*, 28, 821–843.

Fredrickson, J.W., and Iaquinto, A.L. (1989) Inertia and creeping rationality in strategic decision processes, *Academy of Management Journal*, 32 (3), 516–542.

Fredrickson, J.W., and Mitchell, T.R. (1984) Strategic decision processes: Comprehensiveness and performance in an industry with an unstable environment, *Academy of Management Journal*, 27 (2), 399–423.

Goll, I., and Rasheed, A.A. (2005) The relationships between top management demographic characteristics, rational decision making, environmental munificence, and firm performance, *Organization Studies*, 26 (7), 999–1023.

Goll, I., and Sambharya, R.B. 1998. Rational model of decision making, strategy, and firm performance, *Scandinavian Journal of Management*, 14 (4), 479–492.

Gottschalk, P. (1999) Implementation of formal plans: the case of information technology strategy, *Long Range Planning*, 32 (3), 362–372.

Hambrick, D.C., and Mason, P.A. (1984) Upper echelons: The organization as a reflection of its top managers, *Academy of Management Review*, 9 (2), 193–206.

Hickson, D., Butler, R., Cray, D., Mallory, G.R., and Wilson, D. (1986) *Top Decisions: Strategic decision-making in Organizations*, San Francisco, CA: Jossey-Bass.

Hickson, D.J., Miller, S.J., and Wilson, D.C. (2003) Planned or prioritized? Two options in managing the implementation of strategic decisions, *Journal of Management Studies*, 40 (7), 1803–1836.

Hodgkinson, G.P., and Sparrow, P.R. (2002) *The Competent Organization*. Buckingham: Open University Press.

Hough, J.R., and Ogilvie, D. (2005) An empirical test of cognitive style and strategic decision outcomes, *Journal of Management Studies*, 42 (2), 417–448.

Hough, J.R., and White, M.A. (2003) Environmental dynamism and strategic decision-making rationality: An examination at the decision level. *Strategic Management Journal*, 24 (5), 481–489.

Huber, G.P., and Power, D.J. (1985) Retrospective reports of strategic-level managers: Guidelines for increasing their accuracy, *Strategic Management Journal*, 6 (2), 171–180.

Huff, A.S., and Reger, R.K. (1987) A review of strategic process research, *Journal of Management*, 13 (2), 211–236.

Hutzschenreuter, T., and Kleindienst, I. (2006) Strategy-process research: What have we learned and what is still to be explored, *Journal of Management*, 32 (5), 673–720.

Judge, W.Q., and Miller, A. (1991) Antecedents and outcomes of decision speed in different environmental contexts, *Academy of Management Journal*, 34 (2), 449–463.

Ketchen, D.J., Thomas, J.B., and McDaniel, R.R. (1996) Process, content and context: Synergistic effects on organizational performance, *Journal of Management*, 22 (2), 231–257.

Khatri, N., and Ng, H. (2000) The role of intuition in strategic decision making, *Human Relations*, 53 (1), 57–86.

Kilduff, M., Angelmar, R., and Mehra, A. (2000) Top management-team diversity and firm performance: Examining the role of cognitions, *Organization Science*, 11 (1), 21–34.

Kim, W.C., and Mauborgne, R. (1998) Procedural justice, strategic decision making, and the knowledge economy, *Strategic Management Journal*, 19, 323.

Kukalls, S. (1991) Determinants of strategic planning systems in large organizations: a contingency approach, *Journal of Management Studies*, 28, 143–160.

Kumar, N., Stern, L.W., and Anderson, J.C. (1993) Conducting interorganizational research using key informants, *Academy of Management Journal*, 36 (6), 1633–1651.

Langley, A. (1989) In search of rationality: The purposes behind the use of formal analysis in organizations, *Administrative Science Quarterly*, 34 (4), 598–631.

Lawrence, B.S. (1997) The black box of organizational demography, *Organization Science*, 8 (1), 1–22.

Lohrke, F.T., Bedeian, A.G., and Palmer, T.B. (2004) The role of top management teams in formulating and implementing turnaround strategies: A review and research agenda, *International Journal of Management Reviews*, 5–6 (2), 63–90.

Lu, Y. (1997) 'Strategic Investment Decisions in China,' in V. Papadakis, and P. Barwise (eds) *Strategic Decisions*. Boston: Kluwer Academic Publishers, 127–143.

Mallory, G.R., Butler, R., Cray, D., Hickson, D., and Wilson, D. (1983) Implanted decision-making: American owned firms in Britain, *Journal of Management Studies*, 20, 191–211.

Maritan, C.A., and Schendel, D.E. (1997) 'Strategy and Decision Processes: What is the Linkage?' in V. Papadakis and P. Barwise (eds) *Strategic Decisions*. Boston Kluwer Academic Publishers, 259–266.

Martinsons, M.G., and Davison, R.M. (2007) Strategic decision making and support systems: Comparing American, Japanese and Chinese management, *Decision Support Systems*, 43 (1), 284–300.

Miller, C.C. (2008) Decisional comprehensiveness and firm performance: towards a more complete understanding, *Journal of Behavioral Decision Making*, 21 (5), 598–620.

Miller, C.C., Burke, L.M., and Glick, W.H. (1998) Cognitive diversity among upper-echelon executives: Implications for strategic decision processes, *Strategic Management Journal*, 19 (1), 39–58.

Miller, C.C., and Ireland, R.D. (2005) Intuition in strategic decision making: Friend or foe in the fast-paced 21st century? *Academy of Management Executive*, 19 (1), 19–30.

Miller, D. (1989) Matching strategies and strategy making: Process, content, and performance, *Human Relations*, 42 (3), 241–260.

Miller, D., and Friesen, P.H. (1983) Strategy making and environment, *Strategic Management Journal*, 4, 221–235.

Miller, S., Wilson, D., and Hickson, D. (2004) Beyond planning: Strategies for successfully implementing strategic decisions, *Long Range Planning*, 37 (3), 201–218.

Molloy, S., and Schwenk, C. (1995) Effects of information technology on strategic decision making, *Journal of Management Studies*, 32, 283–311.

Mueller, G.C., Mone, M.A., and Barker, V.L. (2007) Formal strategic analyses and organizational performance: Decomposing the rational model, *Organization Studies*, 28 (6), 853–883.

Nooraie, M. (2008) Decision magnitude of impact and strategic decision-making process output: The mediating impact of rationality of the decision-making process, *Management Decision*, 46 (4), 640–655.

Nutt, P. (1997) Better decision-making: A field study, *Business Strategy Review*, 8 (4), 45–52.

Nutt, P.C. (1998a) Leverage, resistance and the success of implementation approaches, *Journal of Management Studies*, 35 (2), 213–240.

Nutt, P.C. (1998b) Evaluating alternatives to make strategic choices, *Omega*, 26 (3), 333–354.

Nutt, P.C. (1999) Surprising but true: Half the decisions in organizations fail, *Academy of Management Executive*, 13 (4), 75–90.

Nutt, P.C. (2000a) Decision-making success in public, private and third sector organisations: Finding sector dependent best practice, *Journal of Management Studies*, 37 (1), 77–108.

Nutt, P.C. (2000b) Context, tactics, and the examination of alternatives during strategic decision making, *European Journal of Operational Research*, 124 (1), 159–186.

Nutt, P.C. (2002) *Why Decisions Fail: Avoiding the Blunders and Traps that Lead to Debacles*. San Francisco, CA: Berrett-Koehler.

Nutt, P.C. (2005) Search during decision making, *European Journal of Operational Research*, 160 (3), 851–876.

Nutt, P.C. (2007) Intelligence gathering for decision making, *Omega*, 35, 604–622.

Nutt, P.C. (2008) Investigating the success of decision making processes, *Journal of Management Studies*, 45 (2), 425–455.

Olson, B.J., Bao, Y., and Parayitam, S. (2007) Strategic decision making within Chinese firms: The effects of cognitive diversity and trust on decision outcomes, *Journal of World Business*, 42 (1), 35–46.

Olson, B.J., Parayitam, S., and Yongjian, B. (2007) Strategic decision making: The effects of cognitive diversity, conflict, and trust on decision outcomes, *Journal of Management*, 33 (2), 196–222.

Papadakis, V.M. (1998) Strategic investment decision processes and organizational performance: An empirical examination, *British Journal of Management*, 9 (2), 115–132.

Papadakis, V.M. (2006) Do CEOs shape the process of making strategic decisions? Evidence from Greece, *Management Decision*, 44 (3), 367–394.

Papadakis, V.M., and Barwise, P. (2002) How much do CEOs and top managers matter in strategic decision-making? *British Journal of Management*, 13 (1), 83–95.

Papadakis, V.M., and Barwise, P. (1997) 'Research on Strategic Decisions: Where Do We Go From Here?' in V. Papadakis and P. Barwise (eds), *Strategic Decisions*. Boston: Kluwer Academic Publishers, 289–301.

Papadakis, V.M., Kaloghirou, Y., and Iatrelli, M. (1999) Strategic decision making: From crisis to opportunity, *Business Strategy Review*, 10, 29–37.

Papadakis, V., and Lioukas, S. (1996) 'Do Early Perceptions of Strategic Decisions Influence Strategic Processes? An Empirical Investigation.' Paper presented at the Academy of Management Proceedings.

Papadakis,V.M., Lioukas, S., and Chambers, D. (1998) Strategic decision-making processes: the role of management and context, *Strategic Management Journal*, 19 (2), 115–147.

Pettigrew, A.M. (1992) On studying managerial elites, *Strategic Management Journal*, 13, 163–182.

Pettigrew, A. (2003) 'Strategy as Process, Power and Change' in S. Cummings, and D.C. Wilson (eds) *Images of Strategy*. Oxford: Blackwell Publishing, 301–330.

Pettigrew, A., and Whip, R. (1991) *Managing Change for Competitive for Competitive Success*. Oxford: Basil Blackwell.

Podsakoff, P.M., MacKenzie, S.B., Lee, J.-Y., and Podsakoff, N.P. (2003) Common method biases in behavioral research: A critical review of the literature and recommended remedies. *Journal of Applied Psychology*, 88 (5), 879–903.

Pondy, L.R. (1987) 'The Union of Rationality and Intuition in Management Action. Introduction: Common Themes in Executive Thought and Action,' in S. Srivastava et al. (eds), *The Executive Mind*. San Francisco, CA: Jossey-Bass.

Priem, R.L., Lyon, D.W., and Dess, G.G. (1999) Inherent limitations of demographic proxies in top management team heterogeneity research, *Journal of Management*, 25 (6), 935–953.

Priem, R.L., Rasheed, A.M.A., and Kotulic, A.G. (1995) Rationality in strategic decision processes, environmental dynamism and firm performance, *Journal of Management*, 21 (5), 913–929.

Rajagopalan, N., Rasheed, A.M.A., and Datta, D.K. (1993) Strategic decision processes: Critical review and future directions, *Journal of Management*, 19 (2), 349–384.

Rajagopalan, N., Rasheed, A.A., Datta, D.K., and Speitzer, G.M. (1997) 'A Multi-Theoretic Model of Strategic Decision Making Processes,' in V. Papadakis and P. Barwise (eds) *Strategic Decisions*. Boston: Kluwer Academic Publishers, 229–249.

Sadler-Smith, E. (2004) Cognitive style and the management of small and medium-sized enterprises, *Organization Studies*, 25 (2), 155–181.

Schwenk, C.R. (1995) Strategic decision making, *Journal of Management*, 21 (3), 471–493.

Schwenk, C.R. (1997) 'Diversity Eccentricity and Devil's Advocacy,' in V. Papadakis and P. Barwise (eds) *Strategic Decisions*. Boston: Kluwer Academic Publishers, 85–94.

Sharfman, M.P., and Dean, J.W. (1997) Flexibility in strategic decision making: Informational and ideological perspectives, *Journal of Management Studies*, 34 (2), 191–217.

Shook, C., Ketchen, D., and Hult, D. (2004) An Assessment of the use of Structural Equation Modeling in Strategic Management Research, *Strategic Management Journal*, 25 (4), 397–404.

Simon, H.A. (1987) Making management decisions: The role of intuition and emotion, *Academy of Management Executive*, 1 (1), 57–64.

Simons, T., Pelled, L.H., and Smith, K.A. (1999) Making use of difference: Diversity, debate, and decision comprehensiveness in top management teams, *Academy of Management Journal*, 42, 662–673.

Spanos, Y.E., and Lioukas, S. (2001) An examination into the causal logic of rent generation: Contrasting Porte's Competitive Strategy Framework and the resource-based perspective, *Strategic Management Journal*, 22 (10), 907

Szulanski, G., Porac, J., and Doz, Y. (2005) 'Strategy Process: Introduction to the Volume,' in G. Szulanski, J. Porac, and Y. Doz (eds) *Advances in Strategic Management*, Vol. 22. JAI, xiii–xxxv.

Van De Ven, A.H. (1992) Suggestions for studying strategy process: A research note, *Strategic Management Journal*, 13, 169–188.

Wally, S., and Baum, J.R. (1994) Personal and structural determinants of the pace of strategic decision making, *Academy of Management Journal*, 37 (4), 932–956.

Walter, J., Lechner, C., and Kellermanns, F.W. (2008) Disentangling alliance management processes: Decision making, politicality, and alliance performance, *Journal of Management Studies*, 45, 530–560.

Walters, B.A., and Bhuian, S.N. (2004) Complexity absorption and performance: A structural analysis of acute-care hospitals, *Journal of Management*, 30 (1), 97–121.

Wilson, D.C. (2003) 'Strategy as Decision Making,' in S. Cummings and D.C. Wilson (eds) *Images of Strategy*. Oxford: Blackwell Publishing, 383–410.

Part II

KEY THEORETICAL PERSPECTIVES

3

Decision Making: It's Not What You Think

HENRY MINTZBERG AND FRANCES WESTLEY

Sloan Management Review Spring 2001, Copyright © 2001 by the Massachusetts Institute of Technology, Reprinted with permission.

Sometimes decisions defy purely step-by-step logic. To be effective, companies also should embrace intuitive or action-oriented forms of decision making.

How should decisions be made? Easy, we figured that out long ago. First define the problem, then diagnose its causes, next design possible solutions, and finally decide which is best. And, of course, implement the choice.

But do people always make decisions that way? We propose that this rational, or "thinking first," model of decision making should be supplemented with two very different models — a "seeing first" and a "doing first" model. When practicing managers use all three models, they can improve the quality of their decisions. Healthy organizations, like healthy people, have the capacity for all three.

Consider how a real decision was made, a personal one in this case. It begins with a call from an aunt.

"Hi, kiddo. I want to buy you a housewarming present. What's the color scheme in your new apartment?"

"Color scheme? Betty, you've got to be kidding. I'll have to ask Lisa. Lisa, Betty wants to know the color scheme of the apartment."

"Black," daughter Lisa says.

"Black? Lisa, I've got to live there."

"Black," she repeats.

A few days later, father and daughter find themselves in a furniture store. They try every desk, every chair: Nothing works. Shopper's lethargy sets in. Then Lisa

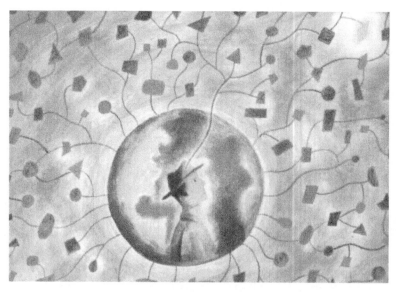

FIGURE 3.1

spots a black stool: "Wouldn't that look great against the white counter?" And they're off. Within an hour, they have picked out everything — in black, white and steel gray.

The extraordinary thing about this ordinary story is that our conventional theories of decision making can't explain it. It is not even clear what the final decision was: to buy the stool; to get on with furnishing an apartment; to do so in black and white; to create a new lifestyle? Decision making can be mysterious.

THE LIMITS OF "THINKING FIRST"

Rational decision making has a clearly identified process: define → diagnose → design → decide. However, the rational approach turns out to be uncommon.

Years ago, one of us studied a host of decisions, delineating the steps and then laying them out. A decision process for building a new plant was typical. The process kept cycling back, interrupted by new events, diverted by opportunities and so on, going round and round until finally a solution emerged. The final action was as clear as a wave breaking on the shore, but explaining how it came to be is as hard as tracing the origin of that wave back into the ocean.

Often decisions do not so much emerge as erupt. Here is how Alexander Kotov, the chess master, has described a sudden insight that followed lengthy analysis:

"So, I mustn't move the knight. Try the rook move again. ... At this point you glance at the clock. 'My goodness! Already 30 minutes gone on thinking about whether to move the rook or the knight. If it goes on like this you'll really be in

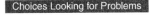

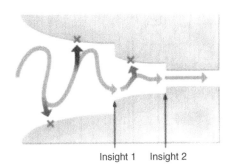

Insight 1   Insight 2

FIGURE 3.2

time trouble.' And then suddenly you are struck by the happy idea — why move rook or knight? What about B-QN1? And without any more ado, without analysis at all, you move the bishop. Just like that."

Perhaps, then, decision making means periods of groping followed by sudden sharp insights that lead to crystallization, as A. Langley and co-authors suggested in a 1995 Organizational Science article. (See "Insight: Groping Precedes Zeroing In.")

Or perhaps it is a form of "organized anarchy," as Stanford professor James March and colleagues have written. They characterize decision making as "collections of choices looking for problems, issues and feelings looking for decision situations in which they may be aired, solutions looking for issues to which they might be an answer, and decision makers looking for work." (See "Choices Looking for Problems.")

But is the confusion, as described by those authors, in the process, or is it in the observers? Maybe messy, real-life decision making makes more sense than we think, precisely because so much of it is beyond conscious thought.

"SEEING FIRST"

Insight — "seeing into" — suggests that decisions, or at least actions, may be driven as much by what is seen as by what is thought. As Mozart said, the best part about creating a symphony was being able to "see the whole of it at a single glance in my mind." So, understanding can be visual as well as conceptual.

In W. Koehler's well-known 1920s experiment, an ape struggled to reach a banana placed high in its cage. Then it *saw* the box in the corner — not just noticed it, but realized what could be done with it — and its problem was solved. Likewise after Alexander Fleming really *saw* the mold that had killed the bacteria in some of his research samples (in other words, when he realized how that mold could be used), he and his colleague were able to give us penicillin. The same can be true for strategic vision. Vision requires the courage to see what others do not — and that means having both the confidence and the experience to recognize the sudden insight for what it is.

A theory in Gestalt psychology developed by G. Wallas in the 1920s identifies four steps in creative discovery: preparation → incubation → illumination → verification.

Preparation must come first. As Louis Pasteur put it, "Chance favors only the prepared mind." Deep knowledge, usually developed over years, is followed by incubation, during which the unconscious mind mulls over the issue. Then with luck (as with Archimedes in the bathtub), there is that flash of illumination. That eureka moment often comes after sleep — because in sleep, rational thinking is turned off, and the unconscious has greater freedom. The conscious mind returns later to make the logical argument. But that verification (reasoning it all out in linear order for purposes of elaboration and proof) takes time. There is a story of a mathematician who solved a formula in his sleep. Holding it in his mind's eye, he was in no rush to write it down. When he did, it took him four months!

Great insights may be rare, but what industry cannot trace its origins to one or more of them? Moreover, little insights occur to all of us all the time. No one should accept any theory of decision making that ignores insight.

"DOING FIRST"

But what happens when you don't see it and can't think it up? Just do it. That is how pragmatic people function when stymied: They get on with it, believing that if they do "something," the necessary thinking could follow. It's experimentation — trying something so that you can learn.

A theory for "doing first," popularized in academia by organizational-behavior professor Karl Weick, goes like this: enactment → selection → retention.

That means doing various things, finding out which among them works, making sense of that and repeating the successful behaviors while discarding the rest. Successful people know that when they are stuck, they must experiment. Thinking may drive doing, but doing just as surely drives thinking. We don't just think in order to act, we act in order to think.

Show us almost any company that has diversified successfully, and we will show you a company that has learned by doing, one whose diversification strategy emerged through experience. Such a company at the outset may have laid out a tidy strategy on the basis of assessing its weaknesses and strengths (or, if after 1990, its "core competencies"), which it almost certainly got wrong. How can you tell a strength from a weakness when you are entering a new sphere? You have no choice but to try things out. Then you can identify the competencies that are really core. Action is important; if you insist on "thinking first" and, for example, doing formalized strategic planning (which is really part of the same thing), you may in fact discourage learning.

MAKING DECISIONS THROUGH DISCUSSION, COLLAGE AND IMPROVISATION

Thus the three major approaches to decision making are "thinking first," "seeing first" and "doing first." They correlate with conventional views of science, art and craft. The first is mainly verbal (comprising words in linear order), the second is visual, the third is visceral. Those who favor thinking are people who cherish facts, those who favor seeing cherish ideas and those who favor doing cherish experiences. (See "Characteristics of the Three Approaches to Making Decisions.")

We have for some years conducted workshops on the three approaches with mid-career managers sent by Asian, European and North American companies to our International Masters program in Practicing Management (www.impm.org). We begin with a general discussion about the relationship between analysis, ideas and action. It soon becomes evident that practicing managers recognize the iterative and connected nature of those elements. We then ask small groups first to discuss an issue for about an hour (one of their own or else what we call a "provocative question." For example: "How do you manage customer service when you never see a customer?" or "How do you organize without structure?"), summarize their conclusions on a flip chart and report back to the full group. Next we give the groups colored paper, pens, scissors and glue. Each small group must create a collage about the issue they discussed in the thinking-first session. At the end of that second workshop, the groups view one another's images and compare "seeing first" with "thinking first" — in terms of both process and results. Finally, each group, with only a few minutes of preparation time permitted, improvises a skit to act out its issue. Again, the groups consider the results.

Reactions to the approaches are revealing. Participants note that in the thinking-first workshop, the initial discussions start off easily enough, no matter what the mix of nationalities or work backgrounds. Participants list comments on flip charts and spontaneously use bulleted items and numbers — with the occasional graph thrown in. Almost no time is spent in discussing *how* to go about analyzing the problem. Groups quickly converge on one of several conventional analytic frameworks: cause and effect, problem and solution, pros and cons, and so on.

Characteristics of the Three Approaches to Making Decisions

"Thinking first" features the qualities of	*"Seeing first" features the qualities of*	*"Doing first" features the qualities of*
science	art	craft
planning, programming	visioning, imagining	venturing, learning
the verbal	the visual	the visceral
facts	ideas	experiences

Many participants observe that such frameworks, particularly when adopted early, blunt exploration. Quality and depth of analysis may be sacrificed for process efficiency. Thinking-first workshops encourage linear, rational and rather categorical arguments. All too often, the result is a wish list, with disagreements hidden in the different points. In other words, there may be less discipline in thinking first than we believe. Thinking comes too easily to most of us.

But when a group must make a picture, members have to reach consensus. That requires deeper integration of the ideas. "We had to think more to do this," a participant reported. The artistic exercise "really forces you to capture the essence of an issue," another added. People ask more questions in the seeing-first exercise; they become more playful and creative.

"In 'thinking first,' we focused on the problems; in 'seeing first,' we focused on the solutions," one person said. One group believed it had agreement on the issue after the thinking-first workshop. Only when the picture making began did its members realize how superficial that agreement was — more of a compromise. In contrast, when you really do see, as someone said, "The message jumps out at you." But to achieve that, the group members have to find out more about one another's capabilities and collaborate more closely. "I felt it became a group project, not just my project," said a participant who had chosen the topic for his group. The seeing-first exercise also draws out more emotions; there is more laughter and a higher energy level. This suggests that being able to see a trajectory — having a vision about what you are doing — energizes people and so stimulates action. In comparing the seeing-first exercise with the thinking-first discussion, a participant remarked, "We felt more liberated." The pictures may be more ambiguous than the words, but they are also more involving. A frequent comment: "They invite interpretation."

One particularly interesting observation about the pictures was that "the impression lasts longer." Studies indicate that we remember pictures much longer and more accurately than words. As R. Haber demonstrated in Scientific American in 1970, recall of images, even as many as 10,000 shown at one-second intervals, is nearly 98% — a capability that may be linked to evolution. Humans survived by learning to register danger and safety signals fast. Emotion, memory, recall and stimulation are powerfully bundled in "seeing first." Contrast that with one comment after the thinking-first workshop: "Twenty-four hours later, we won't remember what this meant."

In fact, although many participants have not made a picture since grade school, the art produced in the seeing-first workshops is often remarkable. Creativity flows freely among the managers, suggesting that they could come up with more creative ideas in their home organizations if they more often used symbols beyond words or numbers.

Our multicultural groups may like the art workshop for overcoming language barriers, but groups of managers from the same company, country or language group have responded equally well. One British participant who was working on a joint venture with an American partner found that out. He met with his U.S. counterpart a few days after the workshops. "We talked past each other for two hours," he

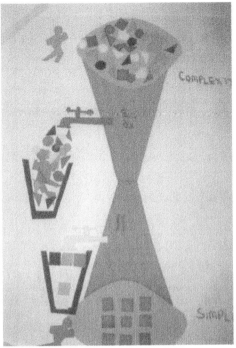

In the "seeing first" workshop, midcareer managers find making a picture of problems required deeper integration of ideas.

FIGURE 3.3

reported. When he suggested they create a picture of their common concerns, they finally were able to connect.

The improvisation skits — "doing first" — generate more spontaneity. Participants respond to one another intuitively and viscerally, letting out concerns held back in conversation and even in artwork. For example, turf battles become evident in the way people stand and talk. Humor, power, fear and anger surface. (M. Crossen and M. Sorrenti discuss improvisation at length in a helpful article published in 1997 in *Advances in Strategic Management*.)

Weick has suggested that a key aspect of effective action in organizations is the ability to remain open to signals from others, even under extreme pressure. He believes that such heedfulness, as he calls it, is a finely honed skill among group improvisers such as jazz musicians. Organizations that recognize opportunities for improvisation — and hone the skills required — increase their capacity for learning. In improvisation, people have to respond with a speed that eliminates many inhibitions. "Having to just act gets rid of the fears," a participant said. Another added, after watching a colleague play the role of a frustrated bank customer, "The output can be scarily real."

Mere words, in contrast, feel more abstract and disconnected — numbers, even more so — just as the aggregations of marketing are more abstract than the experience of selling. The skits bring out what the words and numbers do not say — indeed, what problems they cause. "Not everything is unsayable in words," claimed playwright Eugène Ionesco, "only the living truth." Or as Isadora Duncan, the modern-dance pioneer, insisted, "If I could say it, I wouldn't have to dance it." Thus "doing first" facilitates the dancing that is so lacking in many of today's organizations.

ENOUGH THINKING?

The implications for our large, formalized, thinking-obsessed organizations are clear enough: not to suspend thinking so much as put it in its place, alongside seeing and doing. Isn't it time we got past our obsession with planning and programming, and opened the doors more widely to venturing and visioning? A glance at corporate reports, e-mail and meetings reveals that art is usually something reserved for report covers — or company walls. And when organizations separate the thinking from the doing, with the former coming from the heads of powerful formulators and the latter assigned to the hands of ostensibly docile implementers, those formulators lose the benefits of experimenting — and learning.

Each approach has its own strengths and weaknesses. (See "When Each Decision-Making Approach Works Best.") "Thinking first" works best when the issue is clear, the data reliable and the world structured; when thoughts can be pinned down and discipline applied, as in an established production process. "Seeing first" is necessary when many elements have to be combined into creative solutions and when commitment to those solutions is key, as in much new-product development. The organization has to break away from the conventional, encourage communication across boundaries, bust up cerebral logjams and engage the heart as well as the head. "Doing first" is preferred when the situation is novel and confusing, and things need to be worked out. That is often the case in a new industry — or in an old industry thrown into turmoil by a new technology. Under such circumstances, complicated specifications get in the way, and a few simple relationship rules can help people move forward in a coordinated yet spontaneous manner.

That suggests the advantages of combining all three approaches. In order to learn, a company group might tackle a new issue first by craft, which is tied to doing; then, in order to imagine, by art, which is tied to seeing; finally, in order to program, by science, which is tied to thinking. In ongoing situations, art provides the overview, or vision; science specifies the structure, or plan; and craft produces the action, or energy. In other words, science keeps you straight, art keeps you interested, and craft keeps you going. No organization can do without any one approach. Isn't it time, then, to move beyond our narrow thinking about decision making: to get in *touch*, to *see* another point of view?

When Each Decision-Making Approach Works Best

"THINKING FIRST" WORKS BEST WHEN:

+ the issue is clear;
+ the data is reliable,
+ the context is structured;
+ thoughts can be pinned down; and
+ discipline can be applied

as in an established production process.

"SEEING FIRST" WORKS BEST WHEN:

+ many elements have to be combined into creative solutions;
+ commitment to those solutions is key; and
+ communication across boundaries is essential as in new-product development.

"DOING FIRST" WORKS BEST WHEN:

+ the situation is novel and confusing;
+ complicated specifications would get in the way; and
+ a few simple relationship rules can help people move forward

for example, when companies face a disruptive technology.

Henry Mintzberg and Frances Westley are professors of management at McGill University in Montreal. Contact them at mintzber@management.mcgill.ca and westley@management. mcgill.ca.

4

Organizing and the Process
of Sensemaking

Karl E. Weick and Kathleen M. Sutcliffe[1]

David Obstfeld[2]

Organization Science Vol. 16, No. 4, July–August 2005, pp. 409–421

ISSN 1047-7039 |EISSN 1526-5455|05|1604|0409 © 2005 the

Institute for operations Research and the Management Sciences, 7240 Parkway Drive,

Suite 300, Hanover, MD21076, USA. Reprinted with permission.

Sensemaking involves the ongoing retrospective development of plausible images that rationalize what people are doing. Viewed as a significant process of organizing, sensemaking unfolds as a sequence in which people concerned with identity in the social context of other actors engage ongoing circumstances from which they extract cues and make plausible sense retrospectively, while enacting more or less order into those ongoing circumstances. Stated more compactly and more colorfully, "[S]ensemaking is a way station on the road to a consensually constructed, coordinated system of action" (Taylor and Van Every 2000, p. 275). At that way station, circumstances are "turned into a situation that is comprehended explicitly in words and that serves as a springboard to action" (p. 40). These images imply three important points about the quest for meaning in organizational life. First, sensemaking occurs when a flow of organizational circumstances is turned into words and salient categories. Second, organizing itself is embodied in written and spoken texts. Third, reading, writing, conversing, and editing are crucial actions that serve as the media through which the invisible hand of institutions shapes conduct (Gioia et al. 1994, p. 365).

The emerging picture is one of sensemaking as a process that is ongoing, instrumental, subtle, swift, social, and easily taken for granted. The seemingly transient

[1]Department of Management and Organizations, Ross School of Business, University of Michigan, 701 Tappan, Ann Arbor, Michigan 48109-1234 {karlw@umich.edu, ksutclif@umich.edu}

[2]Organization and Strategy, University of California, Irvine, Irvine, California 92697, dobstfel@uci.edu

Handbook of Decision Making. Edited by Paul C. Nutt and David C. Wilson
© 2010 John Wiley & Sons, Ltd

nature of sensemaking ("a way station") belies its central role in the determination of human behavior. Sensemaking is central because it is the primary site where meanings materialize that inform and constrain identity and action (Mills 2003, p. 35). When we say that meanings materialize, we mean that sensemaking is, importantly, an issue of language, talk, and communication. Situations, organizations, and environments are talked into existence.

Explicit efforts at sensemaking tend to occur when the current state of the world is perceived to be different from the expected state of the world, or when there is no obvious way to engage the world. In such circumstances there is a shift from the experience of immersion in projects to a sense that the flow of action has become unintelligible in some way. To make sense of the disruption, people look first for reasons that will enable them to resume the interrupted activity and stay in action. These "reasons" are pulled from frameworks such as institutional constraints, organizational premises, plans, expectations, acceptable justifications, and traditions inherited from predecessors. If resumption of the project is problematic, sensemaking is biased either toward identifying substitute action or toward further deliberation.

Sensemaking is about the interplay of action and interpretation rather than the influence of evaluation on choice. When action is the central focus, interpretation, not choice, is the core phenomenon (Laroche 1995, p. 66; Lant 2002; Weick 1993, pp. 644–646). Scott Snook (2001) makes this clear in his analysis of a friendly fire incident over Iraq in April 1994 when two F-15 pilots shot down two friendly helicopters, killing 26 people. As Snook says, this is not an incident where F-15 pilots "decided" to pull the trigger.

> I could have asked, "Why did they *decide* to shoot?" However, such a framing puts us squarely on a path that leads straight back to the individual decision maker, away from potentially powerful contextual features and right back into the jaws of the fundamental attribution error. "Why did they decide to shoot?" quickly becomes "Why did they make the *wrong* decision?" Hence, the attribution falls squarely onto the shoulders of the decision maker and away from potent situation factors that influence action. Framing the individual-level puzzle as a question of meaning rather than deciding shifts the emphasis away from individual decision makers toward a point somewhere "out there" where context and individual action overlap.... Such a reframing—from decision making to sensemaking—opened *my* eyes to the possibility that, given the circumstances, even *I* could have made the same "dumb mistake." This disturbing revelation, one that I was in no way looking for, underscores the importance of initially framing such senseless tragedies as "good people struggling to make sense," rather than as "bad ones making poor decisions" (pp. 206–207).

To focus on sensemaking is to portray organizing as the experience of being thrown into an ongoing, unknowable, unpredictable streaming of experience in search of answers to the question, "what's the story?" Plausible stories animate and gain their validity from subsequent activity. The language of sensemaking captures the realities of agency, flow, equivocality, transience, reaccomplishment, unfolding, and emergence, realities that are often obscured by the language of variables, nouns, quantities, and structures. Students of sensemaking understand that the order in organizational life comes just as much from the subtle, the small, the relational, the oral, the particular, and the momentary as it does from the conspicuous, the large, the substantive, the written, the general, and the sustained. To work with the idea of sensemaking is to appreciate that smallness does not equate with insignificance. Small structures and short moments can have large consequences.

We take the position that the concept of sensemaking fills important gaps in organizational theory. We reaffirm this idea and take stock of the sensemaking concept first by highlighting its distinctive features descriptively, using an extended example of pediatric nursing. Next we summarize the distinctive features of sensemaking conceptually and discuss intraorganizational evolution, instigations, plausibility, and identity. Finally, we summarize the distinctive features of sensemaking prospectively and examine future lines of work that may develop from ideas about institutions, distributed sensemaking, power, and emotion. We conclude with a brief description of gaps in organizational theory that the concept of sensemaking fills.

THE NATURE OF ORGANIZED SENSEMAKING: VIEWED DESCRIPTIVELY

Organizational sensemaking is first and foremost about the question: How does something come to be an event for organizational members? Second, sensemaking is about the question: What does an event mean? In the context of everyday life, when people confront something unintelligible and ask "what's the story here?" their question has the force of bringing an event into existence. When people then ask "now what should I do?" this added question has the force of bringing meaning into existence, meaning that they hope is stable enough for them to act into the future, continue to act, and to have the sense that they remain in touch with the continuing flow of experience.

While these descriptions may help delimit sensemaking, they say little about what is organizational in all of this. The answer is that sensemaking and organization constitute one another: "Organization is an attempt to order the intrinsic flux of human action, to channel it toward certain ends, to give it a particular shape, through generalizing and institutionalizing particular meanings and rules" (Tsoukas and Chia 2002, p. 570). We need to grasp each to understand the other. The operative image of organization is one in which organization emerges through sensemaking, not one in which organization precedes sensemaking or one in which sensemaking is produced by organization.

A central theme in both organizing and sensemaking is that people organize to make sense of equivocal inputs and enact this sense back into the world to make that world more orderly. Basic moments in the process of sensemaking are illustrated in the following account, where a nurse describes what she did while caring for a baby whose condition began to deteriorate (Benner 1994, pp. 139–140)[1]:

Nurse: I look care of a 900-gram baby who was about 26 or 27 weeks many years ago who had been doing well for about two weeks. He had an open ductus that day. The difference between the way he looked at 9 a.m. and the way he looked at 11 a.m. was very dramatic. I was at that point really concerned about what was going to happen next. There are a tot of complications of the patent ductus, not just in itself, but the fact that it causes a lot of other things. I was really concerned that the baby was starting to show symptoms of all of them.

Interviewer: Just in that two hours?

Nurse: You look at this kid because you know this kid, and you know what he looked like two hours ago. It is a dramatic difference to you, but it's hard to describe that to someone in words. You go to the resident and say: "Look, I'm really worried about X, Y, Z," and they go: "OK." Then you wait one half hour to 40 minutes, then you go to the Fellow (the teaching physician supervising the resident) and say: "You know, I am really worried about X, Y, Z." They say: "We'll talk about it on rounds."

Interviewer: What is the X, Y, Z you are worried about?

Nurse: The fact that the kid is more lethargic, paler, his stomach is bigger, that he is not tolerating his feedings, that his chem strip (blood test) might be a little strange. All these kinds of things. I can't remember the exact details of this case; there are clusters of things that go wrong. The baby's urine output goes down. They sound like they are in failure. This kind of stuff. Their pulses go bad, their blood pressure changes. There are a million things that go on. At this time, I had been in the unit a couple or three years.

Sensemaking Organizes Flux

Sensemaking starts with chaos. This nurse encounters "a million things that go on" and the ongoing potential for "clusters of things that go wrong"—part of an almost infinite stream of events and inputs that surround any organizational actor. As Chia (2000, p. 517) puts it, we start with "an undifferentiated flux of fleeting sense-impressions and it is out of this brute aboriginal flux of lived experience that attention carves out and conception names." As the case illustrates, the nurse's sensemaking does not begin de novo, but like all organizing occurs amidst a stream of *potential* antecedents and consequences. Presumably within the 24-hour period surrounding the critical noticing, the nurse slept, awoke, prepared for work, observed and tended to other babies, completed paper work and charts, drank coffee, spoke with doctors and fellow nurses, stared at an elevator door as she moved between hospital floors, and performed a variety of formal and impromptu observations. All of these activities furnish a raw flow of activity from which she may or may not extract certain cues for closer attention.

Sensemaking Starts with Noticing and Bracketing

During her routine activities, the nurse becomes aware of vital signs that are at variance with the "normal" demeanor of a recovering baby. In response to the interruption, the nurse orients to the child and notices and brackets possible signs of trouble for closer attention. This noticing and bracketing is an incipient state of sensemaking. In this context sensemaking means basically "inventing a new meaning (interpretation) for something that has already occurred during the organizing process, *but does not yet have a name* (italics in original), has never been recognized as a separate autonomous process, object, event" (Magala 1997, p. 324).

The nurse's noticing and bracketing is guided by mental models she has acquired during her work, training, and life experience. Those mental models may help her recognize and guide a response to an open ductus condition or sickness more generally. Such mental models might be primed by the patient's conditions or a priori permit her to notice and make sense of those conditions (Klein et al., in press). Some combination of mental models and salient cues calls her attention to this particular baby between the hours of 9 to 11 with respect to a bounded set of symptoms.

The more general point is that in the early stages of sensemaking, phenomena "have to be forcibly carved out of the undifferentiated flux of raw experience and conceptually fixed and labeled so that they can become the common currency for communicational exchanges" (Chia 2000, p. 517). Notice that once bracketing occurs, the world is simplified.

Sensemaking Is About Labeling

Sensemaking is about labeling and categorizing to stabilize the streaming of experience. Labeling works through a strategy of "differentiation and simple-location, identification and classification, regularizing and routinization [to translate] the intractable or obdurate into a form that is more amenable to functional deployment" (Chia 2000, p. 517). The key phrase here is "functional deployment." In medicine, functional deployment means imposing diagnostic labels that suggest a plausible treatment. In organizing in general, functional deployment means imposing labels on interdependent events in ways that suggest plausible acts of managing, coordinating, and distributing. Thus, the ways in which events are first envisioned immediately begins the work of organizing because events are bracketed and labeled in ways that predispose people to find common ground. To generate common ground, labeling ignores differences among actors and deploys cognitive representations that are able to generate recurring behaviors: "For an activity to be said to be organized, it implies that types of behavior in types of situation are systematically connected to types of actors. . . . An organized activity provides actors with a given set of cognitive categories and a typology of actions" (Tsoukas and Chia 2002, p. 573).

A crucial feature of these types and categories is that they have considerable plasticity. Categories have plasticity because they are socially defined, because they have to be adapted to local circumstances, and because they have a radial structure. By radial structure we mean that there a few central instances of the category that have all the features associated with the category, but mostly the category contains peripheral instances that have only a few of these features. This difference is potentially crucial because if people act on the basis of central prototypic cases within a category, then their action is stable; but if they act on the basis of peripheral cases that are more equivocal in meaning, their action is more variable, more indeterminate, more likely to alter organizing, and more consequential for adapting (Tsoukas and Chia 2002, p. 574).

Sensemaking Is Retrospective

The nurse uses retrospect to make sense of the puzzles she observes at 11:00. She recalls "what he looked like two hours ago. It's a dramatic difference." Symptoms are not discovered at 11:00. Instead, symptoms are created at 11:00 by looking back over earlier observations and seeing a pattern. The nurse alters the generic sensemaking recipe, "how can I know what I think until I see what I say," into the medically more useful variant, "how can I know what I'm seeing until I see what it was."

Marianne Paget (1988, p. 56) has been especially sensitive to the retrospective quality of medical work as is evident in her description of mistakes in diagnosis: "A mistake follows an act. It identifies the character of an act in its aftermath. It names it. An act, however, is not mistaken; it becomes mistaken. There is a paradox here, for seen from the inside of action, that is from the point of view of an actor, an act becomes mistaken only after it has already gone wrong. As it is unfolding, it is not becoming mistaken at all; it is becoming." When people bracket a portion of streaming circumstances and label them as a concern, a bad sign, a mistake, or an opportunity, the event is at an advanced stage; the label follows after and names a completed act, but the labeling itself fails to capture the dynamics of what is happening. Because mistakes and diagnoses are known in the aftermath of activity, they are fruitfully described as "complex cognitions of the experience of now and then. They identify the too-lateness of human understanding" (Paget 1988, pp. 96–97). So, "the *now* of mistakes collides with the *then* of acting with uncertain knowledge. *Now* represents the more exact science of hindsight, *then* the unknown future coming into being" (Paget 1988, p. 48).

Sensemaking Is About Presumption

To make sense is to connect the abstract with the concrete. In the case of medical action, "instances of illness are concrete, idiosyncratic, and personal in their expression, and the stock of knowledge is abstract and encyclopedic. Interpretation and experimentation engage the concrete, idiosyncratic, and personal with the abstract and impersonal" (Paget 1988, p. 51). It is easy to miss this linkage and to portray sensemaking as more cerebral, more passive, more abstract than it typically is. Sensemaking starts with immediate actions, local context, and concrete cues, as is true for the worried nurse. She says to the resident, "Look, I'm really worried about X, Y, Z."

What is interesting about her concerns is that she is acting as if something is the case, which means any further action tests that hunch but may run a risk for the baby. To test a hunch is to presume the character of the illness and to update that presumptive understanding through progressive approximations: "The [medical] work process unfolds as a series of approximations and attempts to discover an appropriate response. And because it unfolds this way, as an error-ridden activity, it requires continuous attention to the patient's condition and to reparation" (Paget 1988, p. 143).

Sensemaking Is Social and Systemic

The nurse's sensemaking is influenced by a variety of social factors. These social factors might include previous discussions with the other nurses on duty, an offhand remark about the infant that might have been made by a parent, interaction with physicians—some of whom encourage nurses to take initiative and some who do not—or the mentoring she received yesterday.

However, it is not just the concerned nurse and her contacts that matter in this unfolding incident. Medical sensemaking is distributed across the healthcare system, and converges on the tiny patient as much through scheduling that involves cross-covering of one nurse's patients by another nurse (and through multiple brands of infusion pumps with conflicting setup protocols) as it does through the occasional appearance of the attending physician at the bedside. If knowledge about the correctness of treatment unfolds gradually, then knowledge of this unfolding sense is not located just inside the head of the nurse or physician. Instead, the locus is systemwide and is realized in stronger or weaker coordination and information distribution among interdependent healthcare workers.

Sensemaking Is About Action

If the first question of sensemaking is "what's going on here?," the second, equally important question is "what do I do next?" This second question is directly about action, as is illustrated in this case, where the nurse's emerging hunch is intertwined with the essential task of enlisting a physician to take action on the case. The talk that leads to a continual, iteratively developed, shared understanding of the diagnosis and the persuasive talk that leads to enlistment in action both illustrate the "saying" that is so central to organizational action. In sensemaking, action and talk are treated as cycles rather than as a linear sequence. Talk occurs both early and late, as does action, and either one can be designated as the "starting point to the destination." Because acting is an indistinguishable part of the swarm of flux until talk brackets it and gives it some meaning, action is not inherently any more significant than talk, but it factors centrally into any understanding of sensemaking.

Medical sensemaking is as much a matter of thinking that is acted out conversationally in the world as it is a matter of knowledge and technique applied to the world. Nurses (and physicians), like everyone else, make sense by acting thinkingly, which means that they simultaneously interpret their knowledge with trusted frameworks, yet mistrust those very same frameworks by testing new frameworks and new interpretations. The underlying assumption in each case is that ignorance and knowledge coexist, which means that adaptive sensemaking both honors and rejects the past. What this means is that in medical work, as in all work, people face evolving disorder. There are truths of the moment that change, develop, and take shape through time. It is these changes through time that progressively reveal that a seemingly correct action "back then" is becoming an incorrect action "now." These changes also may signal a progression from worse to better.

Sensemaking Is About Organizing Through Communication

Communication is a central component of sensemaking and organizing: "We see communication as an ongoing process of making sense of the circumstances in which people collectively find ourselves and of the events that affect them. The sensemaking, to the extent that it involves communication, takes place in interactive talk and draws on the resources of language in order to formulate and exchange through talk ... symbolically encoded representations of these circumstances. As this occurs, a situation is talked into existence and the basis is laid for action to deal with it" (Taylor and Van Every 2000, p. 58). The image of sensemaking as activity that talks events and organizations into existence suggests that patterns of organizing are located in the actions and conversations that occur on behalf of the presumed organization and in the texts of those activities that are preserved in social structures.

We see this in the present example. As the case illustrates, the nurse's bracketed set of noticings coalesce into an impression of the baby as urgently in need of physician attention, but the nurse's choice to articulate her concerns first to a resident and then to a Fellow produces little immediate result. Her individual sensemaking has little influence on the organizing of care around this patient as this passage shows (Benner 1994, p. 140):

> ... At this time, I had been in the unit a couple or three years. I was really starting to feel like I knew what was going on but I wasn't as good at throwing my weight in a situation like that. And I talked to a nurse who had more experience and I said, "Look at this kid," and I told her my story, and she goes: "OK." Rounds started shortly after that and she walks up to the Attending [Physician in charge of patient] very quietly, sidles up and says: "You know, this kid, Jane is really worried about this kid." She told him the story, and said: "He reminds me about this kid, Jimmie, we had three weeks ago," and he said: "Oh." Everything stops. He gets out the stethoscope and listens to the kid, examines the kid and he says: "Call the surgeons." (Laughter) It's that kind of thing where we knew also what had to be done. There was no time to be waiting around. He is the only one that can make that decision. It was a case we had presented to other physicians who should have made the case, but didn't. We are able in just two sentences to make that case to the Attending because we knew exactly what we were talking about. ... this particular nurse really knew exactly what she was doing. [The Attending] knew she knew what she was doing. ... She knew exactly what button to push with him and how to do it.

What we see here is articulation (Benner 1994, Winter 1987), which is defined as "the social process by which tacit knowledge is made more explicit or usable." To share understanding means to lift equivocal knowledge out of the tacit, private, complex, random, and past to make it explicit, public, simpler, ordered, and relevant to the situation at hand (Obstfeld 2004). Taylor and Van Every (2000, pp. 33–34) describe a process similar to articulation: "A situation is talked into being through the interactive exchanges of organizational members to produce a view of circumstances including the people, their objects, their institutions and history, and their siting [i.e., location as a site] in a finite time and place." This is what happens successively as the first nurse translates her concerns for the second more powerful nurse, who then rearticulates the case using terms relevant to the Attending. The second nurse absorbs the complexity of the situation (Boisot and Child 1999) by holding both a nurse's and doctor's perspectives of the situation while identifying an account of the situation that would align the two. What is especially interesting is that she tries to make sense of how other people make sense of things, a complex determination that is routine in organizational life.

Summary

To summarize, this sequence highlights several distinguishing features of sensemaking, including its genesis in disruptive ambiguity, its beginnings in acts of noticing and bracketing, its mixture of retrospect and prospect, its reliance on presumptions to guide action, its embedding in interdependence, and its culmination in articulation that shades into acting thinkingly. Answers lo the question "what's the story?" emerge from retrospect, connections with past experience, and dialogue among people who act on behalf of larger social units. Answers to the question "now what?" emerge from presumptions about the future, articulation concurrent with action, and projects that become increasingly clear as they unfold.

The Nature of Organized Sensemaking: Viewed Conceptually

Sensemaking as Intraorganizational Evolution

The preceding overview of early activities of sensemaking and organizing that mobilize around moments of flux needs to be compressed if it is to guide research and practice. One way to do that is to assume that "a system can respond adaptively to its environment by mimicking inside itself the basic dynamics of evolutionary processes" (Warglien 2002, p. 110). The basic evolutionary process assumed by sensemaking is one in which retrospective interpretations are buiit during interdependent interaction. This framework is a variant of Donald Campbell's application of evolutionary epislemology to social life (1965, 1997). It proposes that sensemaking can be treated as reciprocal exchanges between actors (Enactment) and their environments (Ecological Change) that are made meaningful (Selection) and preserved (Retention). However, these exchanges will continue only if the preserved content is both believed (positive causal linkage) and doubted (negative causal linkage) in future enacting and selecting. Only with ambivalent use of previous knowledge are systems able both to benefit from lessons learned and to update either their actions or meanings in ways that adapt to changes in the system and its context. For shorthand we will call this model "enactment theory," as has become the convention in organizational work (e.g., Jennings and Greenwood 2003). Graphically, the ESR sequence looks like Figure 4.1.

If we conceptualize organizing as a sequence of ecological change-enactment-selection-retention with the results of retention feeding back to all three prior processes, then the specific activities of sensemaking fit neatly into this more general progression of organizing. The reciprocal relationship between *ecological change* and *enactment* includes sensemaking activities of sensing anomalies, enacting order into flux, and being shaped by externalities. The organizing process of *enactment* incorporates the sensemaking activities of noticing and bracketing. These activities of

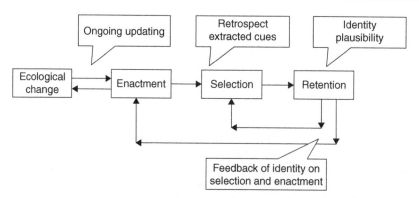

FIGURE 4.1 The Relationship Among Enactment, Organizing, and Sensemaking
Source. Jennings and Greenwood (2003; adapted from Weick 1979, p. 132).

noticing and bracketing, triggered by discrepancies and equivocality in ongoing projects, *begin* to change the flux of circumstances into the orderliness of situations. We emphasize "begin" because noticing and bracketing are relatively crude acts of categorization and the resulting data can mean several different things. The number of possible meanings gets reduced in the organizing process of *selection.* Here a combination of retrospective attention, mental models, and articulation perform a narrative reduction of the bracketed material and generate a locally plausible story. Though plausible, the story that is selected is also tentative and provisional. It gains further solidity in the organizing process of *retention.* When a plausible story is retained, it tends to become more substantial because it is related to past experience, connected to significant identities, and used as a source of guidance for further action and interpretation. The close fit between processes of organizing and processes of sensemaking illustrates the recurring argument (e.g., Weick 1969, pp. 40–42) that people organize to make sense of equivocal inputs and enact this sense back into the world to make that world more orderly. The beauty of making ESR the microfoundation of organizing and sensemaking is that it makes it easier to work with other meso- and macro-level formulations that are grounded in Campbell's work (e.g., Aldrich 1999, Baum and Singh 1994, Ocasio 2001).

Instigations to Sensemaking

The idea that sensemaking is focused on equivocality gives primacy to the search for meaning as a way to deal with uncertainty (e.g., Mills 2003, p. 44). Thus, we expect to find explicit efforts at sensemaking whenever the current state of the world is perceived to be different from the expected state of the world. This means that sensemaking is activated by the question, "same or different?" When the situation feels "different," this circumstance is experienced as a situation of discrepancy (Orlikowski and Gash 1994), breakdown (Patriotta 2003), surprise (Louis 1980), disconfirmation (Weick and Sutcliffe 2001), opportunity (Dutton 1993), or interruption (Mandler 1984, pp. 180–189). Diverse as these situations may seem, they share the properties that in every case an expectation of continuity is breached, ongoing organized collective action becomes disorganized, efforts are made to construct a plausible sense of what is happening, and this sense of plausibility normalizes the breach, restores ihe expectation, and enables projects to continue.

Questions of "same or different" tend to occur under one of three conditions: situations involving the dramatic loss of sense (e.g., Lanir 1989), situations where the loss of sense is more mundane but no less troublesome (e.g., Westley 1990), and unfamiliar contexts where sense is elusive (e.g., Orton 2000). Methodologically, it is hard to find people in the act of coping with disconfirmations that catch them unawares (see Westrum 1982 for a clear exception). Such outcroppings can be found, however, if we examine how everyday situations sometimes present us with either too many meanings or too few. For example, managing any kind of process (e.g., a production routine) with its interconnected processes of anticipation and retrospection (Patriotta 2003) creates equivocality of lime (e.g., is this a fresh defect, or has it happened for some time?) and equivocality of action (e.g., do I have the resources to correct this defect?). Regardless of whether there are too many meanings or too few, the result is the same. Actors are faced with fleeting sense impressions that instigate sensemaking.

While scholars have a strong interest in conscious sensemaking and in making the sensemaking process more visible, they also agree with Gioia and Mehra (1996, p. 1,228), who suggest that much of organizational life is routine and made up of situations that do not demand our full attention. As they note, people's sense can be "modified in intricate ways out of awareness via assimilation of subtle cues over time" (p. 1,229). Acknowledgement of this facet of sensemaking is important if only to avoid the impression that "routine organizational life is devoid of sense" (Gioia and Mehra 1996, p. 1,229).

Plausibility and Sensemaking

Sensemaking is not about truth and getting it right. Instead, it is about continued redrafting of an emerging story so that it becomes more comprehensive, incorporates more of the observed data, and is more resilient in the face of criticism. As the search for meanings continues, people may describe their activities as the pursuit of accuracy to get it right. However, that description is important mostly because it sustains motivation. People may get better stories, but they will never get *the* story. Furthermore, what is plausible for one group, such as managers, often proves implausible for another group, such as employees. In an important study of culture change, Mills (2003, pp. 169–173) found that stories tend to be seen as plausible when they tap into an ongoing sense of current climate, are consistent with other data, facilitate ongoing projects, reduce equivocality, provide an aura of accuracy (e.g., reflect the views of a consultant with a strong track record), and offer a potentially exciting future.

The idea that sensemaking is driven by plausibility rather than accuracy (Weick 1995, p. 55) conflicts with academic theories and managerial practices that assume that the accuracy of managers' perceptions determine the effectiveness of outcomes. The assumption that accuracy begets effectiveness builds on a long stream of research on environmental scanning, strategic planning, rational choice, and organizational adaptation (e.g., Duncan 1972, Pfeffer and Salancik 1978) and persists, for example, in current theorizing on search and adaptive learning (e.g., Gavetti and Levinthal 2000) and strategic decision making (e.g., Bukszar 1999).

However, studies assessing the accuracy of manager's perceptions are rare (see Sutcliffe 1994, Starbuck and Mezias 1996 for exceptions), and those studies that have been done suggest that managers' perceptions are highly inaccurate (Mezias and Starbuck 2003). This may explain why some scholars propose that the key problem for an organization is not to accurately assess scarce data, but to interpret an abundance of data into "actionable knowledge" (Bettis and Prahalad 1995). These critiques have raised the question of the relative importance and role of executives' perceptual inputs relative to their interpretations of these inputs. Kruglanski (1989) argues, for example, that perceptual accuracy should be treated as pragmatic utility, judged only by its usefulness for beneficial action.

A focus on perceptual accuracy is grounded in models of rational decision making: A given problem is evaluated in relation to stable goals and a course of action chosen from a set of alternatives. In this model, accurate information is important in evaluating the feasibility and utility of alternative actions, and accurate perceptions increase decision quality. However, actual organizations do not fit this conception. Problems must be bracketed from an amorphous stream of experience and be labeled as relevant before ongoing action can be focused on them. Furthermore, managers with limited attention face many such issues at the same time, often evaluating several situations, interpretations, choices, and actions simultaneously. Thus, inaccurate perceptions are not necessarily a bad thing, as Mezias and Starbuck (2003) conclude. People do not need to perceive the current situation or problems accurately to solve them; they can act effectively simply by making sense of circumstances in ways lhat appear to move toward general long-term goals. Managerial misperceptions may not curtail effective performance if agents have learning mechanisms and operate in a context where there are incentives to improve performance (Mezias and Starbuck 2003, p. 15; Winter 2003, p. 42).

The important message is that if plausible stories keep things moving, they are salutary. Action-taking generates new data and creates opportunities for dialogue, bargaining, negotiation, and persuasion that enriches the sense of what is going on (Sutcliffe 2000). Actions enable people to assess causal beliefs that subsequently lead to new actions undertaken to test the newly asserted relationships. Over time, as supporting evidence mounts, significant changes in beliefs and actions evolve.

Identity and Sensemaking

Identity construction is seen by many to be one of the two basic properties that differentiate sensemaking from basic cognitive psychology (Gililand and Day 2000, p. 334). The other property is the use of plausibility as the fundamental criterion of sensemaking. Mills (2003) made a similar point when she organized her study of culture change at Nova Scotia Power around identity construction, which "is at the root of sensemaking and influences how other aspects, or properties of the sensemaking process are understood" (Mills 2003, p. 55).

Discussions of organizational identity tend to be anchored by Albert and Whetten's (1985) description of identity as that which is core, distinctive, and enduring about the character of the organization. From the perspective of sensemaking, who we think we are (identity) as organizational actors shapes what we enact and how we interpret, which affects what outsiders think we are (image) and how they treat us, which stabilizes or destabilizes our identity. Who we are lies importantly in the hands of others, which means our categories for sensemaking lie in their hands. If their images of us change, our identities may be destabilized and our receptiveness to new meanings increase. Sensemaking, filtered through issues of identity, is shaped by the recipe "how can I know who we are becoming until I see what they say and do with our actions?"

The pathway from image change to identity change is demonstrated in Gioia and Thomas (1996). Their work suggests that if managers can change the images that outsiders send back to the organization, and if insiders use those images to make sense of what their actions mean, then these changes in image will serve as a catalyst for reflection and redrafting of how the organization defines itself. The controversy implicit in Gioia and Thomas's findings is the suggestion that identity may not be nearly as enduring as first thought, and may be more usefully conceptualized as a variable, mutable continuity (Gioia et al. 2000). If this were found to be the case, then identity would turn out to be an issue of plausibility rather than accuracy, just as is the case for many issues that involve organizing and sensemaking.

Gioia and Chittipeddi (1991) set the stage for many of the current concerns with identity and image in their early finding that sensemaking is incomplete unless there is sensegiving, a sensemaking variant undertaken to create meanings for a target audience. The refinement of this demonstration is the finding that the content of sensegiving (present versus future image) and the target (insider versus outsider) affect how people interpret the actions they confront. Yet to be examined is the effect of efforts at sensegiving on the sensemakers. In the sensemaking recipe "how can I know what I think until I see what I say?" sensegiving corresponds to the *saying*. However, notice that the saying is problematic, you do not really know what you think until you *do* say it. When you hear yourself talk, you see more clearly what matters and what you had hoped to say. Sensegiving therefore may affect the sensemaker as well as the target. For example, in Gioia and Chittipeddi's study, those administrators trying to move a university's identity and image into the category "top 10 university" may themselves have thought differently about this issue as they articulated their campaign to improve the university's reputation.

It is clear that the stakes in sensemaking are high when issues of identity are involved. When people face an unsettling difference, that difference often translates into questions such as who are we, what are we doing, what matters, and why does it matter? These are not trivial questions. As Coopey et al. (1997, p. 312, cited in Brown 2000) note,

Faced with events that disrupt normal expectations and, hence, the efficacy of established patterns of meaning and associated behavior, individuals attempt to make sense of ambiguous stimuli in ways that respond to their own identity needs. They are able to draw creatively on their memory—especially their personal experience—in composing a story that begins to make sense of what is happening while potentially enhancing their feelings of self-esteem and self-efficacy. The story is a sufficiently plausible account of "what is happening out there?" that it can serve as a landscape within which they and others might be able to make commitments and to act in ways that serve to establish new meanings and new patterns of behavior.

The outcomes of such processes, however, are not always sanguine. This was the case in Bristol Royal Infirmary's (BRI) continuation of a pediatric cardiac surgery program for almost 14 years in the face of data showing a mortality rate roughly double the rate of any other center in England (Weick and Sutcliffe 2003, p. 76). The board of inquiry that investigated this incident concluded that there was a prevailing mindset among people at BRI that enabled them to "wish away their poor results" as a "run of bad luck" even though "there *was* evidence sufficient to put the Unit on notice that there were questions to be answered as regards the adequacy of the service" (Kennedy 2001, pp. 247–248). That mindset prevailed partly because surgeons constructed their identity as that of people learning complex surgical procedures in the context of unusually challenging cases. The dangerous omission in this identity was that the resources they used for learning were minimal. They did not collect detailed data about their own prior performance, solicit input from other members of the surgical team, or observe the work of other surgeons who were more skilled at this procedure until formal complaints were filed against pediatric surgeons.

THE NATURE OF ORGANIZED SENSEMAKING: VIEWED PROSPECTIVELY

Considering the modest amount of empirical work on sensemaking that has accumulated so far, the question of "future directions" pretty much takes care of itself. Almost any kind of work is likely to enhance our understanding of a largely invisible, taken-for-granted social process that is woven into communication and activity in ways that seem to mimic Darwinian evolution. We briefly discuss institutionalization, distributed sensemaking, power, and emotion to illustrate a few of the many ways in which present thinking about sensemaking might be enhanced.

Sensemaking and Institutional Theory

We have treated organizing as activity that provides a more ordered social reality by reducing equivocality. A crucial question is whether that reality gets renegotiated in every social interaction or whether, as Zucker (1983) puts it, "institutionalization simply constructs the way things are: alternatives may be literally unthinkable" (p. 5). The tension inherent in these otherwise "cool" positions is evident when Czarniawska (2003, p. 134) observes that "Intentional action never leads to intended results, simply because there is a lot of intentional action directed at different aims in each time and place. Institutionalization, like power, is a post factum description of the resultant of all those efforts combined with the random events that accompanied them."

Discussions of sensemaking often include words like "construct," "enact," "generate," "create," "invent," "imagine," "originate," and "devise." Less often do we find words like "react," "discover," "detect," "become aware of," or "comply with." This asymmetry suggests that people who talk about sensemaking may exaggerate agency and may be reluctant to assume that people internalize and adopt whatever is handed to them, as Zucker suggests. An example of such exaggeration might be the statement, "sensemaking is the feedstock for institutionalization" (Weick 1995, p. 36). Institutionalists might well argue that the causal arrow in this assertion points in the wrong direction. The causal arrow neglects evidence showing that organizational members are socialized (indoctrinated) into expected sensemaking activities and that firm behavior is shaped by broad cognitive, normative, and regulatory forces that derive from and are enforced by powerful actors such as mass media, governmental agencies, professions, and interest groups (Lounsbury and Glynn 2001). In other words, "no organization can properly be understood apart from its wider social and cultural context" (Scott 1995, p. 151).

These diverse positions can begin to be reconciled if we focus on mechanisms that link micro-macro levels of analysis and if we pay as much attention to structuring and conversing as we do to structures and texts. One way to further such reconciliation is lo follow the lead of Hedstrom and Swedberg (1998), who argue that when we want to explain change and variation at the macrolevel of analysis, we need to show "how macro states at one point in time influence the behavior of individual actors, and how these actions generate new macro states at a later time" (p. 21). Sensemaking can provide micromechanisms that link macrostates across time through explication of cognitive structures associated with mimetic processes, agency, the mobilization of resistance, alternatives to conformity such as independence, anticonformity, and uniformity (Weick 1979, p. 115), and ways in which ongoing interaction generates the taken for granted. Examples of such mechanisms are found in Elsbach's (2002) description of institutions within organizations and in descriptions of "conventions" in the French Convention School of institutionalists' thought (Storpor and Salais 1997, pp. 15–43).

The juxtaposition of sensemaking and institutionalism has been rare, but there are recent efforts to correct this (see the important integration proposed by Jennings and Greenwood 2003). For example, Klaus Weber's (2003) study of globalization and convergence specifically connects the sensemaking and macroinstitu-tional perspectives. Weber focuses on the content rather than the process of sensemaking. He argued that the media provides corporate vocabularies, and that corporate social structures direct the distribution of these vocabularies among actors. His findings suggest that while institutions in the form of public discourse define and impose the problems to which corporate actors respond, those public institutions do not appear to direct the solutions. Thus, public discourse appears to direct corporate attention, set agendas, and frame issues, but it is less critical for supplying response repertoires. Weber concludes that the relationship between institutions and corporate sensemaking is not linear; the use of corporate sensemaking vocabularies tends to be triggered by institutions, but institutions have less influence over what happens subsequent to triggering.

Distributed Sensemaking

The rhetoric of "shared understanding," "common sense," and "consensus," is commonplace in discussions of organized sensemaking. However, the haunting questions remain: Are shared beliefs a necessary condition for organized action (Lant 2002, p. 355), and is the construct of collective belief theoretically meaningful (Porac et al. 2002, p. 593)? The drama associated with such questions is demonstrated by Hughes et al. (1992) in their study of reliability in the UK air traffic control system:

> If one looks lo see what constitutes this reliability, it cannot be found in any single element of the system. It is certainly not to be found in the equipment... for a period of several months during our field work it was failing regularly.... Nor is it to be found in the rules and procedures, which are a resource for safe operation but which can never cover every circumstance and condition. Nor is it to be found in the personnel who, though very highly skilled, motivated and dedicated, are as prone as people everywhere to human error. Rather we believe it is to be found in the cooperative activities of controllers across the "totality" of the system, and in particular in the way that it enforces the active engagement of controllers, chiefs, and assistants with the material they are using and with each other (cited in Woods and Cook 2000, p. 164).

Promising lines of development would seem to occur if work on distributed cognition (Hutchins 1995), heedful interrelating (Weick and Roberts 1993), and variable disjunction of information[2] (Turner 1978, p. 50) were focused less on the assembling and diffusing of preexisting meaning and more on collective induction of new meaning (see Laughlin and Hollingshead 1995 for laboratory investigations of this issue). When information is distributed among numerous parties, each with a different impression of what is happening, the cost of reconciling these disparate views is high, so discrepancies and ambiguities in outlook persist. Thus, multiple theories develop about what is happening and what needs to be done, people learn to work interdependently despite couplings loosened by the pursuit of diverse theories, and inductions may be more clearly associated with effectiveness when they provide equivalent rather than shared meanings.

Sensemaking and Power

Sensemaking strikes some people as naïve with regard to the red meat of power, politics, and critical theory. People who are powerful, rich, and advantaged seem to have unequal access to roles and positions that give them an unequally strong position to influence the construction of social reality (Mills 2003, p. 153). Sensemaking discussions do tend to assume that meanings survive as a result of voting (e.g.,

Weick 1995, p. 6), with the proviso that sometimes ihe votes are weighted equally and sometimes they are not.

Enhancements of sensemaking that pay more attention to power will tend to tackle questions such as how does power get expressed, increase, decrease, and influence others? Preliminary answers are that power is expressed in acts that shape what people accept, take for granted, and reject (Pfeffer 1981). How does such shaping occur? Through things like control over cues, who talks to whom, proffered identities, criteria for plausible stories, actions permitted and disallowed, and histories and retrospect that are singled out. To shape hearts and minds is to influence at least seven dimensions of sensemaking: the social relations that are encouraged and discouraged, the identities that are valued or derogated, the retrospective meanings that are accepted or discredited, the cues that are highlighted or suppressed, the updating that is encouraged or discouraged, the standard of accuracy or plausibility to which conjectures are held, and the approval of proactive or reactive action as the preferred mode of coping.

Sensemaking and Emotion

Magala (1997, p. 324) argued that perhaps the most imporiant lost opportunity in the 1995 book *Sensemaking in Organizations* was fuller development of a theory of organizational sentiments. Such a theory was "hinted at but ignored." The opening for further development of emotional sensemaking was the property that projects are ongoing, and when interrupted generate either negative emotions when resumption is thwarted or positive emotions when resumption is facilitated. If emotion is restricted to events that are accompanied by autonomic nervous system arousal (Berscheid and Ammazzalorso 2003, p. 312; Schachter and Singer 1962), if the detection of discrepancy provides the occasion for arousal (Mandler 1997), and if arousal combines with a positive or negative valenced cognitive evaluation of a situation (e.g., a threat to well-being or an opportunity to enhance well-being), then sensemaking in organizations will often occur amidst intense emotional experience. Consider the case of high task interdependence. As the interdependent partners "learn more about each other and move toward closeness by becoming increasingly dependent on each other's activities for the performance of their daily behavioral routines and the fulfillment of their plans and goals, the number and strength of their expectancies about each other increase. As a result, their opportunities for expectancy violation, and for emotional experience also increase" (Berscheid and Ammazzalorso 2003, p. 317). When an important expectancy is violated, the partner becomes less familiar, less safe, and more of a stranger. In the face of an emotional outburst, people often ask in disbelief "what did I do?!" That is the wrong question. The better question is "what did you expect" (Berscheid and Ammazzalorso 2003, p. 318)? Expectations hold people hostage to their relationships in the sense that each expectancy can be violated, and generates a discrepancy, an emotion, and a valenced interpretation. If I expect little, there is little chance for discrepancy and little chance for emotion. However, when "an outside event produces negative emotion for an individual in a close relationship, the individual's partner may be less likely lo remain tranquil and supportive than a superficial partner might be because the partner is likely to be experiencing emotion him or herself; the partner's emotional state, in turn, may interfere with the partner's ability to perform as the individual expects" (Berscheid and Ammazzalorso 2003, p. 324).

Further exploration of emotion and sensemaking is crucial lo clear up questions such as whether intraorganizational institutions are better portrayed as cold cognitive scripts built around rules or as hot emotional attitudes built around values (Elsbach 2002, p. 52).

CONCLUSIONS

To deal with ambiguity, interdependent people search for meaning, settle for plausibility, and move on. These are moments of sensemaking, and scholars stretch those moments, scrutinize them, and name them in the belief that they affect how action gets routinized, flux gels tamed, objects get enacted, and precedents get set. Work to date suggests that the study of sensemaking is useful for organizational studies because it (fills several gaps. Analyses of sensemaking provide (1) a micro-mechanism that produces macro-change over time; (2) a reminder that action is always just a tiny bit ahead of cognition, meaning that we act our way into belated understanding; (3) explication of predecisional activities; (4) description of one means by which agency alters institutions and environments (enactment); (5) opportunities to incorporate meaning and mind into organizational theory; (6) counterpoint to the sharp split between thinking and action that often gets invoked in explanations of organizational life (e.g., planners versus doers); (7) background for an attention-based view of the firm; (8) a balance between prospect in the form of anticipation and retrospect in the form of resilience; (9) reinterpretation of breakdowns as occasions for learning rather than as threats to efficiency; and (10) grounds to treat plausibility, incrementalism, improvisation, and hounded rationality as sufficient to guide goal-directed behavior.

Analyses of sensemaking also suggest important capabilities and skills that warrant attention and development. For example, the concept of enacted environments suggests that constraints are partly of one's own making and not simply objects to which one reacts; the concept of sensemaking suggests that plausibility rather than accuracy is the ongoing standard that guides learning; the concept of action suggests that it is more important to keep going than to pause, because the flow of experience in which action is embedded does not pause; and, the concept of retrospect suggests that so-called stimuli for action such as diagnoses, plans for implementation, and strategies are as much the products of action as they are prods to action.

Taken together, these properties suggest that increased skill at sensemaking should occur when people are socialized to make do, be resilient, treat constraints as self-imposed, strive for plausibility, keep showing up, use retrospect to get a sense of direction, and articulate descriptions that energize. These are micro-level actions. They are small actions, but they are small actions with large consequences.

ACKNOWLEDGMENTS

The authors thank two anonymous reviewers. Senior Editor Alan Meyer, and Gary Klein for constructive comments on previous versions of this paper.

NOTES

1. The terms "open ductus" and "complications of the patent ductus" referenced by the nurse in her description refer to a condition formally known as patent ductus arteriosus. Patent ductus arteriosus is a condition where the ductus arteriosus, a blood vessel that allows blood to bypass the baby's lungs before birth, fails to close after birth. The word "patent" means open. If the patent ductus is not closed, the infant is at risk of developing heart failure or a heart infection.
2. "... a complex situation in which a number of parties handling a problem are unable lo oblain precisely the same information about the problem so that many differing interpretations of the problem exist" (Turner 1978, p. 50).

REFERENCES

Albert, S., D. Whetten. 1985. Organizational identily. L. L. Cummings, R. M. Staw, eds. *Research in Organizational Behavior*, Vol. 7. JAI Press, Greenwich, CT, 263–295.

Aldrich, H. 1999. *Organizations Evolving*. Sage, Thousand Oaks, CA.

Baum, J. A. C., J. V. Singh. 1994. *Evolutionary Dynamics of Organizations*. Oxford University Press, Oxford, UK.

Benner, P. 1994. The role of articulation in understanding practices and experience as sources of knowledge in clinical nursing. J. Tully, ed. *Philosophy In An Age of Pluralism: The Philosophy of Charles Taylor In Question*. Cambridge University Press, New York, 136–155.

Berscheid, E., H. Ammazzalorso. 2003. Emotional experience in close relationships. G. J. Fletcher, M. S. Clark, eds. *Blackwell Handbook af Social Psychology: Interpersonal Process*. Blackwell, Malden, MA, 308–330.

Bettis, R. A., C. K. Prahalad. 1995. The dominant logic: Retrospective and extension. *Strategic Management J.* 16 5–14.

Boisot, M., J. Child. 1999. Organizations as adaptive systems in complex environments: The case of China. *Organ. Sci.* 10 (3) 237–252.

Brown, A. 2000. Making sense of inquiry sensemaking. *J. Management Stud.* 37 45–75.

Bukszar, E., Jr. 1999. Strategic bias: The impact of cognitive biases on strategy. *Canadian J. Admin. Sci.* 16 105–117.

Campbell, D. T. 1965. Variation and selective retention in sociocuitural evolution. H. R. Barringer, G. I. Blanksten, R. Mack, eds. *Social Change in Developing Areas*. Schenkman, Cambridge, MA, 19–49.

Campbell, D. T. 1997. From evolutionary epistemology via selection theory to a sociology of scientific validity. *Evolution Cognition* 3 (1) 5–38.

Chia, R. 2000. Discourse analysis as organizational analysis. *Organization* 7 (3) 513–518.

Czarniawska, B. 2003. Constructionism and organization studies. R. I. Westwood, S. Clegg, eds. *Debating Organization: Point-Counterpoint in Organization Studies.* Blackwell, Malden, MA, 128–139.

Duncan, R. B. 1972. Characteristics of organizational environments and perceived uncertainty. *Admin. Sci. Quart.* 17 313–327.

Dutton, J. E. 1993. The making of organizational opportunities: An interpretive pathway to organizational change. L. L. Cummings, B. M. Staw, eds. *Research in Organizational Behavior,* Vol. 15. JAI Press, Greenwich, CT, 195–226.

Elsbach, K. D. 2002. Intraorganizational institutions. J. A. C. Baum, ed. *The Blackwell Companion to Organizations.* Blackwell, Malden, MA, 37–57.

Gavetti, G., D. Levinthal. 2000. Looking forward and looking backward: Cognitive and experiential search. *Admin. Sci. Quart.* 45 113–137.

Gililand, S. W., D. V. Day. 2000. Business management. F. T. Durso, ed. *Handbook of Applied Cognition.* Wiley, New York, 315–342.

Gioia, D. A., K. Chittipeddi. 1991. Sensemaking and sensegiving in strategic change initiation. *Strategic Management J.* 12 433–448.

Gioia, D. A., A. Mehra. 1996. Book review: *Sensemaking in Organizations. Acad. Management Rev.* 21 (4) 1226–1230.

Gioia, D. A., J. B. Thomas. 1996. Identity, image, and issue interpretation: Sensemaking during strategic change in academia. *Admin. Sci. Quart.* 41 370–403.

Gioia, D. A., M. Schultz, K. Corley. 2000. Organizational identity, image, and adaptive instability. *Acad. Management Rev.* 25 63–81.

Gioia, D. A., J. B. Thomas, S. M. Clark, K. Chittipeddi. 1994. Symbolism and strategic change in academia: The dynamics of sensemaking and influence. *Organ. Sci.* 5 363–383.

Hedström, P., R. Swedberg. 1998. Social mechanisms: An introductory essay. P. Hedström, R. Swedberg, eds. *Social Mechanisms: An Analytical Approach to Social Theory,* Ch. 1. Cambridge University Press, Cambridge, UK, 1–31.

Hughes, J., D. Randall, D. Shapiro. 1992. Faltering from ethnography to design. *Comput. Supported Cooperative Work (CSCW) Proc.,* Toronto, Ontario, Canada, 1–8.

Hutchins, E. 1995. *Cognition in the Wild.* MIT Press, Cambridge, MA.

Jennings, P. D., R. Greenwood. 2003. Constructing the iron cage: Institutional theory and enactment. R. Westwood, S. Clegg, eds. *Debating Organization: Point-Counterpoint in Organization Studies.* Blackwell, Malden, MA, 195–207.

Kennedy, I. 2001. *Learning from Bristol: The Report of the Public Inquiry into Children's Heart Surgery at Bristol Royal Infirmary 1984–1995.* Her Majesty's Stationer, London, UK.

Klein, G., J. K. Phillips, E. L. Rall, D. A. Peluso. In press. A data/frame theory of sensemaking. Unpublished manuscript. R. R. Hoffman, ed. *Expertise Out of Context: Proc. 6th Internat. Conf. Naturalistic Decision Making.* Erlbaum, Mahwah, NJ.

Kruglanski, A. W. 1989. The psychology of being "right": The problem of accuracy in social perception and cognition. *Psych. Bull.* 106 395–409.

Lanir, Z. 1989. The reasonable choice of disaster—The shooting down of the Libyan airliner on 21 February 1973. *J Strategic Stud.* 12 479–493.

Lant, T. K. 2002. Organizational cognition and interpretation. J. A. C. Baum, ed. *The Blackwell Companion to Organizations.* Blackwell, Oxford, UK, 344–362.

Laroche, H. 1995. From decision to action in organizations: Decision-making as a social representation. *Organ. Sci.* 6 (1) 62–75.

Laughlin, P. R., A. B. Hollingshead. 1995. A theory of collective induction. *Organ. Behavior Human Decision Processes* 61 94–107.

Louis, M. R. 1980. Surprise and sensemaking: What newcomers experience in entering unfamiliar organizational settings. *Admin. Sci. Quart.* 25 226–251.

Lounsbury, M., M. A. Glynn. 2001. Cultural entrepreneurship: Stories, legitimacy, and the acquisition of resources. *Strategic Management J.* 22 (6) 545–564.

Magala, S. J. 1997. The making and unmaking of sense. *Organ. Stud.* 18 (2) 317–338.

Mandler, G. 1984. *Mind and Body.* Free Press, New York.

Mandler, G. 1997. *Human Nature Explored.* Oxford, New York.

Mezias, J. M., W. H. Starbuck. 2003. Managers and their inaccurate perceptions: Good, bad or inconsequential? *British J. Management* 14 (1) 3–19.

Mills, J. H. 2003. *Making Sense of Organizational Change.* Routledge, London, UK.

Obstfeld, D. 2004. Saying more and less of what we know: The social processes of knowledge creation, innovation, and agency. Unpublished manuscript, University of California-Irvine, Irvine, CA.

Ocasio, W. 2001. How do organizations think? T. K. Lant, Z. Shapira, eds. *Organizational Cognition: Computation and Interpretation.* Erlbaum, Mahwah, NJ, 39–60.

Orlikowski, W. J., D. C. Gash. 1994. Technological frames: Making sense of information technology in organizations. *ACM Trans. Inform. Systems* 2 174–207.

Orton, J. D. 2000. Enactment, sensemaking, and decision making: Redesign processes in the 1976 reorganization of US intelligence. *J. Management Stud.* 37 213–234.

Paget, M. A. 1988. *The Unity of Mistakes.* Temple University Press, Philadelphia, PA.

Patriotta, G. 2003. Sensemaking on the shop floor: Narratives of knowledge in organizations. *J. Management Stud.* 40 (2) 349–376.

Pfeffer, J. 1981. *Power in Organizations.* Pitman, Marshfield, MA.

Pfeffer, J., G. R. Salancik. 1978. *The External Control of Organizations: A Resource Dependence Perspective.* Harper and Row, New York.

Porac, J. F., M. J. Ventresca, Y. Mishina. 2002. Interorganizational cognition and interpretation. J. A. C. Baum, ed. *The Blackwell Companion to Organizations.* Blackwell, Malden, MA, 579–598.

Schachter, S., J. E. Singer. 1962. Cognitive, social, and physiological determinants of emotional state. *Psych. Rev.* 69 379–399.

Scott, R. W. 1995. *Institutions and Organizations.* Sage, Thousand Oaks, CA.

Snook, S. 2001. *Friendly Fire.* Princeton University, Princeton, NJ.

Starbuck, W. H., J. Mezias. 1996. Opening Pandora's box: Studying the accuracy of managers' perceptions. *J. Organ. Behavior* 17 99–117.

Storpor, M., R. Salais. 1997. *Worlds of Production: The Action Frameworks of the Economy.* Harvard, Cambridge, MA.

Sutcliffe, K. M. 1994. What executives notice: Accurate perceptions in top management teams. *Acad. Management J.* 37 1360–1378.

Sutcliffe, K. M. 2000. Organizational environments and organizational information processing. F. M. Jablin, L. L. Putnam, eds. *The New Handbook of Organizational Communication.* Sage, Thousand Oaks, CA, 197–230.

Taylor, J. R., E. J. Van Every. 2000. *The Emergent Organization: Communication as Its Site and Surface.* Erlbaum, Mahwah, NJ.

Tsoukas, H., R. Chia. 2002. Organizational becoming: Rethinking organizational change. *Organ. Sci.* 13 (5) 567–582.

Turner, B. 1978. *Man Made Disasters.* Wykeham Press, London, UK.

Warglien, M. 2002. Intraorganizational evolution. J. A. C. Baum, ed. *The Blackwell Companion to Organizations.* Blackwell, Malden, MA, 98–118.

Weber, K. 2003. Does globalization lead to convergence? The evolution of organizations' cultural repertoires in tlte biomedical industry. Unpublished dissertation, University of Michigan, Ann Arbor, MI.

Weick, K. 1969. *The Social Psychology of Organizing.* Addison-Wesley, Reading, MA.

Weick, K. E. 1979. *The Social Psychology of Organizing*, 2nd ed. Addison-Wesley, Reading, MA.

Weick, K. E. 1993. The collapse of sensemaking in organizations: The Mann Gulch disaster. *Admin. Sci. Quart.* 38 628–652.

Weick, K. E. 1995. *Sensemaking in Organizations*. Sage, Thousand Oaks, CA.

Weick, K. E., K. H. Roberts. 1993. Collective mind in organizations: Heedful interrelating on flight decks. *Admin. Sci. Quart.* 38 357–381.

Weick, K. E., K. M. Sutcliffe. 2001. *Managing the Unexpected*. Jossey-Bass, San Francisco, CA.

Weick, K. E., K. M. Sutcliffe. 2003. Hospitals as cultures of entrapment: A re-analysis of the Bristol Royal Infirmary. *California Management Rev.* 45 (2) 73–84.

Westley, F. R. 1990, Middle managers and strategy: Microdynamics of inclusion. *Strategic Management J.* 11 337–351.

Westrum, R. 1982. Social intelligence about hidden events. *Knowledge* 3 381–400.

Winter, S. 1987. Knowledge and competence as strategic assets. D. Teece, ed. *The Competitive Challenge—Strategies far Industrial Innovation and Renewal.* Bollinger, Cambridge, MA, 159–184.

Winter, S, 2003. Mistaken perceptions: Cases and consequences. *British J. Management* 14 39–45.

Woods, D. D., R. I. Cook. 2000. Perspectives on human error: Hindsight biases and local rationality. F. T. Durso, ed. *Handbook of Applied Cognition*. Wiley, New York, 141–172.

Zucker, L. G. 1983. Organizations as institutions. S. B. Bacharach, ed. *Research in the Sociology of Organizations*, Vol. 2. JAI Press, Greenwich, CT, 1–48.

5

The Political Aspects of Strategic Decision Making

John Child, Said Elbanna, and Suzana Rodrigues

Introduction

The present chapter examines the political perspective on strategic decision making in organizations. This perspective is concerned with the ways in which involved parties can affect the process and outcomes of strategic decision making either through the power they possess or through measures they take to exert influence. Strategic decisions are those which have a significant impact on the organization and its long-term performance (Hickson, Butler, Cray, Mallory, and Wilson, 1986). The political perspective focuses on how and why individuals, groups, and organizations exercise power or accrue influence so as to shape the strategic decisions that are made on behalf of organizations.

Strategic decisions are particularly likely to stimulate political actions because they are complex, significant, and subject to uncertainty. Their complexity legitimates multiple views as to appropriate outcomes or solutions, as well as providing a power base for those groups which possess special knowledge or skills to deal with the complexity (Butler, Davies, Pike, and Sharpe, 1991). While all strategic decisions are, by definition, relatively significant, some may be particularly so because they are critical for an organization's survival and/or may carry major implications for the distribution of resources within the organization. The significance of strategic decisions means that there is more at stake for those who stand to gain or lose from the decisions in terms of material or reputational consequences. Pettigrew (1973: 20–21) argued that

> as long as organizations continue as resource-sharing systems where there is an inevitable scarcity of those resources, political behaviour will occur ... such political behaviour is likely to be a special feature of large-scale innovative

Handbook of Decision Making. Edited by Paul C. Nutt and David C. Wilson
© 2010 John Wiley & Sons, Ltd

decisions. These decisions are likely to threaten existing patterns of resource-sharing.

Strategic decisions involve a political problem of reconciling divergent interests as well as a technical problem of attempting to calculate the best decision given a number of parameters (Hickson *et al.*, 1986). They generally look forward over the long term, and authorize innovations or other moves into imperfectly known conditions. This lends an ambiguity and uncertainty to the arguments and calculations through which they can be justified, which in turn allows for a range of competing proposals and preferences to claim credibility. Competing proposals are made on the basis of selective perception and identification with sub-goals and interests (March and Simon, 1958). This situation encourages political behaviour between the competing parties. At the same time, political behaviour adds to the uncertainty of decision making because it is at variance with formal decision rules and may subvert them (Mumford and Pettigrew, 1975).

There are a number of issues to which a political perspective draws attention and which this chapter considers with reference to the available literature. What specifically is the concept of political behaviour in decision making? How does it contrast with the normative model of rational decision making? What kinds of political behaviour manifest themselves in the process of making strategic decisions? Are there certain conditions that favour the presence of such behaviour? What are the consequences of the incursion of politics into strategic decision making, for the quality of decisions and for organizational performance? Broadening the horizon, do the political aspects of strategic decision making carry implications for the wider issue of corporate governance and accountability for organizational power? This chapter considers these issues in turn before concluding with an integrating framework and suggestions for further research.

THE CONCEPT OF POLITICAL BEHAVIOUR IN DECISION MAKING

Political behaviour is behaviour by individuals or groups which involves the use of power or exercise of influence. The origin of the political perspective on strategic decision making lies in the political science literature of the 1950s, when various authors developed a view that the conflicting goals and interests of people affect decision making in government (Eisenhardt and Zbaracki, 1992). This view assumes that decisions are the result of a process in which decision makers have different goals, form alliances to achieve their goals, and in which the preferences of the most powerful prevail (Stone, 2002). Lindblom (1959), for example, developed the theory of incrementalism or 'muddling through' in decision making within society. In this view, decision making evolved through small steps, each one representing the consequence of competition and bargaining between elite groups in politics and in the marketplace. He argued that the balance between competing interests would help to ensure democracy and a reasonably equitable distribution of benefits. Later on, Lindblom (1977) came to warn that if certain groups gained more power than others, or started to collude rather than compete, then exploitation of the less powerful and suppression of any discussion of alternatives was likely to follow. This warning remains apposite to the abuse of power by corporate strategic decision makers, of which there have been a number of well-publicised examples.

Various strands within the literature on management also began to provide fertile ground for a political perspective. Close examination of managers at work provided insights into the political nature of their behaviour (e.g. Dalton, 1959) and how it frequently departed from rationality (e.g. Mintzberg, 1973). The realization that the organization is typically a political arena raised doubts about the validity of the rational strategic planning model (Mintzberg, 1985; 1994). Cyert and March (1963) incorporated this political realism into their behavioural theory of the firm, seeing conflicts of interest based on differences in the goals held by different organizational groups as normal aspects of organizational life. They therefore regarded decision making as very much a political process. Building partly on Cyert and March's notion of the dominant coalition, and also informed by his previous industrial experience, Child (1972; 1997a; 1997b) argued that attention had to be given to 'strategic choice'. This was defined as the process whereby power-holders within organizations decide on courses of strategic action. 'Strategic choices were seen to be made through initiatives within the network of internal and external organizational relationships – through *pro-action* as well as *re-action*' (Child, 1997a: 45–6).

Interaction between people is one of the underlying features of the strategic decision-making process. 'Since strategic decisions are made among people by people for people they are a welter of action, interaction, and counteraction' (Hickson *et al.*, 1986: 54). An organization comprises distinct groups of people with different motivations for getting involved in decisions (Butler, 2002). Political behaviour is essentially generated by the combination of differentiation and interdependence among these individuals and groups. Each has its own specialized functions and responsibilities, but they have to relate to other subunits and work interdependently with them. They compete for scarce resources which can generate conflict between them (Mumford and Pettigrew, 1975). Strategic decisions in particular involve the allocation of such resources. The interplay of interests, conflict, and power between individuals and groups means that the strategic decision-making process can be characterized as political in nature (Wilson, 2003).

Hence, interest groups practice political tactics to influence decisions which affect their positions and interests in the organization. Also, top management's need to balance its goals with the expectations of lower echelons to get their support leads to many trade-offs which affect the direction of the organization (Quinn, 1980). Hickson *et al.* (1986) argue that the decision-making processes is influenced by a specified set of interest units or executives – the 'decision-set'. The decision-set of interests introduces political tactics into decision making in an attempt to exert influence over the decision to ensure that it encompasses their objectives.

There is a lack of uniformity in defining politics. Gandz and Murray (1980: 237) divide definitions of politics into two categories. In the first category, politics are defined in 'a "neutral" fashion as the occurrence of certain forms of behaviour associated with the use of power or influence'. Some consider these behaviours to be political if they involve conflict over scarce resources or specific decisions, while others extend the definition to include any use of power or influence. The second category defines politics in terms of consciously self-serving behaviours against others in the organization.

Traditionally, political behaviour has been regarded as a negative use of power in pursuit of sectional interest, even to the point where it contravenes organizational or social rules. For example, Lyndall Urwick, a major exponent of classical organizational principles, considered organizational politics of any kind to be incompatible with a 'scientific' approach to management (Urwick, 1945). Political behaviour can be divisive and conflictive, often pitting people against other 'approved' systems of influence, such as formal authority, accepted ideology, or recognized expertise, or else against each other (Mintzberg and Waters, 1985). Political behaviour in decision making seeks to 'get others to do what we want, when they might not elect to do so' (MacMillan and Jones, 1986: 1). Such organizational behaviour is sometimes depicted as game-playing (Allison, 1971). Game-playing constitutes normal behaviour for ambitious executives because it gives them a greater ability to influence events according to their interests and to enhance their power and position.

In strategic decision making, researchers see political behaviour from several perspectives. One perspective examines politics inside organizations and consists of broadly two approaches. The first approach focuses on individual organizational members. It investigates political tactics among actors and their attempts to affect the outcomes of decision processes to serve their self-interests. In addition, it examines the relationship between political dynamics and some types of organizational outcomes, such as organizational performance and decision effectiveness (e.g. Dean and Sharfman, 1996; Eisenhardt and Bourgeois, 1988; Elbanna and Child, 2007). The second approach investigates politics among organizational units, and the acquisition by these units of power to influence the decision process (e.g. Pfeffer and Moore, 1980; Salancik and Pfeffer, 1974). Another perspective is broader and includes all kinds of influence on decision processes exercised by both internal actors – organizational members and/or organizational units – and external parties such as government agencies, unions, and customers (e.g. Hickson *et al.*, 1986; Mintzberg, Raisinghani and Theoret, 1976; Pettigrew, 1973). What links these perspectives is the recognition that people, whether they are located inside or outside the organization, believe they will be affected by the outcomes of its decisions. For this reason, they attempt to satisfy their personal or institutional needs by influencing the decision process using political tactics.

Politics cannot be addressed without considering its relation to power. Harrison (1999) suggests that decision politics can be seen as a process of actual influence, whereas power is a reservoir of potential influence. The relationship between politics and power is relatively straightforward, though the ways in which power is exercised are not. A power base facilitates the use of influence to protect the self-interest of decision makers. Effective strategic decision makers are aware of the power they possess, but use it judiciously as they seek to influence and determine the outcome of choices. However, power is not synonymous with political behaviour in strategic decision making as some authors tend to assume (e.g. Pfeffer, 1981). Thus political behaviour results from the use of power, but it may also be an attempt by those without power to exercise some influence through persuasion. Moreover, power is not a given. It can be enhanced or compromised by other tactics such as persuasion and by the legitimacy that others grant the person or unit in question. It is uncommon to find political behaviour limited only to one tactic. In addition to the use of power (Dean and Sharfman, 1993a; Elbanna and Child, 2007; Krishnan and Park, 2003; Pfeffer, 1981), decision makers may employ other tactics such as coalition formation (Bacharach and Lawler, 1980; Child and Tsai, 2005; Eisenhardt and Bourgeois, 1988; Elbanna and Child, 2007; Narayanan and Fahey, 1982; Stevenson *et al.*, 1985); agenda control (Eisenhardt and Zbaracki, 1992; Elbanna and Child, 2007; Papadakis and Barwise, 1997); tactics of timing affecting communications and meetings (Elbanna and Child, 2007; Hickson *et al.*, 1986; March and Olsen, 1982); the use of outside expert consultants (Dean and Sharfman, 1993a; Mumford and Pettigrew, 1975; Papadakis and Barwise, 1997; Pfeffer, 1992); negotiation or bargaining (Bacharach and Lawler, 1980; Elbanna and Child, 2007; Nutt, 1998; Papadakis, 1998); and tactics concerning the manipulation and control of crucial information (Cyert and March, 1963; Eisenhardt and Zbaracki, 1992; Elbanna and Child, 2007; Pettigrew, 1973; Pfeffer and Salancik, 1974).

POLITICAL BEHAVIOUR AND RATIONAL DECISION MAKING

'Rationality is the reason for doing something and to judge a behaviour as reasonable is to be able to say that the behaviour is understandable within a given frame of reference' (Butler, 2002: 226). Rational processes have long been recognized as a central aspect of strategic decision making and have been intensively subjected to both theoretical and empirical investigation in the literature on the subject. However, exponents of a political model of decision making dismiss the notion that organizational members, taken as a whole, can be rational (Eisenhardt, 1997). They argue that members may share some objectives, such as the welfare of the organization, but that they have conflicting preferences and interests which arise from different expectations of the future and different positions inside the organization. Thus some may attach a priority to growth while others may favour profitability (Allison, 1971). So the question arises as to how the political aspects of strategic decision making contrast with rationality and impinge on it.

Although strategic decisions are likely to stimulate political behaviour because they are significant and subject to uncertainty, paradoxically decision makers may feel a greater need to demonstrate rationality for such decisions rather than for decisions of less consequence. There are symbolic as well as functional reasons behind this (Dean and Sharfman, 1993a). Rational procedures such as collecting and analysing information are used to symbolize capable management (Langley, 1989; Mueller, 1998). Economic arguments suggest that more attention should be allocated to issues involving the highest cost or risk (Winter, 1981). Executives are expected to be more rational when making decisions crucial to the success of their organizations (Hickson *et al.*, 1986). Papadakis, Lioukas, and Chambers (1998) lend empirical support to this argument, finding that decision makers act more rationally when decisions imply important consequences. Although the evidence is limited, the balance of findings points to a positive relationship between the use of rational procedures and decision-making effectiveness (Dean and Sharfman, 1996) and organizational performance (Janis, 1989; Miller and Cardinal, 1994; Schwenk and Shrader, 1993).

Hence there is reason to expect that political behaviour and a use of techniques for rational analysis may typically both be found in strategic decision making. Political behaviour may shape the assumptions that are fed into rational analysis as well as the information it employs. Even under these conditions, rational analysis may still prove to be superior to its absence because it is systematic and synthetic, and because it may also point to certain practical limits to strategic choice. However, a tension will remain between making decisions that represent sound rational options for the organization as a whole and those which serve one or more sectional interests. This dilemma ultimately reflects the question of whether an organization's goals are oriented to the interests of one group, such as the shareholders of a firm, or to a wider set of stakeholders.

The rational synoptic formalism model and the political incrementalism model pervade the literature on the strategic decision-making process (Elbanna and Child, 2007). Synoptic formalism is considered an extension of the traditional rational decision-making model, and its basic feature is analysis leading to a comprehensive strategy. Contrasting with synoptic formalism are various depictions of incrementalism as the way in which strategic decisions are actually made in organizations. Incrementalism is essentially the taking of decisions in small cumulative steps as opposed to the idealized rational model of comprehensive planning. These limited steps can be made in response to the limited information that is available or affordable at one point in time, and they can also be addressed to resolving points of conflict one by one. Some exponents of incrementalism regard it as a more realistic way of injecting rationality into decision making, and all would regard it as closer to the reality of how strategic and policy decisions are usually made. It is consistent with the perspective of strategy as an emergent process (Mintzberg and Waters, 1985). Early expositions of incrementalism regarded it as 'muddling through' – a fragmented process of serial mutual adjustments around specific issues with little coordination between them (Braybrooke and Lindblom, 1970; Lindblom, 1959; 1979; Mintzberg, 1973). Later Quinn (1978) suggested that strategy involves a process of 'logical incrementalism' in which senior managers integrate incremental processes towards an overall strategic logic that is rational for the organization. More recently, a greater appreciation of how organizational politics is involved in incremental decision making has led to political incrementalism (Elbanna and Child, 2007; Goll and Rasheed, 1997). The three terms – incrementalism, logical incrementalism, and political incrementalism – are therefore not identical. Quinn's 'logical incrementalism' differs from Lindblom's incrementalism or 'muddling through' in that it combines elements of rational planning with elements of incrementalism (Papadakis and Barwise, 1997). Although there are some differences between these three terms, they are often offered as the antithesis to synoptic formalism or as simply a more accurate characterization of the way that organizations in reality make strategic decisions.

Eisenhardt and Zbaracki (1992) conclude that the political perspective provides a compelling description of the way in which managers actually make decisions. Reviewing the strategic decision-making literature, they conclude that the strategic decision-making process is best described as an 'interweaving' of both bounded rationality and political processes. The rationality of decision-making processes has received a central place in strategic decision-making theory and practice. Political behaviour among decision makers has also for some time been recognized as an intrinsic aspect of decision making and has received a great deal of attention from researchers. More recent research has emphasized how executives make decisions using political processes in addition to rational procedures (Butler, 2002). For example, two studies in two different settings, the USA and Egypt, offer convincing evidence that rationality and political behaviour are distinct characteristics of the strategic decision-making process (Dean and Sharfman, 1993b; Elbanna and Younies, 2008). They conclude that decision makers can be rational and/or political at the same time.

FORMS OF POLITICAL BEHAVIOUR IN STRATEGIC DECISION MAKING

Since interaction between people both within organizations and across their formal boundaries is one of the underlying features of the strategic decision-making process, forms of political behaviour affecting that process can be categorized according to their source and the relations involved. Some political actions arise primarily from the exercise of formal authority by those in superior hierarchical positions. Others amount to politicking between people or organizational units occupying similar hierarchical levels, but often oriented toward persuading strategic decision makers higher up. There are also instances in which political behaviour amounts primarily to the exercise of upward influence. Finally, there is political activity between organizations, including community and institutional bodies, which can also have a considerable impact on the strategic decisions that are made. This last category is of increasing importance as organizations extend the networks to which they belong as well as finding their strategic decisions increasingly judged by reference to social criteria.

1 Political behaviour deriving from hierarchical power

The principal forms of political intervention in strategic decision making deriving from hierarchical power are determination of the premises for such decisions, control of the financial allocations required to implement strategic decisions, control over key appointments, and a general power of veto.

The British Steel Corporation Korf Contract case (Harvard Business School, 1985) is a good illustration of how action taken by a chief executive can alter the basis of an ostensibly rational approach to strategic decision making. It actually provides one of the best records of the process whereby a strategic decision was taken in a large corporation. In this instance, the Chairman of BSC changed the assumptions entering into a major investment decision when they failed to produce the outcome he sought. He was committed to investment in one or two new plants in Scotland using a new alternative 'direct reduction' technology together with building a new related terminal facility. The alternative of not investing in any direct reduction plant was kept off the agenda. The chairman's judgement was partially informed by the political desirability of investing in Scotland at a time when Scottish nationalism was on the rise. The first round of rational modelling indicated that the proposed investment was not viable on the basis that alternative cheaper sources of steel from blast furnaces would be available. The chairman then ordered that the calculations should henceforth assume that a larger number of blast furnaces would be taken out of commission, with the consequence that the investment now appeared to be justified. In the event, the investment was a failure and the port facility was never used for its original purpose. The case illustrates the use of hierarchical power to affect strategic decision making in two ways. One is that identified by Bachrach and Baratz (1962), namely preventing an issue or option – no investment in direct re-duction plants – being considered in the first place. A similar tactic is to lay down the order in which issues are considered so that initial decisions are likely to pre-clude certain options being considered later on (Pfeffer, 1992). The other use of hierarchical position illustrated by this case is the power to change the premises of rational calculations when the results do not conform to what is desired.

A more recent example of how hierarchical power was used to push through a misguided strategic decision concerns the acquisition by the Royal Bank of Scot-land of the Dutch bank ABN Amro. On this occasion, the result was even more disastrous for the company, leading to the failure of RBS and its rescue by the State. The decision was taken very much at the insistence of the RBS chief executive, Sir Fred Goodwin, despite little prior due diligence and warnings that the acquisition would overstretch the bank's capital. Goodwin is reported to have exercised control though daily morning meetings at which senior managers were often humiliated. One former executive said that 'it wasn't a positive or healthy atmosphere. You have to wonder about the decisions people made in that environment.' The misjudge-ment over ABN Amro arose in large part because centralized political power was used to drive the decision through (Larsen, 2009).

Other studies of investment decision making and of resource allocation have shown how in a multi-level corporation this typically proceeds through a process of iterated negotiation between subsidiary or divisional level and the corporate level (e.g. Bower, 1970; Noda and Bower, 2007). Final approval, however, rests with top management. Indeed, despite the view that bounded rationality obliges CEOs to 'guide' a bottom-up process whereby divisional or subsidiary managers propose strategies for review and approval by the corporate level, there is reason to believe that CEOs tend to play a more decisive role in some circumstances, such as when integration between divisions or major capital investment is at issue (Eisenmann and Bower, 2000). Control of the financial allocations for key investment and of ap-pointments to head them up normally rests with a CEO or top management team and top management. It provides a power base from which to steer decisions and their implementation in desired directions.

2 Politicking between organizational units oriented towards strategic decisions

It has been somewhat easier to research political behaviour oriented towards strate-gic decisions among actors located below the highest levels of management than it has to access top managers. Consequently, more studies are available and some have been able to follow the process of decision making closely through participant observation. Such studies indicate that differentiation within an organization between departments or units tends to encourage political activity between these groups because each seeks to make a claim on the resources of the organization (Pettigrew, 1973). Some are likely to form coalitions if they perceive that they share an affinity of interests and that an alliance enhances their possibility of achieving enough power to dominate the decision-making process (Pfeffer, 1981).

The political tactics that the members of organizational units employ to generate or exercise power over major decisions respectively concern the use of information and knowledge, and the manipulation of reputation and credibility. Pettigrew (1973) observed how an established group of computer programmers maintained their power vis-à-vis a newer group of systems analysts in decision making over investment in a new large-scale computer installation. An important factor in this process was the role of the head of the programmers as a 'technical gatekeeper'. His control over the communication of information to top management gave him the ability to bias information in favour of his own demands as well as to feed negative information about the demands of his opponents (Pettigrew, 1972). Feldman's study (1988) of the struggles between line and staff groups for control over the high revenue-generating Phone Stores unit of a Bell Telephone company provides a fascinating insight into how information was manipulated and distorted through secret violations of normal organizational behaviour. The vice-president of the staff group secretly accessed the company's CEO and deceived him into thinking that the line vice-presidents had approved a document making the Phone Stores part of the staff organization before any discussion took place in the formal meeting convened to consider the issue. Moreover, the staff group immediately made the decision public so as to make it difficult to reverse. By violating organizational norms and manipulating information, an interest group within the organization was able to secure higher level approval for a major decision that advanced its interests and status within the company.

The social construction and capitalization of reputation within an organization, and its converse, the denial of reputation and competence to others, is another tactic in the struggle between groups within an organization to secure the power to influence strategic decisions. Pettigrew's study shows clearly how critical the 'assessed status' of the head of programmers was for his own and his department's ability to secure access to the directors and to use this to influence their thinking. At the same time, the programmers were outspoken in their denial that rival O & M and systems analyst groups possessed the knowledge necessary to making, or advising on, informed decisions. The programmers also fostered a protective myth that they were especially well qualified. This tactic was again assisted by secrecy: the programmers withheld information that might have reduced the uncertainty or mystique of their work. Pettigrew notes other studies that have illustrated how secrecy is used by defined groups within organizations to protect their positions and augment their power (Pettigrew, 1973: 152).

3 The exercise of upward influence over strategic decisions

As organizations grow they tend to become vertically differentiated. Within a unitary structure, differentiation may simply take the form of more hierarchical levels. If growth is also fostered by geographical and/or business diversification, it will often be accompanied by the delineation of corporate from divisions or business units, and the establishment by companies of affiliates such as subsidiaries and joint ventures. Vertical differentiation tends to expand the scope of the strategic decision-making process so that it is no longer confined to the ambit of top management. While top management may continue to set the general strategic direction of a firm, it will under these circumstances increasingly need to rely upon proposals and detailed knowledge provided by managers in lower-level positions. A similar trend is to be expected with the development of knowledge-based organizations in which the knowledge and judgement essential to informing strategic decisions becomes more widely dispersed throughout the organization's various levels and constituent units. These developments increase the scope, and indeed the necessity, for the exercise of upward influence over strategic decisions.

The case studies conducted by Feldman and Pettigrew have provided examples of the exercise of upward influence on major decisions that had significant resource and status allocating implications. In these examples, organizational groups used various manoeuvres to influence major decisions with the intention of maintaining or extending their claims on organizational resources against those of rival groups. In an internally pluralistic organization, competition between groups is always likely to involve attempts on their part to exercise upward influence. Further research offers additional detailed insights into the methods these actors may employ so as to exercise effective upward influence. One such study was conducted of elementary school principals reporting to school district superintendents (Mowday, 1978). Another examined the case of a joint venture general manager reporting to a majority-owning parent company (Lyles and Reger, 1993).

Mowday (1978) examined the effectiveness of five methods of upward influence: (1) threats, (2) legitimate authority (e.g. reference to school board policies), (3) persuasion, (4) rewards or exchange of favours, and (5) 'manipulation' – providing information in such as way that the recipient is not aware he or she is being influenced. Although there was some variation between three types of decision that school district principals commonly faced, manipulation was the method of influence that most consistently differentiated between the influence of the principals as rated by their immediate superiors. In other words, manipulation – the most subtle method of exercising upward influence – appeared to be the most effective, followed by persuasion in the case of one type of decision. By contrast, threats, reference to legitimate authority and rewards tended to be less effective. Mowday notes the complimentarity between his findings and Pettigrew's (1972; 1973) in that 'while his [Pettigew's] research demonstrated that the ability to control the content of information selectively is an important aspect of effectiveness in exercising influence, the results of the present study suggest the way in which information is transmitted is also an important strategic consideration' (p. 154).

An advantage of covert methods of influence such as manipulation lies in the fact that the organizational actors seeking to exert influence over a decision retain a greater degree of credibility and flexibility insofar as their intentions are not known and they are not perceived to be self-serving.

The case of a joint venture general manager studied by Lyles and Reger (1993) throws further light on how managers can influence higher-level decision making that is of strategic consequence for their units. The general manager deployed a variety of measures that enhanced his upward influence despite having a relative disadvantage in the organizational power structure. Some of these enabled the joint venture to increase its independence from parent firms, such as generating a self-sufficient resource base, developing superior products, and achieving good performance. Others were individual initiatives by the manager himself, such as informal personal interactions with parent firm managers and gaining cooperation from people outside the formal authority structure. These initiatives appear to have been facilitated by the manager's previous track record (credibility) and the overall success of the joint venture.

In short, informal methods such as manipulation of information and personal persuasion, together with personal credibility, can assist organizational members to influence strategic decisions even when their formal position lies outside the top decision-making group.

4 Inter-organizational political influence on strategic decisions

Strategic decision making within an organization can be influenced by other actors in the relevant community of organizations. Equally, in order to create conditions favourable to their preferred strategies, organizational decision makers may seek to shape external conditions through political actions. We are reminded here that strategic choice operates through initiatives taken within the network of internal and external organizational relationships (Child, 1997a). Traditionally, decision-making studies have focused on how organizations adapt to environmental demands through internal changes. Much less is known about how organizational decision makers may shape the fields in which they operate (Lewin and Carroll, 1999; Volberda and Lewin, 2003; Rodrigues and Child, 2008). Yet the concept of inter-organizational fields suggests that in order to be able to carry out their preferred strategies, organizations collude, make alliances with each other and are embedded within a web of relationships with other organizations, institutions, and players. An inter-organizational field consists of a recognized community of actors with which an organization interacts and from which it receives inputs that regulate how it functions and influence the values it adopts (DiMaggio and Powell, 1991; Greenwood and Hinings, 1986; Scott, 2001). Bourdieu (1973) first used this concept to describe the logic of knowledge production. His idea that social actors create and reproduce positions of power through socially constructed criteria of recognition by, and entry into, social groups, has been developed further by organizational theorists (DiMaggio and Powell, 1991; Scott, 2001; Fligstein, 2001).

Three theoretical perspectives focusing respectively on resources, institutions, and co-evolution, importantly inform an understanding of inter-organizational political influences on strategic decisions. Resource-based theory points to the conditions in which organizational actors have the capacity to change the external environment and are motivated to do so. The theory starts from a recognition that firms are bundles of heterogeneous resources. It argues that while large firms with considerable resources are individually able to influence their environments, small firms can only hope to have an effect if they act collectively (Penrose, 1979). Research on corporate political behaviour suggests that firms possessing greater resources are more likely to be politically active (Hillman and Hitt, 1999). In a similar vein, it has been argued that firms with high levels of organizational slack tend to engage more frequently in political behaviour (Schuler, 1999; Schuler, Rehbein, and Cramer, 2002). In addition to lobbying, this may involve cooptation and making alliances with other organizations (Pfeffer, 1992). Slack provides the wherewithal to engage in external political behaviour, whereas its opposite – resource scarcity and dependence on external resource providers – can severely constrain such initiative (Pfeffer and Salancik, 1974). Situations that involve competition for resources and their allocation, both within and between organizations, generate conflict and encourage political behaviour (Pettigrew, 1973; Zald, 1970).

Firms are embedded in institutional settings which are usually defined by a close interdependence between government and firms. Because of the kind of resources they possess, large firms may play an active role in restructuring that setting. Conversely, governments are able to influence business outcomes in a variety of ways. Public policy makers can increase or decrease the power of actors in the market place through a number of policies and interventions, such as by reducing or increasing barriers of entry and exit, by imposing environmental and quality standards. Furthermore, governments may alter the size of markets through purchasing decisions that create alternative markets for complementary products (Hillman and Hitt, 1999). Multinational corporations [MNCs], on the other hand, may impact on issues which are strategic for the State, such as levels of employment, investment, and tax revenues, through their ability to relocate economic activities in different countries. Governments and MNCs thus operate in a political arena where policy outcomes are largely dependent on each other's bargaining power and negotiation skills, including the ability to mobilize support for their respective strategies (Boddewyn, 1998; Boddewyn and Brewer, 1994).

Large corporations attempt to influence governments in numerous ways (McLaughlin, Jordan, and Maloney, 1993). In order to create strategic opportunities and reduce competitive threats, they are increasingly creating professional structures to deal with governments and institutions that regulate their activities (Lord, 2000; Armey, 1996; Getz 1997). Political behaviour by organizations is therefore recognized as strategic in obtaining comparative advantage. In lobbying governments and institutions, and building political capital (Frynas, Mellahi, and Pigman, 2006), organizations may be able to influence the conditions of trade and regulation. They can also help shape the ecology of the market – its size, its players, and the rules of interaction within their industries (Fligstein, 1996).

McLaughlin, Jordan, and Maloney (1993) suggested that governments in turn shape the way in which companies exert influence on their institutions. For example, governments can decide to listen to the representations of whole industries rather than those of individual companies. In these circumstances, organizations may increase their bargaining power if they can influence the views of the relevant community (Hadjikham, 2000). Corporate actors can enhance their bargaining power if they are able to bring opponents onside through 'constituency building' (Lord, 2000). In order to have an impact on public policies, large players need to reconcile needs of those who are small or have different views. Such political skills may help large players to gain legitimacy for their own claims. As Allison (1969) pointed out some time ago, political advocacy, persuasion, and diplomacy help to reconcile fragmented and divergent interests.

Institutional theory provides insights into inter-organizational political influence on strategic decisions, by addressing the issue of self-regulation versus institutional regulation (DiMaggio and Powell, 1991; Meyer and Rowan, 1977; Scott, 2001). Institutions are seen to establish boundaries on the possible courses of action by setting norms and rules to govern interaction within and between organizations. Once these are in place they take on a life of their own and impose limits on implementation as well as strategy. Considerations of legitimacy, norms, and culture become more important in the process of choosing strategic alternatives than rationality and efficiency (Greenwood and Hinings, 1986). Thus, institutional theory offers insights into the reasons why decisions are not implemented, and why some decisions are interrupted and not implemented at all (Oliver, 1991; 1992). Mintzberg *et al.* (1976) illustrate how external organizations, often public authorities, can block strategic decisions. Norms and rules may take a long time to fall into disuse and they may persist even if they adversely affect innovation or threaten organizational survival. Institutionalized rules may impede the making of strategic decisions, and even inhibit initial discussions.

However, even very established norms may suffer deinstitutionalization if they lose their utility and credibility. Oliver (1991; 1992) has developed this insight, and in so doing has enlightened institutional theory by incorporating a political perspective. Thus deinstitutionalization can be a response to a redistribution of power and change in dependencies among major players – both firms and public agencies. These situations may encourage political decisions or equally non decisions. Under conditions of dysfunctional norms or a lack of consensus, non decision making may be perceived as the most sensible course of action (Rodrigues and Hickson, 1995). One of Oliver's main contributions is to suggest that political behaviour does not necessarily involve exerting pressure for change. On the contrary, doing nothing – acquiescence, compromise, and avoidance – also implies a political choice (Oliver, 1991). In such circumstances, decisions that change the status quo may only occur through the mobilization of those who feel that prevailing norms and rules conflict with their interests (Rodrigues, 1980). When norms cease to be instrumental for large players, they may withdraw their support in order to secure their own interests and agendas. Oliver cites the example of how cartels may be dismantled because a main player realizes it will be better off withdrawing from the collective. According to the institutional perspective, neither regulation nor deregulation are seen as necessarily being the product of a fair and rational decision processes.

The third perspective relevant to inter-organizational political influences on strategic decision making is that of co-evolution between organizations and their environments (Lewin and Carroll, 1999; Volberda and Lewin, 2003). Despite its origins in the study of natural selection, analyses of co-evolution have recently come to recognize and illustrate the part played by conscious political action in the evolving relationships between organizations and external agencies (e.g. Rodrigues and Child, 2008). This allocates a central role to politics in the processes of strategic decision making, and broadens that role to include the outcomes of interaction

between organizational and external actors through the specific social arrangements or 'relational frameworks' (Meyer and Scott, 1983) that may exist between
them. Joint business–governmental committees are an example of such frameworks,
which permit networks or coalitions to form. Such networks are institutionally
sanctioned arrangements that connect actors through participation in a common
discourse. They cross system levels by involving people who occupy strategic
decision-making roles within both institutional agencies and organizations (Castilla
et al., 2000). These links can be especially effective in conveying and articulating
expectations about the policies of organizations that are highly dependent upon
institutional approval and resource provision because of a regulatory regime and/
or public ownership (Gould, 1993; Mische, 2003).

Relational frameworks are potentially relevant to the process of accommodation
between public policy priorities and firms' preferred strategies. They provide channels through which institutional bodies can express approval or otherwise of particular corporate strategies. At the same time, they can also provide a conduit for
corporate executives to express their point of view, and through which leading firms
may have an opportunity to shape institutional regulations so as to better accommodate the strategic decisions that corporate leaders seek to make.

The political action view of organizational co-evolution suggests that the concept of interest group is pivotal to understanding inter-organizational influences
on strategic decision making. Interest groups are social collectivities whose members perceive that they have a strong commonality of interests and who therefore
tend to act together to negotiate and exert pressure (Rodrigues and Child, 2008).
In order to shape strategic decisions, organized interest groups that span system
levels may compete simultaneously for control within organizations and for positions of influence over the institutional rules that are likely to be laid down for the
operation of the markets within which the organization operates (Fligstein, 1996).
For example, the senior managers of large firms may be involved in a government's
project to re-organize an industry, such as through privatization. The outcomes of
such decision arenas may be unpredictable once competing interests seek to capture or influence the decision process for their own ends or for the benefit of their
own organizations (McLaughlin *et al.*, 1993).

ANTECEDENT CONDITIONS FAVOURING POLITICAL BEHAVIOUR IN STRATEGIC DECISION MAKING

Available research suggests that the intensity and form of political behaviour associated with strategic decision making can be predicted by a number of antecedent
conditions. These conditions fall into three categories: (1) relations with external
organizations, (2) organizational characteristics, and (3) the nature of the strategic
decision in question. The greater the dependence on external organizations for resources and/or for approvals from governmental agencies and other institutions,
the greater is likely to be the effort made by organizational leaders to lobby, co-opt
or otherwise influence the external parties. Organizational characteristics likely to

encourage political behaviour in strategic decision making are the centralization of power, the degree of horizontal differentiation within the organization, and the presence of groups with the ability to control the handling of strategic contingencies. Features of the decision itself that are likely to intensify political behaviour include its significance for organizational survival and for resource allocation within the organization, as well as the scope given to politicking by ambiguity and uncertainty surrounding the issue to be decided.

We noted in the previous section that resource or institutional dependence on external organizations is liable to bring them into an organization's strategic decision-making arena. Dependence on external parties places an organization in a subsidiary relationship which makes the objectives and values of those external units become highly relevant to that organization's strategy. Insofar as external parties can withdraw their resource support, or block decisions through legal, regulatory or orchestrated public pressure, they play a political role in strategic decision making. It therefore becomes a matter of priority for the leaders of an organization placed in this dependent position to endeavour to secure the support of the external parties. The actions that they can take are well recognized by political scientists. One is the lobbying of external agencies in an attempt to elicit support for the organization's preferred strategy (Bentley, 1908; Berry, 1997). A second commonly used device is to co-opt influential people from external bodies into an organizational role such as advisor and/or onto one of the organization's policy making bodies (Selznick, 1949). A third possibility is to develop political capital such as through providing expert assistance and other acts of goodwill. This last approach may be particularly effective for multinational corporations seeking to obtain governmental support for their preferred strategies in emerging economies (Frynas *et al.*, 2006). Through such initiatives, senior managers or particular interest groups within an organization seek to gain the support of significant external parties for a favoured strategic decision, or to avoid their opposition to the decision. Sometimes, the support of outside consultants is engaged in order to strengthen the case for a particular decision outcome by adding to it the weight of expertise.

Three organizational characteristics have been identified as relevant to the intensity of politics around strategic decision making. One is the hierarchical centralization of power, the impact of which may depend on contingent conditions. In general, power centralization is expected to reduce the scope for political behaviour because it submerges conflict (Pfeffer, 1981). On the other hand, in organizations such as high technology firms where relevant knowledge is distributed among middle-level staff, centralized power can become dysfunctional and political behaviour arises in an attempt to counter or by-pass it (Eisenhardt and Bourgeois, 1988).

The second relevant organizational characteristic is the degree of horizontal differentiation. Mumford and Pettigrew (1975: 57) point out that 'a characteristic of modern industry is the proliferation of groups of specialists within large firms'. Such groups perform specialized tasks subject to their own criteria of performance and their members may well differ in their occupational cultures, values, and career interests. Therefore the more that individuals and groups within the organization are differentiated in these characteristics, the greater is the likelihood of rivalry and conflict between them (Pettigrew, 1973). This conflict will stimulate attempts on their part to influence strategic decisions through political action.

The third organizational feature is the presence of certain occupational groups that have a large degree of control over strategic contingencies. Such contingencies are events that could seriously impact on the organization's performance such as plant failure, the inappropriate purchase of expensive equipment, and a failure in cash-flow management. When specialist groups have exclusive competencies to evaluate and deal with such contingencies, and senior management cannot readily substitute for them, they are in an enhanced position to influence strategic decisions relating to their areas of specialized expertise. Crozier (1964) identified the power that maintenance workers and technical engineers may have to set limits on what it is feasible for management to decide through possessing the expertise to deal with contingent uncertainties. If and when the procedures for dealing with contingencies can be converted into explicit routines, this power will be curtailed. Hickson, Hinings, Lee, Schneck, and Pennings (1971) later developed a formal theory of how the control by organizational subunits of strategic contingencies augmented the power of those units under conditions of uncertainty, especially when it was difficult to substitute for their activities.

A further antecedent of political behaviour in strategic decision making is the nature of the decision itself. The intensity of politicking associated with a strategic decision is expected to increase the more significant the decision is perceived to be for the survival of the organization and/or the more significance it has for the allocation of resources within the organization (or between the organization and its stakeholders). Pettigrew (1973) argued that because strategic decisions involve the allocation of scarce resources, they are especially liable to exhibit political behaviour between individuals and units competing for such resources. Ambiguity about the parameters of the issue being decided and uncertainty surrounding its consequences also open the door for political behaviour. Ambiguity and uncertainty limit the scope for identifying a rationally optimum decision and allow for a range of competing proposals and preferences to claim credibility (Lyles, 1981). As March and Simon (1958) noted, under conditions of complexity and imperfect information, decisions are made on the basis of selective perception and identification with sub-goals.

THE CONSEQUENCES OF POLITICAL BEHAVIOUR IN STRATEGIC DECISION MAKING

Most previous research has concluded that political behaviour adversely affects the quality of decision making and/or organizational performance (e.g. Bourgeois and Eisenhardt, 1988; Dean and Sharfman, 1996; Elbanna and Child, 2007; Gandz and Murray, 1980; Zahra, 1987). Elbanna (2006) provides a comprehensive review of this research. The following reasons may help to account for this negative relationship.

First, we have already seen that many of the political tactics that are successful in exerting influence over strategic decision making, such as manipulation and secret communication, lead to a selective and biased disclosure of relevant information (e.g. Pettigrew, 1973). Organizational politics is therefore likely to distort the information required for effective decision making (Cyert and March, 1963; Pfeffer, 1992; Pfeffer and Salancik, 1974). This behaviour contrasts with open and straightforward methods of eliciting opinion in favour of the best outcome, which rely on open discussion and the sharing of information among decision makers (Eisenhardt and Bourgeois, 1988; Elbanna and Child, 2007). The consequence is that organizational politics may lead managers to make decisions based on incomplete information, giving rise to disappointing outcomes (Dean and Sharfman, 1996).

Second, political decision processes are divisive. This divisiveness may inhibit agreement on key strategic concepts and on the allocation of responsibilities to carry out strategies effectively (Maitlis and Lawrence, 2003). Zahra (1987) found in a study of American manufacturing companies that more intense organizational politics was associated with less consensus among managers over their organization's mission. Moreover, they are time-consuming. They may delay decisions, with the possible loss of opportunities and profits (Pfeffer, 1992). This problem will be more obvious in competitive and rapidly changing environments in which decisions need to be made speedily (Eisenhardt, 1989). Some therefore regard political behaviour as a waste of organizational resources which could instead be directed towards achieving the organization's objectives (e.g. Eisenhardt and Bourgeois, 1988; Mintzberg and Waters, 1985).

Third, as argued by Dean and Sharfman (1996), political behaviour may lead to incomplete understanding of the environmental constraints, resulting in the undermining of strategic decision quality in two ways. One is that political tactics are directed towards serving the interests, power bases, and positions inside the organization rather than on what is feasible, given the prevailing environmental forces. Hence, decisions which result from such processes are less likely to consider environmental constraints. The other way in which strategic decision quality can be undermined is that political processes may exclude some feasible alternatives because they conflict with the interests of powerful individuals.

Political processes are unlikely to encourage a complete and accurate analysis of strategic decisions; consequently, they increase the possibility of poor performance and unsuccessful decisions. This is because political behaviour leads to many shortcomings in the strategic decision-making process, such as distortion and restriction of information; waste of time; and a failure to focus on environmental constraints. Pfeffer (1992) wonders why, if the political aspects of decision making inject all these shortcomings, do people not treat the cases advanced for particular strategies with greater wariness? Moreover, why does feedback not correct some of these shortcomings? For example, if executives misuse information and prefer to pursue their self-interest, they should expect to suffer when this comes to light. His answer is that the decision makers who use political tactics are rarely concerned about these matters, and this may be due to a number of reasons. Strategic decisions are generally long-term, complex, and taken under conditions of high uncertainty. There is a time lag between the decision-making process and the availability of its results. The outcomes of strategic decisions are affected by multiple factors, which can introduce indeterminacy into their evaluation. So there is no way to know if the right decision was made – at least before a considerable period of time has elapsed. This limits the ability to hold executives accountable for making strategic decisions that were compromised by their pursuit of sectional or personal self-interest. Moreover, apart from very small organizations, there is collective responsibility for strategic decisions. This means that it is difficult to assign responsibility for error to a particular individual and there is a collective unwillingness to determine who is responsible for the failure.

Although most previous studies take a negative view of politics, some authors argue that politics may be harmful in some situations but helpful in others (Gray, 1989; Janis, 1989; Pfeffer, 1992; Stevenson *et al.*, 1985). Eisenhardt, Kahwajy, and Bourgeois (1997), for example, argue that in a rapidly changing environment, politics may be beneficial because they serve as an important mechanism for organizational adaptation. Although Zahra (1987) found a negative association between intensity of organizational politics and overall company performance, he also found that it was associated with some positive aspects of the strategic process, including quality of long-range planning, effective selection of a strategy, and effective strategy implementation. It appears that political behaviour can encourage multiple perspectives and assumptions to be examined resulting in better decisions. Mintzberg (1998) points out that politics should be evaluated according to their effect on the ability of an organization to pursue the appropriate mission efficiently in the long term. He suggests some functional roles for politics over the different stages of strategic decision making. In the preparation stage, politics can ensure that all sides of the decision are fully debated. Then, in the decision-making stage, politics can work as a kind of 'invisible underhand' to promote a necessary change blocked by the legitimate systems of influence. Lastly, in the execution stage, politics can ease the path for the implementation of a strategic decision. Other authors argue that political behaviour can be expressed in two ways, namely competitive and collaborative (Baum, 1989; Frost, 1987; MacMillan and Jones, 1986). As described by Simmers (1998: 38), competitive politics 'correspond to traditional politics, the politics of win-lose competition, self-interest, and unsanctioned means and ends'; while collaborative political activities 'begin with the assumption that people will continue to support each other despite conflicts. Interests are asserted vigorously but securely, openly, and with win-win competition'.

Political behaviour can be seen as commonplace in strategic decision making. A good understanding of such behaviour could serve to forestall its negative manifestations and instead be used to widen discussion and debate in the long-term best interests of both decision makers and the organization itself. For example, the risk of information distortion through manipulation and secrecy can be offset by protocols that offer an open and equal voice to all interested groups and individuals. In other words, there is a need for competence in the use of politics in strategic decision making in order to (1) limit the adverse consequences likely to result from the irresponsible use of politics and (2) enhance the functional benefits of politics (Drory and Romm, 1988). Similarly, Hayes (1984) asserts that decision makers need to develop political competence to operate effectively.

Moreover, it appears that past research may have overstated the negative aspect of political behaviour. Organizational politics has a negative connotation in the minds of most researchers and practitioners. However, Mintzberg (1985) identified the potential functional benefits of political behaviour for both the decision-making process and the organization as a whole. Hence, we need to adopt a more balanced view of political behaviour and to take its multi-dimensional nature into account. While traditionally political behaviour has been defined by reference to serving sectional interests, it can also widen and enrich a debate over the best strategic paths to follow in the interest of the organization as a whole. In other words, political behaviour can be defined as 'action(s) taken by decision makers in order to serve their own interests *or* these of the organisation'. This broad definition of political behaviour reflects both aspects of political behaviour: the constructive or positive aspect and the destructive or negative aspect. It opens a promising arena for future research to address both aspects of political behaviour in strategic decision making. In conjunction with this, there is an opportunity for researchers to develop new constructs of political behaviour, which can provide a more dynamic and eclectic view of political behaviour and uncover the unsystematic side of reality. This recommendation is consistent with that of Hutzschenreuter and Kleindienst (2006) in repeating the call of Fredrickson (1983: 572) that 'investigators should place greater emphasis on evolving concepts into constructs and developing measures of those constructs'.

In conclusion, rather than assuming, as do many authors on the subject, that political behaviour in strategic decision making is automatically dysfunctional or destructive (Harrison, 1999), we argue that political behaviour can sometimes be functional to the strategic decision. The consequences of political behaviour may vary from one decision to another (Hickson *et al.*, 1986; Elbanna and Child, 2007). We also need to consider the unit of analysis more carefully, and in particular to distinguish between the quality of a given decision from organizational performance as a whole. For example, a decision on innovation normally involves many unknowns and often requires contributions from a range of specialists. A lively political process may improve the quality of that decision so long as the process is conducted openly. However, it is equally possible that if this political process lends an exaggerated prominence to innovation within the strategy making process, the organization may end up with an unbalanced strategy. It may invest too much in innovation at the expense of its shorter term financial survival.

THE POLITICS OF STRATEGIC DECISION MAKING AND CORPORATE GOVERNANCE

How to make business leaders accountable through good corporate governance has been a subject of concern for over a hundred years. The concern arises from the possibility of a conflict of interest between such leaders and other stakeholders, and it has been amplified by the development of large powerful corporations and evidence of abuse on the part of their senior executives. Thorstein Veblen foreshadowed the problem when he claimed that a major feature of modern capitalism lay in a conflict of interests between waste-making business 'financiers' and engineers who represented the pursuit of true wealth-creation in the interests of the whole community through production and workmanship (Veblen, 1904; 1914). Veblen was exercised by the wasteful exploitation of resources by powerful oligopolistic owners who increasingly absented themselves from the productive process. However, the present day focus of corporate governance was largely set by Berle and Means (1932). They drew attention to the 'divorce of ownership from control,' resulting from the increasing dispersion of the ownership of large corporations which left their control effectively in the hands of managers who often held relatively little stock ownership themselves. Berle and Means feared that the divorce of ownership from control undermined the ability to hold managers to account and to prevent them from pursuing their own sectional interests. They were concerned that the separation of ownership from control not only held the danger of a lack of managerial accountability to investors but also a lack of accountability to society in general (Mizruchi, 2004). In this way, the question of whose interests shape the strategic decisions of corporations and through which political processes lies at the heart of corporate governance.

However, studies of corporate governance have evolved in isolation from those of strategic decision making. There has been little dialogue between these two streams of scholarship. Corporate governance is primarily concerned with how organizations allocate resources and its effects on stakeholders. Questions on who is best equipped to establish the goals of the corporation and about who has the legitimacy to determine performance criteria and the allocation of returns are pivotal to corporate governance inquiries (O'Sullivan, 2000). It is axiomatic that those who govern corporations and other organizations are supposed to be closely involved in decisions on strategic issues, and the way these are taken. Nevertheless, corporate governance research has so far adopted a more limited frame of reference which overlooks the process of strategic decision making and its political dynamics. It has mostly formulated hypotheses concerning the limits to shareholder control over managerial agents and its practical recommendations have focused on board composition and structure.

In this vein, the analysis that Berle and Means offered focused on formal rights as expressed in share ownership or in official positions such as directorships. This focus on formal provisions and 'codes' of good corporate governance has carried through to most debate and research on corporate governance ever since, as witnessed both in reports on the subject (e.g. Cadbury, 1992) and comparative studies (e.g. Clarke, 2007; Zattoni and Cuomo, 2008). Without denying the importance of codes and regulations, and the sanctions attached to their breach, they are limited by their very formality. They do not deal with the informal processes through which corporations are actually governed and their strategic decisions made. Studies of how politics actually enter into strategic decision making, of the kind reviewed in this chapter, can offer insights that are essential to understanding how corporate governance really works.

A political perspective on strategic decision making draws attention to the limitations of purely formal provisions as the means of safeguarding against socially irresponsible corporate behaviour. As we have noted in this chapter, much of the political behaviour associated with strategic decision making is informal. This informal character applies not only to political behaviour within organizations; it also characterizes much 'behind the scenes' activity between organizational members and external parties. We have seen that political behaviour can be underhand, relying on secrecy and even deceit. This clearly presents difficulties for identifying who is actually responsible for the decisions that are made and for attributing accountability. It may be argued that attributing formal responsibility for strategic decisions, such as to the CEO and/or members of the board, and backing this up with sanctions, will encourage these persons to take more care to ensure that their decisions are not based on distorted information or their own self-serving interests. Even so, this usually leaves plenty of scope for such decisions to be justified through the selective release of information and arguments that in reality cloak a pursuit of sectional interests. The significance of the contribution that a political perspective on strategic decision making can offer lies in the way that it cautions against too sanguine a reliance on purely formal governance provisions.

Attention to the politics of strategic decision making also reminds us that the quality of decision outcomes, and their impact on organizational performance, will depend significantly on the processes through which those decisions are reached. This point is also often missed in discussions of corporate governance, which tend to concentrate their attention on accountability for decision outcomes. Evidence has been cited suggesting that the quality of those outcomes may be enhanced by an active political process, so long as certain conditions apply. Thus it appears that political behaviour can encourage multiple perspectives and assumptions to be examined, which in turn provides a wider range of considerations and relevant information to feed into better decisions. Under conditions of rapid change and uncertainty this provision of more, rather than less, information and viewpoints can improve the quality of strategic decisions so long as the necessary speed can be maintained through effective conflict management and integration of inputs (Eisenhardt, 1989). The implication is that a broadening of participation in strategic decision making, at least to those with relevant knowledge and insight, is a positive corporate governance provision. Another more challenging requirement for political processes to enhance strategic outcomes is that they should be open rather than secretive. Information distortion, leading to decisions that are poorly informed and/or serve narrow interests, is more likely when the decision process is secretive. This again is an insight arising from political studies of strategic decision making which has the potential to inform corporate governance policies. Transparency is generally considered to be an essential requirement for good corporate governance. A significant issue for further investigation is whether, and under what conditions, political behaviour in strategic decision making encourages transparency and open discussion rather than the opposite.

DISCUSSION AND CONCLUSION

Strategic decision making is a process for which normative models and techniques based on rationality have been proposed, but which is in practice always infused with political behaviour. However, the sensitivity of the behaviour, and its often devious and secret nature, renders its study subject to severe methodological problems. It is clearly problematic to gain access to valid information on political behaviour when it may well include underhand manoeuvres and the deliberate distortion of information. Moreover as Allison (1971) argued, in searching for an understanding of how a strategic decision was reached one has to put oneself in the place of the various participants. However, this is likely to provide a number of explanations for a given decision outcome rather than a coherent picture of what took place and why. Different people and groups may have only a partial involvement in a decision process. They also act on different and potentially conflicting premises, and understand the decision process in the light of their own selective interpretations. They may well rationalize the part they played after the event, and the more politically charged the decision process the more this is likely to happen. So even if the participants in a decision-making process are willing to talk about it, the researcher may still be presented with divergent information.

Problems of confidentiality, partial involvement, and post hoc rationalization make it particularly difficult to uncover the political aspects of strategic decision making through convenient and conventional methods of undertaking organizational research, namely self-administered questionnaires and interviews. Direct real-time observation is a far more adequate method, which can be supplemented by conversations and interviews, but it requires a very intense level of access that is time-consuming and for which it is very difficult to obtain permission. It is therefore no accident that after half a century of interest in the subject we have only a handful of studies that provide a vivid insight into the politics of strategic decision making.

The paucity of good empirical evidence places limits on our ability to model the role of politics on strategic decision making. It is in any case a complex process liable to proceed through several stages, and to experience interruptions and recursive loops (Mintzberg et al., 1976). There is still no parsimonious set of concepts that captures much of what occurs in the political processes of strategic decision making (Maitlis and Lawrence, 2003).

Any modelling of the politics of strategic decision making will therefore necessarily be suggestive rather than definitive. Two forms of modelling offer a way forward, one being oriented towards variance analysis and the other towards process analysis (Mohr, 1982). Variance analysis is concerned with the prediction of variance in phenomena of theoretical interest. Applied to the subject of this chapter, it directs attention to the antecedents of political behaviour in strategic decision making and, in turn, is concerned with predicting and explaining the effects of political behaviour on outcomes such as decision-making quality and organizational performance. Process analysis, by contrast, would direct attention to the sequence of events in a decision process. Applied to the subject of this chapter, it would focus on, for example, how the political initiatives taken by certain organizational members generate reactions from others. Process analysis could also be directed towards the ways in which political behaviour impacts on decision quality and organizational performance through features such as agenda control, information rationing, and distortion.

Variance analysis

The model shown in Figure 5.1 presents a variance analysis that builds upon the concepts and research presented in this chapter. It categorizes the factors we have

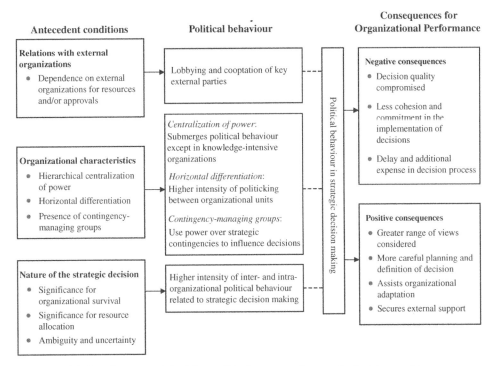

FIGURE 5.1 A variance model of the political aspects of strategic decision making.

discussed into antecedent conditions, political behaviour and consequences for organizational performance.

The first stage in the model identifies antecedent conditions that are likely to promote political behaviour in strategic decision making. Our review has suggested that variance in the form and intensity of political behaviour associated with strategic decision making is likely to be predicted by (1) relations with external organizations, (2) organizational characteristics, and (3) the nature of the strategic decision in question. Political behaviour, in turn, may be characterized in terms of (1) its form, such as lobbying, cooptation, and the use of power over strategic contingencies, and (2) its intensity.

The second stage in the variance model concerns the impact that political behaviour has on the outcomes of strategic decision making. Does more intense politicking improve or deteriorate the quality of strategic decisions and hence organizational performance, or can it actually have positive consequences? The evidence discussed earlier in this chapter points to a generally negative impact of politics on both decision quality and organizational performance, due to features such as the manipulation of information and the delays and additional costs incurred. However, some results also suggest important qualifications to this conclusion. One qualification is that it depends on whether managers have the skills to handle conflict and political behaviour constructively so that it produces a diversity of arguments while preserving a collaborative culture. If they have such skills, active organizational politics may assist an organization to learn and adapt. By stimulating greater interest in the process of strategic decision making, an active political process may also lead to a more careful definition and planning of an organization's strategy. Also proactive political moves towards consequential external parties may secure support for an organization's strategy.

Process analysis

Only a few writers have advanced models of the process whereby political behaviour enters into strategic decision making. Process here refers to the sequence of events leading up to a decision. Mintzberg *et al.* (1976: 246) define a 'decision process' as 'a set of actions and dynamic factors that begins with the identification of a stimulus for action and ends with the specific commitment to action'. These authors developed a general model of the strategic decision process that incorporated a number of phases: recognition of a problem or opportunity, diagnosis, search, design, selection, screen, evaluation-choice, and authorization. They note from their study of 25 strategic decision processes that political activities could enter into any of these phases. In two cases, principals within the organization even disputed the need to recognize the issue in the first place. These were instances of an attempt to influence the strategic agenda. In two other cases, political bargaining took place during the development and selection phases. Here the political behaviour was directed at influencing the design or choice of solutions. In four cases, outside parties confronted and temporarily blocked proposed decisions late in the final selection phase. The authors provide other examples of how political 'impasses' led to delays in the decision process. The responses to political opposition by those driving the decisions included cycling back in the process to redesign the proposal or find an alternative one, and in some instances taking action to undermine the power of the antagonists.

Political dynamics either carry strategic decision making towards a decision outcome that commands consensus and/or overrides opposition, or towards a failure to take and implement a decision at all. The outcome of this process is seen to depend on whether there is a progression from the different 'initial preferred outcomes' [IPOs] held by participating actors to a position in which they are prepared, or obliged, to modify their preferred outcomes [MPOs] (Abell, 1975). This modification could result from various factors such as coercion by superior power holders, bargaining or the persuasive influence of new information. In a rather similar way, Mumford and Pettigrew (1975) view the process of deciding on innovations as moving forward from preliminary goal-seeking and goal-setting to a decision choice, driven by a combination of technical information and political bargaining.

A central issue in the strategic decision process is how power and influence is brought to bear on the content and progress of proposed decision outcomes. Table 5.1 summarizes some of the possibilities. The table suggests that the use of superior power, rather than free discussion, to resolve conflicts between IPOs is likely to lead to poor results. If there is an application of hierarchical power within the organization, the consequences may well be a poorly informed solution and one

TABLE 5.1 Decision process conditions and likely outcomes

Parties involved	Resolution of conflicts/ move from IPOs to MPOs	Implication for quality of decision
Top management	Through fiat by top management	Poor implementation due to resentment by organizational members, technical inadequacy of the decision, etc.
	Through discussion with subordinates and generation of consensus	Good quality, well informed decision, with strong backing for implementation
Middle management and staff groups	Through political manoeuvres such as subterfuge, secrecy, myth creation	May lead to inadequate decisions due to information distortion. Also reluctance of some individuals or groups to implement the decision
	Through mutual discussion between groups and creation of consensus	Good quality, well informed decision, with strong backing for implementation – especially in a knowledge-based organization
Key external resource providers or regulators	External parties block proposed decisions	Possibility that a strategic opportunity for the organization will have been missed
	External parties persuaded to accept proposed solutions or to accept modifications to them	A decision that is informed by the concerns of external parties, and has their consent, should encounter fewer problems of implementation

that middle managers and staff groups are not motivated to implement. If the application of power comes from external parties, the result could be a sub-optimum compromise or the missing of an opportunity due to the blocking of the decision. The implications are that an open discussion of the political issues associated with a strategic issue is likely to produce a more satisfactory result than an attempt either to force the issue through the use of power, or to make a decision based on information that is inadequate or false due to political artifice.

Avenues for further research

There are many issues concerning the political aspects of strategic decision making that deserve further research. Although we have noted the practical difficulties of investigating this subject, its intrinsic importance warrants efforts to overcome these. We now identify some promising avenues.

The strategic decision process cannot be properly understood unless we take adequate account of its setting. The national context is likely to be very relevant because it is accompanied by specific institutional arrangements that vary in the extent to which officials and external agencies can influence major organizational decisions. However, there is still only limited research on strategic decision making outside the USA and the UK. Future research needs to examine the extent to which the results of research concerning political behaviour conducted in those countries apply elsewhere. There is reason to expect, for example, that the politics of strategic decision making in China will tend to involve government officials to a much greater extent than in the so-called Anglo-Saxon countries (Child and Lu, 1996, Child and Tse, 2001).

Another aspect of the decision setting that has not been taken into account very systematically is the type and function of the organization. Although many authors argue that both business and public organizations must deal with similar managerial problems (Schwenk and Huff, 1986), decision makers' perceptions of the appropriate way of dealing with these problems may significantly vary in the two types of organizations (Schwenk, 1990). For example, the management of private business firms has different objectives and far more clear cut criteria for success (Chandler, 1962). Pfeffer (1981: 77) has observed that:

> Business organizations are, for the most part, less overtly political than organizations in non-profit or public sectors such as governmental agencies, hospitals, and universities. The reason is not that businessmen are more rational, more analytical, or less political than administrators in these other organizations. Rather, business organizations have a reasonably agreed upon goal of profit maximization, and this goal consensus negates much of the need for the use of power that might otherwise exist.

Hence, in organizations with the relatively clear goal of profit maximization, political behaviour may be viewed with some suspicion. This does not mean that decision makers in these organizations do not behave politically. Rather, it suggests that business executives may not be receptive to some kinds of political behaviour. By contrast, those who manage public organizations may be more concerned with meeting the multiple interests of stakeholders. In order to reconcile these interests and integrate them into the final decision, decision makers may use a wider range of political tactics (cf. Schwenk, 1990).

A further promising issue for future research is how managers can overcome the negative effects of political tactics. One answer may be through improved mutual trust (Papadakis and Barwise, 1997). For example, Dean and Sharfman (1993b) reported that a high level of interpersonal trust was effective in encouraging managers to limit their political behaviour. Another potential answer is provided by Eisenhardt (1999), who suggests that common goals, clear areas of responsibility and humour make managers see themselves as players on the same team, rather than as competitors. This helps to prevent executives from slipping into political tactics.

The relationship between political behaviour and decision quality is not a simple one and more attention needs to be directed toward the role of the 'third factor' or moderating variables on this relationship. For example, previous research suggests that several intervening variables may moderate the relationship between political behaviour and organizational outcomes (e.g. Elbanna and Child, 2007; Wooldridge and Floyd, 1990). It appears that one important requirement for political behaviour in strategic decision making to have constructive results is that efforts are made to reconcile valid differences in viewpoints through a process of participative integrative problem-solving of the kind advocated by Mary Parker Follett (Graham, 1995).

We have also argued that discussions of corporate governance could benefit from an awareness of research into the political processes around strategic decision making in organizations. This breaks down into several lines of further inquiry. First, students of corporate governance should inquire beyond formal provisions and recognize the significance of informal processes for the taking of major corporate decisions. Second, they need to extend their attention beyond the present almost exclusive focus in the governance literature on relations between top executives and owners or other stakeholders to take into account the processes inherent in relationships within an organization that may also shape top decisions in a significant way (Child and Rodrigues, 2003). Third, there is a need to understand better how decision makers deal with key governance dilemmas such as confidentiality versus transparency, and efficiency versus inclusion within a politically charged decision process.

There are several methodological limitations in most previous research on the political aspects of strategic decision making that offer opportunities for improvement. Often the data collected are cross-sectional; they are collected after the decisions were made and their outcomes were clear; and analyses are post hoc. A more accurate understanding of the causal relationships and processes between political behaviour and decision outcomes requires the adoption of research designs that combine longitudinal scope, ideally with real-time investigation. This is a demanding requirement, but one that is necessary if we are to uncover how the links between political behaviour and decision outcomes unfold over time.

Moreover, in the field of strategic management, scholars prefer to concentrate on examining interrelationships between variables instead of defining and measuring the variables themselves (Priem et al., 1995). Conceptualization and measurement still remains an under-developed area (Bowman et al., 2002), and measures have been criticized for the weakness with which they address the issues of validity and reliability. Montgomery et al. (1989) identify loosely defined variables as a major problem in the field of empirical strategic decision research. A key requirement for the development of the field is to improve measurement. In particular, a clear opportunity for future research lies in better conceptualization of political behaviour in order to reflect its multiple aspects.

Last but not least, it would be timely to examine the relationships between political behaviour and rationality more closely in order to understand better the whole strategic decision-making process, including its antecedents and its outcomes. Despite the potential value of combining different characteristics of decision making, studies that investigate multiple strategic decision-making process characteristics are still rare (Elbanna and Younies, 2008). There is a need to offer a more integrated picture of decision making through the simultaneous examination of its various features.

References

Abell, P. (1975) *Organizations as Bargaining and Influence Systems.* London: Heinemann.

Allison G.T. (1969) Conceptual models and the Cuban missile crisis, *The American Political Science Review*, 63, 689–718.

Allison, G.T. (1971) *Essence of Decision: Explaining the Cuban Missile Crisis.* Boston, MA: Little, Brown.

Armey, D. (1996) 'How Taxes Corrupt.' *Wall Street Journal*, A20.

Bacharach, S.B., and Lawler, E.J. (1980) *Power and Politics in Organizations.* San Francisco, CA: Jossey-Bass.

Bachrach, P., and Baratz, M.S. (1962) Two faces of power, *American Political Science Review*, 56, 947–952.

Baum, H.S. (1989) Organisational politics against organisational culture: A psychoanalytic perspective, *Human Resource Management*, 28, 191–206.

Bentley, A.F. (1908) *The Process of Government.* Chicago: University of Chicago Press.

Berle, A.A. and Means, G.C. (1932) *The Modern Corporation and Private Property.* New York: Macmillan.

Berry, J.M. (1997) *The Interest Group Society.* London: Longman, 3rd edition.

Boddewyn, J. (1988) Political aspects of MNE theory, *Journal of International Business Studies*, 15, 341–363.

Boddewyn, J., and Brewer, T. (1994) International business political behaviour: new theoretical directions, *Academy of Management Review*, 19, 119–143.

Bourdieu, P. (1973) 'Cultural Reproduction and Social Reproduction,' in R. Brown (ed.) *Knowledge, Education and Cultural Change.* London: Tavistock.

Bourgeois, L.J., and Eisenhardt, K.M. (1988) Strategic decision processes in high velocity environments: Four cases in the microcomputer industry, *Management Science*, 34, 816–835.

Bower, J.L. (1970) *Managing the Resource Allocation Process.* Boston, MA: Harvard Business School Press.

Bowman, E.H., Singh, H., and Thomas, H. (2002) 'The Domain of Strategic Management: History and Evolution', in A. Pettigrew, H. Thomas, and R. Whittington (eds) *Handbook of Strategy and Management.* London: Sage, 31–51.

Braybrooke, D., and Lindblom, C.E. (1970) *A Strategy of Decision: Policy Evaluation as a Social Process.* New York: Free Press.

Butler, R. (2002) 'Decision Making', in A. Sorge (ed.) *Organization.* London: Thomson Learning, 224–251.

Butler, R., Davies, L., Pike, R., and Sharp, J. (1991) Strategic investment decision making complexities, politics and processes, *Journal of Management Studies*, 28, 395–415.

Cadbury, A. (1992) *The Financial Aspects of Corporate Governance: A Report of the Committee on Corporate Governance.* London: Gee & Co.

Castilla E., Hwang, H. Granovetter, E., and Granovetter, M. (2000) 'Social Networks in Silicon Valley', in W. Miller, H. Rowen, C. Lee, and M. Hancock (eds) *How Silicon Valley Works.* Stanford, CA: Stanford University Press.

Chandler, A.D. (1962) *Strategy and Stucture.* Cambridge, MA: MIT Press.

Child, J. (1972) Organizational structure, environment and performance: The role of strategic choice, *Sociology*, 6, 1–22.

Child, J. (1997a) Strategic choice in the analysis of action, structure, organizations and environment: Retrospect and prospect, *Organization Studies*, 18 (1), 43–76.

Child, J. (1997b) 'From the Aston Programme to Strategic Choice: A Journey from Concepts to Theory', in T. Clark (ed.) *Advancement in Organizational Behaviour.* Aldershot: Ashgate.

Child, J., and Lu, Y. (1996) Institutional constraints on economic reform: The case of investment decisions in China, *Organization Science*, 7, 60–77.

Child, J., and Rodrigues, S.B. (2003) Corporate governance and new organizational forms, *Journal of Management and Governance*, 7, 337–360.

Child, J., and Tsai, T. (2005) The dynamic between firms' environmental strategies and institutional constraints in emerging economies: Evidence from China and Taiwan, *Journal of Management Studies*, 42, 95–125.

Child, J., and Tse, D. (2001) China's transition and its implications for international business, *Journal of International Business Studies*, 32, 5–21.

Clarke, T. (2007) *International Corporate Governance: A Comparative Approach.* London: Routledge.

Crozier, M. (1964) *The Bureaucratic Phenomenon.* Chicago: Chicago University Press.

Cyert, R.M., and March, J.G. (1963) *A Behavioural Theory of the Firm.* Englewood Cliffs, NJ: Prentice-Hall.

Dalton, M. (1959) *Men who Manage.* New York: Wiley.

Dean, J.W., and Sharfman, M.P. (1993a) Procedural rationality in the strategic decision making process, *Journal of Management Studies*, 30, 587–610.

Dean, J.W., and Sharfman, M.P. (1993b) The relationship between procedural rationality and political behaviour in strategic decision making, *Decision Sciences*, 24, 1069–1083.

Dean, J.W., and Sharfman, M.P. (1996) Does decision process matter? A study of strategic decision making effectiveness, *Academy of Management Journal*, 39, 368–396.

DiMaggio, P., and Powell, W.W. (1991) Introduction, in P. DiMaggio and W.W. Powell (eds) *The New Institutionalism in Organizational Theory.* Chicago: University of Chicago Press.

Drory, A., and Romm, T. (1988) Politics in organization and its perception within the organization, *Organization Studies*, 9, 165–179.

Eisenhardt, K.M. (1989) Making fast strategic decisions in high velocity environments, *Academy of Management Journal*, 32, 543–576.

Eisenhardt, K.M. (1997) Strategic decisions and all that jazz, *Business Strategy Review*, 8, 1–3.

Eisenhardt, K.M. (1999) Strategy as strategic decision making, *Sloan Management Review*, 40, 65–72.

Eisenhardt, K.M., and Bourgeois, L.J. (1988) Politics of strategic decision making in high-velocity environments: Toward a midrange theory, *Academy of Management Journal*, 31, 737–770.

Eisenhardt, K.M., Kahwajy, J.L., and Bourgeois, L.J. (1997) Conflict and strategic choice: How top management teams disagree, *California Management Review*, 39, 42–62.

Eisenhardt, K.M., and Zbaracki, M. (1992) Strategic decision making, *Strategic Management Journal*, 13, 17–37.

Eisenmann, T.R., and Bower, J.L. (2000) The entrepreneurial M-Form: Strategic integration in global media firms, *Organization Science*, 11, 348–355.

Elbanna, S. (2006) Strategic decision making: Process perspectives, *International Journal of Management Reviews*, 8, 1–20.

Elbanna, S., and Child, J. (2007) Influences on strategic decision effectiveness: Development and test of an integrative model, *Strategic Management Journal*, 28, 431–453.

Elbanna, S., and Younies, H. (2008) The relationships between the characteristics of the strategy process: Evidence from Egypt, *Management Decision*, 46, 626–639.

Feldman, S.P. (1988) Secrecy, information, and politics: An essay on organizational decision making, *Human Relations*, 41, 73–90.

Fligstein, N. (1996) Markets as politics: a political-cultural approach to market institutions, *American Sociological Review*, 61, 656–673.

Fligstein, N. (2001) *Organizations: Theoretical Debates and the Scope of Organizational Theory*. Department of Sociology, University of California Berkeley.

Fredrickson, J.W. (1983) Strategic process research: Questions and recommendations, *Academy of Management Review*, 8, 565–575.

Frost, P.J. (1987) 'Power, Politics, and Influence,' in F.M. Jablin (ed.), *Handbook of Organisational Communication*. Newbury Park: Sage, 503–548.

Frynas, J.G., Mellahi, K., and Pigman, G.A. (2006) First mover advantages in international business and firm-specific political resources, *Strategic Management Journal*, 27, 321–345.

Gandz, J., and Murray, V.V. (1980) The experience of workplace politics, *Academy of Management Journal*, 23, 237–251.

Getz, K. (1997) Research in corporate political action: integration and assessment, *Business and Society*, 36, 32–72.

Goll, I., and Rasheed, A.A. (1997) Rational decision making and firm performance: The moderating role of environment, *Strategic Management Journal*, 18, 583–591.

Gould, R. (1993) Collective action and network structure, *American Sociological Review*, 58, 182–196.

Graham, P. (ed.) (1995) *Mary Parker Follett – Prophet of Management: Writings from the 1920s*. Boston, MA: Harvard Business School Press.

Gray, B. (1989) *Collaborating: Finding Common Ground for Multiparty Problems*. San Francisco, CA: Jossey-Bass.

Greenwood, R., and Hinings, C.R. (1986) Understanding radical organizational change: bringing together the old and the new institutionalism, *Academy of Management Review*, 21, 1022–1054.

Hadjikham, A. (2000) The political behavior of business actors: The case of Swedish MNCs and the EU, *International Studies of Management and Organization*, 30, 93–117.

Harrison, E.F. (1999) *The Managerial Decision Making Process*. Boston, MA: Houghton Mifflin.

Harvard Business School (1985) British Steel Corporation: the Korf contract. Case no. HBS 9-481-110. See also accompanying video HBS 9-882-020.

Hayes, J. (1984) The politically competent manager, *Journal of General Management*, Autumn, 24–33.

Hickson, D.J., Butler, R.J., Cray, D., Mallory, G.R., and Wilson, D.C. (1986) *Top Decisions:Strategic decision making in organizations*. Oxford: Basil Blackwell.

Hickson, D.J., Hinings, C.R., Lee, C.A., Schneck, R.E., and Pennings, J.M. (1971) A strategic contingencies theory of intraorganizational power, *Administrative Science Quarterly*, 16, 216–229.

Hillman, A., and Hitt, M. (1999) Corporate political strategy formulation: A model of approach participation and strategy decisions, *Academy of Management Review*, 24, 825–842.

Hillman, A., Keim, G.D., and Schuler, D. (2004) Corporate political activity: a review and research agenda, *Journal of Management*, 30, 838–857.

Hutzschenreuter, T., and Kleindienst, I. (2006) Strategy-process research: What have we learned and what is still to be explored, *Journal of Management*, 32, 673–720.

Janis, I.L. (1989) *Crucial Decisions: Leadership in Policy and Crisis Management*. New York: The Free Press.

Krishnan, H.A., and Park, D. (2003) Power in acquired top management teams and post-acquisition performance: A conceptual framework, *International Journal of Management*, 20, 75–80.

Langley, A. (1989) In search of rationality: The purposes behind the use of formal analysis in organizations, *Administrative Science Quarterly*, 34, 598–631.

Larsen, P.T. (2009) 'Goodwin's undoing.' *Financial Times*, 25 February, p. 11.

Lewin, A.Y., and Carroll, T.N. (1999) The coevolution of new organizational forms, *Organizational Science*, 1, 535–550.

Lindblom, C.E. (1959) The science of muddling-through, *Public Administration Review*, 19, 79–88.

Lindblom, C.E. (1977) *Politics and Markets: The world's Political-economic Systems*. New York: Basic Books.

Lindblom, C.E. (1979) Still muddling, not yet through, *Public Administration Review*, 39, 517–526.

Lord, M.D. (2000) Corporate political strategy and legislative decision making, *Business and Society*, 39, 76–93.

Lyles, M.A. (1981) Formulating strategic problems: Empirical analysis and model development, *Strategic Management Journal*, 2, 61–75.

Lyles, M.A., and Reger, R.K. (1993) Managing for autonomy in joint ventures: A longitudinal study of upward influence, *Journal of Management Studies*, 30, 383–404.

McLaughlin A.M., Jordan, G., and Maloney, W.A. (1993) Corporate lobbying in the European Community, *Journal of Common Market Studies*, 31, 191–212.

MacMillan, I.C., and Jones, P.E. (1986) *Strategy Formulation: Power and politics*. St Paul: West Publication.

Maitlis, S., and Lawrence, T.B. (2003) Orchestral manoeuvres in the dark: Understanding failure in organizational strategizing, *Journal of Management Studies*, 40, 109–139.

March, J.G., and Olsen, J.P. (1982) *Ambiguity and Choice in Organisations*. Bergen: Universitetsforlaget.

March, J.G., and Simon, H.A. (1958) *Organizations*. New York: John Wiley & Sons, Inc.

Meyer, J., and Rowan, B. (1977) Institutionalized organizations: formal structure as myth and ceremony, *American Journal of Sociology*, 83, 340–363.

Meyer, J.W., and Scott, W.R. (1983) *Organizational Environments: Ritual and Rationality*. Beverly Hills, CA: Sage.

Miller, C.C., and Cardinal, L.B. (1994) Strategic planning and firm performance: A synthesis of two decades of research, *Academy of Management Journal*, 37, 1649–1665.

Mintzberg, H. (1973a) *The Nature of Managerial Work*. New York: Harper and Row.

Mintzberg, H. (1973b) Strategy making in three modes, *California Management Review*, 16, 44–53.

Mintzberg, H. (1985) The organization as political arena, *Journal of Management Studies*, 22, 133–154.

Mintzberg, H. (1994) *The Rise and Fall of Strategic Planning: Reconceiving the roles for planning, plans, planners*. New York: Free Press.

Mintzberg, H. (1998) *Strategy Safari: A Guided Tour Through the Wilds of Strategic Management*. London: Prentice-Hall.

Mintzberg, H., Raisinghani, D., and Theoret, A. (1976) The structure of 'unstructured' decision processes, *Administrative Science Quarterly*, 21, 246–275.

Mintzberg, H., and Waters, J.A. (1985) Of strategies, deliberate and emergent, *Strategic Management Journal*, 6, 257–272.

Mische, A. (2003) Cross-talk in movements: Rethinking the culture-network link. in M. Diani and D. McAdam (eds), *Social Movements and Networks: Relational approaches to collective action*. New York: Oxford University Press, 258–280.

Mizruchi, M.S. (2004) Berle and Means revisited: The governance and power of large US corporations, *Theory and Society*, 33, 579–617.

Mohr, L.B. (1982) *Explaining Organizational Behavior*. San Francisco, CA: Jossey-Bass.

Montgomery, C.A., Wernerfelt, B., and Balakrishnan, S. (1989) Strategy content and the research process: A critique and commentary, *Strategic Management Journal*, 10, 189–197.

Mowday, R.T. (1978) The exercise of upward influence in organizations, *Administrative Science Quarterly*, 23, 137–156.

Mueller, G.C. (1998) Strategic decision-making and performance: Decision processes and environmental effects. Unpublished PhD thesis. The University of Wisconsin: Milwaukee.

Mumford, E., and Pettigrew, A. (1975) *Implementing Strategic Decisions*. London: Longman.

Narayanan, V.K., and Fahey, L. (1982) The micro-politics of strategy formulation, *Academy of Management Review*, 7 (1), 25–34.

Noda, T., and Bower, J.L. (2007) Strategy making as iterated processes of resource allocation, *Strategic Management Journal*, 17, 159–192.

Nutt, P.C. (1998) Evaluating alternatives to make strategic choices, *Omega*, 26, 333–354.

Oliver, C. (1991) Strategic responses to institutional processes, *Academy of Management Review*, 16, 145–179.

Oliver, C. (1992) The antecedents of deinstitutionalization, *Organization Studies*, 13, 563–588.

O'Sullivan, M. (2000) *Contests for Corporate Control: Corporate governance and economic performance in the United States and Germany*. Oxford: Oxford University Press.

Penrose, E.T. (1979) *The Theory of the Growth of the Firm*. Oxford: Blackwell.

Papadakis, V.M. (1998) Strategic investment decision processes and organizational performance: An empirical examination, *British Journal of Management*, 9, 115–132.

Papadakis, V.M. and Barwise, P. (1997) 'What Can We Tell Managers about Making Strategic Decisions?' in V.M. Papadakis and P. Barwise (eds) *Strategic Decisions*. London: Kluwer, 267–287.

Papadakis, V.M., Lioukas, S., and Chambers, D. (1998) Strategic decision making: The role of management and context, *Strategic Management Journal*, 19, 115–147.

Pettigrew, A.M. (1972) Information control as a power resource, *Sociology*, 6, 187–204.

Pettigrew, A.M. (1973) *The Politics of Organizational Decision Making*. London: Tavistock.

Pfeffer, J. (1981) *Power in Organizations*. London: Pitman.

Pfeffer, J. (1992) *Managing with Power: Politics and Influence in Organizations*. Boston, MA: Harvard Business School.

Pfeffer, J., and Moore, W.L. (1980) Power in university budgeting: A replication and extension, *Administrative Science Quarterly*, 25, 637–653.

Pfeffer, J., and Salancik, G.R. (1974) Organisational decision making as a political process: The case of a university budget, *Administrative Science Quarterly*, 19, 135–151.

Pfeffer, J., and Salancik, G.R. (1978) *The External Control of Organizations: A Resource Dependence Perspective*. New York: Harper & Row.

Powell, T.C. (2001) Competitive advantage: logical and philosophical considerations, *Strategic Management Journal*, 22, 875–888.

Priem, R.L., Rasheed, M.A., and Kotulic, A.G. (1995) Rationality in strategic decision processes, environmental dynamism and firm performance, *Journal of Management*, 21, 913–929.

Quinn, J.B. (1978) Strategic change: 'Logical incrementalism', *Sloan Management Review* 20, 7–19.

Quinn, J.B. (1980) *Strategies for Change: Logical Incrementalism*. Homewood: Irwin.

Rodrigues, S.B. (1980) Processes of Successful Decision Making in Organizations. Unpublished PhD Thesis, University of Bradford, UK.

Rodrigues, S.B., and Child, J. (2008) *Corporate Coevolution: A Political Perspective*. Chichester: John Wiley & Sons, Ltd..

Rodrigues, S.B. and Hickson, D.J. (1995) Success in decision making, *Journal of Management Studies*, 32, 655–678.

Salancik, G.R., and Pfeffer, J. (1974) The bases and use of power in organisational decision making: The case of a university, *Administrative Science Quarterly*, 19, 453–473.

Scott, W.R. (2001) *Institutions and Organizations*. Thousand Oaks, CA: Sage.

Schuler, D.D. (1999) Corporate political action: rethinking the economic and organizational influences, *Business and Politics*, 1, 83–97.

Schuler, D.D., Rehbein, K., and Cramer, R. (2002) Pursuing strategic advantage through political means: A multivariate approach, *Academy of Management Journal*, 45, 659–672.

Schwenk, C.R. (1990) Conflict in organizational decision making: An exploratory study of its effects in for-profit and not-for-profit-organizations, *Management Science*, 36, 436–448.

Schwenk, C.R., and Huff, A. (1986) 'Argumentation in Strategic Decision Making', in R. Lamp (ed.) *Advances in Strategic Management*. Greenwich, CI: JAI Press.

Schwenk, C.R., and Shrader, C.B. (1993) Effects of formal strategic planning on financial performance in small firms: A meta-analysis, *Entrepreneurship Theory and Practice*, 17, 53–64.

Selznick, P. (1949) *TVA and the Grass Roots*. Berkeley, CA: University of California Press.

Simmers, C.A. (1998) Executive/board politics in strategic decision making, *Journal of Business and Economic Studies*, 4, 37–56.

Stevenson, W., Pearce, J., and Porter, L. (1985) The concept of 'coalition' in organisation theory and research, *Academy of Management Review*, 10, 256–268.

Stone, D. (2002) *Policy Paradox: The Art of Political Decision Making*. New York: Norton.

Urwick, L.F. (1945) *Business Administration. A Series of Five Lectures*. London: Institute of Industrial Administration.

Veblen, T. (1904) *The Theory of Business Enterprise*. New York: Scribners.

Veblen, T. (1914) *The Instinct of Workmanship*. New York: Macmillan.

Volberda, H., and Lewin, A.Y. (2003) Co-evolutionary dynamics within and between firms: from evolution to co-evolution, *Journal of Management Studies*, 40, 2111–2236.

Wilson, D. (2003) 'Strategy as Decision Making,' in S. Cummings, and D. Wilson (eds) *Images of strategy*. Oxford: Blackwell, 383–410.

Winter, S. (1981) Attention allocation and input proportions, *Journal of Economic Behaviour*, 2, 31–46.

Wooldridge, B., and Floyd, S.W. (1990) The strategy process, middle management involvement, and organizational performance, *Strategic Management Journal*, 11, 231–241.

Zahra, S.A. (1987) Organizational politics and the strategic process, *Journal of Business Ethics*, 6, 579–587.

Zald, M.N. (1970) 'Political Economy: A Framework for Comparative Analysis,' in M.N. Zald (ed.) *Power in Organizations*. Nashville, TN: Vanderbilt University Press, 221–261.

Zattoni, A., and Cuomo, F. (2008) Why adopt codes of good governance? A comparison of institutional and efficiency perspectives, *Corporate Governance: An International Review*, 16, 1–15.

6

Organizational Identity and Strategic Decision Making

AIMEE L. HAMILTON AND DENNIS A. GIOIA

Consider the following now famous exchange on the floor of the US Senate in July of 2005: Senator Jeff Sessions, a staunch Republican and defender of the Bush administration's policies in Iraq, spoke out against legislation that would have expressly prohibited cruel, inhumane or degrading treatment of prisoners in the custody of the US Army. Senator Sessions argued that there was no need for the legislation because, as he characterized it, the prisoners were not prisoners of war, 'they are terrorists!' Senator John McCain, another Republican and decorated former Prisoner of war, argued strongly that '[i]t's not about who *they* are. It's about who *we* are!' A follow-up letter from Senator McCain argued that '[t]he abuse of prisoners ... is anathema to the values Americans have held dear for generations.'

In more scholarly, if less provocative terms, Barney *et al.* (1998) have summed up the essence of this stance by noting that the 'theory of what we should do follows pretty quickly from the theory of who we are' (p. 113). In straightforward terms, the 'theory of who we are as an organization' is a set of beliefs and claims about the deeply-held values, ideals, principles, beliefs, etc., that constitute an organization's identity (Albert and Whetten, 1985) – an identity that *should* guide fundamental decisions and actions. Within the charged context of the Sessions/McCain exchange lies the essence of the relationship between organizational identity and strategic decision making: if we (as a society, a nation, an organization, etc.) are consistent in aligning 'who we are' with 'what we do,' then organizational identity should exert a potentially governing influence over the strategic choices we make and the strategic actions we take – 'governing' in the sense that identity is an influential precursor to organizational functioning, such that function follows from identity.

Concern with the relationship between identity and strategic decision making has never been greater than in the present era. This relationship is implicitly prevalent in much of contemporary business writing. As Elgin (2007: 46) noted:

Handbook of Decision Making. Edited by Paul C. Nutt and David C. Wilson
© 2010 John Wiley & Sons, Ltd

With rising consumer anxiety over global warming, businesses want to show that they're part of the solution, says Chris Hunter,... who works for the environmental consulting firm GreenOrder. 'Ten years ago, companies would call up and say 'I need a digital strategy.' Now, it's 'I need a green strategy.'

Yet, as will become apparent below, in the modern era, 'needing a green strategy' first implies 'needing a green identity'. For many, even most organizations, that sort of challenge also implies two different, difficult, and simultaneous enterprises: organizational identity change and strategic change.

Organizational Identity as Progenitor of Organizational Decision Making

Our fundamental stance in this chapter is that organizational identity matters. It matters most when the most major of organizational decisions are made – which implies that identity plays its most crucial role when strategic decisions are contemplated. Furthermore, identity matters more than most executives are aware, because identity tends to reside at the deepest and most tacit levels of understanding. So, what matters from a scholarly perspective – especially a perspective that is oriented toward affecting practice – is that executives be sensitized to the subtle, but profound ways in which identity influences their major decisions.

Arguably, no concept is more fundamental to strategic decision making than the organization members' implicit theory of 'who we are as an organization.' Identity is central to both personal and organizational self-conceptions. As such, it tends to reside in the background, unquestioned, for most routine or unproblematic decisions, but identity infuses every aspect of consequential organizational decision making, and perhaps especially strategic decision making. It serves as a deep-level frame for interpretation, understanding, and action. Yet, despite its essential role, organizational identity has been generally underplayed as a factor in major decisions by both scholars and practitioners. Perhaps, there is no great surprise here because organizational identity is typically 'assumed away' by organizational members. Identity only enters the overt conversation when the subject is big decisions – for instance, divestments, mergers or acquisitions, new product development, and perhaps especially changes in strategy. As Whetten (2006: 226) put it, identity only becomes explicit when organizations face 'fork-in-the-road' decisions.

These are the kinds of decisions that prompt members to reflexively examine themselves as an organization before deciding whether a contemplated course of action is consistent with who they take themselves to be as an organization. These kinds of decisions are almost inevitably strategic decisions or decisions with strategic implications. For our purposes, then, our main conceptual exhortation to scholars is to recognize that organizational identity provides the substrate for strategic decision making. Our main pragmatic exhortation to practicing executives is to recognize that organizations need an explicit awareness of 'who they are' before taking consequential decisions and actions. That means that the practical problem often becomes one of making tacit identity explicit.

We operate on the premise that the best way to 'see' the role of identity is to provide an overview of the concept of organizational identity and describe work on the topic that most directly pertains to decision making in organizations. Our review is selective, so we refer the interested reader to Hatch and Schultz (2004) for a more complete consideration of the topic of organizational identity. In the short time since that compendium was published, however, organizational identity research has only gathered momentum. Some of this recent work is directly germane to our discussion, and in this chapter we devote some attention to it.

We seek not only to illustrate the importance of organizational identity in strategic decisions processes, but also to encourage greater integration of the concept into various perspectives on decision making. Therefore, the chapter closes with suggestions for future decision-making research that accounts for the role of organizational identity. We believe that the consideration of organizational identity lends itself to a variety of perspectives, levels of analysis, and methodological approaches in the study of decision making.

WHAT IS ORGANIZATIONAL IDENTITY?

We introduced our topic and our main thesis with a rather minimalist definition of organizational identity. To move our discussion forward, we add some detail to this definition and also point out some important nuances in the way the concept has been interpreted by various theorists and researchers. To do so, it is best to start at the beginning, 1985, when Albert and Whetten first explicitly articulated the notion of identity as an organization-level concept. These authors drew upon the concept of *personal* identity that has been a topic of intellectual discourse since ancient times (cf. Gioia, 1998). In the modern era, personal identity has been the focal concept in several important works from sociology (e.g. Goffman, 1959) and psychology (e.g. Erickson, 1968) that influenced Albert and Whetten's conceptualization of organizational identity. Erickson described personal identity as one's sense of self and 'selfsameness' over time and one's perception that this selfsameness is recognized by other people (1968: 22). In extending the notion of identity to organizations, Albert and Whetten melded the concept with ideas from organization theory, such as resource dependency (Pfeffer and Salancik, 1978), contingency theory and path-dependency (Thompson, 1967), institutionalization (Meyer and Rowan, 1977; Selznick, 1957), and loosely coupled systems (Weick, 1976). It was their distinctive insight to make apparent the linkages between these disparate concepts.

Albert and Whetten described organizational identity as the answer that organizational members provide to the 'self-reflective question' (1985: 264) 'Who are we as an organization?' They proposed that the answer to this question will consist of what members believe are the core features of their organization. Albert and Whetten theorized that those features would meet three necessary and sufficient criteria: (1) organizational identity consists of what members perceive to be *central* or essential characteristics of their organization; (2) it is what members believe to be *enduring* about their organization, i.e. a current attribute that has maintained some continuity over time and is expected to be stable into the future; and (3) it is what members take to be *distinctive* about their organization as compared to others. This triad of central, enduring, and distinctive features has come to be known as the 'CED definition' of organizational identity (Whetten, 2006), a nearly parallel application of the personal identity concept to organizations. Like individuals, organizations 'define who they are by creating or invoking a classification scheme and locating themselves within it' (Albert and Whetten, 1985: 267). Similar to individual identity, organizational identity is inherently relational and comparative; organizations answer the question of 'who we are' by identifying what about them is different from (and similar to) other organizations. What a given organization (or subgroup of the organization) considers to be central, enduring, and distinctive may vary depending on the situation. Further, the CED definition imposes no requirement that an organization's various identity statements be compatible – in fact they might be unrelated or even contradictory.

The answer to the identity question is taken for granted by members under ordinary decision-making conditions. It is such a weighty and difficult matter to question organizational identity that organizational members tend to avoid it if at all possible. Organizational members invoke CED characteristics as an explicit decision-making guide only when all other 'easier, more specific, more quantifiable solutions have failed' (Albert and Whetten 1985: 267). It is for this reason that identity-referencing discourse is most noticeable during organizational crises or on those relatively rare occasions when *bona fide* strategic decisions must be made – i.e. those deemed essential to an organization's welfare.

In general, organization members actively defend their collective identity. On those rare occasions when strategic decisions are at issue, organization members are likely prompted to (re)consider identity explicitly and might decide that accomplishing a strategic change necessitates a revision in the organizational identity (Gioia and Thomas, 1996). Such a decision is a decision with *gravitas*. These occasions not only make organizational identity precarious, however, they might also actually make the organization more adaptable – by conferring an 'adaptive instability' that enables necessary adjustments to environmental demands (Gioia, Schultz, and Corley, 1996). Gagliardi (1986) has even noted, in engagingly paradoxical terms, that organizations sometimes must change to remain what they have always been, implying that changes to identity are made in a fashion that allows members to maintain the sense that their core values and founding assumptions are intact, even though times have changed. How might such a process occur? Gioia *et al.* (2000) and Corley and Gioia (2004) noted that although the descriptive labels that members use to describe 'who they are' remain stable over time, the meanings associated with those labels change, such that identity appears much more stable than it actually is, thus allowing identity to adapt to changing circumstances.

When contemplating consequential decisions, decision makers rely on the core identity of the organization to anchor their deliberations. Thus, identity issues will be most apparent and influential during 'profound organizational circumstances' (Whetten, 2006: 226). Albert and Whetten proposed that these situations would include life-cycle transitions such as: an organization's creation, loss of the founder or other important 'identity sustaining element,' achievement of the organization's essential goal, rapid growth (internally generated or through mergers and acquisitions), and restructuring and downsizing (Albert & Whetten, 1985: 274).

Albert and Whetten noted that the organizational identity concept is used both by researchers and organizational members. That the concept of identity is meaningful to both investigators and their informants has been called a 'rare and fortunate' circumstance (Gioia, Schultz, and Corley, 2002: 270) and has generated a substantial body of qualitative research (e.g. Corley and Gioia, 2004; Dutton and Dukerich, 1991; Elsbach and Kramer, 1996; Ravasi and Schultz, 2006). At the same time, the dual applications of the concept might have obscured its usefulness as a scientific construct in quantitative studies (an exception is Gioia and Thomas (1996), which combines qualitative and quantitative methods). Indeed, in the interest of clarification and to encourage more studies of a hypothesis-testing nature, Whetten has recently suggested a constitutive definition of the organizational identity construct as 'the central and enduring attributes of an organization that distinguish it from other organizations' (Whetten, 2006: 220).

Whetten (2006) noted that a degree of 'ambiguity' in the original presentation of organizational identity spawned multiple perspectives on the concept among organizational scholars. One perspective is that organizational identity is a property of an organization as a 'social actor' that society imbues with powers and responsibilities, such as the right to enter into contracts (Whetten, 2006; Whetten and Mackey, 2002). Organizational identity in this view can be inferred only from the official claims and formal commitments made by the organization as a social actor/entity. These 'identity referents' (Whetten, 2006) signify the organization's self-determined and self-defining position in a social field. The social actor perspective, therefore, treats organizational identity as a set of institutional claims that are explicitly articulated and supply a consistent and legitimated narrative to internal and external stakeholders. These claims facilitate the construction of a collective sense of an organizational self (Whetten and Mackey, 2002). Ravasi and Schultz (2006) note that this conception emphasizes the *sensegiving* function of organizational identity as a guide for members' decision making and how other organizations should relate to them. From the social actor perspective, organizational identity is a tractable scientific construct that is amenable to model-building and hypothetico-deductive reasoning.

In contrast to the social actor perspective is the view of organizational identity as social construction. From this perspective, organizational identity is 'an organization's members' collective understanding of the features presumed to be central and relatively permanent and that distinguish the organization from other organizations' (Gioia *et al.*, 2000: 64). As a social construction, organizational identity is subject to periodic revision as members interact with each other and with outsiders and renegotiate their collective interpretation of organizational experiences. Ravasi and Schultz (2006) have suggested that this view emphasizes the *sensemaking* processes associated with the social construction of organizational identity as a shared interpretive scheme among organizational members.

It has been pointed out that the two perspectives are rooted in fundamentally different ontological assumptions about the nature of the social world (cf. Corley *et al.*, 2006). Ravasi and Schultz (2006) suggested that the two perspectives emphasize distinct yet important aspects of organizational identity and are therefore quite complementary. In their study of the *avant garde* Danish electronics firm, Bang & Olufsen, Ravasi and Schultz developed a model that brought these two perspectives together, suggesting that organizational identity is the dynamic 'interplay between identity claims and understandings' (2006: 436).

All these previous considerations, taken together, imply a central role for organizational identity in the life of members of an organization and in the life of the organization itself. Identity helps to supply an understanding and explanation for the organization's past; identity provides the substrate for the present claims made, and understandings held, by the organization and its members; identity is also the point of departure for the organizational future. When things change, identity circumscribes not only what can change, but also specifies what will *not* change (cf. Gagliardi, 1986). Overall, organizational identity is the foundation on which organization members make sense of their experience and give sense to others about how to interpret their organizational experience (via the public claims they make about who they are and what they are attempting to do with their strategy).

Organizational identity, then, provides both an impression and an expression of an organization's reason for being, what it stands for, and its basic approach to action (Ravasi and Schultz, 2006), whether as a business enterprise, a nonprofit organization, a government entity, an NGO, or a volunteer organization. Identity not only lends continuity to an organization's own narrative; it supplies the basis on which both thought and action are guided; it is the basis for claims made by and to its own members and to external stakeholders; as such, identity is the basis on which organizations are judged as 'acting in character' (Czarniawska, 1997). When an organization acts out of character, it can be wrenchingly difficult for internal and external stakeholders to come to grips with the situation – as was the case in our introductory epigram, wherein observers found it difficult to accept the atrocities of American soldiers who had violated strongly-held American identity ideals concerning the treatment of prisoners.

ORGANIZATIONAL IDENTITY RESEARCH THROUGH A DECISION-MAKING LENS

A considerable body of organization theory and research describes *how* decision-making processes unfold (e.g. Cohen, March, and Olsen, 1972; Fredrickson and Iaquinto, 1989; Mintzberg, Raisinghani, and Theoret, 1976; Nutt, 1998; Thompson, 1967; Wilson, Hickson, and Miller, 1996). The concept of organizational identity provides a basis for investigating the corollary questions of *why* and *when* these processes are likely to be triggered and *what* is likely to guide members through their deliberations. We have already alluded to the foundational Albert and Whetten (1985) work, which introduced and initially developed the concept for organizational application. Highlighted below are a selected group of empirical studies of organizational identity that are particularly relevant to an understanding of strategic decision-making processes. We present the existing research in roughly chronological order to convey a sense of how this relatively young field has developed, as well as its many exciting potential extensions to decision-making theory, research, and practice.

In their classic study of the Port Authority of New York and New Jersey, Dutton and Dukerich (1991) demonstrated how organizational identity filtered and constrained the Authority's interpretations of an issue (i.e. homeless people inhabiting their facilities), as well as choices of action in response to the problem. In addition, the study showed how organizational identity supplied the criteria by which the Authority decided the success and failure of its initiatives to deal with the problem – a problem that became consequential enough to harbor strategic implications. Dutton and Dukerich also drew a connection between organizational identity and 'construed external image' i.e. the way organizational members believe outsiders see their organization, (see also Dutton, Dukerich, and Harquail, 1994), demonstrating how perceived deterioration in external image prompted changes in issue interpretation, a reconsideration of organizational identity, as well as some tactical and strategic actions that were intended to bring image back into alignment with identity.

Gioia and Chittipeddi (1991), under the rubrics of 'sensemaking and sensegiving' also accounted for organizational identity in their study of a large university that was attempting a strategic change effort. They showed that the introduction of a 'top 10 public research university' strategic vision had important implications for the university's identity. Later, Gioia and Thomas (1996) in an integrated qualitative/quantitative study investigated the interplay of identity and image, demonstrating that both concepts were critical perceptions that influenced interpretation and strategic action at a broad spectrum of universities. Their qualitative study also provided evidence that a decision to initiate strategic change can imply the need for a change in organizational identity. Further, they showed that a 'desired future image' is a crucial symbolic means for management to effect a change in identity necessary to accomplish strategic change. In addition, the study also suggested that organizational identity cannot be enduring in any absolute sense if *bona fide* strategic change is to be accomplished, but rather must strike a balance between change and stability so that organizational members maintain a connection with past conceptions of who they were.

Elsbach and Kramer (1996) investigated the responses of university stakeholders to the rankings published in *Business Week*. They explored how the leaders of eight highly ranked business schools dealt with the perceived threat represented by a ranking that challenged their core beliefs about who they were. Elsbach and Kramer's analysis suggested that the rankings posed two particular threats to schools' identities: first, by calling into question members' perceptions of core identity attributes; and second, by challenging beliefs about their school's relative standing with other schools. In response, faculty members were inclined to affirm their positive perceptions of their school's preferred identity by emphasizing their school's membership in particular, selected strategic reference groups and also by highlighting comparisons along dimensions not recognized by the rankings. This study not only demonstrated the impact of an external identity threat on an organization, but also documented the way in which organizational leaders actively work to manage organizational identity.

Czarniawska and Wolff (1998) applied the concept of organizational identity to the choices made by two new European universities attempting to establish themselves in highly institutionalized environments. Their analysis was structured around three main concepts: 1) the influence of the organization field, 2) 'action nets', used by the two organizations to influence their fields, and 3) the influence of organizational identity. The study showed how the different organizational identities constructed by the two new organizations resulted in the success of one and failure of the other, implying that identity was critical to the strategic choices made and, ultimately, the survival of the organization.

Glynn (2000) considered the impact of hybrid organizational identity – when the central/enduring/distinctive features do not ordinarily go together and may actually conflict – in affecting the use of strategic resources and capabilities. She investigated the impact of the conflicting identity referents of 'artistic excellence' and 'fiscal solvency' within a symphony orchestra during a musician's strike. Her study revealed embedded and latent identity conflicts and demonstrated how definitions of resources and core capabilities, generally considered unproblematic by strategic management researchers, can actually be affected by an organization's identity and members' sense of who they are. For example, members who more strongly identified with the aesthetic mission and identity tended to see the orchestra's resources in terms of musical talent, while those who identified with the business mission and identity defined resources in terms of donors and customers. Competing claims about the institutional identity thus affected strategic decisions and actions of the organization.

Foreman and Whetten (2002) also investigated the case of 'hybrid' organizations in a study of rural cooperatives that have both 'business' and 'family' identities. They found that conflicting identities can have significant impacts on organizational members. For example, in identifying with both aspects of the organizational identity, members can end up holding paradoxical expectations and beliefs about the organization. Their analysis also showed that congruence between the two organizational identities affected member commitment, but also perceived cognitive and pragmatic legitimacy, lending support to the notion that identity should be construed as a viable multilevel construct.

Elsbach and Bhattacharya (2001) explored the relationship between organizational identity and identification (how people identify with organizations), using the provocative example of the National Rifle Association. Their findings suggested that people 'dis-identified' with an organization when they experienced an inconsistency between their own identity and that expressed by the organization (i.e. the NRA). They noted that disidentification seemed to be motivated by people's tendencies to simultaneously want to affirm positive distinctiveness and avoid negative distinctiveness by distancing themselves from incongruent values and negative stereotypes attributed to an organization like the NRA. Their findings imply that any organizational strategic decision-making efforts need to try to achieve congruency between constituents' beliefs and values and those expressed by the organization.

Fiol (2002) investigated the decisions and actions made by the top management of a large company as it attempted to guide a strategic transformation in response to major changes in the company's industry and markets. Fiol found that a strong and highly stable organizational identity presented a difficult challenge to change efforts and that, similar to the findings of Gioia and Thomas (1996), transformation necessitated a change in identity. Though identity might serve as a glue that binds people together behind the change initiative, a strong organization-wide identity often inhibits their ability to see and commit to new possibilities. Fiol investigated the processes by which individual and organizational levels of identity interact and identified rhetorical techniques that leaders can use to guide people through the strategic change process when identity is a potential inhibitor of the process.

Corley and Gioia (2004) used organizational identity as a focal concept for understanding the profound organizational circumstance of a corporate spin-off (i.e. the case in which a corporate parent made a strategic decision to spin off a subunit into a free-standing entity). They found that the spin-off prompted 'identity ambiguity' and that leaders were compelled to resolve this ambiguity so that the new organization was not paralyzed. They also examined the processes by which the labels and meanings associated with the organizations' identity underwent changes during and after the spin-off, and concluded that ambiguity could be resolved by changing both the identity-referent label as well as the meaning of that label. This study constituted another example that identity issues were central to strategic decision making.

Brickson (2005) investigated the connection between organizational identity and the ways that organizations relate to various internal and external stakeholders. She introduced and employed the construct of identity orientation and proposed that organizations have three distinct identity orientations: individualistic, relational, and collectivistic, finding that an organization's identity orientation was an important part of organizational identity, with implications for understanding various strategic decisions. Another intriguing finding of the study was that fairly specific organizational-level factors (e.g. type of client and cooperative structure) explained more variance in identity than did more general factors (e.g. organizational age) or more individual-level factors (e.g. employee traits).

Hannan *et al.* (2006) applied organizational identity to an understanding of the hazard of failure and the growth prospects of a group of nascent high tech companies. They noted that firms were likely to be affected by two kinds of major organizational changes: an alteration in the 'founders' blueprints' for an employment relation and replacing a founding CEO with an outsider. Either event can destabilize organizations, but they found that changes that affected the core identity of the organization (e.g. changes in the founders' 'blueprints' for employee relations) were more predictive of organizational failure and lower growth than were replacing the CEO. That is, they found that changes in employment blueprints were more tightly tied to the organization's identity and thus were more destabilizing, so a change in the employment blueprint increased the hazard of failure. They discussed their finding in terms of ecological and institutional perspectives on organizations, demonstrating that identity has strong implications, even at these levels of analysis.

Ravasi and Schultz (2006) conducted a long-term, longitudinal study of organizational responses to environmental changes that prompt organization members to question their organization's identity. They looked at the role of organizational identity over time as Bang & Olufsen adapted to three different and significant changes in the market for audio/video products and found evidence of a dynamic relationship among organizational culture, identity, and image. They argued that organizational culture served to support 'sensemaking' action carried out by leaders as they worked to reevaluate the way they understood who their organization was, and as a platform for 'sensegiving' action aimed at influencing internal perceptions. These authors then developed a theoretical framework to explain how the interplay of construed images and organizational culture shapes changes in organizational claims and shared understandings about the identity of an organization. As noted earlier, this study's findings suggested that the social actor and social construction perspectives on identity are complementary.

Nag *et al.* (2007) investigated the way in which organizational identity affected a strategic change effort that was intended to transform a high-tech company from a technology-oriented to a market-oriented organization by 'grafting on' new, non-technological knowledge. The strategic transformation did not succeed because of the ways that organizational identity, knowledge, and practice were closely interrelated. These authors found that the way knowledge was actually used in the organization played a crucial role in organizational identity, suggesting that identity was not retained just in the language and symbols that constitute formal claims and collective understandings of organizational members, but actually infuses their daily practices. The failure of the knowledge graft revealed a relationship between identity and knowledge that manifested itself in organization members' efforts to preserve the collective practices that characterized how they used knowledge in accomplishing their work, which undermined the strategic change effort itself.

In summary, these studies provide an overview of the many and diverse connections between organizational identity and decision making. In the first place, an organization's identity fundamentally influences what will (and will not) be recognized by an organization as a situation calling for strategic decision making. Further, organizational identity serves as an important trigger for strategic choice and action – often in response to an external threat to that identity. In addition, identity change can be an essential precursor to strategic change, and, in turn, strategic change can bring about modifications to an organization's identity. These changes can be subtle, as when the labels used to describe the identity stay the same, but the meaning changes, or striking, as when the labels and the meanings both change. In this light, organizational identity change and strategic change are companion concepts that should be considered in concert. At minimum, these ideas drawn from studies of organizational identity suggest interesting directions for future research.

Organizational Identity and Strategic Decision Making

Future directions

To date the empirical research streams of organizational identity and strategic decision making have been fairly independent; however, a few theoretical pieces have made conceptual linkages between the topics. One of the earliest explicit considerations of organizational identity implications for decision making was a wide-ranging 'strategy conversation' (Barney *et al.*, 1998) held during the 1997 Conference on Organizational Identity. The participants in this particular conversation – all theorists and researchers in strategic management – considered the potential of organizational identity as a source of sustained competitive advantage, and discussed the implications of organizational identity for organizational learning and renewal efforts. They also contemplated the management challenges presented by hybrid or multiple-identity organizations (Barney *et al.*, 1998). Overall, they concluded that accounting for identity in studying strategic decision making was a fruitful avenue for future research (although relatively little research has been done to date).

More recently, Santos and Eisenhardt (2005) have theorized that organizational identity is an important factor in boundary decisions made by organizations. They suggested that organizational members' core beliefs about who they are may help explain 'make or buy' choices that transaction costs economics and other existing theories have not entirely addressed. The authors also proposed that organizational identity is 'coevolutionary' or reflexive with other important aspects of organizations including efficiency, power, and competence. This proposal echoes the linkages between organizational identity and power found by Nag *et al.* (2007). Miller and Wilson (2006) have called for more study of the role of power in decision-making processes; organizational identity offers a fruitful potential framework for such inquiry.

Organizational identity has many other potential applications within the realm of decision-making research. For example, as noted above, organizational identity can be thought of as a perceptual lens, affecting what environmental features will be attended to and viewed as salient by organizational members (e.g. Gioia and Thomas, 1996). Cognitive biases (cf. Bazerman, 2003) and managerial attention (Cho and Hambrick, 2006) are examples of strategic decision-making concepts that can be understood within an identity framework. In addition, organizational identity might provide greater understanding for the types of search strategies (Nutt, 2005) that organizations use during decision making and how these strategies might be improved. Organizational identity might also help explain why decision rules are often inappropriately applied (Nutt, 2002).

At the individual level, when we consider the ways in which organization members use their organizational identity to help them to make decisions, we discover that the ways that they define themselves often disclose what they are trying to achieve. A similar argument seems particularly relevant to our consideration of top management team (TMT) members. When we consider the ways in which TMT members use their organization's identity to help them to make strategic decisions, we discover that the ways that they define 'who they are as an organization' disclose what they are trying to achieve on behalf of their organization (and gives us some good insight into one of the primary bases for their chosen strategic decisions and actions). In some significant sense, then, organizational identity is the fountainhead of organizational strategy. In that light strategy and decision making *must* be consistent with identity or the organization soon becomes incoherent, not only to its stakeholders, but even to itself.

Another important area for research is the role of organizational identity in *failed* decision making and implementation. Reger *et al.* (1994) theorized that identity played a major role in the failure of Total Quality Management initiatives. Similarly, Nutt (2004) has proposed that organizational identity considerations are the key to the success or failure of downsizing. He introduced the notion of 'de-evolution' or slow and deliberate downsizing guided by a new identity that retains the core competencies of the organization. Elsewhere, Nutt (1999; 2003) has described the astoundingly high failure rate of decisions in organizations, and Wilson, Hickson, and Miller (1996) coined the term 'decision overreach' to describe a particularly calamitous form of decision failure. Organizational identity holds some promise for helping to explain such decision failures and why some firms are more susceptible to decision overreach than others.

Finally, organizational identity has tremendous potential for shedding light on what has been called 'micro-strategizing' (Johnson, Melin, and Whittington, 2003) – the micro-level processes that support macro-level outcomes. The concept of micro-strategy contains within it the assumption that strategizing is not context-free (Wilson and Jarzabkowski, 2004). An organizational identity framework provides a way to conceptualize and understand the context in which micro-strategy takes place. This type of work is also inherently multi- or cross-level, and the concept of organizational identity lends itself to such analyses. In addition, scholars taking the strategy-as-practice turn (e.g. Jarzabkowski, Balogun, and Seidl, 2007; Jarzabkowski and Wilson, 2006) have called for theory that is more actionable in practice. As noted above, the concept of organizational identity has meaning to both informants and researchers. This 'rare and fortunate' circumstance makes organizational identity an ideal bridge between theory and practice. In this sense, organizational identity could be an important enhancement to the strategy-as-practice perspective and indeed could serve to make strategy and decision-making research more actionable in practice.

REFERENCES

Albert, S., and Whetten, D.A. (1985) Organizational identity, *Research in Organizational behavior*, Vol. 7. Greenwich, CT: JAI Press, Inc., 263–295

Barney, J., Bunderson, J.S., Foreman, P.O., Gustafson, L.T., Huff, A.S., Martins, L.L., Reger, R.K., Sarason, Y., and Stimpert, J.L. (1998) 'A Strategy Conversation on the Topic of Organization Identity', in D.A. Whetten and P.C. Godfrey (eds) *Identity in Organizations: Building Theory through Conversations*. Thousand Oaks, CA: Sage, 99–168.

Bazerman, M.H. (2004) 'Common Biases', in B.M. Staw (ed.) *Psychological Dimensions of Organizational Behavior*. NJ: Prentice Hall, 3rd edition, 181–20.

Brickson, S.L. (2005) Organizational identity orientation: Forging a link between organizational identity and organizations' relations with stakeholders, *Administrative Science Quarterly*, 50 (4), 576–609.

Cho, T.S., and Hambrick, D.C. (2006) Attention as the mediator between top management team characteristics and strategic change: The case of airline deregulation, *Organization Science*, 17 (4), 453–469.

Cohen, M.D., March, J.G., and Olsen, J.P. (1972) A garbage can model of organizational choice, *Administrative Science Quarterly*, 17, 1–25.

Corley, K.G., and Gioia, D.A. (2004) Identity ambiguity and change in the wake of a corporate spin-off, *Administrative Science Quarterly*, 49 (2), 173–208.

Corley, K.G., Harquail, C.V., Pratt, M.G., Glynn, M.A., Fiol, C.M., and Hatch, H.J. (2006) Guiding organizational identity through aged adolescence, *Journal of Management Inquiry*, 15 (2), 85–99.

Czarniawska, B. (1997) *Narrating the Organization: Dramas of Institutional Identity.* Chicago: University of Chicago Press.

Czarniawska, B., and Wolff, R. (1998) Constructing new identities in established organization fields, *International Studies of Management & Organization*, 28 (3), 32–56.

Dutton, J.E., and Dukerich, J.M. (1991) Keeping an eye on the mirror: Image and identity in organizational adaptation, *Academy of Management Journal*, 34 (3), 517–554.

Dutton, J.E., Dukerich, J.M., and Harquail, C.V. (1994) Organizational images and member identification, *Administrative Science Quarterly*, 39 (2), 239–263.

Elgin, B. (2007) 'Little green lies.' *BusinessWeek*, 44–52.

Elsbach, K.D., and Bhattacharya, C.B. (2001) Defining who you are by what you're not: Organizational disidentification and the National Rifle Association, *Organization Science*, 12 (4), 393–413.

Elsbach, K.D., and Kramer, R.M. (1996) Members' responses to organizational identity threats: Encountering and countering the Business Week rankings, *Administrative Science Quarterly*, 41 (3), 442–476.

Erickson, E.H. (1968) *Identity, Youth, and Crises.* New York: Norton.

Fiol, C.M. (2002) Capitalizing on paradox: The role of language in transforming organizational identities, *Organization Science*, 13 (6), 653–666.

Foreman, P., and Whetten, D.A. (2002) Member's identification with multiple-identity organizations, *Organization Science*, 13 (6), 618–635.

Fredrickson, J.W., and Iaquinto, A.L. (1989) Inertia and creeping rationality in strategic decision processes, *Academy of Management Journal*, 32 (3), 516–542.

Gagliardi, P. (1986) The creation and change of organizational cultures: A conceptual framework, *Organization Studies*, 7 (2), 117–134.

Gioia, D.A. (1998) 'From Individual to Organizational Identity', in D.A. Whetten and P.C. Godfrey (eds) *Identity in Organizations: Building Theory through Conversations.* Thousand Oaks: Sage, 17–31.

Gioia, D.A., and Chittipeddi, K. (1991) Sensemaking and sensegiving in strategic change initiation, *Strategic Management Journal*, 12 (6), 433–448.

Gioia, D.A., Schultz, M., and Corley, K.G. (2000) Organizational identity, image, and adaptive instability, *Academy of Management Review*, 25 (1), 63–81.

Gioia, D.A., Schultz, M., and Corley, K.G. (2002). On celebrating the organizational identity metaphor: A rejoinder to Cornelissen, *British Journal of Management*, 13 (3), 269.

Gioia, D.A., and Thomas, J.B. (1996) Identity, image, and issue interpretation: Sensemaking during strategic change in academia, *Administrative Science Quarterly*, 41 (3), 370–403.

Glynn, M.A. (2000) When cymbals become symbols: Conflict over organizational identity within a symphony orchestra, *Organization Science*, 11 (3), 285–298.

Goffman, E. (1959) *The Presentation of Self in Everyday Life.* New York: Doubleday.

Hannan, M.T., Baron, J.N., Hsu, G., and Koçak, Ö. (2006) Organizational identities and the hazard of change, *Industrial and Corporate Change*, 15 (5), 755–784.

Hatch, M.J., and Schultz, M. (eds) (2004) *Organization Identity: A Reader.* Oxford, England: Oxford University Press.

Jarzabkowski, P., Balogun, J., and Seidl, D. (2007) Strategizing: The challenges of a practice perspective, *Human Relations*, 60 (1), 5–27.

Jarzabkowski, P., and Wilson, D.C. (2006) Actionable strategy knowledge:* A practice perspective, *European Management Journal*, 24 (5), 348–381.

Johnson, G., Melin, L., and Whittington, R. (2003) Guest editor's introduction: Micro strategy and strategizing: Towards an activity-based view, *The Journal of Management Studies*, 40 (1), 3–22.

Meyer, J.W., and Rowan, B. (1977) Institutionalized organizations: Formal structure as myth and ceremony, *American Journal of Sociology*, 83 (2), 340–363.

Miller, S.J., and Wilson, D.C. (2006) 'Perspectives on Organizational Decision-making', in S.R. Clegg, C. Hardy, T.B. Lawrence, and W.R. Nord (eds) *The Sage Handbook of Organization Studies*. London: Sage, 2nd edition, 469–484.

Mintzberg, H., Raisinghani, D., and Theoret, A. (1976) The structure of 'unstructured' decision processes, *Administrative Science Quarterly*, 21 (2), 246–275.

Nag, R., Corley, K.G., and Gioia, D.A. (2007) The intersection of organizational identity, knowledge, and practice: Attempting strategic change via knowledge grafting, *Academy of Management Journal*, 50 (4), 821–847.

Nutt, P.C. (1998) Framing strategic decisions, *Organization Science*, 9 (2), 195–216.

Nutt, P.C. (1999) Surprising but true: Half the decisions in organizations fail, *The Academy of Management Executive*, 13 (4), 75–86.

Nutt, P.C. (2002) Selecting decision rules for crucial choices: An investigation of the Thompson Framework, *The Journal of Applied Behavioral Science*, 38 (1), 99–131.

Nutt, P.C. (2003) Why decisions fail: Avoiding the blunders and traps that lead to debacles, *The Academy of Management Executive*, 17 (1), 130–132.

Nutt, P.C. (2004) Organizational de-development, *The Journal of Management Studies*, 41 (7), 1083–1103.

Nutt, P.C. (2005) Search during decision making, *European Journal of Operational Research*, 160 (3), 851–876.

Pfeffer, J., and Salancik, G.R. (1978) *The External Control of Organizations: A resource-dependence perspective*. New York: Harper & Row.

Ravasi, D., and Schultz, M. (2006) Responding to organizational identity threats: Exploring the role of organizational culture, *Academy of Management Journal*, 49 (3), 433–458.

Reger, R.K., Gustafson, L.T., Demarie, S.M., and Mullane, J.V. (1994) Reframing the organization: Why implementing total quality is easier said than done, *The Academy of Management Review*, 19 (3), 565–584.

Santos, F.M., and Eisenhardt, K.M. (2005) Organizational boundaries and theories of organization, *Organization Science*, 16 (5), 491–508.

Selznick, P. (1957) *Leadership in Administration*. Berkeley, CA: University of California Press.

Thompson, J.D. (1967) *Organizations in Action: Social science bases of administrative theory*. New York: McGraw-Hill.

Weick, K.E. (1976) Educational organizations as loosely coupled systems, *Administrative Science Quarterly*, 21 (1), 1–19.

Whetten, D.A. (2006) Albert and Whetten revisited: Strengthening the concept of organizational identity, *Journal of Management Inquiry*, 15 (3), 219–234.

Whetten, D.A., and Mackey, A. (2002) A social actor conception of organizational identity and its implications for the study of organizational reputation, *Business and Society*, 41 (4), 393–414.

Wilson, D.C., Hickson, D.J., and Miller, S. (1996) How organizations can overbalance: Decision overreach as a reason for failure, *The American Behavioral Scientist*, 39 (8), 995–1010.

Wilson, D.C., and Jarzabkowski, P. (2004) Thinking and acting strategically: New challenges for interrogating strategy, *European Management Review*, 1 (1), 14–20.

Part III

CONCEPTUALIZING STRATEGIC DECISION MAKING

7

Building a Decision-making Action Theory

Paul C. Nutt

Introduction

Failed decisions in organizations have disastrous outcomes with long-term effects (Nutt, 1999). Examples include ill-advised products, questionable acquisitions, and botched product recalls, such as the launch of New Coke, Ford's purchase of Jaguar, and Beechnut's stonewalling a recall of their apple-less apple juice (Nutt, 2002). Failure poses questions. Is failure caused by bad luck or by faulty decision making practices? Are there other practices more apt to succeed? This chapter draws on a quarter of a century of research that sought answers to such questions. A series of studies that were undertaken to uncover how key people in organizations go about decision making and the success realized will be drawn upon to provide answers (Nutt, 2002). In these studies, more than 400 decisions were collected to uncover the practices of decision makers, accounting for the situation being confronted and documenting success. Many of the decisions were made by first-rate managers in well-run companies. They included acquisitions, buildings, new products, revamped services, promotions, and recalls. Decision making practices that were employed were correlated with the results realized in which responsible parties either bore burdens or reaped benefits. Linking decision results to decision making practices, accounting for content and context, provided a telling appraisal of the practices. The decisions, both good and bad, offered a first hand account of events and circumstances allowing me to probe for why some practices work, and others go awry, looking for recommendations.

The findings are unequivocal. Failure occurs more often than leaders realize. Half fail: making failed decisions a commonplace event in organizations (Nutt, 1999). Failure plagued both the best and brightest and the more novice manager working in organizations with strong and more modest track records. Some were discarded before an implementation attempt, others after concerted but fruitless

Handbook of Decision Making. Edited by Paul C. Nutt and David C. Wilson
© 2010 John Wiley & Sons, Ltd

effort. In either case, no benefits are realized. Considering the wasted resources and forgone benefits, uncovering the causes of failure and ways to improve matters seemed vital. This pointed to another key finding. Decision makers are not at the mercy of the situation being confronted. The practices followed have *far* more influence on success than abrupt changes in customer tastes, the cost of money, draconian regulations, and other situational constraints that can erect barriers and pose difficulties. Some decision making practices yield good results; others poor results.

This chapter highlights best practice and practices prone to failure. To uncover each, successful (adopted with sound benefits) decisions and unsuccessful (questionable benefits and not adopted) decisions in my database were studied to find how the practices used in successful decisions differed from those applied in unsuccessful decisions. (The mixed cases of non-adopted beneficial decisions and non-beneficial adopted decisions are not considered here.) Success rates double when decision makers follow best practices.

Both best practices and the failure-prone practices will be illustrated by AEP's pollution control fiasco, CompuServe's failed attempt to acquire AOL, and the Perrier and Fen-Phen recall debacles. Table 7.1 provides an overview of the key events in the village purchase, failed acquisition, and recalls how they lead to the pivotal decision. Failed decisions provide an ideal vehicle to reveal failure-prone practices, why they are apt to fail, and what can be done to improve the prospects of success. Failure brings to light failure-prone practices. This sets the stage to look for how things could have been done differently. Examining real decisions in this way has considerable president, such as Snyder and Page (1958) and their study of the Korean War, Allison (1971) and his exploration of the Cuban missile crisis, Hall's (1984) exposure of the Bay Area Rapid Transit fiasco, Mckie's (1973) study of London's aborted third airport, and my study of the Snapple acquisition by Quaker (Nutt, 2002).

AEP's Purchase of Cheshire, Ohio

American Electric Power (AEP) is a multinational company and the largest energy producer in the United States.[1] AEP owns and operates more than 80 energy-producing plants worldwide. The Gavin plant, located on the Ohio River in southeast Ohio, is a coal burning facility that began operations in 1974. The plant provides 26 000 mega watts of power. The facility's smoke stacks sit within yards of Cheshire, Ohio, a village of 221 people located in a low-income area of Ohio, with high unemployment.

There were complaints about ash fallout lodged with the Environmental Protection Agency soon after operations began at the Gavin plant. The EPA took no overt enforcement action but asked AEP to voluntarily reduce its nitrogen oxide emissions. This prompted AEP officials to study the situation. The study found that pollution abetments would be ineffective during the summer months and company officials decided against an investment in pollution control. In the years that followed, widespread concerns about air quality and heightened public awareness about the adverse effects of air pollution led to a renewed interest

TABLE 7.1 Flow of events in the decisions

Events	PERRIER RECALL	FEN-PHEN RECALL	AEP PURCHASE OF CHESHIRE	COMPUSERVE'S ACQUISITION OF AOL
Before	'Premium' product develops 24 % market share. Plans to market a low-end product using healthful image. NC health department finds benzene traces in Perrier. Contend incident caused by improper cleaning of filling equipment.	Weight loss drug (Fen-Phen) counteracts side effects when taken as a cocktail. Wyeth acquires rights to drugs. Approved by FDA for use by high risk patients due to continued questions about side effects (VHD). Mayo clinic reports 30 % VHD in studies of Fen-Phen.	Gavin plant established in southern Ohio. Ash fallout prompts complains by Cheshire residents. EPA asks for study, but no corrective action. AEP invests $ 7 million, only to exchange ash fallout for acid rain. Cheshire residents contact lawyers who suggest village buyout for $ 20 million.	CompuServe founded as a time-sharing service for companies. Growth financed by H&R Block buyout. Introduce CIS for high-end users to utilize late night capacity. CompuServe founder fired after buy back attempt. Huge growth in mass market forecasted. Three options explored to meet mass market online information (ignore, build, & buy). Select buy option and identified targets. Offer to buy Quantum Computing (AOL). Approach H&R Block board with a proposal to buy Quantum for $ 60 million.
Pivotal decision	Worldwide recall of Perrier bottled water	Continue to market Fen-Phen	Purchase village	

(Continued)

TABLE 7.1 (Continued)

Events	PERRIER RECALL	FEN-PHEN RECALL	AEP PURCHASE OF CHESHIRE	COMPUSERVE'S ACQUISITION OF AOL
After	Forecast no time off market; revised to 2 to 3 months. More benzene found; off market 5 months. Announced that benzene occurs naturally in the water and not removed due to a filter failure. Critics note that carbonation was added, contradicting labeling. $ 25 million Ad campaign to reintroduce product. Market share falls to 14 %; Losses $ 263 million.	FDA withdraws the drugs Lawsuits filed. Side effects verified Class action settlements Losses estimated at $ 40 billion.	10 % of Cheshire residents refuse to sell. Negative publicity on a national scale. Complaints continue and EPA issues citations. AEP's proposal for a demonstration of a clean coal-fired plant rejected by DOE. Courts rule updated plants as well as new plants must have most up-to-date pollution control. AEP's request to bill customers for pollution control rejected by courts.	Block board conducts additional studies. Board calls for a $ 55 million purchase price. Lower offer rejected. CompuServe looks for 'White Knight'. Division reorganized. High-end service purchased from Block by AOL.

in pollution control. To respond, Congress enacted more stringent regulations. This prompted the EPA to call on AEP to reduce the ash fallout produced by its plants, including Gavin. As a result, AEP was confronted with a number of pollution-related complainants and the associated negative publicity. This coaxed AEP to spend $ 7 million to install a previous shelved plan. The selective catalytic reduction (SCR) system was installed at the Gavin plant to reduce the nitrogen oxide emissions (ash fallout). The new system also moved the plant's boundary even closer to the village.

The SCR system proved to be ineffective, merely decreasing one type of pollution by increasing another. The new pollutant came from SRC exhaust plumes that emitted sulfur trioxide, causing a blue haze of sulfuric acid to engulf the village. Residents experienced burning eyes, headaches, sore throats and white burns on their bodies. The EPA was alerted and called on AEP to correct the blue haze problem. AEP conducted engineering studies seeking to reduce the sulfur trioxide, hoping to eliminate or at least reduce the blue haze. No solution was found after considerable effort, prompting company officials to abandon pollution abatement attempts. AEP officials believed they had made an investment of $ 7 million only to intensify the pollution problem, which argued that further investments would be foolhardy. Negative publicity intensified. Unanswered complaints prompted a group of Cheshire residents to engage a battery of lawyers. The lawyers came up with a solution, suggesting the AEP be approached with an offer to buy the village. The residents agreed and asked the attorneys to present an offer to sell the village to AEP for $ 20 million.

After reviewing the lawyers' proposal, AEP's top management agreed to purchase the village for the asking price. Company analysts found that the purchase price would pay the villagers more than the market value of the homes. Company officials reasoned that this would appease the villagers. As part of the agreement, residents were to wave their right to sue for any medical problems resulting from the blue haze. Corporate press releases suggest that AEP officials saw the buyout as addressing the concerns of Cheshire in a responsible manner. They also claimed that the land acquired would be used to build a dock to unload barges that bring coal to the plant (AEP, April, 16, 2002). There were to be no negotiations with individuals. Payments were to be coordinated through the attorneys. Later, company officials conceded that they had no plans to use the land.

If AEP management was attempting to eliminate liabilities, then a single resident who refused to sell would render the decision a failure. Yet, top management never asked who was being represented by the attorneys. It turned out that the attorneys had been hired by a majority block of villagers who wanted to sell their properties. A smaller group of Cheshire residents were not represented and had no interest in selling. After the deal had been agreed to 21 (10 %) of the residents refused to sell and stated their intent to keep the village intact. Other complications arose. Many residents were underage and thus unable to wave their rights. Subsequently, a probate court ruled that the deal was in the best interests of the children but that liability from haze-related health problems could not be removed by the agreement. All this attention brought the village and its blue haze into the national spotlight. National news stories appeared. The *New York Times* and the *Washington Post* as well as local papers kept the story line alive with periodic updates, making connections to Love Canal and other high profile pollution debacles. By deciding it was cheaper to buy a village than to deal with pollution, AEP appeared to be disinterested in environmental protection. The media questioned whether AEP had made any attempt to comply with federal laws. Negative publicity persists to the present day. The village still exists, with the remaining residents forming the village council. The residents continue to complain about pollution and sue for medical problems caused by the blue haze. This has prompted people in neighboring villages to take legal action, claiming that the blue haze made them ill as well. By ignoring surrounding areas, which contained several public schools affected by the blue haze, more potential liabilities were created.

Assuming that AEP officials sought to stifle complaints, the actions taken were flawed. Company officials failed to uncover stakeholder concerns and interests. Instead, the urge to resolve the controversy prompted company officials to agree to a seemingly workable remedy that, for the most part, preempted due diligence. There was little study of the plan beyond a cursory examination of costs. The decision took shape as either accepting or rejecting an offer to buy what turned out to be most, but not all, of the village. Company officials failed to determine the extent of liability for the blue haze and made no attempt to identify other options. There are several, depending on the results desired. If the objective was to deal with pollution several options can be identified. They include: searching for other pollution abatement options, turning off the SRC in summer months, reducing the burning of low sulfur coal, trying other coal mixtures or exploring the ramifications of shuttering the plant. If the objective was to deal with adverse publicity, the company could determine the extent of pollution and the people affected and negotiate directly with affected parties to educate them, using proactive media and public relations to publicize the AEP position. Failing to work with residents to uncover their concerns ruled out these options. Company officials did none of these searches. Instead, actions were limited to investigating the proposal's costs. There was no attempt to understand potential legal liabilities, the scope of negative publicity or the downstream damage to the company of a village purchase as response to pollution.

The public airing of the village purchase became an embarrassment. Ten per cent of the residents stayed, but the village was essentially destroyed. AEP officials squandered $ 20 million, failed to eliminate their liabilities and managed to grow negative publicity from a local flap into a nationwide fiasco. Neighboring communities became aware of the situation and sued. Treating pollution as a real estate deal tarnished the company image. AEP appeared to be another business bullying the small guy while dodging their responsibilities. By appearing to use subterfuge to avoid compliance with clean air standards, AEP officials became poster boys for poor corporate citizens. There is no barge loading anticipated or being planned, suggesting that company press releases contained misrepresentations.

AEP officials made a rushed judgment. There was no urgency to act on the buyout proposal. The EPA had not set a time table, nor had the Cheshire residents. AEP officials had ample time to sort out their obligations and their costs. This would have allowed company officials to explore ramifications of the buyout such as company risks, costs and obligations, and to look for other options. Also, there was no clarity on what was wanted as a result. Did company officials seek to limit liability, publicity, complaints, cost or responsibility? Without clarity here any proposed action is apt to provoke objections.

The decision produced long-term negative fallout for the company. AEP responded to a Department of Energy request to US power companies, asking for a demonstration of the latest in pollution-free coal-burning plants. AEP's proposal was not taken seriously. The courts have ruled that AEP can not make modifications to older coal-burning plants without first installing up-to-date air-pollution technology. AEP responded by asking regulators for permission to charge customers for the new pollution control. A court challenge overturned the rate increase. AEP now faces fat penalties unless the latest in pollution control is installed in *both* planned and previously modified plants. This prompted the company to delay site work at two new coal-burning plants along the Ohio River until the middle of the next decade, seeking to cut costs. This will cause delays of more than four years. Up-to-date pollution control technology captures many of the emissions from burning coal as well as carbon dioxide, a chief cause of global warming. New federal rules are in the works that will cap carbon dioxide and other emissions. Disregarding pollution control is no longer an option. AEP's cavalier approach to pollution control in Cheshire has brought on more stringent requirements and additional regulation.

CompuServe's Failed Acquisition of AOL

CompuServe was founded in 1969 to provide computerized business applications to businesses, such as accounting and payroll.[2] At the time, many companies were unable to bear the cost of computer mainframes, making it desirable to contract out data-intensive applications to specialists. CompuServe's founder, Jeff Wilkins, initiated computer time sharing to provide subscribers with the latest computer technology. The company became very profitable. In a decade, CompuServe's services had become worldwide, with networking that connected many far-flung clients with electronic communication, product demand tracking, procurement and other cutting-edge applications. Wilkins believed that CompuServe could make better use of its capacity. Day time use was fully subscribed but there was significant unused capacity at night. To sell this capacity, Wilkins developed 'CompuServe information service' or CIS that offered an electronic mail service to the public for the first time, as well as research databases such as Nexus, technical online discussion forums, newswires, online games and other high-end online resources. CIS was offered in 1979 to high-income computer enthusiasts and sold at a premium price. CIS had considerable initial success but was hampered by the lack of investment capital. To grow the service, the company had to develop banks of modems in major metropolitan areas that allowed many more subscribers to dial up CIS and to develop additional cutting-edge online content.

There was a limited amount of technology-related venture capital available at the time but cash-rich companies were looking for investment opportunities. After some study, Wilkins contacted H&R Block; a mature publicly traded but closely held firm specializing in income tax preparation. The board of H&R Block saw a potential synergy with their new and extremely lucrative rapid refund service, which required considerable computing capacity. In exchange, Wilkins would receive the capital needed to develop CIS. To cement the deal, Wilkins sold out to H&R Block and became CompuServe's CEO. By 1985, CIS was an enormous success. Its subscriber base was growing rapidly and the service had become very profitable. H&R Block, in contrast, was experiencing slow growth and declining profitability. The luster of rapid refund had slipped away and H&R Block's long history of ever-improving earnings had ended. CompuServe's profits now sustained its parents' bottom line. With the need for capital met, Wilkins tried to buy his company back and was fired on the spot.

In the next decade CompuServe became the industry leader for high-end online services. Then the computer market began to change. Many more households had become interested in online services, suggesting a huge potential for growth. The services required, however, needed to be value-priced with less emphasis on high-tech. CompuServe insiders believed that the time was ripe to move into the mass market with scaled-down versions of their high-end products. Several options were considered including limiting focus to the high-end market, developing a dumb-down version of CIS or acquiring another consumer information service that could be mass marketed. CompuServe insiders feared that their highly profitable high-end users would be alienated by modifications to CIS sold to a mass audience. They also feared that company engineers would over-engineer an internal offering. With these considerations in mind, the 'buy' option was selected over the 'ignore' and 'build' options.

CompuServe insiders identified firms with small online services that seemed acquirable. After study, Quantum Computing, which later became America Online, emerged as the leading candidate. In the spring of 1990, CompuServe officials entered into negotiations with Quantum to find an acquisition price. At the time Quantum was small, with less than $ 1 million annual profit, but was backed by an ambitious and competent board and financed by Kleiner Perkins, one of the country's best known venture capital firms. After negotiation, a price of $ 60 million was agreed to by CompuServe and Quantum. The proposal was taken to H&R Block's board for their approval. The board rejected the offer and countered at $ 55 million. The offer was rejected and Quantum became AOL, a $ 100 billion company, within a decade. Without the capacity to compete in the explosion of the mass information market, CompuServe sank into obscurity. By 1998, AOL acquired CompuServe's high-end subscriber base at a steep discount, effectively ending this part of their business.

Officials at Block and its CompuServe subsidiary saw things very differently. CompuServe sought to become a market leader while Block wanted steady cash flows to sustain profitability. The Block family, which held one-third of the company's stock, was vitally concerned with protecting their wealth. CompuServe provided 75 % of company profit, but had no representation on the board of directors. CompuServe insiders chafed under the conservative Block management style and wanted a larger role in corporate decisions, particularly strategic choices that influenced the sustainability of their competitive advantage. The Block board questioned whether future growth depended on a mass market and that $ 60 million was required to realize it.

CompuServe insiders were making claims about growth, Block claims about sustaining wealth. These expectations were conflicting.

To make matters worse, CompuServe's insiders had acted without consulting the board. To position for growth, they presented a fully developed plan to the board, expecting approval. This alienated the board, making any proposal a hard sell. To save face, the board conducted some hurried and flawed studies. To give the appearance of control the board demanded a price reduction, which scuttled the deal. CompuServe insiders believed that they had gone to extreme lengths to be heard. However, some of their moves were absurd. At one point, CompuServe sought Time Warner's intervention as a 'white knight' to purchase the division from H&R Block, hoping to save the deal. At the same time, the voices of other key stakeholders were not heard. Quantum's management and investors were ignored, overlooking that either could pull the deal from the table at any time. Clients of CompuServe and Quantum were not consulted although either group could put the deal a risk. Quantum management turned down a 55 to 1 price–earnings ratio, a figure unheard of for an acquisition at the time. Company officials rejected an offer that was 92 % of its asking price. This hardly seems in the best interest of their shareholders.

H&R Block was confronted with a 'buy–no buy' decision to position the company to realize growth in the information mass market. Risk-averse board members were asked to pony up $ 60 million. Their analysis of the deal made no attempt to project best and worse case revenues. A worst case projection would have covered the investment. My analysis of the data available at the time shows a very positive discounted return, assuming the most conservative revenue estimates imaginable.

H&R Block failed to realize an historic opportunity, and a huge payoff. The decision was doomed by an incompatibility of the goals of CompuServe and Block. Block was unwilling to incur a very small risk to realize a huge gain. Such conservative postures had alienated CompuServe insiders who decided to act in their own interests. Doing so, they ignored lines of authority and doomed their idea. CompuServe researched and engaged in discussion with an online provider about the possibility of purchasing its assets without the knowledge and permission of its parent. After agreeing in principle to the purchase, CompuServe had to approach the Block board to finalize the deal. Not surprisingly, the board reacted negatively. Even so, the board did not break off the discussions. There was an attempt to separate a business decision from the deceitful actions used to propose it. CompuServe insiders believed in their vision and were convinced that Block would be reluctant to let them pursue it. A combination of their foresight and hubris drove them to pursue secrecy. They went behind the backs of their superiors to put together an iron-clad case, which they thought could not be refused. However, their due diligence provided no assurance that the ossified, family-controlled Block board would buy into the proposed deal. In the negotiations, there was no attempt to cater to the Block leadership or to their values of long-term wealth-building. Negotiation could have catered to Block's conservative culture, and offered assurances. This seems vital as Block was known to be provincial, risk-averse and slow to adopt change. CompuServe had a vastly different culture that called for an agile and flexible posture, which was required to adjust to a rapidly changing industry. This fostered an entrepreneurial spirit that encouraged educated risks. Such different cultures demanded careful and candid dealings to avoid misunderstandings. Despite this, neither the Block nor the CompuServe faction made an attempt to develop a mutually agreeable working relationship.

THE FEN-PHEN AND PERRIER RECALLS

Recalls cost firms billions. Understandably, company officials fear them. To make a recall decision, leaders must balance fiscal responsibilities with public safety, which is often riddled with uncertainty. Both a recall and failure to recall can backfire if leaders are blind to facts or if they act rashly with limited information. Fen-Phen and Perrier illustrate how each can arise and lead to a fiasco.

American Home Products or AHP is a diversified health care firm made up of acquired companies: Wyeth, Lederle, and AH Robins.[3] (AHP changed its name to Wyeth following its recall debacle.) Wyeth marketed Fen-Phen, a combination of two drugs called a drug cocktail. Phentermine is a central nervous system stimulant designed to control appetite. Fenfluramine is a serotonin blocker that also suppresses appetite but acts centrally to depress the central nervous system. The negative side effects of the two drugs were, theoretically, offsetting. The FDA approved both drugs in the 1970s. The company obtained rights to both drugs with its acquisition of the Lederle division of American Cyanamid. As patents were expiring on the basic compounds in the mid 1990s Wyeth, following longstanding practices in the pharmaceutical industry, developed a related compound to extend the patient called Dexfenfluramine, an isomer of Fenfluramine. A combination of Dexfenfluramine and Phentermine was approved by the FDA in 1996 as a *short-term treatment* for *severe* cases of obesity. The new version of Fen-Phen was marketed as Redux. (As the drugs are chemically identical, the Fen-Phen name will be used.) The approval decision was controversial. The FDA's advisory panel initially voted against the safety of the drug, but for its efficacy. Two months later the panel approved it with a one-vote margin. The WSJ (September 4, 1997) reported that members were swayed by the 'obesity epidemic in America' and the belief that something should be done to curb it.

Instructions for the Fen-Phen drug cocktail limit its use to a few weeks for high-risk patients, participating in a weight-loss program. Enrollment in a formal weight reduction program that restricted caloric intake was required. Help to maintain a realized weight loss was also allowed. Fen-Phen was limited to people with risk factors, such as diabetes and hypertension. Warnings mentioned pulmonary hypertension and concerns with cardiac arrhythmias, but did not mention valvular heart disease (VHD). The instructions also warned against combining the drug with other weight loss agents because such combinations had not been studied.

Initially, investigators found the side effects of Phentermine, like Fenfluramine, were counteracted by Dexfenfluramine. Following a four-year study of 121 patients, an average weight loss of 32 pounds was reported for patients with an average starting weight of more than 200 pounds. The fact that nearly 60 million Americans are more than 20 % overweight coupled with endless reports about how health problems are made worse by obesity prompted a strong demand for Fen-Phen. Fen-Phen was embraced by physicians, storefront diet clinics and diet programs such as Jenny Craig and Nutrisystem, leading to widespread use. In 1996 alone, 18 million prescriptions were written by 11 000 physicians (WSJ, May 16, 2003). Over 6 million patients ware taking the new (Redux) or the original version (Fen-Phen) of the drug. Many prescriptions were obtained at a diet center. David Crossen of Montgomery Securities, a security analyst, claimed it the fastest ever launch of a drug. In the first 11 weeks sales hit an annualized rate of $ 220 million. By 1996, annual sales were at $ 352 million and were predicted to reach $ 1 billion.

As sales grew, evidence was mounting that Fen-Phen caused VHD and primary pulmonary hypertension. Wyeth received such reports from European investigators as early as 1995, but the company resisted adding warning labels to their packaging. By March 1997, investigators in the US were reporting the same side effects, suggesting an incidence as high as 30 %. Federal rules require that adverse effects be reported to the FDA. At this time, Wyeth was suffering from acquisition pains in assimilating the Lederle division of American Cyanamid. FDA inspectors found an understaffed safety department and a faulty computer infrastructure. (WSJ, September 28, 1999). Wyeth had added temporary employees, but they were unable to cope. The new cases of VHD were entered as 'adverse events' but labeled as premature and ignored. Relations between the FDA and Wyeth became strained; the FDA contended that the company did not follow up on reports of VHD. In 1997 several studies appeared in the *New England Journal of Medicine* that linked VHD cases to Fen-Phen. During the 1996 and 1997 period, Wyeth continued to market Fen-Phen, spending $ 52 million in advertising. Mounting concerns prompted the FDA to require a 'black box' warning of possible heart and lung complications to be put on the drug package. This caused prescriptions to fall by more than 50 %. By late summer of 1997, health insurance companies restricted prescriptions to patents taking part in clinical trails. Diet clinics such as Jenny Craig dropped the drug. The American Medical Association called for a moratorium on its use (WSJ, September 4, 1987). In September of 1997, the FDA summoned Wyeth to a meeting and presented evidence that 92 of 291, nearly 30 %, of the patients taking Fen-Phen, had developed serious heart abnormalities and withdrew the drug from the market. Wyeth anticipated a charge of $ 200 to $ 300 million or 20 to 30 cents a share to cover recall costs (WSJ, September 16 1997).

Wyeth did not publicize early reports of health problems, was slow to report required data to the FDA, and did not pull Fen-Phen from the market until forced to by the FDA. Like many recall debacles, Wyeth management blinded themselves to bad news. Thinking they could ill afford to scuttle a winner, company officials refused to recall the drug or even acknowledge that it was being prescribed inappropriately. This may stem from a 'profit drives principle' posture or from an unwillingness to confront an out-of-control situation. The huge losses Wyeth incurred might have been averted or moderated by several actions. Wyeth could have adopted warning labeling when the issue first arose. This was likely to drastically reduce sales (ultimately the warning reduced sales by 50 %) but would have prevented hundreds of cases of VHD and limited company liability. A promotional campaign to physicians, calling attention to instructions that limited Fen-Phen to the high-risk patients, could have been mounted. Sales could be expected to plummet here as well, but harm to patients would have been minimized, and with it company liability. Instead, Wyeth officials sought to protect their huge profits and the prospects of even more, ignoring the risks that accompanied them. The decision not to recall Fen-Phen reflects uncertainty in estimating the incidence of an injury, the extent of the injury, the relationship of use with the injury, the magnitude of damage and the cost of litigation. Only by carefully monitoring drug safety can firms hope to appreciate such uncertainties. And there are vital interests at stake. Wyeth management served the interests of its stockholders by offering a profitable drug. These interests are also served by avoiding costly litigation and by being a responsible corporate citizen. Selling products for human consumption holds firms to a standard of doing no wrong, offering only products known to be safe. Pharmaceutical companies are held to an even higher standard, being expected to offer products that are safe *and* work as advertised. Becoming caught up in windfall profits enticed Wyeth to ignore corporate social responsibility and put its future profit at risk.

Of the 6 million patients who took the drug, 18 000 filed lawsuits prior to a class action. A 1999 settlement required Wyeth to compensate people in pending cases, but some 70 000 potential plaintiffs have opted out to pursue their own law suits. The 1999 settlement cost $ 3.75 billion to provide regular cardiogram monitoring, reimburse for the drugs purchased, medical education and a database for all claimants. The plaintiffs who opted out have cost the company some $ 13 million more. By 2003, notes in Wyeth financial reports suggest that the no-recall decision has cost the company $ 15 billion. Industry observers claim the toll could climb to $ 40 billion (Forbes, September 1, 2003), for drugs that grossed a total of $ 800 million in revenues.

Bottled water became a craze in the 1980s.[4] Products quickly sprang up to meet the demand. In response to this demand a French company, Source Perrier, gathered water from a spring in Vergaze France, bottled it, and distributed it worldwide. Perrier established a strong strategic position for a high-end product by offering 'pure water with a fizz', stemming from 'natural carbonation in the water'. The company claimed that gas in volcanic rock created the fizz and used the word 'natural sparkling' on its label to promote this feature of the product. In a decade, sales increased from $ 800 million to $ 40 billion. Perrier captured 24 % of the bottled water market in the US. As a differentiated product, it was in high demand in bars and restaurants. Its success prompted others such as PepsiCo, Coca Cola and Anheuser Busch to offer their version of bottled water. By this time, Perrier had become 'chic'. Its market was made up of customers willing to pay a premium price for image. At this point, company president, Ronald Davis, wanted to enter the mass market, both to increase sales and to establish Perrier as a household name. Davis came up with a 'healthy choice' image to strategically position Perrier in the larger mass market.

Prior to the mass market launch, Perrier experienced a set back. A laboratory run by the North Carolina agriculture and health department found traces of benzene, a cancer-causing agent, in some of the Perrier bottles and issued a health advisory. The advisory noted traces of benzene in several bottles of water but did not find the amounts to be a health hazard or issue a recall. The advisory was a precautionary step to allow more testing to determine what, if any, dangers were posed. Davis reacted immediately, seeking to protect the aura of pure spring water and its 'healthy image' to be used to capture the mass market. He removed all Perrier from the US market, recalling a total of 70 million bottles. He informed the media thorough the French parent company, contending that the contamination occurred accidentally during the cleaning of a bottling line and that the company had halted the production line that produced the faulty batch. The company was to bear a cost of $ 30 million to carry out the recall, which Davis used to drive home how far the company would go to protect the public.

A month later, reports trickled out that benzene was found in Perrier sold in Denmark and Holland as well. Investigating, local managers found that a warning light on a control panel, indicating need to change the benzene filter, had gone undetected for six months. The carbon filter had become clogged, allowing impurities to pass. In response, Davis extended the recall worldwide recalling 160 million bottles. In a news conference, company officials said that the benzene occurs naturally in the water and that clogged benzene filters caused this contamination. This prompted questions about the purity of the water and its alleged natural ingredient.

Actions to protect product image became a fiasco. First, Davis claimed that a cleaning source had erroneously been applied to machinery in the American plant. He further claimed that shelves would be restocked immediately. Davis then corrected the off-market time to two to three months. Additional reports of benzene were met with a new explanation, involving benzene filters. Additional findings of benzene in Europe and Japan pushed the restocking to five more months. This prompted critics to question whether Perrier had any understanding of the contaminant's source. Perrier's officials saw all media attention as an opportunity to promote its health image, indicating that the company had issued a recall even though the amount of benzene in the water did not pose a health problem. Perrier then attempted to answer its critics at a press conference. This got them into even more trouble. A company spokesperson noted that spring water has a number of impurities, including trace amounts of benzene, and that filters were used to remove the benzene contamination. The filtering also removed natural gasses that are reintroduced after the filtering step. Clearly the fizz did not occur naturally, as Perrier had claimed. The hope for positive PR evaporated with the contradictory statements and with the inadvertent disclosure that a key ingredient had been misrepresented.

Perrier officials were confident that their reputation would sustain them through a period of questioning. Just to be sure, the company budgeted $ 25 million for advertising as they re-launched their product. But during the five months Perrier was off the market, bars and restaurants found that customers had little product loyalty and had substituted cheaper products offered by competitors for Perrier. As a result, many customers were not willing to pay a premium for the Perrier brand. Sales plummeted. Perrier had to resort to discounting and still more marketing. The company had even more difficulty with public relations when the FDA required them to remove 'Naturally Sparkling' from its label. Perrier never attained their pre-recall dominance, with sales only reaching 60 % of historic levels.

In the aftermath, top management continued to believe their actions were prudent. To support this position, a London-based public relations firm was retained to prepare releases that commended the firm's recall, ignoring that no recall was required by health officials. In doing so, company leaders disregarded their deceptive recall justifications and their misrepresentation of a key product ingredient. A five-month market absence allowed customers to try other products and find that Perrier was no different than the less costly brands. This delivered a devastating blow to Perrier's alleged competitive advantage of differentiation. Losses were huge, placed at nearly $ 263 million ($ 198 million for the product to be recalled and destroyed, $ 48 million for related communications, and $ 18 million for consultants and financial assistance).

Davis's actions were bizarre. If one knows that traces of benzene occur naturally in spring water, why lie and attribute it to a cleaning agent? If he did not know, why not consult with company staffers and get the facts? Why make contradictory public statements sure to provoke fallout? And why allow a 'benzene filter argument' to be made when it was certain to reveal that the 'natural fizz' was artificial? Why hold the product off the market for five months when inventories could be sampled to see which lots had been compromised by the clogged filters? Why misrepresent a key ingredient and then make it obvious that there had been a misrepresentation? Davis acted impulsively and failed to consult others in the company. These actions kept the firm from regaining consumer confidence and market share and avoiding colossal financial losses.

How Decision Makers Behave in Failed Decisions

When decisions fail, decision makers have made premature commitments and wasted their resources (Nutt, 2002; 2004). Both a rush to judgment and misused resources lure decision makers into using failure-prone practices. This chain of events is surprising in how often each is observed and the magnitude of their consequences. Failure doubles when this chain of events is set in motion. First, let's see how premature commitments and misused resources arise, drawing on the village purchase, the attempted acquisition, and the recalls for illustrations.

Premature commitments

Decision makers felt pressured to act quickly, which often coaxed them to embrace the quick fix found in a ready-made plan. In the acquisition, village purchase and recalls there was no need to rush. The offer for Quantum (AOL) had no time limit. No one was courting them. Making AOL officials wait would have made the $ 55 million offer seem more attractive. AEP also had ample time to consider what to do. The EPA had set no time limit for pollution abatement. There was no expiration date on the offer presented by the villagers' attorneys. Top management had the time to sort out their obligations, their costs, and to search for options. A recall had not been suggested by health officials. Davis acted impulsively. He had ample time to consult with company experts to locate the source of the benzene contamination, and its prospect of becoming a health hazard. Wyeth officials ignored warning signs that arose long before the FDA removed Fen-Phen from the market. Following the initial warnings, the company had nearly three years to study drug safety and company liability and to call on physicians and weight-loss clinics to follow product-use protocols. Only after this time had slipped away did things become urgent.

Premature commitments stem from a desire to appear decisive, from fear and from personal interests. Many view acting quickly as both pragmatic and shrewd. These virtues are more apparent than real (Cooperrider and Srivastra, 1987). Empirical evidence finds that embracing a quick fix provides neither rapid action nor beneficial outcomes (Nutt, 2002). The ready-made plan poses questions about conflicts of interest and typically requires considerable adaptation. Delays result as attempts are made to convince interested parties that the company's interests, not the decision makers', are being served (Brunsson, 1982; Starbuck, 1983). Retrofits are often more costly and time consuming as well as less effective than expected (Nutt, 2005). Like most human beings, decision makers fear the unknown. Making a tough decision can be a lonely endeavor in which a longing to meet responsibilities and worries about the time required to do so elicits fear. Delays and uncertainties entice decision makers to embrace the available, if not ideal, solution found in a ready-made plan. This sets aside fears, but prompts a rush to judgment. Decision makers are also drawn to personal gains stemming from ego, lust for power and greed, as in the Quantum (AOL) acquisition and the failure to recall Fen-Phen. Posturing to appear decisive, attempting to garner rewards or acting to manage fears makes it hard for a decision maker to step into the unknown and remain there until insight emerges. AEP wanted rid of a nuisance, and its bad publicity. The offer from the villagers' attorneys seemed to offer a quick way out. The urge to adopt a quick fix found in a ready-made plan mounts with perceived urgency. As pressure to deal with the blue haze grew so did the seeming merits of the village buyout.

Misused resources

Decision makers believe they should conserve resources. This urge to be frugal leads to limiting expenditures. My studies show that this stance is maintained, until a quick fix emerges (Nutt, 2002). The prospect of a solution coaxes the decision maker to release funds to determine its virtues, often spending considerable time and money to collect data and testimonials. Little is spent on anything else. To make matters worse such evaluations become defensive (Nutt, 2002), carried out to support the idea and show that it will work (March, 1994; Eisenhardt, 1997). Pressure to show that the idea is both useful and do-able often grows until it becomes intense (Starbuck, 1983; Nutt, 1998a). This creates the appearance of a vested interest, even if there is none. This gets the attention of critics. The critic labels the evaluation as wasteful as well as pointless, carried out to defend what someone wants to do. To silence critics, responding to their concerns as they are voiced, decision makers are drawn into round after round of evaluations that lead to spending far more than was believed to be necessary.

CompuServe's projection of payback for the Quantum (AOL) acquisition was seen as overly optimistic by the Block board, carried out to promote CompuServe's interests. Instead of relieving suspicions, the evaluation raised questions about motives. To answer these questions more evaluation was undertaken. The Block board carried out their own assessment with very conservative assumptions, which scuttled the deal. This is typical. Controversy requires additional expenditures for evaluation; expenditures rapidly grow as more and more justification is demanded.

Even if a defensive evaluation is avoided, decision makers seldom do more than cost an idea. Decision makers spend vast sums on cost studies, but little on anything else (Nutt, 2002). AEP allocated funds to find the value of the homes, but spent little to investigate other issues of importance. This is typical. In failed decisions little time or money is spent to investigate claims, set objectives, search for ideas or manage social and political forces that can derail a decision. Surprisingly, evaluations that measure the benefits and risks of options are rarely attempted. Decision makers who fail to see any of this as a worthy investment have little to steer them away from making fatal errors.

These behaviors are often reinforcing. The urge to make a premature commitment seems to conserve resources. The push to save money can prompt a rush to judgment. Both conspire to entice the decision maker to use failure-prone practices. These practices appear to be efficient so following them is thought to save money.

AVOIDING TRAPS WITH BEST PRACTICES

Table 7.2 shows how premature commitments and misused resources set a series of traps, which are sprung when decision makers apply failure-prone practices (Nutt, 2002; 2004). This includes embracing a claim without study, ignoring interests and interest groups, leaving directions ambiguous, limiting search, misusing evaluations, overlooking ethical questions and failing to learn. Table 7.3 shows how these failure-prone practices mislead company officials in the CompuServe, AEP, Perrier, and Fen-Phen decisions.

My studies show that the prospect of success nearly doubles when decision makers take steps to avoid the traps by applying best practices, found in the actions of successful decision makers (Nutt, 2008). Best practice takes place when decision makers reconcile the claims of stakeholders and network with people who can block a decision. This is done to uncover and appreciate the interests of stakeholders as well as their ideas. The intent is to create a deeper understanding of the issues that merit management and new insights into how this can be done. Search requires a purpose. To envision 'what might be' people elicited in a quest must know 'for what'. Speculation about the future requires a direction indicating what would constitute a useful idea. Such speculations open up new avenues, suggesting what an 'ideal' solution would look like (Nadler and Chandon, 2003). Questioning then asks how to make the vision real. Search tactics of innovation, soliciting and benchmarking follow, incorporating what has been uncovered. Best practice allocates resources to uncovering and reconciling claims, implementation and direction setting and puts them at the forefront of the decision-making effort. Uncovering what the decision is about, barriers to action and desired results place a premium on learning. Learning can take place when an honest appraisal of outcomes is encouraged.

TABLE 7.2 How bad practices stem from decision-maker behavior

Premature Commitments	Misused Resources	Traps (Failure-prone Practices)
Buy into a claim (or claimant) without due diligence	Fail to use resources to look for hidden concerns and the more pressing claims they suggest	Fail to reconcile claims (Select a claim according to the power of the claimant)
Overlook social and political forces provoked by the claim	Little or nothing spent to identify the interests and commitments of stakeholders	Ignore interests and interest groups (Use power and persuasion to implement)
Infer expected results from benefits attributed to a ready-made plan	Little or nothing spent to identify expected results	Ambiguous directions (Use idea or problem-based directions)
Pressure for a quick fix makes a conspicuous solution seem timely and pragmatic	Little or nothing spent for search or innovation	Limited search (Adopt ready-made plans or adapt existing practices)
Defensive assessment carried out to justify a ready-made plan	Resources used to defend ideas and not to explore their benefits and risks	Misusing evaluation (Demonstrate the value of ready-made plans)
See all decisions as ethically neutral	Little or nothing spent to uncover and reconcile values	Overlook ethical issues (Ignore ethical positions of critics and the values behind these positions)
Demand good outcomes and allow no failures	Little or nothing spent to uncover and remove perverse incentives	Fail to learn (Ignore perverse incentives that encourage cover-ups of failures)

Best practice recommendations will be illustrated with multiple perspectives (Linstone, 1984). Technical, personal, and organizational perspectives examine a decision from different angles, illuminating new possibilities. The technical (T) perspective calls for facts and economic realities provided by statistical comparisons, quantitative measures and countable attributes. Projecting savings, estimating profits and measuring quality is emphasized. Not everything that can be counted counts and things that resist measurement often matter, calling for additional perspectives.

TABLE 7.3 Traps in failed decisions

The Traps	PERRIER RECALL	FEN-PHEN RECALL	AEP PURCHASE OF CHESHIRE	COMPUSERVE'S FAILED AOL ACQUISITION
Claims	Benzene contamination requires a recall	Need for effective weight-loss drug justifies the product	Negative PR a potential threat	Need a mass market information product
Concerns Recognized	Product safety issues	Need for product	Keep power on Acid rain	Mass market potential
Hidden	Product vulnerable to shifts in customer taste Mass market plan at risk if health image eroded	Product not being used as intended Drug has dangerous side effects Potential liability Protect windfall profits	Inability to limit acid rain Resident's motivations EPA's possible enforcement actions Potential liability	Block family aims Distrust of Block faction No CompuServe board presence Growth limited by conservative Block board CompuServe products key to company profitability
Inferred Direction	Protect image for mass marketing	Maintain profits	Eliminate negative PR	Increase market share
Options considered	Worldwide recall	Resist recall	Purchase village	Considered ignore, build, and buy; but offered only the buy option to board
Extent of search & innovation	None	None	None	Considered several acquisition targets
Use of evaluation	Estimate time off market	Find safety issues to be unwarranted	Estimate value of property in village to validate cost	Discounted cash flows for Quantum (AOL)

Impact of evaluation	Overly optimistic off-market estimates	Recall justification labeled questionable	Misleading costs that excluded negative publicity and extent of pollution	Market growth seemed uncertain so returns appeared to be overly optimistic
Barriers to Action	Extent of product loyalty Likelihood PR could overcome management misadventures	Distraction from assimilating new division Protecting profits	Extent of public and resident support Experience with real estate deals EPA's position	Extent persuasion could get board support Appearance of behind-the-back dealings Challenges to board authority Block faction's aim to protect wealth Limited board participation in finding options
Ethical Concerns	Harmful levels of benzene Misrepresenting reasons for the recall and product ingredients	Problems with improper drug use Failing to report known safety issues to FDA	Ignoring pollution issues Discounting resident's health concerns Company image more important than public safety Ignoring other parties with legitimate interests	Disloyalty by CompuServe faction
Barriers to Learning	Poor company image can not be fully erased by PR	Commercial expediency	Focus on removing a complaining nuisance	Power and value imbalances between the factions Image of bad faith

The organizational (O) perspective looks at a decision through the eyes of the organization. To do so acknowledges that organizations must protect their interests as internal and external stakeholders assert theirs. Rules and unwritten treaties are put in place to guide decision processes through periods of questioning and controversy as differences arise. Organizational procedures are set in place to ensure that this is done. In the O perspective, following these procedures is as important as measuring things. Rules, codes, agreements, and policies ensure that checks and balances function to preserve organizational interests. The personal (P) perspective looks at the decision through the eyes of the key people who are affected by a decision. This is important because organizational interests can swamp personal concerns such as job security, opportunities to demonstrate competence, and avenues for advancement. The P perspective speculates about individuals who see themselves as benefactors or victims, doers or users, as well as gatekeepers, power brokers, and policy makers who write SOPs with the power to slow, or even block, a decision.

In failed decisions, one of the perspectives dominates (Nutt, 2002). Decision makers who view a decision from all three perspectives can expand their horizons. Tables 7.4, 7.5, and 7.6 show the dominate perspective for the village purchase, recall, and acquisition decisions and how the other perspectives identify additional possibilities. Steps that make these possibilities visible are found in best practice decision making. Table 7.7 summarizes the best practices.

Selecting the arena of action

A decision is set in motion when a stakeholder makes a claim and seeks an endorsement (Cyert and March, 1963). The claim specifies what the stakeholder believes the decision is about, its *arena of action*. A trap is set when decision makers embrace such a claim to appease a powerful stakeholder or to cater to an interest he/she represents, without considering other claims. Selecting an arena of action in this way can mislead the decision-making effort and provoke opposition. Interested parties are apt to question the claim's justification and ponder what the decision *should* be about.

Davis claimed that benzene contamination justified a recall (Table 7.3). CompuServe insiders claimed that investing in Quantum was the key to future growth. AEP saw the negative PR directed at the company as a threat. Wyeth officials cited a desire for a weight-loss drug to justify marketing Fen-Phen. Note how the claim has, or allows one to infer, a remedy. Davis settled on a recall, CompuServe offered an acquisition target as a way to serve a new market, AEP officials saw the village buyout as eliminating a tiresome nuisance, and Wyeth management resisted a Fen-Phen recall. Each remedy was seen as timely and pragmatic by decision makers. In each case, there was no attempt to analyze the claim, to uncover competing claims or to make the concerns behind each explicit, although gathering this kind of intelligence is recommended (e.g. Simon, 1977). Instead, influential supporters were required to make a claim actionable (Cyert and March, 1963; Pfeffer, 1992; Pfeffer and Salancik, 1974).

Decision makers in failed decisions selected among claims according to claimant power without checking to see if other interested parties agree and, if not, why not.

TABLE 7.4 AEP's purchase of Cheshire

PERSPECTIVE/TRAPS	TECHNICAL	ORGANIZATIONAL	PERSONAL
Core Concerns	Expensive technology caused new problems	**Keep power flowing with minimal interference**	Safety issues; Who wants to sell because of pollution and who just wants out.
Objectives Criteria	Reduce blue haze EPA compliance Removal of contaminants Extent of blue haze poses a health hazard	**Eliminate negative PR** **Eliminate bad press and avoid EPA scrutiny**	Placate resident worries Resident priorities
Alternatives	Study 'bad' summer days Improve SCR Switch coal types Technology fixes	**Purchase village for $ 20 million**	1. Identify what each faction wants; Cost and feasibility of the wants 2. Work with Cheshire and other neighbors to improve relationships 3. Have third parties demonstrate limits of technology
Consequences of Alternatives	If unable to remove blue haze company will seem incompetent	**More complaints; further damage to company image**	Extent possible to satisfy complaints and eliminate health risks
Implementation Barriers	Technology not well understood and very expensive	**Changing perceptions of the public; Spent $ 7 million with no effect**	Many individuals are affected and collective demands may be impossible to meet

TABLE 7.5 CompuServe's attempted purchase of AOL

PERSPECTIVE/TRAPS	TECHNICAL	ORGANIZATIONAL	PERSONAL
Core Concerns	**By-passing a potentially huge mass market for information services (CompuServe faction)**	Deal with market realities for most important division to protect its long-term profitability	Wealth protection (Block faction)
Objectives	**Grow market share**	Appropriate rate of growth for division	Protect retained earnings
Criteria	**1. EPS; Profitability** **2. Market Share**	Amount of capital to be put at risk and extent of risk to be tolerated	1. Risk to wealth 2. Protect division's wealth-generating potential
Alternatives	**Options of ignore, buy or develop capacity internally to serve mass market considered. Presented as buy/no buy of Quantum to board**	1. Other possible acquisitions. 2. Internal development with new engineering group 3. Contract out development	1. Wait 2. Pilot to test market 3. Internal development
Consequences of Alternatives	**Put retained earnings at risk; merge mass market with existing system may put off high-end customers; engineers have no experience with mass market customers.**	Conservative posture may cause company to miss huge market; CompuServe lacks expertise in mass market information development;	Unable to diversify holdings; growth limited; company profitability stagnates; miss mass market take off
Implementation Barriers	**Block's risk aversion; difficult and contentious relationships; purchase price; extreme measures of looking for 'white knight' and limiting options make proposal appear disingenuous**	Develop alternative appears less costly but has PR and skill issues; must balance cost and risk for the buy option	Board seen as unrealistic and overly risk-averse by most profitable division; limit key division's future; disheartened people will leave; high-end product's viability threatened

TABLE 7.6 The Perrier recall

PERSPECTIVE/TRAPS	TECHNICAL	ORGANIZATIONAL	PERSONAL
Core Concerns	Contamination sources; benzene occurs naturally in the water and its removal also removes natural carbonation	Protect product image by limiting time off market; Recall costs	**Mass market plan at facilitated by bolstering health image with a recall (Davis)**
Objectives	Limit contamination liabilities	Maintain customer base	**Preserve mass market plan**
Criteria	Extent of contamination; Degree of health hazard posed	Maintain image of high-end product	**Cultivate mass appeal of product**
Alternatives	1. Quantify hazard 2. Isolate sources of contamination 3. Have FDA issue opinion on need for recall. 4. Sample and release unaffected product	1. Expedite market re-entry 2. Internal inquiry into nature and scope of benzene problem 3. Study recall costs	**Recall**
Consequences of Alternatives	May be seen as risking public safety to further study the issue	Criticism for delaying recall and for concealing truth about the source of contamination and product ingredients	**Customer confidence eroded by recall;** **Possibility of product substitution;** **Misrepresenting motivations reveals key product ingredient**
Implementation Barriers	Hazard not well understood; source of contamination misrepresented by management making it hard to offer a technical defense	Need for rapid action to manage image issues	**Time to recall and replace product in market; PR limitations to maintain product loyalty**

TABLE 7.7 Best practices

Traps	Practices that Avoid Traps	What is Required
Fail to take charge by reconciling claims	Network with stakeholders	Involve stakeholders to uncover and reconcile concerns to formulate a claim
Ignore barriers to action	Intervention or Participation	Demonstrate the need to act and ways to consider the interests and commitments of key stakeholders
Ambiguous direction	Set an objective	Indicate expected results
Limited search	Search with innovation	Increase the number of options considered and those with potential first mover advantages
Misused evaluation	Compare the risk and benefits of the options	Expose options with unacceptable risk and validate the choice
Overlooking ethical questions	Look for important values and offer mediation	Uncover and confront the ethical questions of internal and external stakeholders
Failing to learn	Create win-win situations for all stakeholders	Find and remove perverse incentives to encourage honest appraisal of actions

A claim selected in this way seldom reveals claimant motivation. Even when motivation is understood, a claim's importance may not be agreed to by others. Did AEP management understand villager concerns, the concerns of villagers not a party to the lawsuit, or the concerns people in the surrounding areas? Did the CompuServe faction appreciate concerns of the Block board about amassing wealth? Were Wyeth officials tuned into the motivations of investigators who were concerned about Fen-Phen's misuse and its side effects? Did Davis have any idea what had built Perrier's consumer loyalty or the leverage inherent in the product's health persona, if there was any?

None of this seems to have been understood by the decision makers. As a result, concerns behind counter claims were hidden and not understood. The corrective action inferred from a claim does little to deal with such concerns, leaving others to speculate about what the decision maker's motivations might be (Starbuck, 1983; March, 1994). Without clarity about these concerns, the *arena of action* (the village purchase, resisting a recall, or the Quantum acquisition target) appears suspect (Pounds, 1969). This prompts interested parties to become suspicious, setting a trap for the decision maker. Skeptics and those who have something to lose are handed a platform to raise objections. Opponents call attention to errors, faulty logic, and misrepresentations to discredit the decision and the decision maker. The decision maker must then counter the allegations with defensive assertions about the need to act.

Successful decision makers uncover the claims of key stakeholders, looking for hidden concerns. Key stakeholders may include: top management teams, leaders of vital departments, technical experts, staffers with relevant experience (e.g. salespeople and engineers), unions, suppliers, stockholders, creditors, customers, current and future alliance partners, supportive sister organizations, competitors, communities in which the organization operates, environment groups, and the general public. Each constituency offers important cues. Uncovering the concerns behind the claims of each constituency enhances credibility and mobilizes support. Amalgamating the views from these sources identifies a range of plausible claims. The concerns behind these claims suggest the arena of action.

CompuServe people saw the arena of action as capturing a potentially huge market. Block officials saw the arena of action as wealth creation. Limiting risk was their key concern. So Block would approve only low risk and thus low payoff projects. This was obvious in past dealings but not recognized in current negotiations. AEP officials paid little attention to the pollution complaints until the clamor created a PR problem. They believed that their responsibility to the public and to public utility regulators called on them to keep affordable power flowing. Consequently, they ignored complaints that would limit their capacity or increase costs. The prospect of installing another costly and largely ineffective pollution control measure to placate a few villagers galvanized concerns about more cost and regulation, which posed threats to maintaining the flow of affordable power. The immediate concern of finding a way to make a PR problem disappear created a trap that kept the company officials from looking for deeper concerns about pollution and the prospect of stricter and more oppressive regulations, if their actions were seen as irresponsible. AEP officials defined their stakeholders narrowly, which limited what they could learn about their PR nightmare. Blinded by these beliefs, they overlooked the public stakeholder and the public's concerns about pollution and expectations of corporate social responsibility.

To avoid this trap, consider the amalgamated concerns of stakeholders to determine the arena of action. Was the Perrier decision about protecting a healthful image to facilitate mass marketing, as suggested by the P perspective of Davis (Table 7.6)? What about O concerns of protecting the market share of its high-end product by limiting time off market and the associated recall costs and T concerns about the source of the benzene contamination? Should the CompuServe faction merely offer an acquisition target, uncovered with a T perspective (Table 7.5)? Or should the Block faction be offered an opportunity to partner in a search for ways to capture a market (O) *and* protect stockholder wealth (P)? Should AEP focus on silencing complaining nuisances (O) or should company leaders confront technical problems (T) and enhance safety by reducing acid rain (P)?

AEP officials never reconciled their 'keep the power on' mentality with the pollution that was being created (Table 7.4). Ruminating about concerns derived from each perspective questions what the decision should be about – its arena of action.

Allocate resources to explore such claims and their underlying concerns from several points of view (Table 7.7). Decision makers who uncover and reconcile such concerns are more apt to be successful. Demonstrating an awareness of many views provides legitimacy. Stakeholders who understand the decision maker's arguments and see how they point to a particular arena of action are more apt to be support- ive. When people see the arena of action as valid, or at least defensible, momentum is created as word spreads to others with interests (Coch and French, 1948; Cray *et al.*, 1988; Beyer and Trice, 1982). Decision makers who consult in this way show that a variety of concerns have been considered. Such a show of good faith demon- strates the importance of the decision and a commitment to get to the bottom of things. Buy-in is more likely, making momentum easier to sustain. Such insights also broaden the decision maker's views of possible arenas of action and their compara- tive merits (Cooperrider and Srivastra, 1987; Kolb, 1983; Fredrickson, 1985).

Deal with interests and interest groups

In failed decisions, decision makers often use their power and influence to promote a remedy implied by the claims of powerful claimants. Implementing in this way requires either an edict (do this) or persuasion (do this because). Both are failure- prone because interests stirred up by the decision are ignored (Nutt, 1986; 1998b). CompuServe's initial approach to its parent had the appearance of an edict, offer- ing both an issue and a way to deal with the issue. Edicts were also used by Wyeth officials to resist reports of Fen-Phen's health hazards and by AEP in their imple- mentation of the village buyout. Even those unaffected by a decision often resist an edict because they do not like being forced and worry about the precedents that yielding to force can set (Nutt, 2002). When using an edict, the best a decision maker can hope for is indifference: People do not care enough to resist (French and Raven, 1959). Often this is not the case. Using an edict to roll over interested parties produces resentment and token compliance in the powerless and resistance from others, which my studies show leads to failure in two out of three decisions (Nutt, 1998b).

Persuasion is also failure-prone (Nutt, 1986; 1998b). For persuasion to work, par- ties to a decision must be open to rational arguments (Quinn, 1980; Huysmans, 1970; Doktor and Hamilton, 1974). Had Davis known the source of contamination, he could have approached the health department with a plan and may have headed off his recall debacle. Endorsement seems likely had Davis offered a reasonable ex- planation for the benzene contamination and a plan to contain it. Instead, Davis used the media in an attempt to persuade the public that the company was acting responsibly. Persuasion has little effect on people who believe they have something to lose, failing in half of the decisions in which it is attempted (Nutt, 1998c).

Edict and persuasion are often linked. If an edict fails, decision makers resort to persuasion – now trying to explain why the decision has merit (Churchman, 1975;

Schultz and Slevin, 1975; Ginsberg and Schultz, 1987), which has limited success. CompuServe insiders acted as if they had no idea what had put off the board. Their initial power play assumed that the board's conservative nature required extreme measures. When this failed, a compelling argument was then thought to be all that was needed. By overlooking the impact of their power play and by failing to articulate joint interests the CompuServe faction angered board members, which put their plan at risk. In addition, organizational leaders applying power implicit in an edict make it futile for insiders to offer their insights about a decision as it unfolds (Nystrom and Starbuck, 1984). The unwillingness to recall Fen-Phen troubled insiders as did the company's indifferent approach toward consolidating its new division. Seeking insights from knowledgeable people from the newly acquired division could have brought out the risks in stonewalling a recall (Denhardt, 2000).

Decision makers become trapped when they do little to explore the interests and commitments of people affected by a decision (Nutt, 2002). Being more forthcoming about reasons and motives, early in the effort, helps to neutralize opposition (Beyer and Trice, 1978; Leavitt, 1987). Involving potential critics in the decision-making process clarifies their views. Involvement may also shift the critic from a position of opposition to one of support (Table 7.3). Had AEP officials done this, the views of their critics could have been uncovered making them understandable and potentially manageable. CompuServe and Wyeth decision makers fell into the same trap.

Social and political issues arise from the interests of people (Hickson *et al.*, 1986 Rodrigues and Hickson, 1995), as shown by the implementation barriers in Tables 7.4, 7.5, and 7.6. Opposition can be expected when these interests are threatened. If a mass marketing of Perrier is desirable how can Davis convince key players that the opportunity is real and that his plan is reasonable? If a weight loss drug is needed, how can Wyeth officials demonstrate that it is being used safely? Will negotiation with regulators help decision makers at Perrier and Wyeth facilitate an action plan? Would the general public and AEP's critics see the company's side of the 'pollution problem?' What is the prospect of removing the issue with educational efforts?

Successful decision makers put implementation at the front of their decision-making efforts, seeking to uncover and then manage interests (Table 7.7). If power can be shared, teams can be created, involving people with interests in making the decision (Beyer and Trice, 1982; Downs, 1967; Eisenhardt, 1989). People are more apt to disclose their interests in a team-like setting (Nutt, 2002). The act of uncovering an issue and finding a remedy promotes ownership in the remedy and increases its prospect of adoption. Even when not forced to do so, savvy decision makers use participation in this way because it improves their chance of success (Hackman, 1990). Another useful approach, called 'intervention', extends the networking approach in claim/concern identification to demonstrate the need to act (Nutt, 1998b). Current performance is documented and credible performance norms identified. Using this information, key parties are shown the importance of the decision by decision makers, collecting and managing interests with each encounter. People are more likely to be supportive when networking makes them aware of performance shortfalls and the level of performance that is possible, making the need to act credible. Use participation when interested parties are localized, such as the CompuServe faction asking for recommendations from the Block board to exploit a potentially lucrative market and Wyeth insiders looking for ways to integrate a new division. Use networking when dealing with influential stakeholders, such as AEP officials meeting with regulators and consumer factions to identify interests and preferences.

Directing search with expected results

Directions and their expected results were ambiguous in failed decisions (Nutt, 1999; 2004). An ambiguous direction confuses key players and squanders resources (Brunsson, 1982; Mintzberg *et al.*, 1976; Pounds, 1969; Locke and Latham, 1990). AEP officials were silent about their expectations. Did company officials seek to limit liability, publicity, complaints, cost or responsibility? Or was AEP trying to resist government regulation? Perhaps the aim was to make a contentious situation go away? Each could be inferred from the actions and statements of officials. When directions are ambiguous any proposed action can appear misguided. Insiders at AEP had no idea what was motivating the real estate deal and saw it squandering company funds. Clarifying the direction eliminates misunderstandings and focuses search. Had AEP officials asked insiders to look for low-cost ideas that limit pollution key people would be empowered to offer options, such as coal mixes that reduce the blue haze. By keeping their desired result under wraps, AEP officials denied themselves access to such ideas. AEP officials substituted a solution, buy the village, for thinking about ways to reduce acid rain. The remedy, the purchase, eliminated discussion about ways to reduce pollution.

When decision makers adopt a ready-made plan the implied merit of the remedy becomes a stand-in for desired results. To complicate things people often see different merits in a remedy, which entices them to form different impressions about the desired result. Misunderstandings arise when people offer courses of action that deal with their idiosyncratic notion of an expected result. The merits of alternatives are debated, not the hoped-for results prompting them. The ensuing dispute is a chief source of conflict in decision making (Nutt, 1989).

A demand for rapid action makes direction setting difficult. When attempting to cope with such a pressure, it is hard to delay action-taking to explore directions. Admitting that one has doubts can be dangerous (Nystrom and Starbuck, 1984). But doubt coupled with clarity about a desired result, such as minimal cost, can be a powerful force that prompts all involved to think deeply about possibilities. The failure to clarify direction brings with it many such difficulties, setting a trap for the decision maker.

To avoid the ambiguous direction trap, delay search until hoped-for results can be agreed upon. This requires a move from thinking about solutions to thinking about expected results. Davis sought to mass market a new version of Perrier. The solution is clear but what was the desired result? Was it profit, market share or brand protection? Actions that protect a brand and those that grow a market for a new product are quite different. Lacking clarity in hoped-for results, interested parties had a hard time understanding what Davis was up to and how to help. Typically, failed decisions had ambiguity about intent. Was AEP seeking to reduce the blue haze, eliminate a PR problem or improve resident safety? Each direction points to a different type of solution (Table 7.4).

The hoped-for result provides an objective. Objective candidates can be inferred from the perspectives, offering several to consider. AEP decision makers implicitly considered an objective derived from an O perspective of maintaining the flow of power (Table 7.4). The T perspective suggests an objective of reducing pollution. Such an objective points to solutions such as new coal mixes, bad day management, and SCR (the earlier attempt at pollution control) fine tuning. The P perspective suggests placating resident worries as an objective, pointing to working with key consumer groups to identify their concerns. This suggests actions to placate unfounded worries. The Perrier decision could limit liabilities (T) or retain key product customer base (O). The T objective (limit liabilities) suggests actions to quantify the benzene hazard and the O objective (retain customers) ways to expedite market reentry (Table 7.6). The CompuServe faction overlooked objectives from the O perspective, such as risk management, and the P perspective of protecting wealth (Table 7.5). Options include internal product development (O) and pilot testing (P). Setting an objective by selecting among those suggested by the three perspectives or from other sources (Nutt, 2002), indicates desired results and clears away ambiguity (Table 7.7). Being clear about what is wanted also mobilizes support and guides a search. Clarity about what is wanted is a powerful tool that eliminates confusion and focuses effort.

Search broadly and encourage innovation

Four out of ten decisions consider only one alternative; and this alternative is innovative in less than one of ten decisions (Nutt, 1993b; 2002). Search is set aside when remedies are plucked from claims or when the remedy is derived from existing practices. Both discourage search and stifle innovation. Nearly one third of the decisions studied adopted a ready-made plan, making search seem pointless (Nutt, 2002; 2004). Decision makers who became wedded to the remedy in a ready-made plan made no effort to look for other ideas which could be better. AEP officials latched onto a real estate deal; Davis saw a PR opportunity in the benzene contamination; the CompuServe faction offered an acquisition. In each case, the remedy became a trap that preempted search and innovation.

The allure of current practices also limits search (Pettigrew, 1985; Van de Ven *et al.*, 1999). Even when search is attempted, it can be difficult to move away from the familiar to the unknown. One in five decision makers offered remedies derived from minor adaptations of current procedures, arguing that such adaptations reduce both time and cost. Such practices are thought to have value because past use provides the equivalent of a field test, suggesting that adaptations provide a cost-effective if not an innovative solution (Hart and Bogan, 1993: Mintzberg and Westley, 2001).

Both claim-inferred remedies and adaptations of current practices discourage search and stifle innovation, which sets a search trap. This trap is sprung so often that just one in five decision makers conduct a formal search or seek innovative ideas. To dodge the search trap, make a commitment to uncover several options and at least one with innovative features (Table 7.7). A clear direction facilitates search and increases the prospect of success (Nutt, 2002; 2005). Search can be carried out using repeated solicitation, integrated benchmarking and innovation. All have good track records (Nutt, 2005). Repeated solicitation gathers ideas from outsiders. A request for proposal (RFP) is sent to vendors, when needs seem clear, and to consultants, when needs seem vague or uncertain. Vendors or consultants offer prepackaged ideas and show how they meet the organization's need. Decision makers learn about possibilities from the proposals. A new search is then mounted that incorporates what was learned from the initial one. The new RFP incorporates a better understanding of new developments, such as technology. The cycle is repeated until the decision maker has acquired an understanding of the decision to be made, and the scope of useful remedies. At this point, a choice among options is made (Nutt, 2002). Integrated benchmarking is another way to search. High profile organizations are visited to get ideas. Benchmarks are derived from the site visits and from descriptions published in periodicals and books. Decision makers merge the best features of these practices into a plan. The practices and procedures with a good fit to the adopting organization are identified and integrated into a plan.

A custom-made remedy requires innovation. This calls for solutions new to the organization or solutions that are new to the industry, which offer 'first mover' advantage (Damanpour, 1991; Germunden and Hauschildt, 1985; Nadler and Hibino, 1990). Custom-made remedies are successful about half of the time (Nutt, 2004). The prospect of success improves when an objective guides the effort and when multiple options are developed. Objectives clarify what is wanted making the search for a new idea more purposeful. Without this direction the search for a custom-made remedy wanders, which reduces success. Forty per cent of the attempts to find a custom-made remedy lacked a clear objective. Ambiguous objectives make the results expected argumentative. Ambiguous or missing directions lead to a dramatic decline in the success of custom-made plans, which has made innovation seem overly risky to practitioners. Multiple options help as well. At first this may seem foolhardy as the costs and time required would seem to increase for one new idea, let alone several. However, my research shows that multiple options were both efficient and effective. The time to search was no greater than that noted when a single alternative was uncovered and the benefits realized more than justified search costs (Nutt, 2005).

A 'safe space' and a 'new space' facilitate custom-made solutions. A safe space offers a haven that allows speculation. New ideas are more apt to emerge when limits are removed. There are three key moves: protected work environment, finding people with creative urges, and challenging current practices. Protected work environments encourage innovation. Disney has its dream room (no accountants, no criticism) to fashion creative motion picture ideas. Limited stores have breakout sessions to make important decisions. Motorola pioneered the use of self-managed work groups. Ford and the automotive industry have their 'platform teams'. Peters and Waterman (1982) credit a 'skunk works' with finding creative ideas. 'Leaderless organizations', such as Orpheus, the symphony that operates without a conductor, also indicates how to empower. Orpheus gets good quality without sacrificing the satisfaction of its players, something that is rare with the domineering despots that lead many of the world's symphonies. Each takes people from their jobs on a temporary basis to offer ideas and puts them into a new space that simulates an 'adhocracy' (Mintzberg, 1985). The expected results are made clear but not the means to produce the results. This allows teams to gravitate toward new ideas and feel the pull of their attraction. A team-like self-managed work group will increase the chance of finding innovative ideas.

Team make-up is crucial. A team member's creative instinct is more important than knowledge of the decision to be made. People with creative instincts 'think outside the box'. Such individuals set the tone and prompt others to do the same. People with inhibitions that limit their creativity should be avoided. The extrovert who must talk to think is a poor choice as a team member as are people whose training and inclinations coax them to evaluate, such as accountants. A person's behavior is also telling. The best predictor of future behavior is past behavior. People who exhibit an affinity for coming up with new ideas are the best candidates for a creative team. Also, look for right-brain thinkers with this trait and avoid left-brain thinkers that approach everything with a critical posture. People with the MBTI type of NFP are also good candidates (Nutt, 1989).

Draw the team away from existing practices by challenging them (Miller, 1990). To break from the past, allow the team to shed some existing activities that are strongly identified with the organization. This 'letting go' will allow people to discard defensive routines and sever ties to old ways of doing things. It is both symbolic and instrumental (Jantsch, 1975). The letting go signals that the current practices can be questioned. Discarding old commitments opens people to new ideas, such as partnering with a different set of customers or suppliers to produce new strategic alliances. Questioning activities that maintain current suppliers (e.g. purchasing agreements or sole-sourcing with strategic partners) and customers (e.g. dealers and franchises) challenges the value of an old commitment. Savvy facilitators put all such practices up for discussion and possible modification.

A cognitive 'new space' provides a mental state conducive to finding new ideas. Let's consider what works. Just ask. People are more apt to move away from current practices and the conventional to the novel and unconventional if asked to be creative (Stein, 1975). Studies of creativity stress incubation. Anything that puts people in a reflective mode can have this effect. Before convening a meeting, skilled facilitators conducting a retreat encourage people to take a walk, without their cell phones, and reflect on key issues. Putting people in an information-rich environment, in which they can neither write nor talk, allows information to be considered in a unique way and creative ideas to emerge. Such an arrangement frees the mind to roam and limits intrusions that drive out creative thoughts. Devises such a Storyboarding, night notes and similar vehicles have these qualities. The longer the incubation and the more frequent its use, the better the result. Devices that encourage this create a new space for ideas to emerge. People who study creativity in individuals (e.g. de Bono, 1990) find that the emotive safe space coupled with the cognitive new space draw people toward innovative ideas.

Use evaluation wisely

Defending remedies found in ready-made plans consumes most of the resources al-located to decision making (Nutt, 2002). More is spent doing defensive evaluations than on *all* the other decision-making activities combined (Nutt, 2002). A defen-sive evaluation is mounted when information is collected only to *support* an idea (Mintzberg *et al.*, 1976: Langley *et al.*, 1997). Block was eager to fund evaluations to verify the data presented by the CompuServe faction but spent little on anything else. At Perrier, Davis focused on the cost of inventory to document recall losses. When evaluation is used in this way, important questions will not be addressed. AEP officials knew the purchase price of the village, but little else. Company offi-cials made no attempt to understand the cost of negative publicity or the cost of an ill-conceived approach to pollution control. Analysis was limited to factual data collected to reconcile a purchase price with the market value of the homes, which was used to defend the plan.

Defensive evaluations are easier to mount when directions are vague. Without a clear direction, an 'idea champion' can focus on the idea, slanting information collection toward justifications, and ignore other issues. In the AEP village purchase decision, the lack of a clear direction led to a preoccupation with price; this drew company officials away from questions about pollution issues and future liability. The CompuServe proposal was muddied by a conflict about direction. CompuServe insiders identified a huge potential payoff but the Block board saw the payoff as risky, given their wealth maintenance expectations.

Defensive evaluations find what the idea champion expects to find – offering shal-low and predicable results (McKie, 1973; Brunsson, 1982; Pinfield, 1986). The in-formation collected is frequently tainted, offering bloated estimates of sales and the like to justify what a decision maker wants to do or must do to satisfy others (Nutt, 2002). Even when decision makers have the organization's interests at heart, as in the CompuServe acquisition, evaluations that appear self-serving provoke suspicion. Additional evaluation is required to deal with the suspicions. This often poses new doubts and more evaluations. Each round of evaluation prompts more questions and still more evaluations to answer them until costs become excessive. This cycle of suspicion and doubt grows until huge sums are spent on evaluation, setting the evaluation trap.

To dodge the evaluation trap, collect information that compares the benefits of alternatives to objectives and determines the risk in realizing these benefits (Ta-ble 7.7). This kind of evaluation is feasible if and only if expected results have been made clear in an objective, offering a way to norm the benefits identified. The ob-jective specifies what is wanted, such as better quality, which would make defects a defensible criterion to measure the benefits of alternatives. (This connection of criteria that measure benefits to direction is shown in Tables 7.4, 7.5 and 7.6.) An objective makes a defensive evaluation carried out to support a pet idea untenable. When the objective is clear, the only justifiable way to do an evaluation is to docu-ment the benefits of alternatives and the risk to realize them. In the CompuServe ac-quisition, only an evaluation of plans to mass market information services, compar-ing the risks and profits of the Quantum acquisition with other alternatives, would be justifiable.

Decision makers in my studies were found to take very different risk positions. Some ignore risk, others fear it. Because they were very risk-averse, the Block faction was unwilling to incur a comparatively small risk to realize a huge gain. Other decision makers ignore risk; as in Wyeth Stonewalling, a recall of Fen-Phen, and Quaker's acquisition of Snapple (Nutt, 2002). To deal with risk, uncertainly must be understood. To illustrate, using the CompuServe acquisition proposal with a profit objective, best and worst case assumptions about revenues are estimated to bracket risk (Keeney and Raiffa, 1985; Nutt, 1989; 2002). This brings to light factors that lower revenue projections and the likelihood of turning a profit. Such an evaluation uncovers the level of risk in the acquisition decision and strips away ambiguity about what to do for the Block faction. Factors that drive revenues, and the like, upward and downward were often ignored in failed decisions. These hide risk and prompt an unrealistic posture toward it by decision makers, either magnifying or dismissing uncertainty. Evaluations that measure objective-connected benefits coupled with a risk assessment improve the prospect of success (Table 7.7).

Confront ethical questions

Decisions often pose ethical questions to stakeholders and onlookers (Johnson, 1993; Bardaracco, 1997). Questions arise from the preferred course of action and how it is viewed by others. To sustain sales, Wyeth management stonewalled a recall. AEP officials acted on a real estate deal that brushed aside concerns about air pollution. Davis saw a Perrier recall as a PR move that would help his planned product's marketing. CompuServe offered a buy or no buy choice to their board, hoping to capitalize on a market opportunity. In each case, the proposed course of action posed ethical questions to stakeholders and onlookers. Opposition materializes when such questions are ignored.

Ethical questions arise from values, which are often misunderstood (Nutt, 2002). This occurs because critics seldom reveal values prompting their questions. Oversight bodies, such as the FDA, believed that a 'profit drives principle' value prompted Wyeth officials to resist the recall of Fen-Phen. But Wyeth officials were selling a profitable drug, which served the interests of stockholders. These interests are also served by avoiding costly litigation and by being a responsible corporate citizen. Wyeth officials saw the FDA as having their own agenda. The values behind their actions were seen as validating the FDA's mission by overreacting to minor incidents. Wyeth officials saw uncertainties, not ethical issues, which stemmed from the difficulty of estimating the incidence of an injury, the extent of the injury, the relationship of drug use with the injury, the magnitude of damage and the cost of litigation. AEP officials saw objections to the village purchase as stemming from unrealistic beliefs about the challenges to keeping power flowing in an industrial society. To make this point, AEP officials postured to look like a victim. The prospect of being seen as a villain was never considered. Note how both critics and AEP officials failed to disclose their values. Davis saw his marketing plan, hidden in the recall, as pragmatic. He also misrepresented a key product ingredient but saw this as harmless hyping. Others saw his actions as blatant lying to make the company loads of money. Again, the values of insiders and outsiders were not apparent to one another.

An ethical trap is set when decision makers fail to understand values that are motivating questions. Ignoring these questions can prompt whistle-blowing by insiders and contentious relationships with outsiders. Outsiders who oppose an action are enticed to boycott products and insiders are motivated to leak or to engage in whistle-blowing. Even if boycotts and whistle-blowing are avoided, there will be a loss of trust that can taint future dealings.

Appearances are also important. An ethical trap can be set when a decision seems to create inequities among stakeholders. Opposition is likely when there is a misalignment in who pays, who benefits, and who decides (Nutt, 2002). By buying the village, AEP appeared to be using subterfuge to avoid compliance with clean air standards. Company officials wanted to avoid paying for pollution abatement while they benefited and decided. In the recalls, regulators found that company decisions were not being made in the best interest of paying consumers. Products were being sold that failed to perform as promised. When this occurs, regulators can be expected to step in and set things straight by protecting consumers. The Block faction held up the acquisition decision until they could reassert control and ensure that the benefits *they* were seeking could be realized. An ethical trap is set when a critic exposes such misalignments to create controversy.

Uncovering values behind 'ethical positions' allows decision makers to reconcile ethical controversies in which both parties see the other's position as self-serving, as in the Block and CompuServe clash. Uncovering value-based differences among key stakeholders allows decision makers to shift discourse from the lowest to the highest denominator. Ethical questions can be resolved by finding actions that embrace values key stakeholders believe to be crucial. To do this, encourage people to pose ethical questions (Table 7.7). Create forums for ethical questions to be voiced as *claims* and *alternatives* are uncovered in the decision-making effort, and offer mediation to those who disagree. The forum allows a decision maker to look for values behind the positions of people who express opposition. The decision maker can often affirm these values and make minor modifications in a claim or a preferred course of action and carry on much as before. Had AEP officials affirmed the values of the groups that questioned them in the media by addressing pollution questions they would have cut the ground from under their critics. AEP could have listened to residents to find out what they were after. Had the values of pollution abatement been affirmed and endorsed, AEP officials could explain their plans (if they had any) and perhaps get backing for them. If this fails, offer mediation. AEP officials could have held hearings and town meetings to find out what their critics were saying, looking for unwarranted criticisms and misunderstandings that could be diffused. At best, new insights can develop. If not, AEP officials would have to demonstrate a willingness to hear out their critics – a position that is apt to boost the legitimacy of a subsequent decision. Companies with mediation win lawsuits involving whistle-blowing. Companies without it lose them.

Align who pays, benefits and decides. Had AEP officials allowed critics a voice in the decision, such an alignment was possible. Officials contemplating a recall must find links between product use and injury and protect those without a voice in the decision. When proposing capital projects, ensure that the prerogatives of key stakeholders are protected and that the benefits to all are understood.

Promote a culture of learning

Learning, as it is used here, seeks to guide a decision maker away from failure-prone practices (Argyris *et al.*, 1987). Such learning is thwarted by unrealistic expectations that arise when people in power insist on success. When failed decisions are not tolerated, learning is blocked. In such an environment, people conceal bad outcomes. This should be expected, and is even rational, because chance events make decision outcomes uncertain. As a result, it is difficult to separate good decisions with bad outcomes from bad decisions with good outcomes (Nisbett and Ross, 1989). The best decision-making practices do not guarantee a good outcome, because of chance events. To illustrate, the demand for SUVs and gas-efficient hybrids depend upon gas prices, which are notoriously difficult to predict. The lengthy development time for such vehicles makes a new launch risky. A turn on gas prices can make a good design look bad and a poor design look good. Here bad luck can be mistaken for bad decision-making practices. Good luck, such as windfall profits, due to favorable turn on consumer interest in a product, can cover up failure-prone decision-making practices, as in the Quaker acquisition of Gatorade (Nutt, 2002).

When good outcomes are demanded, brushing aside their chancy nature, people caught up in a failed decision reveal as little as possible (Nutt, 1989; 2002). Davis continued to trumpet the wisdom of his recall in media releases, but said little about its rationale or his mistaken assumptions about the market for bottled water. AEP officials fainted surprise when critics mounted a national expose. This prompted them to label their critics 'utility bashers', saying little about considerations that prompted the village purchase. Wyeth officials contended that they were startled by the litigation that followed disclosures of fatal compilations associated with using Fen-Phen, but said nothing about how they failed to ensure proper drug use and delayed action after health hazards had been uncovered. The CompuServe faction ignored their considerable history with the Block faction. They knew that the block board was risk-averse and apt to equate high cost with high risk, no matter what the potential payback.

Decision makers who can be held accountable for a failure find themselves in a no-win situation. Some failure is inevitable, but there is no tolerance for failure. There are but two options: own up or cover up. An own-up makes the day of atonement today; a cover-up makes it tomorrow and, with some luck, never. Put in this bind, it is rational to delay atonement. This creates even more trouble because several acts of deception are now required (Nutt, 1989; 2002). Offsetting bad news with good news sidetracks threatening questions. The cover-up is two tiered: the distorted good news and the creation of misleading information. These games of deception become 'undiscussable' because to reveal them would also reveal the 'lose-lose position' it creates (Argyris and Schon, 1978). There must be a cover-up of the cover-up to cover ones tracks. In this way, failed decisions and decision-maker actions become undiscussable.

Like many recall debacles (Nutt, 2002), Wyeth officials believed they had a winner and blinded themselves to bad news. Officials refused to acknowledge that Fen-Phen was being prescribed inappropriately and that they had turned a blind eye to this practice. This may have stemmed from a desire to protect a profitable product or from an unwillingness to confront an out-of-control situation. Whatever the reason, a cover-up was required. Once there is a cover-up this has to be covered up. Company officials could not admit wrongdoing and had to take steps to cover their tracks. Both become undiscussable to hide company failures to monitor drug safety. To create good news in the aftermath of massive market share loss at Perrier, Davis insisted his actions were prudent. He retained a London-based public relations firm to prepare press releases to commend his recall. This ignored the fact that no recall had been called for by health officials. The PR also said nothing about the deceptive recall justifications and the misrepresentation of a key product ingredient. At this point, how each came about has been covered up and is not discussable. It is unlikely Perrier has any idea how to cope with a product contamination should one occur in the future. AEP continues to believe that their village purchase was justified and fails to connect it with the company's subsequent string of misfortunes in securing federal grants to pilot pollution control ideas, rate negotiations, court rulings and coal plant construction plans.

The culprit here is the *perverse incentive* of undiscussability. If truth-telling results in punishment there is very little truth-telling. A perverse incentive always has this effect, making it difficult for people to come forward with their insights about what happened and why (Nutt, 2002). Subordinates often know why things went badly but are not inclined to share what they know in a punishment-driven environment. If higher ups make it clear they will tolerate no opposition to a proposed product, don't expect product defects to be revealed by subordinates. In both cases, a perverse incentive creates an effective barrier to learning why a decision went wrong and how to avoid a similar fate in a future decision. To learn, organizational leaders must create an environment that avoids the blame trap.

Uncovering what worked, what didn't, and why, avoids the learning trap. Environments that tolerate no failure have perverse incentives to hide information essential to make such assessments. The perverse incentive can be implicit, buried in the social fabric of an organization, or explicit in a wrong-headed reward system. Both can be subtle and destructive. Organizational leaders ask for quality, measure cost and lament that people pay no attention to their quality quest. To change this state of affairs the wrong-headed rewards being dispensed must be identified and altered.

To eliminate a perverse incentive, leaders must demonstrate that it no longer applies. This is both time-consuming and difficult. To show that quality mattered at Harley-Davidson, a new CEO had to show that old company practices were no longer in force (Tichy and Devanna, 1990). The cost-based incentives inherent in fast-running production lines had been drummed into the work force over many years. To root them out, the CEO called on Harley's workers to stop the production line if they spotted a quality problem. It took six months of bad quality before someone stopped the line to fix a quality problem. The CEO had to wait until this happened before he could recognize the action with a bonus and set in motion a new understanding about what counts. After perverse incentives have been rooted out, a quest for quality can be set in place in which quality issues can be revealed. The trap set by perverse incentives must be removed before a learning environment can be established (Table 7.7).

LESSONS FOR DECISION MAKING AND DECISION MAKERS

My research identified principles and practices found in successful decision making. A key principle is to stay 'issue centered' (Delbecq, 1989), using an exploratory mindset, to cope with pressure to take action. Cooperrider and Srivastra (1987) use the notion of a 'mystery' to make this point. A decision does not pose a problem to be solved but a mystery to be embraced. The urge to 'fix' something is at odds with a mystery, which calls for skillful questioning to get to the bottom of things.

A claim that captures the fancy of a protagonist makes up one part of the puzzle. A knee-jerk diagnosis with such a claim runs considerable risk of missing the point. Important decisions justify taking time to uncover what is 'at issue with the issue', much like the retreat embraced by many in management consulting. Appreciative inquiry places considerable emphasis on this kind of discovery (Cooperrider and Srivastra, 1987). An investment is made to discover what gives life to the issue being confronted. Pause in claim reconciliation with open meetings and other forums in which stakeholders representing various points of view can do a 'data dump' to indicate what they know about the situation. Have others gather to listen. Challenge those listening to reflect, seeking to make sense of what is heard. Ask them to look for what is most appreciated, what has given life to the issue, before doing anything else.

Pausing to reflect suggests an openness in which answers can be revealed and wisdom gained (Delbecq et al., 2004). The attitude toward judgment is one of 'indifference'. The indifference is to which action, not that action is needed. No commitment is made until there is time to reflect to gain insight. Instead of embracing a quick fix, judgment is suspended until understanding can be gained. To do so, let go of the push for a quick fix. This dispels the urge to calm the chaos, get people 'off my back', relax the tension and act in the many other subtle ways as pressure mounts to give up freedom of choice. Realize that a quick fix is often motivated by fear, greed or a lust for power. These anxieties are often present but usually exaggerated. Fears get amplified and greed and power needs stay unfulfilled because the quick fix is overrated. The recommended contemplation sets aside the quick fix until the true reasons for acting materialize and insights can emerge.

Freedom of choice calls for a decision maker to listen to stakeholders and avoid precipitous actions. Decision failures that become debacles stem from the dysfunctional behavior provoked by fear, greed and needs for power (Nutt, 2004). Confront each position 'in the decision', accepting the uncertainty of not knowing what is best, agreeing not to screen out messages and engaging in reflective listening. Look for deep feelings about what is right and listen for an inner voice. Take on the commitment to manage an exploratory dialogue with many stakeholders. Manage the dialogue with coaching and facilitation roles. Give up directing events to demonstrate power and control. Seek a picture of relevant interests and how competing interests can be handled.

As the cases illustrate, the pressure for action can become intense. Pausing to reflect in the face of such pressure is difficult. When challenged to act remind people of the alternative. Ask them to recall the last time people in the organization quickly found a way to 'fix the problem with (fill in the blank)'. Ask how many meetings were called *after* the fix? How many of the quick fix solutions turned out to be bad ideas? How many required extensive retrofits? And how long did all this take? Who got blamed and what did all that blame accomplish? Ask the critic to visualize the chaos, the squandered energy, and the smoldering resentment. Ask if it seems wise to spend some time to pause and reflect today to avoid all this chaos tomorrow? To avoid all this, use resources to deal with stakeholders and interest groups up front. Stay issue centered by uncovering and exploring claims and the concerns that prompt them. Such an investment today will pay many future dividends.

There are several practices that improve a decision maker's chance of success. Suggestions are all drawn from my research findings that uncovered best practices and tips on how to manage a decision-making effort. Following them has very little cost, compared to the cost of failure. Personally manage the decision-making effort. The prospects of success improve when the decision maker takes charge. Delegation to experts or others expected to champion your ideas gives time for other things, but has an unfortunate result. The individual getting the hand-off lacks a proponent's zeal for effort, which lowers the chance of success.

Make ethics an ongoing consideration. Empower people to apply their 'standards of justice' to the decision and how it is being made If areas of sensitivity are noted, look for values provoking the sensitivities and try to incorporate these values into proposed actions. This gives ethical rationality, as suggested by standards of justice, equal standing with political, logical and economic rationality. Considering people's values, as given by their justice standards, has at least as much power as what is suggested by logic and facts. Finding actions that embrace these values paves the way for success.

Find an arena of action. Signals that capture a decision maker's attention can be symptomatic, misleading or more urgent than important. Careful probing of the claims offered by stakeholders provides a window that opens up on a landscape with useful insights into what needs attention. The time spent in reflecting on these needs to find what is at issue in an issue can pay handsome dividends. A deeper understanding of the issues that merit attention suggests what the decision is about and provides a defense for the course of action that is ultimately selected.

Allocate time and money to deal with the barriers to action. Use groups or network with people who can block the decision to find out their interests and ways to manage them. This puts implementation questions into the mix early on, introducing one to political realities so political rationality can be incorporated in proposed actions. Intervention is the best way to manage barriers that can sidetrack a decision. Participation can be recommended when using intervention would draw attention away from other, more important activities. Avoid edicts and persuasion, even when the decision is urgent.

Set a direction to indicate what is wanted as a result before encouraging people to offer an 'answer'. Knowing what is wanted clarifies expectations and makes a search more effective *and* more efficient. Direction is given by an objective. The objective directs a search and opens it up to new ideas. Objectives also make evaluations more meaningful, easier too carry out and less costly. Inserting logical and economic rationality into the mix in this way ensures that a decision will benefit the organization.

Stress political *and* logical rationality. A decision maker should think about desired actions and how to take action. Many decision makers are pulled toward idea development or managing the politics of the situation, seeing the importance of one but not the other. There is no substitute for clear thinking *or* for diplomatic action. Both thoughtful idea development and adroit promotion are essential. Coupling ethical rationality with the political and economic rationality positions the decision maker to find a win-win remedy that is valuable as well as beneficial to those that must be catered to.

Do not limit search. When decision makers embrace an idea-driven effort that promotes a single idea, a limited search trap is set. Idea-driven efforts reduce the prospect of success by 50 % (Nutt, 2008). To dodge the trap, invest time and money to identify a pool of alternatives, some with innovative features.

To uncover a pool of alternatives, guide a search with an objective given by each of the three perspectives. Be wary of the remedies found in the claims of influential stakeholders. Identify more than one alternative. Several competing alternatives improve results. The discarded alternatives are not wasted. They help confirm the value of a preferred course of action and frequently offer ways to improve it. Employ the more effective option development tactics to do this. Consider developing one alternative with integrated benchmarking, one with repeated solicitation search, *and* one with innovation. Also develop alternatives from the T, P, and O perspectives. This opens up the search process to a variety of ideas from different sources. The best one or a combination of best features suggests a plan with compelling attributes. Often it is useful to combine the best features of several alternatives. All this will make it impossible to mount a defensive evaluation. The moneys spent on defensive evaluations can be allocated to uncovering additional alternatives.

Insist on learning. Treat all decisions as a learning experience. Insist on making failures discussable. This will open up information about outcomes that you need to learn. Creating a safe space for people to operate is essential before things become discussable. Discussability is essential before learning can occur.

NOTES

1. The information for the AEP case was gleaned from anonymous interviews with current and former employees, Newspaper accounts, and corporate press releases dated April 16, 2002 and September 24, 2002.
2. The information for the CompuServe case was gleaned from anonymous interviews with former employees and from company financial statements.

3. The information for the AHP case was gleaned from the *Wall Street Journal*, September 4, 16, and 28, 1997; May 16, 2003; *Financial Times*, November 21, 2003; Forbes, 'Bad Medicine,' vol. 174, pa 48; company financial statements, and Appellants v. John R. Stafford *et al.* and American Home Products Corporation (No 99-5184).

4. The information for the Perrier case was gleaned from Hartley, R., *Marketing Mistakes*, New York: John Wiley & Sons, Inc., 2004; *ADWEEK*, March 12, 1990. Source Perrier, February 10, 1990 (explaining the source of benzene contamination, the steps taken by the company to remove it, the magnitude of the recall, and costs) and from company financial statements.

REFERENCES

Allison, G.T. (1971) Conceptual models and the Cuban Missile Crisis, *American Political Science Review*, 63, 968–1718.

Argyris, C., and Schon, D. (1978) *Organization Learning: A Theory of Action Perspective*. Reading, MA: Addison-Westley.

Argyris, C., Putnam, R., and Smith, D.M. (1987) *Action Science*. San Francisco, CA: Jossey-Bass.

Bardaracco, J.L. (1997) *Defining Moments: How Managers Must Choose Between Right and Right*. Cambridge, MA: Harvard University Press.

Beyer, J.M., and Trice, H.M. (1978) *Implementing Change: Alcoholism Policies in Work Organizations*. New York: Free Press.

Beyer, J.M., and Trice, H.M. (1982) The utilization process: A conceptual framework and synthesis of empirical findings, *Administrative Science Quarterly*, 27 (4/5), 591–622.

Brunsson, N. (1982) The irrationality of action and action rationality: Decisions, ideologies, and organization action, *Journal of Management Studies*, 19, 29–44.

Churchman, C.W. (1975) 'Theories of Implementation,' in R.L. Schultz and D.P. Slevin, *Implementing Operations Research/Management Science*, New York: Elsevier.

Coch, L., and French, Jr, J.R. (1948) Overcoming resistance to change, *Human Relations*, 1, 512–532.

Cooperrider, D., and Srivastva, R. (1987) 'Appreciative Inquiry in Organizational Life,' in *Research in Organizational Change and Development*, JAI Press, Vol. 1.

Cray, D., Mallory, G.B., Butler, R.J., Hickson, D.J., and Wilson, D.C. (1988) Sporadic, fluid, and constricted processes: Three types of strategic decisions in organizations, *Journal of Management Studies*, 26 (1), 13–40.

Cyert, R.M., and March, J.G. (1963) *A Behavioral Theory of the Firm*. Englewood Cliffs, NJ: Prentice Hall.

Damanpour, F. (1991) Organizational innovation and preference: The problem of organizational lab, *Administrative Science Quarterly*, 29, 392–409.

de Bono, E. (1990) *Lateral Thinking: Creativity Step by Step*. New York: Harper and Row (revised edition).

Delbecq, A.L. (1989) *Sustaining Innovation as an America Competitive Advantage*, College Park. M. Institute of Urban Studies, University of Maryland.

Delbecq, A.L., Nutt, P.C., Liebert, E., Mostyn, J., and Walter, G. (2004) 'Discernment and Strategic Decision Making, Reflections for a Spirituality of Organizational Leadership,' in Moses L. Pava, (ed.), *Spiritual Intelligence at Work: Meaning, Metaphor, and Morals*, San Francisco, CA: Elsevier JAI Ltd.

Denhardt, J. (2000) *Business, Institutions, and Ethics*. Oxford: Oxford University Press.

Doktor, R., and Hamilton, W. (1974) Cognitive style and the acceptance of management science recommendations, *Management Science*, 19 (8), 889–894.

Downs, A. (1967) *Inside Bureaucracy*. Boston, MA: Little, Brown.

Eisenhardt, K. (1989) Making fast decisions in high velocity environments, *Academy of Management Journal*, 32, 543–576.

Eisenhardt, K. (1997) Strategic decisions and all the jazz, *Business Strategy Review*, 8 (3), 1–3.

Fredrickson, J.W. (1985) Effects of decision motive and organizational performance on strategic decision processes, *Academy of Management Journal*, 28, 821–843.

French, J., and Raven, B. (1959) 'The Bases of Social Power,' in D. Cartwright (ed.), *Studies in Social Power*. Ann Arbor, MI: Institute for Social Research.

Germunden, H., and Hauschildt, J. (1985) Number of alternatives and efficiency of different types of management decisions, *European Journal of Operational Research*, 22 (2), 178–190.

Ginzberg, M., and Schultz, R. (1987) Special issues in implementation, *Interfaces*, 17 (3).

Hackman, L. (1990) *Groups the Work*. San Francisco, California: Jossey-Bass.

Hall, P. (1984) *Great Planning Disasters*. Berkeley: University of California Press.

Hart, G., and Bogan, A. (1993) *The Baldrich Prize*. New York: McGraw-Hill.

Hickson, D., Butler, R., Gray, D., Mallory, G., and Wilson, D. (1986) *Top Decisions: Strategic Decision-Making in Organizations*. San Francisco, CA: Jossey-Bass.

Huysmans, J. (1970) *The Implementation of Operations Research*. New York: John Wiley & Sons, Inc..

Jantsch, E. (1975) *Design for Evolution: Self Organization and Planning in the Life of Systems*, New York: Brasilia.

Johnson, M. (1993) *Moral Imagination*. Chicago, University of Chicago Press.

Keeney, R., and Raiffa, H. (1985) *Decisions with Multiple Objectives*. New York: John Wiley & Sons, Inc.

Kolb, D. (1983) 'Problem Management: Learning from Experience,' in S. Srivastra (ed.), The *Executive Mind*. San Francisco, CA: Jossey-Bass, 109–143.

Langley, A. (1989) In search of rationality: The purpose behind the use of formal analysis in organizations, *Administrative Science Quarterly*, 34, 598–631.

Langley, A., Mintzberg, H., Pitcher, P., Posada, E., and Macary, J. (1997) Opening up decision-making: the view from the black stool, *Organization Science*, 6 (3), 260–279.

Leavitt, H.L. (1987) *Corporate Pathfinders*, New York: Penguin.

Linstone, H. (1984) *Multiple Perspectives for Decision Making: Bridging the Gap Between Analysis and Action*, New York: North Holland.

Locke, E.A., and Latham, G.P. (1990) *A Theory of Goal Setting and Task Performance*. Englewood Cliff, NJ: Prentice Hall.

March, J.G. (1994) *A Primer on Decision Making: How Decisions Happen*. New York: Free Press.

McKie, D. (1973) *A Sadly Mismanaged Affair: The Political History of the Third London Airport*. London: Croon Helm.

Miller, D. (1990) *The Icarus Paradox: How Excellent Companies Bring About Their Own Downfall*. New York: Harper.

Mintzberg, H. (1985) *Structure in Fives*. Englewood Cliffs, NJ: Prentice Hall.

Mintzberg, H., Raisinghani, D., and Theoret, A. (1976) The structure of unstructured decisions,' *Administrative Science Quarterly*, 21 (2), 246–275.

Mintzberg, H., and Westley, F. (2001) Decision-making: It's not what you think, *MIT Sloan Management Review*, 41 (3), 89–93.

Nadler, G., and Chandon, W. (2003) *Ask the Right Questions*. Los Angeles: Center for Breakthrough Thinking Press.

Nadler, G., and Hibino, S. (1990) *Breakthrough Thinking*. Rocklin, CA: Prima.

Nisbett, R., and Ross, L. (1989) *Human Inferences: Strategies and Shortcomings of Human Judgments.* New York: John Wiley & Sons, Inc. (revised edition).

Nutt, P.C. (1986) The tactics of implementation, *Academy of Management Journal,* 29 (2), 230–261.

Nutt, P.C. (1989) *Making Tough Decisions.* San Francisco, CA: Jossey-Bass.

Nutt, P.C. (1993b) The identification of solution ideas during organizational decision making, *Management Science,* 39 (9), 1071–1085.

Nutt, P.C. (1998a) Evaluating complex strategic choices, *Management Science,* 44 (8), 1148–1166.

Nutt, P.C. (1998b) Leverage, resistance, and the success of implementation approaches, *Journal of Management Studies,* 35 (2), 3–240.

Nutt, P.C. (1999) Surprising but true: Half of organizational decisions fail, *Academy of Management Executive,* 13 (4), 75–90.

Nutt, P.C. (2002) *Why Decisions Fail.* San Francisco, CA: Berrett-Koehler.

Nutt, P.C. (2004) Expanding search during strategic decision making, *Academy of Management Executive,* 18 (4), 13–28.

Nutt, P.C. (2005) Search and decision making, *European Journal of Operational Research,* 160 (3), 851–876.

Nutt, P.C. (2008) Investigating decision making processes, *Journal of Management Studies,* 45 (2), 425–455.

Nystrom, P., and Starbuck, W. (1984) To avoid organizational crises, unlearn, *Organizational Dynamics,* 12 (4), 53–65.

Peters, T.J., and Waterman, R.H. (1982) *In Search of Excellence: Lessons from America's Best Run Companies.* New York: Harper and Row.

Pettigrew, A. (1985) *The Awaking Giant,* New York: Blackwell.

Pfeffer, J. (1992) *Managing with Power: Politics and Influence in Organizations.* Boston, MA: Harvard University Press.

Pfeffer, J., and Salancik, G. (1974) Organizational decision making as a political process: The case of a university budget, *Administrative Science Quarterly,* 19, 135–151.

Pinfield, L. (1986) A field evaluation of perspectives on organizational decision making, *Administrative Science Quarterly,* 31, 365–388.

Pounds, W. (1969) The process of problem finding, *Industrial Management Review,* Fall, 1–19.

Quinn, J.B. (1980) *Strategies for Change: Logical Incrementalism.* Homewood, IL: Dow Jones-Irwin.

Rodrigues, S., and Hickson, D. (1995) Success in decision-making: Different organizations, different reasons for success, *Journal of Management Studies,* 32 (5) 654–679.

Schultz, R.L., and Slevin, D.P. (1975) *Implementing Operations Research/Management Science,* New York: Elsevier.

Simon, H.A. (1977) *The New Science of Management Decision.* Englewood Cliffs, NJ: Prentice Hall (revised edition).

Snyder, R.C., and Page, G.D. (1958) The United States decision to resist aggression in Korea: The application of an analytical scheme, *Administrative Science Quarterly,* 3, 341–378.

Starbuck, W.H. (1983) Organizations as action generators, *American Sociological Review,* 48, 91–102.

Stein, M.I. (1975) *Stimulating Creativity: Volume 2 Group Procedures.* New York: Academic Press.

Tichy, N., and Devanna, M. (1990) *Revisiting The Transformational Leader.* New York: John Wiley & Sons, Inc.

Van de Ven, A., Polley, D.E., Garud, R., and Venkataraman, S. (1999) *The Innovation Journey.* New York: Oxford University Press.

8

A Decision Process Model to Support Timely Organizational Innovation

Andre L. Delbecq, Terri L. Griffith, Tammy L. Madsen, and Jennifer L. Woolley

Innovation as a Critical Organizational Concern

Ask any group of organizational leaders from any business sector what keeps them awake at night and arguably 'managing the pace of change' will appear at the top of the list. The concern does not focus on one or two strategic changes. Rather the concern is whether every program, unit, department, and functional area, as well as the organization as a whole can continue to operate at the cutting edge relative to its competitors.

There was a time when a few organizational elites could gather once every several years to identify needed changes and formulate a strategic plan to introduce innovation into their organization (Mintzberg, 2000). That day has passed. Now organizations face the need for continuous improvement in every organizational unit and function even as they face frequent disruptive radical changes affecting the organization as a whole. The causes are many. We will mention but a few.

The growth in the worldwide population has a major impact on organizations. More people than ever before contribute to the forces that create change. Similarly, the trend towards globalization increases the access to and pressures from worldwide stakeholders. The contemporary company faces potential competition from major global international corporations as well as small third world entrepreneurs funded through micro financing; from small un-bundled specialty organizations to large multi-product firms. Not only do new generations of information technology and cyberspace allow ideation from these multiple sources to flow through global information exchange, but also Internet marketing brings competitive opportunities quickly to the attention of customers and users.[1] Furthermore, systems of micro, angel, venture, internal and public financing rapidly enable dispersed competitive

Handbook of Decision Making. Edited by Paul C. Nutt and David C. Wilson
© 2010 John Wiley & Sons, Ltd

endeavors. Additionally, contemporary innovation often combines superior features with lower costs. For example, the week we wrote this Apple announced their new 3G iPhone – 'Twice as fast. Half the price'.[2]

The result is an organizational world that has no enduring changeless 'safe space'. This new innovation rich environment requires that organizational arrangements and capacities be widely distributed throughout the organization to assure that each unit maintains timely innovation. A lack of innovation in one sector of an organization creates a problem for timely achievements in other functions. Particularly in areas of the organization's core capabilities, processes must be in place to ensure that it creates the future to which competitors must respond (Leonard-Barton, 1995). Otherwise, an organization lives in a crisis mode constantly responding to an uncertain future imposed externally.

We believe that these contemporary realities require embracing a continuous cycle of decision making that supports unfolding and timely innovation. There must be an 'organizational capacity' beyond the response of select and isolated enterprising individuals. Whether the responsible parties in a particular organizational unit are concerned with process, product, service, or large-scale organizational change, there should be a way of proceeding to both read the signs of the time and to experiment with and implement bold and timely change efforts. Unless this organizational capacity is unleashed, profits and the competitive position of the organization suffer. But it is not simply economic advantage that is at stake. A decision process that supports organization-wide innovation also enables the creative energies of all the organization's cadres. Encouraging such co-creation provides an important aspect of human dignity in the workplace that contributes to both individual and organizational meaning even as it better serves organizational clients (Cherns, 1975; Davis, 1973).

Organizational leaders can see their current environmental context either as an unwanted and disruptive state of affairs or as a creative energy field. We see the modern environment of rapid change in the latter sense and believe there is reason for confidence. The essential elements of an organization-wide discipline to support timely innovation are identifiable and even well known. Still, our experience is that only a fraction of organizations in most industry sectors successfully manage a continuing organization-wide internal innovation process. A complicating factor is that some firms associate innovation exclusively with research and development (R&D), but this is only one relevant type of innovation. Other forms such as process innovation and organizational change are consequently ignored. Thus, often the innovation process and implementation are poorly enacted beyond R&D. Drawing from the authors' combined 109 years of discussions with managers involved in innovation and change, we offer a decision process model to guide innovation. In the model we discuss the four steps of the process, participants involved in each step, and some of the barriers often spoken of by professional managers.

A DECISION PROCESS MODEL TO GUIDE INNOVATION

The purpose of this chapter is to set forth a step-process decision sequence that can be utilized across organizational units for varied innovation challenges. This model of innovation decision making is understandable to a practicing organizational leader, is theoretically defensible, and can be enacted by an average participant in the modern organization. As such, this is a normative position paper setting forth the authors' understanding of one useful approach. It is not an encyclopedic treatment of innovation, but rather our best counsel at this particular point in time. (This paper builds on earlier expressions. See, Delbecq, 1994; Delbecq and Weiss, 1988; 2000.) There are other defensible points of view, other interpretations of the literature, and other prescriptive processes. Here we claim only to offer our interpretation on how leaders might proceed to embed innovation within their organizations.

A caveat: step-process models are recursive as behavior at one phase of an innovation effort tends to bleed into behavior at other stages. Nevertheless, without the conceptual clarity of such a model, important steps are commonly skipped or truncated which reduces innovation effectiveness. The model we propose consists of the following sequence:

1. Visioning
2. Feasibility Studies
3. Design and Pilot Testing
4. Implementation.

Figure 8.1 guides our presentation of this sequence. The left hand column delineates the action and general goals. The right hand column highlights the suggested participants. The center column suggests possible outcomes. We also provide examples for each stage of the model based on a fictitious boat-building enterprise, 'Beluga Boats'.

Step One: Visioning

The first step of the proposed model is 'Visioning', during which a heterogeneous group seeks to holistically map both consumer trends and the competitive landscape to generate a basket of propositions for innovation. The Visioning process stimulates an awareness of the need for and potential features of possible future innovations. Visioning is based on the exchange of ideas and insights among internal participants and includes scanning for information across external informants. During this step the participants deal with complex problems, the dimensions of which are not yet fully identified; and with solutions, the component elements of which are not yet understood. The result is a set of specific potential options for innovation, each of which warrants a more detailed Feasibility Study.

At the individual level of analysis, 'vision' is one of the pillars of contemporary leadership theory and defined as 'a sense of direction and concern for the future' (Kouzes and Posner, 2007). However, current theory neglects to explain how a vision comes into being. For example, we remember Mohandas Gandhi and Eleanor Roosevelt as leaders of vision. However, we often are less aware of the processes that led to their vision. Gandhi's vision unfolded over time through many preparatory steps. These include his study in England where he learned an appreciation for the positive features of English culture and law that allowed him to be a skilled and sensitive negotiator; his first experimental experience with protest in South Africa;

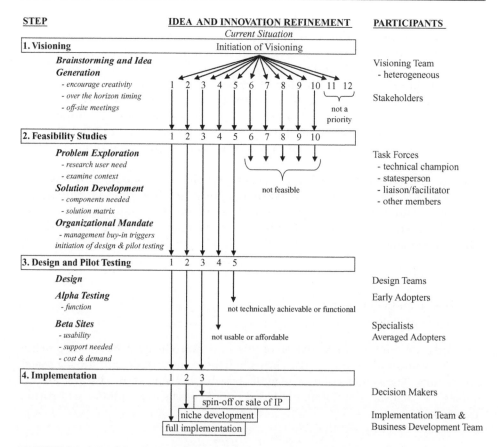

FIGURE 8.1 A Decision Process Model to Support Timely Organizational Innovation

* This figure is intended to be illustrative, but not a description of reality. These steps are not separate, but flow into one another. Additionally, the process for examining each idea will happen simultaneously, but the steps may not be completed at the same time.

his preparatory travels throughout India to deeply understand the people and their needs and his in-depth study and prayerful reflection on religious wisdom. Likewise, Eleanor Roosevelt's preparation to become an advocate for many features of her husband's 'New Deal' involved a long path of personal preparation and then discoveries regarding the needs of her nation's poor. In sum, a careful reading of biography and history shows (Gardner and Laskin, 1995) that 'vision' is not arrived at in solitary reflection by an isolated individual with a clever mind. It is formulated through an interactive process that includes both prospective stakeholders and potential solution designers. We believe Visioning, in the context of organizational innovations, should likewise be a dialogical discovery process.

As stated earlier, every business unit at every level within an organization should consider Visioning as an imperative managerial activity (Tushman and O'Reilly III, 2002). The experience of quality improvement teams demonstrates that line workers can envision innovative ways of working when given the opportunity. The same value can be achieved in every organizational function, laboratory, unit, and program. Indeed, arguments regarding high involvement management (Lawler, 1986, e.g. quality circles, self-managing work teams, Kaizen) and decentralization more generally, are based on a common perception that organizational members who are closest to a particular genre of a problem and to a particular customer or user group have insights regarding continuous improvement (and sometimes radical innovation) that elites, who are separated by space, information filters, and alternative conceptual maps, do not possess. Similarly, marketing, financial, and other support functions need to engage in Visioning to discover how better to enable the organizational members they serve and to avoid overlooking novel opportunities. For instance, when marketing caters to an organization's established customers it may discount or ignore innovations that do not align with the established customers' needs, but are highly valuable to potential customers (Christensen, 1997).

This does not eliminate elites from Visioning. Elites at the headquarters level must engage in high-level Visioning beyond product and process innovation and examine strategic issues such as the fit between organization structure and strategy, new avenues for garnering resources, timely capital investments, partnerships, alliances and mergers. In short, Visioning for innovation must be pervasive throughout the organization (Gupta, Tesluk and Taylor, 2007; Miller, Fern, and Cardinal, 2007). Unless timely innovation and well understood vision emerges within each function and at each level, top-level innovations may simply shuffle around increasingly arcane activities (Dougherty, 1992).

Guidelines for leaders initiating a group Visioning process.   How can an organizational leader initiate a group process that parallels experiences that are evident in exemplary individual Visioning? We identify four components as critical: enabling creativity and flexibility, long-term preemptive planning, using large blocks of time for off-site meetings, and involving heterogeneous team composition. First, Visioning requires creativity and flexibility. A lack of either limits the number and value of the innovation propositions and hinders the potential of the process. To enable creative Visioning, a leader must implement a process with few constraints. For example, participants should be encouraged to generate ideas during brainstorming, even those that seem unreasonable or outlandish.

Second, time and place also matter. Regarding time, if Visioning is to proceed in a playful and creative fashion, it is best undertaken 'over the horizon' and before a technological/competitive threat emerges. Some scholars argue that organizations primarily respond to threats and that a crisis should be the stimulus to Visioning (see Mintzberg and Westley, 1992 for a discussion of change catalysts). We disagree. Visioning that is preemptive and anticipatory holds greater promise for building a competitive advantage. In our experience, successful Visioning typically concerns a future at least 18 months to three years out from the present time, which varies by industry. It seeks to preempt a future space that competitors might otherwise occupy when a market becomes more generally apparent (e.g. through the emergence of a better understanding of market needs or the availability of technologically superior solutions). Organizational units that devote specific periods for reflection on the future are more likely to be prepared for repositioning their unit for innovation. It is not unreasonable to expect that organizational units engage the Visioning process at least annually and even more frequently during periods of rapid change.

Third, off-sites with lumpy blocks of time for Visioning provide a more powerful venue for reflecting on the future than short on-site meetings. In the latter case, it is difficult for participants to transition their thinking away from current challenges and agendas and focus on long-term organizational needs. Indeed, the majority of on-site conversations are preoccupied with current short-term concerns and re-actionary thinking. Holding the conversation in a time and space removed from settings devoted to the present tense supports the binocular adjustment to a future.

Fourth, who should be involved? Visioning in the past was seen solely as the pre-rogative of those occupying leadership roles. Yet, if the organization is dealing with the future, the Visioning team benefits from being more heterogeneous. A diversity of insights from multidisciplinary viewpoints and even external resource stakehold-ers (consultants, industry experts, association professionals, etc.) can enhance the ability of a Visioning team to think broadly and 'outside the box'. Using a more diverse set of stakeholders also may yield a more diverse set of options (Gallupe et al., 1992). Thus, discipline-based heterogeneity improves team creativity and the quality of the outcomes.

Visioning is also enhanced not only through sifting and winnowing diverse in-ternal dialog, but also through conversations with future users and providers of possible technological solution approaches residing outside the firm. Groups that send members of the Visioning team to visit the jobsites of potential users or places where pieces of the future are already unfolding (e.g. research centers, universities, high performing organizations in parallel industries) will gain much from such cos-mopolitan search. This essay will not deal with further details of either group com-position or creative process techniques for aggregating judgments that are available elsewhere (see for example, Delbecq, Van de Ven, and Gustafson, 1986).

Visioning then is an intuitive analysis of targets of opportunity felt to be worthy of exploration as potential innovations. Typically, Visioning is accomplished by a team through a series of meetings that unfold somewhat as follows:

Meeting 1: Group formation, preliminary environmental assessments, and iden-tification of stakeholder and potential users groups to survey.

Meeting 2: Reports of visits by group members with varied stakeholders and po-tential users, early discussion of insights obtained, and determination of needs for further information and clarification.

Meeting 3: Preliminary listing of potential innovation opportunities and pooling judgments regarding a rank ordering of those innovation opportunities that seem to warrant future Feasibility Studies.

Meeting 4: Preliminary report of these evolving intuitions of the Visioning team to stakeholders.

Meeting 5: Refinement of priorities for Feasibility Studies following stakeholder feedback and development of recommendations for membership composition of Feasibility Study task forces.

When the results of the Visioning conversations are shared across stakeholders, functional silos, and authority groupings, more serendipitous linkages and valuable insights can be discovered (Merton and Barber, 2004). However, there is an inverse relationship between formalization and centralization with innovation at this stage. The role of authority figures and functional mandarins is restricted to sharing ideas that might improve ideation. It is not their role to either dominate or override the decisions of a Visioning team. At this stage of the discovery process, formal organizational approval regarding innovation priorities must be held in abeyance until after Feasibility Studies are completed.

In our step-process model, the Visioning team should not refine the details of either the problem or solution designs. Rather, its charge is to identify target potential innovations that hold promise and should be explored in detail by future project teams with specialized expertise. Thus, the output of a Visioning process is a set of potential innovations that warrant investigation either because they were discovered as important to serve future client needs (market pull), or because the technology seems to hold promise of a more elegant solution (technology push) than is presently available.

At this first stage in the step-process sequence, Visioning, team participants must not attach rigid expectations to any of the possibilities and must avoid premature anchoring to any potential innovation. Further, participants are likely to assess innovation opportunities with different values. This strengthens the process. The intent of Visioning is not to narrowly specify organizational priorities or to drive a premature consensus. Additionally, Visioning should not focus on constraints or resource barriers, but rather on identifying a number of areas worthy of investigation through future Feasibility Studies. This includes areas that are not a priority in discussions with stakeholders.

Barriers to Visioning.   Table 8.1 lists the barriers to Visioning that are typically encountered by practicing managers in our experience as consultants. These barriers are mainly related to process, resources, timing, managerial attention, and organizational leadership. For example, managerial attention must recognize that as a team shifts from homogeneous composition and leader dominated planning to heterogeneous composition admissive of many different points of view, facilitation skills are crucial (Tsui and O'Reilly, 1989). An outside group process specialist is particularly helpful for avoiding undue individual dominance and stimulating creativity (Griffith, Fuller, and Northcraft, 1998).

Three prominent areas of difficulty for the Visioning process are maintaining focus on the problem at hand, using judgment pooling, and using creative problem solving. First, it is important for the group to remain problem centered until the many dimensions of the future are better understood. Second, techniques for pooling judgments through ranking and rating also are superior to casual consensus. Third, structured creative problem solving is superior to basic idea exchange for a more unique basket of innovation ideas.

There are even more subtle forces at work, however, that demand a consciously enacted and disciplined decision process to avoid premature closure. Often, strategic decisions fail (Nutt, 2002). Causes include making assumptions from past

TABLE 8.1 Examples of barriers encountered during visioning

Barriers Related to:

Process	Resources (Stocks & Allocation)	Timing	Managerial Attention	Organizational Leadership
– Lack of focus. – Not using judgment pooling. – Not using creative problem solving. – Visioning based on the exchange of opinions of an internal group committed to existing ideas/opinions. – Engaging in Visioning infrequently. – Premature closure around preferred innovation choices preempts creative Feasibility Studies of other viable and important options.	– Core rigidities and competence traps. – Locating Visioning meetings on-site. – Visioning Team Homogeneity.	– Time is not provided for meetings devoted to the future. – Proceeding without full brainstorming. – Proceeding too quickly through the process.	– Lack of process facilitation so personalities and roles distort open discussion.	– No common expectation or norm that innovation & Visioning are part of each organizational member's job. – Only using Visioning when facing crisis (e.g. serious threats or performance lags threaten survival). – Dominance by leaders curtails exploration from the bottom up. – Using traditional resource allocation rules to guide the Visioning process.

practices and successes, unwillingness to engage and listen to voices outside the current set of dominant decision makers, reluctance to break away from traditional resource allocation rubrics (Christensen, 1997), truncating search and uncritically promoting an early solution (Simon, 1957), reinforcing competence traps (Levitt and March, 1988) and/or core rigidities (Miller, 1990), and failing to bring to bear values, ethical concerns, emotional, and spiritual insights (Mittroff and Linstone, 1993). There is a tendency toward an all-too-tidy consistence marked by narrow thinking rather than by the necessary expansive ideation. Almost unconsciously, leaders are moved by impulses of which they are vaguely aware, and the biases with which they interpret reality are quite imperceptible to them. The result is linear thinking, a tendency to extrapolate along current trends and be conceptually constrained by present budget and resource practices. These are not problems associated with broken leaders in poorly performing organizations. These are problems manifested by highly respected leaders in high performing organizations.

Visioning must be more than a rational/technical sequence in that attention to ontological questions is necessary for productive innovation. Such questions evoke emotional and spiritual intelligence that jars complacence and, in turn, provokes a different order of thinking. Examples of such questions include: What would ...

- ◆ be more in line with our mission?
- ◆ serve our customers more generously?
- ◆ be attentive to customers with the greatest needs and least resources?
- ◆ honor our deepest commitments?
- ◆ be congruent with our values?
- ◆ provide the greatest dignity?

These important probing questions stimulate thinking beyond the immediately expedient and conventional. The evolving vision must be judged by its expansiveness, its ability to break out of prior conceptual boxes, and its ability to speak to both mind and heart.

Case Study 1

It's January 2008 and Beluga Boats is a small boat building enterprise[3] located in Vallejo, California, in the San Francisco Bay waterway. Its product offering has focused on performance racing sailboats (fast, high-tech, speed over comfort and price). While Beluga has been both technically and financially successful, the market is saturated for high-end race boats. Family recreational boating, at about a tenth the annual operating cost of racing, is a stronger force in the market – especially in the local San Francisco Bay area, which, like most industrial complexes, is being hit by an economic downturn. Though the leadership team has more boat racing than management expertise, market pressures and changes in the economy are pushing them towards an innovation process similar to that described here. Their relatively small size (owner, three area leads with an assistant each, and 20 craftspeople of varying expertise) allows us to see the process in a simplified way. We urge readers to not take this simplification as appropriate for more complex organizations.

Their first step is to create a diverse eight-person Visioning team composed of both internal and external members. From Beluga Boats: the owner and Beluga marketing lead (both are hard-core racers and unfamiliar with more recreational boating), a newly hired assistant in the production area (he came from fiberglass RV production, not a boater), a younger member of the sales force (she has excellent listening skills and has been bringing back feedback from customer calls). From outside of Beluga: a customer (he is both a sail-boat racer and owns a recreational powerboat), the editor of a major boat magazine (she has covered trends on different market segments), a local yacht broker who sells across customer segments, and a racing buddy who provides process facilitation consulting to businesses.

The owner tasks the group with Visioning around other kinds of recreational boats that would compliment Beluga's competencies and allow for horizontal growth. Their brainstorming and idea generation meeting (off-site) produces five alternatives: pilothouse motorsailer (cruising sailboat with family amenities), entry-level outboard-driven powerboat, heavy cruising trawler yacht (again with family amenities), sportfishing/charter cruising powerboat, and a ferry/water taxi multi-passenger powerboat.

They next prioritize with their competencies and the local market in mind. The outcome is that three of the possibilities are clearly out: sportfishing powerboats (variabilities in the fishing industry and high fuel costs make this market less attractive), ferry/water taxis (federal regulations and the size of the crane needed are beyond Beluga's expertise), and entry-level outboard powerboats (Beluga's expertise is in hulls that cut through, rather than plane across, the water – and inboard engines). After more discussion, the team decides to focus on the pilothouse motorsailer and the trawler yacht (see Figure 8.2).

Step Two: Feasibility Studies

In the Feasibility Study step, a task force examines each of the potential innovation opportunities identified in the Visioning step in light of the current and prospective context in which the end-user functions. Visioning ends and Feasibility Studies begin when the Visioning team agrees that a set of options for potential innovation opportunities is worthy of further exploration (e.g. options 1 through 10 in Figure 8.1, the options available at the end of the Visioning phase, and the pilothouse motorsailer and trawler yacht in the Beluga example). These innovation options might encompass various forms including product, service, continuous process improvement, paradigm shift, or organizational change. In some cases, one potential innovation option might compete with another. In other instances, innovation options might be complementary to each other or of an entirely different order and kind (in the Beluga example, consider the different subcategories of innovation – both type of vessel and then subcategories of different systems or process innovations involved in the design and construction of the candidate vessels).

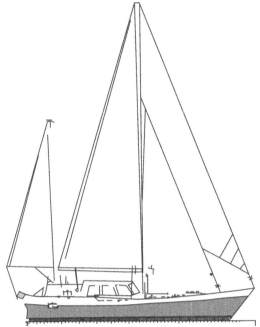

Pilothouse Motorsailer

Cruising Trawler

FIGURE 8.2 Vessel Designs

To ensure the efficacy of the process, each highly rated potential innovation opportunity that emerges from Visioning should be investigated through a Feasibility Study with appropriate attention. Each of the Feasibility Study task forces must explore an innovation option with an open mind and without prejudice to guard against anchoring bias (Tversky and Kahneman, 1974), inertia (Hannan and Freeman, 1984), and the innovator's dilemma (Christensen, 1997). Each Feasibility

Study seeks to uncover potential strengths, possible ways to overcome weaknesses, and the strategic practicality of an innovation option.

Feasibility Study task forces.   The Feasibility Study begins by identifying task forces of volunteers who have passion, interest, and belief in the particular innovation options. Each task force conducts a Feasibility Study for a different option defined in Visioning. At this stage of the innovation step-process, opponents, or those who hold serious doubts, are not appropriate task force members.

The task force should be organized using a tripartite leadership structure to increase the likelihood of its success. A technical champion who believes in the potential innovation and has logistics expertise leads the Feasibility Study task force. Two complementary leadership roles are a statesperson who serves as a boundary spanner of the vertical power structure and authority matrix, and a liaison/facilitator who brings horizontal boundary spanning capability and internal group facilitation skills.

The technical champion is the logistic leader of the Feasibility Study process (Delbecq and Mills, 1985; Howell and Higgins, 1990). This person typically focuses on problem solving and task design. As a result, the technical champion often under-attends both horizontal and vertical communication challenges. Importantly, the technical champion propels the study forward and organizes tasks, but does not assess quality or judge the study.

The statesperson is chosen to sponsor the project within the corridors of power. Given this role, the statesperson should be well networked within the organization's authority matrix. The statesperson need not hold a hierarchical position, but should be an influential opinion leader among current authority elites. In addition, the statesperson should not compete with the technical champion on design and task leadership.

The facilitator manages task force member relations as well as horizontal boundary relations with other organizational units that may be impacted by the innovation option under review. Internal task force facilitation is critical. Highly performing heterogeneous task forces require careful attention to internal processes and group maintenance. Likewise, sizeable projects involve communication across multiple horizontal group boundaries. Vertical and horizontal communication at formal review points, and through informal conversations, paves the way for organizational acceptance. Indeed, communication failures underlie the demise of innovation efforts even more than deficiencies in technical design. At this point in the process, relevant individuals within different horizontal organizational units are typically only loosely coupled. Yet, the cooperation of these individuals is crucial to the effectiveness of late stages of the innovation process. As a result communication across these horizontal organizational units must be managed from the beginning.

These three complementary leadership roles are critical to long-term success of complex innovation efforts. Relative to classical power source typologies (French and Raven, 1959; Pfeffer, 1992), the influence base of the technical champion is expert logistics power, that of the statesperson is referent power, and that of the facilitator is relational power. By using these tripartite leadership roles, the ability of the task force to manage the complex unfolding of the innovation process increases.

The remaining members of the Feasibility Study task force bring a matrix of relevant multidisciplinary expertise to the effort. Since Feasibility Studies take the task force into areas of investigation beyond current organizational experience, participants from outside the organization are often helpful (e.g. consultants, industry or customer experts, etc.). This implies that task force composition to support successful Feasibility Studies requires thoughtful attention to a skill matrix and meticulous recruiting.

Problem Exploration.   It is helpful to separate Feasibility Study investigations into two phases: Problem Exploration and Solution Development. To stimulate more creative and robust solution designs, the goal of the first phase of the Feasibility Study, Problem Exploration, is to understand the context, world view, and needs of the user. A critical aspect of successful Problem Exploration is patience in coming to a detailed understanding of the need that the innovation option seeks to satisfy. Exploratory methods are called for to enter deeply into the mindsets of potential users. These methods might include:

- Shadowing potential users to understand the context in which the innovation will be embedded.
- Conducting focus groups and unstructured interviews that do not lead user responses, but rather allow for the discovery of subtle aspects of need, even by the users themselves.
- Utilizing surveys later in the exploratory sequence when dimensions of user needs have been discovered and the task force seeks to understand the distribution of preferences among potential users.

The anthropological methodologies[4] appropriate for discovering client needs during Problem Exploration are often not part of the skill sets of the engineering, scientific, or technical team members. This suggests the importance of creating a multidisciplinary task force as discussed earlier. Outside technical support may be useful in structuring the discovery processes of this phase.

The Problem Exploration process uncovers user-preferred and user-friendly features important for eventual adoption of the innovation. Understanding these features allows the Feasibility Study task force to incorporate a flexible solution architecture into their recommendations. Patience and thoroughness in Problem Exploration avoids the error in which an ineffective solution is designed based on the task force's preferences instead of user need.

Communication is crucial to success. For example, it is important to return to user informants for verification of the task force's interpretations of their responses. This provides an opportunity for additional clarification and feedback. Sharing the emerging understanding of user needs with the authority matrix and horizontal functional groups is also critical because their collaboration will be needed in subsequent steps of the innovation process. This approach aids conceptual unfreezing and avoiding surprises when these stakeholders later are asked to analyze solution recommendations.

Case Study 2

Beluga's team splits into two at this stage in the offsite meeting. They get on their cell phones and use the Internet to do the basic research. The owner, editor, and new assistant take on the Problem Exploration for the motorsailer. The marketing lead, customer, new assistant, and salesperson take on the trawler. The process facilitator consults with both groups.

The motorsailer group decides to speak with couples that have recently purchased cruising sailboats. They identify these couples through the local yacht clubs. They also discover that Northern Europe is historically the expert in the design and construction of motorsailers. One of the group members uses professional contacts to arrange for phone interviews with two firms there.

The trawler group concludes that their customer base is best accessed in the 'Delta'. This is the favorite vacation area for many families with this style of boat. By talking with families while they are actually engaged in trips they are able to get vivid examples of the use characteristics the customers prefer.

Two weeks later, the two groups reconvene (again, offsite) to present their findings.

Motorsailer:

- Good for families who don't want to be constrained by basic weather (temperature, rain) and who want some control over their schedule (big inboard engine allows for motoring when wind isn't available).
- Ability to raise three smaller sails is easier than worrying about the strength required to raise two larger sails.
- Interior accommodations, even in a smaller 35' version, are family friendly – the craft is easy to maintain yet has sufficient space (two bathrooms, a sizable galley, and three births/sleeping areas).
- Use of a wheel versus a tiller is easier for non-sailors to master and takes up less space.
- Navigation can be controlled via GPS and/or from inside an enclosed steering station; electronic 'roller' furling of the forward sail is possible given battery and engine support.
- Size and set up (e.g. swim ladder and steps) make it easy to launch water toys (and children).
- Anchoring is power assisted by a high power engine (supported by enough diesel to travel 400 miles).
- Water makers are available and should be contrasted to large water tanks.
- Innovations are suggested for using: modularized cabinets versus custom joinery (cabinetry and wood fittings); modularized electronics; and electronic fuel controls to support fuel efficiency.

Trawler:

- The emphasis is on living conditions versus nautical design, but the boat has to be stable in sea conditions to avoid seasickness.

◆ Less skill required than for a sailboat and some owners will take on a professional skipper to move the boat from seasonal locations (making navigation support less an issue).

◆ Basically a floating vacation apartment.

◆ The boat has walk around beds in the main stateroom.

◆ The focus is on beautiful joinery that keeps the below decks area dry.

An additional process innovation is the use of 3D electronic goggles and computer simulation to design and evaluate a prototype. Design of the 3D model is low cost as it can be done in Second Life (http://www.secondlife.com) versus using naval architecture tools.

Solution Development.   Once the problem dimensions are fully understood, a search for solution elements for each innovation option begins. Normally, Problem Exploration uncovers a set of user needs, each requiring their own Solution Development. This phase of the process advances by creating a solution matrix to address these needs as appropriate for the user context. The overall strength of the Feasibility Studies results from the combination of learning Problem Exploration and Solution Development, both of which help to avoid premature selection of inappropriate solution features. Discovery of the entire array of user and organizational concerns usually reveals the need for a package of multiple solution components. Avoiding premature movement toward a preferred overall solution architecture before all elements are explored is critical to creating a balanced, useful, and adoptable innovation.

Before finalizing a composite design through internal dialog, the Feasibility Study task force needs to search outward to discover solution elements that have already been tried or developed and that relate to the overall solution matrix (Rosenkopf and Nerkar, 2001). This provides an opportunity to find prior innovations that have failed originally, but that may be valuable in the current context (Hargadon and Sutton, 1997). To do so, the task force should contact technical gatekeepers to identify sources of prior knowledge, techniques, and experience that can stimulate open and creative thinking about solution elements. Gatekeepers are individuals who occupy a pivotal point in a network of potential informants. (Examples might be journal editors, association officers, key industrial or consumer group leaders, etc.) Gatekeepers should be asked to nominate useful informants for further discussions regarding Solution Development. Follow up in-person interviews and site visits serve as important stimuli to avoid truncating Solution Development for several reasons. For example, actual physical visits allow the task force members to avoid a premature sense that they understand the experience of others. Such visits also create a dual form of confidence: within the team in their own results and external validation of the Feasibility Study task force. This dual confidence promotes organizational acceptance of the innovation since their unfolding insights regarding solution components are grounded in experience, not simply speculation.

It is important to emphasize that often the solution elements in successful innovation design are discovered through contact with outside sources as opposed to being conceived of solely through internal dialog (Aldrich and Kim, 2007; March, 1991). This is increasingly so given the worldwide knowledge explosion and sub-specialization that makes it impossible for any group within a single organization to possess all aspects of knowledge surrounding the solution to a new challenge. This holds notwithstanding the bench strength of a particular organization. (Indeed, one reason that small organizations often innovate more effectively than large orga-nizations is that they understand that their internal personnel do not encompass all the necessary knowledge. This stimulates small organizations to engage in robust ex-ternal search behavior.) Further, exploring solution elements through contact with external sources helps to calibrate high standards for success and provokes creative possibilities for recombination and re-invention (Fleming, 2001; Kogut and Zander, 1992). Finally, the external search guides prudential decisions regarding whether to develop a particular solution component internally, to externally partner, or out-source the design. Such choices occur whether the decision focuses on a bundled solution or is restricted to one or more specific solution components.

Solution Development encompasses variables that increase a user's perceived value, reduce the organization's costs of producing a good or service, or both. A final preferred innovation solution should combine superior user value while low-ering the organization's cost of producing that value. Issues of both organizational and user acceptability must be addressed when formulating solution recommen-dations. In the review processes, the statesperson and the liaison/facilitator play an important role in communicating the task forces' evolving insights. Again, the Feasibility Study task force needs to bring early conceptualizations from their evolving Solution Development back to informants for review and comment. They also should again seek commentary from the authority matrix and functional groups that subsequently will be impacted. The Feasibility Study task force should seek feedback while their thinking is still tentative and fluid. Involving various stakeholders in the process will result in additional insights regarding modifications that might improve the design. It also stimulates a broad base of understanding across stakeholders that will shape future decisions regarding whether to go forward with the innovation process.

Case Study 3

The Beluga group decides to use additional field research to assist their solu-tion search. The subgroups use their contacts to get out for a day on the Bay – each in a boat similar to the one that they are considering and owned by a peo-ple like the customers they envision. By watching the owners interact with the boats they gain insights that as racers they never would have had on their own. At the end of the day they use their newfound camaraderie with the cruising owners of their test boats to go over some of the group's conclusions from the Problem Exploration phase as well as their nascent solutions. They find great value in 'reality testing' their views with people from their potential customer base. They return to Beluga's conference room with some solution ideas.

Motorsailer: Fuel costs push for reduced weight. Recent innovations enable lighter weight designs including: using a lighter cored hull versus solid epoxy;

installing a water-maker versus having larger water tanks; using smaller fuel tanks enabled by modern, more efficient electronic fuel injection; and an understanding that shorter trips are the goals of their likely market. They also decide to focus on a commodious, modularized kitchen. Electronic sail furling is downgraded given reliability concerns. Lastly, they conclude that the inside and outside finishes are important to likely customers; thus quality, as well as value, will be important on that dimension.

Trawler: As they think about the viability of the trawler option, their discovery process points to strengths and weaknesses of Beluga Boat's current capabilities. They find that the performance characteristics of a trawler are more similar to commercial fishing vessels than their current offering of racing sailboats. Developing these characteristics in a boat exceeds Beluga's competencies. Additionally, the interior and systems of a trawler, what they now see as a 'luxury water apartment', is not Beluga's strength or their joy.

Organizational Mandates.   Feasibility Studies should unfold as a search and dialogical process. Feasibility Study task forces must not retire into isolated conversation that results in a 'surprise' recommendation at the end of a relatively hidden process. An organizational mandate to go forward with further innovation design following reclusive decision making is a doubtful outcome.

Feasibility Studies end when a general understanding of a set of practical solutions to an important potential innovation has been determined and rough financial and strategic implications of proceeding are understood. It is important not to over-promise at this point. A detailed design has not been worked out and actual performance outcomes, costs, and user acceptance have not been tested. The results of a Feasibility Study are still a conceptual artifact, that is a best guess.

When the results of the Feasibility Study are presented to organizational decision makers there are many possible outcomes. To mention but a few:

- ◆ Enthusiastic embrace of the conceptualization and a mandate to go forward with a vigorous design and pilot test effort.
- ◆ Hesitant approval, but willingness to at least go forward with a pilot as a form of organizational learning.
- ◆ Recommendation of partial adaptation, perhaps incorporating some elements into continuous improvement efforts.
- ◆ A decision not to go forward.

Review processes used to arrive at the decision at the end of the Feasibility Studies are important. Reviewers should discuss the strengths of a proposal and the ways in which the proposal echoes the earlier Vision. Next, the group should discuss modifications that might improve the proposal. Only then should weaknesses be discussed. Returning to ontological questions discussed in Visioning (i.e. what is in keeping with mission and values, what would be nobler, what would be more generous in serving the needs of society, etc.) helps to keep the decision from becoming simply a critics' feast on technical details. The final decision is more accurate when numeric ratings and rankings are used to pool judgments as opposed to verbal consensus (Huber and Delbecq, 1972).

Barriers to Feasibility Studies.   Table 8.2 lists barriers to Feasibility Studies that are frequently cited by practicing managers. Above all, the classical error is hubris. There is a tendency for organizations experiencing recent success to minimize (if not to skip entirely) Feasibility Studies thereby proceeding from Visioning directly to Design and Implementation. Recent success often leads organizations to overestimate provider expertise and omniscience. All of the earlier mentioned psychological traps (e.g. attending to the voices of a few, prematurely narrowing choices; advocating for a preferred solution rather than exploring multiple possibilities, etc.) and all of the reasons strategic decision processes are truncated are the enemy of the careful listening and discovery processes encompassed in the disciplines of Feasibility Studies. Therefore, it is misguided to trust that the high degree of psychological and spiritual maturity required for careful listening to the voices of others is in place. An organization does well to normatively require a thorough Feasibility Study protocol as the prelude to proceeding to Design and Pilot Testing.

The two mantras for a Feasibility Study should be: (1) search behavior is more important than brilliance and (2) transparency creates trust. Feasibility Studies end when the organization decision makers mandate the initiation of Design and Pilot Testing. Design and Pilot Testing only focus on the remaining feasible set (in Figure 8.1 we show options 6–10 dropping out at the conclusion of the Feasibility Studies). The broader this mandate is the better. Ideally, the formal and informal leaders, as well as the rank and file, will support the decision.

Case Study 4

Beluga again goes offsite to develop an organizational mandate that will lead to an initial design. The full set of the team first formed during the Visioning step is recombined for this stage of the process. Given their focus on Problem Exploration and Solution Development, this is a relatively easy step for the recombined group. After sharing pictures of their day on the Bay and discussing the results of their solution search efforts, they easily decide to drop the trawler from the solution set since it is a less feasible option than the motorsailer. They choose to move forward with a design of a pilothouse motorsailer, keeping in mind that sales of cruising boats have softened in the current economy. It is agreed that cost per value will be a critical feature. This approach is in line with the desires of young families.

They also get a mandate to move forward on the process innovation of using computer simulation for the first stage of design and prototyping. After serious research into formal computer aided design simulations as well as retail on-line simulation possibilities, they see that the cost, speed, and technical issues are within their feasible set if they stick to retail versus marine architecture versions.

TABLE 8.2 Examples of barriers encountered during feasibility studies

Barriers Related to:

Process	Resources (Stocks & Allocation)	Timing	Managerial Attention	Organizational Leadership
– Focusing on 1–2 preferred innovations vs. conducting a Feasibility Study for each of the priority options. One implication is missing serendipitous opportunities that may not have been known at the time of Visioning. – Relying on filtered information from select informants regarding user perceptions and needs. – Distorting user information by asking users to react to a pre-determined solution vs. using exploratory methods to discover subtle user preferences that may shape an innovative solution. – Failing to return to informants for verification of the task force's interpretation of their input. – Missing the two pivotal early feedback opportunities for bringing stakeholders into the evolving understanding.	– Insufficient discipline-based heterogeneity in task force composition.	– Proceeding to detailed design before organizational mandate to proceed. – Rushing through Problem Exploration before full understanding user needs. – Skipping Solution Development.	– Expecting the Champion to fulfill internal task force facilitation and all boundary-spanning roles. – Lack of all three leadership roles.	– Premature attachment to an idea prior to full study.

Step Three: Design and Pilot Testing

The Design and Pilot Studies step of the model includes additional conception of the innovation options that the organization has mandated for further exploration at the end of the Feasibility Studies. As with prior steps, the Design and Pilot Studies are undertaken by a multidisciplinary task force. Norms supportive of creative playfulness and avoidance of premature closure remain critical.

First, each innovation option is designed in light of the information gathered from the Feasibility Studies and conversations with potential users and external stakeholders. Second, each innovation option is examined for technical achievability, functionality, usability, and cost through thorough *Alpha testing* and *Beta sites*. The Design and Pilot Studies step concludes with a robust analysis of each innovation option on which well-informed implementation decisions are made.

Design.   The Design step of the process involves the Design team exploring each innovation option. When we arrive at the Design stage of the step-process model, most engineers, scientists, and functional experts feel more at home. They are drawn to this arena of creative effort. Of course, the danger is that as members of the Visioning Team or Feasibility Task Force, they may have truncated prior steps because they are anxious to turn their attention to the creative design details. However, if the earlier steps have been patiently completed, the Design team will find themselves in the presence of rich heuristics that stimulate design creativity due to the exploration and data collection involved in each step.

Since design is specific to each innovation, limits exist regarding what we can say except to suggest process guidelines. Perhaps most importantly, we continue to stress the need for a dialogic and transparent process. The purpose of the Design stage is to create a solution that adequately addresses as many aspects of the problems that stakeholders raised as possible. In this regard, the Design team must constantly test the emerging design against the needs and preferences that emerged during prior conversations with stakeholders: users, outside experts, and authority figures. This does not imply the need to continually seek re-approval. The task force already possesses a mandate for Design and Pilot Testing. Once the Design and Pilot Testing phase begins, it should not be controlled or arbitrarily stopped by organizational stakeholders. Rather, frequent communication continually affirms that the unfolding design is responsive to earlier articulated concerns – and also is a step towards developing commitment to the outcomes (Salancik, 1977). Returning to the ontological questions (how is the design in keeping with mission, high standards, generous response to more vulnerable users, etc.) brings to bear emotional intelligence and wisdom on technical considerations. Failing to consider stakeholder preferences or ontological questions increases the temptation to slip back into a narrow technocratic perspective.

The Design team should not constrain the design process too early; however, over time, the design inevitably will be narrowed by choices and constraints. As these tradeoffs are considered, a desire for design perfection should not prevent timely action learning. For example, it is important to go forward with Pilot Testing to resolve design questions and conflicts. Delaying until there is consensus, independent of experience, on every design feature is unwise. 'Perfect' designs prior to Pilot

Testing are seldom achieved in innovation efforts. Instead, designs are refined through experiential learning; star users often improve upon the initial design (Jasperson, Carter, and Zmud, 2005). Importantly, a penchant toward action assures timely forward progress.

Pilot Testing.   The Pilot Testing phase of the process involves testing the innovation options. At this point, each of the options has been designed for user needs, preferences, and technical feasibility. During the Pilot Tests, the solutions are tested for function, usability, support, training, cost, and demand. Pilot Tests are conducted in two phases: *Alpha testing* and *Beta sites.*

Alpha Tests.   *Alpha Tests* are the starting point for assessing the actual use parameters of the solution based on functionality. In this stage the Design team engages a specific group of potential users called early adopters. If one thinks of a bell shaped curve of potential technological innovation users, the left hand tail is composed of 'innovators' and 'early adopters' (Moore, 1995; 1999; Rogers, 1987). In this case, innovators are those who have taken part in the design process. Early adopters are potential users who are as excited as the designers regarding the new possibilities implied by the innovation. Early adopters are anxious to try a new approach and delighted to contribute to the discovery of what works. The center of the bell curve represents average adopters (called the early and late majority). These individuals do not strongly oppose the innovation, but, they are intelligently skeptical about the risks of early involvement with the attendant disruption to what is already in place. Finally, the right side tail of the bell curve includes 'laggards' or users who strongly prefer the present way of doing things and who remain very resistant to the potential innovation. Both average adopters and laggards are engaged later in the *Beta Site* testing and *Implementation* planning (if implementation is executed).

An important organizational lesson for assuring timely change in innovation efforts is the value of partnering with early adopters during *Alpha Tests* to refine and hone (debug) a preliminary design. Early adopters are not offended by imperfection. Indeed, they delight in contributing to the refinement of a design. Because *Alpha Test* design refinement is based on actual experience rather than speculation, unanticipated learning is uncovered. Different preliminary design features also are tested comparatively in different iteration cycles during an *Alpha Test* period. This yields an ability to discover how the design might be varied to fit differentiated preferences among future users. Particular features (e.g. option 5 in Figure 8.1) are discarded at this stage based on technical feasibility and/or functionality.

Case Study 5

While Alpha Tests are based on actual experience rather than speculation, the Beluga team determines that given the costs of prototypes, they are better off with experiences gained in virtual reality. The combination of computer aided design (CAD) and virtual world simulations allows them to address systems integration issues (how the systems fit together physically), and to demo the new model with possible buyers.

The implementation of the new technology brings its own complexity. Their first attempt to import their design documents into a 'free' virtual world site fails. They quickly discover that addressing this process change as a separate innovation process would have had value. Not all solutions are the same and they spend some time scrambling for a feasible outcome as a result. Eventually they begin to work with a technical expert who is able to help them import their design information into the virtual world site.

Given their market in the tech-savvy San Francisco and Seattle areas, the demos are well received even though the computer interface is sometimes slow and jerky on screen. Valuable information is gained about how to more effectively run the plumbing and electrical systems, but also about color schemes and monitor/TV screen placements. They also discover by watching customers play what comes to be known as the 'sailing game', that none of the families intend to take long trips under motor (especially given current high diesel prices). As a result, the team decides to build the prototypes with 200-gallon tanks, saving on space and weight.

Beta Sites.   While the *Alpha Test* focuses on the functionality of the design solution, another dimension remains to be tested – usability. The *Beta Site* shifts the focus to usability: how the user will engage the innovation, ways the end user can be best introduced to the innovation, and systems to enable full use of all solution design functions. Ease of use is the primary concern. Secondary concerns include production cost, customer value, demand projections, and return estimates.

To assess the usability of the solution, the *Beta Site* engages average adopters who remain skeptical, want a design that 'works' without flaws, need training to learn how to utilize the innovation, and value technical support when problems occur. Designers and *Alpha Test* participants are often poor teachers to *Beta Site* users. For designers and early adopters, the innovation is so intuitive and error correction reflexes so automatic that they have little empathy for, or understanding of, problems the average user encounters. So, typically, there is a need to hand-off the *Beta Site* implementation to educator/trainers/service specialists who are sensitive to the learning curve of the average adopter. Trainers who can interpret the 'beginner's mind' are also charged with recording and codifying average client concerns. This approach facilitates the development of user manuals and technical support protocols that are necessary for implementation.

When estimating the potential use of an innovation, researchers often simply find current use data and demographics and extrapolate these to the broader market. Not surprisingly, estimations using *Alpha Test* results, and based solely on demographics, generally overestimate average users' future demand. They also seriously underestimate the education, training, and service support required for large-scale innovation adoption. Therefore, in addition to assessing usability, *Beta Sites* provide data regarding overall potential demand of the innovation from those most intimate with the setting: the average users.

In the end, it is often not the perfection of the design but the user friendliness and technical support refined in *Beta Sites* that best predicts successful broad-scale innovation implementation. Furthermore, *Beta Sites* often generate new knowledge about the features or applications average users actually prefer, desire, engage, and/or frequently utilize. This knowledge can be applied to the design to refine the solution for maximum usability. (For example, option 4 drops out at this stage in Figure 8.1.) *Beta Site* trainers must not over-sell or push, but instead, seek to discover the degree of desire for the solution(s) offered, improvements that would make the solution more user-friendly, and the type of support desired. Conducted in such a manner, the information gathered in the *Beta Sites* allows for a more accurate assessment of user demand than from *Alpha Test* data alone.

In summary, *Beta Site* learning contains critical insights on how to facilitate market pull as opposed to solo reliance on technology push. For example, later, the testimony of satisfied *Beta Site* participants will be much more convincing than advocacy by either designers or *Alpha Test* participants. As a consequence, it is useful to fish bowl *Beta Sites* by allowing both organizational stakeholders and future users to observe the innovation process in action and to listen to the experience of *Beta Site* users.

Case Study 6

Beluga spends the Fall and Winter producing two full-scale, full-detail prototype pilothouse motorsailers; one for San Francisco and one for Seattle. Both are given to brokers focused on the family cruising market. Luckily, the timing is right and the San Francisco version is able to be 'test sailed' at the annual Strictly Sail boat show. A charity raffle is run with the prize being an overnight sail to Angel Island. In Seattle, the broker takes a local family on an overnight to the San Juan Islands. Both test trips yield changes in fine details (e.g. lifeline netting to keep children and pets from sliding under the lifelines is added as a standard feature; removable dustbins are incorporated into the bilge areas for easy clean up; the carbon-fiber steering wheel is switched out for a cheaper, though slightly heavier stainless steel one). The changes are handled at Beluga for the San Francisco boat, and by a local boatyard in Seattle for the other vessel. Given new market information from the now very knowledgeable brokers, Beluga scales production to build hull numbers 1 through 5 of the new model.

Barriers to Design and Pilot Testing.   Table 8.3 summarizes common barriers to Design and Pilot Testing encountered by practicing managers. The barriers suggest the importance of ground rules to avoid premature freezing of design decisions. Indeed, an effective organization continuously engages in double loop learning throughout the innovation process and during implementation, should it occur.

To summarize, the step-process approach to Design and Pilot Testing assures that Design is not a technocratic end game by a group of technical providers who hope for market acceptance. Rather, it is an orchestrated dialogic process where designers select 'state of the art' features, but users adjust the state of the art into a 'system in

TABLE 8.3 Examples of barriers encountered during design and pilot testing

Barriers Related to:

Process	Resources (Stocks & Allocation)	Timing	Managerial Attention	Organizational Leadership
– Failing to view **Design & Pilot Studies** as an iterative exercise in problem solving unfolding in partnership with different constituents. – Regressing to a specialist point of view and forgetting what has been learned in the Feasibility Study. – Moving directly from Alpha Tests to recommendations for full-scale implementation. – Skipping Alpha Tests; often occurs when a design team assumes that the solution functionality is optimal and moves to gathering demand and usability data from Beta Site testing. – Failing to leverage Beta sites for information on the innovation experience.	– Lack of resources committed to testing.	– Moving too quickly to Design before all the information available in Feasibility Studies is gathered and processed. – Moving too slowly to Alpha Tests due to debates within the design team regarding 'one best way'.	– Lack of commitment to testing.	– Absence of a clear mandate that assures organizational commitment to the design team that they are authorized to complete Alpha and Beta testing unless some unusual unforeseen event arises.

use' that meets their needs. At the end of Design and Pilot Testing, the functionality of the solution design is proven and realistic cost parameters regarding production, implementation, training, and support are established. *Beta Site* responses refine the solution's usability and provide a reasonable basis for demand estimates. At the end of the *Beta Site* Testing, any innovation options that are not technically achievable, functional, usable, or affordable are dropped from the solution set (Options 4 and 5 in Figure 8.1). At this point, organizational decision makers hold all of the data necessary to make well-informed implementation choices from the remaining innovation options. We now turn to critical decisions regarding whether to go forward with implementation, and if so, in what fashion.

Step Four: Implementation

Implementation is the final step in the process and involves determining which innovation option to pursue and in what capacity. This is the second pivotal decision point that is truly organizational. Once a Visioning priority is established, the first pivotal organizational decision is made – to mandate an innovation effort and to see the effort through Pilot Testing unless strong contrary evidence requires an early discontinuation. When such a mandate is given, a preferential option to proceed in support of organizational learning remains in place.

Of course, circumstances earlier in the process might contribute to a decision to discontinue an innovation's investigation. For example,

- ◆ Problem Exploration might disclose user preferences that are outside the organization's interests or are not feasible.
- ◆ Solution Search might suggest that the requirements for an adequate technical design to address user needs require capabilities the organization does not possess and does not desire to acquire.
- ◆ Alpha Tests might show that a technically adequate design is not achievable at this stage of engineering know-how.
- ◆ Beta Sites may indicate that user technology support will be too expensive to implement.

Thus, innovation efforts may be discontinued at earlier stages in the step-process sequence. Healthy organizations, which place faith in human creativity and the passion of those driving intrapreneurship, usually bring innovation investigation through the *Beta Site* testing sequence. *Ceteris paribus,* proceeding this far should be the norm.

Progressing from the *Beta Site*, an innovation must satisfy an appropriate organizational decision appraisal. The essential question is whether the responses from the *Beta Site* sufficiently predict performance effectiveness, market acceptance, and adequate economic returns to warrant an implementation strategy. Here, the prudence of proceeding with *Beta Sites* becomes evident. If an organization bases its decision on the *Alpha Test* experience, advocacy and enthusiasm often distort organizational choices. By contrast, *Beta Site* results allow the decision to focus on evidentiary criteria.

Implementation Decisions.   Depending on *Beta Site* results, numerous possible decision outcomes exist.

A. Abort.   *Beta Site* evidence may suggest insufficient demand by average users to warrant moving forward. In this case, one choice is to discontinue the innovation effort, trusting that lessons gained from exploratory learning will be retained and, in turn, benefit a future related effort. (A visit to the Dayton, Ohio Air Museum provides a wonderful portrayal of experimental aircraft that benefited future generations of aircraft design.)

B. Niche implementation strategies.   *Beta Site* evidence may suggest limited mainstream market demand and that a small niche market exists, but that a major market thrust is not timely. For example, this might occur when the innovation is new to the world rather than just new to the firm's core industry or to the firm's operations. Here several options can be considered.

- The organization may allow members of the innovation group to form a small business unit to serve this limited demand, thereby holding the organization's place in markets until there is greater public readiness for the innovation.
- The organization might spin off the intellectual capital by selling the design and knowledge learned from the innovation effort to an outside entity. Alternatively, the organization, while maintaining partial or full ownership of the innovation idea, can identify a customer who might benefit from the innovation and embed the project within their firm (e.g. Christensen, 1997). In this case, the organization should target a small firm that is enthusiastic about small opportunities and small wins.
- Members of the innovation team may wish to initiate a start up enterprise believing in the offering's future potential. The economic expectations for a small start-up are not the same as those for a publicly traded firm. By taking an equity position in the start-up, the organization shares in future possible returns on the learning it sponsored. It also supports innovation team members who have invested deeply in the exploration of the innovation and wish to continue to develop its potential.

There are numerous variations on the above theme: joint ventures, alliances, etc. We suggest one final caveat where a full implementation strategy is not the decision. One demoralizing characteristic of North American culture is superstitious attribution of success or failure as being the result of a 'great champion/team' or a 'failed champion/team' based upon the decision to implement their innovation solution. Organizational cultures that wish to sustain continuing innovation endeavors must avoid the traps of over-celebrating successful *Beta Sites* and under-celebrating less successful outcomes. Innovation deals with discovery processes that cannot be predicted and uncertainties that cannot be controlled. Innovation therefore, must always be managed as experimentation and discovery with equal kudos to all good faith efforts. Myths that superior persons generate superior results must be avoided. Otherwise, a risk-averse culture emerges.

C. Full-scale Implementation – new products and services.   Given promising *Beta Site* results, the process shifts to the challenges associated with full-scale implementation of new products and services. In one sense, the innovation process ends with *Beta Site* testing. Implementation brings us into the arena of business development that involves separate disciplines. However, we briefly address some of the challenges associated with implementation since innovation failures often stem from implementation failure. Business history is replete with examples where organizations developed a pioneering innovation, but failed to harvest the benefits from its breakthrough (e.g. Betamax versus VHS, and now Blu-ray versus HD-DVD, Lewis, 2006). Indeed, it is our experience that most innovations fail not for design reasons, but because of implementation failure.

Full-scale implementation of product or service innovations seeks to capture first-mover advantages for a pioneering firm. The pioneer's intent is to preempt the market by positioning a superior new offering within the market before competitors can develop their own alternative. This positioning forces the competition to play catch-up. While rivals design their competitive offering, the pioneering firm is able to shift its focus to continuous design refinements, process improvements, and complementary skill investments leading to user benefits and production efficiencies. The pioneering firm's established market lead provides an income stream that enables it to stay ahead of rivals' learning curves and resource investments.[5] This seems a self-evident strategy for harvesting the benefits of a promising innovation. Why is it so often not the lived history of pioneering efforts? Table 8.4 summarizes some of the barriers to full implementation encountered by managers.

The first error is failing to hand-off the implementation effort to a business development implementation team. 'Hand-off' refers to a transition process; this process may involve some degree of overlap among the teams and is not intended as a 'throw it over the wall and we're done' action. That said, often a timely hand-off is thwarted by possessiveness of the champion and the innovation team. Sometimes the organization is distracted by other concerns and relies on the innovation team to engage in business development even though it lacks the full complement of business skills. Under these conditions, clumsy business development delays movement into an effective market-capture strategy.

Another common error occurs when the pioneering firm lacks financial, marketing, and/or manufacturing capacities and is unwilling to enter into partnerships or alliances to achieve the market capture strategy. (It is for this reason that most start-up firms in incubator industrial complexes such as Silicon Valley cease to exist. Their 'end game' is acquisition by a mature firm because they recognize resource limitations that prevent a smaller business entity from sufficiently penetrating the market in a timely fashion.) For these and similar reasons, unless the pioneering firm is willing to bring sufficient business development resources to bear, competitors may displace the pioneer however superior its original design might be. Unfortunately this is an all-too-typical story of invented here, but harvested by others.

TABLE 8.4 Examples of barriers encountered during implementation

Barriers Related to:

Process	Resources (Stocks & Allocation)	Timing	Managerial Attention	Organizational Leadership
– Failure to pass the baton from a design and development team to an implementation team with requisite development support skills. – Overly ambitious/unrealistic market entry efforts that inadequately supports each new set of users. Mid-course corrections are not made, leaving dissatisfied customers and decreasing market enthusiasm. – Zero to few incentives to adopt the innovation.	– Insufficient staff and/or budget allocation → failure to harvest a first mover advantage.	– Missing learning opportunities by moving too quickly.	– Senior management devoting inadequate attention and commitment to a well thought out strategy → lack of momentum to garner enthusiasm.	– Over-celebrating successful Beta Site innovations outcomes which creates a risk-averse culture.

Assume a contrary case. An innovation emerges within a strong host organization. After the *Beta Site* testing, the innovation is transferred to a business development team for implementation. The innovators are justly compensated for their efforts and retain some form of gain sharing as a reward for their development (e.g. Arthur and Huntley, 2005). The business development team is fully supported by the organization's core business leaders who believe in the innovation's potential based on *Beta Site* data. The leaders are willing to bring the gravitas of their organizational resources to bear: investment capital, manufacturing ramp-up capabilities, marketing and branding competencies, training and development skills, etc. Where the organization lacks the resources, it engages in creative alliances and partnerships to support the development effort.

Even under these favorable circumstances, the story of successful business development is rarely an easy path. We mention only one other classic paradox, the matter of scale. Overly ambitious attempts to enter markets too rapidly tend to fail (Camerer and Lovallo, 1999). One reason is a lack of careful attention to each new customer segment that is required to ensure that each is provided the same educational and service support that the initial implementation target market received. Education, training, and service support resources often rapidly reach their limit. Therefore, the business development team must struggle with the antinomy between haste and care. The pioneering firm has only one chance to make a positive first impression with each customer segment. *Beta Sites* help to calibrate the magnitude of required customer support, but pioneering organizations often find it difficult to accept the high cost of providing this support for each new market penetration effort.

There is a delicate dance between doing it right and doing it in a timely fashion. If existing organizational resources are over-stretched, customer satisfaction often plummets. This provides an opening to competitors and leaves the door open for value transfer to these firms rather than value capture by the focal firm. Frequently, it is not the technically superior offering that wins, but the organization that provides the user with the most comfortable and supportive experience.

This is just a flavor of the implementation challenges organizations face. Further elaboration is beyond the scope of this chapter as it concerns the dimensions of establishing and running a successful business line. Instead, we proceed to the last probable outcome: full implementation of organizational innovation.

D. Full-scale Implementation – organizational change innovations.   Many innovations are not new products or services, but rather new organizational processes. In these instances, successful *Beta Site* results serve as a prelude to introducing an important change within an organization. In this section, we turn to full-scale implementation of process innovations, which lead to organizational change.

Here the issue is not the 'free choice' of dispersed users. Rather, organizational process innovation requires adaptation by organizational cadres who express varying degrees of resistance to a given innovation. In this type of innovation effort, the implementation team often faces a paradox regarding readiness. When the innovation is being tested as a possibility, organizational members often take insufficient notice thinking (hoping) that the experiment may fail or that it will have limited implications for them personally. But just as the innovators feel the evidence from the *Beta Sites* should largely eliminate resistance, organizational members faced with the change increase their resistance as they realize the inherent inconveniences of change.

Under these conditions, not only do the burdens regarding preparation for incorporating the innovation increase, but also, the previously identified stakeholders' concerns shift subtlety. (We refer you to Table 8.4 for a summary of potential implementation barriers.) This requires that the implementation team reiterate the innovation's original purpose(s), (re)clarify the benefits evidenced in *Beta Sites*, remain open to further modifications to enhance differentiated user fit, and patiently support a rollout plan that provides for education and technical support. Once again, shifting the responsibility to an implementation team is critical since the original innovation design group is typically impatient with teaching new users. Internal innovation requires careful and patient implementation with each new adapting organizational group. Boundary communications and the degree of support for late adopters are more predictive of organizational acceptance than technical design quality. Effectiveness requires answering critical questions for each adopting group:

Why do we have to do this?

* Requires careful documentation of the real user needs.
* Sharing the robust results of the *Beta Sites* and the testimony from Beta Users.

How will it impact me?

* Requires careful attention to fears and felt inadequacies of adapters.
* Avoiding any implied criticism of prior practices based on earlier knowledge.
* Adequate training, learning time, and technical support.

Do I really have to do this?

* Requires top management clarity regarding commitment and support of the innovation as an organizational priority.
* Frequent reiteration of the reasons for the change including connection with key organizational values and overall strategy.
* An implementation schedule with a clear date for the death and discontinuance of prior practices.
* Align incentives with effective use of implemented innovation.

The preferred strategy is small, well-supported incremental wins through rollouts with iterative organizational units. Massive efforts are inevitably doomed as they are almost always under-resourced and uncoordinated.

Case Study 7

Spring has arrived in the Vallejo area. The local marina hosted the largest sailboat race of the season and Beluga Boats took the opportunity to announce they would have five of their new pilothouse motorsailers available for the next year's season. The Beluga boatyard team (joiners/cabinet specialists, fiberglass experts, engine installers, electricians, and riggers) is invited to a special kickoff as the first production hull is laid into its mold. Jackets with the new design stitched on the back are handed out and it looks like a good kickoff.

As the team works out how to transition from prototype to production models, a couple of issues become clear: the hull design will need some adjustments to the order in which the structural elements are incorporated – they need to find a new way to build in the connections that allow the modular galley and electronics components. This is especially important as it allows customers to install less expensive versions initially, with the possibility to upgrade later – this feature also is key in keeping the prices in line with the current economy. The need for these additional innovations is met as a challenge and actually excites most of the team members who were not as involved in the early steps of the innovation process.

Less excitement, however, is evident amongst the joiners. They find the focus on modular, which they call 'pre-fab' and liken to building cheap house trailers, as a restriction of their professional skill set and development. Beluga management realizes that this resistance is a common symptom of change and works to negotiate an outcome. The joiners are not against the new design, or the addition to the Beluga product line. Instead, they are concerned that their expertise will decline over time, and that their expertise will be less valuable to the organization. Through meetings where these issues are directly addressed, the joiners and management work to resolution by stepping through the innovation steps on this particular topic. The resolution provides the joiners with more control over the CAD process, while allowing them to market their skills to boat owners interested in retrofitting their boats to the new modular designs (it turns out that the modular design has safety and maintenance benefits).

A similar innovation process begins with a focus on how to best work with the local boat brokers. Whenever the economy takes a downturn, brokers are inundated with used boats to sell. Used boats, like cars, lose much of their value the minute they are put into use. Yet, they often offer excellent value and, in turn, market demand exists. As a result, Beluga needs to find a way to incent the brokers to spend time marketing the new model.

CONCLUSION

In this chapter, we propose a decision process model to guide timely innovation. Four steps are discussed: Visioning, Feasibility Studies, Design and Pilot Testing, and Implementation. We offer that the innovation process is no longer, if it ever was, the domain of management elites. Instead, organization-level product and process innovation involves all segments of the organization, and is a requirement for the effective functioning of the segments themselves. This form of innovation is a continuous process and required skill throughout the organization. We also take a strong stand on moving through the steps in order (acknowledging activities may bleed across steps, and that the steps are often recursive) and avoiding the temptation to skip ahead to design, and/or to assume that implementation will take care of itself. Each step is important and provides needed knowledge, commitment, and sometimes, marketing opportunities that support innovation into the future. Using such a step-wise innovation model will help an organization design creative, usable, functional, and data-driven innovations that are motivated by the organization's vision.

NOTES

1. Here we use 'users' to designate those whom the innovation seeks to ultimately serve. Thus the reference may be to customers, but in other instances the reference would be to internal organizational users when an innovation focuses on organizational change.
2. http://www.apple.com/iphone/ accessed June 20, 2008.
3. Fictional.
4. An excellent example of this methodology is described in the 1999 Nightline presentation of IDEO's 'Deep Dive' approach. The documentary is available online at http://www.ideo.com/media/nightline.asp.
5. First mover advantages vary in duration and, under certain conditions, may be short-lived Lieberman, M., and Montgomery, D. (1998) First-mover (dis)advantages: Retrospective and link with resource-based view, *Strategic Management Journal*, 19, 1111–1125.

REFERENCES

Aldrich, H.E., and Kim, P.H. (2007) Small worlds, infinite possibilities? How social networks affect entrepreneurial team formation and search, *Strategic Entrepreneurship Journal*, 1 (1–2), 147–165.

Arthur, J.B., and Huntley, C.L. (2005) Ramping up the organizational learning curve: Assessing the impact of deliberate learning on organizational performance under gainsharing, *Academy of Management Journal*, 48 (6), 1159–1170.

Camerer, C., and Lovallo, D. (1999) Overconfidence and excess entry: An experimental approach, *American Economic Review*, 89 (1), 306–318.

Cherns, A. (1975) *The Quality of Working Life*. New York: The Free Press.

Christensen, C.M. (1997) *The Innovator's Dilemma*. Cambridge, MA: Harvard Business School Press.

Davis, L. (1973) *Work in America*. Cambridge, MA: MIT Press.

Delbecq, A.L. (1994) Innovation as a Silicon Valley obsession, *Journal of Management Inquiry*, 3 (3), 266–275.

Delbecq, A.L., and Mills, P. K. (1985) Managerial practices that enhance innovation, *Organizational Dynamics*, 14, 24–34.

Delbecq, A.L., Van de Ven, A.H., and Gustafson, D.H. (1986) *Group Techniques for Program Planning*. Madison, WI: Greenbriar Press, 2nd edition.

Delbecq, A.L., and Weiss, J. (1988) 'The business culture of Silicon Valley: Is it a model for the future?' in J. Hage (ed.) *Futures of Organizations*. Lexington, MA: Lexington Books.

Delbecq, A.L., and Weiss, J. (2000) The business culture of Silicon Valley: A turn of the century reflection, *Journal of Management Inquiry*, 9 (1), 37–44.

Dougherty, D. (1992) Interpretive barriers to successful product innovation in large firms, *Organization Science*, 3 (2), 179–202.

Fleming, L. (2001) Recombinant uncertainty in technological search, *Management Science*, 47, 117–132.

French, J.R.P., and Raven, B. (1959) 'The bases of social power,' in D. Cartwright and A. Zander (eds) *Group Dynamics*. New York, NY: Harper and Row, 150–167.

Gallupe, B.R., Dennis, A.R., Cooper, W.H., Valacich, J.S., Bastianutti, L.M., and Nunamaker, J.R., Jr. (1992) Electronic brainstorming and group size, *Academy of Management Journal*, 35 (2), 350–369.

Gardner, H.K., and Laskin, E. (1995) *Leading Minds: An Anatomy of Leadership*. New York: Basic Books.

Griffith, T.L., Fuller, M.A., and Northcraft, G.B. (1998) Facilitator influence in group support systems: Some intended and unintended effects, *Information Systems Research*, 9 (1), 20–36.

Gupta, A.K., Tesluk, P.E., and Taylor, M.S. (2007) Innovation at and across multiple levels of analysis, *Organization Science*, 18 (6), 885–897.

Hannan, M. T., and Freeman, J. (1984) Structural inertia and organizational change, *American Sociological Review*, 49 (2): 149-164.

Hargadon, A., and Sutton, R. I. (1997) Technology brokering and innovation in a product development firm, *Administrative Science Quarterly*, 42 (4), 716–749.

Howell, J.M., and Higgins, C.A. (1990) Champions of technological innovation, *Administrative Science Quarterly*, 35, 317–341.

Huber, G., and Delbecq, A.L. (1972) Guidelines for combining individual judgments in decision conferences, *Academy of Management Journal*, 15 (2), 161–174.

Jasperson, J., Carter, P.E., and Zmud, R.W. (2005) A comprehensive conceptualization of the post-adoptive behaviors associated with IT-enabled work systems, *MIS Quarterly*, 29 (3), 525–557.

Kogut, B., and Zander, U. (1992) Knowledge of the firm, combinative capabilities, and the replication of technology, *Organization Science*, 3 (3), 383–397.

Kouzes, J.M., and Posner, B.Z. (2007) *The Leadership Challenge*. San Francisco, CA: Jossey-Bass, 4th edition.

Lawler, E.E.I. (1986) *High Involvement Management*. San Francisco, CA: Jossey-Bass.

Leonard-Barton, D.A. (1995) *Wellsprings of Knowledge: Building and Sustaining the Sources of Innovation*. Boston, MA: Harvard Business School Press.

Levitt, B., and March, J. (1988) Organizational learning, *Annual Review of Sociology*, 14, 319–340.

Lewis, P. (2006) The war at home, *Fortune*, 154 (2), 194–196.

Lieberman, M., and Montgomery, D. (1998) First-mover (dis)advantages: Retrospective and link with resource-based view, *Strategic Management Journal*, 19, 1111–1125.

March, J.G. (1991) Exploration and exploitation in organizational learning, *Organization Science*, 2 (1), 71–87.

Merton, R.K., and Barber, E. (2004) *The Travels and Adventures of Serendipity: A Study in Sociological Semantics and the Sociology of Science*. Princeton, NJ: Princeton University Press.

Miller, D. (1990) *The Icarus Paradox*. New York: Harper Business.

Miller, D.J., Fern, M.J., and Cardinal, L.B. (2007) The use of knowledge for technological innovation within diversified firms, *Academy of Management Journal*, 50 (2) 308–326.

Mintzberg, H. (2000) *The Rise and Fall of Strategic Planning*. New York: Prentice Hall.

Mintzberg, H., and Westley, F. (1992) Cycles of organizational change, *Strategic Management Journal*, 13 (Winter), 39–59.

Mittroff, I.I., and Linstone, H.A. (1993) *The Unbounded Mind: Breaking the Chains of Traditional Business Thinking*. New York: Oxford University Press.

Moore, G. (1995) *Inside the Tornado*. New York: Harper Business.

Moore, G. (1999) *Crossing the Chasm*. New York: Harper Business.

Nutt, P.C. (2002) *Why Decisions Fail*. San Francisco, CA: Barrett-Koehler.

Pfeffer, J. (1992) *Managing with Power and Influence in Organizations*. Boston, MA: Harvard Business School Press.

Rogers, E. (1987) *The Diffusion of Innovations*. New York: Free Press.

Rosenkopf, L., and Nerkar, A. (2001) Beyond local search: Boundary spanning, exploration, and the impact in the optical disk industry, *Strategic Management Journal*, 22, 287–306.

Salancik, G.R. (1977) 'Commitment and the Control of Organizational Behavior and Belief,' in B.M. Staw, and G.R. Salancik (eds) *New Directions in Organizational Behavior*. Chicago, IL: St Clair Press.

Simon, H. (1957) *Models of Man: Social and Rational*. New York: John Wiley & Co, Inc.

Tsui, A.S., and O'Reilly, C.A. (1989) Beyond simple demographic effects: The importance of relational demography in superior-subordinate dyads, *Academy of Management Journal*, 32, 402–423.

Tushman, M.L., and O'Reilly III, C.A. (2002) *Winning Through Innovation*. Boston, MA: Harvard Business School Press.

Tversky, A., and Kahneman, D. (1974) Judgment under uncertainty: Heuristics and biases, *Science*, 185, 1124–1131.

9

Decision Making in Groups: Theory and Practice

COLIN EDEN AND FRAN ACKERMANN

INTRODUCTION

The purpose of this chapter is twofold: (i) to focus attention descriptively on some important aspects of decision making in teams – namely, the sense-making process, the nature of multiple perspectives and interpretations, the interdependency of problems that make up a difficult and messy situation, the nature of purposeful behaviour – goals systems, and perspectives on psychological and social negotiation; and (ii) to explore ways of translating these descriptions into prescriptions that might reduce the probability of decision failures.

The description of decision making and problem solving processes presented in the chapter links directly with some of the aspects of decision making that might decrease the probability of failures. Theories from psychology, social psychology, group processes, the nature of problems, and psychological and social negotiation are used as a basis for description.

The chapter introduces cognitive and causal mapping as a method for describing and managing decision situations including: sense making, multiple perspectives, and goals systems. The chapter also considers the use of causal mapping as a tool for facilitating negotiation in teams and so aiding the reaching of agreements about how to act. In addition the chapter discusses the role of Group Support Systems (GSS) and operational research in addressing aspects of decision failure. In particular the use of a GSS is argued to address delivering a balance between the potential benefits and potential dangers accrued from drawing multiple stakeholders into decision-making situations.

The chapter draws particularly upon the research of Nutt that led to his analysis of failed decisions (Nutt, 2002).

Handbook of Decision Making. Edited by Paul C. Nutt and David C. Wilson
© 2010 John Wiley & Sons, Ltd

SENSE MAKING

An obvious and crucial aspect of group decision making is the process of people *changing their mind* – their way of making sense of the situation. As members of a group discuss, argue, and make claims about the nature of the situation and actions that should be taken, they seek to shift the points of view of others in the group. There are, of course, other important aspects of group decision making relating to the use of power, including social pressures, consolidating personal trading agreements, charisma, and personality. Each of these aspects is important in its own right, and the use of them affects the way in which a person thinks about the situation. Thus, it is appropriate to consider the way in which any one person uniquely makes sense of the situation they believe the group is facing.

A personal 'definition of the situation' (McHugh, 1968) relates to the psychological acts of both perception and construal. Perception is to do with what we see or don't see, and construal is about giving meaning to what we see. It is important to note that we do not perceive things by filtering out from the mass of data around about us, but rather from filtering in, by seeing the world through our own set of spectacles (Neisser, 1976). The set of spectacles is often referred to as our mental schema (Walsh, Henderson, and Deighton, 1988).

Cognitive psychology should, therefore, play a role in helping our understanding of decision-making groups. But, what sort of cognitive psychology? With what sort of focus? There are a number of important requirements for choosing a helpful theory of cognition that can inform group decision making and sense making. Most importantly the chosen theory of cognition should have practical implications for influencing the process of group decision making, and in particular making better decisions. We are also interested in decision making within an organizational setting where conversation is an important currency of organizational life. We regard the process of construal, giving meaning and making sense, as significant, and so we are interested in the processes of socially negotiating new meanings (Weick, 1995).

One body of cognitive psychology theory meets these requirements well. Personal Construct Theory, developed, explained, and used by George Kelly (Kelly, 1955) is undoubtedly helpful. Not only did Kelly develop and explain the theory but as a practitioner he made use of it. He used it by translating the theory, as best he could, into a technique he was able to use to understand how people construed their world. In essence Kelly was interested in how we made sense of the world *in order to act it*. He was also very interested in how that sense making changed. Therefore, he saw people as problem solvers (in his terms – 'scientists', experimenting and learning). He thought of people making sense of the world through the use of a system of constructs: these constructs enabled people to construct a definition of the situation they faced. It thus became important for him to learn about the constructs people used.

The technique he invented, called the *Repertory Grid* (Fransella and Bannister, 1977), was designed to elicit these constructs. Because he believed that we made sense of our world through contrast and similarity he reckoned that we would reveal constructs by articulating a view of the differences and similarities across a triad of elements. The elements could be people, objects, or other descriptors. For example, we might ask a production manager what she thought about three different markets within which her products were sold (the elements). She might respond by stating that Japan and Hong Kong tended to send products back for the tiniest of faults, whereas Italy was very accepting of products. The response suggests a single construct that is: send products back for the tiniest of faults, in contrast to very accepting. Having established an acceptable number of constructs (typically about 12) he was able to understand the relationship between these constructs, as a system, by seeing how a person used them with respect to each of the elements. The grid, therefore, captured a matrix of how each construct was used in relation to each element. An analysis of this matrix would allow a depiction of the relationships between the contructs – as a construct *system* (Bannister and Fransella, 1971). How people change their mind, thus, can be understood as the process of the construct *system* changing – the relationship between constructs, and through elaboration of the system – losing and gaining constructs.

This very brief introduction to personal construct theory is designed to set out some important principles that can be used to understand and influence decision making and problem solving. These principles are: group decision making involves each member of the group changing their mind; each member of the group seeks to manage the meanings attributed to aspects of the situation; meanings are derived from each person's unique construct system; meanings change as the construct system is changed and elaborated; meanings derive from making sense of the situation through contrast and similarity, and seeking explanations for the situation and understanding why it matters. In essence personal construct theory simply reflects the notion that 'if men define situations as real, they are real in their consequences' (Thomas and Thomas, 1928).

Although the use of Repertory Grids (and the later introduction of *Implication Grids*, Hinkle, 1965) introduced an instrument for listing personal constructs, it was hardly naturalistic. As members of a group discuss, argue, and make claims that seek to persuade others towards a particular course of action they do so through the use of arguments constructed using natural language. Although these arguments are not necessarily full in their explication of explanations and consequences, they do give clues. In particular, the personal values, goals, or objectives that are driving the arguments may not be made explicit. At the simplest level this may be because there is not enough time to state them before a person is interrupted. More subtly, personal values may be in conflict with occupational values and so a person may not want to make clear their goals, or they might not be sufficiently aware of them. Nevertheless, the arguments presented map out, in part, contrasts and similarities, explanations and articulated outcomes, that can give clues to goals or values that are sometimes implicit, not stated, and at other times unknown. Thus, rather than use grids to explicate a theory of personal constructs, it is likely to be more effective to record the way a person makes sense of a situation by seeking to understand how they suggest acting and why they believe these actions might be appropriate. In other words, directly apply the theory.

Sense making, misunderstandings, different meanings

We have discussed above the way that construal is related to giving meaning to constructs and that meaning is derived from making sense of the world *in order to act it* – that is, it is action oriented. Figure 9.1 shows an example of 'maps' of how two managers construe the need for 'increased motivation' in their organization. In discussion they may quickly agree that increasing motivation is critical for the future of their organization. However, if they were to expand on this apparent agreement we would see two very different action oriented meanings. If we were to listen carefully to their view of the current situation, one would be talking of motivation as against laziness (a unique contrast), and the other, motivation rather than no energy – they perceive different 'events' implying apparently the same response. However, after further discussion we understand they have different objectives: one focuses on service and errors, the other on creativity and retention of staff. Also each sees different types of actions that they believe would increase motivation: one sees the work environment and overtime rates as drivers, and the other 'softer' drivers.

Of course, it is possible through conversation that they might reach some mutual understanding where each changes their views (meanings) by encompassing the views of the other. This would lead to an elaboration of each other's construct system. In particular there is an important 'dialectic between the individuality of reality and reality as a "social construction" (see particularly Berger and Luckmann, 1966) in which meanings are "socially sustained" and experienced "as social facts" (Silverman, 1970) and it is this dialectic which gives rise to the complicated notion of intersubjectivity' (Eden, Jones, S., Sims, D., and Smithin, 1981: 40) and so encourages a negotiated meaning.

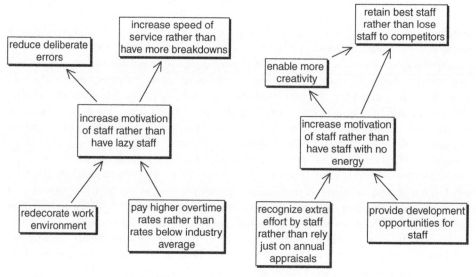

FIGURE 9.1 An example of different, action-oriented, meanings.

Another cause of misunderstanding is that a person might not be clear about what they think until they talk about it. As Huw Wheldon of the BBC said 'How can I know what I think until I hear what I say?' (quoted in David Attenborough (2002) *Life on the Air*, London: BBC Books, p. 216), and notably paraphrased by Weick as – 'how do I know what I think until I see how I act' (Weick, 1979). Seeking to persuade others can often enable a person to understand and develop their own views. Thus, misunderstandings arise because a person misunderstands themselves – their own thinking about an issue is muddled! So, a construct system is clarified, modified, and elaborated through the process of 'thinking out loud'. The process is annoying for others leading to accusations of 'you're always changing your mind' and 'that isn't what you said earlier'.

Contribution of operations research modelling: Qualitative models of a problem situation

Figure 9.1 introduced the idea of representing somebody making sense of their world by using a *causal map*. To the extent that the map represents somebody's thinking, it may be called a *cognitive map*. By representing causality (the arrows), they indicate how someone might envisage changing their world, and with what intent. Thus, a 'cognitive' map seeks to represent the beliefs and values of a person. The person's beliefs (causality: arrows) and constructs (nodes) are captured as a model of *a part of* the person's construct system.

In sympathy with personal construct theory the action orientation means that argumentation about issues is coded to reveal, or highlight, the implications for 'managing and controlling the future' through the way the issues are 'anticipated'. Arrows (illustrating chains of argument) show the implied possible actions and possible outcomes as suggested by the 'theories' a person uses to explain the world as they see it. In building the map, the central questions guiding the coding of the map are 'what are the implications of *using* the belief about the world as a basis for intervening in the world so as to protect or support values?' and 'what might explain or support the assertion?' (see Appendix 1 for the full set of mapping guidelines).

Presented assertions, or 'facts', about the nature of the world are assumed to have significance for the person. Thus, rather than an assertion being simply a statement of 'what is', understanding a person's construct system demands seeking to make sense of why the fact or assertion is presented. The map will show that assertions are taken to have consequences or implications. Thus, an assertion is elaborated by considering why the person is stating it – 'what does the person expect someone to do as a result of knowing the assertion?' For example, a person might assert that 'helping the customer solve problems is one important aspect of getting the right relationship instead of always treating the customer to a sales pitch, as some of our less intelligent sales staff do'. Another example might be when a person makes an assertion such as 'most of our customers are well qualified'. In each of these cases it becomes important to review the context of the assertion, within the holistic sense of the person's construal, to discover, and so state in the map, the way in which this statement is regarded as significant. Clues derive from other contextual statements such as those made above and others such as 'many of our salesmen can only discuss football – the last thing they might do is hold together a conversation about what's going on with the technology our customers deal with'. In each case the assertion implies consequences.

Perhaps the most interesting property of a cognitive map is the way in which it hints at, or expresses, a possible value system. Providing the map has been constructed properly, where means lead to valued ends and options for change lead to outcomes, then the top part of the map hierarchy might reveal the value *system* of the person. It is a system because it will usually be represented as a network of values – where each value informs others and is, in turn, informed by others. Thus, values will be defined both by the property of the words making up the construct and by the position of the construct within the hierarchy of values.

Constructing cognitive and causal maps of construal

We have implied above that the maps must always be written down artefacts. But, the principles of mapping can facilitate an understanding of how other people are making sense of situations by 'mapping in the head'. This process of mapping in the head allows a listener to understand better the way in which another person uniquely defines the situation.

We have been discussing the process of making sense as if we were only ever trying to understand how someone else makes sense of their world. Oftentimes we wish to try and help ourselves make sense of our own world and provide an opportunity for reflection. Constructing our own cognitive map, following the principle of 'how can I know what I think until I hear what I say?', can help us make sense of a situation as *we see it*. The formalities of causal mapping facilitate the construction of a cognitive map that helps develop an understanding of the situation we are facing. In doing so the map becomes a model – something that can be roughly analysed, because of its formal structure. This analysis provides a deeper understanding of the definition of the situation – at the simplest level the process of understanding the 'top' of the hierarchy as the best expression of values or goals is a form of analysis. The effectiveness of this analysis depends totally upon the creation of a map that follows the formality of option to outcome.

As we shall argue later, many failed decisions arise from an inadequate exploration and understanding of the goals we seek to attain, or the values that drive action. Because the principles of mapping explore meanings, personal values gradually emerge from the exploration of why we see the situation as problematic. The process of using a map for self reflection often leads us to 'finishing' with a problem rather than feeling a need to solve it (Eden, 1987). The map may help us understand that the situation we feel to be problematic does not in fact attack values that really matter to us, or the situation is more manageable than we had thought (see Bryson, Ackermann, Eden, and Finn, 2004: chapters 3–5 for examples of self reflection maps).

Figure 9.2 shows an example of developing thinking about a situation through mapping. The numbers indicate the order in which statements arose. Links with a –ve sign attached to them show how one assertion drives out the opposite of another

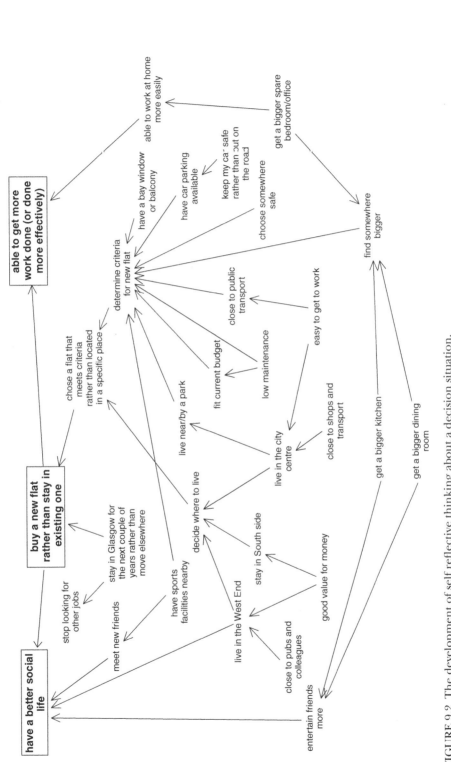

FIGURE 9.2 The development of self reflective thinking about a decision situation.

Reprinted from Visible Thinking, Bryson et al., 2004

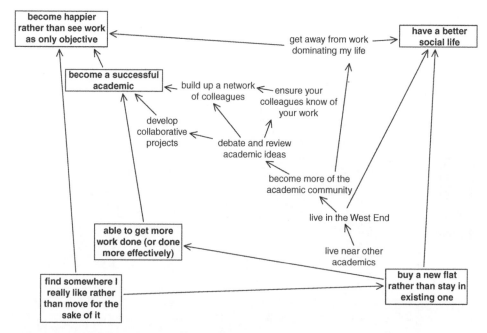

FIGURE 9.3 An example of mapping consequences of options to conflicting values.
Reprinted from Visible Thinking, Bryson *et al*, 2004

assertion. Figure 9.3 shows how conflicting values become clearer and show why the situation is problematic for the person elaborating the map.

The process of self reflective mapping may indicate that the situation that concerns us is indeed too complex for simple solutions. Real decision-making situations that have important consequences are invariably complex situations. There are usually multiple and conflicting objectives. And there is no right answer, but rather, better answers. Recipes can rarely be used to determine the solution to problems. Difficult situations are riddled with personalities, politics, and power. So-called rational solutions are impossible to implement because the people involved in implementation are never as perfect as in an ideal world. In these circumstances, it is possible that we might wish to involve others in helping us to resolve the situation by offering their expertise, by offering alternative perspectives, by involving them so that they are more likely to satisfactorily implement a solution. In other words, group decision making becomes the appropriate way of addressing the problem situation.

In the remaining parts of this chapter we consider a number of important aspects of group decision making that build on this use of mapping:

- managing multiple perspectives: developing a group definition;
- gaining substantive outcomes from group mapping – the process outcomes and input to *negotiating* the definition of the situation;

- ◆ managing the complexity of decision situations by understanding structure: complexity derives from interdependent decision areas (clusters – busyness); and by goal *systems* (hierarchy);
- ◆ enabling politically feasible agreements: what is a group?;
- ◆ and negotiating agreements.

In the next section, we focus on the implications, and reasons for, seeking out multiple perspectives.

MULTIPLE PERSPECTIVES

Organization theorists realize that organizations do not have mechanisms separate from individuals to set goals, process information, or perceive the environment. People do these things. The distinctive feature of organizational-level information activity is sharing. A piece of data, a perception, a cognitive map, is shared among managers who constitute the interpretation system. Passing a startling observation among members, or discussing a puzzling development, enables managers to converge on an approximate interpretation. Managers may not fully agree about their perceptions (Starbuck 1976), but the thread of coherence among managers is what characterizes organizational interpretations. Reaching convergence among members characterizes the act of organizing (Weick, 1979).

The above notwithstanding, it is to state the obvious that members of a team have different perspectives on any apparently similar situation! Indeed the main purpose of having a team is to bring to bear different perspectives on any problem. Typically in a commercial organization, for example, we would expect the finance person to have a different view from the production person, from the marketing person, etc. We expect them to bring to the discussion different experiences and different expert knowledge, as well as different personal stances.

However, oftentimes we get upset by the complexity that arises from hearing views different from our own view. Consequently we close down discussion that might enable different perspectives to surface. And, of course, we close down discussion because we want our own view to prevail.

Multiple perspectives can provide a significant potential for ensuring that possible promising options are not missed, that beneficial outcomes can be realized, and undesirable outcomes protected against. But, at the cost of increased complexity and the surfacing of personally disagreeable views that might lead to decisions we do not approve of.

However, to further complexify the situation, it is not enough that one member sees an external signal in order for the organization to be able to take appropriate action. Organizational action requires a critical mass of agreement; therefore weak signals must first enter the conversation before they can be acted upon. Without the individual mental models of members in the organization having a degree of overlap strategic conversation is not possible, and the signal does not enter the 'collective consciousness'. At the end of this road lies fragmentation which leads to paralysis due to lack of basic agreement on what things mean, and therefore what needs to be done.

Institutions can use the diversity in mental models of their members to extend their zone of proximal development, and in doing so see and perceive more. Differentiation in thinking increases the range of vision of the group.

If multiple perspectives are surfaced and discussed then a process of both social and psychological negotiation might occur. Two aspects of negotiation in a group are particularly important (Eden and Ackermann, 1998: 48–49): the creation of a new negotiated social order (NSO) where the relationships between team members change, and a new socially negotiated order (SNO) where the conversations and behaviours of team members lead to a new situation – aspects of the problem situation change as a result of agreements and actions that seek to change things. This negotiation *may* lead to a level of consensus that allows for coordination and cooperation in the implementation of a decision.

But, there is an important pathology in organizational cognition – Group Think. Group think is associated with the consequences of a group's need for cohesion, alignment of ideas, pressure towards uniformity, and so suppression of dissent. In contrast – differentiation allows for heterogeneity of opinions, airing views, and not closing too quickly

Although Janis (1972; 1989) is the key writer about group think, Harrison (1987) usefully added to the dangers of group think by discussing the following failures: belief in group morality disregards ethical consequences, outsiders are stereotyped (for example, evil, weak, stupid), sense of invulnerability in the group, over rationalization that leads to ignoring warnings, a felt threat of being seen as disloyal silences people, doubts about group wisdom suppressed, assumptions that silence signifies agreement, and information held back to protect cohesion.

There is a significant dilemma here for organizations. There is a need to develop differentiation for perception and awareness, but also integration for organizational dissemination and action (Eden and Ackermann, 1998: 48). But while developing differentiation there is a danger of fragmentation, and while developing integration there is a danger of group think. Thus if a group is left to its own devices it may move to either extreme: fragmentation, and action paralysis, or group think, and boxed-in mental models resulting in poor perception.

For the manager, in amongst her team, there is a further dimension that matters. A manager would like to have high levels of ownership of the decision outcome. To gain ownership she needs to attend to what is known as 'procedural justice' (Korsgaard, Schweiger, and Sapienza, 1995; Kim and Mauborgne, 1995; Thibaut and Walker, 1975): providing team members with an opportunity to express their views and be listened to. Team members are significantly more likely to go along with the decision if they believe that the process of reaching it was fair and just. This means implementation is likely to be more effective. Thus attending to multiple perspectives opens up the problem and makes it less likely that important options are missed, demonstrates procedural justice and so increases the chance of effective implementation, decreases the chance of misunderstandings, but on the other hand significantly increases complexity. Opening up the issue means the group can address the problem of limiting the search (Nutt, 2002: 43). The complexity from conflicting claims means there will need to be a process issue of reconciliation. Failure to reconcile claims – negotiation – leads to poor ownership and poor implementation (see Nutt, 2002: 24–25).

Developing a group problem definition

Most significantly the above considerations suggest a total lack of separation between process and content in seeking to surface multiple perspectives. Without addressing process issues it is unlikely that multiple perspectives will be made explicit. Thus, in developing a group problem definition attention must be paid to achieving both substantive and process outcomes – where process outcomes are an end in themselves but also significantly influence the extent to which substantive outcomes can be achieved.

Substantive Outcomes:

- Surface multiple perspectives: the issues (both positive and negative) that reflect current and future potential concerns of the group's participants with respect to the situation.
- Structure the resultant issues in a hierarchical structure by understanding how one issue might support, or be supported by another – building a group map – 'if you buy into a claim without understanding its motivating concerns, you can misdirect effort' (Nutt, 2002: 62).
- Elaborate the group map by building on the views of others and 'explaining yourself' through causality.
- Detect patterns within the resultant hierarchical group map to reveal emergent properties.
- Enabling a more 'creative' and shared outcome.

Process Outcomes:

- Address the realities of life – individuals have their own concerns/issues and will claim that these are the important ones for the group to address. These issues are a part of their individual perspectives on the situation. This attends to the need to 'understand claims' (Nutt, 2002: 42).
- Catharcism – a release of anger, tension, and frustration – 'getting an opportunity to make your point' and so move on.
- 'Open up the problem and avoid edicts' (Nutt, 2002: xx). Encouraging divergence before a process of convergence begins.
- Listening – gain ownership of the issues from the entire group – as members are involved in the process and therefore more committed to the outcomes.
- An appreciation of 'fairness'.
- Shared understanding and joint learning.
- Self reflection.
- Developing relationships to enable continuing joint working.

DEVELOPING A GROUP DEFINITION:
SUBSTANTIVE OUTCOMES FROM GROUP MAPPING

Group mapping can be seen as similar to brainstorming in seeking to surface contributions from all those attending. However, group mapping used for group decision making has a number of important differences from brainstorming. To begin with the focus is on surfacing issues and concerns – usually those activities or events that are potentially attacking or supporting aspirations – rather than on creativity as an aim in its own right. The aim is to surface current wisdom and experience rather than 'off-the-wall' ideas.

Starting with issues enables group participants to put on the table the events, activities, and concerns that they expect will demand their attention and time and will have an impact on dealing with the situation as they see it (the realities of organizational life). This not only gets at what is seen to be important – as these issues are the focus of attention – but also allows group participants to experience some relief as they bring them out into the open and can begin to explore and understand them (another important difference from brainstorming). Until these are openly presented and discussed, attention on the rest of the decision-making processes will be clouded by their continual presence, as group participants seek to find ways of making coherent links between their day-to-day concerns and the future. Realistic group decision making thus starts with issue surfacing.

Group mapping encompasses not only the surfacing of issues, but also assumptions, concerns, facts, assertions, and constraints along with their relationships. This enables the material to be structured by reflecting causality (a key difference from traditional brainstorming). As we discussed above, structuring through causal mapping gives meaning to each statement by setting it within a context: why it matters (consequences), and what needs to be done to change it (explanations). Instead of interpreting the statement by reference to a dictionary, meaning is determined by action and purpose. Encouraging participants to avoid arguing over the precision of the words and concentrate instead on the action context of a statement helps with the development of a shared understanding. It provides some clarity in terms of next steps – answering the 'so what?' question – and so further *elaborates the map*.

The process of detecting how issues impact upon one another is found by most participants to be an activity that they can easily relate to – this is because we all use causality in order to make sense of our world. Group mapping thus aims to release deep knowledge and wisdom to get beyond the apparently similar descriptions of situations and into the subtle, but important, differences of what has to be done and why. The process raises alternative formulations and therefore opens up new options and new understandings.

Causal mapping provides a structure to the merging of perspectives and avoids the danger of reducing the complexity by focusing on a small number of considerations. Group maps comprising in excess of 100 issues (claims) can represent effectively a merging of the views of many people.

The network's ability to help groups become more creative by not having to close down avenues of thought avoids the dangers of a limited search and no innovation (quick fix) (Nutt, 2002: 33). By seeing the different concerns and their context in one structured space participants are able to build on the views, adapt ideas, and as a group craft possible new solutions. This opening up of the situation facilitates *creativity*. In essence the members of the group are 'piggy backing' off one another (Shaw, 2003). In addition, the process supports negotiation towards an agreed decision as the 'device' of the causal map, with its inherent ability to act as a visual interactive model, allows changes to be made – as group members amend, adapt, and extend different ideas giving rise to decisions that contain elements of many of those involved rather than just one.

Finally, the process of explicating the relationships allows the group to move from a set of divergent perspectives to a more shared understanding. The process of not just surfacing the issue but also capturing the consequences of the issue and some of its explanatory text enables both added value in terms of managing the complexity and additional insight and learning. The process of linking issues or risks together also helps those participating to gain a better understanding of the whole picture rather than their own idiosyncratic part. As such not only is a better understanding derived from seeing the whole and thus a better outcome but a better appreciation of the organization's context is also elicited. Participants learn more about the full situation.

Contribution of operational research modelling: Introducing the contribution gained from using a Group Support System (GSS)

The use of a Group Support System (GSS) enables group participants to enter their claims/issues/concerns directly into a developing set of views about the situation through the use of an individual laptop computer that is a part of a computer network of other laptops that are the input device for other participants. As well as seeing their own contributions on their laptop, the system, using a data projector, shows all of the contributions on a public screen and does so without any reference to the proponent (see Figure 9.4).

There are three well established GSSs: *Group Systems* (Nunamaker, Dennis, Valacich, and Vogel, 1991) which organizes ideas, *Group Explorer* (Ackermann and Eden, 2001) which uses causal maps, and *Meetingworks* (Lewis, 1993; 2010) which evaluates options against multiple criteria. The data capture and structuring processes differ with some working off lists and categories and others adopting a more graphical form of representation such as the use of causal mapping. Each uses similar equipment, namely individual participant laptops, a computer as a 'server', a central computer with projector, and either a wireless or wired local area network.

The use of a GSS encourages divergence, and openness in contribution. However, in addition the systems enable the group to move between the periods of divergence supported by the anonymous contributions, and periods of convergence where the interconnections between contributions are discussed, amendments made, and further elaboration captured – the beginnings of a group problem definition. This helps manage the two different pressures mentioned above – the anonymity facility manages the conformity or social pressures, and the convergence stage through its discursive focus facilitates the shared development of views.

FIGURE 9.4 A Group Support System in use showing participants with networked laptops, and public screen displaying their developing causal map.

However, developing a group problem definition depends upon being able to get a group together. Later in this chapter we consider the issues in choosing group membership, but here we consider the issues of getting a group 'around the table'. Intended participants may not wish to be involved due to, for example, time constraints. For many the call to 'yet another meeting' leads to excuses for not attending. Finding more productive ways of managing meetings can set a climate where there is a higher likelihood of attendance. The well proven productivity gains that are possible through the use of a GSS can be an important incentive to group decision making and to enlarging the group size. A GSS allows group participants to 'speak' simultaneously. The additional air time gained allows quieter members to contribute to defining the situation. It also enables each participant to more carefully craft their point of view – expressing it in a way that more thoughtfully reflects their concerns. A GSS, in effect, creates a 'safe space' (Nutt, 2002: 148) that enables increased creativity as well as more openness without the potential for social punishments arising from alternative views being expressed.

The use of a GSS enables the group causal map to become the group definition of the situation. The developing map can be in continual transition because the GSS facilities allow continuous editing of both statements and arrows as the meeting progresses. In addition, the use of a computer-based system creates a developing group memory – a continuously created set of minutes that are produced by the group rather than by a single individual.

Figure 9.5 illustrates, through a real example, the initial collecting of views as they are scattered across the public screen. In this case the group were invited to 'dump' views before suggesting causal links. Figure 9.6 shows the first stage of transition to a cause map. Although the figure shows a very complicated set of links that could be displayed with fewer crossing arrows, the group participants are able to work with the map's apparent messiness because the map grew gradually through their own interaction with it. The group subsequently, and gradually, 'tidy up' the display.

Needless to say, much of the above can be attained using a non-computer supported GSS. The maps can be created through using 'post-its', 'hexagons', 'ovals', or 'sno-cards' (see Bryson, Ackermann, Eden, and Finn, 1995; Eden and Ackermann, 1998; Hodgson, 1994; Nutt and Backoff, 1992) to capture the different views. These can then be linked with hand drawn arrows (see Figure 9.7). Whilst this way of working reduces the demand on resources, anonymity of views is more difficult to achieve – although providing identical pens does help. Manual methods also make the transition from a set of individual views to a group held view difficult as editing is tedious and changing arrows messy.

THE PROCESS OUTCOMES AND INPUT TO NEGOTIATING THE DEFINITION OF THE SITUATION

In the previous section we considered the substantive outcomes from group mapping. We acknowledged that the development of substantive content is influenced by the designed process, and similarly the group decision making success is influenced by process outcomes. Content management and process management are integrally related (Eden, 1990). In this section we focus on some of the important process issues in group decision making.

Ensuring 'procedural justice'

Adopting a procedurally just process is expected to increase the likelihood of an increase in ownership of the outcomes and subsequently implementation of the outcomes that might occur.

Procedural justice focuses on the 3 Es of (i) clear *explanations* of the decision-making processes, (ii) setting realistic *expectations*, and (iii) ensuring *engagement* (Kim and Mauborgne, 1995). Clear explanations and the setting of expectations encompass not only what will occur and what are the objectives but also who will be involved and why.

Managing explanations and expectations is relevant during the meeting and also at the beginning of the meeting when the rules of engagement are made clear. However, establishing and communicating realistic expectations prior to getting participants together is also important (Eden and Ackermann, 1998: 55). The process of providing clear expectations and explanations are a part of well established facilitation practices (Ackermann, 1996; Phillips and Phillips, 1993).

29 deal with uncertain but GROWING dementia - future demographics

8 resource shortage - ageing population versus diminishing workforce and finite resources

20 expected changes in family and societal structures

49 recognise the changing the expectations of the "caring agencies"

10 reduce reliance on GPs for access to services

16 increase the possibilities of early access for carers to services and support

39 resolve difficulties around early diagnosis & support where diagnosis is uncertain

51 gather and make better use of statistics, activity levels and demographics to plan appropriate services

3 ensure expected development keeps pace with demographic change

37 appropriate recognition, support and services for carers

22 meet increased User/Carer expectations

40 information and education for carers

12 greater availability of specialist dementia care

33 debate the BALANCE of provision of specialist vs well supported generic services

46 secure clarity of 7 gain more funding funding, transparency re budgets, managing the budget with increasing demand

34 use more imaginative approaches to funding including private sector

42 increasing numbers of people with dementia in the future

32 reduce delays in accessing home care services

59 deliver range of care options to a dispersed population in a rural area

35 reduce waiting times specialist health services

13 equity of service both specialist and generic support

52 lack of on-going input after diagnosis

44 more emphasis on information, early diagnosis and supportive services

11 provide more support in early stages of disease

63 dementia becomes part of older person's services -

27 public understanding-access to info, overcoming stigma

18 dementia regarded as poor relation of Mental/Physical Illhealth and Social Care services

56 support and supervision for frontline staff/carers

53 develop robust systems to ensure the safety and wellbeing of vulnerable adults

62 Capacity of SW teams to assess and deliver services

21 good detailed multi-disciplinary assessments to ensure complex needs are met

24 respond and manage the needs and impact of patients with dementia in general & community hospitals

54 develop new models of care for people with dementia- rehab, intermediate care

61 STOP inadequate choice of a variety of good quality long term care homes in all areas

25 continuing care aspires to/ provides more than custodial care

28 training and development to enable enlightened care, more community across organisations

23 provide robust specialist training packages for staff

6 develop clear shared objectives 41 shared vision are where we want to go talking about the with dementia same thing services

38 communications across the organisation [which], particularly from management, more bottom up

31 increase ability of care homes to respond to both physical and behavioural problems

47 services work in partnership to provide holistic support to users and carers

48 more holistic and person centred approach to meeting integrated care needs

30 deliver comprehensive range of services that are reliable and flexible- home care long term care

19 promoting knowledge, skills and understanding amongst service providers, family carers and the public

58 monitor and review appropriateness of service provision and ability to change if not working

26 improve skills in care home sector

9 overcome culture differences

57 (dare to) review building based services and dispose of what isn't needed

45 increase feeling of shared responsibility for range of services between SWD and NHS

5 availability of good and varied dementia care in the Borders

17 broadening the range of accommodation options for people with dementia

50 disregard the assumption that everyone wants to stay at home isn't necessarily right

60 don't be inhibited by what we have now as a basis for planning - aspire to what we need

36 improve seamless working- broadening assessment, IT, full integration

15 less bureaucracy more seamless pathway for people - agreeing the pathway

43 develop systems of care which respond to the changing needs of PWD with the minimum of disruption and the maximum well-being

55 improving working systems between statutory services and the private sector

64 respect the rights of PWD to be treated with dignity and to have the same choices of care provision to maintain their abilities

14 increase quality of care in private sector

65 deal with underperforming care providers

FIGURE 9.5 Initial views from a group of 10 participants (after 22 minutes) – reference numbers in front of statements show the order in which these surfaced.

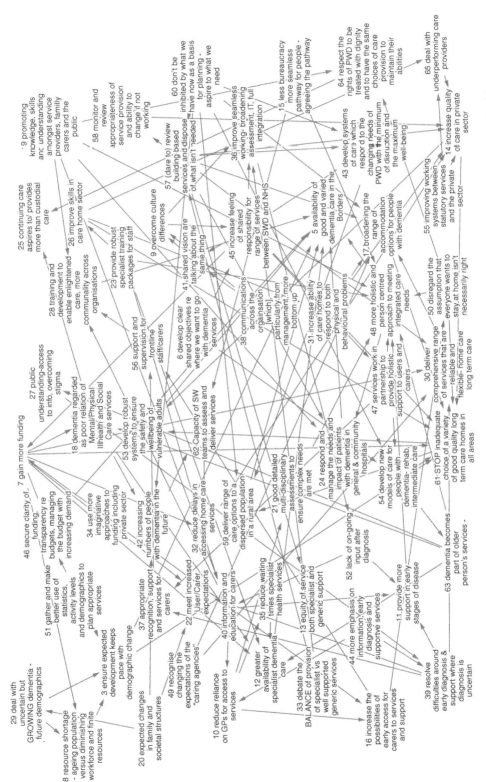

FIGURE 9.6 Developing a group definition through causal linking – the first stage after 37mins of surfacing statements and linking.

FIGURE 9.7 Using a technology free 'Group Support System'.

The significance of engagement

However, the third 'E' – that of engagement – is a significant consideration in the provision of group support through good facilitation and, when possible, the use of a Group Support System.

Engagement depends, in part, on the ability to express views that are thought to be important for others to consider. One of the well established inhibitors to raising issues, claims, and counterclaims are concerns about the consequences of conformity pressures. These pressures are encapsulated in the theories of Risky Shift (Stoner, 1968), Group Think (Janis, 1989), and the Abilene Paradox (Harvey, 1988). All describe situations where the 'decision makers are silent about their concerns' (Nutt, 2002: 25). Engagement and procedural justice also demand ensuring that those attending get listened to effectively rather than only one or two members dominating the air space. Providing a means for allowing all to speak simultaneously ensuring contributions can be heard and captured ensures this demand is met.

There are a number of different facilitation methods for reducing the likelihood of these behavioural problems. One well used method is the Nominal Group Technique (Delbecq, Van de Ven, and Gustafson, 1975) where each member contributes their views independently of one another and then considers the whole before contributing further. Other facilitation methods include the *Delphi technique* (Dalkey and Helmer, 1963; Van de Ven and Delbecq, 1974) and *Brainwriting* (Buzan & Buzan, 1993) (also see von Oech, 1982).

These processes however can often be lengthy and do not lead to a particularly integrated and well understood representation.

The contribution from group support: Facilitation and/or Group Support System (GSS)

One of the major gains from using a GSS is not only the ability to allow those involved to be able to speak 'simultaneously' but also anonymously. As such participants can surface anything that they consider an issue or risk without being concerned by conformity pressures (Jessup and Valacich, 1993). Anonymity reduces the tendency towards conformity. Anonymity reinforces the provision of a 'safe space' in which participants are able to risk expressing views that they might judge to be 'out-on-a-limb'. In addition, although group participants might assert that they can 'guess' which of them contributed particular statements, our experience suggests that these guesses are often wrong and that participants can therefore be more open in their views. Consequently, not only is there likely to be a greater range of views presented but also there will be less need for participants to feel concerned about the need to defend their views. The GSS reduces the likelihood of decisions being 'failure prone because defensiveness is stirred up by the problem' (Nutt, 2002: 122).

Whether dysfunctional pressures on group participants exist or are just perceived to exist is of no concern – they have the same effect of a reduction in engagement. Moreover, not only does directly entering the contributions into the GSS help surface a wide range of views but also viewing a wide range of perspectives on a public screen facilitates psychological and social negotiation. Separating the proponent from the contribution and allowing a claim to be viewed in its own right rather than 'claims being offered according to their proponents' leverage' (Nutt, 2002: 25) helps build a more comprehensive and robust understanding.

As the contributions – claims – from group participants are made and viewed, new views – often the amalgam of existing views – are created by participants. This gives rise to streams of argument that are 'owned' by more than one member of the group as they are a combined product. This process of amalgamation and 'piggybacking' helps reduce the likelihood of falling into the trap where 'pressure goads you into selecting among competing claims instead of finding concerns suggesting a claim all could agree to' (Nutt, p. 76).

The use of natural language as the basis of modelling facilitates a positive role for equivocality. Equivocality in this sense means the provision of sufficient degrees of 'fuzziness' to encourage negotiation. The fuzziness allows for gentle shifts in thinking and positions that are imperceptible to others (and sometimes to the participant themselves). This transitional process is more likely when the modelling process is visually interactive and so the publicly displayed causal map becomes a 'transitional object' (de Geus, 1988; Winnicott, 1953).

The map projected on a public screen allows participants to have time to 'mentally pause' rather than feeling pressured to respond emotionally to face-to-face and verbal communication. This avoids the 'knee jerk' – often poorly considered – response being made public. For example, a particular perspective being put forward by one participant flies in the face of the views of another. However, because there is less pressure to respond immediately the member who disagrees is able to listen more to the contribution, and as the mapping process reveals the context, appreciate in more depth the contribution and its value. As a result, it might be that the potential antagonist is either persuaded or at least sees merit in the views of the other member. In addition, by not contradicting or arguing publicly the member is able to change their mind imperceptibly to the rest of the group and thus avoid the issue of being stuck defending a position that they may no longer subscribe to. They are thus able to listen better. This reduces the likelihood of group members responding physiologically with a solely emotional rather than cognitive response and therefore being caught in the position of having to defend (or back down from) a view that, after hearing more of the discussion, they no longer wish to hold.

The brief vignette (Figure 9.8) exemplifies the role of a GSS in tackling the process issues discussed above.

A sticky problem faced the newly appointed Chief Executive. . . . The organization he was managing was a new merged composite of two previous organizations. However, as with many mergers the combined Top Management Team (TMT) was proving to be unmanageable – a consequence of including TMT members from both organizations. It was simply too big to work! This situation was not helped by the fact that members were geographically spread around the country, and that some TMT members disliked to varying degrees other members. Each meeting was a battlefield. He needed to reduce the size – but how could he make this decision in a manner that would be supported by the other members?

He was aware that many of the other TMT members felt the same, that there was a shared sense of frustration but that no-one wanted to raise the issue for fear of causing offence, being penalized, or ridiculed. He needed a way to involve his TMT that allowed the issues to be surfaced but not publicly. One late afternoon, whilst talking with a friend over a beer, he mentioned the situation. His friend suggested he use a Group Support System which allowed members to anonymously state their concerns but would also through using a public screen provide the means of viewing the various contributions. This way the issues could be 'put on the table' and discussed more openly. This sounded ideal.

The Chief Exec set about arranging for a meeting with the TMT to be held using the GSS (on a neutral site). The session would start with anonymous gathering of views before focussing on how the different contributions supported/influenced one another. A more comprehensive *and owned* picture would emerge. The process would switch between
periods of time spent generating material anonymously and periods of time working together on structuring – helping to weave the different views together and develop a sense of shared understanding. A full and frank (well as much as was possible) discussion could be held.

FIGURE 9.8 Anonymity to the rescue! – a vignette.

Another way of surfacing different claims and appreciating different viewpoints comes from using 'role-think' (Eden and Ackermann, 1998: 133). Here group members may be separated into subgroups and asked to consider the possible perspectives emerging from the point of view of a stakeholder different from themselves. For example, when considering some of the options open to a police force, senior decision makers took on the role of 'disenfranchised youth', 'vulnerable elderly community', and 'local politicians'.

Figure 9.9 shows an example of the police beginning to 'role-think' the issues the police should address through the eyes of the elderly.

Group definition of the situation and options for resolving it gradually develop when, although there is not an expectation of agreement, there is likely to be more agreement about the nature of the situation, with each participant having elaborated their own views (constructs). In this way 'trans-subjective knowledge' is created (Ward, 1920).

As we acknowledged earlier, paying attention to multiple perspectives is expected to increase an awareness of the complexity of the situation. This complexity can be debilitating for the group (Eden *et al.*, 1981):

> [T]he need to take account of intersubjectivity seems overwhelming. It is also clear that the deliberate attempt that it involves to address complexity can appear both to a consultant and members of teams to be a debilitating process, the outcome of which can be potentially destructive to a team. Most particularly an awareness of complexity can sap the desire or felt capacity to act. The world is complicated enough, it may be argued, without seeking to make even more of the complexity explicit and, thus, even more of the difficulties of acting effectively in the world apparent. This is particularly so when whatever one does can be simulated to have both good and bad consequences for somebody in the team. Encouraging members of a team to listen both caringly and analytically to each other is inevitably consuming of both time and energy. (p. 43)

Increasing complexity, if encouraged, must be managed. If it can be managed then it will more likely be encouraged. In the next two sections we address two powerful ways of managing, rather than reducing, complexity: through analysis of the structure of the map and so generating overviews without losing richness, and through categorization of the map content.

Using the mapping hierarchy that implies options seeking to address decision areas which in turn supports goals (purpose) (see Figure 9.10) suggests a categorization of decision areas (a variety of 'clustered' views of the situation, and of goals or purpose and direction).

In the next two sections we are not just seeking to manage complexity for its own sake, but also enabling a structure for reaching agreements: ideally seeking to resolve each of the interacting decision areas and doing so with a goal orientation.

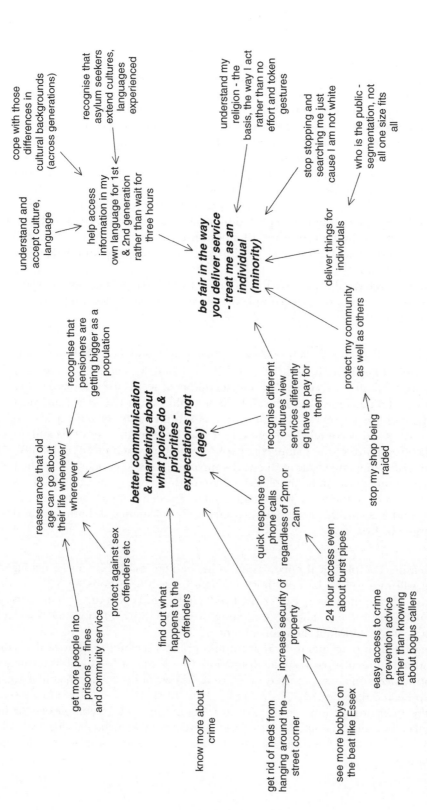

FIGURE 9.9 Using 'role think' to extend perspectives – the imagined views of the elderly.

FIGURE 9.10 The structure of options, decision areas, and goals.

MANAGING THE COMPLEXITY OF DECISION SITUATIONS BY UNDERSTANDING STRUCTURE: COMPLEXITY DERIVES FROM INTERDEPENDENT DECISION AREAS

Complexity and the ability to address it, rather than pretend it does not exist, is an important component for decision making. Cognitive complexity is seen as one way of addressing complex situations. But what do we mean by complex situations? The sorts of situations of interest to us in this chapter are those where the word 'problem' is an inadequate descriptor. Issues that are complex are made up of many problems. Some have referred to these issues as 'wicked problems' (Rittel and Webber, 1973) and 'messy' problems (Ackoff, 1981), and others call them a problematique (Ozbekhan, 1974). Wicked problems are a network of interacting and interconnected decision areas (Friend and Hickling, 1987).

But how do we identify these interconnected decision areas? The easiest and per- haps most common way of doing this is to collect statements and organize them in to thematic headings. So, for example, in a commercial organization we might use the well established thematic headings of finance, operations, human resource management, etc., and allocate each statement to one of these headings. However, by doing so, we ignore the action orientation implied by the way in which people make statements in order to persuade others to act in particular ways. In causal map- ping this is reflected through the linkage between statements – the arrows. There is no a priori reason why the links between claims and proposed actions should be thematic. Indeed, there is a reasonable expectation that messy problems involve implications across many themes.

The network of linked statements will have structural properties – clusters – where statements are tightly linked to each other and yet relatively isolated from other tightly linked statements. In the extreme these clusters may be 'islands', implying that within the situation there are a series of independent problems. In such an extreme case each problem can be dealt with as if they were separate enti- ties, having no implications for one another. However, because this is not a typical situation, at the very least, attention to multiple perspectives will have generated intersubjectivity and so interdependence. Nevertheless, in order to help manage complexity, and the potentially debilitating nature of it, identifying interacting clusters is likely to be helpful to the group. It is difficult to attend to the requirement that 'best practice calls for a comparison of competing ideas to select the one that comes closest to providing the hoped for results' (Nutt, 2002: 58) without seeking to manage complexity.

Thus, identifying clusters is, in itself, problematic because there are many ways of doing so. Using a simple, and visually attractive, way of doing so, rather than a more statistically 'accurate but opaque' method, can avoid arguments within the group about what the clusters should be rather than addressing the substantive situation. As groups gradually identify a group definition of the situation, using a causal map, they easily and naturally identify with 'busy' parts of the map – some statements have many links with other statements.

Interacting decision areas: 'busyness' and an overview

The mapping process not only facilitates examination of the issues (claims) but also how they impact upon one another. The map provides a structure which is amenable to analysis. Thus, those issues that are 'central' or 'busy' (Bryson *et al.*, 2004; Eden, 2004) gain significance in terms of their importance as the numerous relationships either linking into or out of them suggest that paying attention to the central statements and the statements linked to them is likely to be important in resolving at least one aspect of the situation.

Nevertheless, it is difficult to identify a theoretically robust body of argument about why busyness should correlate with importance. Indeed, a single isolated statement (minimum busyness) may describe the most important part of the situation. And it may be most important simply because nobody in the group has been able to elaborate its explanations and consequences! However, as we shall see below, at least a crude form of cluster analysis would identify this isolated statement as one of many problems making up the definition of the situation.

Figure 9.11 shows how, in a real example, identifying a range of busy statements can provide an easy and early indication of the situation described as a system of interdependent problems. Focusing attention, temporarily, on the busy statements and the network of interconnections between them provides an initial overview of the defined complex situation. Thus, Figure 9.12, illustrates this overview of the more complex problem definition shown in Figure 9.11. In this overview, the links between the busy statements represent a path of causality, a sequence of arguments, existing between the busy statements.

Interacting decision areas: problem clusters and an overview

The notion of interacting decision areas was noted earlier: 'the "problem" to be solved was in fact a whole series of "nested" problems, each alternative solution to a problem at one level leading to a new set of problems at the next level' (Cyert, Simon, and Trow, 1956: 247).

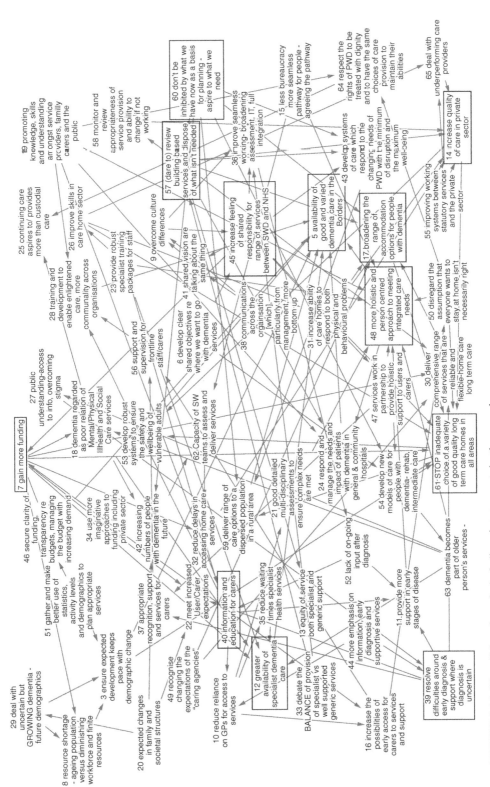

FIGURE 9.11 Identifying the relatively 'busy' statements in the causal map.

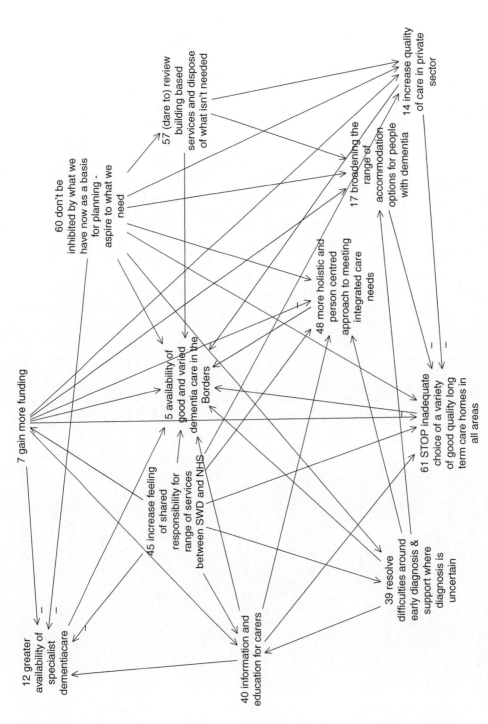

FIGURE 9.12 An overview of the issue map shown in Figure 9.11 based on link paths between 'busy' statements.

Using busy statements as a way of indicating possible interdependent problems is an intuitively attractive way of establishing the nesting of problems. However, simply working with the visually attractive 'busy' statements is to ignore other statements that are beyond one level of explanation in consequence. The identification of clusters of statements, where each cluster is small enough to ensure that the group is not overwhelmed by debilitating complexity, provides for an alternative way of identifying interacting problems. Inevitably, each cluster is highly likely to encompass at least one busy statement. But, importantly, the labelling of the cluster will be derived from the total content of the cluster, rather than simply from the busy statements. The interdependence of these clusters derives from the links ('bridges') between them.

The process of a group identifying and labelling clusters is an important part of the group participants listening to one another. By asking the group to suggest clusters, each participant will listen to others through the process of reading statements other than those contributed by themselves. Nevertheless, as we suggested above, there is a danger that the group argues unproductively about the clusters rather than the substance of the situation. But, the process of identifying an overview is also a crucial part of defining the situation.

Dynamic interactions: the significance of vicious, virtuous, and self-correcting cycles

Recognizing the interdependence of problems leads to the possibility of problems being connected so that they feed off each other. Looking at the network's structure will reveal whether there are self-sustaining feedback cycles where potentially vicious or virtuous dynamic behaviour might be a significant description of part of the problem. The complexity of a situation is typically increased considerably when there are dynamic behaviours in the situation, and whilst these might not be not understood, they are felt. Identifying and understanding the cycles, when they exist, can make a significant contribution to managing complexity and the situation.

Sometimes one group participant will seek to persuade others that a vicious or virtuous cycle exists. However, more typically the group begins to realize the existence of a self-sustaining situation through the merging of the beliefs of a number of participants. The identification of a feedback loop in this way does not necessarily imply the group participants can agree about whether the self-sustaining nature of the feedback is vicious or virtuous. Viciousness or virtuousness is a point of view, whereas the existence of self-sustaining feedback may be agreed by all.

The existence of feedback is likely to be of significance for the group. Two possibilities for feedback exist: positive or self-sustaining feedback – either as a vicious cycle or virtuous cycle; and negative controlling feedback – where any action taken results in a tendency for the situation to return to its original state. Feedback is of significance because it represents the potential for dynamics in the situation – changes over time.

Figure 9.12 shows a real example of a group considering how to react to increasing demands on the police. The figure shows 10 feedback loops that represent

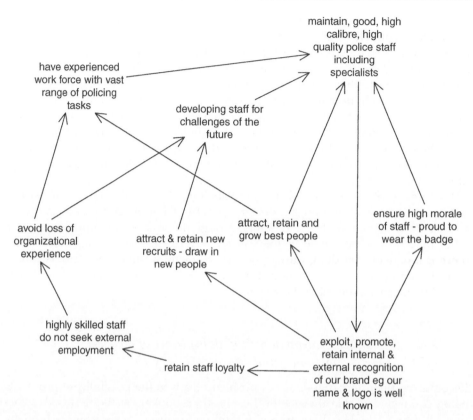

FIGURE 9.13 Feedback – a real example of a group considering how to react to increasing demands on the police.

virtuous self-sustaining cycles. These loops were not obvious or easily apparent to the group. Notably they realized, from the summary map (Figure 9.12), that the causal link from 'maintain high quality staff' to 'recognition of the brand' drives all of the loops. This realization, of course, became obvious to the group after they had noticed it!

In complicated messy situations the identification and realization of feedback can be difficult. Even though a causal map, as opposed to other representations, will be more likely to capture feedback, it may not be identified. As we have seen, the causal map which represents multiple perspectives is likely to be complex. Identifying feedback through visual inspection is often impossible.

The contribution of operations research modelling

The existence of feedback loops implies a dynamic. These dynamics can be modelled quantitatively by using simulation modelling techniques. The behaviour of these dynamics can often be counterintuitive, and such behaviour is difficult to understand without the support from the computer simulation model. There is reasonable evidence that human beings find it very difficult to grasp the implications of dynamic behaviour (Sterman, 1989), and it is for this reason that the formal quantitative modelling may be particularly helpful. Such models can be constructed using a group model building approach, where participants are extensively involved in specifying the nature of the simulation model. By using this approach group participants have a greater ownership and understanding of the output of the simulation model and are more likely to pay attention to its conclusions. The construction of such a model, however, can be very time consuming and is open to criticism. This is related to the need to estimate in quantitative terms the nature of many subjective beliefs represented by the causal arrows.

This approach to understanding the nature of feedback is called system dynamics simulation modelling (Coyle, 1996; Forrester, 1961; Richardson and Pugh, 1981; Sterman, 2000), and it has been used with great success in a variety of fields.

MANAGING THE COMPLEXITY OF DECISION SITUATIONS BY UNDERSTANDING STRUCTURE: GOAL *SYSTEMS* (HIERARCHY)

Determining the goals and clarifying direction addresses one of the key 'traps' that result in failed decisions. Nutt's studies show that groups often have ambiguous directions that lead to problems which occur when 'directions were either misleading, assumed but never agreed to, or unknown' (Nutt, 2002: 31).

However, goals do not stand alone; they support and interact with one another – as a system.

Understanding and developing direction

Negotiating an agreed goals *system* implies not only identifying the goals but also the means by which they support one another. The goals system can usefully be depicted using a causal diagram/map. One of the benefits from representing the goals in this manner is that those involved in both the direction setting and implementation are able to understand the synergistic effects of meeting any single goal.

Agreeing a goals system is not a simple activity because of the reasons identified above in relation to capturing multiple perspectives – there will be differing views about what outcomes are desired. There are likely to be a range of different and possibly conflicting goals manifested and espoused across group participants. Disagreement about goals and the means of achieving goals are an important source of conflict (Schwenk, 1984) (although the role of conflict appears to vary between for-profit and not-for-profit organizations, with not-for-profit groups valuing conflict (Schwenk, 1990)).

However, whilst the need to discuss desired outcomes, purpose, or goals is obvious, there is little clarity regarding what actually constitutes a goal. Not only is there a multitude of terms including, but not limited to, goals, aspirations, objectives, intentions, values, purposes, etc., but also little agreement about what each of these terms mean. Goals may usefully be considered as desired outcomes that are 'good in their own right' (so much so that they are hardly seen as optional by the person stating it). These 'goals' may be an expression of personal values, and personal values may be expressed as if they should be goals of the group. Sometimes expressions of goals of the group coincide with personal values. Very often goals are not explicitly known until the issues are explored and the goals, and negative goals, emerge from a reflective understanding of the issues a person or group see themselves as facing. But what must also be taken into account is that when a team is facing a messy problem they are often seeking to protect themselves from a bad outcome that is 'bad in its own right' – a 'negative goal'. In other words, regardless of the other goals that might support it or be supported by it, the single goal is a matter of concern in its own right.

Constraints are often stated as if they were goals, but they are not good (or bad) outcomes, rather they are subordinate to all the goals and have consequences that constrain actions, the achievement of goals, and the resolution of issues. For example: 'attaining minimum levels of shareholder return' may act as a constraint on management behaviour, rather than act as a goal (even though shareholders would wish to see it expressed as a goal).

Whilst most argue for the importance of goal identification or direction setting, there is less clarity in terms of how to determine them, how to gain agreement for them, and how link them. Typically it is presupposed that goals are known rather than discovered, the implication being that any member of a decision-making group should be able to state, at the outset of decision making, what goals are being attacked by a problem situation (classically Kepner and Tregoe, 1965, but also many other more recent instruction texts in decision making). Also, the notion that problem situations might arise because of a fear of negative outcomes – outcomes that would rarely be expressed if someone were asked for their goals – is not considered. These views imply that goal discovery does not follow from developing an understanding of the decision situation. And yet, as Nutt's research reinforces (following Wildavsky, 1979), it is a common experience that 'many decision makers see a direction as a solution because they do not know what they want until they see what they can get' (Nutt, 2002: 121). Goals (and negative goals), therefore, are often emergent and become formulated, clarified, and negotiated, as discussion about the situation, encompassing multiple perspectives, is undertaken.

The contribution from operations research modelling and a Group Support System

Goals may more usefully be discovered through firstly defining the situation – identifying the interdependent problems and so opening up the problem. The failure to reconcile claims can often lead to a failure to discover goals – in particular negative goals. Exploring what the consequences of each of the problems are helps generate a set of goals (and negative goals) that are grounded in the organization's reality. In the same way, exploring the consequences of resolving problems helps discover positive goals. This process of 'laddering up' avoids settling on a solution too early and attends to the demand that 'decision makers must uncover and reconcile the concerns and considerations of people whose support they need to be successful' (Nutt, 2002: 29). Linking the process of goal identification to problem surfacing makes intuitive sense to managers as they focus much of their time on the myriad problems facing them, and by so doing they are implicitly identifying goals that are under attack. A manager will more easily articulate the problems she is facing rather than talk of goals. 'Being clear about expected results is set aside in the rush to find a remedy and also sidetracks direction setting' (Nutt, 2002: 32).

Starting with surfacing the issues (and their impacts upon one another) and laddering up to consequences helps to develop an *emergent goals* system. The process works most naturally by starting with what is taken to be a high priority problem or issue and asking 'what would happen if nothing was done about this issue' and/or 'what would happen if something was done about it' (see Ackermann, Eden, with Brown, 2005: 80 for further discussion of this process). The answers might be further problems as well as goals or negative goals. The process therefore enables a chain of argument linking issues to goals to be elicited – allowing those involved to elicit and consider the unfolding argument. In addition, the process emphasizes the need to explore the many consequences that might emerge from each issue rather than focusing purely on the most obvious/important/critical one. The resultant network then reveals each problem having a range of outcomes which branch out potentially further to more problems before supporting a set of goals which weaves the different branches together – as a system of interacting problems and goals.

Alongside goals, the process can also identify negative goals. These are ramifications that emerge typically from doing nothing about a particular issue and are seen as bad outcomes. To illustrate this point along with the laddering up process Figure 9.13 shows how the issues presented in Nutt (2002: 201) reveal a map of alternative consequences and interacting problems. As can be seen from the Figure the issue 'huge investment in urban transit systems' leads to 'introduce mass transit' which in turn results in 'reduce pollution and noise' finally culminating in not contributing to 'degrade downtown areas'. The negative link (minus sign at the head of the arrow) represents the fact that 'reducing noise and pollution' has a negative effect on 'degrading downtown areas'. The example also shows how 'reduce energy dependence' contributes towards the not-goal of 'reduce our dependence on foreign oil'. Not-goals are used to highlight those objectives that are at best peripherally within the sphere of control of the organization – they suggest that this goal is 'not my goal, and I am not prepared to be accountable for attaining it, but I am prepared to make a contribution towards it'. Finally following up from the chain 'huge investment in urban transit systems' leads to 'introduce mass transit' results in a further goal of 'provide people with access to downtown jobs and services'.

As these examples show, one important contributor derives from an acknowledged realization of multiple goals or criteria. Within the field of operations research there have been developed a series of techniques for helping groups address multiple criteria: multiple criteria decision analysis or modelling, using on some occasions software support – *VISA: visual interactive sensitivity analysis* (MCDA and MCDM) (Belton, Ackermann, and Shepherd, 1997), analytical hierarchy process (AHP) (Saaty, 1980; Vargas, 1990); Strategic Choice (Friend and Hickling, 1987);

Decision Conferencing using a type of GSS called *HiView* (Phillips, 1987; Andersen and Rohrbaugh, 1983). These can be combined with the mapping process by using the emergent goals system and options created by the group as the basis for multiple criteria analysis (Belton *et al.*, 1997).

Much of this process of considering the consequences and detecting the emergent goals system contributes to a shared understanding both of the ramifications and ultimate potential goals, negative goals, and not-goals.

The conversation about a messy problem also takes the form of exploring the options that are proposed for the resolution of the problems. This 'laddering down' extends the hierarchy further and enables options to be linked to decision areas and subsequently to goals. This hierarchy is similar to that suggested by Nutt when he suggests using 'a laddering technique to create a hierarchy of objectives and interpret it to find the most appropriate objectives to follow. This technique helps address two difficulties: i) people who become fixated on a particular objective and ii) arranging a large number of objectives, uncovered by a group process, to reveal their relationships' (Nutt, 2002: 126–127). In Figure 9.14 above, statements 5 and 11 represent initial options although it is likely that there are considerably more available.

ENABLING POLITICALLY FEASIBLE AGREEMENTS: WHAT IS A GROUP?

Involving many group participants meets, (i) the need to tap into a range of different areas of expertise and perspectives, and (ii) the importance of gaining ownership for the outcome(s) among all those who can influence the implementation of agreements. Therefore include everyone who has an informed view and everyone who is potentially affected by the possible outcomes! But, we do not know in advance what will be decided, so we do not know who will be affected, and we do not know in advance what the definition of the situation is, and so who can offer an informed view – after all 'decision makers must uncover and reconcile the concerns and considerations of people whose support they need to be successful' (Nutt, 2002: 29). And, in addition, this approach is likely to lead to the involvement of too many people.

For the above reasons the membership of any group considering a decision situation becomes critical. As we argued earlier, there will always be a tension between keeping it small to reduce complexity and enlarging it to include many participants and their perspectives. Those who are affected are stakeholders, and stakeholders are those who 'focus their attention on events that have meaning for them' (Nutt, 2002: 78).

In noting the above two considerations – increasing the scope and contribution rate, along with gaining ownership and commitment – there is the inevitable consequence that the resultant groups become large and therefore more difficult to manage. In particular one counterproductive consequence can be that the decision-making process becomes fragmented with some members feeling isolated (this may or may not be the case), subgroups forming, and side conversations emerging. Each

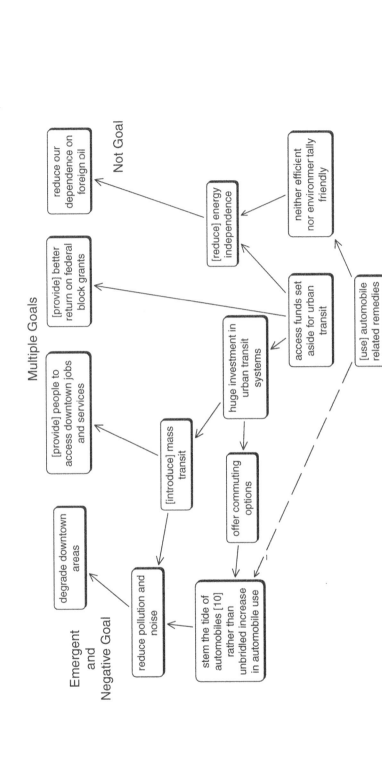

FIGURE 9.14 Laddering up from issues – multiple goals, negative goals, and not-goals.
Assertions taken from Nutt (2002: 201)

of these may work against some of the benefits of being involved. For example, if airtime (the chance to be able to contribute) is traded off against gaining support to ensure group ownership, the benefits from involving members will not be achieved.

Following from the issues raised above, determining which bodies of expertise (wisdom, expertise, or knowledge) to tap into initially appears to be a relatively straightforward task. The choice of which knowledge or discipline areas are necessary to include in the process might not be universally agreed by all (for political as well as intellectual or time paucity reasons). Even if there is agreement over which areas, there is still the question of specifically who from the different constituencies/areas should represent the views. This difficulty arises because of the varying personalities and power bases brought to the decision-making arena.

Thus, some clear and agreed rationale needs to be found for helping decide who should be around the table.

Beyond gaining expertise, perspectives, gaining ownership for the outcomes is designed to attend to the need to ensure that there is commitment (and understanding) regarding the decision outcome. This is because 'there is nothing more difficult than to achieve a new order of things with no support from those who will not benefit from the new order, and only lukewarm support from those who will' Machiavelli, *The Prince* (1514). This quote from Machiavelli is echoed by Nutt (2002) who notes: 'persuasion is dependent upon the indifference of stakeholders and has little success when people have something to lose' (Nutt, 2002: 99). As such decision makers need to pay attention to understanding who will benefit and who is likely to lose from the decision. And so, whilst it is important to ensure that the resulting decision is analytically sound, it is also important to pay attention to those who might support or sabotage the outcome. Therefore, some appreciation of who is going to take notice and why (what is the basis of their interest) is fundamental to ensuring an outcome that has a reasonable chance of being implemented.

How to decide who to involve?

Who decides who is to decide who shall be involved? It is likely to be those who define a situation as urgent, interesting, and maybe strategic – recognizing that some situations are tedious but require immediate attention. The extent of 'pain' is an important determinant – an attack on personal and/or organizational values – highlighting issues of real concern and working to distract from other duties. The formation of decision-making groups often follows as a coalition of interests come together where there appears to all in the group, at that time, to be a common perspective. However, the group can be very fragile – each of the participants sits within other teams of powerful actors, each with a stake in the outcome of other problem situations. These stakeholders have a social life within which each situation is one, often small, part of the conversations that affect the dynamics of each problem definition. Usually, in addition, there are other key actors who influence the formation of the initial group who will decide group membership. They will have some ownership of the initial problem definition and are likely to wish to protect it.

Thus, there are a number of different ways this initial group might consider who it is necessary to involve. Firstly, they may consider carefully who is likely to be interested in the decision-making topic and who has the power to influence, positively or negatively, the desired outcomes. Thinking carefully about all of the variety of different stakeholders that are either interested and/or powerful helps prioritize who might be involved (Ackermann and Eden, 2010).

In the identification of a set of stakeholders, there will always be a question about the level of disaggregation of stakeholders. When considering the stakeholders it is usually the case that negotiations involve some *one*, or at least a negotiating party, rather than a reified entity. Of course, in some instances, the negotiation will take place with a categorized mass of people (as with categories of consumers), but often the stakeholders who can most powerfully and deliberately influence the outcomes of the decision are specific individuals and groups. This suggests the use of a grid with the two dimensions of power and interest.

The grid, with the stakeholders categorized, then reveals insights into who to involve. Those that are both very powerful and interested make up a powerful first set to consider. In addition, those that are powerful and potentially positive could be considered as potential supporters and so may be involved at some stage to increase their interest and support. Likewise those that are very interested and supportive might be considered to see if there are ways of increasing their power base to support the decision outcome.

Another way to consider who to involve is to look at those being considered and review the list below of potential roles for group participants. This might give a deeper understanding of who should attend.

- Anticipated Loser. Nutt (2002: 142) also reflects on the need to be aware of those that are potentially winners or losers as these will enter the fray).
- Anticipated Winner.
- Genuine Cynic (often a senior and powerful person who has 'been through this sort of thing before, and nothing comes of it'). Where these individuals can be persuaded of the legitimacy and efficacy of the outcome they can become powerful advocates
- Opinion Former (when this person expresses a view in the organization it tends to be followed by many others without their investigating the validity of the view. They might, for example, assert that the strategy making is a 'good thing' and so influence many others in the organization to think positively about it).
- Ideas Generator. This person stimulates creativity, often thinking at a tangent and providing new viewpoints.
- Saboteur (this person often overlaps with the anticipated loser).
- Sit back and 'wait and see' before jumping (this person often literally sits at the back in group sessions and does not become involved. They might overlap with a genuine cynic).

Two further roles suggested by Nutt (2002) include:

- Insiders.
- Sceptics (who could be seen as a cynic).

A more 'sophisticated' way of considering group participant roles follows from studies by Belbin (1981) that suggest eight roles – where a participant may adopt a repertoire of several roles. In evaluating the roles, the chosen participants may form the ideal circumstance where all roles are covered. In addition, as we suggested above, personality influences the choice of group participants. Research using the Myers-Brigg type indicator (MBTI) suggests that, for example, more creativity arises from people with the MBT of 'intuitive-feeling-perception' (Nutt, 2002: 150).

Dealing with those not involved

'Whose interests are being served and whose are neglected will always pose an ethical issue' (Nutt, 2002: 200). Earlier we discussed the role of 'role think' as one way of understanding the perspectives of others and so how they might support or sabotage agreements. More instrumentally, an understanding of the perspectives of those not involved permits stakeholder management – the deliberate formation of coalitions and the manipulation of the power base and interests of these others to support agreements. Without an understanding of the perspectives of others there is little likelihood of effective manipulation.

NEGOTIATING AGREEMENTS

We stated at the beginning of this chapter that

> an obvious and crucial aspect of group decision-making is the process of people *changing their mind* – their way of making sense of the situation. As members of a group discuss, argue, and make claims about the nature of the situation and actions that should be taken, they seek to shift the points of view of others in the group. There are, of course, other important aspects of group decision making relating to the use of power including; social pressures, consolidating personal trading agreements, charisma and personality. Each of these aspects is important in its own right, and the use of them affects the way in which a person thinks about the situation.

Negotiating agreements that will be implemented depends upon gaining at least a minimum level of ownership of the agreement – indeed it cannot be regarded as an agreement unless there is some degree of ownership. The essence of reaching agreement is recognizing that agreement occurs through a process of psychological and social negotiation and that full consensus is rare.

Reaching agreement requires a process to do so. Thus, any analysis technique that is intended to ensure rational decision making must only be seen as one particular lens on the world – a contribution to an informed process. A number of such techniques have been referred to in this chapter: causal mapping, multiple criteria decision analysis, and system dynamics simulation modelling. In addition this chapter has made reference to the role of the Group Support System to aid the *process* of decision making, or reaching agreement.

The technique of causal mapping does not lead to a recommended decision, however it does focus attention on causality and words and arrows. For many the process of seeing a public view that shows evidence that a particular participant has been listened to facilitates involvement and ownership. For others a picture in the form of words connected by arrows can be puzzling. The purpose of the causal map in group decision making is primarily to link multiple perspectives and provide a structure that can explore the consequence of options for goals.

The technique of multiple criteria decision analysis focuses attention on evaluating the impact of options on each of several goals. The technique assumes that criteria can be differentially weighted and that it is appropriate to multiply differential impacts by the differentially weighted goals and then add the products together in order to determine the best option. The main contribution of such an exercise is to promote an informed discussion, however many believe that it suggests a decision outcome. Unfortunately, such a rational process will often leave participants unable to argue with the recommended outcome, and so a false consensus arises. In such circumstances successful implementation is unlikely.

The technique of system dynamics simulation modelling seeks to protect a group from making a decision that will not work over the long term. The technique demands that the participants are able to reach agreement about the nature of causal beliefs: their quantitative impact on one another. Such agreements are often not easy to reach and the simulation model cannot be run without this quantification. Nevertheless, as with the other techniques above, by looking at decision consequences through the lens of feedback dynamics, long-term consequences can usefully inform discussion. In the 1970s modellers constructed a system dynamics computer simulation that was expected to address the *limits to growth* of the world (Meadows and Meadows, 1972). Many argued that this was an overambitious and preposterous activity; however, its significance was to promote an informed debate about the assumptions built into the model, and those who argued for its inadequacy to express their reasons. In recent times, system dynamics modellers have promoted the process of group model building (GMB) (Andersen, Richardson and Vennix, 1997; Vennix, 1996) and the view that the process of model building is as important, or more important, than the model itself.

This chapter has argued that the potential for better decision making is more likely to be realized through the use of a system that supports process: a Group Support System. However, it is important to realize that such systems are not widespread across organizations and make significant, and extensive, demands on facilitators (Eden, Ackermann, Bryson, Richardson, Andersen and Finn, 2009). There is never likely to be an oversupply of experienced facilitators able to use sophisticated Group Support Systems. However, in recent years, the newly developing field of collaborative engineering (Briggs, de Vreede, and Nunamaker, 2003) is seeking to create a set of simple group support episodes that can be put together to make a sensible group support process for a particular situation. The use of a portfolio of episodes (known as 'ThinkLets' (Briggs *et al.*, 2003) creates a script that reduces the need for an experienced facilitator.

Appendix: Creating a Helpful Map?

There are some useful formalities (rules) that enable the creation of a map that can communicate purposefulness (goals), options, and meanings. The formalities also, of course, derive from considerations of personal construct theory.

- The direction of an arrow should indicate the direction of causality and influence: means to ends, options/actions to outcomes.
- One person's means can be another person's ends:
  - For example: A→B might be what one person thinks, while another person may think B→A is correct.
  - For example: 'turning things around means we have to win every battle in the next 5 years' may be coded with 'winning every battle' as the desired outcome from 'turning things around', or alternatively 'winning every battle' is required in order to 'turn things around', depending on the desired ends of the interviewee.
  - But, bear in mind some 'objective' truths might be subject to debate.
  - For example: 'putting more policemen on the beat will reduce crime' may be an objective truth to one person; nevertheless, another person might argue the objective truth is that more crime leads to more policemen on the beat.
  - Sometimes A→B can be treated as so consensual that it need not be debated e.g. 'obvious' arithmetical relationships.
  - For example: More sales causes more sales revenue.
- Means to ends are most difficult to judge when considering a hierarchy of criteria – that is, values and goals:
  - For example: is 'be unhappy and upset much of the time' more disastrous than 'crawl into my shell and give up'? That is, does 'be unhappy' lead to 'into shell' or vice versa? This can only be judged by the person being mapped, or at least this choice must be open to consideration.
  - It sometimes helps to work with a hierarchy of goals, such as 'objectives' lead to 'goals,' which lead to 'ideals or values'. So objectives are shorter term and more easily measurable; whereas goals are expressive of desirable longer term outcomes; whereas ideals or values are unlikely ever to be attained but guide purposeful behaviour.[1]
  - Avoid mapping time sequences which are not causal relationships (as this will produce flow diagrams or process maps that are not amenable to the same sort of analysis or meaning as cause maps).

Getting linking right: Avoiding duplicate and double headed arrows

- Ensure that the map does not contain duplication of links
  - For example where the map shows A→B→C→D along with A→C and C→D and A→D – ensure that the latter three links show different causal chains (through additional material).

- ◆ Avoid double headed arrows as these are implicit feedback loops suggesting either:
  - ◆ Muddled thinking that can be resolved by determining means and ends
  - ◆ A legitimate feedback loop consisting of additional statements that might provide more intervention options.

We shall utilize these formalities throughout this chapter with respect to the entire example maps presented.

NOTE

1. Based upon the Ackoff and Emery typology in *On Purposeful Systems* Wiley (1972); see also discussion on 'values' in Eden *et al.* (1979) *Thinking in Organisations* Macmillan.

REFERENCES

Ackermann, F. (1996) Participants' perceptions on the role of facilitators using group decision support systems, *Group Decision and Negotiation*, 5, 93–112.

Ackermann, F., and Eden, C. (2001) Contrasting single user and networked group decision support systems for strategy making, *Group Decision and Negotiation*, 10, 47–66.

Ackermann, F., and Eden, C. (2010) Strategic management of stakeholders: Theory and practice. *Long Range Planning*, forthcoming.

Ackermann, F., Eden, C., and with Brown, I. (2005) *The Practice of Making Strategy*. London: Sage.

Ackoff, R.L. (1981) The art and science of mess management, *Interfaces*, 11, 20–26.

Ackoff, R.L., and Emery, F. (1972) *On Purposeful Systems*. London: Tavistock.

Andersen, D.F., Richardson, G.P., and Vennix, J.A.M. (1997) Group model building: Adding more science to the craft, *System Dynamics Review*, 13, 187–201.

Andersen, D.F., and Rohrbaugh, J. (1983) Specifying dynamic objective functions: problems and possibilities, *Dynamica*, 9.

Bannister, F., and Fransella, F. (1971) *Inquiring Man: The Theory of Personal Constructs*. Harmondsworth: Penguin.

Belbin, R.M. (1981) *Management Teams: Why they succeed or fail*. Oxford: Heinemann.

Belton, V., Ackermann, F., and Shepherd, I. (1997) Integrated support from problem structuring through to alternative evaluation using COPE and V.I.S.A., *Journal of Multi-Criteria Decision Analysis*, 6, 115–130.

Berger, P.L., and Luckmann, T. (1966) *The Social Construction of Reality*. New York: Doubleday.

Briggs, R.O., de Vreede, G.J., and Nunamaker, J.F. Jr (2003) Collaboration engineering with thinklets to pursue sustained success with group support systems, *Journal of Management Information Systems*, 19, 31–63.

Bryson, J., Ackermann, F., Eden, C., and Finn, C. (2004) *Visible Thinking: Unlocking Causal Mapping for Practical Business Results*. Chichester: John Wiley & Sons, Ltd.

Bryson, J.M., Ackermann, F., Eden, C., and Finn, C. (1995) 'Using the "Oval Mapping Process" to Identify Strategic Issues and Formulate Effective Strategies,' in J.M. Bryson (ed.)

Strategic Planning for Public and Nonprofit Organisations. San Francisco, CA: Jossey-Bass, 257–275.

Buzan, T., and Buzan, B. (1993) *The Mind Map Book.* London: BBC Books.

Coyle, R. (1996) *System Dynamics Modelling: A Practical Approach.* London: Chapman & Hall.

Cyert, R.M., Simon, H.A., and Trow, D.B. (1956) Observation of a business decision, *Journal of Business,* 29, 237–248.

Dalkey, N., and Helmer, O. (1963) An experimental application of the Delphi Method to the use of experts, *Management Science,* 9, 458–467.

de Geus, A. (1988) Planning as learning, *Harvard Business Review,* March–April, 70–74.

Delbecq, A.L., Van de Ven, A.H., and Gustafson, D.H. (1975) *Group Techniques for Program Planning.* Glenview, IL: Scott Foresman.

Eden, C. (1987) 'Problem Solving or Problem Finishing?' in M.C.K.P. Jackson (Eds.), *New Directions in Management Science.* Hampshire: Gower, 97–107.

Eden, C. (1990) 'The Unfolding Nature of Group Decision Support,' in C. Eden and J. Radford (eds) *Tackling Strategic Problems: The Role of Group Decision Support.* London: Sage, 48–52.

Eden, C. (2004) Analyzing cognitive maps to help structure issues or problems, *European Journal of Operational Research,* 159, 673–686.

Eden, C., and Ackermann, F. (1998) *Making Strategy: The Journey of Strategic Management.* London: Sage.

Eden, C., Ackermann, F., Bryson, J., Richardson, G., Andersen, D., and Finn, C. (2009) Integrating modes of policy analysis and strategic management practice: Requisite elements and dilemmas, *Journal of the Operational Research Society,* 60, 2–13.

Eden, C., Jones, S., and Sims, D. (1979) *Thinking in Organisations.* London: Macmillan.

Eden, C., Jones S., Sims D., and Smithin, T. (1981) The intersubjectivity of issues and issues of intersubjectivity, *Journal of Management Studies,* 18, 37–47.

Forrester, J. (1961) *Industrial Dynamics.* Cambridge, MA: MIT Press.

Fransella, F., and Bannister, D. (1977) *A Manual for Repertory Grid Technique.* London: Academic Press.

Friend, J., and Hickling, A. (1987) *Planning Under Pressure: The Strategic Choice Approach.* Oxford: Pergamon.

Harrison, F.E. (1987) *The Managerial Decision-Making Process.* Boston, MA: Houghton Mifflin.

Harvey, J. (1988) The Abilene Paradox: the management of agreement, *Organizational Dynamics,* Summer, 17–34.

Hinkle, D.N. (1965) 'The Change in Personal Constructs from the Viewpoint of a Theory of Implications.' Ohio State University, PhD Thesis.

Hodgson, A.M. (1994) 'Hexagons for Systems Thinking', in J.D.W. Morecroft and J. Sterman (Eds.), *Modeling for Learning Organizations.* Portland, OR: Productivity Press.

Janis, I.L. (1972) *Victims of Group Think.* Boston, MA: Houghton Mifflin.

Janis, I.L. (1989) *Crucial Decisions.* New York: Free Press.

Jessup, L., and Valacich, J. (1993) *Group Support Systems: New Perspectives.* New York: Macmillan.

Kelly, G.A. (1955) *The Psychology of Personal Constructs.* New York: Norton.

Kepner, C.H., and Tregoe, B.B. (1965) *The Rational Manager: A Systematic Approach to Problem Solving and Decision Making.* New York: McGraw Hill.

Kim, W.C., and Mauborgne, R.A. (1995) A procedural justice model of strategic decision making, *Organization Science,* 6, 44–61.

Korsgaard, M.A., Schweiger, D.M., and Sapienza, H.J. (1995) Building commitment, attachment, and trust in strategic decision making teams: the role of procedural justice, *Academy of Management Journal,* 38, 60–84.

Lewis, F. (1993) 'Decision-aiding Software for Group Decision Making,' in S. Nagel (ed.), *Decision-Aiding Software and Decision Analysis: Theory and Applications.* Westport: Quorum Books.

Lewis, F. (2010) 'Group Support Systems: Overview and Guided Tour,' in D.M. Kilgour and C. Eden (eds.), *Handbook of Group Decision and Negotiation.* Dordrecht: Springer.

McHugh, P. (1968) *Defining the Situation.* New York: Bobbs-Merrill.

Meadows, D., and Meadows, D. (1972) *The Limits to Growth.* London: Earth Island.

Neisser, U. (1976) *Cognition and Reality.* San Francisco, CA: Freeman.

Nunamaker J.F., Dennis, A.R., Valacich, J.S., and Vogel D.R. (1991) Electronic meeting systems to support group work, *Communications of the ACM,* 34, 40–61 .

Nutt, P.C. (2002) *Why Decisions Fail: Avoiding the blunders and traps that lead to debacles.* San Francisco, CA: Berrett-Koehler Inc.

Nutt, P.C., and Backoff, R. (1992) *Strategic Management of Public and Third Sector Organizations.* San Francisco, CA: Jossey-Bass.

Ozbekhan, H. (1974) Thoughts on the emerging methodology of planning, *Fields within Fields,* 10.

Phillips, L. (1987) 'People-centred Group Decision Support,' in G.I. Doukidis, F. Land, and G. Miller (eds) *Knowledge Based Management Support Systems.* Chichester: Ellis Horwood, 208–224.

Phillips, L., and Phillips, M.C. (1993) Facilitated work groups: Theory and practice, *Journal of the Operational Research Society,* 44, 533–549.

Richardson, G., and Pugh, A.L.I. (1981) *Introduction to System Dynamics Modeling.* Boston, MA: Productivity Press.

Rittel, H.W.J., and Webber, M.M. (1973) Dilemmas in a general theory of planning, *Policy Sciences,* 4, 155–169.

Saaty, T.L. (1980) *The Analytic Hierarchy Process.* New York: McGraw Hill.

Schwenk, C. (1984) Cognitive simplification processes in strategic decision making, *Strategic Management Journal,* 5, 111–128.

Schwenk, C.R. (1990) Conflict in organizational decision making: An exploratory study of its effects in for-profit and not-for-profit organizations, *Management Science,* 36, 436–448.

Shaw, D. (2003) Evaluating electronic workshops through analysing the 'brainstormed' ideas, *Journal of the Operational Research Society,* 54, 692–705.

Silverman, D. (1970) *The Theory of Organizations.* London: Heinemann.

Starbuck, W.H. (1976) 'Organizations and their environments,' in M.D. Dunnette (ed.) *Handbook of Industrial and Organizational Psychology.* Chicago: Rand McNally, 1069–1123.

Sterman, J.D. (1989) Modeling managerial behavior: Misperceptions of feedback in a dynamic decision making experiment, *Management Science,* 35, 321–339.

Sterman J.D. (2000) *Business Dynamics: Systems Thinking and Modeling for a Complex World.* Chicago: Irwin McGraw-Hill.

Stoner, J.A.F. (1968) Risky and cautious shifts in group decisions: The influence of widely held values, *Journal of Experimental Social Psychology,* 4, 442–459.

Thibaut, J., and Walker, L. (1975) *Procedural Justice: A Psychological Analysis,* Hillsdale, NJ: Lawrence Erlbaum.

Thomas, W.I., and Thomas, D.S. (1928) *The Child in America: Behavior Problems and Programs.* New York: Knopf.

Van de Ven, A.H., and Delbecq, A.L. (1974) The effectiveness of nominal, Delphi, and interacting group decision making processes, *Academy of Management Journal,* 17, 605–621.

Vargas, L.G. (1990) An overview of the analytic hierarchy process and its applications, *European Journal of Operational Research,* 48, 2–8.

Vennix, J. (1996) *Group Model Building: Facilitating Team Learning Using System Dynamics*. Chichester: John Wiley & Sons, Ltd.

von Oech, R. (1982) *A Whack on the Side of the Head*. Menlo Park, CA: Creative Think.

Walsh, J.P., Henderson, C.M., and Deighton, J. (1988) Negotiated belief structures and decision performance: An empirical investigation, *Organization Behavior and Human Decision Processes*, 42, 194–216.

Ward, J. (1920) *Psychological Principles*. Cambridge: Cambridge University Press.

Weick, K.E. (1979) *The Social Psychology of Organizing*. Reading, MA: Addison-Wesley.

Weick, K.E. (1995) *Sensemaking in Organizations*. Thousand Oaks, CA: Sage.

Wildavsky, A. (1979) *Speaking Truth to Power*. Boston, MA: Little, Brown.

Winnicott, D.W. (1953) Transitional objects and transitional phenomena: A study of the first not-me possession. *The International Journal of Psych-Analysis*, XXXIV Part 2, 89–97.

Part IV

FACTORS AND CONSIDERATIONS THAT IMPINGE ON DECISION MAKING

10

Decision Making in Professional Service Firms

Tim Morris, Royston Greenwood, and
Samantha Fairclough

Introduction

Understanding how organizations reach decisions is a well-established research theme within organization theory (e.g. Simon, 1957, 1979; March & Simon, 1958; Cyert and March, 1963; Cohen, March, and Olsen, 1972). Equally well-established is that processes of organizational decision making are contingent upon an organization's context, form, and tasks (e.g. Thompson and Tuden, 1959; Lawrence and Lorsch, 1967) (see Figure 10.1). Relations between these sets of variables are neither linear nor straightforward, but complex and reciprocal. Nevertheless, they provide an ordering framework.

This chapter examines decision making within professional service firms ('PSFs'), taking account of the managerial challenges and organizational tensions which they routinely face. Existing conceptualizations of organizational decision-making processes have failed to recognize that PSFs differ in unique and consistent ways from traditional organizations such as manufacturing firms or other forms of labour- or capital-intensive organization. Although previous research has examined the authority structure, leadership, and strategic goals of PSFs (e.g. Nelson, 1988; Maister, 1993; Lowendahl, 1997; Greenwood *et al.*, 2002), little attention has been paid to the way in which these firms process strategic choices and put their decisions into practice. Researchers have tended to assume that decision-making processes in professional firms mirror those which occur in other forms of organization (but see Hickson *et al.*, 1986 for an exception). PSFs are an exceptional form of knowledge-intensive organization (Alvesson, 1995), with organizational and contextual characteristics which make them extremely challenging to manage. The intention of our discussion is to build upon and expand the small amount of research which

Handbook of Decision Making.   Edited by Paul C. Nutt and David C. Wilson
© 2010 John Wiley & Sons, Ltd

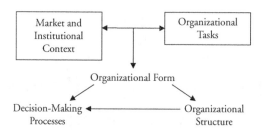

FIGURE 10.1 Contingent factors affecting decision making.

has considered the nature of decision making in professional firms.Our starting point is to outline the defining characteristics of PSFs, paying particular attention to the nature of their work (i.e. the tasks undertaken and resources deployed), the external context (both institutional and technical) within which their work is performed, and the organizational framework of structures and systems which are typically applied. Having established a working definition of what they are and how they operate, we focus upon two themes. *First,* using data gathered from a series of investigations into the issues faced by the managers of professional service firms and the strategies they use to make and implement organizational decisions, we examine and classify the types of decisions which arise from the distinctive characteristics, context, and task dimensions of professional firms. We identify an important distinction between 'strategic' and 'nonstrategic' decisions, the latter having been largely ignored in previous investigations of decision making within organizations. We consider which decisions – whether strategic or not – are the most difficult for these firms to deal with and discuss why this might be. Further, we refine the distinction between strategic and nonstrategic decisions by categorizing them according to whether they are 'easy' or 'hard' for managers to adopt or implement. We speculate that the level of difficulty of a decision is dependent upon whether it is concerned with commercial or economic matters, or if it relates to human, emotional, identity, or client-specific issues. *Second,* we consider how the pattern of decision types affects the general character of decision-making processes in professional firms. We discuss our observations, which suggest that the form and difficulty of decisions undertaken by PSFs may be categorized according to the extent to which they are 'affective' or 'cognitive'. We propose that the most troublesome decisions which a professional firm must take and enact are those which relate to the inherent and unique structural and ownership characteristics of their professional human resources. We also consider how the leadership, structure, and size of PSFs impact upon how these problems are resolved *through* their decision-making processes.

Although much of our discussion focuses upon the largest professional firms, many of the points we make apply equally well to more modest-sized professional organizations. The structural, contextual, and task characteristics we identify as distinctive of PSFs are common currency in all forms of professional organization, no matter what their size. We do, however, speculate on the possible importance of size as a limiting condition in the formulation and enactment of organizational decisions within professional firms.

PROFESSIONAL SERVICE FIRMS: THEIR SIGNIFICANCE

Why study professional service firms? One answer is that they are 'becoming ever more pronounced in economies the world over' (Delong and Nanda, 2003: ix). Aharoni (1993: 11) shows that employment in these firms grew by 53.8 % in the United States from 1978–1986 compared to 13.1 % in the rest of the economy. The largest firms are among the world's biggest and geographically complex business enterprises. PricewaterhouseCoopers ('PwC'), for example, the largest accounting firm* in the world, has over 146 000 employees and generates $US 25.2 billion in revenue. Table 10.1 shows the largest firms in six professional sectors and Table 10.2 shows where these firms would rank on the *Fortune* ranking of the world's 500 largest firms.

Equally impressive is the global scope of such firms. PwC has 766 offices in more than 150 countries worldwide – a greater global reach than the overwhelming majority of corporations. Wal-Mart, for example, operates in approximately 15 countries, Proctor & Gamble in 80, Ford in 111, McDonalds Corporation in 119, and Citigroup in 100. Furthermore, while manufacturing firms' growth patterns are shrinking, the largest PSFs continue to grow. Between 1990 and 2007 Ernst & Young almost doubled its number of employees and increased its revenue more than fourfold. General Motors in the same period has added less than 50 % to its revenue and its employee base actually decreased. Scott (1998: ix) estimated that the professional services industry had revenues of $US 700 billion worldwide in 1997. By 2000, Lorsch and Tierney (2002) suggest the figure was nearer $US 911 billion, although such comparisons are hampered by inconsistencies in defining professional services.

In addition to their size, PSFs play a significant role in societal and worldwide economic activity. Collectively, they are 'knowledge engines for business' (Lorsch and Tierney, 2002: 14) and strengthen the infrastructure for economic exchange. Large law firms negotiate complex commercial deals and help establish and interpret the ground rules of the legal, industrial, and capital market systems. Consulting firms generate and champion new management ideas, and are significant influences on how companies are organized and led. Investment banks are key sources of the venture capital used to generate new companies and projects. Accounting firms define international accounting standards and affect the integrity of financial markets (Levitt, 2000). According to *The Economist,* 'Investors depend upon the integrity of the auditing profession and without it capital markets would lack a vital base of trust.' (November 20, 2004: 16). In fact, such is the importance of professional service firms that, without them, 'business as we know it, would come to a grinding halt' (Sharma, 1997: 758). The fallout from the Enron affair, including the demise of Arthur Andersen and the precipitous fall in stock markets, testifies to Sharma's conclusion.

Given their size and significance it is not surprising that there is a growing interest in how they function (e.g. Greenwood, Suddaby, and McDougald, 2006; DeLong and Nanda, 2003; Lorsch and Tierney, 2002; Morris and Empson, 1998). An often

---

*We refer to PwC as an accounting firm, even though it provides a range of nonaccounting services.

TABLE 10.1 Largest firms in selected professional service sectors (2007)

Sector	Largest Firm	Revenues ($US M)	Personnel	Geographical Scope	
				Countries	Offices
Accounting (2007 figures)	1. PricewaterhouseCoopers	25 200	146 000	148	771
	2. Deloitte	23 100	150 000	140	715
	3. Ernst & Young	21 100	130 000	140	700
Advertising (2007 figures)	1. Omnicom Group Inc.	12 700	70 000	100	N/A
	2. WPP Group Inc.	12 200	100 000	106	2000
	3. Interpublic Group	6430	43 700	130	N/A
Architecture (2006 figures)	1. Gensler	500	3000	6	26
	2. URS	420	2500	7	18
	3. HOK(total employees 29,400)	372	1200	20	322
Engineering (2007 figures)	1. Bechtel Corporation	27 000	42 500	24	40
	2. Fluor Corporation	16 700	46 000	28	54
	3. The Turner Corporation	9400	5800	20	59
Law (2007 figures)	1. Clifford Chance	2600	7400	21	28
	2. Linklaters International	2470	N/A	22	30
	3. Skadden, Aarps, Slate, Meagher & Flom	2170	4500	14	23
Management Consulting (2007 figures)	1. IBM Global Services	47 400	190 000	170	300
	2. Accenture	22 400	178 000	49	110
	3. Cap Gemini	12 005	83 000	36	N/A

TABLE 10.2 Professional service firms[*] and the *Fortune*
Global 500 (2005)

Company	Fortune Global 500	Revenues ($US M)
PricewaterhouseCoopers	345	17 600
Bechtel Corp.	347	17 300
Ernst & Young	355	16 900
Accenture	455	13 674
KPMG	463	13 440

Source: *Fortune* Global 500
Ranking for 2004
[*]IBM Global Services is not separately ranked by *Fortune*: it is
incorporated into the figures for IBM. If treated separately,
IBM Global Services would rank 93rd on the Global 500 list.

implicit and sometimes explicit assumption of this body of work is that professional service firms share highly unusual task characteristics that raise distinctive managerial challenges which, in turn, shape the kinds of organizational arrangements – including governance structures and decision-making processes – that can be used successfully. So, what are these task characteristics and their accompanying managerial challenges?

Tasks

We assert that professional service firms have two distinctive and defining characteristics resulting from the knowledge-based features of their task inputs and outputs. The first arises from their inputs: the need to employ a highly educated (professional) workforce that is able to *customize* complex knowledge to client situations. Even where particular tasks are replicated from one client to another, the delivery of a professional service requires that it be tailored to a client's specific needs and is delivered in the context of a close (i.e. customized) relationship (Morris and Empson, 1998). PSFs 'are forced to attract and retain qualified people who can adapt their repertoires to meet the demands of the task' (Kärreman *et al.*, 2002: 73). The professional workforce thus constitutes *the* critical input of a PSF because it embodies, operates, and translates the knowledge and expertise inherent in the firm's output. PSFs are thus critically dependent on their ability to recruit, motivate, and retain professional employees in order to ensure the survival and growth of the firm.

Balancing the needs of highly educated professionals with a firm's requirements for efficiency, growth, and a coordinated strategy is, however, a complex managerial task. Professionals enjoy high levels of *autonomy* within their working environment, which allows them wide *discretion* and the exercise of personal judgment in the manner in which they carry out their tasks, manage their work, and develop their client relationships. Given this self-determination of professionals, a significant managerial challenge for PSFs is to achieve a standardization of quality of services which is commensurate with the firm's goals and the needs of its clients, and which maintains and/or enhances the firm's reputation, while providing professional employees with sufficient scope to carry out their tasks according to professional norms of discretion and independence. Individual professional discretion must also be balanced with the requirement that the firm as a whole be seen as behaving in a professional manner, in order to preserve the firm's reputational standing in the eyes of its clients and external observers. One need only think of the business scandals which erupted in the US in the early part of this decade to appreciate the implications that unethical behaviour may have on the viability of a professional firm.

Another managerial challenge missing from the nature and criticality of PSFs' inputs is the need for PSF managers to coordinate and control a complex environment in which there may be, in some of the largest PSFs, many thousands of professionals, each of whom have their own realms of expertise, client bases, and career agendas. This tension is particularly apparent when managers attempt to extract value from their internal intellectual capital: the adjacent yet diverse spheres of expertise and client affiliations which exist within and between practice areas and across individual professionals (Morris and Empson, 1998). Market-oriented commercial logics encourage PSFs to exploit the synergies arising from their professional asset base by way of the cross-selling of services to existing clients, and the coordination of expertise from contiguous practice areas in order to better meet the specific needs of clients. However, as Lowendahl (1997: 63) notes, the management of a PSF can be akin to 'herding wild cats' because of the difficulties involved in attempting to coordinate strong-willed and individualistic professionals to deliver a service which conforms to firm strategy. As we discuss below, the structural characteristics of PSFs also contribute to difficulties in harmonizing the direction and culture of a professional firm.

A third managerial issue arising out of the nature of PSFs' knowledge inputs is that their crucial assets are *highly mobile*; as well as being proprietors of a firm's expert knowledge, professionals develop social capital – including close relationships with clients – which they frequently retain and exploit when they leave a firm (Levinthal and Fichman, 1988; Baker et al., 1998; Broschak, 2004). Disruptions to a professional firm's structure, culture, or management can cause its employees to defect in large numbers. Greenwood et al. (2005), for example, provide the illustration of Andersen Worldwide, which purchased the French law firm S.G. Archibald in 1992 but lost almost 80 % of the acquired firm's professionals in the following six years. Therefore, a significant challenge for the managers of PSFs is not only to pursue and secure client work and the professionals who will perform it, but also to secure the commitment and direction of its staff. PSFs must recruit a high proportion of professional staff of appropriate quality, and provide incentives for them to perform well whilst satisfying their need for developmental and promotional opportunities. This challenge is usually addressed by offering them the prospect of becoming a partner or principal and therefore of sharing in the firm's profits (Gilson and Mnookin, 1989; Starbuck, 1992; Sherer, 1995).

The second distinctive task characteristic of PSFs is that their outputs are *intangible applications of complex knowledge*. Typically, a process of creation and innovative solution development results in an intangible artifact such as an advertising concept or a new production process (Lowendahl, 1997). For the managers of PSFs, the intangibility of task output makes it very difficult to develop or apply initiatives to improve service efficiency, and to assess the quality of a firm's output objectively. Consumers of professional services contend with a similar problem: engaging a professional is perceived as high in personal involvement and potential risk (Patterson, 1993) and clients find it difficult to measure the quality of service provided (Nayyar, 1990; Glückler and Armbrüster, 2003), before, during, and after the service event. Clients are often wholly dependent on their professional advisors in the delivery of these services and require reassurance that the professional advisor is competent, reliable, and will not act opportunistically. The traditional view of the professions is that they are populated by individuals who can apply knowledge and skills beyond the capacity of laypeople to understand or perform (Abbott, 1988; Gunz and Gunz, 2006), therefore clients must rely on a professional's fiduciary obligation to act in the best interests of a client (DuPlessis *et al.*, 2005). Without the trust resulting from established social or historic bonds between client and professional, or the indirect trust arising from a PSF's reputation or referrals from trusted personal sources, clients have difficulty assessing the competence of the professional or the quality of the service to be delivered. Yet, trust is difficult to prove or create in the high credibility/intangibility context of the purchase of a professional service. For this reason, a firm's reputation and how it manages its relationships with clients are crucial to its survival and success. One of the major challenges for a professional firm is thus to develop and sustain a superior reputation by *constantly* providing signals of competence and trustworthiness. In addition, it must ensure that client relationships are established and maintained so that problems, should they arise, are dealt with quickly and adeptly.

The importance of reputation was sharply illustrated by the collapse of Arthur Andersen after its implication in the Enron affair. A less dramatic but telling example was the damage to Saatchi & Saatchi after the announcement of its intention to acquire a retail bank. This violated the confidence of investor and clients because the decision signaled a movement beyond the services that observers associated as legitimate for an advertising agency. In Nayyar's terms, the firm incurred 'image contamination costs' (1993: 32).

The notion of image contamination echoes the so-called 'categorical imperative' (Zuckerman, 1999; Benner, 2007), whereby firms incur social 'penalties' for transgressing widely held conceptions of appropriate conduct. Unlike Zuckerman's study, where relations between 'audiences' (in his case, potential stock purchasers) and 'candidates' (companies offering shares) are 'mediated' by analysts, whose assessments (and the likelihood of reduced share prices) reflect the extent to which a company aligns with analysts' cognitive expectations of how companies fit into established product categories, professional service firms are more typically evaluated by sources such as print and on-line media, and via informal network processes amongst industry actors. These appraisal processes result in rankings and critical assessments which categorize PSFs according to, for example, reputation and expertise (Fairclough, 2008). White (1981; 1992; 2001) suggests that these shared assumptions and reference frames formed by categorization are a stabilizing influence on a market, becoming commonly accepted and taken for granted, and creating an explicit market nomenclature. The managerial challenge arising from these assessments is that individual PSFs are expected to conform to taken-for-granted categories in order to maintain their legitimacy and reputational capital; in particular, they must convey particular images of competence and credibility in order to attract and retain clients and employees.

Context

The context in which professional service firms operate has both institutional and commercial dimensions. In terms of the former, the cultural and ideological environment of PSFs is shaped by a taken-for-granted set of norms, standards, assumptions, and codes of conduct which influence the expectations and behaviours of both professionals and clients. Of particular significance in this respect are forms of professional governance, which have become established features of contemporary professions. These typically include legally sanctioned or other formal rules of professional independence, integrity, and confidentiality, which become taken for granted and reproduced through processes such as training, education, recruitment, and other rites of professional passage (Greenwood *et al.*, 2002). Such professionalized elements influence the PSF–client relationship by setting up customs of behaviour and practice which constrain firms' actions and establish 'normatively and coercively sanctioned expectations' (Greenwood, Suddaby, and Hinings, 2002: 62). It has also been suggested that they are an institutionalized way of attesting to the expertise of professionals and professional firms and therefore generate credibility and trust for clients who need their services but have no direct measure of their quality or reliability (Friedson, 1994).

Formal professional standards are usually overseen by professional associations and regulatory bodies. These organizations are key elements in the reproduction and persistence of such institutionalized contextual elements, because they act to secure their members' observance of codes of conduct and ethical rules by insisting that membership is conditional on compliance, and through the administration of disciplinary sanction (Lawrence, 1999; Greenwood *et al.*, 2002).

PSFs are also constrained by a variety of informal – but just as powerful – valorized, mythologized, and deeply embedded professional norms (Lawrence and Suddaby, 2006). In addition, professional firms have themselves established a range of institutionalized organizational controls and incentives to secure the compliant behaviour of their employees (Cardinal *et al.*, 2004). For example, partners are expected to participate in the training and recruitment activities of the firm, to establish a network of interorganizational and interpersonal relationships in order to initiate and develop client engagements, and to participate in the management of the firm and its knowledge resources (Maister, 1993). Non-partners are similarly caught up in a plethora of formal and informal institutionalized behaviours and expectations, conformance with which binds them to the firm and establishes their legitimacy to attain the rewards of partnership (Empson, 2007).

Regarding the commercial environment in which PSFs are rooted, most have consistently operated in highly competitive markets where they are restricted in their ability to distinguish themselves from their rivals. Many professional firms operate in market segments in which there are numerous competitors who appear to offer similar levels of professional service and competence; however, the complex, ambiguous, and unpredictable nature of their service offerings makes it difficult for PSFs to differentiate their services or expertise from competitive rivals in order to realize a competitive advantage. In addition, most professional firms are hindered in their strategic marketing activities by regulatory, professional, or social obligations of client confidentiality, which require that they adopt an 'introverted façade' (Fombrun, 1996) and norms of operation which shun direct publicity or advertising. Given the limited information about professional service quality, PSFs must often trade on the reputations they create through the referral networks of their existing and former clients, their employees, and the formal and informal quality assessments formed.

PSFs have also been increasingly subject to a variety of contextual changes over the past two decades including, *inter alia*, increased market competition, technological changes, the globalization of economic relations, and the deregulation of professional markets (Cooper *et al.*, 1996; Greenwood and Hinings, 1996; Morgan and Quack, 2005). Many of their clients have demanded service improvements or extensions (Greenwood and Suddaby, 2006) and/or have undertaken globalization strategies which a number of the largest PSFs have attempted to follow (Aharoni, 1999; Aharoni and Nachum, 2000). Clients have become more discerning and have become less committed to long-term relationships with their professional advisers (Pinnington and Morris, 2003). Expectations in terms of service delivery and efficiency have increased, which has led to a greater emphasis by PSFs on their technical efficiency, even where this has compromised collegiality, autonomy, and consensus (Morris and Pinnington, 1999).

To summarize, the task and contextual characteristics which are distinctive of PSFs raise important managerial challenges and critical tensions that are not typically found in nonprofessional organizations, or at least not to the same degree.

These managerial challenges and tensions – summarized in Figure 10.2 – have become more demanding in recent years as professional firms have grown in complexity, both through the expansion of their portfolio of services and through international growth. The recent proposal by the accountancy firm of Ernst & Young to merge its separate practices in Europe, the Middle East, India, and Africa into a single business unit is an example of the sort of globalization strategy which international professional firms are adopting in response to the demands of their worldwide clients to provide a 'seamless' cross-border service. Whilst a successfully integrated global network can reap rewards for a PSF in terms of leveraging its core competencies and creating additional value from multinational exchanges of knowledge and skills between interdependent business units, the implementation of such a strategy can create significant structural and operational challenges. Ernst & Young's attempt to create a transnational firm will need to address issues of cross-border integration arising from differences between country offices in, for example, client relationship practices and policies; profitability and compensation policies; levels of competence and expertise; and consistency of practice and service delivery to a centrally set standard. In particular, it is crucial that a globally integrated PSF

Characteristics	Managerial Challenges
Outputs: ♦ intangible ♦ innovative ♦ complex ♦ customized ♦ difficult to assess. Inputs: ♦ professional asset base ♦ autonomous expertise ♦ discretionary effort ♦ mobile assets. Context: ♦ regulation by professional body or law ♦ institutionalized norms of behaviour and practice ♦ commercial pressures to become more bureaucratic and/or international ♦ changing market environment and increased competitive pressures.	♦ signalling competence to clients (e.g. by way of marketing or reputation) ♦ developing and maintaining the firm's reputation ♦ recruiting, motivating, and retaining highly mobile professionals ♦ balancing respect for individual professional discretion with collective (firm-wide) imperatives for coordinated and high quality service provision ♦ balancing respect for individual professional discretion with collective (firm-wide) imperatives for professional behaviour ♦ balancing professionals' need for individual discretion with collective (firm-wide) imperatives to exploit synergies within the firm, i.e. through cross-selling and coordination of complementary assets and/or expertise.

FIGURE 10.2 Distinctive characteristics of PSFs, and their associated managerial challenges.

ensure that its network adheres to common standards of professionalism in order to protect the integrity of the firm's reputation (Fenton and Pettigrew, 2000).

ORGANIZATIONAL FORM AND DECISION PROCESSES

The traditional means of addressing the challenges posed by the professional, institutional, and technical requirements of professional service has been through the use of an organizational form which emphasizes collegial forms of governance rather than more formal systems such as those observed in corporations of equivalent size and complexity.

It would be an oversimplification to assume that all professional firms are the same and that they use the same organizational arrangements. On the contrary, we note below an important distinction between those that are governed as partnerships and those that are incorporated. We also note that some professional firms are more complex than others because of their size and their internal heterogeneity and comment upon how this has affected the formality of their structures. Nevertheless, our starting point here is to describe the traditional organizational form typically associated with professional firms. Having established this form, we then elaborate upon significant changes resulting from increases in litigation against partnerships, and from their growing complexity.

Professional partnerships

PSFs have traditionally organized and governed themselves as professional partnerships. Although not universally used, this organizational form is distinctive of PSFs and remains dominant in some professional industries – notably law and accounting. However, it has been undermined by two developments. First, an increasing number of firms are abandoning the partnership format in favour of more corporate arrangements (Von Nordenflycht, 2007). Second, even firms that have retained the partnership format have found it necessary to adopt more formal structures and bureaucratic controls in order to manage their growing complexity, scope, and sheer size.

Professional service firms constituted as 'partnerships' (Greenwood, Hinings, and Brown, 1990, refer to them as the 'P^2' form), vest ownership in a group of professionals who are also managers and practitioners *within* the firm. It is a form of organizational structure typically seen as an effective governance mechanism for delivering the appropriate degree of autonomy required to motivate senior professionals (Greenwood *et al.*, 1990; Tolbert and Stern, 1991). In contrast with an incorporated organization, traditional partnerships are not separate legal entities but are a collection of their constituent owners (i.e. 'partners'), each of whom is responsible for the business debts, taxes, or other legal liabilities of the partnership, including any misdemeanour of any other partner, even when a partner was not involved in the misdemeanour. Partnerships are also amorphous beasts: they lack hierarchy, are decentralized, and have diffuse authority structures (Greenwood, Hinings, and Brown, 1990). Although some professional organizations, particularly in the consulting and architectural sectors, are constituted as private or publicly quoted corporations, research has found that they often imitate the cultural and governance structures of traditional partnership forms in order to address the managerial challenges associated with knowledge-intensive inputs and outputs (Empson and Chapman, 2006).

In addition, a number of large professional service firms which formerly operated as partnerships have responded to the threat of litigation facing their partners – and the associated exorbitant professional indemnity insurance premiums – by taking advantage of recent changes in the law which allow partnerships to be constituted as limited liability partnerships. The conversion means that members of the firm are able to restrict their personal liability to their capital contribution to the business (unless they are negligent in relation to the work carried out for a client); however, they have the flexibility to organize their internal structure as a traditional partnership, and there is anecdotal evidence to suggest they retain the 'ethos' of a partnership in their internal and external relationships (Empson, 2007).

The partnership format is highly institutionalized in several professional sectors, including law and accounting (see Table 10.3, taken from Greenwood and

TABLE 10.3 Employment in selected professional services, in the United States[2]

Sector NAICS	1990		1993		2000		2002		2004	
	No. empl.	%	No. empl.	%	No. empl.	%	No. empl.	%	No. empl.	%
Accounting	662,000	0.61	668,000	0.60	880,000	0.66	779,000	0.60	841,000	0.65
Advertising	329,000	0.30	371,000	0.33	503,000	0.38	435,000	0.33	428,000	0.33
Architecture & Engineering	926,000	0.85	930,000	0.83	1,265,000	0.96	1,240,000	0.95	1,290,000	0.99
Law 541100	945,000	0.87	968,000	0.86	1,071,000	0.81	1,128,000	0.87	1,164,000	0.90
Management & Tech Consulting	329,000	0.30	398,000	0.36	741,000	0.56	745,000	0.57	790,000	0.61
Professional Services Sector	**10,758,000**	**9.86**	**11,754,000**	**10.48**	**16,833,000**	**12.72**	**15,869,000**	**12.20**	**16,674,000**	**12.82**
Total Non-farm Employment	**109,118,000**	**100**	**112,203,000**	**100**	**132,441,000**	**100**	**130,096,000**	**100**	**138,846,000**	**100**

Source: U.S. Department of Labor, Bureau of Labor Statistics: *Current Employment Statistics Survey* (National)

Empson, 2003), and there are at least two reasons why it is widely used. First, partners' personal liability and their shared ownership is a form of guarantee that the firm will not abuse its position of power *vis-à-vis* the client because each partner will be concerned to maintain the trustworthiness and quality standards of the collective whole, which partners both serve and from which they benefit. In addition, and perhaps of greater relevance today, the partnership form allows professionals to share responsibility for decisions affecting their work. That is, 'partnership' is consistent with notions of *peer* control. Empson (2007) has argued that the ethos of partnership is highly symbolic as a unifying concept which establishes strong social norms of mutual support and sanction amongst partners; she claims that the systems, structures, and socialization processes of a professional service firm tend to nurture a philosophy of collective interest whereby the interests of the firm outweigh partners' inclinations to free ride or maximize their individual interests.

The principle of peer control has traditionally been observed throughout a professional organization, and to a considerable extent remains so today, where those in positions of authority are often elected and have limited tenures. Although a PSF may have hundreds of owner-partners, the significant growth of the largest firms has meant that collective decision making has become virtually impossible and thus the delegation of authority to senior professionals, committees, and task forces has become inevitable. However, the holders of these directive and managerial positions typically have circumscribed power relative to corporate CEOs (Lowendahl, 1997; Empson, 2000); legitimacy is based less on formal position than on the ability to secure at least the symbolic appearance of consensus. Indeed, one of the significant challenges for PSFs is to manage '"resources" that make their own decisions' (Lowendahl, 1997: 49).

It would be easy to overemphasize the principle of collegial control. In recent years, as many firms have grown exponentially both in size and complexity, the balance between collegial and more formal bureaucratic mechanisms of control has shifted. In particular, commentators have noted the increasing propensity of PSFs to adopt a new managerial mindset or archetype called the 'managed professional business' ('MPB') as a replacement or addition to the traditional professional partnership (e.g. Cooper *et al.*, 1996; Brock, Powell, and Hinings, 1999; Pinnington and Morris, 2003). Nevertheless, professional service firms still typically embrace the values of peer control and have retained a strong emphasis upon professional self-monitoring. Cooper *et al.* (1996), in their case studies of two Canadian law firms, explain the transition from the P^2 professional partnership to the MPB archetype as a process of 'sedimentation' (ibid: 635), whereby the change process represents not a direct shift, but rather the 'layering' of elements from the new organizational design onto the old foundations. This suggests that archetypes – or elements of them – 'might co-exist alongside the continuity of a traditional professional archetype' (Pinnington and Morris, 2003: 87). Although the sedimented professional firm may exhibit surface changes in its structure and work practices, it also tends to retain a strong collective spirit, which encourages unity and self-regulation amongst its members.

Despite the growth of research into the organizational arrangements of professional service firms (e.g. Nelson, 1988; Greenwood *et al.*, 1990; Maister, 1993;

Lowendahl, 1997; Leicht and Fennel, 2001), there is only a limited understanding of how decisions are made and executed in these organizations. Hickson *et al.* (1986), for example, examined how decisions were made in seven *public* professional organizations, finding that although there was some evidence that the conglomeration of professionals created difficulties in achieving consensus in the making of decisions, the majority of these organizations displayed 'smooth and orderly' decision making (ibid: 219). However, the organizations under examination were quite different in structure and ownership to the PSFs with which we are concerned. As we shall explain, professionals' duality of ownership and production within a professional service firm is a significant influence upon the style of its decision making.

What follows, therefore, is based on an exploratory study to examine the types of decision faced by the managers of PSFs, and the methods used to determine and enact both strategic and nonstrategic choices in professional firms. Our previous professional and research experience has given us considerable insight into the contextual, structural, and operational nature of professional service firms (e.g. Greenwood and Empson, 2003; Pinnington and Morris, 2003; Greenwood and Suddaby, 2006; Anand, Gardner, and Morris, 2007; Fairclough, 2008), and we have built our data and insights from this base. We interviewed managing partners and lead partners of large practices within 16 firms in the legal, advertising, consulting, and accounting sectors. Three of the firms were publicly owned, while the rest were limited liability partnerships. Our interviews were supplemented by documentary and archival data from each firm. Interviews focused on the context in which the managing partner/partner worked, the types of decisions they had made, and how these had been classified and enacted. Once our decision-making schema and conclusions had been sketched out, we revisited a number of our interviewees in order to validate and/or refine our categories and reasoning.

Decision Processes

Our starting point is to classify the types of decisions with which professional firms are engaged into those defined by senior managers as 'Strategic' and those defined as routine ('Non-strategic'). Our interest is to observe whether the strategic decisions of corporations such as (for example) General Motors or Syncrude are the same as those that preoccupy PricewaterhouseCoopers or Clifford Chance or McKinsey. We then explore whether these are the tough (i.e. troublesome) decisions, and why.

Strategic decisions

The existing literature concerning organizational decision making is exclusively concerned with *strategic* decisions, which are defined by Hickson *et al.* (1986: 35) as those 'which can be thought of as lying at one end of a continuum, at the other end of which are the more trivial decisions'. Commentators claim that strategic decisions are likely to be those which are comparatively novel; have few, if any direct precedents; require significant organizational resources; and have decision-making implications for other parts of an organization (Mintzberg *et al.*, 1976, Mintzberg, 1979; Butler *et al.*, 1980). In short, strategic decisions are 'relatively unusual, substantial, and all-pervading' (Hickson *et al.*, 1986: 28). The results of our investigation appear to partially confirm this assertion: professional service firm leaders distinguish between major decisions and other types of organizational judgment on the basis of the level of resources involved in the making and enactment of the decision, and its potential implications for the future of the firm. 'Big' decisions are decisions concerned with developing and communicating a consensus-based vision of the long-term direction of the firm, its goals, and priorities (Lowendahl, 1997). In this sense, PSFs are no different from other organizations in their pattern of decision making.

Examples of strategic decisions in professional service firms include:

- how to compete effectively in the market and to achieve a competitive advantage;
- product choices: the client markets in which the firm should operate (or not) and what should be the range of services it offers;
- how to develop or extend existing practices;
- market choices: the geographic markets in which the firm should operate (or not), and whether to invest in new markets and jurisdictions;
- divestments of practices or of operations in geographic areas;
- alliances and merger options;
- the overall logic of the firm's bundle of services and markets;
- growth objectives and how to achieve them: the mix of organic and other forms of growth and how these will be funded;
- lateral hiring policies; and
- key human resource policies including: promotion criteria and processes, and the remuneration of partners and associates.

This list of strategic decisions is similar to that which would be found in other categories of organization to the extent that it relates to orthodox strategic concerns with product and market decisions that define a firm's external positioning in client and labour markets, and, although these terms were never used to us, the firm's internal resource capabilities and advantages. In particular, many of the strategic decisions listed above concern PSFs' aim to achieve differentiation from other firms in these markets and to link the decisions in each market and business line so that they are coherent: these strategic concerns are manifestations of managers' desire to act commercially, coordinate their firms' service quality, and utilize and leverage their cross-firm resources in a synchronized fashion. The key difference in the range of strategic decisions taken by professional firms as compared with non-PSFs is that they relate less to capital investment decisions, which are relatively light in these firms, and more to investments in human capital. Strategic decisions in professional firms are much more focused upon policies to attract, retain, and create incentives for its human capital. These are crucial in order to nurture competence, creativity, and commitment amongst the firm's most crucial assets, who are the foundations of PSFs' profits, reputation, and strategic expansion into new markets. Indeed, the growth imperative is driven as much by the need to manage the aspirations of professional staff as by external, market-based (especially client) considerations.

PSF managers also made a clear distinction between 'big' strategic decisions, and 'small', non-strategic ones: the latter were described as more routine, without substantial resource implications and, in the view of those interviewed, did not fundamentally affect the overall strategic course of the firm. Although these small ('Nonstrategic') decisions were not of great import for the long-term direction of the organization, they were not always as 'trivial' or inconsequential as implied by the state of existing decision-making research, which has little or nothing to say about non-strategic organizational decision making. We note that there have been a number of previous attempts to categorize strategic decisions and the processes which create them (e.g. Mintzberg *et al.*, 1976; Nutt, 1984; MacCrimmon, 1985; Cray *et al.*, 1991), but none of these attempts have defined decisions in terms of their difficulty or degree of strategic intent. Our findings reveal that these are significant variables and, as we shall outline below, nonstrategic decisions are often those which are most difficult to implement within PSFs.

As well as identifying an important distinction between strategic and nonstrategic decisions, our interviews also revealed a further refinement to the classification of decision types. We found that senior managers in professional firms operate with an implicit distinction between what we call 'Easy decisions' and 'Hard decisions': the former were either logically obvious *or* they were noncontentious. However, in practice there was considerable overlap between these two ways of defining an easy decision, since if a decision was rational and its logic was evident to all concerned, then it was not usually contentious. By contrast, managing partners explained that there were many types of decision which were initially assumed to be easy, but ended up being Hard, i.e. difficult to enact. As one respondent said:

> What surprised me when I came into the job was that the big decisions, which I assumed would be the toughest, were not the same as the hardest ones. For example, we made a strategic decision to open an office in Japan and I assumed that would be a difficult one because it's a big commitment and risky but it went through with hardly a murmur. Often, they (the hard decisions) would be what I would think of as small issues like an individual being asked to move his office to a different part of the same floor.

We organize our findings around these two dimensions of decision making – Easy/Hard: Non-strategic/Strategic – as shown in Figure 10.3, and discuss more fully what sorts of decisions fall into each quadrant, and why.

Types of decision

Quadrant I (Strategic/Easy). In this quadrant, managing partners place typical strategic decisions affecting their firm or one of its major practices. One partner

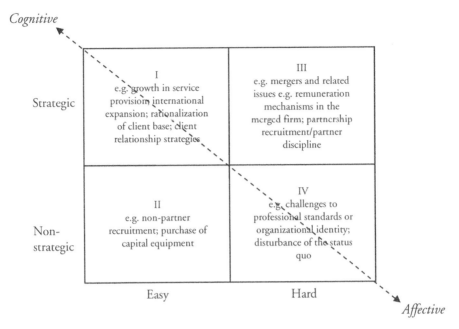

FIGURE 10.3 Typology of decisions in professional service firms.

described the decision to grow his firm's private equity practice across continental Europe from its base in the UK and US as 'straightforward' because:

> It's an area of growth in financial services whether the market declines temporarily or not. We believe that the market will grow globally and we have developed a capability in serving that market so we have decided to put resources into expanding our offices, transferring some key partners and making some hires.

Easy decisions about strategic issues were typically concerned with areas of future growth in services or geographic coverage. These decisions are driven by strong signals from client markets and choices about how to follow key clients as they move into, or expand operations in, different markets. A common theme was the decision to follow clients into China and how to do this – whether by opening an office or forming an alliance with a local firm – and the level of resources to commit to the decision. Firms usually operate with formal but loosely framed strategic plans, which typically cover a three-year period with annual updates. Longer time horizons are rarely used. In partnerships, the three-year plan is generally approved by a meeting of the entire partnership and reviewed at a yearly meeting at which the managing partner provides a commentary on progress and any proposed alterations. This process reveals that strategic decision making is 'rational' and based on market analysis; specifically, it is concerned with linking organizational goals with resourcing decisions, and the allocation of partner, committee, and task group responsibilities in achieving those goals.

The commercial focus of decisions about strategy is also demonstrated by the persistent concern to strengthen client relationships. Firms typically analyse their client base (a practice hardly known before the 1990s!) and formulate strategies designed to, first, classify existing clients by their importance to the firm and, second, to formulate ideas on how to serve key clients more effectively *and*, critically, to develop and strengthen the firm's relationship with key personnel in the client's organization. PSFs go further and identify potential clients in certain industry, product, or geographical sectors. In pursuit of gains from more efficient resource utilization and/or coordination, some of the largest PSFs have decided to rationalize their client list by eliminating the 'tail' of their client bell curve in order to focus on those organizations who they believe generate the best returns on investment, or who possess the greatest potential for fee growth. In many cases these strategic decisions have involved PSFs structurally adapting their internal organization by developing sector or industry groupings that cut across the underlying expertise-based practices. As one managing partner put it:

> We organize ourselves on a practice group basis which is where we budget primarily, but we put in place a form of industry focus . . . trying to bring together lawyers from different disciplines. We're looking at our largest hundred clients who give us sixty per cent of our income and . . . we do it because it drives our activity in terms of where we're going to spend time and resources, otherwise we'd probably spend the same resources to all four thousand clients we work for. So we're looking at the industry groups and revenue planning, saying, well the clients in that industry are responsible for this amount of our income and setting targets for them.

A managing partner of a consulting firm also emphasized the importance of decisions about the allocation of resources:

> A big decision for us is how much budget to put into existing account management and how much to put into developing new relationships because assets are our relationships. So, a big exercise for us every year is who do we know in which accounts, who do we not know and who do we want to introduce and try and get to know. So, which partners are going to try and develop relationships with which clients?

Strategic decisions of this kind are considered Easy to the extent that they are driven by commercial considerations such as client opportunities and the cross-selling of services, and are a coherent means of determining where resources should be allocated across the portfolio of practices in the firm. However, if a firm decides that growth or market extension is best achieved by merger with another firm, these decisions are potentially more difficult because of the risks they pose to the firm's reputation from the process or result of the association, particularly if there is a mismatch of status or culture between the parties. Moreover, mergers disturb the career progression (or the perception of career progression) of non-partners and can unsettle them. In other words, to the extent that mergers involve bringing professionals together into combined practices (departments), or a recombination of the practice portfolio, they run the risk that dissatisfaction will lead to 'asset hemorrhage' i.e. professionals will leave the firm. Given the crucial importance of motivating and retaining professionals to the survival and success of PSFs, managers strive, not always successfully (Greenwood et al., 1990), to handle merger decisions delicately, seeking not only to explain anticipated strategic benefits but also to reassure partners and non-partners about the implications for their own positions and for their client relationships.

One partner illustrated the sensitivity of a merger for him:

> We merged with XXX. The problem for me is that, although the merger was good for the firm as a whole, one of my major clients promptly left because their major competitor was audited by the firm we merged with. They didn't want to risk the leakage of information. The firm had to 'choose' which client to retain, and I lost out. Overnight, my years of investment in that firm were worthless.

Mergers may also give rise to a number of other difficult decision making matters, which would likely fall within quadrant III (Strategic/Hard) of Figure 10.3. These include the issue of how to combine different remuneration models and, in several instances, how to deal with mergers between firms that have different levels of profitability. Unlike other types of mergers, e.g. between publicly traded companies, mergers between professional service firm partnerships directly affect the compensation of senior professionals. Professional partnerships are 'owned' by their partners, *not* external shareholders; this means that a merger between two partnerships which have different levels of profitability per partner requires that, in the short term at least, partners in the more profitable firm will have to subsidize the incomes of partners from the less profitable firm(s). Presenting such an arrangement to a large number of partners who will suffer reduced incomes is a difficult one. *Unless* the situation is managed with the requisite political and rhetorical skills to persuade them of the long-term goals and commercial benefits of the agreement, the merger may fail, senior management positions may be jeopardized, and the viability of the firm itself may be in danger. A striking example is the mergers of the international accounting firms in the 1990s, which did not always go smoothly; in some instances, the firms of a particular country voted *not* to join the proposed international firm and, instead, moved to another one.

Another example involves the merger of a US firm, which did not operate a 'lockstep' profit share system,[1] with a UK law firm that did. To obtain the agreement of its partners to the merger, the firm had to 'ring fence' the profit shares of its US partner firms for a period of seven years and allow them to continue dividing their profits on a revenue-based bonus system rather than the lockstep arrangement of the UK firm. The ring fence was deemed necessary to ensure that key American partners would remain loyal to the merged firm by ensuring continuity of their income expectations. Even so, it provoked opposition amongst the partners of the UK firm because the decision disrupted cultural norms of partner collegiality, as well as ensuring that US partners would earn more than partners located elsewhere, notably those in London. Again, these circumstances demonstrate the distinctive decision-making challenges confronting PSFs in respect of their need to motivate and retain their highly mobile and autonomous professional resources. As a managing partner of another firm wryly observed:

> Mergers are fraught with risk, particularly if the merger partners do not roughly correspond in profitability, because then one group of partners is effectively subsidizing the others, unless you can reflect that difference accurately in the profit share. If you don't get that sorted out, as we did by establishing an exception to our global profit pool and agreeing that certain offices would take a lower cut for the medium term until they had developed their business, you risk breaking up the firm. You have to keep your partners on side or you can unravel all the benefits of the merger.

Managing partners then, by and large claim that their strategic decisions are relatively Easy because they are based on analytical methods and rational, means-ends decision making. There is agreement that strategic planning is driven by a firm's commercial context and is concerned with market and service portfolios, choices about how to grow (but not whether they could grow or not), and the key policies to attract, retain, and reward human capital. In interviews partners said it was crucial to attract and secure the commitment of a highly mobile, expert workforce in realizing the strategic goals of a firm. The major risk which senior partners had to take into account was the internal opposition of their colleagues – as owners and controllers of client relationships – about these decisions; in other words, would changes to the firm's strategy or to key practices such as compensation systems be politically feasible to approve or implement?

Quadrants II (Non-strategic/Easy) and IV (Non-strategic/Hard). Small decisions are routine and functional. Many decisions within PSFs fall into this category and are taken in a conventional, accepted way, making them Non-strategic/Easy (quadrant II). To a large extent they share characteristics with Strategic/Easy decisions, in that they are focused on issues related to the firm's infrastructure and operations, and are adopted and carried out with the intention of maximizing economic performance. Managing partners occasionally become involved in these decisions – such as the purchase of capital equipment, and the replacement of junior or support staff – but mainly delegate them to practice group leaders through budgeting processes. They do not regard them as strategic.

Surprisingly, however, many such apparently Nonstrategic/Easy decisions could, and often do, flare into Hard ones in an unpredictable way (i.e. they move from quadrant II to quadrant IV). One interviewee referred to this effect as being 'blind-sided' by an apparently innocuous decision. He explained that the usual first indication of an impending flare in his firm would be receipt of a large number of emails from senior staff demanding immediate action to rectify an offending decision. Another managing partner recalled how a re-branding exercise in his firm resulted in a decision to re-style ('brand') the firm's name into lower case letters, followed by a full-stop, that would be printed on artifacts such as coffee mugs. He subsequently received over one hundred complaints from partners; meanwhile the main re-branding effort was otherwise ignored. The managing partner was obliged to hold extensive consultations with partners to address their concerns, and eventually agreed to modify the re-branding of the firm's name.

Other examples of routine decisions flaring into time-consuming conflicts included a decision to send a small number of non-partners to a conference which, although entirely consistent with established policy, proved contentious because it was felt to be privileging one practice area of the firm at the expense of others.

Surprisingly, the flaring process was very common and interviewees claimed that it was increasing for two reasons. First, decisions which affect professional values or identities stir emotions and create friction amongst professionals who perceive such changes as an attack upon their own values or identity. The re-branding decision, for example, was deemed offensive to professional standards and damaging to the firm's external image (and thus, by association, to the identity and esteem of the firm's professionals) because it demonstrated weak writing and poor grammar (the complainants argued that a proper noun should start with a capital letter and should not be followed by a full stop as it was not a sentence). Second, flaring occurs when decisions are perceived to be at odds with established norms about status and/or the distribution of resources. In a professional context in which collegiality and equality are institutionalized features, any hint of iniquitous behaviour violates professional and social norms and encourages aggrieved groups to demand equal privilege.

It is worth noting that the willingness and ability of individual professionals to effectively challenge the authority of senior partners over seemingly trivial issues, in a way less likely to occur in a more corporate setting, illustrates three things. First, it underlines our original assertions that professional firms are dominated by autonomous professionals who are given high discretion, *and* demonstrates that they are aware of their firm's dependency upon them. Their position of power permits and perhaps even encourages *prima donna*-like behaviour, which is difficult to control given the persistent state of leadership uncertainty in many PSFs, especially in those which are partnerships. Formal leaders of PSFs are more *primus inter pares* than superiors. Second, partners are able to challenge small decisions because they are owners of the organization, embedded in a highly institutionalized context in which norms of partner equality are symbolically entrenched. The ambiguous nature of the leadership role allows licence to collectively veto management proposals that partners deem unacceptable, even if the managing partner has formally been given the authority to make such proposals. The increase in the volume of small issues that flare into hard ones may reflect this institutionalized norm in the distinctive setting of PSFs, where the influence of senior partners in the implementation of strategic decisions is less significant, and where the professional and social standards of behaviour and practice are both deeply embedded and rigorously applied. Flaring may be an instinctive attempt to assert the 'ethos' of partnership, the culture of collectivity and mutual support described as 'one for all and all for one' (Empson, 2007). Third, professionals' personal ownership stake in their organization ties their own identity closely to that of their firm. Partners in many PSFs are life-long members, recruited, trained, and groomed for partnership in a single firm. Challenges to the organizational identity of a PSF are thus regarded as of greater significance to the self-identification and self-esteem of partners than if these individuals were simply shareholders or managers. Issues which in the corporate world might be of trivial concern often take on a personal and significant quality for the professionals within a PSF.

Quadrant III (Strategic/Hard). Decisions that are difficult and of strategic importance involve substantial resources and/or affect the overall direction of the firm. They are also difficult to make or implement. Two types of strategic organizational decision are usually found in this quadrant: the execution of decisions, and decisions relating to human capital.

The inherent difficulty in effecting Strategic/Hard decisions in PSFs is that managers require the support and commitment of staff in order to put their judgments into practice. Our interviews revealed that even where strategic plans had been agreed by the partnership as a whole, some partners would resist operational implementation. For example, one firm explicitly resolved to limit its client work to innovative and complex transactions in order to sustain its brand image and premium pricing; this meant, however, that many partners were forced to abandon existing client work and reject lucrative existing or potential opportunities. Perhaps inevitably, this led to considerable resistance. Many partners continued to undertake work which did not fit the new strategic profile, arguing that they had to protect long-standing client relationships because it would be 'unprofessional' not to do so (because it would adversely affect the interests of clients). A less remarked but clearly important implicit reason for resistance to the new strategy was that a partner's annual performance targets might be under threat if the work was not accepted. The managing partner became involved in difficult discussions with practice group heads whilst simultaneously attempting to implement the new client policy. Practice group heads, in turn, found themselves in the middle ground – responsible for implementing the new strategy yet at the same time representing upwards the concerns of fellow partners. The firm was only able to implement this decision after extended discussions among the whole partnership about the speed of implementation and agreement on how to handle partners' utilization targets during the adoption of the new policy.

This example again demonstrates how the influence of professional norms and autonomous, discretionary individuals impact upon the decision-making processes within PSFs. Professionals are bound by rules which emphasize the priority of their clients' interests above their own, as well as beliefs about professional courtesy and service which encourage ongoing relationships with clients that are hard to break. In addition, it illustrates how commercial concerns – utilization targets – interact with the professional context to shape how professionals react to organizational decision making.

Another managing partner emphasized the difficulty of executing decisions within a professional partnership, claiming that the major obstacle to their implementation was the need to build consensus among partners (which could be a slow process), combined with the indistinct nature of his authority within the partnership:

But during the course of the year I've got one sanction I can apply to all the partners in a practice group which is that if they haven't managed their working capital properly I can delay the distribution of their cash, their profit share. Everything else here is done by consensus and persuasion rather than coercion.

All of the managing partners interviewed recognized that their authority was essentially 'negotiated' with the partnership as a whole. The distinctive organizational and contextual characteristics of PSFs, and the managerial challenges which accompany them, create a uniquely political environment within which strategic choices are made and implemented. Many traditional professional partnerships are consensus-based democracies but, as such, they are subject to the lobbying, scheming, and bargaining which occurs in any other political arena in order to achieve agreement on decisions amongst diverse individuals and interest groups.

The second type of Strategic/Hard decisions are the so-called 'people decisions', particularly those to do with the hiring of partners, the promotion of non-partners to partnership status, instances of discipline, or dispute over the 'ownership' of clients. These decisions are clearly provocative in the context of PSFs because of their distinctive human-centred asset base which, as we are emphasizing, is both the substance and the engine of a professional firm. As both producers and owners, one might expect partners to be sensitive to decisions which might remove them from their position, dilute their partnership share, or interfere with their client relationships. Any decision on who might become a partner, or that is to do with the conduct of a partner, is perceived by PSF managers as strategically important and hard to manage. Not only is it difficult to take a decision which impacts negatively upon a supposed equal, but it can be problematic to do so without considerable support from colleagues. Hence, despite other strategic decisions being effectively removed from the decision arena of the partnership and given to a small (usually elected) executive, decisions related to the condition or circumstances of partnership frequently continue to require the approval of the whole partnership.

These decisions are very difficult because partners are self-interested individual owners who expect a high degree of autonomy in the management of their work life and of their client engagements, yet the strategic operation of the firm requires that there be an integrated approach to issues such as marketing, reputation management, human resource practices, client care, and the selling of additional services to existing customers. The management of these issues is a major influence upon the future performance and reputation of the entire firm. One managing partner outlined two big decisions made early in his term of office, which illustrate the sensitive nature of decisions concerning professional human resources. The first was to close a group of offices in Asia, a decision which required substantial consultation across the firm before it could be implemented because it carried significant implications for the firm's *perceived* ability to execute work in the region. In particular, partners were concerned that the firm's reputation would be diminished if established client relationships were severed, or that quality standards would be compromised by subcontracting to a local firm. The second decision was to remove a number of underperforming partners. This decision also involved extensive discussion across the whole firm. Although many partners agreed with the dismissals, there were serious concerns about the implications of the release for the idea of tenure for a partner and for the relationship between the firm and its constituent partners. As a result, the decision to downsize the partnership took three years, during which time underperforming partners remained in place and in receipt of full profit shares.

Another managing partner reported substantial resistance from partners to a proposal to instigate a 10 % reduction in the firm's associates (i.e. non-partners) by dismissing those at the tail of the firm's performance distribution. While partners agreed that the firm would perform better as a result and that *their* profits would rise, the majority felt that this behaviour was a breach of a long-standing implied contract between partners and their associates, and that it would also damage the firm's reputation in the labour market. Furthermore, the decision might impact negatively upon the morale of existing associates who, as we have explained, are mobile assets with portable expertise who need to be retained and motivated for the long-term benefit of the firm.

Because managing partners rely upon other partners to undertake management positions in the firm – such as running practice areas and local offices – managing with their consensus is particularly important. Effective managing partners therefore learn and draw upon a range of tactics to build collective agreement and to nurture support. One managing partner described how he had learned to do so:

> I think I probably just didn't understand when I began the sort of nature of decision making processes, and I assumed it was my responsibility to make these difficult decisions and probably people would, you know, accept or not the decisions I made ... You've got all these decisions and it's down to you mate ... The change in approach for me is that our approach is now bottom-up and the critical thing is not so much the quality of the idea but the quality of the person executing it. My real critical question is, 'OK, who is behind this then and where is the energy behind this?' And I've got a pretty acute sense of who is going to deliver. For example we opened up in Eastern Europe and we did our due diligence etc. but ultimately the most important thing you're weighing up is trust and confidence in the individual who's leading it.

In this quadrant there is a clear difference between professional firms that are publicly owned and those that are owner-managed, such as partnerships. In the former, the ability of the leader to control and discipline the activities of their 'partners' or senior colleagues was much more explicit. The chief executive of a consulting firm that had been previously a partnership, but is now publicly owned, highlighted the difference:

> Well, the hard decisions normally involve people, and whether to get rid of a certain competency area because it's not utilized as much or because it's not fitting with where we are going, and therefore what do you do with those people in that area? Do you ask them to leave or do you retrain them ... not complex but difficult. The decision would be on performance because one of the big differences of becoming a public owned company instead of part

of a partnership is that there are just so many metrics you know you have to hit. So, I have a signings target, I have a revenue target and revenue target per quarter, I have a PTI which is profit contribution. All of these are annual and broken down quarterly ... [In the partnership] we had a vague annual target ... The difference is huge. [Partnerships display] a fuzziness and a lack of discipline. We are very centrally driven, its typical command and control, top-down. The targets are set to the level that will maintain or move the stock price I guess. So we have squeezed considerably more out of this business by going into public ownership.

The head of an advertising business, who had previously managed a partnership before moving to his current business within a publicly owned marketing conglomerate, also stressed the difference between public and private ownership:

What drives the chief executive (i.e. my boss) is his share plan, his bonus plan. The culture of the share price is through the organization. The business leaders are on a share scheme as well, it's a retention mechanism and a board control mechanism. I started to miss my targets last May, after thirty months in a row where I hit target, and the first thing they do at the centre is ask 'What are you doing about your headcount?' It's soul destroying because that's the way to ruin the business. The second thing they do [if you keep missing the target before year end] is take your scalp (dismiss you).

While all interviewees said that decisions concerning the management of senior personnel were in the Strategic/Hard category, there was a marked difference in the decision-making approach within different ownership forms of PSF. In traditional partnerships, the possession of a share of the equity in a firm and the consequent diffusion of managerial power means that partners exercise their rights to question, debate, or contest strategic decisions. In particular, they are sometimes prepared to oppose senior partners or majority decisions which attempt to rationalize or reorganize client relationships or professional staff, even if their opposition will have negative consequences for their own earnings by impacting the profit of the whole firm. As a consequence, the process of decision making is often slowed. In publicly owned PSFs, a greater acceptance of senior managerial power by professionals results in faster decision making and less dissent in implementation. The separation of management from ownership results in a decision-making style which emphasizes rationality, efficiency, and defined organizational goals over emotion and consensus via politicking. As compared with partnerships, these firms operate with more defined and enforced financial controls and in ways which are less tolerant of exceptions and challenges to the formal processes of decision making and implementation. Public ownership, in other words, pushes professional service firms towards the corporate model, although the extreme form of that model, as described in the literature, is tempered by the human asset base underlying PSFs' competitive position.

The nature of decision making

The contextual, task, and structural distinctiveness of professional service firms creates complex managerial dilemmas concerning how to balance the autonomy, professional standards, and institutionalized norms of key human capital assets with the need of senior managers to assert control by making and implementing decisions on behalf of the entire firm. The pattern or types of decisions made in professional service firms reflect the kinds of managerial challenges uniquely associated with PSFs. These challenges are particularly pronounced in the case of professional partnerships, where established norms of collegiality, consensus, and equality of ownership undermine the hierarchical authority of appointed managers. The inherent ambiguity of leadership roles within partnerships is amplified by the nature of the work itself, which requires that managers make decisions about the delivery of intangible services performed by autonomous individuals.

Although some PSFs have adopted a corporate form in order to deal with issues resulting from their size, complexity, and vulnerability to litigation, even these firms frequently retain the 'spirit' of a partnership, and are subject to the same distinguishing commercial, institutional, and resource issues as professional firms who have retained a partnership structure (Empson and Chapman, 2006). Publicly owned firms may be able to process and enact decisions more quickly because the power of their senior managers is less ambiguous, but all ownership forms of PSFs must routinely manage unpredictable human resources who have strong opinions and an awareness of alternative employers (Lowendahl, 1997). The decisions made by managers of PSFs are distinguished by their focus on how to motivate their professional workforce in order to realize the goals of the firm.

We have proposed that the decisions made within PSFs may be classified according to their strategic intent, and whether they are experienced as easy or hard to make and implement. Decisions which are Easy – whether strategic or not – appear to be motivated similarly by commercial, market-driven concerns, such as the recruitment of personnel, growth into new markets, or the development of client relationships. These decisions are characterized by their emphasis on economic rationality, the maximization of profits and firm growth, and appear to be largely divorced from emotional or human-centred concerns. By contrast, Hard decisions within professional firms are invariably associated with 'people' issues, which can provoke passion and irrationality amongst the professionals who must submit to, and implement, senior management's difficult mandates. Even apparently Easy decisions about minor aspects of a firm's operation, such as its visual identity, can flare into troublesome (Hard) issues if they resonate with emotionally charged notions of professional identity, self-identification, and equality. The most difficult decisions to make and to enact, and which are of most strategic significance to a PSF, are those associated with a strong affective reaction amongst professionals. Strategic/Hard decisions are problematic to make and to implement because they impact upon professionals' relationships with clients, partners, staff, or other organizations. The choices made by managers in respect of (for example) mergers, remuneration, and the constitution of a partnership must be handled delicately in order not to violate the trust which glues a professional firm together, or to impact negatively upon the reputation of the firm in the eyes of its external and internal audiences.

We suggest that as the strategic content of a professional firm's decision increases, or the perceived difficulty of a decision decreases, decision making becomes more cognitive; in other words, managerial choice and the enactment of decisions proceeds with logic and a regard for the competitive benefits which may accrue to the firm. By contrast, as a decision becomes less strategic, or is perceived as increasing in difficulty, decision making becomes more affective: it is imbued with sentiment, professionals' personal interests and considerations which may be irrelevant to the commercial reasons for the making and taking of the decision. This cognitive-affective dimension is illustrated in Figure 10.3.

Given that all PSFs are populated with professionals who are both constrained by an institutionalized professional environment and are also a diverse set of individuals with differing agendas and allegiances, it is surprising that decisions get made or enacted at all. As Hickson *et al.* (1986: 219) note, it is 'easy to imagine professional organizations as uncontrollable conglomerations in which professionals engage constantly in sterile bickering, whilst the administrative hierarchy tries feebly to hold them together'. The diffusion of power in PSFs could potentially paralyze and undermine the execution of strategies needed for the continued survival and success of a firm (Lorsch and Tierney, 2002), particularly in the largest professional firms where there are hundreds of partners and it is thus impractical to implement collective decision-making structures. As PSFs increase in size, the interests of their constituent owners and producers will likely become more varied, and the opportunity for factions and divisions increases. Furthermore, the heterogeneity of a large and complex organization – often with multiple international outposts – puts collective decision making, collegial 'spirit', and the mutual support of a partnership under strain. Some PSFs have responded to this challenge by adopting a more corporate approach to the management of their firms, including the implementation of more formal bureaucratic controls; that is, the formation of committees and task forces charged with specific decision-making agendas, and the delegation of some managerial roles to non-professional specialists. Although it is a common assumption that 'big is bureaucratic', and therefore size must also affect decision making, there is some evidence to suggest that this is not the case. Hickson *et al.* (1986) examined a number of large organizations and could find no differences in the types of decision process which were explained by size. They said that 'managerial practice is managerial practice whatever the scale of the operation' (ibid: 215). However, even in the large professional partnerships, or in PSFs which have incorporated, managers must still deal with a diverse set of autonomous professionals whose working agreement requires the establishment of consensus by way of negotiation, political rhetoric, and a sensitive approach to issues of professional status, behaviour, or identity. Decision-making processes in these firms may be slower and probably harder to enact, but the principles by which agreement is achieved are similar to those required in firms of more modest size.

The success of a number of the very largest PSFs, which are worldwide organizations with substantial profits and eye-catching numbers of employees, is testament to the fact that many of these organizations have successfully addressed the inherent tensions of the contextual, structural, and operational contingencies described in this chapter. In doing so, we note that many of them are headed by charismatic and effective leaders, who can monitor the political atmosphere within a firm, broker agreements between diverse factions, and build the consensus needed to form agreements about the decisions a PSF needs to make in order to remain competitive, develop and sustain its reputation, and retain a workforce of committed professionals. Like good politicians, the senior managers of a PSF need to be strong negotiators, with a flair for rhetoric and a reputation for integrity. By gaining the trust of their assorted constituents, managers can achieve the support they need to make and implement the operating decisions crucial to the success of a PSF (Alvesson, 1992; Boxall, 1996; Lowendahl, 1997; Fenton and Pettigrew, 2000).

There is much, therefore, to learn from the success of professional firms in determining and operationalizing their strategic and nonstrategic choices. Although human or 'hard' decisions are not exclusive to PSFs, these organizations deal with them more often than other types of organization, and they are frequently of greater significance to success and survival. In particular, the substantial experience of PSFs in managing a diverse set of professionals embedded in a complex institutionalized environment may provide lessons and cautions for other types of organizations who strive to achieve consensus amongst a diverse group of stakeholders whose support, however minimal, is required for the organization to thrive and survive. These may include shareholders, management, employees, unions, customers, suppliers, banks, or other organizations that control access to vital resources. We remain surprised by the ability of professional organizations to deal successfully with the managerial challenges they face, particularly in light of the fact that the senior management of PSFs must integrate a purpose and direction for their firm which is often at odds with the professional autonomy and discretion demanded by the individuals who comprise it.

NOTES

1. Lockstep is a remuneration model whereby partners receive the *same* level of reward, adjusted for length of tenure as a partner. This pattern was once the industry norm but has come under increasing challenge in recent years, giving way to some form of merit-based allocation system.
2. Percentage refers to proportion of total non farm employment.

REFERENCES

Abbott, A. (1988) *The System of Professions.* Chicago: Chicago University Press.
Aharoni, Y. (1993) *Coalitions and Competition: The Globalization of Professional Business Services.* London: Routledge.

Aharoni, Y. (1999) 'Internationalization of Professional Services: Implications for Accounting Firms', in D.M. Brock, M. Powell and C.R. Hinings (eds), *Restructuring the Professional Organization: Accounting, Health Care and Law*. London: Routledge.

Aharoni, Y., and Nachum, L. (2000) *Globalization of Services: Some Implications for Theory and Practice*. London: Routledge.

Alvesson, M. (1992) Leadership as social integrative action: A study of a computer consultancy company, *Organization Studies*, 13, 185–209.

Alvesson, M. (1995) *Management of Knowledge Intensive Companies*. Berlin: Walter de Gruyter.

Anand, N., Gardner, H., and Morris, T. (2007) Knowledge-based innovation: Emergence and embedding of new practice areas in management consulting, *Academy of Management Journal* 50 (2), 406–428.

Baker, W.E., Faulkner, R.R., and Fisher, G.A. (1998) Hazards of the market: The continuity and dissolution of interorganizational market relationships, *American Sociological Review*, 63, 147–177.

Benner, M.J. (2007) The incumbent discount: Stock market categories and response to radical technological change, *Academy of Management Review*, 32 (3), 703–720.

Boxall, P. (1996) The strategic HRM debate and the resource-based view of the firm, *Human Resource Management Journal*, 6, 59–75.

Brock, D., Powell, M., and Hinings, C.R. (eds) (1999) *Restructuring the Professional Organization: Accounting, Health Care and Law*. London: Routledge.

Broschak, J.P. (2004) Managers' mobility and market interface: The effect of managers' career mobility on the dissolution of market ties, *Administrative Science Quarterly*, 49, 608–640.

Butler, R.J., Astley, W.G., and Hickson, D.J. (1980) Strategic decision making: Concepts of content and process, *International Studies of Management and Organization*, ix/4, 5–36.

Cardinal, L.B., Sitkin, S.B., and Long, C.P. (2004) Balancing and rebalancing in the creation and evolution of organizational control, *Organization Science*, 15 (4), 411–431.

Cohen, M.D., March, J.G., and Olsen, J.P. (1972) A garbage can model of organizational choice, *Administrative Science Quarterly*, 17 (1), 1–25.

Cooper, D.J., Hinings, C.R., Greenwood, R., and Brown, J.L. (1996) Sedimentation and transformation in organizational change: The case of Canadian law firms, *Organization Studies*, 17 (4), 623–647.

Cray, D., Mallory, G.R., Butler, R.J., Hickson, D.J., and Wilson, D.C. (1991) Explaining decision processes, *Journal of Management Studies*, 28 (3), 227–251.

Cyert, R.M., and March, J.G. (1963) *A Behavioral Theory of the Firm*. Englewood Cliffs, NJ: Prentice Hall.

DeLong, T., and Nanda, A. (2003) *Professional Services: Text and Cases*. Boston: McGraw Hill Irwin.

DuPlessis, D., Enman, S., O'Byrne, S., and Gunz, S. (2005) *Canadian Business and the Law*. Toronto: Nelson, 2nd edition.

Empson, L. (2000) Mergers between professional service firms: Exploring an undirected process of integration, *Advances in Mergers and Acquisitions*, 1, 205–237.

Empson, L. (2007) 'Surviving and Thriving in a Changing World: The Special Nature of Partnership', in L. Empson (ed.), *Managing the Modern Law Firm*. Oxford: Oxford University Press, 10–36.

Empson, L., and Chapman, C. (2006) 'Partnership versus Corporation: Implications of Alternative Forms of Governance in Professional Service Firms', in R. Greenwood and R. Suddaby (eds) *Research in the Sociology of Organizations: Professional Service Organizations, Vol. 24*. Greenwich, CT: JAI Press, 139–170.

Fairclough, S.J. (2008) 'Magic, Myths and Media: The Maintenance of an Institutionalized Professional Elite.' *Unpublished doctoral thesis*. University of Oxford.

Fenton, E.M., and Pettigrew, A.M. (2000) 'Integrating a Global Professional Services Organization: The Case of Ove Arup Partnership', in A.M. Pettigrew and E.M Fenton (eds) *The Innovating Organization*. London: Sage, 47–81.

Fombrun, C.J. (1996) *Reputation: Realizing Value from the Corporate Image*. Boston: Harvard Business School Press.

Friedson, E. (1994) *Professionalism Reborn: Theory, Prophecy and Policy*. Chicago: The University of Chicago Press.

Galanter, M., and Palay, T. (1991) *Tournament of Lawyers: The Transformation of the Big Law Firm*. Chicago, IL: University of Chicago Press.

Gilson, R.J., and Mnookin, R.H. (1989) Coming of age in a corporate law firm: The economics of associate career patterns, *Stanford Law Review*, 41 (3), 576–595.

Glückler, J., and Armbrüster, T. (2003) Bridging uncertainty in management consulting: The mechanisms of trust and networked reputation, *Organization Studies*, 24, 269–297.

Greenwood, R., and Empson, L. (2003) The professional partnership: Relic or exemplary form of governance? *Organization Studies*, 24 (6), 909–933.

Greenwood, R., Hinings, C.R., and Brown, J. (1990) 'P²-form' strategic management: Corporate practices in professional partnerships, *Academy of Management Journal*, 33 (4), 725–755.

Greenwood, R., and Suddaby, R. (2006) Institutional entrepreneurship in mature fields: The Big Five accounting firms, *Academy of Management Journal*, 49 (1), 1–21.

Greenwood, R., Suddaby, R., and Hinings, C.R. (2002) Theorizing change: The role of professional associations in the transformation of institutionalized fields, *Academy of Management Journal*, 45 (1), 58–80.

Greenwood, R., Suddaby, R., and McDougald, M. (2006) 'Introduction', in R. Greenwood and R. Suddaby (eds) *Research in the Sociology of Organizations: Professional Service Firms, Vol. 24*. Greenwich, CT: JAI Press, 1–16.

Gunz, H.P., and Gunz, S.P. (2006) 'Professional ethics in formal organizations', in R. Greenwood and R. Suddaby (eds) *Research in the Sociology of Organizations: Professional Service Organizations, Vol. 24*. Greenwich, CT: JAI Press, 257–281.

Hickson, D.J., Butler, R.J., Cray, D., Mallory, G.R., and Wilson, D.C. (1986) *Top Decisions: Strategic Decision-Making in Organizations*. San Francisco, CA: Jossey-Bass.

Kärreman, D., Sveningsson, S., and Alvesson, M. (2002) The return of machine bureaucracy? Management control in the work settings of professionals, *International Studies of Management and Organization*, 32 (2), 70–92.

Lawrence, P., and Lorsch, J. (1967) *Organization and Environment*. Cambridge, MA: Harvard University Press.

Lawrence, T.B. (1999) Institutional strategy, *Journal of Management*, 25 (2), 161–188.

Lawrence, T.B., and Suddaby, R. (2006) 'Institutions and Institutional Work', in S. Clegg, C. Hardy, W.A. Nord, and T.B. Lawrence (eds) *The Sage Handbook of Organization Studies*. Thousand Oaks: Sage, 2nd edition, 215–255.

Leicht, K.T., and Fennel, M. (2001) *Professional Work: A Sociological Approach*. London: Blackwell.

Levinthal, D.A., and Fichman, M. (1988) Dynamics of interorganizational attachments: Auditor-client relationships, *Administrative Science Quarterly*, 33 (3), 345–369.

Levitt, A. (2000) Renewing the Covenant of Investors. Speech by US SEC Chairman Arthur Levitt at New York University Centre for Law and Business, May 10, http://www.sec.gov/news/speech/spch370.htm.

Lorsch, J., and Tierney, T. (2002) *Aligning the Stars: How to Succeed When Professionals Drive Results*. Boston: Harvard Business School Press.

Lowendahl, B.R. (1997) *Strategic Management of Professional Service Firms*. Copenhagen: Copenhagen Business School Press.

MacCrimmon, K.R. (1985) 'Understanding Strategic Decisions: Three Systematic Approaches', in J.M. Pennings (ed.) *Organizational Strategy and Change*. San Francisco, CA: Jossey-Bass.

Maister, D. (1993) *Managing the Professional Service Firm*. New York: Free Press.

March, J.G., and Simon, H.A. (1958) *Organizations*. New York: John Wiley & Sons, Inc.

Mintzberg, H. (1979) *The Structuring of Organizations*. Englewood Cliffs, NJ: Prentice-Hall.

Mintzberg, H., Raisinghani, D., and Theoret, A. (1976) The structure of 'unstructured' decisions processes, *Administrative Science Quarterly*, 21, 246–275.

Morgan, G., and Quack, S. (2005) Institutional legacies and firm dynamics: The growth and internationalization of British and German law firms, *Organization Studies*, 26, 1765–1785.

Morris, T., and Empson, L. (1998) Organization and expertise: An exploration of knowledge bases and the management of accounting and consulting firms, *Accounting, Organizations and Society*, 23 (5), 609–624.

Morris, T., and Pinnington, A. (1999) 'Continuity and Change in Professional Organizations: Evidence from British Law Firms', in D. Brock, M. Powell, and C.R. Hinings (eds) *Restructuring the Professional Organization: Accounting, Health Care and Law*. London: Routledge, 200–214.

Nayyar, P.R. (1993) Performance effects of information asymmetry and economies of scope in diversified service firms, *Academy of Management Journal*, 36 (1), 28–57.

Nayyar, P.R. (1990) Information asymmetries: A source of competitive advantage for diversified service firms, *Strategic Management Journal*, 11, 513–519.

Nelson, R. (1988) *Partners with Power: The Social Transformation of the Large Law Firm*. Berkeley, CA: University of California Press.

Nutt, P. (1984) Types of organizational decision processes, *Administrative Science Quarterly*, 29, 414–450.

Patterson, P.G. (1993) Expectations and product performance as determinants of satisfaction for a high involvement purchase, *Psychology and Marketing*, 10 (5), 449–465.

Pinnington, A., and Morris, T. (2003) Archetype change in professional organizations: Survey evidence from large law firms, *British Journal of Management*, 14 (1), 85–99.

Scott, W.R. (1998) *The Intellect Industry: Profiting and Learning from Professional Service Firms*. New York: John Wiley & Sons, Inc.

Sharma, A. (1997) Professional as agent: Knowledge asymmetry in agency exchange, *Academy of Management Review*, 22, 758–798.

Sherer, P. (1995) Leveraging human assets in law firms: Human capital structures and organizational capabilities, *Industrial and Labor Relations Review*, 48 (4), 671–691.

Simon, H.A. (1957) *Models of Man: Social and Rational*. New York: John Wiley & Sons, Inc.

Simon, H.A. (1979) Rational decision making in business organizations, *American Economic Review*, 69 (4), 493–513.

Starbuck, W.H. (1992) Learning by knowledge intensive firms, *Journal of Management Studies*, 29 (6), 713–740.

Thompson, J.D., and Tuden, A. (1959) 'Strategies, Structures and Processes of Organizational Decision', in J.D. Thompson, P.B. Hammond, R.W. Hawkes, B.H. Junker, and A. Tuden (eds) *Comparative Studies in Administration*. Pittsburgh: University of Pittsburgh Press, 195–216.

Tolbert, P.S., and Stern, R.N. (1991) Organizations of professionals: Governance structures in large law firms, *Research in the Sociology of Organizations*, 8, 97–117.

Von Nordenflycht, A. (2007) Is public ownership bad for professional service firms? Ad agency ownership, performance, and creativity, *Academy of Management Journal*, 50 (2), 429–445.

White, H.C. (1981) Where do markets come from? *American Journal of Sociology*, 87, 517–547.

White, H.C. (1992) *Identity and Control: A Structural Theory of Social Action*. Princeton, NJ: Princeton University Press.

White, H.C. (2001) *Networks in Markets*. Princeton, NJ: Princeton University Press.

Zuckerman, E.W. (1999) The categorical imperative: Securities analysts and the illegitimacy discount, *American Journal of Sociology*, 104 (5), 1398–1438.

11

Risk Taking and Strategic Decision Making

PHILIP BROMILEY AND DEVAKI RAU

RISK IN STRATEGY RESEARCH

Risk is a key concept in decision related research. Since Bowman's (1980) seminal study on associations of risk and return in accounting data, numerous researchers in strategy have attempted to explain risk–return relations, often drawing on studies of risk in other fields, such as finance and psychology, to do so. Other researchers have proposed alternative conceptualizations of risk, and examined risk in many different areas such as strategy and organizational learning, as well as examined risk taking at different levels including networks, individual firms, teams and individual decision makers.

This chapter presents an overview of risk in decision-making research. We begin by examining how different decision-making researchers define, measure and use risk to examine different types of organizational outcomes. We then examine treatments of risk by three key strategic decision making approaches, namely, the behavioral theory of the firm (BTOF), behavioral decision theory (BDT) and agency theory. We conclude with an examination of the implications of this research for managers, and identify some future areas of study in risk research.

DEFINITIONS AND MEASURES OF RISK IN DECISION-MAKING RESEARCH

Like many social science terms, risk has various meanings for various research communities. Knight (1921) defined risk as a state of accurate knowledge of the probability distribution of outcomes with probabilities taking values between zero and one. 'Uncertainty' exists if the probability distribution of outcomes is unknown, while 'certainty' exists if probabilities of decision outcomes are either zero or one.

Handbook of Decision Making. Edited by Paul C. Nutt and David C. Wilson
© 2010 John Wiley & Sons, Ltd

However, most strategic decisions involve greater uncertainty than these definitions allow for. Managers can seldom enumerate all the possible permutations of actions they may undertake for a given problem. Likewise, they cannot enumerate all the potential outcomes or assess their likelihood in any serious manner. This kind of problem is associated with the term ambiguity in some literatures.

In the strategy research community, a wide range of constructs have used the term risk. Let us consider some of them. First, researchers often associate risk with the variability of a performance measure, or an indicator of potential variability (Bowman, 1980; Fiegenbaum and Thomas, 1986; Jegers, 1991; Lehner, 2000). Thus, Fiegenbaum and Thomas (1986; 1988) and Bowman (1980) use variance or standard deviation in return on equity or return on assets as risk measures. Bromiley (1991a) uses variance in analyst forecasts of earnings, again to indicate the uncertainty about the income stream. Nutt (2006; 1993) uses this concept in simulations in which practicing decision making selects among options with differing amounts of uncertainty (variance in payoff prospects). This construct has been referred to as income stream uncertainty.

Second, researchers often borrow risk constructs from finance theory and therefore talk about systematic and unsystematic risk. Systematic risk measures the covariance of a firm's stockholder returns with the stockholder returns for the market as a whole. Unsystematic risk refers to the remaining variation in firm stockholder returns that cannot be explained by aggregate movements in the capital market.

Third, following March and Shapira (1987), researchers have attempted to measure a construct of risk associated with only negative potential outcomes. That is, the first and second definitions or constructs treat variation in above average returns the same way they treat variation in below average returns. However, managers and most casual users of the term risk do not associate desirable outcomes as increasing risk. Miller and his students have developed a measure analogous to the first risk constructs but only focusing on negative deviations (Miller and Leiblein, 1996; Miller and Reuer, 1996; 1998a; 1998b). Ruefli (1990; 1991) developed a measure where firms in an industry were ranked by performance, and risk depended on changes in rank.

Fourth, researchers have defined risk taking in terms of actions that reasonably may be seen as increasing firm risk or uncertainty. These actions include increasing research and development expenditures, changing the bank loan portfolio, engaging in activity that results in lawsuits, etc.

Fifth, in a very different approach, some researchers offered various risk measures associated with measuring the risk propensities of individual managers rather than firms. MacCrimmon and Wehrung (1986) offer one of the most complete studies in the literature. This study used a sample of over 500 US and Canadian managers. Each manager completed 16 different indicators of risk propensity. Two of the measures were in-basket exercises with gambles embedded in the cases. One gamble had to do with a lawsuit and the other with a venture. Four of the measures dealt with conventional behavioral decision theory experiments where individuals are given accurate simple gambles and asked to choose among them, with the gambles being both positive and negative in outcomes and with probabilities of success of 10 % and 50 %. Two of the measures had respondents rank gambles in desirability. Five of the measures dealt with the individual's actual real-life behaviors – the extent to which they have or hold risky assets, a fair amount of debt, about whether they have insurance, whether they gamble, and whether they have resigned their job without another job already. Finally, three of the measures follow traditional social psychology measures associated with risk propensity – sensation seeking, internal locus of control and a self rating of risk propensity.

The literature clearly demonstrates that these different measures reflect different underlying constructs. Miller and Bromiley (1990) demonstrate that CAPM, return variation and financial ratio indicators of risk load onto three separate factors in a factor analysis, and the factors have low correlations with each other. Furthermore, each of the factors has different associations with prior performance and subsequent performance. At the individual level MacCrimmon and Wehrung (1986) find essentially no association between different sorts of risk measures. Their two in-basket exercises of risk propensity have risk propensities that only correlate .16 with each other and have statistically insignificant correlations with all 14 other risk indicators. The five natural situation indicators of risk propensity correlate somewhat with one another, but the correlations are as often negative as positive. Furthermore, these five measures have no statistically significant correlations with the other 11 indicators. Finally, of the three social psychology measures, only two statistically significant correlations occur between any of the three measures and the 13 other indicators. The associations between risk measures with one response mode and the risk measures from other response modes clearly are within the bounds one might expect from chance.

While the simple analyses from economics of decision making assume a one-dimensional risk construct (in economics associated with the curvature of the utility function), this lack of a single risk construct in this type of research fits empirical results from other literatures quite well. The behavioral decision theory literature in psychology demonstrates that risk behaviors depend dramatically on how a problem is framed. In corporations, different kinds of 'risk' related issues will be framed differently. Even casual observation suggests the lack of a single risk-propensity construct. Individuals who take risks in one domain (rock climbers, for example) do not necessarily take risks in other domains (financial investments, for example). Furthermore, individuals taking actions that outside observers would consider extremely risky (e.g. walking an elevated tight rope) often claim the actions are not risky because the individual knows what he or she is doing (Simon and Houghton, 2003).

March and Shapira (1987), and Shapira (1994) offer particular insights into managerial perceptions of risk taking. Based on interviews with managers, they find managers define risk in terms of the potential of outcomes below a reference point or aspiration level, and how much or how bad a potential negative outcome is. The potential to do better than expected does not contribute to risk, nor do highly uncertain events that involve trivial outcomes. In addition, managers offer a very active perception of risk taking. They see risk taking as part of their jobs, but also believe they substantially influence the outcome after the risky choice. Thus, in contrast to traditional ideas of risk taking where a decision is followed by a randomly determined outcome, these managers see themselves as taking a decision and then taking the responsibility to make the appropriate outcome occur.

To summarize, despite the apparent attractiveness of a single risk construct, the literature clearly demonstrates that researchers are working with multiple, very different constructs of risk. The problem has at least two levels – the risk construct and the measurement of that construct. Over the years, debate has continued over the appropriate conceptualization and measures for the study of risk in strategic management research. Researchers have questioned the appropriateness of using CAPM and variability measures in decision-making research (Bromiley, 1990; Chatterjee, Lubatkin and Schulze, 1999; Ruefli, 1990; 1991; Ruefli, Collins and Lacugna, 1999). Researchers have also debated whether risk is better measured ex ante (based on say, analysts' forecasts) or ex post (based on historical performance data) (Bromiley, 1991b), whether measuring downside risk is more appropriate for strategy research than measuring variability in earnings (Miller and Reuer, 1996), whether risk measures should reflect the performance of other industry competitors (Woo, 1987; Ruefli, 1990) and whether risk measures are replicable and comparable across firms and time periods. Along with offering criticism, researchers have refined existing measures of risk, and developed novel measures of risk that attempt to address many of the above issues (Bromiley, 1991a; Collins and Ruefli, 1992; 1996; Deephouse and Wiseman, 2000; Miller and Leiblein, 1996; Lubatkin, Schulze, McNulty and Yeh, 2003; Palmer and Wiseman, 1999; Wiseman and Bromiley, 1996; Woo, 1987).

Risk Studies Areas

Risk related research in decision making roughly divides into a number of streams. In addition to the substantial research stream that attempts to explain the associations of firm-level risk and return, researchers have examined the relations between risk and concrete corporate actions such as strategic alliance formation, and attempted to identify how and why senior executives may perceive risks differently. We examine these streams of research in more detail below.

As mentioned at the beginning of this chapter, Bowman (1980) brought risk to the attention of researchers by identifying a negative relation between firm-level variation in returns (risk) and firm-level returns within industries, which contradicted the positive risk–return relation one might expect from conventional economic analyses. A substantial stream of research on the risk–return relations followed this study. Several papers argue that low performance firms take more risks and high performance firms avoid risks, either because of differences in perceptions of gain and loss relative to a reference point (Bowman, 1982; Fiegenbaum and Thomas, 1986), or in an attempt to reach or maintain their performance relative to an aspiration level (Bromiley, 1991a; Wiseman and Bromiley, 1996; Singh, 1986). In either case, we should expect to observe the risk–return paradox. While substantial empirical support exists for the general patterns predicted (Bromiley, 1991a; Fiegenbaum and Thomas, 1988; McNamara and Bromiley, 1997; Park, 2007), less research has successfully differentiated between the two underlying theories.

Another stream of research argues that some patterns of corporate diversification may simultaneously reduce risk and increase returns (Bettis and Hall, 1982; Bettis and Mahajan, 1985; Chang and Thomas, 1989). This argument has mixed empirical support. Bettis and Hall (1982) find a negative association between risk and return for firms engaged in related-linked diversification, a positive association for unrelated diversifiers, and no association for related-constrained diversifiers, but Bettis and Mahajan (1985) find that related diversification does not always guarantee a negative risk–return relation. Kim, Hwang and Burgers (1993) extend this research to an international context and argue that global market diversification, which provides international firms with different options and opportunities than domestic firms have, can explain the risk–return paradox. Reeb, Kwok and Baek (1998) temper this argument by presenting evidence that some of the reduction in systematic risk due to global diversification is offset by an increase in systematic risk associated with an increase in the standard deviation of cash flows from internationalization. Tong and Reuer (2007) find a curvilinear relation between multinationality and downside risk; downside risk first declines as a result of increased operational flexibility, but then increases as the firm's portfolio of international investments becomes extensive and coordination costs increase.

Still other studies in this area offer alternative explanations for the risk–return paradox rooted in individual firm and managerial differences. Chatterjee, Wiseman, Fiegenbaum and Devers (2003), for instance, suggest that continuous risk taking by firms may help sustain competitive advantage and lower firm risk. Anderson, Denrell and Bettis (2007) argue that differences in managerial conduct can account for the risk–return paradox such that 'high performance with low variability can be achieved through superior strategic conduct, and that low performance with high variability can be achieved through inferior strategic conduct. More generally, heterogeneity in the effectiveness of strategic management processes can result in an inverse relationship between return and variability of return' (p. 409). They find empirical support for their model through a study of 45 industries over a 10-year time period.

A final category of explanations attributes the risk–return paradox to statistical artifacts (Denrell, 2004; Ruefli, 1990; Ruefli and Wiggins, 1994), or to the choice of risk and return measures used (Baucus, Golec and Cooper, 1993). Bromiley (1991b) and Wiseman and Bromiley (1991) provide analytical and data-based evidence against some of the critiques. However, the original practice of associating the mean return with the variance in return over some time period (often five years) makes several questionable assumptions – that the returns have a normal distribution, that the mean return is constant over time, etc. Researchers have generally moved away from such studies toward more time series-cross sectional analyses using different time periods for risk and return measurements.

Risk research has also examined the influence of risk on other corporate actions, particularly alliance formation and new product development. A significant body of literature on strategic alliances, for instance, examines the role of risk and its management during the alliance formation process (Arino, de la Torre and Ring, 2001; Das and Teng, 2001; Kaufmann and O'Neill, 2007; Korhonen and Voutilainen, 2006; Sengun and Wasti, 2007; Van Mieghem, 2007). Korhonen and Voutilainen

(2006) find that the choice of alliance structure between banks and insurance companies depends on how the risk in the alliance is emphasized. Das and Teng (2001) identify two types of downside risk related to strategic alliances, namely, relational risk (the uncertainties in partner cooperation) and performance risk (uncertainty in alliance formation). Das and Teng (2001) argue that trust and control mechanisms determine risk, and propose a framework to explain how firms in a strategic alliance manage the risk inherent in the alliance. Sengun and Wasti (2007) and Kaufmann and O'Neill (2007) find some empirical evidence support for Das and Teng's (2001) framework.

Another stream of research examines risk in new product development (Cabrales, Medina, Lavado and Cabrera, 2008; He and Mittal, 2007; Keizer and Halman, 2007; Salomo, Weise and Gemunden, 2007). Keizer and Halman (2007), for instance, identify two kinds of risks characteristic of radical innovation projects. Salomo, Weise and Gemunden (2007) find that project risk planning predicts new product development performance. Other work examines the relations among risk, slack, and exploration and exploitation, particularly in new product development (Greve, 2003; Mishina, Pollock and Porac, 2004; Voss, Sirdeshmuk and Voss, 2008). This research builds on March's (1991) idea that decision-maker risk preferences influence the choice between exploration and exploitation, with exploration involving more risk taking than exploitation. Mishina *et al.* (2004) build on March's (1991) idea to argue that ambitious managers with a high risk-taking propensity and a desire for growth will view slack as 'waste', driving it down to minimal levels by investing it in activities that expand a firm's market or product position. In an empirical study of manufacturing firms, they find that different combinations of different types of slack ('sticky' or 'liquid') and different types of expansion uncertainty (predictable or unpredictable) have different effects on product expansion.

Voss *et al.* (2008) identify a conflict between two views on slack and risk taking. One view suggests that slack enables organizations to focus on risky, innovative ventures with potentially high returns (Nohria and Gulati, 1996). In contrast, Levinthal and March (1993) argue that success decreases search and increases slack, thus reducing risk, while failure increases search and decreases slack, thus increasing risk. Organizations with increased amounts of slack should take fewer risks, while organizations with low levels of slack will be more likely to explore, particularly in competitive environments (Katila and Shane, 2005). Voss *et al.* (2008) attempt to resolve this conflict by examining how two dimensions of slack resources – their rareness and absorption in operations – interact with the appraisal of environmental threats to influence product exploration and exploitation.

Still other studies examine other types of risk such as reputational risk (Eccles, Newquist and Schatz, 2007), the mortality risk of new ventures (Shepherd, Douglas and Shanley, 2000), and information risk (Schnatterly, Shaw and Jenning, 2008), their effects on firm performance, and ways to mitigate these risks.

In addition to these studies emphasizing concrete corporate behaviors, several studies examine perceptions of risk taking by senior executives (MacCrimmon and Wehrung, 1985; 1990; Nicholson, Soane, Fenton-O'Creevy and Willman, 2005; Larazza-Kintana, Wiseman, Gomez-Mejia and Welbourne, 2007; Pennings and Smidts, 2000; Simon and Houghton, 2003; Sitkin and Pablo, 1992; Sitkin and

Weingart, 1995). These studies typically examine the link between risk perception and/or risk propensity, and problem framing, decision making, and organizational outcomes such as innovativeness and performance (Calantone, Garcia and Droge, 2003; Hughes and Morgan, 2007). Hughes and Morgan (2007), for instance, find that risk taking negatively influences the performance of young, high-technology firms at an embryonic stage of development. Simon and Houghton's (2003) results from a study of managers in high-technology firms suggest managers taking riskier actions misperceive the riskiness of their actions; they are overconfident about their chances for success and thereby underestimate risk.

Many of these studies attempt to identify the antecedents of risk propensity. It appears managerial risk propensity depends on personality and experience (Dewett, 2007; MacCrimmon and Wehrung, 1990; Nicholson *et al.*, 2005) as well as on organizational factors (Larazza-Kintana *et al.*, 2007). Some studies assume individual risk propensity is a stable trait (MacCrimmon and Wehrung, 1985; 1990; Nicholson *et al.*, 2005; Pennings and Smidts, 2000), while others assume risk propensity is persistent but does change over time (Sitkin and Weingart, 1995).

Researchers disagree on how much managerial risk propensity influences managerial behavior. Nicholson *et al.* (2005) identify three non-exclusive types of risk takers, of which they consider only one, stimulation seekers, as true risk takers, with the other two more accurately characterized as risk bearers. MacCrimmon and Wehrung (1990) find clear differences in risk taking depending on the success and maturity of the executives. MacCrimmon and Wehrung (1985), however, caution that though risk propensity is a stable trait, willingness to take risks varies across contexts, particularly across contexts presented as opportunities rather than threats (see also Kahneman and Lovallo (1993)). Bothner, Kang and Stuart (2007) support this contingency perspective on the willingness to take risks by finding that risk taking by NASCAR drivers depends on the extent of competitive crowding from both below and above. A significant stream of research on entrepreneurship also explores this idea of risk propensity influencing behavior. This research focuses on examining whether differences in risk propensity can account for decision-making differences between entrepreneurs and non entrepreneurs (Brockhaus, 1980; Norton and Moore, 2006; Stewart and Roth, 2001; Wu and Knott, 2006). Other research in this area looks at how other actors in the entrepreneurial process, such as venture capitalists, differ in their perceptions of risk from entrepreneurs (Fiet, 1995).

Many of these studies, particularly those that examine the relations between risk and return, base their arguments for increased or decreased risk taking by firms on either BDT or the BTOF. In addition, many risk studies predict concrete organizational or managerial actions based on agency theory. We now examine these three paradigms that have dominated research on risk taking – BDT, the BTOF and agency theory.

BEHAVIORAL DECISION THEORY

Behavioral decision theory (BDT), based largely in psychology, emphasizes experimental studies of choices under risk. While BDT constitutes an immense literature, most applications in strategy rest on one of two articles. Tversky and Kahneman (1974) present a set of systematic errors individuals make in dealing with uncertainty arguing the errors come from information processing heuristics. Kahneman and Tversky (1979) propose a specific theory, prospect theory, to explain individual choices in risky decision-making situations. Based on experimental studies of individuals' risk preferences, they find that individuals measure outcomes relative to a reference point, and that individuals typically avoid risk in choices where all outcomes lie above the reference point and risk seek for choices where all outcomes lie below it.

Prospect theory directly associates choices with characteristics of the choice, but its operation is most easily explained as a sequential process. First, a reference point is subtracted from each outcome to give an adjusted outcome. Second, each outcome is assigned a value based on a value function. The value function is risk averse for positive adjusted outcomes and risk seeking for negative adjusted outcomes. A one unit change in adjusted outcome has a greater impact on value for negative adjusted outcomes than for positive adjusted outcomes of the same absolute magnitude, i.e. losses carry more weight than gains. The overall value of a choice is the weighted sum of the outcomes possible from the choice, with the weights a function of the outcome probabilities. The weights generally underweight high probability events, and overweight low probability events, but may assign zero weight to extremely low probability events.

Bowman (1982; 1984) uses prospect theory to explain the risk–return paradox; he states that low performing firms will seek more risks than high performing firms. Many other researchers in this line of work make similar arguments (Fiegenbaum, 1990; Fiegenbaum and Thomas, 1986; 1988; 1990). Fiegenbaum, Hart and Schendel (1996) and Bamberger and Fiegenbaum (1996) apply prospect theory to theories of competitive advantage.

Other researchers in strategic management have used prospect theory to examine risk taking by individuals, groups and organizations (Gomez-Mejia, Haynes, Nunez-Nickel, Jacobson and Moyano-Fuentes, 2007; Mullins, Forlani and Walker, 1999; Shimizu, 2007; Whyte, 1998). Mullins, Forlani and Walker (1999), for example, define risk as the degree of uncertainty and potential loss that follows from a given behavior or set of behaviors, and manipulate risk levels in an experiment by varying variables including current performance of the business unit, organizationally imposed goals or aspirations of the decision maker, available resources, and attributions to recent outcomes. They also measure individual risk propensities and find that both organizational and decision-maker factors influence managers' new product development decisions. At the organizational level, Shimizu (2007) uses prospect theory in combination with behavioral theory and the threat rigidity hypothesis to examine organizational decisions to divest or retain formerly acquired units. He claims that ambiguity exacerbates managers' tendency to overweight low probability outcomes and underweight high probability. Under high ambiguity, managers are more likely to divest a poorly performing acquired unit.

Some researchers compare the contradictory predictions made by prospect theory and the threat rigidity hypothesis regarding risk taking (Mone, McKinley and Barker, 1998; Ocasio, 1995). While prospect theory predicts that performance below target increases risk taking, the threat rigidity hypothesis (Staw, Sandelands and Dutton, 1981) proposes that performance below target will decrease risk taking if decision makers perceive the gap between performance and target as a threat to survival. The empirical evidence related to these contradictory predictions is mixed. Chattopadhyay, Glick and Huber (2001) find that, consistent with prospect theory, likely losses lead to riskier externally directed actions, and that, consistent with the threat rigidity hypothesis, threats to corporate control lead to more conservative internally directed actions. Audia and Greve (2006), in the context of the shipbuilding industry, find that risk taking by small firms appears consistent with the threat rigidity hypothesis, while large firms appear to take actions more consistent with prospect theory. Similarly, Gomez-Mejia *et al.* (2007) find that family owned firms may be risk averse and risk willing at the same time. Chattopadhyay, Glick and Huber (2001) and Highhouse and Yuce (1996) suggest that these mixed results stem from different dimensions of threat identified by prospect theory and the threat rigidity hypothesis. They argue that prospect theory focuses on loss or gain dimensions while the threat rigidity hypothesis focuses on the reduction of control.

Some scholars question applications of BDT to organizational contexts. One of the major themes in BDT is that choice under uncertainty is sensitive to a variety of influences. Given that Kahneman and Tversky (1979) developed prospect theory to explain individual behavior, its assumptions may not make sense for firms (Bromiley, Miller and Rau, 2001). Prospect theory assumes a unitary decision maker provided with accurate data on possible outcomes and their probabilities. BDT evidence suggests that prospect theory's predictions do not hold where decision makers must learn probabilities by repeated trials (Barkan, 2002; Barkan, Zohar and Erev, 1998; Hertwig, Weber, Barron and Erev, 2004). Furthermore, some studies that directly compare organizational and BDT predictions find little support for BDT. For example, Bromiley (1987) examines organizationally produced forecasts for conservatism or anchoring-and-adjustment heuristics (Tversky and Kahneman, 1974). If anchoring and adjustment influences the forecasts, organizational forecasts should fall between the anchor and the actual, but instead forecasts reflected clear organizationally justified biases. Likewise, McNamara and Bromiley (1997, 1999) find that organizational effects dominate the psychological in risk assessments on commercial loans.

Part of the difficulty in testing BDT on strategic decisions comes from its lack of single coherent theoretical stance, and the similarities of predictions researchers derive from BDT to the predictions from other theories of organization. While prospect theory stands as a unified model, much of BDT consists of empirical demonstrations of ways experimental subjects systematically deviate from rational (expected utility maximizing) decisions. It constitutes a large inventory of possible effects rather than a theoretical argument. In contrast, while prospect theory offers a unified theory, researchers have largely claimed it predicts risk seeking for firms below a reference point and risk aversion above, which coincides with predictions other scholars have made based on the BTOF.

Bromiley (2008) poses a more fundamental challenge to prospect theory analyses. Almost all strategy applications of prospect theory examine just the value function and refer to the value function to predict risk seeking below and risk aversion above the reference point. However, such an inference assumes all gambles have strictly positive or strictly negative adjusted outcomes. Bromiley (2008) argues that prospect theory predicts extreme risk aversion in mixed gamble situations – arguably, the kinds of situations that managers face on a frequent basis. In addition, the predictions of prospect theory depend on a variety of assumptions regarding the distribution of outcomes on gambles, the parameters of the value function and other factors the strategy literature has ignored.

THE BEHAVIORAL THEORY OF THE FIRM

March and Simon (1958) and Cyert and March (1963) develop the BTOF based on assuming individuals are boundedly rational – they seek goals but with severe limitations of their abilities to process information. Given such limitations, organizations operate largely by routines that save on calculation and allow coordination. Instead of a unified objective function, the firm has a set of goal dimensions and on each dimension it has an aspiration level. These aspiration levels depend on the organization's past performance, past aspirations and the past performance of comparable organizations. If the performance of the firm exceeds its aspiration level on a goal, the organization operates with its established routines. If the firm fails to meet its aspiration levels, however, it looks for alternative courses of action and will change. Researchers assuming change involves more risk than continuity have then argued that performance above aspirations leads to less risk taking and performance below aspirations leads to more risk taking. Slack, i.e. excess resources available to the firm, may moderate its actions. Numerous studies find support for the influence of the gap between performance and aspiration on risk taking (Singh, 1986; Bromiley, 1991a; Wiseman and Bromiley, 1996; Wiseman and Catanach, 1997; Greve, 1998).

March and Shapira (1987; 1992) and Shapira (1994) added several important refinements to the BTOF risk work. Based on interviews with managers, they found that managers defined risk very differently than scholars define it. Risk to managers only applied to returns below some reference point – excessively high returns were not risky. Variance measures of risk include high returns as risk. The amount that could be lost also constituted part of the definition of risk – a very small potential loss was not risky, whereas a large potential loss was a serious risk even if the probability of loss was small. Consistent with prior work, their interviews suggested that when firms are below target they generally take on more risk in an attempt to meet their aspiration levels. However, they add an important caveat – the aspiration level may switch to survival when firms approach bankruptcy. A firm expecting to survive but in real danger of bankruptcy (i.e. just above the survival aspiration level) may take few risks, whereas a firm expecting bankruptcy (i.e. below the survival aspiration level) may take more risks.

Miller and Leiblien (1996) and Miller and Reuer (1998a; 1998b) develop measures of corporate risk as a strictly downside potential based on March and Shapira's (1987) arguments and test these measures. The evidence in support of March and Shapira's (1987; 1992) refinement of the BTOF is mixed. Miller and Chen (2004) find evidence of increased risk taking as firms approach bankruptcy, while

Gomez-Mejia *et al.* (2007) find evidence of decreased risk taking as firms face an increased threat to survival.

Researchers have argued that a variety of corporate behaviors reflect risk taking and so use arguments from the BTOF to explain such behaviors. For example, Chen and Miller (2007) examine how a firm's performance relative to aspirations, proximity to bankruptcy, and slack influence its R&D intensity, where high R&D intensity equates to risk taking. Greve (1998) looks at radio station format changes. One interesting stream of research uses the BTOF to examine organizational change. Park (2007) equates the divergence of a firm's strategy from the strategies of the other firms in the industry as risk taking and argues that this risk taking depends on performance relative to aspirations and executive hubris. Ketchen and Palmer (1999) examine whether poor performing organizations will make strategic changes, as predicted by the BTOF, or whether these organizations will continue with previous actions, as predicted by the threat rigidity hypothesis. Their results find support for the BTOF but no support for the threat rigidity hypothesis.

As noted above, researchers have not carefully distinguished between the predictions of prospect theory and the predictions of the behavioral theory of the firm. Bromiley (2008) argues that many implications researchers have drawn from prospect theory need more careful examination. He points out that the two theories differ in their treatment of outcomes near the reference point/aspiration level. Whereas prospect theory predicts extreme risk aversion for gambles near the reference point (because they will generally have both positive and negative potential outcomes), the behavioral theory of the firm predicts a substantial drop in risk taking between firms just below and just above the reference point. Additional differences might be found to differentiate between the two theories. To advance risk research in decision making, researchers need to distinguish between the predictions of the two theories since they apply to completely different levels of analysis.

Agency Theory

Agency theory deals with how a principal (or owner) can get an agent, who makes critical decisions on behalf of the principal, to take actions that are in the best interests of the principal (Demsetz, 1983; Fama, 1980). Studies based on agency theory assume that principals and agents differ in their risk preferences, often assuming a risk-neutral principal and a risk-averse agent. The theory assumes a perfectly honest principal and an amoral agent. Jensen and Meckling (1976) propose that in cases where there is a separation of ownership and control (Berle and Means, 1932), as in a modern corporation, principals or owners would have to compensate agents (managers) for making risky decisions at the firm level that might expose these individual managers to employment risk. The agency problem thus becomes one of designing appropriate monitoring and control systems that reduce moral hazard on the part of the agents (decision makers).

Several studies have used agency theory to examine the influence of incentive systems, particularly at the top management level, on organizational risk taking, innovation and performance (Cadsby, Song and Tapon, 2007; McGuire and Matta, 2003; Palmer and Wiseman, 1999; Sanders and Hambrick, 2007; Wright, Kroll, Krug and Pettus, 2007; Wu, Lin and Chen, 2007). Wright *et al.* (2007), for instance, find that the type of incentive offered to top management team members (fixed versus variable, stock options, shareholdings) influences subsequent variation in ROA and stockholder returns. Sanders and Hambrick (2007) identify three major elements of managerial risk taking, namely, the size of an outlay, the variance of potential outcomes and the likelihood of extreme loss. They find that CEO stock options may prompt CEOs to make high-variance bets, not simply larger bets.

Recent studies have used agency theory to examine other organizational issues. Goranova, Alessandri, Brandes and Dharwadkar (2007) find some evidence that supports the agency theory prediction that managers may diversify their firm's operations to reduce their individual employment risk. Camuffo, Furlan and Rettore (2007) analyze risk sharing between buyers and suppliers in the Italian air conditioning industry. They find that, consistent with agency theory, the level of risk absorbed by the buyer depends on the characteristics of the supplier, including the extent to which the supplier faces environmental uncertainty, and exhibits risk aversion and moral hazard.

Throughout these studies, empirical work has tested a few general predictions of agency theory, but has not tested the full theory in any detail. That is, no study we know of has examined whether choices are optimal (as the theory requires), but rather simply tests whether decision makers respond to incentives in a sensible manner. In other words, almost all the predictions are equally justifiable under a social psychology view of incentives as they are under the optimizing view of agency theory (Bromiley, 2004).

A number of studies attempt to integrate agency theory with prospect theory. One prominent set of studies in this area examines the 'behavioral agency model' (Wiseman and Gomez-Mejia, 1998). Wiseman and Gomez-Mejia (1998) build the behavioral agency model on the idea that risk preferences of decision makers, and thus, their risk-taking behavior, changes with the framing of problems. They then propose a framework that presents managerial risk taking as a function of risk bearing and problem framing, which are, in turn, influenced by factors such as compensation mix, performance history and evaluation criteria. Researchers have used the behavioral agency model to examine the influence of different forms of risk bearing created by compensation contracts on perceived risk taking (Larazza-Kintana, Wiseman, Gomez-Mejia and Welbourne, 2007), and the designing of contracts to improve supply chain performance when the participants have different risk preferences (Wang and Webster, 2007).

Carpenter, Pollock and Leary (2003) also integrate behavioral and agency perspectives to propose a theory of 'reasoned risk taking', whereby the risks undertaken depend on the interaction between governance mechanisms and stakeholder characteristics. They demonstrate their theory by predicting the association between corporate governance and the degree of international expansion of a firm, a form of strategic risk seeking. Other researchers use concepts from both agency and prospect theories to examine organizational phenomena, without going to the extent of formally integrating the two theories (D'Aveni, 1989; Wiseman and

Catanach, 1997). Wiseman and Catanach (1997), for instance, compare the extent to which the two theories can explain operational risks and firm performance in regulated and unregulated environments.

What Do we Know? What Do we not Know?

A substantial research literature demonstrates several stable findings about risk applicable to decision making. First, organizations take more risk when below an aspiration or reference level, and less when above. Second, top management incentives influence risk taking. Third, risk taking appears in numerous corporate behaviors such as R&D spending, diversification, etc. Fourth, many forms of risk taking influence future performance, but the sign of the relation is not always positive.

In addition to continuing work on specific risky choices and outcomes, some researchers have begun to shift from examining the impact of risk on organizational outcomes to focusing on the risk management process (Bonabeau, 2007; Clarke and Varma, 1999; Fichman, Keil and Tiwana, 2005; Miller and Waller, 2003; Shi, 2007; van Wyk, Dahmer and Custy, 2004). Some scholars in this area have begun to identify and examine the different types of risk that businesses need to manage and control, including complexity risk (Bonabeau, 2007) and the risk associated with business process outsourcing (Shi, 2007). Other scholars in this area examine the use of real options as a risk management tool (Fichman, Keil and Tiwana, 2005; Miller and Waller, 2003).

Of more scholarly concern, we need studies that more carefully distinguish among alternative theoretical explanations. None of the studies we know of distinguish between agency theory (which calls for optimal managerial choices) and simple incentive explanations. The field has failed to distinguish between psychological and organizational theories of risk taking. Indeed, in our experience, referees often demand papers mix the two. This results in citation-based 'theory' sections, rather than the development and testing of tight theories. While risk research has developed an impressive set of empirical results, it has yet to carefully distinguish among such alternative explanations.

Risk has emerged as a major line of research in decision making. Indeed, it has formed the largest stream of work based directly on the BTOF, and is central to both agency theory and BDT arguments. Future work on risk needs to examine how the assumptions behind each of these theories may differentially predict the effects of risk on managerial decisions.

References

Andersen, T.J., Denrell, J., and Bettis, R.A. (2007) Strategic responsiveness and Bowman's risk-return paradox, *Strategic Management Journal*, 28, 407–429.

Arino, A., de la Torre, J., and Ring, P.S. (2001) Relational quality: Managing trust in corporate alliances. *California Management Review*, 44 (1) 109–131.

Audia, P.G., and Greve, H.R. (2006) Less likely to fail: Low performance, firm size, and factory expansion in the shipbuilding industry, *Management Science*, 52 (1), 83–94.

Bamberger, P., and Fiegenbaum, A. (1996) The role of strategic reference points in explaining the nature and consequences of human resource strategy, *Academy of Management Review*, 21 (4), 926–958.

Barkan, R. (2002) Using a signal detection safety model to simulate managerial expectations and supervisory feedback, *Organizational Behavior and Human Decision Processes*, 89, 1005–1031.

Barkan, R., Zohar, D., and Erev, I. (1998) Accident and decision making under uncertainty: A comparison of four models, *Organizational Behavior and Human Decision Processes*, 74, 118–144.

Baucus, D.A., Golec, J.H., and Cooper, J.R. (1993) Estimating risk-return relationships – An analysis of measures, *Strategic Management Journal*, 14 (5), 387–396.

Berle, A., and Means, G. (1932) *The Modern Corporation and Private Property*. New York: Macmillan.

Bettis, R.A., and Hall, W.K. (1982) Diversification strategy, accounting determined risk, and accounting determined return, *Academy of Management Journal*, 25, 254–264.

Bettis, R.A., and Mahajan, V. (1985) Risk/return performance of diversified firms, *Management Science*, 31 (7), 785–799.

Bonabeau, E. (2007) Understanding and managing complexity risk, *MIT Sloan Management Review*, 48 (4), 62–68.

Bothner, M.S., Kang, J.H., and Stuart, T.E. (2007) Competitive crowding and risk taking in a tournament: Evidence from NASCAR racing, *Administrative Science Quarterly*, 52 (2), 208–247.

Bowman, E.H. (1980) A risk/return paradox for strategic management, *Sloan Management Review*, 21, 17–31.

Bowman, E.H. (1982) Risk seeking by troubled firms, *Sloan Management Review*, 23, 33–42.

Bowman, E.H. (1984) Content analysis of annual reports for corporate strategy and risk, *Interfaces*, 14 (1), 61–71.

Brockhaus, R.H. (1980) Risk taking propensity of entrepreneurs, *Academy of Management Journal*, 23, 509–520.

Bromiley, P. (1987) Do forecasts produced by organizations reflect anchoring and adjustment? *Journal of Forecasting*, 6 (3), 201–210.

Bromiley, P. (1990) 'On the Use of Finance Theory in Strategic Management', in P. Shrivastava and R. Lamb (eds), *Advances in Strategic Management, Vol. 6*. Greenwich, CT: JAI Press, 71–98.

Bromiley, P. (1991a) Testing a causal model of corporate risk taking and performance, *Academy of Management Journal*, 34, 37–59.

Bromiley, P. (1991b) Paradox or at least variance found: A comment on 'Mean-variance approaches to risk-return relationships in strategy: Paradox lost', *Management Science*, 37, 1206–1215.

Bromiley, P. (2004) *Behavioral Foundations of Strategic Management*. Oxford: Blackwell Publishers.

Bromiley, P. (2008) A prospect theory model of resource allocation. Working Paper, Merage School of Business, University of California, Irvine.

Bromiley, P., Miller, K., and Rau, D. (2001) 'Risk in Strategic Management Research', in M.A. Hitt, R.E. Freeman, and J.S. Harrison (eds) *The Blackwell Handbook of Strategic Management*. Oxford: Blackwell, 259–288.

Cabrales, A.L., Medina, C.C., Lavado, A.C., and Cabrera, R.V. (2008) Managing functional diversity, risk taking, and incentives for teams to achieve radical innovations, *R & D Management*, 38 (1), 35–50.

Cadsby, C.B., Song, F., and Tapon, F. (2007) Sorting and incentive effects of pay for performance: an experimental investigation, *Academy of Management Journal*, 50 (2), 387–405.

Camuffo, A., Furlan, A., and Rettore, E. (2007) Risk sharing in supplier relations: An agency model for the Italian air-conditioning industry, *Strategic Management Journal*, 28, 1257–1266.

Carpenter, M.A., Pollock, T.G., and Leary, M.M. (2003) Testing a model of reasoned risk-taking: Governance, the experience of principals and agents, and global strategy in high-technology IPO firms, *Strategic Management Journal*, 24, 803–820.

Chang, Y. M., and Thomas, H. (1989) The impact of diversification strategy on risk-return performance, *Strategic Management Journal*, 10 (3), 271–284.

Chatterjee, S., Lubatkin, M.H., and Schulze, W. S. (1999) Toward a strategic theory of risk premium: Moving beyond CAPM, *Academy of Management Review*, 24, 556–567.

Chatterjee, S., Wiseman, R.M., Fiegenbaum, A., and Devers, C.E. (2003) Integrating behavioral and economic concepts of risk into strategic management: The twain shall meet. *Long Range Planning*, 36, 61–79.

Chattopadhyay, P., Glick, W.H., Huber, G.P. (2001) Organizational actions in response to threats and opportunities, *Academy of Management Journal*, 44 (5), 937–955.

Chen, W.R., and Miller, K.D. (2007) Situational and institutional determinants of firms' R&D search intensity, *Strategic Management Journal*, 28 (4), 369–381.

Clarke, C.J., and Varma, S. (1999) Strategic risk management: The new competitive edge, *Long Range Planning*, 32 (4), 414–424.

Collins, J.M., and Ruefli, T.W. (1992) Strategic risk: An ordinal approach, *Management Science*, 38, 1707–1731.

Collins, J.M., and Ruefli, T.W. (1996) *Strategic Risk: A State Defined Approach*. Norwell MA: Kluwer Academic Publishers.

Cyert, R.M., and March, J.G. (1963) *A Behavioral Theory of the Firm*. Englewood Cliffs, NJ: Prentice-Hall.

D'Aveni, R.A. (1989) Dependability and organizational bankruptcy – An application of agency and prospect-theory, *Management Science*, 35 (9), 1120–1138.

Das, T.K., and Teng, B. (2001) Strategic risk behavior and its temporalities: Between risk propensity and decision context, *Journal of Management Studies*, 38 (4), 515–534.

Deephouse, D.L., and Wiseman, R.M. (2000) Comparing alternative explanations for accounting risk-return relations, *Journal of Economic Behavior and Organization*, 42, 463–482.

Demsetz, H. (1983) The structure of ownership and the theory of the firm, *Journal of Law and Economics*, 26, 375–390.

Denrell, J. (2004) Risk taking and aspiration levels: Two alternative null models, Academy of Management Best Paper Proceedings, New Orleans, LA.

Dewett, T. (2007) Linking intrinsic motivation, risk taking and employee creativity in an R&D environment. *R & D Management*, 37 (3), 197–208.

Eccles, R. G., Newquist, S. C., and Schatz, R. (2007) Reputation and its risks, *Harvard Business Review*, 85 (2), 104–114.

Fama, E. (1980) Agency problems and the theory of the firm, *Journal of Political Economy*, 88, 288–307.

Fichman, R.G., Keil, M., and Tiwana, A. (2005) Beyond valuation: 'Options thinking' in IT project management, *California Management Review*, 47 (2), 74.

Fiegenbaum, A. (1990) Prospect theory and the risk-return association: An empirical examination in 85 industries, *Journal of Economic Behavior and Organization*, 14, 187–203.

Fiegenbaum, A., Hart, S., and Schendel, D. (1996) Strategic reference point theory. *Strategic Management Journal*, 17 (3), 219–235.

Fiegenbaum, A., and Thomas, H. (1986) Dynamic and risk measurement perspectives on Bowman's risk-return paradox for strategic management: An empirical study, *Strategic Management Journal*, 7, 395–407.

Fiegenbaum, A., and Thomas, H. (1988) Attitudes toward risk and the risk-return paradox – Prospect theory explanations, *Academy of Management Journal*, 31 (1), 85–106.

Fiegenbaum, A., and Thomas, H. (1990) Strategic groups and performance: The U.S. insurance industry, 1970–1984, *Strategic Management Journal*, 11 (3), 197–215.

Fiet, J. O. (1995) Risk avoidance strategies in venture capital markets, *Journal of Management Studies*, 32 (4), 551–574.

Gomez-Mejia, L.R., Haynes, K.T., Nunez-Nickel, M., Jacobson, K.J.L., and Moyano-Fuentes, J. (2007) Socioemotional wealth and business risks in family-controlled firms: Evidence from Spanish olive oil mills, *Administrative Science Quarterly*, 52 (1), 106–137.

Goranova, M., Alessandri, T.M., Brandes, P., and Dharwadkar, R. (2007) Managerial ownership and corporate diversification: A longitudinal view, *Strategic Management Journal*, 28 (3), 211–225.

Greve, H.R. (1998) Performance, aspirations, and risky organizational change, *Administrative Science Quarterly*, 43 (1), 58–86.

Greve, H. R. (2003) A behavioral theory of R&D expenditures and innovations: Evidence from shipbuilding, *Academy of Management Journal*, 46 (6), 685–702.

He, X., and Mittal, V. (2007) The effect of decision risk and project stage on escalation of commitment, *Organizational Behavior and Human Decision Processes*, 103 (2), 225–237.

Hertwig, R., Weber, E.U., Barron, G., and Erev, I. (2004) Decisions from experience and the effects of rare events in risky choices, *Psychological Science*, 15, 534–539.

Highhouse, S., and Yuce, P. (1996) Perspectives, perceptions, and risk-taking behavior, *Organizational Behavior and Human Decision Processes*, 65 (2), 159–167.

Hughes, M., and Morgan, R.E. (2007) Deconstructing the relationship between entrepreneurial orientation and business performance at the embryonic stage of firm growth, *Industrial Marketing Management*, 36 (5), 651–661.

Jegers, M. (1991) Prospect theory and the risk return relation – Some Belgian evidence, *Academy of Management Journal*, 34 (1), 215–225.

Jensen, M.C., and Meckling, W. (1976) Theory of the firm: Managerial behavior, agency costs and ownership structure, *The Journal of Financial Economics*, 3, 305–360.

Kahneman, D., and Lovallo, D. (1993) Timid choices and bold forecasts – A cognitive perspective on risk-taking, *Management Science*, 39 (1), 17–31.

Kahneman D., and Tversky, A. (1979) Prospect theory: An analysis of decision under risk, *Econometrica*, 47, 263–291.

Katila, R., and Shane, S. (2005) When does lack of resources make new firms innovative? *Academy of Management Journal*, 48, 814–829.

Kaufmann, J.B., and O'Neill, H.M. (2007) Do culturally distant partners choose different types of joint ventures? *Journal of World Business*, 42, 435–448.

Keizer, J.A., and Halman, J.I.M. (2007) Diagnosing risk in radical innovation projects, *Research – Technology Management*, 50 (5), 30–36.

Ketchen, Jr, D.J., and Palmer, T.B. (1999) Strategic responses to poor organizational performance: A test of competing perspectives, *Journal of Management*, 25 (5), 683–706.

Kim, W.C., Hwang, P., and Burgers, W.P. (1993) Multinationals' diversification and the risk-return trade-off, *Strategic Management Journal*, 14, 275–286.

Knight, F.H. (1921) *Risk, Uncertainty, and Profit*. Houghton Mifflin reprint, Chicago: University of Chicago, 1971.

Korhonen, P., and Voutilainen, R. (2006) Finding the most preferred alliance structure between banks and insurance companies, *European Journal of Operational Research*, 175 (2), 1285–1299.

Larraza-Kintana, M., Wiseman, R.M., Gomez-Mejia, L.R., and Welbourne, T.M. (2007) Disentangling compensation and employment risks using the behavioral agency model, *Strategic Management Journal*, 28 (10), 1001–1019.

Lehner, J.M. (2000) Shifts of reference points for framing of strategic decisions and changing risk-return associations, *Management Science*, 46 (1), 63–76.

Levinthal, D.A., and March, J.G. (1993) The myopia of learning, *Strategic Management Journal*, 14, 95–112.

Lubatkin, M.H., Schulze, W.S., McNulty, J.J., and Yeh, T.D. (2003) But will it raise my share price? New thoughts about an old acquisition, *Long Range Planning*, 36 (1), 81–91.

MacCrimmon, K.R., and Wehrung, D.A. (1985) A portfolio of risk measures, *Theory and Decision*, 19, 1–29.

MacCrimmon, K.R., and Wehrung, D.A. (1986) *Taking Risks: The Management of Uncertainty*. New York: Free Press.

MacCrimmon, K.R., and Wehrung, D.A. (1990) Characteristics of risk taking executives, *Management Science*, 36 (4), 422–435.

March, J.G. (1991) Exploration and exploitation in organizational learning, *Organization Science*, 2 (1), 71–87.

March, J.G., and Shapira, Z. (1987) Managerial perspectives on risk and risk taking, *Management Science*, 33, 1404–1418.

March, J.G., and Shapira, Z. (1992) Variable risk preferences and the focus of attention, *Psychological Review*, 99 (1), 172–183.

March, J.G., and Simon, H. (1958) *Organizations*. New York: John Wiley & Sons, Inc.

McGuire, J., and Matta, E. (2003) CEO stock options: The silent dimension of ownership, *Academy of Management Journal*, 46 (2), 255–265.

McNamara, G. and Bromiley, P. (1997) Decision making in an organizational setting: Cognitive and organizational influences on risk assessment in commercial lending, *Academy of Management Journal*, 40, 1063–1088.

McNamara, G. and Bromiley, P. (1999) Risk and return in organizational decision making, *Academy of Management Journal*, 42, 330–339.

Miller, K.D., and Bromiley, P. (1990) Strategic risk and corporate performance: An analysis of alternative risk measures, *Academy of Management Journal*, 33, 756–779.

Miller, K.D., and Chen, W.R. (2004) Variable organizational risk preferences: Tests of the March-Shapira model, *Academy of Management Journal*, 47 (1), 105–115.

Miller, K.D., and Leiblein, M.J. (1996) Corporate risk-return relations: Returns variability versus downside risk, *Academy of Management Journal*, 39, 1, 91–122.

Miller, K.D., and Reuer, J.J. (1996) Measuring organizational downside risk, *Strategic Management Journal*, 17, 671–691.

Miller, K.D., and Reuer, J.J. (1998a) Asymmetric corporate exposures to foreign exchange rate challenges, *Strategic Management Journal*, 19, 1183–1191.

Miller, K.D., and Reuer, J.J. (1998b) Firm strategy and economic exposure to foreign exchange rate movements, *Journal of International Business Studies*, 29, 493–513.

Miller, K.D., and Waller, H.G. (2003) Scenarios, real options, and integrated risk management, *Long Range Planning*, 36 (1), 93–107.

Mishina, Y., Pollock, T.G., and Porac, J.F. (2004) Are more resources always better for growth? Resource stickiness in market and product expansion, *Strategic Management Journal*, 25, 1179–1197.

Mone, M.A., McKinley, W., and Barker, V.L. (1998) Organizational decline and innovation: A contingency framework, *Academy of Management Review*, 23 (1), 115–132.

Mullins, J.W., Forlani, D., and Walker, O.C. (1999) Effects of organizational and decision-maker factors on new product risk taking, *Journal of Product Innovation Management*, 16 (3), 282–294.

Nicholson, N., Soane, E., Fenton-O'Creevy, M., and Willman, P. (2005) Personality and domain-specific risk taking, *Journal of Risk Research*, 8 (2), 157–176.

Nohria, N., and Gulati, R. (1996) Is slack good or bad for innovation? *Academy of Management Journal*, 39, 1245–1264.

Norton, W.I., and Moore, W.T. (2006) The influence of entrepreneurial risk assessment on venture launch or growth decisions, *Small Business Economics*, 26 (3), 215–226.

Nutt, P.C. (1993) Flexible styles of decision making and the choices of top executives, *Journal of Management Studies*, 30 (5), 695–772.

Nutt, P.C. (2006) Comparing public and private sector decision making practices, *Journal of Public Administration Research and Theory*, 12 (2), 289–316.

Ocasio, W. (1995) The enactment of economic adversity – a reconciliation of theories of failure-induced change and threat-rigidity, *Research in Organizational Behavior: An Annual Series of Analytical Essays and Critical Reviews*, 17, 287–331.

Palmer, T.B., and Wiseman, R.M. (1999) Decoupling risk taking from income stream uncertainty: A holistic model of risk, *Strategic Management Journal*, 20, 1037–1062.

Park, K. M. (2007) Antecedents of convergence and divergence in strategic positioning: The effects of performance and aspiration on the direction of strategic change, *Organization Science*, 18 (3), 386–402.

Pennings, J.M.E., and Smidts, A. (2000) Assessing the construct validity of risk attitude. *Management Science*, 46 (10), 1337–1348.

Reeb, D.N., Kwok, C.C.Y., and Baek, H.Y. (1998) Systemic risk of the multinational corporation, *Journal of International Business Studies*, 29 (2), 263–279.

Ruefli, T.W. (1990) Mean-variance approaches to risk-return relationships in strategy: Paradox lost, *Management Science*, 36, 368–380.

Ruefli, T.W. (1991) Reply to Bromiley's comment and further results: Paradox lost becomes dilemma found, *Management Science*, 37, 1210–1215.

Ruefli, T.W., Collins, J.M., and Lacugna, J.R. (1999) Risk measures in strategic management research: Auld lang syne? *Strategic Management Journal*, 20, 167–194.

Ruefli, T.W., and Wiggins, R.R. (1994) When mean square error becomes variance: a comment on 'Business risk and return: a test of simultaneous relationships', *Management Science*, 40, 750–759.

Salomo, S., Weise, J., and Gemunden, H.G. (2007) NPD planning activities and innovation performance: The mediating role of process management and the moderating effect of product innovativeness, *Journal of Product Innovation Management*, 24 (4), 285–302.

Sanders, W.G., and Hambrick, D.C. (2007) Swinging for the fences: The effects of CEO stock options on company risk taking and performance, *Academy of Management Journal*, 50 (5), 1055–1078.

Schnatterly, K., Shaw, K.W., and Jenning, W.W. (2008) Information advantages of large institutional owners, *Strategic Management Journal*, 29 (2), 219–227.

Sengun, A.E., and Wasti, S.N. (2007) Trust, control, and risk: A test of Das and Teng's conceptual framework for pharmaceutical buyer-supplier relationships, *Group and Organization Management*, 32 (4), 430–464.

Shapira, Z. (1994) *Risk taking: A management perspective.* New York: Russell Sage Foundation.

Shepherd, D.A., Douglas, E.J., and Shanley, M. (2000) New venture survival: Ignorance, external shocks, and risk reduction strategies, *Journal of Business Venturing*, 15, 393–410.

Shi, Y.W. (2007) Today's solution and tomorrow's problem: The business process outsourcing risk management puzzle, *California Management Review*, 49 (3), 27.

Shimizu, K. (2007) Prospect theory, behavioral theory, and the threat-rigidity thesis: Combinative effects on organizational decisions to divest formerly acquired units, *Academy of Management Journal*, 50 (6), 1495–1514.

Simon, M., and Houghton, S.M. (2003) The relationship between overconfidence and the introduction of risky products: Evidence from a field study, *Academy of Management Journal*, 46 (2), 139–149.

Singh, J.V. (1986) Performance, slack, and risk taking in organizational decision making, *Academy of Management Journal*, 29 (3), 562–585.

Sitkin, S.B., and Pablo, A.L. (1992) Reconceptualizing the determinants of risk behavior. *Academy of Management Review*, 17 (1), 9–38.

Sitkin, S.B., and Weingart, L.R. (1995) Determinants of risky decision-making behavior: A test of the mediating role of risk perceptions and propensity, *Academy of Management Journal*, 38 (6), 1573–1592.

Staw, B.M., Sandelands, L.E., and Dutton, J.E. (1981) Threat-rigidity effects in organizational behavior: A multilevel analysis, *Administrative Science Quarterly*, 26, 501–524.

Stewart Jr, W.H., and Roth, P.L. (2001) Risk propensity differences between entrepreneurs and managers: A meta-analytic review, *Journal of Applied Psychology*, 86 (1), 145–153.

Tong, T.W., and Reuer, J.J. (2007) Real options in multinational corporations: Organizational challenges and risk implications, *Journal of International Business Studies*, 38 (2), 215–230.

Tversky, A., and Kahneman, D. (1974) Judgement under uncertainty: Heuristics and biases, *Science*, 185, 1124–1131.

van Wyk, J., Dahmer, W., and Custy, M.C. (2004) Risk management and the business environment in South Africa, *Long Range Planning*, 37 (3), 259–276.

Voss, G.B., Sirdeshmukh, D., and Voss, Z.G. (2008) The effects of slack resources and environmental threat on product exploration and exploitation, *Academy of Management Journal*, 51 (1), 147–164.

Wang, C.X., and Webster, S. (2007) Channel coordination for a supply chain with a risk-neutral manufacturer and a loss-averse retailer, *Decision Sciences*, 38 (3), 361–389.

Whyte, G. (1998) Recasting Janis's groupthink model: The key role of collective efficacy in decision fiascoes, *Organizational Behavior and Human Decision Processes*, 73, 185–209.

Wiseman, R.M., and Bromiley, P. (1991) Risk-return associations: Paradox or artifact? An empirically tested explanation, *Strategic Management Journal*, 12 (3), 231–241.

Wiseman, R.M., and Bromiley, P. (1996) Toward a model of risk in declining organizations: An empirical examination of risk, performance, and decline, *Organization Science*, 7, 524–543.

Wiseman, R.M., and Catanach, A.H. (1997) A longitudinal disaggregation of operational risk under changing regulations: Evidence from the savings and loan industry, *Academy of Management Journal*, 40 (4), 799–830.

Wiseman, R.M., and Gomez-Mejia, L.R. (1998) A behavioral agency model of managerial risk taking, *Academy of Management Review*, 23 (1), 133–153.

Woo, C.Y. (1987) Path analysis of the relationship between market share, business-level conduct and risk, *Strategic Management Journal*, 8, 149–168.

Wright, P., Kroll, M., Krug, J.A., and Pettus, M. (2007) Influences of top management team incentives on firm risk taking, *Strategic Management Journal*, 28, 81–89.

Wu, B., and Knott, A.M. (2006) Entrepreneurial risk and market entry, *Management Science*, 52 (9), 1315–1330.

Wu, H.L., Lin, B.W., and Chen, C.J. (2007) Examining governance-innovation relationship in the high-tech industries: Monitoring, incentive and a fit with strategic posture, *International Journal of Technology Management*, 39, 86–104.

12

Decision Errors of the 4th, 5th, and 6th Kind

KIM BOAL AND MARK MECKLER

INTRODUCTION

Most people are familiar with Alpha or Beta errors from statistics or even error of the third kind (Mitroff and Betz, 1972). Alpha errors arise when we reject a true hypothesis and Beta errors arise when we 'fail to reject' a false hypothesis. 'Errors of the third kind' arise because managers, when faced with a decision often solve the 'wrong' problem very precisely. Here we expand on these concepts by drawing attention to errors of the 4th, 5th, and 6th kind.

VISIONING ERROR, CORRELATION ERROR, AND ACTION ERROR

Clawson (2009) describes 'the leadership point of view': seeing what needs to be done; understanding the underlying relationships and forces at play, and having the courage to initiate action. This framework covers the basic things a leader must do. Decision errors can similarly be separated into three kinds that parallel this leader/decision maker model: 'visioning errors', 'correlation errors', and 'action errors'. Firstly, visioning errors may be made when deciding what the main problem is that needs to be fixed. Such meta-level errors are those described by Mitroff and Betz (1972) as errors of the third kind. Secondly, correlation errors may be made when interpreting data and other evidence while figuring out causes of problems, and relationships between the various forces at play. These errors are the classic Type I (α) and Type II (β) errors described by Neyman and Pearson (1928, 1933). Thirdly, action errors may occur when deciding whether or not, and when, to act. These action errors we will describe as errors of the 4th and 5th kind. Finally, a dangerous compound error of the 6th kind may be made when particular combinations of error mistakenly introduce new forces that have unforeseen interactions and impact outside of the field of attention.

Handbook of Decision Making. Edited by Paul C. Nutt and David C. Wilson
© 2010 John Wiley & Sons, Ltd

Visioning errors happen when managers are deciding what the problems or issues are that need to be addressed. When managers do not notice, fail to consider a live hypothesis (James, 1896), or fail to pay attention to main issues and levers, and instead focus attention and effort on subordinate or inconsequential issues, then they have made *visioning errors*. Seeing what needs to be done means discerning which problems are tightly linked to the prioritized outcomes they hope to bring about. When management focuses upon corollary problems that only indirectly impact desired outcomes, or when attention is limited to effects of root problems rather than the root problems themselves, then management is committing errors of vision. Mitroff and Betz (1972) labeled the mistake of working on the wrong problem or issue an 'error of the third kind'.

Correlation errors occur when pondering, testing, and deciding about relationships between variables such as existing forces, possible actions, and potential outcomes related to a problem. Type I (or α) errors occur when the null hypothesis is mistakenly rejected – we mistakenly reject that there is no relationship between the variables. In other words, there is not in fact sufficient evidence to support the hypothesis, but we mistakenly decide that the evidence does support the hypothesis. It is not unusual to find managers believing they have evidence that 'A' is the cause of 'Problem B,' when there is in fact actually not sufficient evidence of a relationship.

Action errors occur when deciding whether to act on a proposed solution. Managers, after deciding what needs to be done, face a decision of whether or not to take action. There are two kinds of action errors: actions that you should have taken and actions that you should not have taken. Action error *does not* occur in cases (1a) when action is taken when action is truly needed, and (1b) when action is not taken when it is not appropriate. Action error *does* occur (2a) when action is taken, when it should not be taken, and (2b) when action is not taken when it should be taken.

Certainly there are multiple possible causes for a manager, having already decided what might be done *about* a problem, to then either act or not act. Sometimes a manager acts on a correct decision about what needs to be done, and the problem gets solved. When managers fail to act, often this is in the belief that systems and procedures are already in place to solve the problem at hand. Sometimes managers decide not to act because they believe that the problem will simply go away, or at least fade into inconsequence, if they exercise patience and wait it out. In either case, the decision to act or to forebear may be the correct decision.

Another possibility is that the decision to act, or the decision not to act, is a mistake that leads to unintended consequences. We introduce these as errors of the 4th and the 5th kind.

CONCATENATION OF VISIONING ERROR, EVIDENCE ERROR, AND ACTION ERROR

There is certainly no guarantee that only one kind of error is committed per problem. After all, there are three possible genres of error, and it is possible for management to make all three kinds of error, none of the errors, or any combination. Poor decision makers (or those with bad luck) might find themselves all too often working on the wrong problem, accepting unfounded cause and effect relationships, and then acting when they shouldn't. What happens when these different kinds of errors interact when working on a problem? There are $2 \times 3 \times 4 = 24$ (twenty-four) possible combinations to examine. The two (2) covers the bimodal situation of 'vision error' and 'no vision error'. The three (3) counts 'no correlation error', 'Alpha error', and 'Beta error'. The four (4) covers the action possibilities: 'no nonaction error', 'no action error', 'action error', and 'nonaction error'.

Below, we use a decision tree (Figure 12.1) to diagram the paths and interactions of this three-part decision-making process. We use the standard binomial notation of '0' for an error and '1' for a correct decision at each of the three levels through the decision tree. The labels 'Right, 1' or 'Wrong, 0' on the first decision stand for the correct decision to work on the *right problem* and the incorrect decision to work on the *wrong problem*. The next level of labels covers possibilities when analyzing evidence, testing for correlations, and possible cause–effect relationships. 'No Error, 1', 'Wrong (α) 0,' and 'Wrong (β) 0' are the labels for the three possible decisions about correlation among the data: a right decision about what the evidence/data shows; a Type I error of believing in a correlation that does not exist; or a Type II error of not believing in a correlation that does exist. The third level of labels stands for the possible action errors. An 'a' stands for acting, and a 'w' stands for waiting. A '1' means that it was the correct action decision, and a '0' indicates an incorrect action decision. Thus a path of '1, 1, 1_a' stands for 'right problem, causes understood, take action that is needed'. A path of '1, 1, 0_a' indicates 'right problem, causes understood, unnecessary action taken'. Other combinations are less simple to understand, but no less likely to occur. For example a '1, 0, 1' combination indicates working on the right problem, then making either an alpha or a beta

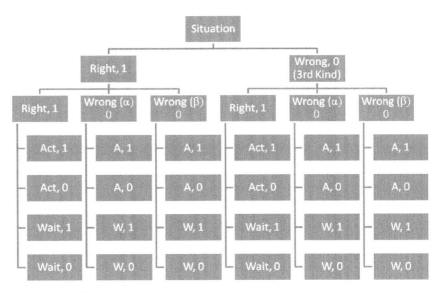

FIGURE 12.1 Decision tree for vision error, correlation error, and action error.

correlation/causation error, and then making a *seemingly* correct action decision, but one that is based upon the mistaken assumption that the causes and effects of the problem are properly understood, even though decisions about the causes were *in fact* in error. For a complete summary of all possible paths, the type of error they are associated with, and what they mean, see Appendix III.

Using this decision tree allows for probabilities to be calculated using the binomial distribution. The odds of each decision path are simply dependent upon the probability that each kind of error is made at each step. For example if there are a host of problems facing a manager, there is a possibility that management will work on the wrong problem. Perhaps a manager quite good at recognizing and prioritizing problems is right 80 % of the time. Further assume that this manager is a stickler for an audit trial, making sure that all the reasonably available evidence is gathered, correctly measured, and tested, so we assign a 0.9 probability that no correlation error will be made when analyzing the evidence, with a 0.05 chance of Type I error and 0.05 chance of Type II error. Finally, assume that this manager is good at knowing when to act, when to withhold action, and has the courage to act when it is indicated. If we then assign a 0.95 probability this good decision maker does not make a Type IV error or a Type V action error then *there is only a 68.4 % chance (0.8 × 0.9 × 0.95) that a very good decision maker like the one we have assumed will make no errors.* One would expect that a more average decision maker would have a lower probability of making the right decision. Nutt (1999) reports that half of the decisions made in organizations fail, and we do not find this claim surprising.

No Error

The ideal situation is when no decision errors are made. There are two paths in the decision tree like this, noted by a 1, 1, 1 score. The first describes the competent take charge leader making no errors. In this cell, the decision may be assumed to be sufficiently solved with no enduring problems connected to the solution.[1] Leadership has done at least three things correctly. Firstly, management is working on the right problem. They have had clear enough macro-vision to see what needs to be done and not get distracted into working on subordinate, associated, or inconsequential problems. Secondly, management has gathered enough of the proper evidence/information to discern fact from belief, desire, and fiction, and to uncover true correlations among the forces involved from apparent but nonexistent correlations, and to locate true causes from among the many effects and correlates. Thirdly, management has acted upon this evidence because there is not another effective curative process already underway.

The second 1, 1, 1 path is similar to the first in all respects except that management has the good judgment to refrain from taking action, even though the causes of the problem are now understood: This might be described as the 'Good decision, no action, problem solved' path. Refraining from action may be the proper decision for a variety of reasons. Firstly, the problem may be the type that just goes away if one waits it out. Dealing with the common cold and or an employee's occasional bad mood seems to fall into this category of problem. Burgelman and Grove

(1996) describe how various instances of dissonance require no action, (unless it is 'strategic dissonance'). Leaders, they say, should know their organizations well enough to discern between ordinary dissonance that is best ignored and will go away, and strategic dissonance that requires action. Boal and Hooijberg (2001) suggest that discernment lies at the heart of managerial wisdom. It involves the ability to perceive variation in both the interpersonal and noninterpersonal environment. In addition, it involves the capacity to take the right action at the appropriate moment. Secondly, there may be structures and processes in place that will solve the problem if you do nothing. The real question is whether or not the manager can yield to the logic of this path given the 'bias for action' that many managers have. Given a problem, managers may need to defend their reputation as a take charge decision maker, and thus act when they would be better off not acting. Some wisdom on the part of the decision maker is called for if they are to be able to discern between 1_A and 0_A. If they cannot, they may create problems of the third kind or iatrogenic solutions.

ERROR OF THE 1ST KIND (TYPE I)

When attention is focused on the right problem, and no action is taken, the problem can escalate if a Type I correlation error has been made. This is modeled as the $1, 0_\alpha, 1_w$ path. Some argue that President George W. Bush erred early in 2002 in just this (Type I) way when he concluded that Iraq was an immediate terrorist threat based upon evidence of weapons of mass destruction ('WMDs'), when the evidence was not in fact sufficient to support that hypothesis. Another example occurred two years before the October 2008 global financial system crisis that sent equity values down over 40 %, and shut down interbank lending. No later than 2006, both Senators Barack Obama and John McCain had separately spoken about the subprime mortgage crisis, especially how it was affecting Fannie Mae and Freddie Mac (mortgage investment companies), and yet nothing was done. One could argue that the right problem *was* brought to attention, and *was* worked on, but then a Type I error was made. The Senate committee gave too much weight to the evidence pushed forth by Fanny and Freddie Mac lobbyists, who demonstrated a strong inverse relationship between the existing controls and the size of the mortgage asset problem. Leaders were therefore convinced that using the existing control systems more would make the problem less. This was not also an error of non action. That is, action was (correctly) not taken on a problem that (it rationally seemed) *should not have been acted upon* because adequate existing resolution systems *seemed* in place. However, while resolution systems *were* already in place, they were not in fact adequate. The adequacy was (incorrectly) established at the correlation error point, not at the action decision point. Errors are often rooted in this kind of bounded rationality. What we mean is that sometimes action and nonaction decisions are rational at the time of the decision, given the problem as presented and the evidence at hand, but in fact wrong due to error caused by complexity, information equivocality, tunnel vision, and so forth.

Error of the 2nd Kind (Type II)

When a decision path takes the form 1, 0_β, 1 it indicates a Type II error. Type II or β errors occur when a hypothesized relationship does in fact exist, but one fails to recognize the truth of the matter. Relying on flawed testing methods, the Union Cycliste Internationale (UCI) erred in just such a way with a series of decisions from 1995 to 2005 that performance enhancing drugs were not significantly influencing the outcomes of races such as the *Tour de France*. The UCI's tests were showing insufficient evidence to claim the presence of illegal performance enhancement supplements when such supplements were in fact present.

In 1985 The Coca-Cola Company decided to abandon their original recipe for Coca-Cola in favor of a new formula. They tested to find out if existing loyal customers would be turned off by the change, and tested if non customers might be more likely to adopt the new product. Unfortunately they made a Type II error, and failed to reject the null hypothesis when testing for an inverse relationship between demand by existing customers and the new coke formula. While they were correct that potential new customers were more willing to adopt new coke than classic coke-cola, they erroneously failed to reject the other null hypothesis, concluding that there was no inverse relationship between changes in the formula and demand from their existing customers. Focused on the right problem (i.e. gaining new customers), Coca-Cola tested for the relevant correlates and made an error, then rationally acted, abandoning the original recipe and launched New Coke $(1, 1, 0_\beta, 1_a)$. Type II error can cause serious damage.

Error of the 3rd Kind (Type III)

Ian Mitroff's famous 'Error of the Third Kind' (1972) occurs when the manager is trying to solve the wrong problem very precisely. The manager may be a take charge person, but with blinders on. S/he misdiagnoses the situation, and thinks the problem is one thing when it is in fact another. We call this 'vision error' because it is the result of incorrectly seeing what needs to be done, leaving the 'true' problem outside of the attention of the decision makers. As a result organizational resources are used to solve something (another problem or a non problem), but not *The Problem*. As a result, the original problem lingers. It may do so benignly still requiring a solution, but it may fester requiring greater resources to solve. Organizational decline is often characterized by the process of denial, followed by action involving errors of the third kind, which do not stop the decline. Finally, the real problem is addressed and further action taken. Unfortunately, when the organization gets around to solving the real problem, the problem has festered requiring greater organizational resources to solve but which the organization no longer has, and decline continues.

When there has been an error of the 3rd kind, the solution is at best only indirectly effective, on average irrelevant, and at worst iatrogenic. In the best case, there are already effective administrative structures in place to deal with the true problem, and the problem gets solved even though it was not addressed by decision makers. In the average case, the true problem remains unaddressed and lingers, yet perhaps remains more or less in check because action is being taken on a related, but wrong problem. In worse cases, the lingering true problem festers, perhaps becoming more difficult to remove. In even worse cases, no action is even taken on related (yet wrong) problems. (This compound situation we describe below as an error of the 6th kind.) An error of the 3rd kind can be quite serious.

ERROR OF THE 4TH KIND (TYPE IV)

Acting to solve a problem, be it the right problem or the wrong problem, can create other difficulties. Sometimes solutions are 'iatrogenic,' meaning that they create more, or bigger, problems than they solve. Faced with such a possibility the decision maker should thoroughly examine all the potential system effects, and perhaps refrain from action.

In the case that it was an attempted solution to the right initial problem, one important problem is now replaced by another, perhaps worse, problem. We might call one who takes this path 'the Iatrogenic Decision Maker'.

Iatrogenic Decision Maker: Here the decision maker takes charge, makes a decision, but the solution to the original problem creates more and greater problems to be solved. This often occurs when the manager can not anticipate the interconnections between elements, especially nonlinear interactions. This may occur because the manager compartmentalizes the decision not foreseeing how the effects may set up other, more difficult problems, or because the manager's time frame is too limited. A classic example is Three Mile Island (Osborn and Jackson, 1988). There was a leak in the coolant system and the valve froze up. They decided to fix the problem by draining the coolant, and this led to the disaster in which the plant went south in a major meltdown. While this is a dramatic example of an iatrogenic outcome, such outcomes are more prevalent than we realize. For example, most medicines give lists of contraindications, i.e. don't use this medicine with that medicine. However, drug companies rarely look past two-way interactions. One of the authors takes five different medications per/day. Yet none of his doctors can tell him if he should be taking the five medications together or not. People who suffer from multiple ailments are always at risk from unknown drug interactions. Some solutions have unknown consequences, but some solutions can be anticipated to cause other problems. Sometimes, because decision makers do not anticipate the futurity of their decisions, focusing on too short a time period, problems that could reasonably be anticipated are ignored. Sometimes, the decision maker might realize his solution will cause other problems, but because he thinks the immediate problem is more important, or he believes the anticipated problem is a bridge to be crossed when it happens, or the stakeholder group is too weak to worry about, s/he will go ahead and make a decision that they know will create more and greater problems for the organization. But, that will be someone else's headache.

Some have argued that President George W. Bush committed this kind of action error of the 4th kind in March of 2003 by initiating (military) action in Iraq when he should not have. The critic's argument is that even if there were no α-error and Iraq was in fact gathering WMDs, the decision to *act* upon it was in error because broad and powerful international diplomatic systems and control processes were already in place that would have solved or at least contained the problem. Critics point out that President Bush acting when he should not have acted created an iatrogenic outcome, that is, his solution made the problem worse instead of better.

ERROR OF THE 5TH KIND (TYPE V)

Deciding to take no action, when no action is called for, is the correct solution. However, falsely believing that the problem will either solve itself or simply go away is an error of the 5th kind. Such errors allow the situation to linger, at best, or to fester and worsen requiring greater resources to solve. The decision maker on path 1, 1, 0_W might be described as 'the wishful non action taker'. This person mistakenly thinks that if they do nothing the problem will either go away or resolve itself through existing processes and network externalities. What they don't realize is that the problem either will not go away or that the original problem will metastasize and require great resources to solve the longer organization waits. Collins (2001) discusses how the Great Atlantic and Pacific Company (A&P) went from dominating the grocery business in the first half of the twentieth century to an also ran behind Kroger's in the second half of the twentieth century. Despite data that consumers wanted superstores, and that they had a model that worked (Gold Key stores), A&P failed to act because it did not fit their identity. As Ralph Burger, then CEO of A&P said, 'you can't argue with 100 years of success'. Fox-Wolfgramm, Boal, and Hunt (1998) discuss how an organization's identity can lead to resistance to change. Boal (2007) notes that the rules and routines that make up an organization's transactive memory inhibit search, and lead to a misdiagnosis of the problem or non action. Such was the case with Sony when it could not let go of its cathode ray tube (CRT) technology for making televisions, while Sharp, Samsung, and LG Electronics forged ahead producing liquid crystal display (LCD) televisions. Finally, Wetzel and Johnson (1968) discuss how organizational failure and decline is almost always preceded by a denial of reality leading to non action.

While not taking action may be the correct decision, in many managers' eyes a worse outcome is a reputation of lack of courage or initiative to take action. This would be an especially powerful fear if a boss incorrectly believes that you were aware of the problem but chose not to act thereby risking the creation of a bigger problem. This reinforces the schema that managers are problem solvers/decision makers and action takers creating a general bias for action. For the manager/decision maker, there exists a risk management dilemma: which is worse, making an action decision that turns out bad or not making a nonaction decision that allows a problem to evolve into a disaster? In organizational cultures with a bias for action, we would likely find more errors of the 4th kind than errors of the 5th kind. In organizational cultures or structures with a bias for inaction, we would likely find more errors of the 5th kind than errors of the 4th kind.

Sometimes a Type V error takes the form of waiting too long for action. Often it is hoped that not taking action will allow the problem to solve itself or become a non problem. If the decision maker is wrong, s/he hopes that merely delaying the decision will not be fatal and that the problem will stay of the same shape and form requiring the same resources to solve. In other words, the decision makers act as if the problem does not have a time dimension. Often by delaying the decision, greater resources may be needed to solve the problem, but the needed resources are manageable. As long as management's attention is on the problem, it probably will not get too bad before action is prioritized.

ERRORS OF THE 6TH KIND (TYPE VI)

Errors of the 6th kind are compound errors that may occur in three circumstances. Two of them are indicated when an error of the 3rd kind has already been made, and then an action error is made. For example, there is the '0, 1, 0' situation, in which a Type III error has already been made, then the initial problem is still outside of the attention, and so possible negative interactions with it may not have been considered when a manager acts. Not only does the real problem lie untreated and festering, but mistaken action on the wrong problem may introduce new correlates that may create forces that did not previously exist. This compound decision error situation is a Type VI Error ('error of the 6th kind'). In this case action creates more problems than it solves and allows other problems to combine in new ways and morph into a qualitatively different problem.

The other Type VI error circumstance takes the 1, 0, 0 form. For example '1, 0a, 0a,' notes a decision path of working on the right problem, seeing a cause that does not exist, and then acting when one shouldn't. By introducing new forces into a group of previously uncorrelated forces, new correlations and unexpected outcomes occur. It is possible that the US-led war in Iraq initiated by President George W. Bush on March 21, 2003 followed this particular path. In terms of our model, a Type I error (of believing in the existence of WMDs) combined with the Type IV error (acting when he should have allowed existing processes to solve the problem) resulted in a Type VI Error. This 'error of the 6th kind' may have introduced new forces that combined with existing variables in unforeseen ways. The outcome provides possible evidence that this was a Type VI error: a morphing of the initial hidden terrorism cell problem into a major occupation style war, foreign government building initiatives, massive dept increases, economic hardship, and a global loss of power and influence for the USA.

In cases when one of the two action errors (non action, when action should have been taken, or action when action should not have been taken) are made on the 'wrong' problem, the true problem will likely morph into something unrecognizable in terms of the original problem. Unlike errors of the 4th kind, which cause escalation of the problem, or errors of the 5th kind, which give problems time to fester, these 'error of the 6th kind' paths allow problems to grow qualitatively as well. Errors of the 6th kind often result in situations where the problem resolution does not just require more resources, but entirely different resources altogether.

If the right problem is not noticed, and no action is taken, the problem can morph into a new shape and form if a Type I correlation error has also been made. This would be the 0, 0a, 1_W path situation. Expanding on our Type 1 error example from above, when senators Barack Obama and John McCain brought to the US Senate the issue of how sub-prime loans might negatively affect Fannie Mae and Freddie Mac and nothing was done, one might argue that not only were they wrong that the VaR (value at risk) model was inadequate (Rickards, 2008) and other control systems would solve the problem (as lobbyists reportedly convinced them), but that they were working on the wrong problem altogether. The senate worried about Fannie Mae and Freddie Mac, and did not focus on the root: mortgage brokers selling and then under-disclosing loan default risk, and consumers and businesses engaging in loans that they could not afford if even a small downturn were to occur, either in their lives or in the general economy. A problem was brought to attention, and worked on. Then the subsequent Type I error was of believing in a strong inverse relationship between the existing control systems and the problem was made, so that leaders thought just using the existing control systems more would make the problem less. The US Senate did not attend to the bigger or root problem, and furthermore erroneously concluded that the existing control systems were adequate for this (wrong) problem. They then made the rationally correct decision not to act.

The above kind of situation shows how complicated an error of the 6th kind can be, and how easy it is for leaders to make them. The error was (a) vision: did not consider the broader macro-systems effects combined with (b): did not have enough clear and relevant information about forces and relationships involved.

Another example, related to the 2008 financial crisis was when no one knew that Lehman was shorting firms, and covering the short sales with treasury stock it had just taken as collateral for lines of credit to those very firms it was shorting. Even the firms who gave them the collateral did not know Lehman was going to float those shares on the market, desperate to make some money to hold them over. This Type VI error is decision error of the 3rd kind combined with error of the 5th kind $(0, 1, 0_w)$. Regulators (a) did not have vision to see that unethical short-selling was not the important problem, it was firms desperate for cash and about to default on payments; (b) lacked information that Lehman Brothers were short-selling their own clients backed with treasury stock that was collateral they had no right to float, leading to (c) non action resulting in new and worse problems. As a result, Lehman Brothers was eventually left to fail, and many experts in the weeks that followed, including the French Minister of Finance, claimed that this was the event that led most directly to the global financial meltdown of October, 2008. When a Type VI error is made, the resulting problem may no longer be recognizable in its original form. The problems are not easily diagnosable, the resources and choices available become less sufficient or desirable, the solution is not readily apparent, and the solution not so attainable.

Error of the 6th kind creates 'wicked' as opposed to 'tame' problems. Tame problems may be very complex, but they are solvable such as sending a man to the moon. It was a very complex problem, but the individuals could agree upon the definition of the problem and a solution could be found. Wicked problems are ones for which either the problem cannot be defined or *no* agreement on the solution can be found. Think about the problem of unwed teenage pregnancy. What is the underlying problem? Hormones? Morality? Both? Neither? What is the solution? Birth Control? Abstinence? Where individuals cannot agree on the problem, much less the solution, non action is the likely outcome.

DECISION ERRORS LEADING TO POSITIVE OUTCOMES

We find two decision error combinations that can lead to positive outcomes. These are an error of the 4th kind in the presence of an error of the 2nd kind (β), and an error of the 5th kind in the presence of an error of the 1st kind (α). '1, 0_α, 0_w' describes a situation in which leadership mistakenly believes they have identified some causal relationship that if acted upon will solve the problem. If action were taken, the decision maker would be committing an error of the 4th kind. Here however, management mistakenly does not act even when they believe they are supposed to act. Perhaps management is lacking the courage to act, the incentive to act, or just has too much else going on to work on another implementation. Unknown to the decision maker, the evidence was wrong, and by mistakenly not acting, an error of the 4th kind is avoided. Holcombe (2006) details a poignant example of such a situation. He brings to attention decisions regarding global climate change problems circa 1950–1980. Holcombe points out that if we had acted 30 years ago to stem global climate change based upon the best scientific evidence and overwhelming consensus among our best scholars, we would have tried to *warm* the planet, not cool it. By not acting, even when all evidence said we should have, we probably averted making a huge mistake and making the current warming trend worse.

Decision makers in taking the 1, 0_β, 0_a path take action on some hypothesized cause of a problem even when there is no apparent evidence that this cause or correlation exists. Flying in the face of the apparent evidence, they act anyway. Perhaps we can describe this kind of decision maker as the 'intuitive contrarian' because the evidence was in fact wrong, the causal relationship did exist but was missed (Type II error), and action was actually needed. Through luck, intuition, and perhaps even recklessness an error of the 5th kind is avoided.

Playing off of Holcombe's global climate change in the 1970s decision example, we may at the time of this writing (2008) be in this situation. That is given the complexity of the earth's environment and interacting forces, it is very difficult to gain certainty about what action should be taken to fix the global warming problem, or if action is appropriate at all. However, many now agree that despite not yet being certain that atmospheric CO_2 reductions will solve climate change problems we should nonetheless act aggressively. Despite the live hypothesis that Earth has natural cycles and systems that allow it to take care of itself, most agree that it would be irresponsible and in error not to act. Sometimes, despite the lack of complete information, evidence, and understanding, we decide to act anyway 'before it is too late' – before the problem morphs into new and worse problems. Going with intuition about causes, and taking action without full understanding, we sometimes end up with a positive outcome.

CASE STUDIES

We next summarize two cases in which a number of decisions and decision error possibilities present themselves. The first case study is the financial markets and systems crisis of 2008, as observed no later than October 12, 2008. This means that at the time of writing (October 12, 2008), outcomes of the situation after the stock market(s) crash are unknown, as are many of the details which will later no doubt come to light. Therefore predictions will be made, and decision error possibilities suggested, but the truth will not be known until well after this chapter goes to print. It will hopefully be informative to compare in retrospect the decision errors we proposed were being made (at the time of this writing), with the decision errors that will be borne out by history to be true to the facts. Data for the 'World Financial Crisis, October 2008' case study was collected from the extensive ongoing newspaper, web, and television media coverage of the event as it occurred.

The second case study 'Meltdown in the Tropics' occurred on Tuesday evening, March 3, 1992, making it possible to look backward and analyze the decision paths and errors. On that evening, a manager was involved in an operations 'meltdown'. Fifteen years later, he said, 'I still don't like thinking about it' and it was 'my worst day of work, ever'. Data reported for this case is based upon first hand recollections of the event gathered from the manager involved in the case.

The Appendix contains a table summarizing the possible decision paths and error(s) that we have established above. We refer to this table during our discussion of each case study.

Case 1: World Financial Crisis, October 2008

On July 15, 2008, US Treasury Secretary Hank Paulson and Securities and Exchange Commission Chairman Christopher Cox took radical steps: they created an emergency order limiting short-selling in shares of Fannie Mae, Freddie Mac, Lehman Brothers, Goldman Sachs, Merrill Lynch, and Morgan Stanley. They did this to stop a growing problem that seemed suspiciously close to insider trading, and that was creating unnecessary and unfounded worry among all shareholders that the biggest investment banks in the world were in trouble. VaR (value at risk) models were double checked, and no bank had more at risk than the balance of their assets could easily cover.

Two and a half months later, In October of 2008, the United States Federal Reserve faced a major decision. Should they commit about $ 1 trillion of the public's money to bail out investment banks holding mortgage and real estate backed assets whose values had plummeted over the last year. Investment banks and mortgage banks were failing at an alarming rate. Morgan Stanley, Fanny Mae, Freddy Mac, and Washington Mutual had already been closed down then sold. Lehman Brothers had been allowed to fail altogether, as no buyer could be found. The other major investment and mortgage banks were on the brink of failure. Even worse, the firms that sold insurance to these banks providing a hedge against downside risk were also about to declare bankruptcy. AIG, one of the largest of those, had already been rescued; purchased by the US Government to prevent its failure. Leaders of nations and of financial markets gathered and had meetings 24 hours a day in order to figure out what was going on, understand what might be done, and decide what to do, and what not to do about it. The life blood pressure of modern financial systems, the liquidity of assets, and the flow of cash had dropped precariously. The system was on the brink of failure.

On October 9, 2008, the Dow Jones Industrial average had fallen to 8579.19, down from 14 164.53 exactly one year earlier, a 38 % decline. 'On paper' losses for the year, measured by the Down Jones Wilshire 5000 Composite index which represents almost all of the stocks traded in the USA, added up to $ 8.3 trillion lost, an almost incomprehensible figure. The US stock market had declined 21 % (2338 points) in just four weeks following the bankruptcy of Lehman Brothers investment bank. Much of this decline (17 %) came in the days *after* October 5, *after* a much debated and passionately defended credit market bailout solution had been announced and enacted. The next day, Friday October 10 the slide continued, dropping another 128 points, down 1874 for the week after the solution was announced.

The US Federal Reserve and EU central banks had agreed to purchase devalued assets, mostly mortgage back securities, held by banks and investment firms and had coordinated a global lowering of interest rates on government loans to banks.

On October 6, the day after the solution had been enacted, the Associated Press' Tom Raum and Jeannine Aversa begin their front page article with: 'On Day One, the $ 700 billion plan didn't help, just the opposite. The government's huge rescue package, aimed at rebuilding economic confidence in the US and around the world, instead sounded a global alarm. The trading day after Congress approved the measure and President Bush signed it into law (with much fanfare on a Friday), US and world stock markets dropped approximately 7 %' (Raum and Aversa, 2008). There were now pointed questions about how this would all be paid for. The Treasury Department reported it would increase its bond sales to help pay for the bailout, and the Federal Reserve immediately responded by announcing an expansion of the loan bailout program to $ 900 billion and that it would pay interest on reserves that banks kept at the Federal Reserve.

Raum and Aversa continued: 'Bush sought to reassure panicking markets. "It's going to be awhile to restore confidence in the financial system. But one thing people can be certain of is that the bill I signed is a big step toward solving this problem," he said in San Antonio. Nobody seemed reassured. Chaos in the financial system seemed to grow by the minute.' (Raum and Aversa, 2008: 7) When the Dow Industrial average plunged below 10 000 for the first time in four years that day, all sectors were being sold off en masse, and not just financial and related stocks. 'The crisis has morphed from a near shutdown in lending to a new, more dangerous phase in which financial and other companies face greater chances of insolvency', suggested University of

Chicago Professor of economics and finance Amil Kashyap (Raum and Aversa, 2008: 7).

Three days later, on October 9, when further 'helpful' bailout measures were announced by the federal government, the market dropped another 7 % (679 points), down a full 17 % in the four days since the *solution* to the problem had been announced (Paradis and Crutsinger, 2008).

On October 10, Luis Uchitelle of the *New York Times* News Service wrote:

> The Federal Reserve and congress are pushing out close to $ 1 trillion to repair the nation's financial systems and to encourage lending. But that is not enough to revive the economy. Spending has to resume. Consumers, however have cut back sharply on their spending, in what will be the first quarterly decline in 17 years when the government tally is in for the third quarter. 'We have to prop up consumption,' Rep Barney Frank, D-Mass., chairman of the House Financial Services Committee said in an interview.

Uchitelle's *New York Times* article continued:

> The rationale for another stimulus package, particularly one that helps states and cities, is compelling for many economists. The nearly $ 1 trillion that Congress and the Federal Reserve are making available to the financial system is intended to make credit more available. That props up the supply side. But to make the economy grow, or stop contracting, demand is required. Consumers, businesses and governments need confidence to spend their own incomes or tap credit from a repaired financial system. Uchitelle then quoted Princeton University economist Alan Blinder: 'Deciding not to cut spending is the functional equivalent of spending more. Either one leads to more spending that you otherwise would have.' (Uchitelle, 2008)

Discussion: World Financial Crisis, October 2008

Firstly, note that the problem got worse, twice, not better after action was taken, leading us to believe that at the least, Type IV action errors were made. The first time action was taken, it was to limit, and then to disallow short-selling on financial institutions. This error of the 4th kind (action that should not have been taken) led to financial firms holding risky loans and investments in other banks, and at the same time being unable to hedge against devaluation of those assets. The SEC did not consider that the other primary financial hedge tool, the Chicago credit default swaps market (derived from the credit default insurance contracts), was at the same time becoming unstable (as AIG and other insurers began lacking the capital to back up the policies). With no reliable direct hedges available, financial firms decided they had to sell their un-hedged assets immediately. Unfortunately, with everyone needing to sell, there were almost no buyers and the finance industry asset values dropped faster than anyone predicted. The problem of (seemingly) unethical short-selling had morphed into a massive devaluation of assets on the balance sheets of investment banks and mortgage institutions, and then a complete unwillingness of banks to make loans to each other. The life blood pressure of modern financial systems, the liquidity of assets, and the flow of cash dropped precariously, and then stalled.

The second time the situation worsened when action was taken was just after the stimulus package was enacted. Global stock markets dropped precipitously and nearly crashed entirely. Perhaps President Bush made it even worse on October 7 when he took action by announcing 'It's going to be awhile to restore confidence in the financial system.' For the financial markets, this was a self-fulfilling statement, with everyone realizing that they should not have confidence *now* (since it's going to take awhile). Furthermore, recall that the market stabilized and even began to recover during the days when the US Senate and House of Representatives rejected the bailout. That is, the problem dissipated *when no action was taken,* then immediately worsened when action was taken.

Secondly, note that the problem actually morphed into a new different problem, requiring more and qualitatively different resources. At the time of this writing (October 12, 2008), it is not at all clear what resources will be needed, or indeed what is the extent of the problem.

Thirdly, it is clear that the problem focused upon changed twice, and it is still not clear that the governments are even now working on the right problem. We think they are still working on the wrong problem.

Two years before this crisis, both Barack Obama and John McCain (the two presidential candidates at the time) had separately spoken about the sub-prime mortgage crisis, especially how it was affecting Fannie Mae and Freddie Mac, and yet nothing was done. Unfortunately, leadership in neither the US Senate nor the executive branch (the Bush administration) worked on this problem or acted on this problem. This may be understood as a $0, 1, 0_w$ path. It is also possible that this was a $1, 0_\beta, 0_w$ path. Perhaps the problem *was* worked on by leadership, but no significant relationship between Fannie Mae's and Freddie Mac's struggles and the greater financial system was identified, and furthermore, it was assumed that free financial market forces would take care of the problem, so there was no need to act. By the time the Bush administration recognized the problem it had already escalated into a crisis that was bringing down many Wall Street firms, and other investment banks around the world, causing a liquidity shortage crisis, requiring the government to step in for an estimated $ 1 trillion.

If this was an error of non action on a problem that should have been acted upon, then it was a $1, 1, 0_w$ error of the 5th kind, with the outcome being a more severe problem of the same kind.

On the other hand, this may also have been other kinds of error: a $1, 0_\alpha, 1$ or a $0, 0_\alpha, 1$. That is, a Type I error of believing in a strong inverse relationship between the existing control systems and the problem, so that leaders thought just using the existing control systems more would make the problem less. Unfortunately, it may have been the case that the existing control systems were not adequate for the problem. For example, there is good reason to doubt that the VaR model (value at risk), used by the finance industry to assess appropriate portfolio risk, applies in extreme or complex situations (Rickards, 2008).

Case 2: Meltdown in the Tropics

On Tuesday evening, March 3, 1992, A manager, (we've changed his name to 'Mike'), was involved in an operations meltdown at Valentino's, a 120-seat 4-star restaurant at a resort in the Caribbean. He said it was 'his worst day of work, ever'.

Mike's goals for the evening were simple: smooth service, keeping the guests moving forward at the proper 1:45 minute pace per table, turning the tables over about 1.5 times. This would hopefully result in serving about 150 guests at the $ 60 per person check average, yielding expected revenue of $ 9000.

It was the last day of Mardi-Gras, the day of the grand parade. At 4:30 pm, two waiters and the cashier, all scheduled to begin at 3:30 pm, had not yet shown up. At a table in the back of the dining room, Mike remained un-fazed. He and the chef had planned ahead for the possibility that some of the staff might skip work in favor of the carnival parade. The number of guest reservations was 100, well short of the usual. This meant that operations would be covered even with no-shows, and even if there was the typical good handful of walk-ins (no reservations). Days earlier, Mike had asked the hotel's front desk cashier to be available to cover the restaurant cashier's spot, just in case he needed him. The regular cashier had negotiated to come in for just two hours so she could be with her family. Mike had said yes to her because family is more valued in that country than a job. She would have simply been forced to skip work altogether and get fired. Mike figured two hours was a good com-promise, since she could teach the front desk guy, then he could take over when she left. In the end, she was one of the 'no shows' anyway.

Mike said it didn't matter because the backup cashier had been able to come in an hour early and was already organizing his station. It looked like he knew his stuff. It seemed like the problem was solved. Scheduled employees not showing up could be a serious problem, so foresight on those matters is a good thing to have. With the backup cashier already there, and only 100 reservations, the missing servers and cook would barely be missed.

Neither Mike nor the chef nor any of the staff had any idea just how bad that evening would turn out to be. Mike's belief, that the problem was having no shows on the kitchen and the service staff, was wrong. Not only was he solving the wrong problem, he also wasn't solving that wrong one well. Despite acting properly in advance by over-scheduling and under-booking, he missed two critical factors. First, because of the carnival parade, a lot of other restaurants were closed. All that overflow was directed by the taxis to Valentino's, so there were going to be a huge number of walk-ins. He didn't tell the receptionist about his planning and he didn't say not to seat too many walk-ins. He just never saw it coming. Second, Mike was focusing on the wrong problem. He should have been focused on the critical expertise held by the cashier who did not show up, and worried that the replacement he'd arranged might not know what to do if things got busy.

At 6pm, early walk-in food sales were keeping the line cooks busy and the chef was forced to set up a work station for himself aiding the effort to get ready for the dinner rush. Five tables of walk-ins showed up at about 6:30 pm. Because the reservation book was only half full, and the main rush was scheduled to start around 7:15 pm, the receptionist seated everyone without a second thought. At that point everyone was working as hard and fast as they could.

Fast-forward to 8:25 pm. The manager had just been called to the restaurant ten minutes earlier, and had come quickly from his back office. At the building entrance impatient guests with reservations were lined up out the front door. The bar and restaurant entrance was jammed too. To Mike, it didn't make sense – the reservation system was supposed to take care of guest flow. It provided a regular, even flow in 15-minute cycles. When he asked the receptionist and the bartender 'what happened?' they said 'hopi-hopi walk-ins' and that the cashier was slow.

Upstairs the main dining room was full of irate customers, waiting to pay their bills. There were waiters and section captains looking panicked and lost. After kind of keeping up when things were slow, the back-up cashier had floundered, then panicked under the rush. The few guest checks that got to customers were wrong. To make things worse, he didn't tell anyone he was having any trouble until waiters starting asking for the first guest checks at about 7:45 pm. First wave guests couldn't pay and therefore couldn't leave. The main rush of guests was already waiting for those tables, many for 30 minutes or more. To make matters worse, those guests who wanted to hail a taxi to take them elsewhere found that there were no taxis. Everyone was at the parade.

The cashier had lost track of things under the flood of orders that came in when the rush started. When things were slow, from 6 to 7 pm, he'd been OK, slowly finding buttons and opening tables, adding orders to the system, and letting them print out in the kitchen. After seven o'clock, though, he quickly fell behind and then lost track of things. Nobody found out until he had panicked and told one of the floor captains at about eight o'clock.

He had no idea what items had been ordered or served. Even after realizing he was drowning, he had continued to attempt to use the cash register, hoping that somehow it would work itself out. When waiters learned that there was no written record of what people had ordered they decided to start asking the guests and hope for honesty. It was going to take a long time and the backup of guests had already created a log jam impossible to unravel.

The guests had long since started raising their voices and demanding service. One of the most difficult things about retail work is having clearly unhappy and damaged customers, and no idea what to do to make things right.

That is when Mike realized that not one person in the whole establishment knew how to run the cash register. Mike directed the cashier to stop trying to use the electronic cash register and to organize the receipts and billing by hand. Mike then distributed three-part order pads to the waiters (replacing the two part forms they were using), so that they could drop off a copy of each order in the kitchen. It didn't help.

It was too late for solutions on how to run the cashier's station. The problem had become toxic and had morphed into a different one. The new problem was massive backup at all stations, initially caused by a clogged bottleneck at the cashier's station, but not solvable by unclogging that bottleneck. Now every station was a bottleneck. To get things flowing fast and move inventory forward out of each station to the next, it would require that guests eat faster. Unfortunately, that's not really a viable option.

Mike resigned himself to the fact that neither he nor anyone else knew what to do to stop or even control this building disaster. When people saw Mike give up, organization crumbled. The staff panicked and everyone started working only for themselves. At the end of the night, servers went home with a lot of undisclosed tips, Mike sat numbed and crestfallen, and the chef cried, never having been through such a thing. Some of the staff looked like they'd seen Dante's inferno itself. The little problem of predictable employee 'no show' had turned into an avalanche – it had been a full-scale operations meltdown.

In the days that followed, the accounting department calculated a 60 % shortfall on payments by the 80 guests they managed to serve that night. There were reservations for about 150, all of whom showed up. Two months later the manager was looking for another job.

Discussion: meltdown in the tropics

Mike made a Type III error right from the start and as he focused his attention on that, he ignored the importance of that hour or two of on the job training the backup cashier was supposed to receive from the main cashier, who did not show up. This was a 0, 1, 1 error. Mike correctly saw that there was a relationship between the carnival and no shows, and acted correctly by lowering the number of reservations and overstaffing for that reduced level of service. However, when the cashier did not show up, he added a Type I error, believing that the front desk cashier was a solid substitute for the everyday cashier. That hypothesis, assumed to be true, was not. He was now on a $0, 0_\alpha, 1$ decision path. The compounding of Type III error and Type I error, and correctly taking action, (because action certainly was needed), created a Type VI error, and the problem morphed into a complete operations meltdown. Introducing a bad cashier into an otherwise working-as-normal system combined in all kinds of ways to create chaos. Had the replacement cashier not been brought in, service staff would have worked manually from the start, and everyone would have known that things were going to move slowly. The bartender and the receptionist would have known that they were going manual, and that this would present a challenge. Therefore they would have turned away rather than seated many of those walk-ins.

Mike made at least one other vision error. He did not envision the tidal wave of customers who had gotten into taxis, headed out to dinner houses that turned out to be closed, and ended up as walk-ins at the more costly Valentino's. With basic environmental scanning, he would have known that many of his competitors were going to be closed during the final day of Carnival. These unplanned for guests were promptly seated at tables not yet reserved for that time slot. With the backed-up cashier, operations could not move the early walk-ins and early reservations out of the late reserved slots. The restaurant, because of the massive influx of walk-in guests, was operating at full capacity, and people were still showing up, and would keep showing up en masse for a few hours.

Conclusion

There are six different kinds of decision error spanning three levels of decision. Type I and Type II error take place at a middle level of decision making when figuring out the forces and relationships involved in a problem. We call these kinds of errors 'correlation errors'. Type III error occurs at a more macro level, when deciding what the problems are and what problem to work on. We call this level of error 'vision error'. We then introduce Type IV and Type V errors (errors of the 4th and 5th kind) as 'action errors.' Action error can occur when deciding whether or not to act on a possible solution to a chosen problem. Type IV error is acting when action was uncalled for, and Type V error is not acting when action was called for. Finally, Type VI error (error of the 6th kind) is a compounding vision, correlation, and action error.

A decision maker goes through these three levels of decision: the vision decision, the hypothesis test decision, and the action decision. The first level is where either the right problem is identified and worked on, or a Type III error occurs. At the next level there are three possibilities. Either the evidence/data is correctly analyzed, or a Type I (α) or Type II (β) error is made. At the third level, where a decision about action must be made, there are four possibilities. Two of the possibilities are correct and two are in error. Correct action may take the form of acting when action is called for, or not acting when waiting or doing nothing is called for. The two action errors are the opposites of these.

All six kinds of error may have serious consequences, and error of the 6th kind is the most dangerous. Interactions among variables in complicated contexts, such as financial systems, business operations, political arenas, global climates, and so forth often exist in precarious balance and chaotic order. The introduction of even a single new force, or the withholding of an expected force, can lead to massive disorder, unforeseen outcomes, and a transformation of one problem into brand new and completely different problems.

We have also detailed out a binomial decision tree that tracks the 24 decision sequence possibilities implied by our three-level system and summarized the implications of each pattern. Using this decision tree, and applying 'what if' prior probabilities, one can derive resulting probabilities for each of the outcomes. When we apply 'good decision maker' prior probabilities, we find that that even a good decision maker will probably have about a 70 % success rate.

Appendix I

SUMMARY OF DECISION COMBINATIONS

Decision Path	Error Type	Description
$1, 1, 1_a$:	No error.	Right Problem, causes understood, take action, action solves problem.
$1, 1, 0_a$:	IV	Right Problem, causes understood, unnecessary action taken, problem worsens.
$1, 1, 1_w$:	No error.	Right Problem, right causes, do not act, problem solves itself.
$1, 1, 0_w$:	V	Right Problem, right causes, do not act, problem worsens.
$1, 0_\alpha, 1_a$:	I	Right Problem, evidence wrong, there was no correlation, take action on mistaken correlation. Can make problem worse or make problem morph by introducing new forces.
$1, 0_\alpha, 1_w$:	I	Do damage done. No action is taken on mistaken correlation.
$1, 0_\alpha, 0_a$:	VI	By introducing new forces into a group of previously uncorrelated forces, new correlations and unexpected outcomes occur.
$1, 0_\alpha, 0_w$:	I & V	Double negative avoids damage. Mistaken inaction avoids damage of α error and wasted resources.
$1, 0_\beta, 1_a$:	N/A.	Action is not a rational path if no correlation evidence is found.
$1, 0_\beta, 1_w$:	II	Right Problem, evidence was wrong, there was a correlation, do not act. Problem likely festers and gets worse.
$1, 0_\beta, 0_a$:	II & IV	Results in No Error. Mistaken action solves problem.
$1, 0_\beta, 0_w$:	N/A.	Mistakenly waiting not a rational path if no correlation evidence is found.
$0, 1, 1_a$	III	Action solves wrong problem. May help contain/check 'true' problem if action is on a related problem. May be irrelevant to 'true' problem.
$0, 1, 0_a$	VI	Inappropriate action on wrong problem introduces new correlates and new worse problems are created.
$0, 1, 1_w$	III	Systems and processes already in place solve the 'wrong' problem. 'True' problem festers.

(Continued)

$0, 1, 0_w$	III & V	Resources are not wasted working on the wrong problem and no confounding correlates are introduced.
$0, 0_\alpha, 1_a$	VI	Evidence was wrong, shouldn't have acted. Action creates new unexpected correlates and outcomes.
$0, 0_\alpha, 1_w$	N/A	Not a rational possibility.
$0, 0_\alpha, 0_a$	III & I & IV	Results in Type VI. Mistaken action on assumed relationship that does not in fact exist, working on the wrong problem. New potential correlates are needlessly introduced. Both problems may get worse and/or morph.
$0, 0_\alpha, 0_w$	III	Results in Type III. Double negative limits damage. Mistaken inaction avoids damage of α error and wasted resources, initial problem festers.
$0, 0_\beta, 1_a$	N/A	N/A. Action is not a rational path if no correlation evidence is found.
$0, 0_\beta, 1_w$	III & II	Results in serious Type V. Working on wrong problem, evidence was wrong, should have acted. Both problems fester.
$0, 0_\beta, 0_a$		Mistaken Action solves the wrong problem. **Error of 3rd kind.**
$0, 0_\beta, 0_w$		N/A. Not a rational path.

NOTES

1. When saying sufficient we make no claims to the decision being optimal in outcome or optimal in process. It is our perspective that many fine decisions are suboptimal, as managers satisfice in order to move forward. Sufficient resolution also does not mean that the decision maker went through all of the steps normative decision-making models would describe, i.e. problem identification, diagnosis, idea generation, criteria sieve, alternative selection, and implementation. Competent decision making also does not necessarily mean following an optimal search pattern. For example Simon's satisficing model follows a different search pattern than does Einhorn's Elimination by Aspects model and both wind up with a decision, often different and often suboptimal, but not necessarily. A successful decision and successful action simply means that the decision and the action work in terms of the problem.

REFERENCES

Boal, K.B. (2007) 'Strategic Leadership of Knowledge-based Competencies and Organizational Learning', in Robert Hooijberg, James G. Hunt, John Antonakis, and Kim Boal, with Nancy Lane (eds) *Being There Even When You Are Not: Leading through Strategy, Structures, and Systems, Monographs in Leadership and Management, Vol. 4.* Amsterdam: Elsevier, 73–90.

Boal, K.B., and Hooijberg, R.J. Winter, 2001. Strategic leadership research: Moving on, *Yearly Review of Leadership: A Special Issue of The Leadership Quarterly*, 11, 515–550.

Burgelman, R.A., and Grove, A.S. (1996) Strategic dissonance, *California Management Review*, 38 (2), 8–28.

Clawson, J.G. (2009) *Level Three Leadership.* Upper Saddle River, NJ: Pearson-Prentice Hall, 4th edition.

Collins, J. (2001) *Good to Great.* Harper Business.

Fox-Wolfgramm, S.J., Boal, K.B., and Hunt, J.G. (Jerry) (1998) Organizational adaptation to institutional change: A comparative study of first-order change in prospector and defender banks. *Administrative Science Quarterly*, 43, 87–126.

Holcombe, R.G. (2006) Should we have acted thirty years ago to prevent global climate change? *The Independent Review*, Fall 2006, 11 (2), 283.

James, W. (1896) 'The Will to Believe', in William James, *Essays in Pragmatism.* New York: Hafner Publishing Company, 1948, 88–109. Originally an address to the Philosophical Clubs of Yale and Brown Universities first published in *New World*, June 1896.

Mitroff, I., and Featheringham, T.R. (1974) On systemic problem solving and the error of the third kind. *Behavioral Science*, 19, 383–393.

Neyman, J., and Pearson, E.S. (1967) 'On the Use and Interpretation of Certain Test Criteria for Purposes of Statistical Inference, Part I', reprinted at 1–66 in J. Neyman and E.S. Pearson, *Joint Statistical Papers*, Cambridge: Cambridge University Press (originally published in 1928).

Neyman, J., and Pearson, E.S. (1967) 'The Testing of Statistical Hypotheses in Relation to Probabilities a Priori', reprinted at 186–202 in J. Neyman and E.S. Pearson, *Joint Statistical Papers*, Cambridge: Cambridge University Press (originally published in 1933).

Nutt, P. (1999) Surprising but true, half the decisions in organizations fail, *Academy of Management Executive*, 13 (4), 75–90.

Osborn, R.N., and Jackson, D.H. (1988) Leaders, riverboat gamblers, or purposeful unintended consequences in the management of complex, dangerous technologies, *Academy of Management Journal*, 31, 924–947.

Paradis T., and Crutsinger, M. (2008) 'Familiar factors and plain old fear drop the Dow 679 points', The Associated Press, printed in *The Oregonian*, October 10, pp. 1, 11.

Raum T. and Aversa, J. (2008) 'Financial Alarm spread even as U.S races to enact rescue', The Associated Press, printed in *The Oregonian*, October 7, pp. 1, 7.

Rickards, J.G. (2008) 'How risk models failed Wall Street, U.S.', *The Washington Post*, Guest Opinion. October 4, 2008.

Uhcitelle, L. (2008) 'Congress considers a new stimulus plan', New York Times News Service, in *The Oregonian*, October 10, pp. 1, 10.

Weitzel, W., and Jonsson, E. (1989) Decline in organizations – A literature integration and extension, *Administrative Science Quarterly*, 34, 91–109.

13

Decision Making in Public Organizations

HAL G. RAINEY, JOHN C. RONQUILLO,
AND CLAUDIA N. AVELLANEDA

Decisions in government organizations can have broad impacts on the public interest, so the decision-making processes in public organizations merit analysis. Yet, while major scholars have contributed important essays and observations, very few empirical studies have focused on distinctive aspects of decision making in public organizations as contrasted with other organizations such as business firms. Actually, major scholars have asserted that they differ very little from business in organizational processes such as decision making. This chapter will first address this matter of whether the public sector presents a distinctive context for decision making. We will discuss the meaning of a 'public' organization as a decision context, and the claims people make about the characteristics of this context that affects decision making. Then the chapter reviews scholars' observations and evidence from empirical studies about the distinctive nature of decision making in public organizations. We will describe how people in public organizations often engage in 'rational' decision processes in well-structured and routine situations, and these decisions resemble those in similar situations in business firms. Then the chapter addresses the limits of rationality assumptions for public organizations, and the need for contingency perspectives. Such perspectives, exemplified by James Thompson's framework, take into account such factors as the level of goal agreement and technical knowledge. Then we review additional alternatives for contingency perspectives, including prospect theory and poliheuristic theory that analysts have applied to some governmental settings. In addition, we examine research indicating the importance of issue type and salience, and internal and external constraints on decision processes. Then we review major topics in the literature on public sector decision-making. These include the debate over incrementalism and Lindblom's 'Science of Muddling Through', Etzioni's 'mixed

Handbook of Decision Making. Edited by Paul C. Nutt and David C. Wilson
© 2010 John Wiley & Sons, Ltd

scanning' proposal, and the relevance of the 'Garbage Can' perspective. We then consider prescriptive frameworks and empirical research on strategic decision making in public organizations because it has taken on such importance due to its wide application in governments at all levels and in multiple nations, and laws that require it in US federal agencies and many state government agencies.

THE DISTINCTIVE CONTEXT OF PUBLIC ORGANIZATIONS

The generic perspective: There's not much difference

What is the public sector and what do we mean when we refer to a public organization? Leading scholars and experts on organizations have often taken the position that the commonalities between public and private organizations are greater than the differences (e.g. Simon, 1995; 1998; Thompson, 1962). Researchers also point out that such concepts as public, private, and nonprofit sectors do more to confuse than to clarify matters. One cannot draw a clear line between such 'sectors' because they are interwoven and 'blurred' in many ways. Through laws, ordinances, and regulations, government heavily influences decisions in private firms. Through contracting-out of government services, government shares responsibilities with private firms and nonprofit organizations. Government and private organizations often do the same things, involving the same types of people (attorneys, scientists, accountants, teachers, clerical personnel, custodial personnel) and organizations (hospitals, schools, utilities, universities, railroads, financial organizations, retirement pension organizations). Thus, decision makers in government, business, and nonprofit organizations frequently face decisions that are very similar. In fact, some decision procedures widely used in business were largely developed by government. Some of the decision procedures in Operations Research and Management Science were originally developed for military applications. Strategic decision processes as part of strategic planning have become virtually ubiquitous in organizations of all types, as these procedures become more assimilated across sectors. How can one claim that public sector organizations make distinctive types of decisions under unique circumstances?

What's public? Identifying the public sector context

Organizational scholars have justification for warning about the indistinctiveness of public, private, and nonprofit sectors and organizations. At the same time, the political economies of the United States and numerous other nations are founded and designed on the principle that government and business differ. While the blurring of the sectors makes distinctions difficult, that mixing of the sectors often draws sector distinctions into sharper focus. At the time of writing, the US federal government has begun procedures and payments to support major financial institutions that face collapse without government intervention. The President has proposed, and Congress has approved, plans to provide loans to major investment banks and other institutions, and possibly to buy stock or invest in partial ownership of others. Congress included in some of this legislation sharp limits on the use of these financial resources to support bonuses and financial compensation packages for leaders and employees of these foundering financial institutions. In the media and through other channels, critics berated the massive bonuses and compensation that these institutions had paid, even as the organizations failed. The President and Members of Congress had publicly objected to having the taxpayers' money go to pay high bonuses for the executives of the 'private' firms. While the federal investment in the private companies blurred the distinction between the public category (i.e. the government category) and the private business category, at the same time it brought the public versus private distinction into sharper focus. With public money came more public control, including government intervention into the compensation decisions in the business firms.

Still, we face a challenge in clarifying the meaning of public and private organizations. (We will focus on this distinction and leave the nonprofit category out of the discussion for present purposes.) The 'generic' perspective among many organization theorists fails to recognize the observations of numerous authors in economics and political science who treat government agencies as fundamentally distinct from private firms. As one of many examples, in his very widely cited book, *Inside Bureaucracy*, Anthony Downs (1967: Chapter IV) raised the question of why 'nonmarket' organizations must perform important social functions in modern societies, and why business organizations that sell goods on markets cannot do so. Government organizations such as regulatory agencies must deal with 'externalities' such as air and water pollution, which impose costs and benefits external to an exchange between a business firm and its customers. Government organizations have to provide collective or public goods such as national defense and enforcement of contracts. Such goods provide benefits or costs to everyone in the area in which they are provided. Thus they cannot be sold to individuals at a market price, and government funds them with some of the taxes that citizens pay. Government also must provide protection for consumers in certain instances (for example, by ensuring the safety of foods and drugs), create a framework of law and order, deal with instabilities and deficiencies in the market economy (see the example above about government intervening to support failing private firms), and other essential goods and services.

Prominent authors have analyzed such distinctions between government functions and roles as contrasted with those of private firms. Over half a century ago, Dahl and Lindblom (1953), two of the most prominent political scientists of their era, distinguished between 'enterprises' (private firms) and 'agencies' (government agencies). They pointed out that in modern political economies agencies and enterprises represent two poles or extremes of a complex continuum of organizations that mix characteristics of business firms and government agencies. These 'hybrid' forms include business firms heavily regulated by government (e.g. electric utilities), or enterprises in which government holds some stock. Others include state-owned enterprises such as government-owned banks and transportation organizations (airlines, railroads). While these hybrid forms complicate the distinction between agencies and enterprises, there are still plenty of examples of these two types of organizations, which present no confusion over whether they are government or business organizations.

Wamsley and Zald (1973) offered an additional clarification of the distinction. They pointed out that the public–private distinction actually includes two major component distinctions – ownership and funding. We can think of public organizations as those that government owns and pays for. If there is a nation in which government does not 'own' and operate the equivalent of the US Department of Defense, and does not pay for it from governmental revenues gathered through taxes or other authoritative governmental methods, it is hard to locate that nation. In the US and many other nations, government-owned and funded organizations provide the police and fire fighting functions and major elements of the retirement pension system (The Social Security Administration), collect the taxes, produce the currency, regulate private organizational activities, and perform other major functions. Of course these patterns involve exceptions such as the Defense Department (DoD) relying on private contractors and obtaining a very small proportion of DoD revenues through sales (of surplus equipment, for example). There are private pension, policing, and fire fighting services, as well, but even for these exceptions, we can easily clarify what is 'public' or government funded and operated, and what is not. We can consider private organizations to be those owned by private, nongovernmental owners and/or stockholders, and which receive most of their revenues from sales to customers at a price. We really do not have to puzzle over whether a great many organizations, such as IBM, Microsoft, and Procter and Gamble, are private in this sense. Between these two types of organizations, there are organizations owned by government but funded mainly through private sources such as sales to customers (for example, the U.S. Postal Service). Other organizations, such as defense contractors, are privately owned but get a very large proportion of their financial resources from government contracts. Again, these two types of organizations render inadequate a simple distinction between public and private organizations, but they do not obviate such a distinction. Bozeman (1987) took an additional step by treating government ownership and funding as continua of 'publicness' and pointing out that all organizations have some degree of publicness.

Ultimately, all of these methods of distinguishing between public and private organizations lead to similar conclusions. We can designate public organizations as those organizations that government 'owns' in the sense that they are established and operated under the authority of government, and that they receive most of their financial resources from governmental sources such as legislative allocations from taxes that citizens pay. Private organizations are privately owned and receive most of their financial resources from sales to customers or donations. When we generalize about public and private organizations we are referring to these two types, recognizing the existence of the hybrid and intermediate forms as complications. Whether generalizations about the public and private categories apply to those organizations will depend on the level of public authority and public funding for the particular organization, and becomes an empirical question.

What difference do such differences make? As previously mentioned, in general, public organizations operate under the authority of government and receive authorization and funding for their activities from government officials with ultimate authority over them. Private firms must sell products and services to customers and hence purportedly become subject to 'consumer sovereignty' (Lindblom, 1977). In general they are constrained to sell products that consumers will buy. They have more autonomy in deciding what they will produce, and to whom they will sell it and where. This means that the two types of organizations are subject to different patterns of external and internal control, direction, and oversight. Public organizations are more subject to control and direction by politically constituted governmental authority, while private organizations are less subject to such authority and more constrained to find ways to use their relative autonomy to sell goods and services to customers.

In turn, these general differences in control and direction relate to a variety of differences in conditions that establish the context for organizational decision making. Various authors have delineated these different conditions, with Nutt and Backoff (1992: 27–34) serving as an excellent example.

Concerning markets for organizational outputs, Nutt and Backoff point out that private organizations' markets consist of buying behaviors by customers, while the 'market' for a public agency consists of oversight bodies and officials. Private organizations usually must compete with other providers in their markets, while public organizations often receive mandates to collaborate with other service providers. Public organizations receive their finances from budget allocations, while private organizations must make money through fees and charges for goods and services. In turn, these differences make market information and signals weaker and less available for public organizations than for private organizations, which have more access to market information such as prices, sales, and profits.

External constraints also differ. Public organizations are more subject to mandates that limit their autonomy, while private organizations' leaders tend to have more flexibility and autonomy in strategic decisions about organizational domains of operation and other major decisions. At the same time, the external oversight and direction of public organizations embeds them in the processes of governmental institutions and political processes, that shape the authoritative decisions that direct public organizations.

Transactions with their environments and stakeholders are distinctive, in that public organizations tend to have a more coercive relationship with citizens since citizens must pay for the public organizations' activities with their taxes and usually have to obey authoritative decisions and have little choice among providers. Consumption by customers and participation by stakeholders tends to be more voluntary for private organizations. Decision makers who have had experience in both sectors often report that decisions in public organizations have a broader scope of impact, in that decision makers have to consider implications for broad populations and constituencies, such as those of a nation or a broad jurisdiction. Concomitantly, public organizations and their leaders often become subject to more public scrutiny, as the media, interest groups, and others feel authorized to review and criticize their activities and decisions. They do so in part because in essence citizens and their official representatives and less official gadflies and critics 'own' the government organizations. For private firms, ownership is vested in private owners and stockholders.

These conditions in turn influence organizations' structures and processes. In the absence of market indicators and influences, and in the presence of political control and oversight, public organizations' goals are often more difficult to specify and measure, more complex and multifaceted, and more conflicting than the goals of private organizations. The authority of leaders in public organizations tends to be more limited, by external political interventions and controls and shifts in the election results, and through structures of constraints such as constitutional limitations, and system-wide personnel and purchasing rules that limit administrative authority. These administrative constraints lead to differences in incentive structures and processes within public organizations. For example, numerous studies have now produced evidence that survey respondents in public organizations, as compared to private respondents, perceive greater constraints on administration of such incentives as pay and disciplinary actions, and a stronger role for incentives to serve the public interest and provide services beneficial to society (e.g. Feeney and Rainey, 2009).

Assertions and evidence about decision making in public organizations

As the observations about differences between public and private organizations suggest, public organizations should have distinct decision-making processes because of factors such as political interventions and constraints and more diverse, diffuse objectives. Evidence supports such assertions. Although it shows that the general decision-making processes of public organizations often resemble those of private organizations, it also indicates that major decisions in public organizations involve more complexity, dynamism, intervention, and interruption than those in their private counterparts. At the same time, however, public employees engage in much routine decision making that can be highly standardized and that may differ little from decisions in private firms. There is nothing unusual or contradictory about this. Many contemporary organizational scholars (e.g. Daft, 2007) analyze decision-making processes according to a contingency perspective. Under some contingencies or conditions, managers can successfully adopt highly rationalized decision-making processes. Others involve too much uncertainty for such structured approaches and require more complex, intuitive decision making. This sort of distinction can help to explain how decision processes can be both similar and different in public organizations, as compared to private organizations.

Rational decision-making models and public organizations. Where decision processes can be more 'rational', they may be very similar in public and private organizations. Rationality has various meanings and dimensions, but we can specify that a strictly rational decision-making process would involve the following components.

Decision makers know all the relevant goals clearly, and they also know their preferences among the goals and can rank order the goals. They examine all alternative means for achieving the goals, and choose the means that maximize attainment of the goals with minimum expenditure of resources.

These strict conditions are seldom met except in simple situations, but we know that such situations require decisions all the time. Public agencies apply such techniques when they have consultants or in-house experts analyze work processes to design more efficient, effective work procedures. Public Service Centers of the Social Security Administration, for example, needed a system for keeping track of the huge number of file folders for clients as the folders move around to various employees who process the clients' claims. Consultants working with the agency developed a system for putting bar codes on the file folders, so that the codes could be read into the computer with a scanner wand at each work location. This recorded the folder's location and created a record of the location of each file within the system.

Similarly, 'management science' techniques have wide applications in government (Downs and Larkey, 1986). These techniques involve mathematical models or other highly structured procedures for decision making about design of work flows and queuing processes. Over the years, discussions of such techniques emphasize the greater difficulty of achieving successful applications in government because of such factors as vague performance criteria and political interventions (Drake, 1972; Morse and Bacon, 1967). For many technical areas of government work, however, these techniques have applications that are just as useful as those in industry. Some have led to prize-winning, highly successful applications (Bell, 2003). These include a Yale University professor's development of the diagnostic related groups (DRGs) that provide product definitions for the output of hospitals. In 1983, Medicare adopted DRGs that by 1990 saved more than $50 billion in Medicare hospital payments. The HASTUS bus crew scheduling system is now used in 200 cities around the world. Other highly successful applications have enhanced needle exchange programs used in drug addiction programs, organizing and scheduling of military aircraft operations such as refuelings, and a system for controlling traffic flows on expressways in Japan.

Many of the proposals for improving government operations over the past several decades advocated approaches that involve elements of rational decision making (Downs and Larkey, 1986). Lyndon Johnson issued a presidential directive ordering that the planning and program budgeting system (PPBS) be implemented in the budgeting processes of federal agencies. PPBS involves a systematic process of organizing budget requests according to major programs, with the plans and objectives for those programs specified and justified. The Department of Defense had used the system with some success prior to President Johnson's order. Problems in implementing PPBS more widely led to the order's cancellation a few years later, however.

When Jimmy Carter campaigned for president, he proposed the use of zero-based budgeting (ZBB) techniques as a way of exerting greater control over federal spending. This technique involves looking at the requests for funding of various activities as if their funding levels were zero. The idea is to force a very systematic, rational review of major commitments and possible reallocations rather than simply taking existing programs for granted. The procedure never came into use in any significant way.

Others have proposed that the public sector can use management by objectives (MBO) techniques as well as the private sector does (Rodgers and Hunter, 1992). These techniques involve careful negotiation and specification of primary objectives for individuals and units, with performance evaluations concentrating on whether those objectives have been achieved (Swiss, 1991). The Government Performance and Results Act of 1993 is still in effect, and requires federal agencies to produce strategic plans and performance plans stating their objectives, with reports on their success in accomplishing the objectives. As with the techniques discussed previously, debate goes on over prospects for such a systematic and explicit technique in public organizations (Moynihan, 2008).

Where conditions are conducive to such techniques, highly 'rational' decision processes can clearly succeed in the public sector. Under some circumstances, however, such as broad implementation of budgeting and planning programs, the public sector conditions of diffuse goals, political complications, and highly complex programs often overwhelm such highly rationalized procedures.

Rationality assumptions and the behaviors of public managers and officials.   Another role that the concept of rationality has played in analyzing public organizations revolves around its use to interpret the behavior of public managers and other government officials. 'Public choice' economists have developed a body of theory using approaches typical in economics to analyze how citizens and officials make political decisions. They argue, for example, that in political just as in economic contexts, individuals rationally maximize utility. Voters vote in their own self-interest, and political officials in essence try to buy votes by providing the government programs and services voters want. Since no market process ensures that one has to pay directly for the goods and services one receives, groups of voters use the political system to benefit themselves at the expense of others. They demand that their elected officials give them services and subsidies that they need, sometimes shifting much of the burden of paying for them to other voters. When these theorists turn to the public bureaucracy, they suggest similar problems. In some of the most prominent, widely cited academic works on public bureaucracies, they suggest that government organizations strive for ever greater budgets (Niskanen, 1971) and tend toward rigidity (Downs, 1967) and information distortion (Tullock, 1965). Evidence about these assertions has accumulated, and some of it supports them but some also indicates that they are oversimplified and, as depictions of many 'bureaucrats' and public bureaucracies, are simply inaccurate (Blais and Dion, 1991; Bendor and Moe, 1985).

The limits of rationality and public sector decision making.   To understand research on decision making in public organizations described below, one needs to be aware of ideas about the limits of rationality advanced by Herbert Simon (1948) and others. In one of the genuinely influential insights in the history of the social sciences, Simon emphasized constraints on managers' ability to follow highly rational procedures, especially in complex decision-making settings (see also Jones, 1999). Simon argued that for large-scale, complex decisions, the deluge of information and uncertainty overloads decision makers' cognitive capacity to process it. Decision makers strive for rationality – they are intendedly rational. Cognitive limits, uncertainties, and time limits, however, cause them to decide under conditions of 'bounded rationality'. They do not maximize in accordance with rationality assumptions; they 'satisfice'. They undertake a limited search among alternatives and choose the most satisfactory of them after as much consideration as they can manage within the constraints imposed by their situation. Cyert and March (1963) studied business firms and found that they approached major decisions largely as Simon had suggested. Rather than making decisions in highly rational modes, managers in the firms followed satisficing approaches. They engaged in 'problemistic searches' – that is, they started searching for alternatives and solutions in relation to problems that came up rather than in a systematic, explicitly goal-oriented way. They also engaged in 'sequential attention to alternatives', turning from possibility to possibility, looking at one alternative until they saw some problem with it and then turning to another. They tended to use benchmarks and rules of thumb rather than a careful explication of goals and a strategy for maximizing them.

While Cyert and March found support for Simon's conception of bounded rationality in business firms, we will see below that some evidence indicates that such conditions more often pertain in government organizations. The discussion above about the distinctive contexts and characteristics of public organizations provides numerous explanations for why this should be the case.

Contingency perspectives on decision making.   In significant part because of Simon's and his colleagues' insights and research, current views of management typically follow this pattern of regarding highly rational approaches to decision making as applicable where the tasks and the operating context afford stable, clear conditions. As conditions become more complex and dynamic, however, high volumes of information and uncertain conditions overwhelm highly explicit statements of goals and painstaking analysis of numerous alternatives. James Thompson (1967; Daft, 2007: 426) suggested a contingency framework to express these variations. Decision-making contexts vary along two major dimensions: the degree to which the decision makers agree on goals, and the degree to which they understand means–ends or cause–effect relationships – that is, the degree to which they have well-developed technical knowledge about how to solve the problems and accomplish the tasks. Where both goal agreement and technical knowledge are high, very rational procedures apply. The Internal Revenue Service deals each year with the problem of receiving a flood of tax returns and extracting and sorting them correctly. State departments of motor vehicles and the US Social Security Administration process many routine applications and claims every day. In decisions about activities such as these, management science techniques and other forms of highly rationalized analysis have valuable applications (as long as they are properly implemented, in a humane and communicative fashion). At the other end of the scale, where decision makers have no clear consensus on goals and little clarity as to the technical means of achieving them, one can hardly follow a simple blueprint. Managers engage in more 'satisficing' behaviors, such as bargaining and political maneuvering and more intuitive, judgmental decision making. As noted above, evidence reviewed below suggests that such conditions occur more often in the public sector as compared to the private sector.

Additional alternatives for contingency theories: Prospect and poliheuristic theories.   Some additional theoretical perspectives have been developed and applied largely in analyses of foreign policy decision making. They represent, however, interesting alternatives for analysis of decisions in public organizations more generally. These perspectives include Prospect Theory (PT), Poliheuristic Theory (PH), and considerations of issue type and salience, and of external context and constraints.

As do other contingency theories, Prospect Theory (PT) also assumes that decision makers have cognitive limitations that play an essential role in decision-making process. Kahneman and Tversky (1979) proposed PT as an alternative to expected utility theory for understanding risky decision making. Expected utility theory holds that decision makers maximize expected value; PT rejects this assumption of maximization and contends that decision makers exhibit suboptimal behavior. PT holds that people frame a problem around a reference point rather than in terms of the net gains. Usually, the reference point is the status quo, around which people frame losses and gains. PT also holds that people tend to overemphasize losses in relation to gains (framing effects); when faced with loss, people tend to accept risk to avoid the loss, but when in pursuit of gains, people tend to be risk-averse (Levy, 1992; 1994; 1996; 1997). For example, an attempt at persuasion will tend to have a stronger influence on a decision if it is framed in terms of avoiding a loss than it would if framed as offering the chance of a gain (Farnham, 1994: 3). In both cases, with losses and gains, the decision maker leaves the status quo (or reference point); however, the consequences of doing so vary. This occurs because the disadvantages of leaving the status quo due to a loss outweigh the advantages of leaving the status quo due to a gain (Levy, 1992: 284).

Although PT has been applied to questions about deterrence, crisis stability, bargaining behavior, military action, and diplomatic disputes, it has potential explanatory power for analysis of public managers' decisions about possible losses of budget, reputation, credibility, a program, and/or human resources. The idea is that leaders/managers behave differently when they are bargaining over gains than when they are bargaining over losses. PT's theoretical underpinnings – framing effects and risk acceptance to avoid loss – have been assessed in case studies and experimental analyses.

Despite its wide applicability, critics contend that PT suffers from conceptual and methodological problems. According to Levy (1992: 292–295), PT exhibits problems such as the following: (1) Research on PT often relies on experimental analysis, and this leads to research designs that present decision makers with highly structured choice conditions instead of the highly unstructured conditions of real world decisions. (2) Experimental analyses assign a concrete value and probability to each alternative. In real world decisions, however, values and probabilities are uncertain, making difficult the comparison of alternatives. (3) While in experimental analysis conditions are usually static, in real life conditions continuously change along multiple dimensions. Finally, in order to test how framing influences behavior, PT needs to rule out that the forces determining reference points also influence risky behavior (Levy, 1992: 292–295). Despite these methodological and analytical problems, PT offers an alternative for understanding the process of risky decisions in the public sector.

Like prospect theory, poliheuristic theory (PH) also explains decision making by assuming that it employs both screening processes and more rational processes. In the work of Mintz (1993), subsequently extended by Mintz *et al.* (1997), Mintz and Geva (1997), Reed (2003), and Brule (2005) among others, PH focuses on development of alternatives and choice. The term *poliheuristic* combines the prefix *poly*, which connotes both 'many' and the 'political' nature of decision making, and the word *heurisitic*, which denotes 'shortcuts' (Mintz and Geva, 1997: 82, 84). The PH assumes that the decision-making process consists of two stages. In the first one, the decision maker cognitively screens the alternatives to discard some of them, thus simplifying the decision matrix. Left with fewer choices, the decision maker compares the alternatives' expected utility to make a more rational decision (Mintz, 1993; Mintz and Geva, 1997; Reed, 2003).

In doing so, the decision maker performs five sequential processes (Mintz, 1993; 2004; Mintz and Geva, 1997; Reed, 2003; Stern, 2004). (1) Initially, decision makers employ a 'nonholistic search' by using a 'heuristic decision rule' rather than a full comparison of alternatives. (2) Because decision makers favor certain dimensions over others, they conduct 'dimension-based processing' to discard those alternatives that fail to meet their minimum requirements on key dimension(s). (3) Decision makers follow a 'noncompensatory decision rule', that is, an alternative's high ranking on an irrelevant dimension(s) does not compensate for its failure to fulfill the requirements on key dimension(s). Usually, the noncompensatory principle is to avoid political loss, that is, the political dimension. (4) The decision maker adopts a 'satisfying behavior', stopping the search when an alternative satisfies them. Finally, (5) the above process is characterized by an 'order-sensitive search' because decisions are sensitive to the order and the manner in which the alternatives are presented (Mintz, 1993; 2005; Mintz and Geva, 1997; Reed, 2003; Stern, 2004).

In addition to its extensive application in foreign policy decision making, PH has been applied to state and local decisions (Christensen and Marlowe, 2004), national security decisions, foreign economic decisions, as well as domestic decisions (Astorino-Courtois and Trusty, 2000; DeRouen, 2003; Sathasivam, 2003). PH research has employed a variety of methodologies ranging from case studies (Mintz, 1993), large-N comparative studies (DeRouen and Sprecher, 2004), and experimental analysis (Mintz and Geva, 1997).

PH also receives criticism. Stern (2004), for example, highlights its failure to explain how problems are detected, when problems are framed in term of gains and losses. He also points out that PH neglects consideration of the impact of contextual and institutional variables on the elimination of alternatives. Stern (2004) further objects to its overemphasis on the constraining role of domestic political factors, such as political support. Hence, for Stern (2004) domestic factors act as moderators rather than inhibitors. Finally, the PH neglects the role of transformational leaders, as they can change constraints into opportunities (Stern, 2004; 110–111).

The criticisms of PH should not discourage public sector scholars from testing its propositions when analyzing policymaking process. The idea of a two-stage process and the claims of a noncompensatory dimension are among many factors that merit more research in explaining decision making.

OTHER FACTORS INFLUENCING PUBLIC DECISION-MAKING

Issue type/salience

The debate on whether issue type influences decision making has received attention in foreign policy decision making. As Mansbach and Vasquez (1981) state: 'behavior [or decisions] in world politics may vary significantly according to the issues under contention' (p. 874). Gochman and Leng (1983) articulate issue type to explain decision making in managing conflict behavior. They divide issues into two categories – vital and not vital. The idea is that when facing vital interests (such as preservation of, and control over, one's own territory in the face of a serious threat), decision makers are more likely to choose militarized actions than when facing interests that are not vital (such as minor economic issues). This contention is equally supported by Hensel and Diehl (1994) and Bennett (1996) who explain nonmilitarized and long-lasting disputes as a function, among other factors, of issue salience.

The centrality of issue type, however, extends beyond being vital or not vital. For example, Rosenau (1966) developed an alternative issue typology, classifying it into tangible and intangible. The rationale is that unlike intangible issues, tangible issues facilitate cooperation because they are divisible (Rosenau, 1966; Vasquez, 1983). This issue type discussion suggests that decision making can be influenced by the salience and/or nature of the issue. Yet, the decision-making literature for the most part ignores the role of issue type in explaining choice. Public managers, for example, might choose differently when facing budget allocations (highly salient and tangible/divisible) than when facing allocation of responsibilities (low salience and intangible/indivisible).

Context: Environmental/external constraints

Like issue type, external contexts can influence decision making. The influence of the environment in which an organization operates on managers' decisions has been analyzed by scholarship on organizational performance in the public (Boyne, 1996) and private sectors (Bourgeois, 1984; Capon et al., 1990; Hansen and Wernerfelt, 1989; Hrebiniak and Joyce, 1985; Lenz, 1981; Pettigrew, 1987). These works study the effects of external constraints on leaders' decision making. According to Boyne and his colleagues (2001), 'theories that emphasize the importance of external constrains imply that "force of circumstances" leaves managers with limited room for manoeuvre' (Boyne, 2001: 859–860; see also Andrews et al., 2005). Consequently, given the external constraints, leaders are left with limited choices because organizations are swept along by events that are beyond their control. Some analysts do not accept this limiting role of constraints, however. Hambrinck and Finkelstein (1987) for example, propose a voluntaristic view that suggests that organizational leaders can make qualified decision making in their response to external events, as they continue having substantial discretion.

Nevertheless, there exists considerable support for the constraints–choice relationship (Hrebiniak and Joyce, 1985; Pettigrew, 1987). Some studies of English local governments indicate that constraints have an impact on inter-localities' variations in expenditure decisions (Danziger, 1978; Sharpe and Newton, 1984; Barnett *et al.*, 1992; Boyne et al., 2001) and on inter-localities' variations in public policy, too (Boyne 1996). The work of Andrews *et al.* (2005) also supports the constraint-organizational behavior relationship by suggesting that organizational performance is not only attributable to decisions made by local policymakers but also to the external constraints. They test their proposition across several English local governments demonstrating that external constraints – such as social diversity, size, and economic propensity of the population – affect localities' decisions and, in turn, their performance. Specifically, localities with diverse service needs find it more difficult to perform well, while large size and economic prosperity are conducive to high performance (Andrews *et al.*, 2005: 653). Others, such as Hannan and Freeman (1984), argue that environmental pressure alter the organizational 'periphery' while leaving the 'core' intact. That is, external constraints affect organization's structure and processes but not its values nor strategies. Besides issue type and context, decision making also varies depending on the process employed by public managers. The next section describes some of these processes.

DECISION-MAKING PROCESSES IN PUBLIC ORGANIZATIONS

Incremental decision-making processes in public management and public policy

Probably because of the higher frequency of bounded rationality conditions in government, political scientists have debated whether government decision-making processes follow an incremental pattern. This perspective on public sector decisions has features similar to those of the bounded rationality perspective and has similar intellectual origins. Incrementalism in decision making means concentrating on increments to existing circumstances, or relatively limited changes from existing conditions. Those who contend that the policymaking process has this characteristic argue that major changes to federal budget categories seldom receive much consideration. Instead, the officials formulating the budget concentrate on the limited increments, up and down, proposed in any given year. Policymakers restrict the size of the changes that they propose. The bigger the change, the more opposition it stirs up and the more complex the task of analyzing the change. Political scientists have debated whether incrementalism accurately characterizes the policymaking and budgeting processes. In addition, they debate its desirability. Some argue that incremental processes stimulate useful bargaining among active political groups and officials and guard against ill-considered radical changes. Others complain that they make the policymaking and budgeting processes too conservative and shortsighted and too supportive of existing coalitions and policies.

The debate became mired in difficulties about what is meant by an increment – how large a change has to be to be large. It has led to the conclusion, however, that policy and budgetary changes tend to be incremental but are not always. Fairly drastic cuts in some portions of the federal budget during the Reagan administration, along with fairly sharp increases in military spending, illustrate that however one identifies an increment, cuts or increases can greatly affect public managers and their agencies (Rubin, 1985). More generally, however, the decision-making processes of public organizations play out within these larger incremental policy-making processes. Policy changes that agencies initiate or that influence them involve a complex interplay of political actors tugging and hauling over any significant change.

In fact, these aspects of the governmental context led to prescriptions for using incremental approaches as the most feasible alternative. In a classic contribution to the literature on public administration and policy, Charles Lindblom's article 'The Science of Muddling Through' (1959; 1979) expressed this perspective. He contended that the requirement for political compromise results in vague goals for public policies and programs. Public administrators carrying out such policies must maintain political support through public participation and consensus building. They have to remain accountable to elected officials, who usually have less experience than they do. As a result, stated goals and ends for policies provide little clarity, and means become inseparable from ends. Administrators find it difficult or politically unacceptable to state a precise societal impact for which a program aims. They must identify a package of means and ends that can achieve political consensus and support. Far-reaching, original procedures and goals evoke strong opposition and usually must be modified if support is to be maintained. In addition, the need for political support often outweighs such criteria as efficiency and substantive impact. Thus, in formulating their packages of means and ends, administrators must strive for satisfactory decisions – that is, they must satisfice – after examining a relatively limited set of alternatives. Often they rely heavily on past practice. A good deal of intelligence may enter the decision-making process through the involvement of many groups, experts, and officials. Generally, however, the approach involves avoiding major departures and concentrating on relatively limited, politically feasible steps. Some critics worry about the implications of such an approach (Rosenbloom, Kravchuck, and Rosenbloom, 2001). It can lead to unduly conservative decisions and it can favor politically influential groups over disadvantaged and less organized groups.

An incremental model of decision-making processes within organizations.   Political scientists usually apply the concept of incrementalism to the process of creating public policy. Mintzberg, Raisinghani, and Theoret (1976), on the other hand, studied 25 major decisions in organizations and formulated an incremental model of decision-making processes within organizations. Their study provides a framework for a comparison of business managers' decisions to those of public and nonprofit managers, described in the next paragraph below. The model depicts decisions as involving numerous small, incremental steps, moving through certain general phases. 'Decision interrupts' can occur at any of the stages, causing the process to cycle back to an earlier point. The identification phase involves recognizing and diagnosing the problem. Then, in the development phase, a search process identifies alternatives, followed by the design of a particular solution. Finally, in the selection phase, the solution is evaluated, and the organization makes a formal commitment to the decision. This process seldom flows smoothly. Decision interrupts make the decision-making process choppy and cyclical. An internal interruption may block diagnosis of a problem. Even when a solution has been designed, a new option may pop up and throw the process back. For example, a new executive may come in and refuse to authorize a decision that is otherwise ready for implementation. An external interruption such as a government mandate may cause higher executives to push a proposal back for further development.

This incremental decision-making model has been used in research comparing private managers with managers from public and nonprofit organizations. Schwenk (1990) used it to analyze the managers' perceptions about decision processes in their organizations. He found that compared to the private business managers, public and nonprofit managers reported more interruptions, recycling to earlier phases, and conflicts in the decision processes in their organizations. This finding is consistent with other studies of decision making (e.g. Hickson *et al.*, 1986) that have found that executive-level decisions in government organizations are more 'public'. More different authorities (chief executives, legislators) and interests (e.g. advocacy groups) can influence the decision process. Legal and institutional constraints influence the process. For example, laws sometimes mandate the participation of interest and advocacy groups in the decision process. The political appointment process provides chief executives with authority to appoint top executives in many government agencies. These executives tend to have shorter tenure in office than business executives. This calls to mind Mintzberg *et al.*'s (1976) example of a new top executive taking charge, as a source of decision interrupts.

Mixed scanning

The value of rational decision processes in some conditions, but their inapplicability in others, creates an obvious tension. So does the trade-off between incrementalism, and more approaches that are more rational in the sense of setting and pursuing long-term, broadly strategic goals. Etzioni (1967; 1986) proposed an approach aimed at reaching a balance between incremenatalism and long-term, large-scale goal setting. He argued that administrators and other officials make both decisions that have large-scale, long-term implications and decisions of more limited scope. The latter often follow major directions already selected by the former. Etzioni suggested that decision makers strive, through 'mixed scanning', to recognize the points at which they concentrate on broader, longer range alternatives and those at which they focus on more specific, incremental decisions that are a part of larger directions. Decision makers need to mix both perspectives, taking the time to conduct broad considerations of many major issues and alternatives to prevent the shortsightedness of incrementalism. Yet such broad scans cannot involve all the comprehensive analysis required by highly rational models; thus more intensive analysis must follow on decisions within areas of pressing need.

The garbage can model

The tendency to regard major organizational decisions as complex and dynamic rather than smoothly rational now dominates the management literature, as reflected by the garbage can model, among other ways. The garbage can metaphor comes from the observation that decisions in organizations have a diverse array of material cast into them in a disorderly fashion. As noted above, James March partici-pated in research validating Simon's observations about bounded rationality (Cyert and March, 1963). March and his colleagues also observed that organizational deci-sions involve more internal political activity than generally supposed, with extensive bargaining and conflict among coalitions (March, 1962).

These observations evolved into the garbage can model. It holds that in orga-nizational decision making, participation, preferences, and technology (know-how, techniques, equipment) are ambiguous, uncertain, and rapidly changing. These conditions occur especially in 'loosely coupled' organizations such as universitites and government agencies (Weick, 1979; March and Olsen, 1986). The members and units have loose connections with one another. It is often unclear who has the authority over decisions. People may loosely engage even with very important issues, because other matters preoccupy them. People come and go in decision-making settings such as committees. Problems and potential solutions come and go as well, as conditions change. Choice opportunities also come up – a committee may look for decisions to make, or a manager may look for work to do. A solu-tion may go looking for a problem: a promising alternative may become available that virtually begs for some type of application, or a person or group may have a pet technique that they want to find a way to use. Problems, participants, solu-tions, and choice opportunities flow along in time relatively independently of one another.

Decision making occurs when the right problem arises, when the right decision-making participants are receptive to an available solution, all coming together in a choice opportunity. The linkages between these elements are more temporal than consequential; that is, they result as much from coincidence as from rational calcu-lation (March and Olsen, 1986).

March and Olsen (1986) stress that they intend the model not as a replacement for other perspectives on decision making but as a supplement to them. They do not rule out rational approaches in certain instances. They point out that the model does not imply that all decisions involve unavoidable chaos. Leaders with a firm sense of mission and other factors can guide decisions in systematic ways.

The proponents of the model do not state clearly where and when it applies. Early in their theoretical work, they suggested (without explaining) that the model applies mainly to public and educational organizations (March and Olsen, 1976; Cohen, March, and Olsen, 1972). Most of the applications have concentrated on educational and military organizations and courts. Yet at times they also suggest that it applies to business firms and to all organizations (March and Olsen, 1986: 12). Critics have attacked the model for remaining too metaphorical, imprecise, and internally contradictory (Bendor, Moe, and Shotts, 2001), although the devel-opers of the perspective disagree (Olsen, 2001). Still, the model has important im-plications for public management. As discussed below, Hickson and his colleagues (1986) found that this type of decision-making process occurs more frequently in public organizations than in private firms.

Strategic management

In some ways representing a trend countervailing the emphasis on incremental or chaotic processes in other perspectives, the topic of strategic decision making in the public sector has advanced prominently in recent decades, and government agencies at all levels engage in it (Berry and Wechsler, 1995; Bryson, 2004). In the US, the Government Performance and Results Act requires all federal agencies to publish strategic plans that specify goals and performance measures that reflect upon progress towards those goals. Many state governments have similar mandates for state government agencies. Many states governments also undertake kindred processes of specifying performance measures that involve goal-setting, or performance budgeting initiatives (see Moynihan, 2008; Melkers and Willoughby, 2005). Debates and controversies swirl around issues of how meaningful these activities are, as opposed to amounting to ceremonial exercises (Moynihan, 2008). The strategic decision-making processes do require decision making about long term goals or strategic issues, and about means for pursuing them. Hence they become important as decision processes within government agencies. The growth in interest and practice has spawned two streams of activity, one that involves the development of prescriptive frameworks to guide strategic decision making, and another that involves research on the nature and effects of strategic decision processes.

Prescriptive frameworks for strategic management. Management consultants and experts propose a variety of approaches for developing strategy (Bryson and Roering, 1996). Bryson (2004) concludes that managers can apply them in the public sector (although with several provisos, discussed below). Some of the models, such as that of the Boston Consulting Group, focus on high-level corporate decisions about the relative priority of the corporation's business activities. The Boston Consulting Group's 'portfolio model' exhorts executives to treat the mix of business units in a large corporation as if they represented stocks in an individual's portfolio of assets. Executives assess the business units in the corporation on two dimensions – market growth and size of market share. The units high on both of these dimensions are 'stars'; they should receive priority attention and reinvestment of profits. Units with small shares in slow-growing markets – low on both key dimensions – are 'dogs' and candidates for divestiture. Mixed situations provide opportunities for strategic shifting of resources. A unit with a high market share in a slowly growing market brings in a lot of money but does not have strong growth prospects. These activities should be treated as 'cash cows' and used to provide resources for units that provide growth opportunities. Units that are in a rapidly growing market but are not yet in command of a large share of it should be considered for infusions of resources from other units, especially the cash cows.

Ring (1988) applied a modified portfolio model to public sector strategy making. He used 'tractability of the problem' and 'public support' as the key dimensions. Where problems are manageable and public support is high, public managers can seek to gain resources that they can then use to deal with more difficult policy problems in settings where public support is high but the problem is very difficult to solve. Where public support and tractability are both low, public managers simply seek to shift the priority away from those problems. Similarly, Rubin (1988) suggests that strategic patterns will differ according to whether the time horizon for the policy issue is long or short and whether the policy plays out within a disruptive or an anticipated environment.

Other approaches emphasize different levels and issues (Bryson, 2004). Stakeholder management approaches, for example, analyze how key stakeholders evaluate an organization and form strategies to deal with each stakeholder. (Stakeholders include individuals or groups who have a major interest in an organization, such as unions, customers, suppliers, and regulators.) Competitive analysis approaches analyze major forces acting on an industry, such as the power of buyers and suppliers, to gain competitive advantage through such strategies as differentiating oneself from competitors (Porter, 1998). Strategic issues management focuses on identifying major issues that appear crucial to an organization's ability to achieve its objectives and deciding how a working group in the organization will respond to these issues and resolve them. (For more detail, see Bryson, 2004, and Bryson and Roering, 1996.)

Applications of strategic management in the public sector.   Numerous frameworks for strategic management in the public sector are now available (Bryson, 2004; Nutt and Backoff, 1992). They tend to focus on such procedures as strategic issue management, stakeholder analysis, environmental scanning, and SWOT analysis (described below). The procedures typically begin with a planning and organizing phase. A 'strategic management group' (SMG) typically manages the process and must agree on who will be involved, how the strategic analysis will proceed, and what they expect to achieve. Usually the procedure requires a structured group process and a facilitator – a consultant skilled in helping groups make decisions. The SMG usually begins with a preliminary assessment of the history and current status of the organization to produce a general statement of the organization's mission. Bryson (2004) suggests that for public organizations, this step requires a careful review of the organization's mandates – the requirements imposed by external authorities through legislation and regulations. This review can clarify what external authorities dictate and can also provide insights about new approaches. For example, representatives of a public hospital who interpret their mandate as forbidding competition with private health services may find upon review that they have the authority to do so.

Working toward the mission statement, the SMG reviews trends in the operating environment. It may also conduct a stakeholder analysis and develop visions of how it wants the organization to be in the future. Ultimately the mission statement expresses the general purpose of the organization and its major values and commitments. Next, the SMG members conduct a SWOT analysis, in which they assess the strengths and weaknesses of the organization and look outward to the environment to identify opportunities and threats facing the organization. The SMG can choose from an array of techniques for this analysis (Nutt and Backoff, 1992). From the SWOT analysis, the SMG develops a list of strategic issues – conflicts among opposing forces or values that can affect the organization's ability to achieve a desired future (Nutt and Backoff, 1992). Then the group develops plans for managing these issues (Nutt and Backoff, 1992). A wide variety of public sector organizations have used this approach to strategic planning (Bryson, 2004; Boschken, 1988).

Analytical research on managerial strategies in the public sector. In addition to recommending procedures, researchers have studied the strategies that public organizations pursue and how their strategic decisions actually develop. Some of these studies show the effects of 'public' status on strategy. In their study of strategic decisions in 30 British organizations, Hickson and his colleagues (1986) found that strategic decision-making processes in publicly owned service and manufacturing organizations differed from those in private service and manufacturing firms. The public organizations follow a 'vortex-sporadic' decision-making process. This involves more turbulence, more shifting participation by a greater diversity of internal and external interests, more delays and interruptions, and more formal and informal interaction among participants. The type of decision made a great difference, but so did the distinction between service and manufacturing organizations. The results indicate that the public sector context does impose on strategic decision making the sorts of interventions and constraints described earlier in this chapter. The findings are consistent with other analyses of the distinctive context of strategic planning in the public sector, which observe that strategic planners in the public sector must consider a broader scope of impact and a more diverse and attentive set of stakeholders (Nutt and Backoff, 1995). Considerations of market volatility and competition that apply in the private sector need to be replaced by considerations of need for governmental action and responsiveness (Nutt and Backoff, 1995). Nutt (1999) has also identified distinctive patterns of assessing alternatives in the public sector.

Berry and Wechsler (1995) conducted a national survey of state agencies and found that even by the early 1990s the majority of agencies, about 60 %, employed strategic planning. The leaders of the agencies had initiated the process at their level rather than due to directives from a higher level such as a governor, primarily to set program and policy direction. Berry and Wechsler concluded that the evidence indicated that strategic planning was a successful public sector management innovation.

Mascarenhas (1989) studied 187 public and private offshore drilling firms in 34 countries to analyze their strategic domains (markets served, product type, customer orientation, and technology applied). The government-owned firms operated mainly in domestic markets, with narrow product lines and stable customer bases. Publicly traded private firms (those whose stock is traded on exchanges) were larger, operated in many geographical markets, and offered a wider range of products. Privately held firms were more like the state-owned firms but had less stable customer bases. The results indicate that public organizations have greater constraints on their strategic domains.

Other studies have analyzed important variations in strategy within the public sector. Wechsler and Backoff (1986) studied four state agencies in Ohio and found that they pursued four types of strategies. The Department of Natural Resources followed a developmental strategy of enhancing the capabilities, resources, and general performance of the organization. In the transformational strategy of the Department of Mental Retardation, professional experts and legal rights groups advocated deinstitutionalization of the mentally retarded – getting them out of large hospitals and into normal living conditions. The agency transformed itself from a manager of hospitals to a regulator of client services delivered through community-based programs. The Department of Public Welfare received intense criticism in the media and from legislators, so its managers followed a protective strategy. They strengthened internal controls, lowered the agency's public profile, mended relations with legislators, and worked to protect funding levels. The Public Utilities Commission, which regulates utility pricing decisions, adopted a political strategy to make agency decisions more acceptable to consumers.

The Miles and Snow typology.   The Miles and Snow strategy typology is one of the widely cited and utilized classifications of business-level strategies. It is based on the idea that managers seek to formulate strategies that are congruent with the external environment that their organization confronts (Miles and Snow, 1978; Zahra and Pearce, 1990; Daft, 2007).

Described in more detail, the four orientations of the Miles and Snow typology include:

- *Prospectors*: organizations that 'continually search for market opportunities, and ... regularly experiment with potential responses to emerging environmental trends' (Miles and Snow, 1978: 29). Prospectors often stress product development, have a keen learning orientation and are strong in research, and tend to adopt flexible organizational structures (Zahra and Pearce, 1990; Boyne and Walker, 2004; Daft, 2007).
- *Defenders*: organizations that emphasize controlling secure and premium niches in their respective industries and 'seldom need to make major adjustments in their technology, structure or methods of operation ... [and] devote primary attention to improving the efficiency' of their operations (Miles and Snow, 1978: 29). They engage in little or no product development, work under centralized authority, and have little employee empowerment (Zahra and Pearce, 1990; Boyne and Walker, 2004; Daft, 2007).
- *Analyzers*: organizations that typically exhibit characteristics of both Prospectors and Defenders. They 'operate in two types of product market domains, one relatively stable, the other changing' (Miles and Snow, 1978: 29). Analyzers balance efficiency and learning, use tight cost control with flexibility and adaptability, and often have efficient production for stable product lines while yet maintaining an emphasis on research, creativity, and innovative risk-taking (Zahra and Pearce, 1990; Daft, 2007).
- *Reactors*: organizations 'in which top managers frequently perceive change and uncertainty occurring in their organizational environments, but are unable to respond effectively' (Miles and Snow, 1978: 29). Reactors have a general lack of consistent strategy and have no clearly defined organizational approach. They are generally viewed as dysfunctional (Zahra and Pearce, 1990; Daft, 2007).

Boschken (1988) found this framework useful in analyzing the strategic behaviors of port authority organizations for various cities on the West Coast. More recent research applies the typology to public sector organizations (Boyne and Walker, 2004; Andrews, Boyne *et al.*, 2005; Meier, O'Toole *et al.*, 2007). Boyne and Walker (2004) emphasize the importance of a clearer understanding of the strategies of public service organizations and point out that expectations for more strategic focus are evident in examples such as the National Performance Review in the United States (Thompson, 2000) and the 'Modernisation Agenda' in the United Kingdom (Boyne, Kitchener, and Kirkpatrick, 2001). The purpose of their research was to develop a framework to classify strategies pursued by public organizations. They define strategy content as patterns of service provision that are selected and implemented by organizations. They posit that strategy does not need to be viewed as a 'weapon' that is used to defeat rivals in competitive struggles (Greer and Hoggett, 1999: Boyne and Walker, 2004). Boyne and Walker (2004) asserted that a framework that has applicability to public organizations will make it possible to identify and measure their strategy content. As a dependent variable, their classification scheme could be used to understand why particular strategies are adopted, and as an independent variable it can be used in models of organizational performance. They then asserted that the Miles and Snow (1978) typology corresponded closely with their concept of strategic 'stance', although Boyne and Walker's typology of strategic stance includes only Prospectors, Defenders, and Reactors (Boyne and Walker, 2004). Boyne and Walker did not attempt to place public organizations exclusively into one of those categories, but rather their expectation was that public organizations would pursue a mixture of those strategies and that the mix would change over time as agencies confront new opportunities and challenges. They believe that their criteria are not mutually exclusive, but that they are exhaustive (Boyne and Walker, 2004).

Boyne and Walker joined with other colleagues in additional research wherein they applied the Miles and Snow (1978) typology in other research situations (Andrews, Boyne *et al.*, 2005; Andrews, Boyne and Walker, 2006; Walker and Boyne, 2006; Meier, O'Toole *et al.*, 2007, Andrews, Boyne *et al.*, 2008a, 2008b; Enticott and Walker, 2008). The first of these studies focused on the issue of representative bureaucracy and workforce diversity. Representative bureaucracy is likely to benefit the Prospector types and further enhance their performance (Andrews, Boyne *et al.*, 2005). Because strategies of employee involvement are central to the Prospector's achievement of higher levels of organizational performance, Prospectors are then expected to be able to take advantage of an ethnically diverse workforce that brings alternative perspectives on agency goals and strategies. The results did show that Prospector strategic stances related more positively to service performance measures than did Defender or Reactor strategies (Andrews, Boyne *et al.*, 2005).

The influence of strategic management on public organizational performance. Andrews, Boyne and Walker (2006) reported the first empirical test of the proposition that strategy content is a key determinant of organizational performance in the public sector. In the UK, every local authority reports regularly on a battery of performance measures for public service delivery, and the reports are compiled at the national level. This gave the researchers access to performance indicators. The authors posited that strategy content is comprised of strategic stance, or the extent to which organizations act consistently with categories of the Miles and Snow (1978) typology (e.g., Prospector, Defender, Reactor) and strategic action, which is related to changes in markets, services, revenues, external relations, and internal characteristics. Using a survey of English local authorities and the performance indicators, they found evidence that strategy content matters and that organizational performance is positively associated with a Prospector stance and negatively associated with a Reactor stance. This also indicates that public managers can make significant differences through decisions about the strategies they follow (Andrews, Boyne, and Walker, 2006). Additionally, Walker and Boyne (2006) used the data from this same survey to assess empirically the Labour government's public management reform program in the United Kingdom. As in the previous study, the authors find that public managers' decisions about strategies and actions can influence performance (Walker and Boyne, 2006; see also Enticott and Walker, 2008).

Meier, O'Toole *et al.* (2007) analyzed relations between the Miles and Snow strategic orientation categories and performance indicators, using a large sample of administrators of several hundred Texas school districts over a six-year period. The performance indicators included how the students in the districts scored on statewide standardized tests, dropout rates, and other measures. Unlike previous research, they found that the Defender strategy is the most effective for achieving high stakes objectives such as pass rates on the state standardized tests, which are heavily emphasized by governmental officials in the state. The Prospector and Reactor strategies work best in regard to goals of more politically powerful elements of the organization's environment (e.g. higher SAT scores for college bound students). The researchers interpreted this pattern as more variegated than previous findings showing that Prospectors outperform Defenders, and Defenders outperform Reactors. Instead, the different strategic orientations can have different advantages and disadvantages in different contexts (Meier, O'Toole *et al.*, 2007: 373).

Andrews, Boyne *et al.* (2008a, 2008b) continued this stream of research on strategy and public service performance. They examined centralization as a measure of the hierarchy and authority and the degree of participation in decision making. Again utilizing the Miles and Snow (1978) typology, they found centralization has no independent effect on service performance, even when controlling for prior performance, service expenditure, and external constraints. The strategic orientation of organizations, however, affects the impact of centralization (Andrews, Boyne *et al.*, 2008a). They also examined the separate and combined effects of specific external and internal variables that have strong effects on success in public sector organizations (Andrews, Boyne *et al.*, 2008b). The authors found that the prospecting strategy is most strongly associated with performance in service provision and that organizations that emphasize innovation and change in service provision are more likely to achieve better results. This is consistent with prior findings in both the public and private sectors.

These studies show that decisions about strategic orientation vary among public organizations, and demonstrate that such decisions about strategy play important roles in the decision making and performance in public organizations. Public managers, like private managers, engage in a variety of purposeful efforts to respond to their environment and achieve their objectives.

CONCLUSION

Decision making in public organizations is often quite similar to decision making in other types of organizations such as business firms, but can involve important differences. The 'generic' argument that public, private, and nonprofit organizations display fundamental commonalities has merit, but one also needs to consider various approaches to distinguishing public and private organizations, such as designating public organizations as those owned and funded by government. These public organizations have distinctive contexts and characteristics that are relevant to decision making. These include such conditions as absence of economic markets for organizational outputs, and distinctive external political and legal influences.

These differences do not make a difference for all decisions. We have described and provided examples of people in public organizations applying highly 'rational' decision procedures, especially in routine or highly structured task settings. In addition, we have described efforts to apply rational decision processes in applications like strategic budgeting initiatives such as PPBS and ZBB. Challenges encountered by those who tried this, as well as challenges to some economists who have claimed that government 'bureaucrats' rationally maximize utility in ways that lead to inefficiency, led to a discussion of the limits of rationality in government. These limits in turn point to the need for contingency theories that take into account different decision contexts. Thompson's theory, we pointed out, posits the feasibility of rational procedures when technical knowledge and goal agreement are high, but where they are not, there is a need and tendency for more satisficing, bargaining, politics, and intuitive decision making. We then reviewed research and thought on two additional theoretical perspectives that can be considered contingency perspectives, prospect theory and poliheuristic theory. In addition, research on contingencies that can influence decisions indicates that issue type and salience, and environmental and internal constraints, can exert important influences.

We then described several major perspectives on decision making in the public sector. A major debate in political science and public administration has contested the degree to which governmental decisions about budgets and policies are 'incremental'. Charles Lindblom applied incrementalist ideas in an essay on the 'science of muddling through' that came to be regarded as a classic. He said that public administrators must maintain political support for their decisions, and avoid opposition from among the many groups and authorities in the political process, by avoiding major departures and far-reaching goals. They must decide on limited means and ends that can maintain political consensus. Mintzberg and co-authors developed a very different application of the concept of incremental decisions, in a depiction of organizational decisions in all types of organizations as involving incremental phases and steps, subject to interrupts and cycling back to previous phases. Lindblom's perspective emphasizes the political forces that move the decision process towards incrementalism. That makes it interesting that a study by Schwenk found that the more generic Mintzberg *et al.* incremental model applied more to public organizations than to private firms. In the study, the government managers described decisions in their organizations as subject to more interventions and interrupts than did the business firms. We then described additional perspectives, such as mixed scanning and the garbage can model. Developers of the garbage can model posited its greater applicability to public organizations than private ones, and a study in the UK supported this observation. The study found that top decisions in public organizations, as compared to private organizational decisions, involved more open participation and influence by multiple stakeholders, leading to a process more akin to a garbage can process than in private firms.

Strategic planning has amounted to a movement in the public sector in the US, mandated by federal and state legislation and widely practiced. This has led some experts to develop guidance and procedures for conducting strategic planning, and others to conduct empirical research on it. We described procedures that are fairly typical in governmental strategic planning, and reviewed research that indicates that strategic orientation relates positively to organizational performance in public service delivery in studies in the UK.

Overall, this chapter shows that the generic perspective that sees no important differences between public, private, and nonprofit organizations, and those who believe there are significant differences, can both be right, in a sense. People in public and private organizations often make the same types of decisions in similar ways. Concepts and procedures for decision making in business firms usually apply usefully in government agencies. On the other hand, the limited supply of empirical research cited in this chapter, and the expert and scholarly observations reviewed here, indicate distinctive aspects of decision making in public organizations. Especially for higher level decisions, the conditions that come with government ownership and funding have important influences. These conditions include strong external legal and institutional constraints, more complex and hard-to-specify goals, and multiple authorities and influential groups in the political system. In this context, high level decisions tend to become more open to pluralistic participation. Decision makers must maintain political consensus, while navigating among constitutional and statutory requirements. Decision making tends toward incremental processes, subject to interventions, veto points, and interruptions. Garbage can processes are more likely to characterize the decision processes. This does not necessarily make decision making in public organizations dysfunctional and inferior to those in business. It means that they involve the challenges and virtues of being more 'public'.

REFERENCES

Andrews, R., Boyne, G.A., Meier, K.J., O'Toole, L.J., and Walker, R.M. (2005) Representative bureaucracy, organizational strategy, and public service performance: An empirical analysis of English local government, *Journal of Public Administration Research and Theory*, 15 (4), 489–504.

Andrews, R., Boyne, G.A., and Walker, R.M. (2006) Strategy content and organizational performance: An empirical analysis, *Public Administration Review*, 66 (1), 52–63.

Andrews, R., Boyne, G.A., Law, J., and Walker, R.M. (2008a) Centralization, organizational strategy, and public service performance, *Journal of Public Administration Research and Theory*: Advance Access published on February 29, 2008; doi:10.1093/jopart/mum039.

Andrews, R., Boyne, G.A., Law, J., and Walker, R.M. (2008b) Organizational strategy, external regulation and public service performance, *Public Administration*, 86 (1), 185–203.

Astorino-Courtois, A., and Trusty, B. (2000) Degrees of difficulty: The effect of Israeli policy shifts on Syrian peace decisions, *Journal of Conflict Resolution*, 44, 359–377.

Barnett, R.R., Levaggi, R., and Smith, P. (1992) Local authority expenditure decision: a maximum likelihood analysis of budget setting in the face of piecewise linear budget constraints, *Oxford Economic Papers*, 44 (1), 113–134.

Bell, P.C. (2003) 'Life After Edelman.' OR/MS Today. Available at http://www.lionhrtpub.com/orms/orms-12-03/fredelman.html.

Bendor, J., and Moe, T.M. (1985) An adaptive model of bureaucratic politics, *American Political Science Review*, 79, 755–774.

Bendor, J., Moe, T.M., and Shotts, K.W. (2001) Recycling the garbage can: An assessment of the research program, *American Political Science Review*, 95, 169–190.

Bennett, D.S. (1996) 'Security bargaining and the end of intestate rivalry, *International Studies Quarterly*, 40, 157–184.

Berry, F.S., and Wechsler, B. (1995) State agencies' experience with strategic planning: Findings from a national survey, *Public Administration Review*, 55, 159–168.

Blais, A., and Dion, S. (eds) (1991) *The Budget-Maximizing Bureaucrat.* Pittsburgh: University of Pittsburgh Press.

Boschken, H.L. (1988) *Strategic Design and Organizational Change: Pacific Rim Seaports in Transition.* Tuscaloosa: University of Alabama Press.

Bourgeois, L.J. (1984) Strategic management and determinism, *Academy of Management Review*, 9 (4), 586–596.

Boyne, G.A. (1996) *Constraints, Choice and Public Policies.* London: JAI Press.

Boyne, G.A., Ashworth, R., and Powell, M. (2001) Environmental change, leadership succession and incrementalism in local government, *Journal of Management Studies*, 38 (6), 859–878.

Boyne, G.A., Kitchener, M., and Kirkpatrick, I. (2001) Introduction to the symposium on New Labour and the modernisation of public management, *Public Administration*, 79 (1), 1–4.

Boyne, G.A., and Walker, R.M. (2004) Strategy content and public service organizations, *Journal of Public Administration Research and Theory*, 14 (2), 231–252.

Bozeman, B. (1987) *All Organizations Are Public: Bridging Public and Private Organizational Theories.* San Francisco, CA: Jossey-Bass.

Brule, D. (2005) Explaining and forecasting leaders' decisions: A poliheuristic analysis of the Iran hostage rescue decision, *International Studies Perspectives*, 6, 99–113.

Bryson, J.M. (2004) *Strategic Planning for Public and Nonprofit Organizations: A Guide to Strengthening and Sustaining Organizational Achievements.* San Francisco, CA: Jossey-Bass.

Bryson, J.M., and Roering, W.D. (1996) 'Strategic Planning Options for the Public Sector', in J.L. Perry (ed.) *Handbook of Public Administration.* San Francisco, CA: Jossey-Bass, 2nd edition.

Capon, N., Farley, J., and Hoenig, S. (1990) Determinants of financial performance: a meta-analysis, *Management Science*, 36, 1143–1159.

Christensen, E.J., and Marlowe, J. (2004) 'Poliheuristic Decision-Making and the Character of State–Local Relations.' Paper presented at the Annual Meeting of the Academy of Management, New Orleans, August.

Cohen, M.D., March, J.G., and Olsen, J.P. (1972) A garbage can model of organizational choice, *Administrative Science Quarterly*, 17: 1–25.

Cyert, R.M., and March, J.G. (1963) *A Behavioral Theory of the Firm.* Upper Saddle River, NJ: Prentice Hall.

Daft, R.L. (2007) *Organizational Theory and Design* (9e) Mason, OH: Thomson South-Western.

Dahl, R.A., and Lindblom, C.E. (1953) *Politics, Economics, and Welfare.* New York: Harper Collins.

Danzinger, J. (1978) *Making Budgets.* London: Sage.

DeRouen, K. (2003) 'The Decision Not to Use Force at Dien Bien Phu', in A. Mintz (ed.) *Integrating Cognitive and Rational Theories of Foreign Policy Decision Making.* New York: Palgrave Macmillan, 11–28.

DeRouen, K., and Sprecher, C. (2004) Initial crisis reaction and poliheuristic theory, *Journal of Conflict Resolution,* 48, 56–68.

Downs, A. (1967) *Inside Bureaucracy.* New York: Little, Brown.

Downs, G.W., and Larkey, P. (1986) *The Search for Government Efficiency: From Hubris to Helplessness.* New York: Random House.

Drake, A.W. (1972) 'Quantitative Models in Public Administration: Some Educational Needs', in A.W. Drake, L. Keeney, and P.M. Morse (eds) *Analysis of Public Systems.* Cambridge, MA: MIT Press.

Enticott, G., and Walker, R.M. (2008) Sustainability, performance and organizational strategy: An empirical analysis of public organizations, *Business Strategy and the Environment,* 17 (2), 79–92.

Etzioni, A. (1967) Mixed scanning: a third approach to decision making, *Public Administration Review,* 27, 385–392.

Etzioni, A. (1986) Mixed scanning revisited, *Public Administration Review,* 46, 8–14.

Farnham, B. (1994) 'Roosevelt and the Munich Crisis: Insights from Prospects Theory', in B. Farnham (ed.) *Avoiding Losses/Taking Risks: Prospect Theory and International Conflict,* University of Michigan Press, 41–72.

Feeney, M.K. and Rainey, H.G. (2009) Personnel flexibility and red tape in public and non-profit organizations: distinctions due to institutional and political accountability, *Journal of Public Administration Research and Theory,* doi: 10.1093/jopart/mup027.

Gochman, C., and Leng, R. (1983) Realpolitik and the road to war: An analysis of attributes and behavior, *International Studies Quarterly,* 27, 97–120.

Greer, A., and Hoggett, P. (1999) Public policies, private strategies and local public spending bodies. *Public Administration,* 77 (2), 235–256.

Hambrick, D.C., and Finkelstein, S. (1987) 'Managerial Discretion: A Bridge Between Polar Views of Organizational Outcomes'. in L. L. Cummings and M. Staw (eds) *Research in Organizational Behavior, Vol.* 9. Greenwich, CT: JAI Press, 369–406.

Hannan, M.T., and Freeman, J.H. (1984) Structural inertia and organizational change. *American Sociological Review,* 49, 149–164.

Hansen, G., and Wernerfelt, B. (1989) Determinants of firm performance: The relative importance of economic and organizational factors. *Strategic Management Journal,* 10, 399–411.

Hensel, P.R., and Diehl, P.F. (1994) 'It takes two to tango: Nonmilitarized response in interstate dispute. *Journal of Conflict Resolution,* 38, 479–506.

Hickson, D.J. *et al.* (1986) *Top Decisions: Strategic Decision Making in Organizations.* San Francisco, CA: Jossey-Bass.

Hrebiniak, L.G., and Joyce, W.F. (1985) Organizational adaptation: Strategic choice and environmental determinism, *Administrative Science Quarterly,* 30 (3), 336–349.

Jones, B.D. (1999) Bounded Rationality, *Annual Review of Political Science,* 2: 297–321.

Kahneman, D., and Tversky, A. (1979) Intuitive predictions: Biases and corrective procedures, *TIMS Studies in Management Science,* 12, 313–327.

Lenz, R. (1981) Determinants of organizational performance: An interdisciplinary review, *Strategic Management Journal,* 2, 131–154.

Levy, J.S. (1992) Prospect theory and international relations: Theoretical applications and analytical problems. *Political Psychology,* 13 (2), 283–310.

Levy, J.S. (1994) 'An Introduction to Prospect Theory', in B. Farnham (ed.) *Avoiding Losses/taking Risks: Prospect Theory and International Conflict*, University of Michigan Press, 7–22.

Levy, J.S. (1996) Loss aversion, framing, and bargaining: The implications of prospect theory for international conflict. *International Political Science Review*, 17 (2) 179–195.

Levy, J.S. (1997) Prospect theory, rational choice, and international relations, *International Studies Quarterly*, 41 (1) 87–112.

Lindblom, C.E. (1959) The science of muddling through, *Public Administration Review*, 19, 79–88.

Lindblom, C.E. (1977) *Politics and Markets*. New York: Basic Books.

Lindblom, C.E. (1979) Still muddling, not yet through, *Public Administration Review*, Nov–Dec, 39 (6), 517–526.

Mansbach, R.W., and Vasquez, J. (1981) The effect of actor and issue classifications on the analysis of global conflict-cooperation, *The Journal of Politics*, 43: 862–880.

March, J.G. (1962) The business firm as a political coalition, *Journal of Politics*, 24: 662–678.

March, J.G., and Olsen, J.P. (eds) (1976) *Ambiguity and Choice in Organizations*. Bergen, Norway: Universitetsforlaget.

March, J.G., and Olsen, J.P. (1986) 'Garbage Can Models of Decision Making in Organizations', in J.G. March and R. Weissinger-Baylon (eds), *Ambiguity and Command*. White Plains, NY: Pitman.

Mascarenhas, B. (1989) Domains of state-owned, privately held, and publicly traded firms in international competition, *Administrative Science Quarterly*, 34, 582–597.

Meier, K.J., O'Toole, Jr, L.J., *et al.* (2007) Strategic management and the performance of public organizations: testing venerable ideas against recent theories, *Journal of Public Administration Research and Theory*, 17 (3), 357–377.

Melkers, J., and Willoughby, K. (2005) Models of performance-measurement (PM) use in local governments: Understanding budgeting, communication, and lasting effects, *Public Administration Review*, 65, 180–190.

Miles, R.E., and Snow, C.C. (1978) *Organizational Strategy, Structure and Process*. New York: McGraw-Hill Book Company.

Mintz, A. (1993) The decision to attack Iraq: a noncompensatory theory of decision making, *Journal of Conflict Resolution*, 37, 595–618.

Mintz, A. (2004) How do leaders make decisions? A poliheuristic perspective, *Journal of Conflict Resolution*, 48, 3–13.

Mintz, A., and Geva, N. (1997) The poliheuristic theory of foreign policy decision making', in N. Geva and A. Mintz (eds) *Decision Making on War and Peace: The Cognitive-Rational Debate*, Boulder: Lynne Rienner, 81–101.

Mintz, A., Geva, N., Redd, S., and Carnes, A. (1997) The effect of dynamic and static choice sets on political decision making: An analysis using the decision board platform, *American Political Science Review*, 91, 533–566.

Mintzberg, H., Raisinghani, D., and Theoret, A. (1976) The structure of unstructured decisions Processes, *Administrative Science Quarterly*, 21, 266–273.

Morse, P.M., and Bacon, L.W. (eds) (1967) *Operations Research for Public Systems*. Cambridge, MA: MIT Press.

Moynihan, D.P. (2008) *The Dynamics of Performance Management: Constructing Information and Reform*. Washington, DC: Georgetown University Press.

Niskanen, W.A. (1971) *Bureaucracy and Representative Government*. Hawthorne, NY: Aldine de Gruyter.

Nutt, P.C. (1999) Public-private differences and the assessment of alternatives for decision making, *J-PART*, 9 (2), 305–349.

Nutt, P.C., and Backoff, R.W. (1995) Strategy for public and third-sector organizations, *Journal of Public Administration Research and Theory*, 5, 189–211.

Nutt, P.C., and Backoff, R.W. (1992) *The Strategic Management of Public and Third Sector Organizations*, San Francisco, CA: Jossey-Bass.

Olsen, J.P. (2001) Garbage cans, new institutionalism, and the study of politics, *American Political Science Review*, 95, 191–198.

Pettigrew, A.M. (1987) Context and action in the transformation of the firm, *Journal of Management Studies*, 24 (6) 649–670.

Porter, M.E. (1998) *Competitive Advantage.* New York: Free Press.

Reed, S. (2003) 'The Poliheuristic Theory of Foreign Policy Decision Making: Experimental Evidence', in A. Mintz (ed.) *Integrating Cognitive and Rational Theories of Foreign Policy Decision Making*. New York: Palgrave Macmillan, 101–126.

Ring, P.S. (1988) 'Strategic Issues: What Are They and Where Do They Come From?', in J.M. Bryson and R.C. Einsweiller (eds) *Strategic Planning*. Chicago: Planners Press.

Rodgers, R.R., and Hunter, J.E. (1992) A foundation of good management practice in government: management by objectives, *Public Administration Review*, 52(1), 27–39.

Rosenau, J. (1966) 'Pre-theories and Theories of Foreign Policy', in J. Rosenau (ed.) *Scientific Study of Foreign Policy*. New York: Free Press.

Rosenbloom, D.H., Kravchuck, R.S., and Rosenbloom, D.G. (2001) *Public Administration*. New York: McGraw Hill.

Rubin, I.S. (1985) *Shrinking the Federal Government: The Effect of Cutbacks on Five Federal Agencies.* White Plains, NY: Longman.

Rubin, M.S. (1988) 'Sagas, Ventures, Quests, and Parlays: A Typology of Strategies in the Public Sector', in J.M. Bryson and R.C. Einsweiller (eds) *Strategic Planning*. Chicago: Planners Press.

Sathasivam, K. (2003) 'No Other Choice: Pakistan's Decision to Test the Bomb', in A. Mintz (ed.) *Integrating Cognitive and Rational Theories of Foreign Policy Decision Making*. New York: Palgrave Macmillan, 55–76.

Sharpe, L.J., and Newton, K. (1984) *Does Politics Matter? The Determinants of Public Policy.* Oxford: Clarendon Press.

Simon, H.A. (1948) *Administrative Behavior.* New York: Free Press.

Simon, H. A. (1995) Organizations and markets, *Journal of Public Administration Research and Theory*, 5, 273–294.

Simon, H. A. (1998) Why public administration? *Journal of Public Administration Research and Theory*, 8, 1–12.

Stern, E. (2004) Contextualizing and critiquing the poliheuristic theory. *Journal of Conflict Resolution*, 48 (1), 105–126.

Swiss, J.E. (1991) *Public Management Systems.* Upper Saddle River, NJ: Prentice Hall.

Thompson, J.D. (1962) Common and uncommon elements in administration, *Social Welfare Forum*, 89, 181–201.

Thompson, J.D. (1967) *Organizations in Action.* New York: McGraw-Hill.

Thompson, J.R. (2000) Reinvention as reform: assessing the National Performance Review, *Public Administration Review*, 60 (6), 508–550.

Tullock, G. (1965) *The Politics of Bureaucracy.* Washington, DC: Public Affairs Press.

Vasquez, J. (1983) The test of issues and global conflict: A test of Rosenau's issue area typology, *Journal of Peace Research*, 20, 179–192.

Walker, R.M., and Boyne, G.A. (2006) Public management reform and organizational performance: An empirical assessment of the UK Labour Government's Public Service Improvement Strategy, *Journal of Policy Analysis and Management*, 25 (2), 371–393.

Wamsley, G.L., and Zald, M.N. (1973) *The Political Economy of Public Organizations*. Lexington, MA: Heath.

Weick, K.E. (1979) *The Social Psychology of Organizing*. Reading, MA: Addison-Wesley.

Zahra, S.A., and Pearce, J.A. (1990) Research evidence on the Miles-Snow typology. *Journal of Management*, 16 (1), 751 768.

14

Strategic Decision Making and Knowledge: A Heideggerian Approach

HARIDIMOS TSOUKAS

How did George W. Bush reach this point [to invade Iraq]? I will go to my grave not fully understanding why. There was no meeting or set of meetings at which the pros and cons were debated and a formal decision taken. No, this decision happened. It was cumulative.

—Richard N. Haass, *War of Necessity, War of Choice*

Man proceeds in a fog. But when he looks back to judge the people of the past, he sees no fog on their path. From his present, which was their faraway future, their path looks perfectly clear to him, good visibility all the way. Looking back, he sees the path, he sees the people proceeding, he sees their mistakes but not the fog. And yet all of them Heidegger, Mayakovsky, Aragon, Ezra Pound, Gorky, Gottfried Benn, St-John Perse, Giono – all were walking in fog, and one might wonder who is more blind? Mayakovsky, who as he wrote his poem on Lenin did not know where Leninism would lead? Or we who judge him decades later and do not see the fog that enveloped him? Mayakovsky's blindness is part of the eternal human condition. But for us not to see the fog on Mayakovsky's path is to forget what man is, forget what we ourselves are.

—Milan Kundera, *Testaments Betrayed*

[W]henever people are said to make a decision, what really happens is that they are working retrospectively. When one feels compelled to declare that a decision has been made, the gist of that feeling is that there is some outcome at hand that must have been occasioned by some earlier choice. Decision making consists of locating, articulating, and ratifying that earlier choice, bringing it forward to the present, and claiming it as the decision that has just been made. The decision actually has already been set in motion before people declare that it has been made. The recent history

---

Handbook of Decision Making. Edited by Paul C. Nutt and David C. Wilson
© 2010 John Wiley & Sons, Ltd

is viewed in retrospect, with tentative outcomes at hand, to see what decision could account for that outcome. That plausible decision is the decision people announce. What is crucial about this is that a decision is an act of interpretation rather than an act of choice.

—Karl Weick, *Sensemaking in Organizations*, pp. 184–185

'Strategic decision making' is a problematic concept. What its constituent parts mean is not always clear, since both 'strategic' and 'decision making' have started their conceptual lives in management and organization studies as relatively clear concepts, informing a great deal of empirical research, only to be critiqued later on for poor descriptiveness and ambiguity. 'Strategic' and 'strategy' are often used in a circular manner, which impedes clarity. For example, as Miller and Wilson (2006: 482) note, 'as with the old tautology that arises in the study of managerial work that "management is what managers do" – is strategy what strategists do? Or is it simply that we choose to see it as "strategic"?' Circular definitions are unhelpful. To argue that 'an activity is considered strategic to the extent that is consequential for the strategic outcomes, directions, survival and competitive advantage of the firm' (Jarzabkowski, Balogun, and Seidl, 2007: 8), begs the question.

Similarly, if 'decision' is taken to be 'commitment to action' (cf. Miller and Wilson, 2006: 481), how might one account for situations in which action occurs without explicit commitment (Langley *et al.*, 1995: 265)? And when there are signs of commitment, what is commitment on? Or if 'a decision may be defined as the choice of a course of action to achieve a desired future state' (Butler, 1998: 36), how might one understand situations in which courses of action are not necessarily 'chosen' but emerging from practical situations actors cope with while in the midst of action (as in reflection in action occurring in musical, theatrical, or design im-provisation – see Crossan (1998), Sawyer (2000), Weick (2002), Yanow and Tsoukas (forthcoming))? If strategic decisions 'involve the commitment of significant re-sources, have major long-term consequences and are hard to reverse' (Papadakis and Barwise, 1998: 2), what are we to make of cases in which a pattern of long-term consequences is produced not so much by deliberate decisions as by organizations making do with whatever is historically, culturally, and materially available to them at a point in time, as was the case of Scottish knitwear manufacturers studied by Po-rac, Thomas, and Fuller (1989) and the well-known case of how Honda captured a significant segment of the US motorcycle market in the late 1950s (Pascale, 1984)?

The main problem with notions such as 'strategic' and 'decision making' is the one alluded to by Miller and Wilson above and by Weick's epigraph in this chapter, namely the confusion between the language of the *actor* and the language of the *observer*. Is 'decision' a retrospective attribution of the observer, namely an account of a cognitive community that attempts to form a coherent view of particular orga-nizational outcomes and the processes that led to them, or does 'decision' signify a distinct empirical event, a moment of actors' choice whereby a course of action has been purposefully committed to? The confusion between retrospective attribution (made by an observer) and an unfolding empirical reality (as experienced by an actor) has long generated conceptual difficulties in Management and Organization Studies (MOS).

Thus, as Langley *et al.* (1995: 265) and Chia (1994), among others, have pointed out, such a confusion has often led researchers to focus on distinct organizational outcomes, such as launching a new product, building a new factory, or purchasing an information system, and assume that the particular outcome at hand would not have happened unless there had been a relevant decision committing the organization to a course of action. While there are occasions where this has indeed been the case, especially in machine-like bureaucracies and in formal organizations operating in highly institutionalized environments (e.g. local authorities, public bureaucracies, etc.), such an assumption is not always warranted. Even in machine bureaucracies, what may appear *ex post facto* as a 'decision' may well have been an outcome of nondeliberate coping practices or of interacting routines – 'mechanisms designed after all to allow action while economizing as much as possible on decision' (Langley *et al.*, 1995: 265). Or the commitment to action that is signified by a decision may well have been made at some other time, in some other place.

One can find evidence of decisions in formal organizations. After all, mergers and acquisitions, the purchase of technological systems, the launch of new products, are often the outcomes of some sort of decision. But what they signify, how they are arrived at, and how they are related to action are not always clear. For the traditional school on decision making, decisions are moments of fully rational choice, whereby decision makers identify a problem, search for alternative solutions, prioritize preferences according to certain criteria and, finally, make an optimizing choice (cf. Miller and Wilson, 2006: 469). Even when the unbounded rationality underlying this view has been challenged (March and Simon, 1958; Simon, 1976), suggesting, more realistically, that goal ambiguity is pervasive, information is incomplete and costly to obtain, preferences are often unclear and unstable, and, thus, decision makers opt for 'satisficing' rather than 'optimizing' choices, the basic idea that decision making is, essentially, a cognitive process that can be decomposed into a series of simple, sequential steps has not been abandoned.

The rational model (in its unbounded-rationality and bounded-rationality versions) has been turned on its head by those researchers who have argued that decision making is permeated by ambiguity: ambiguity about preferences, relevance, history, and interpretation (March, 1988; March and Olsen, 1976). Preferences change as a result of exogenous pressures and actors' experience; problems and solutions are less connected by causal relevance and more by simultaneity; linkages between past events are unclear; the gathering and use of information in decision making are symbolic. In other words, rather than decisions rationally solving problems, solutions may well search for problems, thus generating decisions (Cohen, March, and Olsen, 1972). Rather than decisions serving the purpose of choice, they may well serve the purpose of mobilizing organizational action, distribute responsibility, or provide legitimacy (Brunsson, 1990).

Between the two extremes – decision making as a rational process vs. decision making as a chaotic process – there have been several studies exploring the diverse types of decision-making processes (Hickson *et al.*, 1986) as well as the actionability of decisions – how implementation has been carried out (Nutt, 1989). All this is useful but takes for granted the status of decisions as distinct empirical events *necessarily* preceding the taking of action. For critics of this view, such as Langley *et al.* (1995) and Chia (1994), this is unwarranted reification. 'Decision' is observers' construct rather than actors' experienced reality: 'decisions often do not exist; they are merely constructs in the eyes of the observer', note Langley *et al.* (1995: 265). The phenomenology of 'decision making' is different from its conceptual analysis. Mintzberg and his associates find the concept of 'decision' so problematic as to argue for substituting 'action' (Mintzberg and Waters, 1990: 5) or 'issues' (Langley *et al.*, 1995: 276) for 'decisions'. Chia (1994) has similarly argued against reifying decision making, suggesting that it should rather be viewed as a Batesonian 'explanatory principle', namely as a construct created by observers (especially researchers) to help them make coherent sense of aspects of organizational behavior. As Chia (1994: 794) remarks: 'Understanding decision-making as an explanatory principle involves a recognition that it is the product of a *post-hoc* rationalization process in which the cause/effect relationship established has been abstracted, reified and chronologically reversed. "Decision-making" is a conceptual *invention* but one which has been reified and chronologically inverted so as to appear as "event" precede action.'

The critique launched by several detractors of the hitherto mainstream literature on decision making is, either implicitly or explicitly, ontological in character. For March (1988) and Brunsson (1982; 1990), decisions may not be all that important in organizational life after all. What is important is undertaking effective action and how this may be facilitated (Brunsson, 1982: 42). Insofar as decisions exist, they may serve purposes other than rational problem solving and, to the extent that this is the case, decisions are secondary effects of collective processes of sensemaking, interpretation, and politics. Organizations are often too busy to make decisions but they never tire of looking for opportunities for action.

For Hendry (2000), an important distinction needs to be drawn between the *general* concepts of decisions and decision making, which are central means of the social construction of organizational reality and operate mainly at the level of practical consciousness, and the *specific* contents of decisions, which form a main component of organizational discourse and operate at the level of discursive consciousness. Whether strategic decisions are 'made' or not, notes Hendry (2000: 967), they are certainly discussed and invoked to influence the actions of others. As Hendry (p. 967) remarks: "Because of the important structural role played by the concept of decision, the language of strategic decisions pervades organizational discourse and we can readily observe not only where decisions are recorded but also where they are challenged, denied or ignored. In an organizational setting managers have to account discursively both for their actions and for their inactions, both within the organization and to external stakeholders such as customers, shareholders and lenders. By looking at how decisions are invoked in these accounts we can at least draw some reasonable inferences as to the relationships between strategic actions and between actions, decision processes and ideas."

In other words, it is because the language of decisions ontologically structures the way organizational members understand themselves and talk about their actions that specific strategic decisions are important.

Langley *et al.* (1995: 265) and Chia (1994: 795) have explicitly noted that the problem of deciphering the status of 'decision' and 'decision making' is primarily an ontological one. For Langley *et al.*, what fundamentally exists in organizations are interacting 'issue streams' that 'spin off actions, *sometimes* through identifiable decisions' (Langley *et al.*, 1995: 270). Notice that in Langley *et al.*'s ontological scheme of things, it is not that decisions do not exist but that they are not the real stuff organizations are made of: decisions are not viewed as the final points of destination but as 'events that punctuate and modify the flow of issues' (Langley *et al.*, 1995: 276). Although they acknowledge the potential reification of 'issues' (just like 'decisions') in formal organizations, Langley *et al.* do not further specify the ontological status of 'issues'.

Echoing Weick (1979), but drawing on postmodern and process philosophers, Chia (1994) argues that decision making essentially is an ontological act of sense-making, namely carving out a piece of plausible reality for further examination, through punctuating the stream of experience for the purpose of ordering it and making it sensible. As Chia (1994: 800) notes: 'Decision-making is the ontological act of cutting and partitioning off a version of reality from what has hitherto been indistinguishable and then subsequently presenting the former as representative of the latter. [...] Making "incisions", ex-cising or cutting-out a part from the whole of our phenomenal experiences and then finally making that part "stand for" the whole; this is the essential ontological character of decision-making'. What appears as a 'decisional' accomplishment need not be an intentional outcome, but the product of 'incisional acts, interactions and local orchestrations of relationships' (Chia, 1994: 801). Moreover, Chia notes, this way of thinking leads one to inquire about 'how it is that some kinds of actions appear to "succeed" in creating larger scale effects such as "events" of decision-making' (Chia, 1994: 801). On this view, then, 'decisions' are 'events' created by the observer. But decisions are in-cisions, cutting-offs, punctuations, which structure human experience and, therefore, bring forth what we take as real. By insisting that decision making is an ontological act, Chia usefully brings to our attention the structuring propensity of language, the ordering effects of the micro-practices of making distinctions and labeling, and the human participation in bringing forth what is subsequently experienced as an independent pattern. However, what is missing from this account is a further delineation of the sociological basis of the will-to-order as well as of the role of 'decisions' in organizational life. The latter may be already pre-structured through the micro-practices of drawing distinctions but this does not mean that, in formal organizations, decisions are sometimes not self-consciously made.

The challenge is how to take both aspects of decision making into account: on the one hand the deep structuring of reality that takes effect at the level of practical consciousness (decision making as the ontological act of punctuating the flow of experience) *and*, on the other hand, decision making as the discursively conscious process of making explicit commitments to action for various purposes, such as problem solving, motivation, responsibility-distribution or legitimation. Each one of these aspects is connected to different types of knowledge (practical/tacit, discursive/explicit). To do this we need an onto-epistemological framework whose starting point is the flow of human experience and how it is structured.

Below I will present such a framework drawing on Heideggerian phenomenology (Heidegger, 1962), especially as it has been interpreted by Dreyfus (1991a; 1991b; 2000), Spinoza *et al.* (1997), and Schatzki (2000; 2005) (for recent applications of Heideggerian phenomenology in organization and management studies, see Chia and Holt (2006), Sandberg and Targama (2007), Tsoukas (forthcoming), Weick (2003; 2004), and Yanow and Tsoukas (2009)). However, to demonstrate the merits of Heideggerian phenomenology in giving us a better grasp of decisions in organizations it would be useful to present first a relevant case study. The case that will be presented in the next section is an edited version of an article published in *The New Yorker* on May 24, 2004 by the award-winning American journalist Seymour M. Hersh. It concerns the Abu Ghraib prison scandal, namely the physical coercion and sexual humiliation of Iraqi prisoners by American military. This is a particularly relevant case because the American Army is a machine bureaucracy filled with 'decisions'. However, it will be shown how, without getting rid of the concept of 'decision', a Heideggerian phenomenology enables us to better understand the ontological basis of decision making and the importance of issues, discourse, and actions.

A Case Study: The Gray Zone – How a Secret Pentagon Program Came to Abu Ghraib [1]

The roots of the Abu Ghraib prison scandal lie not in the criminal inclinations of a few Army reservists but in a decision, approved last year by Secretary of Defense Donald Rumsfeld, to expand a highly secret operation, which had been focused on the hunt for Al Qaeda, to the interrogation of prisoners in Iraq. Rumsfeld's decision embittered the American intelligence community, damaged the effectiveness of élite combat units, and hurt America's prospects in the war on terror.

According to interviews with several past and present American intelligence officials, the Pentagon's operation, known inside the intelligence community by several code words, including Copper Green, encouraged physical coercion and sexual humiliation of Iraqi prisoners in an effort to generate more intelligence about the growing insurgency in Iraq. A senior C.I.A. official, in confirming the details of this account last week, said that the operation stemmed from Rumsfeld's long-standing desire to wrest control of America's clandestine and paramilitary operations from the C.I.A. [. . .]

The Abu Ghraib story began, in a sense, just weeks after the September 11, 2001, attacks, with the American bombing of Afghanistan. Almost from the start, the Administration's search for Al Qaeda members in the war zone, and its worldwide search for terrorists, came up against major command-and-control problems. For example, combat forces that had Al Qaeda targets in sight had to obtain legal clearance before firing on them. On October 7th, the night the bombing began, an unmanned Predator aircraft tracked an automobile convoy that, American intelligence believed, contained Mullah Muhammad Omar, the Taliban leader. A lawyer on duty at the United States Central Command headquarters, in Tampa, Florida, refused to authorize a strike. By the time an attack was approved, the target was out of reach. Rumsfeld was apoplectic over what he saw as a self-defeating hesitation to attack that was due to political correctness. One officer described him to me that fall as 'kicking a lot of glass and breaking doors.' In November, the *Washington Post* reported that, as many as ten times since early October, Air Force pilots believed they'd had senior Al Qaeda and Taliban members in their sights but had been unable to act in time because of legalistic hurdles. There were similar problems throughout the world, as American Special Forces units seeking to move quickly against suspected terrorist cells were compelled to get prior approval from local American ambassadors and brief their superiors in the chain of command.

Rumsfeld reacted in his usual direct fashion: he authorized the establishment of a highly secret program that was given blanket advance approval to kill or capture and, if possible, interrogate 'high value' targets in the Bush Administration's war on terror. A special-access program, or SAP – subject to the Defense Department's most stringent level of security – was set up, with an office in a secure area of the Pentagon. The program would recruit operatives and acquire the necessary equipment, including aircraft, and would keep its activities under wraps. America's most successful intelligence operations during the Cold War had been SAPs, including the Navy's submarine penetration of underwater cables used by the Soviet high command and construction of the Air Force's stealth bomber. All the so-called 'black' programs had one element in common: the Secretary of Defense, or his deputy, had to conclude that the normal military classification restraints did not provide enough security.

'Rumsfeld's goal was to get a capability in place to take on a high-value target – a standup group to hit quickly,' a former high-level intelligence official told me. 'He got all the agencies together – the C.I.A. and the N.S.A. – to get pre-approval in place. Just say the code word and go.' The operation had across-the-board approval from Rumsfeld and from Condoleezza Rice, the national-security adviser. President Bush was informed of the existence of the program, the former intelligence official said.

The people assigned to the program worked by the book, the former intelligence official told me. They created code words, and recruited, after careful screening, highly trained commandos and operatives from America's élite forces – Navy SEALs, the Army's Delta Force, and the C.I.A.'s paramilitary experts. They also asked some basic questions: 'Do the people working the problem have to use aliases? Yes. Do we need dead drops for the mail? Yes. No traceability and no budget. And some special-access programs are never fully briefed to Congress.'

In theory, the operation enabled the Bush Administration to respond immediately to time-sensitive intelligence: commandos crossed borders without visas and could interrogate terrorism suspects deemed too important for transfer to the military's facilities at Guantánamo, Cuba. They carried out instant interrogations – using force if necessary – at secret C.I.A. detention centers scattered around the world. The intelligence would be relayed to the SAP command center in the Pentagon in real time, and sifted for those pieces of information critical to the 'white,' or overt, world.

Fewer than two hundred operatives and officials, including Rumsfeld and General Richard Myers, chairman of the Joint Chiefs of Staff, were 'completely read into the program,' the former intelligence official said. The goal was to keep the operation protected. 'We're not going to read more people than necessary into our heart of darkness,' he said. 'The rules are "Grab whom you must. Do what you want."'

One Pentagon official who was deeply involved in the program was Stephen Cambone, who was named Under-Secretary of Defense for Intelligence in March, 2003. The office was new; it was created as part of Rumsfeld's reorganization of the Pentagon. Cambone was unpopular among military and civilian intelligence bureaucrats in the Pentagon, essentially because he had little experience in running intelligence programs, though in 1998 he had served as staff director for a committee, headed by Rumsfeld, that warned of an emerging ballistic-missile threat to the United States. He was known instead for his closeness to Rumsfeld. 'Remember Henry II – "Who will rid me of this meddlesome priest?"' the senior C.I.A. official said to me, with a laugh, last week. 'Whatever Rumsfeld whimsically says, Cambone will do ten times that much.'

Cambone was a strong advocate for war against Iraq. He shared Rumsfeld's disdain for the analysis and assessments proffered by the C.I.A., viewing them as too cautious, and chafed, as did Rumsfeld, at the C.I.A.'s inability, before the Iraq war, to state conclusively that Saddam Hussein harbored weapons of mass destruction. Cambone's military assistant, Army Lieutenant General William G. (Jerry) Boykin, was also controversial. Last fall, he generated unwanted headlines after it was reported that, in a speech at an Oregon church, he equated the Muslim world with Satan.

Early in his tenure, Cambone provoked a bureaucratic battle within the Pentagon by insisting that he be given control of all special-access programs that were relevant to the war on terror. Those programs, which had been viewed by many in the Pentagon as sacrosanct, were monitored by Kenneth deGraffenreid, who had experience in counter-intelligence programs. Cambone got control, and deGraffenreid subsequently left the Pentagon. [. . .]

In mid-2003, the special-access program was regarded in the Pentagon as one of the success stories of the war on terror. 'It was an active program,' the former intelligence official told me. 'It's been the most important capability we have for dealing with an imminent threat. If we discover where Osama bin Laden is, we can get him. And we can remove an existing threat with a real capability to hit the United States – and do so without visibility.' Some of its methods were troubling and could not bear close scrutiny, however.

By then, the war in Iraq had begun. The SAP was involved in some assignments in Iraq, the former official said. C.I.A. and other American Special Forces operatives secretly teamed up to hunt for Saddam Hussein and – without success – for Iraqi weapons of mass destruction. But they weren't able to stop the evolving insurgency.

In the first months after the fall of Baghdad, Rumsfeld and his aides still had a limited view of the insurgency, seeing it as little more than the work of Baathist 'dead-enders,' criminal gangs, and foreign terrorists who were Al Qaeda followers. The Administration measured its success in the war by how many of those on its list of the fifty-five most wanted members of the old regime – reproduced on playing cards – had been captured. Then, in August, 2003, terror bombings in Baghdad hit the Jordanian Embassy, killing nineteen people, and the United Nations headquarters, killing twenty-three people, including Sergio Vieira de Mello, the head of the U.N. mission. On August 25th, less than a week after the U.N. bombing, Rumsfeld acknowledged, in a talk before the Veterans of Foreign Wars, that 'the dead-enders are still with us.' He went on, 'There are some today who are surprised that there are still pockets of resistance in Iraq, and they suggest that this represents some sort of failure on the part of the Coalition. But this is not the case.' Rumsfeld compared the insurgents with those true believers who 'fought on during and after the defeat of the Nazi regime in Germany.' A few weeks later – and five months after the fall of Baghdad – the Defense Secretary declared, 'It is, in my view, better to be dealing with terrorists in Iraq than in the United States.'

Inside the Pentagon, there was a growing realization that the war was going badly. The increasingly beleaguered and baffled Army leadership was telling reporters that the insurgents consisted of five thousand Baathists loyal to Saddam Hussein. 'When you understand that they're organized in a cellular structure,' General John Abizaid, the head of the Central Command, declared, 'that ... they have access to a lot of money and a lot of ammunition, you'll understand how dangerous they are.'

The American military and intelligence communities were having little success in penetrating the insurgency. One internal report prepared for the U.S. military, made available to me, concluded that the insurgents' 'strategic and operational intelligence has proven to be quite good.' According to the study:

> Their ability to attack convoys, other vulnerable targets and particular individuals has been the result of painstaking surveillance and reconnaissance. Inside information has been passed on to insurgent cells about convoy/troop movements and daily habits of Iraqis working with coalition from within the Iraqi security services, primarily the Iraqi Police force which is rife with sympathy for the insurgents, Iraqi ministries and from within pro-insurgent individuals working with the CPA's so-called Green Zone.

The study concluded, 'Politically, the U.S. has failed to date. Insurgencies can be fixed or ameliorated by dealing with what caused them in the first place. The disaster that is the reconstruction of Iraq has been the key cause of the insurgency. There is no legitimate government, and it behooves the

Coalition Provisional Authority to absorb the sad but unvarnished fact that most Iraqis do not see the Governing Council' – the Iraqi body appointed by the C.P.A. – 'as the legitimate authority. Indeed, they know that the true power is the CPA.'

By the fall, a military analyst told me, the extent of the Pentagon's political and military misjudgments was clear. Donald Rumsfeld's 'dead-enders' now included not only Baathists but many marginal figures as well – thugs and criminals who were among the tens of thousands of prisoners freed the previous fall by Saddam as part of a prewar general amnesty. Their desperation was not driving the insurgency; it simply made them easy recruits for those who were. The analyst said, 'We'd killed and captured guys who had been given two or three hundred dollars to "pray and spray"' – that is, shoot randomly and hope for the best. 'They weren't really insurgents but down-and-outers who were paid by wealthy individuals sympathetic to the insurgency.' In many cases, the paymasters were Sunnis who had been members of the Baath Party. The analyst said that the insurgents 'spent three or four months figuring out how we operated and developing their own countermeasures. If that meant putting up a hapless guy to go and attack a convoy and see how the American troops responded, they'd do it.' Then, the analyst said, 'the clever ones began to get in on the action.'

By contrast, according to the military report, the American and Coalition forces knew little about the insurgency: 'Human intelligence is poor or lacking ... due to the dearth of competence and expertise. ... The intelligence effort is not coördinated since either too many groups are involved in gathering intelligence or the final product does not get to the troops in the field in a timely manner.' The success of the war was at risk; something had to be done to change the dynamic.

The solution, endorsed by Rumsfeld and carried out by Stephen Cambone, was to get tough with those Iraqis in the Army prison system who were suspected of being insurgents. A key player was Major General Geoffrey Miller, the commander of the detention and interrogation center at Guantánamo, who had been summoned to Baghdad in late August to review prison interrogation procedures. The internal Army report on the abuse charges, written by Major General Antonio Taguba in February, revealed that Miller urged that the commanders in Baghdad change policy and place military intelligence in charge of the prison. The report quoted Miller as recommending that 'detention operations must act as an enabler for interrogation.'

Miller's concept, as it emerged in recent Senate hearings, was to 'Gitmoize' the prison system in Iraq – to make it more focussed on interrogation. He also briefed military commanders in Iraq on the interrogation methods used in Cuba – methods that could, with special approval, include sleep deprivation, exposure to extremes of cold and heat, and placing prisoners in 'stress positions' for agonizing lengths of time. (The Bush Administration had unilaterally declared Al Qaeda and other captured members of international terrorist networks to be illegal combatants, and not eligible for the protection of the Geneva Conventions.)

Rumsfeld and Cambone went a step further, however: they expanded the scope of the SAP, bringing its unconventional methods to Abu Ghraib. The commandos were to operate in Iraq as they had in Afghanistan. The male prisoners could be treated roughly, and exposed to sexual humiliation.

'They weren't getting anything substantive from the detainees in Iraq,' the former intelligence official told me. 'No names. Nothing that they could hang their hat on. Cambone says, I've got to crack this thing and I'm tired of working through the normal chain of command. I've got this apparatus set up – the black special-access program – and I'm going in hot. So he pulls the switch, and the electricity begins flowing last summer. And it's working. We're getting a picture of the insurgency in Iraq and the intelligence is flowing into the white world. We're getting good stuff. But we've got more targets' – prisoners in Iraqi jails – 'than people who can handle them.'

Cambone then made another crucial decision, the former intelligence official told me: not only would he bring the SAP's rules into the prisons; he would bring some of the Army military-intelligence officers working inside the Iraqi prisons under the SAP's auspices. 'So here are fundamentally good soldiers – military-intelligence guys – being told that no rules apply,' the former official, who has extensive knowledge of the special-access programs, added. 'And, as far as they're concerned, this is a covert operation, and it's to be kept within Defense Department channels.'

The military-police prison guards, the former official said, included 'recycled hillbillies from Cumberland, Maryland.' He was referring to members of the 372nd Military Police Company. Seven members of the company are now facing charges for their role in the abuse at Abu Ghraib. 'How are these guys from Cumberland going to know anything? The Army Reserve doesn't know what it's doing.'

Who was in charge of Abu Ghraib – whether military police or military intelligence – was no longer the only question that mattered. Hard-core special operatives, some of them with aliases, were working in the prison. The military police assigned to guard the prisoners wore uniforms, but many others – military intelligence officers, contract interpreters, C.I.A. officers, and the men from the special-access program – wore civilian clothes. It was not clear who was who, even to Brigadier General Janis Karpinski, then the commander of the 800th Military Police Brigade, and the officer ostensibly in charge. 'I thought most of the civilians there were interpreters, but there were some civilians that I didn't know,' Karpinski told me. 'I called them the disappearing ghosts. I'd seen them once in a while at Abu Ghraib and then I'd see them months later. They were nice – they'd always call out to me and say, 'Hey, remember me? How are you doing?' 'The mysterious civilians,' she said, were 'always bringing in somebody for interrogation or waiting to collect somebody going out.' Karpinski added that she had no idea who was operating in her prison system. (General Taguba found that Karpinski's leadership failures contributed to the abuses.)

By fall, according to the former intelligence official, the senior leadership of the C.I.A. had had enough. 'They said, "No way. We signed up for the core program in Afghanistan – pre-approved for operations against high-value terrorist targets – and now you want to use it for cabdrivers, brothers-in-law, and people pulled off the streets"' – the sort of prisoners who populate the Iraqi jails. 'The C.I.A.'s legal people objected,' and the agency ended its SAP involvement in Abu Ghraib, the former official said.

The C.I.A.'s complaints were echoed throughout the intelligence community. There was fear that the situation at Abu Ghraib would lead to the exposure of the secret SAP, and thereby bring an end to what had been, before Iraq, a valuable cover operation. 'This was stupidity,' a government consultant told me. 'You're taking a program that was operating in the chaos of Afghanistan against Al Qaeda, a stateless terror group, and bringing it into a structured, traditional war zone. Sooner or later, the commandos would bump into the legal and moral procedures of a conventional war with an Army of a hundred and thirty-five thousand soldiers.'

The former senior intelligence official blamed hubris for the Abu Ghraib disaster. 'There's nothing more exhilarating for a pissant Pentagon civilian than dealing with an important national security issue without dealing with military planners, who are always worried about risk,' he told me. 'What could be more boring than needing the coöperation of logistical planners?' The only difficulty, the former official added, is that, 'as soon as you enlarge the secret program beyond the oversight capability of experienced people, you lose control. We've never had a case where a special-access program went sour – and this goes back to the Cold War.'

In a separate interview, a Pentagon consultant, who spent much of his career directly involved with special-access programs, spread the blame. 'The White House subcontracted this to the Pentagon, and the Pentagon subcontracted it to Cambone,' he said. 'This is Cambone's deal, but Rumsfeld and Myers approved the program.' When it came to the interrogation operation at Abu Ghraib, he said, Rumsfeld left the details to Cambone. Rumsfeld may not be personally culpable, the consultant added, 'but he's responsible for the checks and balances. The issue is that, since 9/11, we've changed the rules on how we deal with terrorism, and created conditions where the ends justify the means.'

Last week, statements made by one of the seven accused M.P.s, Specialist Jeremy Sivits, who is expected to plead guilty, were released. In them, he claimed that senior commanders in his unit would have stopped the abuse had they witnessed it. One of the questions that will be explored at any trial, however, is why a group of Army Reserve military policemen, most of them from small towns, tormented their prisoners as they did, in a manner that was especially humiliating for Iraqi men.

The notion that Arabs are particularly vulnerable to sexual humiliation became a talking point among pro-war Washington conservatives in the months before the March, 2003, invasion of Iraq. One book that was frequently cited was 'The Arab Mind,' a study of Arab culture and psychology, first published in 1973, by Raphael Patai, a cultural anthropologist who taught at, among other universities, Columbia and Princeton, and who died in 1996. The book includes a twenty-five-page chapter on Arabs and sex, depicting sex as a taboo vested with shame and repression. 'The segregation of the sexes, the veiling of the women ... and all the other minute rules that govern and restrict contact between men and women, have the effect of making sex a prime mental preoccupation in the Arab world,' Patai wrote. Homosexual activity, 'or any indication of homosexual leanings, as with all other expressions of sexuality, is never given any publicity. These are private affairs and remain in private.' The Patai book, an academic told me, was 'the bible of the neocons on Arab behavior.' In their discussions, he said, two themes emerged – 'one, that Arabs only understand force and, two, that the biggest weakness of Arabs is shame and humiliation.'

The government consultant said that there may have been a serious goal, in the beginning, behind the sexual humiliation and the posed photographs. It was thought that some prisoners would do anything – including spying on their associates – to avoid dissemination of the shameful photos to family and friends. The government consultant said, 'I was told that the purpose of the photographs was to create an army of informants, people you could insert back in the population.' The idea was that they would be motivated by fear of exposure, and gather information about pending insurgency action, the consultant said. If so, it wasn't effective; the insurgency continued to grow.

'This shit has been brewing for months,' the Pentagon consultant who has dealt with SAPs told me. 'You don't keep prisoners naked in their cell and then let them get bitten by dogs. This is sick.' The consultant explained that he and his colleagues, all of whom had served for years on active duty in the military, had been appalled by the misuse of Army guard dogs inside Abu Ghraib. 'We don't raise kids to do things like that. When you go after Mullah Omar, that's one thing. But when you give the authority to kids who don't know the rules, that's another.' [...]

The abuses at Abu Ghraib were exposed on January 13th, when Joseph Darby, a young military policeman assigned to Abu Ghraib, reported the wrongdoing to the Army's Criminal Investigations Division. He also turned over a CD full of photographs. Within three days, a report made its way to Donald Rumsfeld, who informed President Bush. [...]

DECISION MAKING REVISITED FROM A HEIDEGGERIAN PERSPECTIVE

How can we make sense of the awful as well as illegal torturing of prisoners at the Abu Ghraib prison? Here is an outcome, a most unpleasant one to be sure, which needs to be accounted. Notice that Hersh's language is replete with terms such as 'decisions' and 'decision making', echoing the general rationalistic discourse that construes outcomes in terms of 'decisions' (Weick, 1995: 184). If, however, we leave this aside, we obtain a better picture of decisions as events that punctuate a flow of issues.

What are the issues at hand? The immediate issue for the American forces is, of course, to obtain better intelligence from Iraqi prisoners. A second, related, issue is to win over the insurgents and, consequently, win the war in Iraq. And a third issue is broader, having to do with defending American interests around the world, through supporting particular projects undertaken by the American military, intelligence, and government at large (in this case, in the aftermath of 9/11 and the Bush Administration's 'war on terror', winning the wars in Afghanistan and Iraq). These issues form at least two interconnected streams – executing successfully the war in Afghanistan and the war in Iraq – which are embedded within the broader history of intelligence operations as well as of American military projects abroad (including military bases, stationing of troops, and active interventions).

For example, SAPs have been in force, with great success, since the days of the Cold War, and were used again, initially in Afghanistan (with alleged success) and later in Iraq. Following 9/11 and the US bombing of Afghanistan, a SAP formed which authorized to kill, capture, or interrogate 'high-value targets' in the Bush Administration's 'war on terror' in Afghanistan. With the 'war on terror' being executed in two fronts, it was only natural that military know-how, interrogation techniques, and personnel would circulate between the two sites of the war. Following two massive terror bombings in Baghdad in August 2003, the Pentagon realized that the war in Iraq was going badly and that intelligence about the insurgence was desperately needed. They turned their attention to those Iraqis in the Army prison system suspected of being (or connected to) insurgents. Interrogation became more intense, especially following a review of the Iraqi prison interrogation procedures by the commander of the detention and interrogation center at Guantanamo, and, crucially, the SAP was extended to Iraq: SAP's rules were applied to the Iraqi prison system, SAP commandos started working in it, and some of the Army military-intelligence officers working in Iraqi prisons were brought under SAP auspices.

From Hersh's account it is clear that interconnected flows of issues should be the core of an account that aims to make sense of the process that led to the outcome subsequently known as the Abu Ghraib prison scandal. But what is the status of 'issues'? An 'issue' is a concern, a disturbance that *matters* to agents whose identity has been constituted in the context of a particular sociomaterial practice. That identity is formed through the normative use of language, body, and equipment (Hardy, Lawrence, and Grant, 2005: 61; Harré and Gillett, 1994: 28–29). To be a member of a sociomaterial practice is to experience one's situation in terms of *already* constituted distinctions and acceptable emotions, articulated through the discourse that defines the practice (Dreyfus, 1991a: ch 5; Taylor, 1985b: 27; Taylor, 1985a: 54–55). Those distinctions situate the agent relative to some standards of excellence, obligations (MacIntyre, 1985: 187–194; Taylor, 1991: 305), or 'normative boundaries' (Kogut and Zander, 1992: 515). It is those ontological distinctions related to what the practice is for and how it is to be achieved that make up Chia's (1994: 803) 'decision making' as the 'primordial urge to order and control [...] human experiences': a chunk of reality is historically made *sensible* by drawing certain distinctions in a particular domain.

Thus, in our admittedly gruesome case, certain ontological distinctions have been drawn in the US military-cum-intelligence domain concerning what an intelligence officer and a prison guard does and does not, how prisoners are to be treated, what is permissible to do to win a war (or a long-standing rivalry with another country), etc. Indeed, ontological in-cisions are in evidence through the Bush Administration's *labeling* of Al Qaeda and other suspected members of illegal international groups to be 'illegal combatants' and, therefore, not eligible for the protection of the Geneva Conventions; and through the setting up of an SAP to pursue 'high-value' targets in Afghanistan, unconstrained by the normal bureaucratic and legal hurdles. Such 'incisions' are ontological in the sense that they define the reality at hand and carve out an identity for the members of a relevant domain, thus delineating their concerns and the ends to pursue.

It is important to realize the reality-constituting effects of the distinctions members of a practice internalize. Fighting in a particular war and interrogating prisoners in certain ways becomes, in the course of time, as unreflective as physicians examining patients (Gawande, 2002) and drivers driving (Dreyfus, 1991a). Through participation in a practice an agent learns to relate to his/her circumstances 'spontaneously' (Wittgenstein, 1980: §699), that is to say non deliberately. The world appears *ready-to-hand*, that is to say unproblematic, possessing a certain familiarity and transparency, thus calling for direct skillful handling without much deliberate thinking. Thus, particular ways of fighting and interrogation techniques cease to be objects of thought for an experienced officer (as the use of medical instruments is no longer an object of reflection for an expert physician) and become, instead, taken-for-granted aspects of his/her setting. The 'spontaneity' with which practitioners relate to their tasks constitutes what Wittgenstein (1979: §94) calls the 'inherited background' against which practitioners make sense of their particular tasks (Shotter and Katz, 1996: 225; Taylor, 1993: 325; 1995: 69). Practitioners are aware of the background but their awareness is largely 'inarticulate' (Taylor, 1991: 308) and implicit in their activity. The background provides the teleoaffective structure that renders their activities sensible, their explicit representations comprehensible, and makes certain emotions acceptable (Dreyfus, 1991a: 102–104; Taylor, 1993: 327–328; 1995: 69–70). Practitioners simply and unproblematically do whatever they have been trained to do (Dreyfus, 1985: 232). The exercise of particular skills within a sociomaterial practice is *nondeliberate* – it consists of an array of spontaneous responses to the developing situation at hand. At the same time, this nondeliberate activity is oriented towards attaining certain *ends* that determine it as the activity it is. Practitioners act purposively without having a purpose in mind (Chia and MacKay, 2007: 235; Schatzki, 2000: 33).

Issues are not isolated events but make up flows or streams. The flow-like character of issues is important in order to understand the actions practitioners undertake – how, over time, ways of addressing one issue may spill over to addressing another one. Practitioners *practically cope* with the situation at hand, that is to say they act *qua* members of a particular sociomaterial practice (e.g. as a teacher, a manager, a physician, or an interrogation officer) in a nondeliberate yet sensible manner, namely by spontaneously as well as appropriately responding to the solicitations of the task at hand. This explains the continuity we often see in practitioners' actions – spontaneous responses to the mild disturbances of the developing situation at hand unreflectively draw on a repository of earlier responses (Klein, 1998). Human action has a strongly improvisational character (Sawyer, 2003; 2007). Practically coping with a current mild disturbance (i.e. a mild issue) unreflectively draws on similar ways of coping with similar issues in the past. In a practical context, the search for, and the evaluation of, alternatives is limited and current judgment choices are made on the basis of past choices (Lindblom, 1959). Although Hersh's account does not aim at describing military and interrogation officers in their routine operations, one easily surmises the kind of tasks undertaken on a routine basis by members of the US forces: policing the streets, fighting insurgents, interrogating prisoners.

Hersh's account becomes conceptually interesting if seen as a description of the 'breakdown' of practical coping, namely when the spontaneous activities undertaken by practitioners encounter obstacles, are disrupted, run into trouble. Then issues are no longer mild disturbances calling for modified forms of practical coping, but appear as breakdowns. In instances of a breakdown the practitioner becomes aware of the activity he/she is engaged in, of the equipment and methods he/she has been using, of what he/she was trying to accomplish. In such a case the practitioner starts acting *deliberately*. He/she is still involved in the activity but now pays attention to what he/she does. His/her awareness is explicit, although oriented to practical ends.

A breakdown occurred in August 2003 in Iraq when, following the terror bombings in Baghdad, the Pentagon realized that the war was going badly and something drastic needed to be done. Fighting the insurgents was the routine activity the US forces had been involved in almost from the start of the war but, following the high-profile deaths of several dozens of civilians (including the head of the UN missions in Baghdad) in 2003, the very activity of putting down the insurgents and, therefore, the need to find out more about them, acquired not only a new urgency but, crucially, it became the *focus* of military planners. The situation now required explicit attention and deliberate thinking, a focused consideration of relevant activities, no mere practical coping. Interrogation techniques required *re*viewing. This was a moment of deliberate choice in the war activities. The prison system in Iraq needed now to become more focused on interrogation; tougher techniques were perhaps required. There was expertise available from other sites of the 'war on terror' – Guantanamo and Afghanistan. Hence, SAP entered the picture.

SAPs, albeit exceptionally employed, had been used by US Administrations at least since the Cold War, with often successful results. Consequently, questions of legitimacy and appropriateness did not arise when their use was deemed necessary by Rumsfeld in the war in Afghanistan; it had been done before and it had proved effective. When putting down the insurgence in Iraq became a focal issue – namely, an explicit concern for those responsible for the war – obtaining information from those held prisoners in Iraqi prisons and suspected of being or linked to insurgents became, in turn, a 'sensible' thing to do – that is sensible against the background of fighting the war. If SAP practices had yielded results in Afghanistan, so they might in Iraq. That meant, among other things, reviewing Iraqi prison interrogation procedures to make them more effective, in the hope of extracting more and better information from detainees. Tough interrogation procedures had already been tried at Guantanamo, and they could apply to Iraq too. And to make the new interrogation procedures even more effective, some US military-intelligence officers working in Iraqi prisons were brought under the auspices of SAP.

One sees here the gradual unfolding of the US Army policies towards obtaining more information about the Iraqi insurgents by using unorthodox means. The SAP mentality and practices spilled over from Afghanistan and Guantanamo to Abu Ghraib. Military actors deliberately responded to the 'breakdown' in their fighting against insurgents through extending SAP, which had already yielded results in Afghanistan, to Iraqi prisons. In the context of winning the war in Iraq, the teleological structure of the sociomaterial practice of the US military made the particular act of extending SAP 'sensible'. Furthermore, the prevailing Orientalist discourse (Said, 1979) within US pro-war neoconservative circles about the 'backwardness' of 'the Arab mind' made plausible the notion that prisoners who would be sexually humiliated would fear exposure of relevant photographs and, therefore, they would be willing to provide tips about impending insurgent action.

However, despite Hersh's rationalistic (i.e. decision-oriented) language, the Abu Ghraib prison scandal was not so much brought about by particular 'decisions' as by the unfolding logic of the practice of the 'war on terror'. Extending SAP from Afghanistan to Iraq late in 2003 was a deliberate, 'sensible' practical choice, following a 'breakdown' in the fight against the insurgents. It was when the process of putting down the insurgents encountered serious problems, best exemplified by the terror bombing of August 2003, that extracting information from Iraqi prisoners became a *focal* issue. American forces had been interrogating Iraqi detainees all along, but, in the aftermath of August 2003, they turned their *explicit* attention on their methods. Their conscious focus on interrogation methods set them to think analogically (Dunbar, 1997) – namely learn from what they did on other, similar occasions, concurrently or in the recent past. Guantanamo and Afghanistan were the most plausible source domains for such analogical reasoning (Dunbar, 1997; Tsoukas, 1991). In the neoconservative intellectual climate of Washington, military planners 'discovered' what makes 'the Arab mind' tick: interrogation methods were thought to be more effective if physical coercion was combined with sexual humiliation.

In the machine bureaucracy of the US Army, such an extension may have been recorded as a 'decision' but the commitment to getting tough with 'enemy combatants' had been made as early as late 2001 with the bombing of Afghanistan and the setting up of SAP there. Moreover, extending SAP to Iraq was not a 'decision' in the traditional sense of rational problem solving (Simon's trio: intelligence, design, choice – see Simon, 1977), but a 'decision' generated by the interaction of particular participants (the Pentagon hawks, especially Rumsfeld and Cambone), solutions (SAP had worked in Afghanistan, interrogation techniques at Guantanamo), problems (extracting more and better information from Iraqi detainees linked to insurgents, following a 'breakdown'), and choice situations (Pentagon review meetings) (Cohen, March and Olsen, 1972). But even 'decision' in the latter sense is not the best way to describe what happened. Not only was it not random as the 'garbage can model' implies (there is a logic in analogically transferring 'solutions' to new 'problems'), but the problems it attempted to address emerged as 'problems' following a breakdown of practical coping. Prior to that the problems were those routine challenges associated with the practice of conducting the war at large, to which practitioners had been spontaneously responding. But the garbage can model has no way of distinguishing between the routine issues a practitioner faces while immersed in a situation, the 'aspects' of a situation when the latter enters actors' consciousness due to a breakdown, and the 'properties' of a situation when looked at in a detached manner. The intentionality denoted by the term 'decision' indicates the presence of mental content indicative of *thematic* intentionality, namely of a context-free mode of consciousness, which, as will be seen below, is different from both practical coping and deliberate coping.

Weick certainly has a point in saying that 'any decision maker is only as good as his or her memory' (Weick, 1995: 185). A good decision maker 'is especially attentive to choice points that could plausibly be punctuated into an earlier flow of events' (ibid.). Using SAP in Afghanistan was such an earlier flow of events and extending it to Iraq was a deliberate choice. It was not, however, a decision per se, insofar as the explicit awareness concerning interrogation methods and what to do about them, following a 'breakdown', was still oriented towards *practical* ends. The agents involved were still *absorbed* in their tasks, although they had now become conscious of what they had been doing. While interrogation methods were transparent before the breakdown, after it they became objects of deliberate attention, giving rise to mental representations about their content and the conditions for their effective employment.

When agents detach themselves from a specific practical situation and look at it from a reflective distance, aiming to know its properties, then the practical situation becomes *occurrent* (the world appears, as Heidegger notes, *present-at-hand*) and agents develop *thematic awareness*. The latter brackets particular, immediate practical concerns and aims at finding out about or reflecting on abstract properties of the situation at hand. Whereas in deliberate coping the language used refers to situated *aspects* of a situation, in thematic awareness it indicates desituated *properties* of the situation – practical understanding gives way to quasi-theoretical understanding. In thematic awareness the language employed is the language of the observer.

In deliberate coping, military officers and Pentagon officials might say 'SAP worked in Afghanistan; let's try it in Iraq'. Such a statement would refer to an *aspect* of the 'war on terror' (i.e. how to obtain more intelligence from Iraqi prisoners in the context of this war) having a practical purpose in mind (i.e. to win the war in Iraq). Actors would become explicitly aware of some aspects of the methods they had been using in another context (i.e. the use of SAP in Afghanistan); they would then retrospectively reframe the practical situation at hand (i.e. 'we have probably been going too much by the book in our interrogation practices in Iraq and that is why we have not been particularly effective') in order to move on (i.e try in Iraq a version of what we have practiced in Afghanistan and Guantanamo).

However, saying 'SAPs work when quick and valuable results are needed without too much concern for the means used' would be a reference to a desituated *property* of this particular military method, which would be made outside the context of a particular practical task. When military planners compare and contrast the use of particular methods, they do so *in abstracto*; they look at the properties of tactics considered not amidst a particular context of action but in terms of their abstracted strengths and weaknesses. The situation they consider is occurrent and their awareness is thematic. This is usually the case in day-away strategy sessions or when planners contemplate the use of particular methods prior to engaging in action. Task-related practical concerns are bracketed in favor of focusing on the abstract properties of the object at hand. This is the closest we come to decisions prior to undertaking action. When objects or situations are looked at *in abstracto* and evaluated, particular de-cisions are made (namely, several alternatives are cut off). Thematic intentionality develops referring to an occurent object and its properties, which are sought to be causally related to desired outcomes. Hersh's account is not revealing in that sense, but we may surmise that such decisions were made by military planners *prior* to the launch of the war in Iraq (Fieth, 2008).

The judicial inquiry into the Abu Ghraib prison scandal, interested in allocating responsibility for the terrible events and aiming to prevent similar ones in the future, employs the language of decision making, namely it construes the events as a consequence of decisions – intentional acts indicating commitment to action – rather than of practical-coping- and deliberate-coping-choices-in-the-midst-of-action. While in deliberate coping actors exhibit intentionality, the latter is, nonetheless, bounded by practical concerns; agents are *in* the situation, not outside it. They act and reframe retrospectively what they do to find out a way of *moving on* in real time. Juries or inquiry boards, however, come *after* the fact and see sequences of already accomplished events; they do not see the fog, the uncertainty, and the open-endedness that necessarily surrounds any concrete streams of action in real time. *Ex post facto* inquirers can talk about 'decisions' since the situation is occurrent, objectively available, and their purpose is to make sense of what happened in order to codify lessons learnt, explain events, and associate particular omissions or actions with particular individuals. Since in our culture we believe in accountability, we generate accounts that link intentional actions to individuals. We intend to see intentionality and we retrospectively find it, or more precisely, construct it and make it the determining factor of human actions.

CONCLUSIONS

Organizations undertake action even in the absence of decisions and make decisions without necessarily following them through with actions. An outcome that may appear to an observer to be the product of a sequence of decisions may not be so if approached from the perspective of the actor. How is that possible? What is the status of 'decisions' in organizational life and what type of knowledge are they associated with? I have argued here that a Heideggerian vocabulary is rich enough to help us answer such questions and reconcile hitherto opposed views. Let me summarize the argument (see Figure 14.1).

'Decisions' address 'problems' but 'problems' emerge as such when the world appears to actors *present-at-hand* and the situation they confront is *occurrent*. Then 'problems' indicate a formal knowledge gap, insofar as they initiate a search for the abstract *properties* of the situation at hand; those properties are sought to be causally related to desired outcomes. Strategic decisions concerning mergers and acquisitions, for example, are usually of that kind. The properties of the organization to be acquired are focused upon and matched with the properties of the acquiring organization, in search of maximizing some sort of utility function. Decisions indicate

	How the world appears to consciousness		
	Actors immersed in a practical context		Actors detached from practical context
	The world appears ready-to-hand	The world appears as a breakdown in a practical activity	The world appears present-at-hand
Type of engagement with the world	Practical coping	Deliberate coping	Thematic awareness - Decision making
Type of rationality	Practical	Deliberate	- Calculative - Abductive
Type of Knowledge	Tacit	Reflective - Analogical	Explicit - Focus on abstract properties

FIGURE 14.1 Strategic decision making and knowledge: A Heideggerian Model.

the development of *thematic intentionality* and of *calculative rationality* towards the situation. Their key feature is not so much commitment to action as detached analysis of the properties of a situation prior to action. How detached analysis is conducted and how its outcomes are used in practical organizational contexts are matters of empirical research.

Moreover, 'decisions' may be discerned *ex post facto*, after the fog has cleared, in the context of public inquiries, judicial inquiries, or reviews. Such contexts, in so far as they programmatically seek to connect individual intentions with actions, are structured in such a way as to make those putative connections possible. In that sense, decisions are indeed, as Langley *et al.* (1995: 265) noted, 'constructs in the eyes of the observer'. This is an instance of *abductive rationality*, namely inference to the best explanation (Paavola, 2004).

When immersed in a practical context, actors undertake actions even without making prior decisions. This takes two forms. First, when actors spontaneously respond to, or practically cope with, the solicitations of the task at hand in a nondeliberate way. The world appears *ready-to-hand* to actors immersed in it; it possesses familiarity and transparency, calling for direct skillful handling without deliberate thinking. Actors possess *tacit knowledge* and exhibit *practical rationality* in their actions. Practical coping – spontaneous, nondeliberate responding – is made possible because actors have been trained to act to the way they do, through their participation in a sociomaterial practice, which is oriented towards the achievement of certain *ends* and makes the performance of certain actions *sensible*. The teleoaffective constitution of the sociomaterial practice, namely the key distinctions in terms of which it defines itself, the ends it specifies, and the affects it enables its members to have, is evidence of already accomplished de-cision making, namely of a set of ontological acts (in-cisions) through which a domain of action is carved out and rendered sensible.

Secondly, when in the already familiar context of practical action a *breakdown* occurs, practitioners are momentarily thrown off-balance, and they become conscious of the activity they have been engaged in as well as of the methods and equipment they have been using. To effectively respond, they act deliberately, although their now explicit awareness is still oriented towards certain practical ends. This is the realm of *deliberative rationality* in which *reflective knowledge* is generated and further used in the midst of action. Reflective knowledge is generated in the midst of action, in dialogue with a developing situation at hand, by questioning the means and tactics hitherto used to carry out a stream of actions. Reflective knowledge may take an analogical form: new responses are initiated by reasoning back to similar cases in the past and reframing the current situation accordingly. Unlike in the case of thematic awareness, however, practitioners take a distance from their activities while still immersed in a practical situation in which they have already had a great deal of experience; they aim at deliberating on it with an eye to further improving their practical coping. And unlike in the case of practical coping, practitioners cannot rely on their nondeliberate, intuitive mode of acting because something unusual has happened (a breakdown) on which they need to reflect. In deliberative rationality, practitioners 'draw on their context-based, intuitive understanding, but check and refine it to deal with the problematic situation' (Dreyfus, 1997: 27); they deal with *aspects* of a situation they are in.

A Heideggerian perspective enables us to accommodate most currently available theories of decision making into a new ontology. De-cisions have *already* occurred in so far as practitioners act within a sociomaterial practice constituted by key distinctions, out of which a sensible piece of reality is cut. Decisions occur prior to action when the abstract properties of a situation or object are focused upon and analyzed in a detached manner. It is here where traditional decision analysis is most helpful. Decisions are *ex post facto* constructions by observers seeking to connect particular outcomes or actions to individual or even collective intentions. But, as we saw in the case of the Abu Ghraib prison scandal, a lot of what ordinarily passes for 'decision making' is nothing else but either practical coping or deliberate coping, both occurring in the midst of action. A great deal of action routinely undertaken in organizations consists of either spontaneous responses to the circumstances at hand or deliberate choices often made in an analogical manner. To simplify somewhat, as the abysmal Abu Ghraib case discussed here has hopefully shown, most of the time organizational actors do not decide; they simply act.

NOTES

1. This section is an edited version of an article, entitled 'The gray zone', by Seymour M. Hersh, published in *The New Yorker*, May 24, 2004.

REFERENCES

Bateson, G. (1972) *Steps to an Ecology of Mind.* Northvale, NJ: Jason Aronson.
Brunsson, N. (1982) The irrationality of action and action rationality: Decisions, ideologies and organizational actions, *Journal of Management Studies*, 19, 29–44.
Brunsson, N. (1990) Deciding for responsibility and legitimation: Alternative interpretations of organizational decision-making, *Accounting, Organizations and Society*, 15, 47–59.

Butler, R. (1998) 'Strategic Decision Making: A Contingency Framework and Beyond', in V. Papadakis and P. Barwise (eds) *Strategic Decisions*. Dordrecht: Kluwer, 35–50.

Chia, R. (1994) The concept of decision: A deconstructive practice, *Journal of Management Studies*, 31, 781–806.

Chia, R., and Holt, R. (2006) Strategy as practical coping: A Heideggerian perspective, *Organization Studies*, 27 (5), 635–656.

Chia, R., and MacKay, B. (2007) Post-processual challenges for the emerging strategy-as-practice perspective: Discovering strategy in the logic of practice, *Human Relations*, 60 (1), 217–242.

Cohen, M.D., March, J.G., and Olsen, J.P. (1972) A garbage can model of organizational choice, *Administrative Science Quarterly*, 17, 1–25.

Crossan, Mary M. (1998) Improvisation in action, *Organization Science*, 9, 593–599.

Dreyfus, H. (1985) 'Holism and Hermeneutics', in Robert Hollinger (ed.) *Hermeneutics and Praxis*. Notre Dame, Indiana: University of Notre Dame Press, 227–247.

Dreyfus, H. (1991a) *Being-in-the-world*. Cambridge, MA: The MIT Press.

Dreyfus, H. (1991b) Reflection on the Workshop on 'The Self', *Anthropology and Humanism Quarterly*, 16, 27–31.

Dreyfus, H. (1997) 'Intuitive, Deliberative and Calculative Models of Expert Performance', in C.E. Zsambok and G. Klein (eds) *Naturalistic Decision Making*. Mahwah, NJ: Lawrence Erlbaum Associates, 17–28.

Dreyfus, H. (2000) 'Responses', in Mark A. Wrathall and Jeff Malpas (eds) *Heidegger, Coping, and Cognitive Science*. Cambridge, MA: The MIT Press, 313–349.

Dunbar, K. (1997) 'How Scientists Think: On-line Creativity and Conceptual Change in Science', in T.N. Ward, S.M. Smith, and J. Vaid (eds) *Creative Thought*. Washington, DC: Amer. Psych. Association, 461–494.

Fieth, D.J. (2008) *War and Decision*. New York: HarperCollins.

Gawande, A. (2002) *Complications: A surgeon's notes on an imperfect science*. New York: Metropolitan Books.

Hardy, C., Lawrence, T.B., and Grant, D. (2005) Discourse and collaboration: The role of conversations and collective identity, *Acad. Management Rev.*, 30, 58–77.

Harré, R., and Gillett, G. 1994. *The Discursive Mind*. Thousand Oaks, CA: Sage

Heidegger, M. (1962) *Being and Time*. New York: Harper and Row.

Hendry, J. (2000) Strategic decision making, discourse and strategy as social practice, *Journal of Management Studies*, 37, 955–977.

Hickson, D.J., Butler, R.J., Cray, D., Mallory, G.R., and Wilson, D.C. (1986) *Top Decisions: Strategic Decision Making in Organizations*. Oxford: Basil Blackwell.

Jarzabkowski, P., Balogun, J., and Seidl, D. (2007) Strategizing: The challenges of a practice perspective, *Human Relations*, 60 (1), 5–28.

Klein, G. (1998) *Sources of Power*. Cambridge, MA: MIT Press.

Kogut, B., and Zander, U. (1992) Knowledge of the firm, combinative capabilities, and the replication of technology, *Organization Science*, 3, 383–397.

Langley, A., Mintzberg, H., Pitcher, P., Posada, E. and Saint-Macary, J. (1995) Opening up decision making: The view from the black stool, *Organization Science*, 6, 260–279.

Lindblom, C.E. (1959) The science of 'muddling through', *Public Administration Review*, 19, 79–88.

MacIntyre, A. (1985) *After Virtue*. London, UK: Duckworth, 2nd edition.

March, J. (1988) *Decisions and Organizations*. Oxford: Basil Blackwell.

March, J., and Olsen, J.P. (1976) *Ambiguity and Choice in Organizations*, Bergen, Norway: Universitetsforlaget.

March, J., and Simon, H. (1958) *Organizations*, New York: John Wiley & Sons, Inc.

Miller, S.J., and Wilson, D.C. (2006) 'Perspectives on Organizational Decision-making', in S.R. Clegg, C. Hardy, T.B. Lawrence, and W.R. Nord (eds) *The SAGE Handbook of Organization Studies*. London: Sage, 2nd edition, 469–484.

Mintzberg, H., and Waters, J.A. (1990) Studying deciding: An exchange of views between Mintzberg and Waters, Pettigrew, and Butler, *Organization Studies*, 11, 2–16.

Nutt, P.C. (1989) Selecting tactics to implement strategic plans, *Strategic Management Journal*, 10, 145–161.

Paavola, S. (2004) Abduction as a logic and methodology of discovery: The importance of strategies, *Foundations of Science*, 9: 267–283.

Papadakis, V., and Barwise, P. (1998) 'Strategic Decisions: An Introduction', in V. Papadakis and P. Barwise (eds) *Strategic Decisions*. Dordrecht: Kluwer, 1–16.

Pascale, R. (1984) Perspectives on strategy: The real story behind Honda's success, *California Management Review*, 26 (3), 47–72.

Porac, J.F., Thomas, H., and Baden-Fuller, C. (1989) Competitive groups as cognitive communities: The case of Scottish knitwear manufacturers, *Journal of Management Studies*, 26, 397–416.

Said, E. (1979) *Orientalism*. London: Vintage.

Sandberg, J., and Targama, A. (2007) *Managing Understanding in Organizations*. London: Sage.

Sawyer, R.K. (2000) Improvisational cultures: Collaborative emergence and creativity in improvisation, *Mind, Culture, and Activity*, 7 (3) 180–185.

Sawyer, R.K. (2003) *Improvised Dialogues*. Westport, CN: Ablex Publishing.

Sawyer, R.K. (2007) *Group Genius*. New York: Basic Books.

Schatzki, T. (2000) 'Coping with Others with Folk Psychology', in Mark A. Wrathall and Jeff Malpas (eds) *Heidegger, Coping, and Cognitive Science*. Cambridge, MA: The MIT Press, 29–52.

Schatzki, T. (2005) The sites of organizations, *Organization Studies*, 26 (3), 465–484.

Shotter, J., and Katz, A.M. (1996). Articulating a practice from within the practice itself: Establishing formative dialogues by the use of a 'social poetics', *Concepts and Transformation*, 1, 213–237.

Simon, H. (1976) *Administrative Behavior*. New York: Free Press, 3rd edition.

Simon, H. (1977) *The New Science of Managerial Decision*. Englewood Cliffs, NJ: Prentice-Hall, 3rd edition.

Spinosa, C., Flores, F., and Dreyfus, H.L. (1997) *Disclosing New Worlds*. Cambridge, MA: The MIT Press.

Taylor, C. (1985a) *Human Agency and Language. Vol. 1*. Cambridge, UK: Cambridge University Press.

Taylor, C. (1985b) *Philosophy and the Human Sciences. Vol. 2*. Cambridge, UK: Cambridge University Press.

Taylor, C. (1991) 'The Dialogical Self', in D.R. Hiley, J.F. Bohman, and R. Shusterman (eds) *The Interpretive Turn*. Ithaca, NY: Cornell University Press, 304–314.

Taylor, C. (1993) 'Engaged Agency and Background in Heidegger', in C. Guignon (ed.) *The Cambridge Companion to Heidegger*. Cambridge, UK: Cambridge University Press, 317–336.

Taylor, C. (1995) *Philosophical Arguments*. Cambridge, MA: Harvard University Press.

Tsoukas, H. (1991) The missing link: A transformational view of metaphors in organizational science, *Acad. of Management Rev.*, 16, 566–585.

Tsoukas, H. (forthcoming) 'Practice, Strategy Making and Intentionality: A Heideggerian Onto-epistemology for Strategy-as-practice', in D. Golsorkhi, L. Rouleau, D. Seidl, and E. Vaara (eds) *The Cambridge Handbook of Strategy as Practice*. Cambridge: Cambridge University Press.

Weick, K.E. (1979) *The Social Psychology of Organizing.* Reading, MA: Addison-Wesley, 2nd edition.

Weick, K.E. (1995). *Sensemaking in Organizations.* Thousand Oaks, CA: Sage.

Weick, K. (2002) 'Improvisation as a Mindset for Organizational Analysis', in K.N. Kamoche, Miguel Pina e Cunha, and J. Vieira da Cunha (eds) *Organizational Improvisation.* London: Routledge, 52–72.

Weick, K. (2003) 'Theory and Practice in the Real World', in H. Tsoukas and C. Knudsen (eds) *The Oxford Handbook of Organization Theory.* Oxford: Oxford University Press, 453–475.

Weick, K. (2004) 'Designing for throwness', in R.J. Bolland, Jr, and F. Collopy (eds) *Managing as Designing.* Stanford, CA: Stanford Business Books, 74–78.

Wittgenstein, L. (1979) *On Certainty.* Edited by G.E.M. Anscombe and G.H. von Wright. Translated by D. Paul and G.E.M. Anscombe. Oxford: Blackwell.

Wittgenstein, L. (1980) *Remarks on the Philosophy of Psychology. Vol. II.* Edited by G.H. von Wright and H. Nyman, Translated by C.G. Luckhardt and M.A.E. Aue. Chicago: University of Chicago Press.

Yanow, D., and Tsoukas, H. (2009), What is reflection-in-action? A phenomenological account, *Journal of Management Studies.* 46 (8), 1339–1364.

15

Challenges of Using IT to Support Multidisciplinary Team Decision Making

MICHAEL BARRETT AND EIVOR OBORN

Over the last decade there has been a significant increase in the development of multidisciplinary teams to improve decision making in organizations across a wide range of sectors (Brodbeck *et al.*, 2007; Mannix and Neale, 2005). Knowledge sharing is often a difficult endeavour in these teams as members have individual knowledge and skills, and different approaches to solving complex problems (Bunderson and Sutcliffe, 2002). In this chapter, we focus on decision making in a multidisciplinary healthcare team, examining the complex role of information technology (IT) in supporting knowledge sharing between different professional groups during the decision-making process. Our findings highlight the importance of knowledge, temporality, and power in the multidisciplinary decision-making process. We begin by outlining the unique context of multidisciplinary knowledge work and decision making prior to elaborating our theoretical perspective. We then present the research methods and case study, followed by our analysis, discussion, and conclusion.

MULTIDISCIPLINARY TEAM DECISION MAKING

Recent literature on work team effectiveness, and in particular multidisciplinary teams, has yielded mixed results (for comprehensive reviews, see Milliken and Martins, 1996; Salas *et al.*, 2004; Mannix and Neale, 2005; Brodbeck *et al.*, 2007). Multidisciplinary teams have been described as 'double edged swords' (Bunderson and Sutcliffe, 2002; Milliken and Martins, 1996) having unique knowledge and skill sets with the potential to increase creativity and breadth of perspective as suggested by the 'value in diversity' hypothesis (Swann *et al.*, 2004; Jehn *et al.*, 1999); yet they

Handbook of Decision Making.   Edited by Paul C. Nutt and David C. Wilson
© 2010 John Wiley & Sons, Ltd

are also more likely to sow dissension (Williams and O'Reilley, 1998). For example, relative to homogeneous groups, members of heterogeneous groups show less commitment (Tsui *et al.*, 1992), experience more conflict (Jehn *et al.*, 1999; Pelled *et al.*, 1999) and take more time to reach decisions (Hambrick *et al.*, 1996). Unique social identities can contribute to diversity of commonly held assumptions, values and priorities across disciplines (Ashforth and Mael, 1989). This can contribute conflict or difficulty in reaching decisions as well as increased uncertainty regarding the decision-making process (Bunderson, 2003; Edmondson *et al.*, 2001; 2003). Thus Milliken and Martins (1996) in their review on heterogeneous teams concluded that while such teams have a cognitive advantage over homogenous teams, there are also greater coordination costs.

Communication has been noted as particularly problematic in inter-disciplinary work (Milliken and Martins, 1996). In the context of new product development, Dougherty (1992) highlighted the interpretive barriers existing between the technical and marketing professionals. Though collaboration was necessary (Dougherty, 1992), it was insufficient or lacking between the diverse groups involved in the production process. These findings concur with the work of Goodstein *et al.* (1994), who found that occupational diversity created interaction difficulties and resulted in low levels of team integration, and this impeded the team in taking action. Similarly, van Aalst and van der Mast (2003) highlight the communication difficulties between artists, graphic designers and engineers working together. Enhancing the social integration of heterogeneous teams has been shown to counteract the communication challenges across disciplinary groups (Smith *et al.*, 1994).

On the other hand there is evidence that heterogeneous groups can produce higher quality solutions than homogenous group in complex decision-making tasks (Hoffman and Maier, 1961; Triandis, Hall and Ewen, 1965). Group members from diverse disciplinary backgrounds can improve creativity and problem solving, lending support for the use of such teams in decision-making contexts (Bunderson and Sutcliff, 2002; 2005; Carpenter *et al.*, 2004). It has been argued (Damon, 1991; Levine and Resnick, 1993) that this advantage is enabled by a divergence of viewpoints and cognitive conflict, as has been demonstrated in controlled laboratory settings (Stasser, Steward and Wittenbaum, 1995). However, for the integration of knowledge, groups need to focus on *information pooling* rather than *negotiation* (Brodbeck *et al.*, 2007), since it is through the process of information pooling that relevant information is made available to the group. Dissent is deemed necessary to contribute to information pooling and processing though it may also result in disengagement (Brodbeck *et al.*, 2002; Schultz-Hardt *et al.*, 2006). In addition to the increased conflict, decreased social integration and leadership challenges (Williams, 2001), the performance of multidisciplinary teams, and their ability to produce superior decisions, has not realised the expected benefits (Mannix and Neale, 2005).

IT AND CLINICAL DECISION MAKING IN HEALTHCARE TEAMS

Multidisciplinary decision making is of increasing importance and prevalence in the context of specialist healthcare delivery (Lanceley *et al.*, 2008; Sidhom and Pousen,

2006; Ford and Kubu, 2006). However, there is little evidence to suggest that multidisciplinary working improves clinical decisions; on the contrary numerous pragmatic barriers to successful team working have been identified (Fleissig *et al.*, 2006; Lancely *et al.*, 2008). Medical work is fundamentally pragmatic, characterised by numerous contingencies which require responses to an ongoing stream of events (Berg, 1997; Strauss *et al.*, 1985) in the process of managing uncertain patient trajectories (Berg, 1999). Hence clinical decision making has been characterised as 'the science of individuals' (Hunter, 2006). This process is rarely accomplished by one individual, but is undertaken by individuals from numerous backgrounds and knowledge bases who make distributed decisions regarding 'what to do next' (Ellingsen, 2003).

Information in various forms (e.g. x-rays, blood results, patient history) is constantly being used to inform the decision-making processes (Christensen and Abbott, 2000). IT can support decision making through enhanced communication, information pooling and information processing (Zigurs and Buckland, 1998). However, distinct information is required and produced by the diverse clinical communities, and one difficulty in effectively using IT is the challenge of combining adequate support for the heterogeneous information needs (Crossan *et al.*, 2005). However, the absence of adequate information sharing limits the ability of the team to make optimal decisions (Christensen and Abbott, 2000).

Electronic patient records are an increasingly common means of structuring and organising data and information concerning patients (Jones, 2004; Wears and Berg, 2005), and support decision making in numerous ways (Berg, 2003; Geissbuhler and Miller, 2000). First, they handle information gathered during the course of a patient's trajectory, providing an overview of the key developments, actions and problems concerning individual patients. Moreover, multiple actors can contribute to the information gathering activity simultaneously. Second, the patient records coordinate work. For example, form structure helps to link the work of several individuals and enable the notes taken by one clinician to be in a recognisable and expected format to that of others. The information structure facilitates how clinicians understand the diverse problems and subsequently decide on an appropriate course of action. Third, computational power can be incorporated into the database structure, so that powerful operations can be undertaken to provide further information in support of decision-making activities. For example, computerisation can provide overviews of workload or disease category outcomes to be searched (Berg, 2003). However, the communication and local decision-making processes need to be considered as part of the implementation process (Crossan *et al.*, 2005).

Despite such promise, recent studies on electronic patient records are less optimistic about current attempts to improve the integration of decision making across a distributed team of healthcare professionals (Jones, 2003; 2004; Vikkelsø, 2005; Crossan *et al.*, 2005). Indeed, the importance of an electronic system supporting/sustaining a common ground across professional groups has been noted as particularly problematic in decision making within multi-professional teams (Beers *et al.*, 2006), as electronic tools and computerised information systems tend to reinforce existing professional boundaries.

Moreover, in a multidisciplinary context, IT use needs to be considered in the context of MDT complexity and the inherent limitation of system capabilities. Further, the actual use of the tool can affect its ability to contribute to decision-making processes. For example, if one group does not routinely fill in information, then the decision-making process is less transparent to members of other disciplinary groups. A tool's ability to provide information and support decision making is thus limited as to how it is actually used in practice (Crossan *et al.*, 2005).

KNOWING-IN-PRACTICE

We use a knowing-in-practice lens to explore how multidisciplinary teams share information and knowledge in making decisions (Orlikowski, 2002; Gherardi, 2000). Such a perspective enables a situated and contextual examination of information use in the context of making decisions. It also examines how disciplinary practice structures the way IT is able to support decision making. 'It leads us to understand knowledge and practice as reciprocally constitutive, so that it does not make sense to talk about either knowledge or practice without the other' (Orlikowski, 2002: 250).

A knowing-in-practice perspective recognises that knowing is inherent in situated activity, rather than cognitively compartmentalised to the mind. Knowledge is acquired through forms of participation and is continually being reproduced and negotiated (Wenger, 1998). This perspective foregrounds the situational and tacitness of knowing as multiple subsidiary clues are drawn on to apprehend meaning (Polanyi, 1968). Drawing on Schon (1983), Orlikowski (2002: 251) suggests 'skillful practice exhibited by professionals [does] not consist of applying some a priori knowledge to specific decision or actions, but rather of a kind of knowing that was inherent in their actions'. Co-workers who engage in different practices, such as pathologists and surgeons, learn to apprehend an aspect of practice (such as a biopsy result) from diverse perspectives.

Polanyi builds a personal view of knowledge, which considers the explicit components of scientific abstractions to be an aspect of knowledge, which need indwelling tacit powers to render their meaning actionable (Polanyi, 1968; 1958). Polanyi's theory of knowledge, popularised in the management literature by Nonaka (1994), emphasises tacit integration as a 'personal coefficient' inherent in all knowledge (1968: 172). Tacit knowing cannot be 'captured' or 'converted' but it can be displayed, discovered or made manifest (Tsoukas, 2003; Polanyi, 1968) in practice.

The extent to which disciplinary groups will be able to share information and build group knowledgeability will depend in part on the extent to which they share tacit coefficients of knowledge and their ability to build common ground (Bechky, 2003). These tacit features render the explicit components of knowledge actionable. Different disciplinary groups will have a unique knowledge base; though these may overlap, the priorities and perspectives given to knowing-in-practice may form a boundary between disciplinary groups (Carlile, 2002; Bechky, 2003; Aram, 2004; Oborn, 2008). Within the context of a specialist healthcare team, members are generally aware of each others' areas of expertise. However, as illustrated in our case study, the focus of this awareness concerns the content of primarily explicit knowledge, such as preferred lines of medication or post operative survival rates.

A practice-based perspective focuses on the communal practices as a site of knowledge and identity development during the decision-making processes. The concept of '*communities of practice*' (Lave and Wenger, 1991; Wenger, 1998) highlights the social and contextual character of knowing and practice. Members of a *community of practice* participate and negotiate understanding whilst learning the skills of their practice. Thus learning to become a surgeon is more than acquiring knowledge and skills of surgery, but also seeing the hospital, patients, nurses etc. through the eyes of a surgeon.

METHODOLOGY

An interpretive research methodology perspective suggests the need to secure an in-depth understanding of the subject matter in its natural setting. However most studies on cross-functional (or multidisciplinary) teams have been cross-sectional, frequently studying accessible student teams rather than those in an occupational context. In a recent summary of research on teams, one of the primary needs identified for future research is to conduct studies 'in the wild' on real teams in their complex day-to-day setting with a focus on team process (Salas *et al.*, 2004). We adopted such an in-depth situated approach in our study.

Multiple primary and secondary sources and interpretations of the phenomenon were gathered to provide richness and multiple insights. Data collection, as summarised in Table 15.1, included formal interviews with team members from all disciplinary groups, meeting attendance, and visits to respective departments to observe interactions. A particular observational focus was the multidisciplinary team (MDT) meeting and subsequent MDT clinics. Frequent informal discussions were used to gain further clarification on ongoing concerns. Data was collected over a period of 13 months by one of the authors.

A number of regular team activities and work spaces other than the MDT meeting were also observed. During multidisciplinary clinics, the researcher was able to sit in the back room staff office, a central location where clinical staff (and occasionally IT staff) 'hung out' during clinic in between seeing their patients.

TABLE 15.1 Summary of data collected

Types of data
23 multidisciplinary meetings
11 other meetings
19 multidisciplinary clinics
24 interviews
regular informal contact and discussions during visits over the 13 months observation
email circulars, documents, protocols

They typically familiarised themselves with the patients' records prior to meeting them and then subsequently wrote their assessments in this room following their consultation. They also discussed their findings with each other and carried on conversations that had begun at the MDT meeting. Multidisciplinary clinics occurred twice weekly, though the oncologists only attended one clinic. Team members were also involved in their own disciplinary specific clinics, such as the oncology clinic and the radiology screening clinic.

Most of the semi-structured interviews were recorded and then transcribed. Some interviewees were not comfortable with a recorded interview, and several individuals asked the researcher to turn the recording off and even visually checked that the machine was not operating, before proceeding to speak about highly sensitive issues. A few individuals offered to be interviewed in locations where recording seemed inappropriate, such as in noisy cafeterias. Most team members were interviewed, as well as relevant office staff, including secretaries who worked closely with the clinicians. IT personnel who were involved in constructing and implementing the new database were also interviewed.

The analyses of the cases involved an iterative process throughout the period of data collection (Mason, 2002). Thus data analysis began shortly after entering the field and continued throughout so that first order and second order concepts were produced (Van Maanen, 1979). These processes involved producing written reflections following site visits and interviews (Golden, Biddle, and Locke, 1997). Written narratives were then reinterpreted through the chosen theoretical perspective of knowing in practice, focusing on elements of knowledge, temporality, and power.

CASE DESCRIPTION

The case concerned a tertiary care university hospital in England. It was a regional cancer centre, and by 1995 the breast cancer specialists formed the flagship MDT (multidisciplinary team) and began weekly meetings to jointly decide on the clinical management of breast cancer patients. In 2001 the surgeons and surgical nurse specialists ceased working from the general surgery clinics and moved into a new location where they, along with radiologists, radiographers and administrative staff were given office and clinic space. The new building made it possible to develop joint 'one-stop' clinics[1] involving oncologists (3), radiologists (4), radiographers (6), surgeons (3), and specialist nurses in surgery and oncology (5). Plastic surgeons (2) were also invited to join the team, and sporadically attended meetings. Senior and junior trainee doctors attended meetings and clinics according to clinical rotas.

Oncology doctors and nurses remained in the greater oncology department, but came over for weekly joint clinics in the new location. The pathologists remained in the pathology department, across from the pathology lab where specimens were dissected and mounted onto slides by lab scientists and technicians. When fieldwork began, the hospital had high national ranking, which was due in part to the high performance of the breast MDT in meeting government waiting targets.

During the fourth month of fieldwork (September) a new web-based clinical information system (SubSys) was implemented over the period of a month. SubSys was used by team members to record cancer related information pertaining to patients seen in the clinics. The system interfaced with the hospital administrative system and enabled all clinicians to have access to the cancer records made by other disciplinary groups. The system was also networked to link into two nearby satellite hospitals where many patients attended for follow up cancer appointments. Five hand held portable 'tablets' were purchased to enable ease of data entry during patient consultations. The surgical theatre used by the breast surgeons were set up for wireless connections to facilitate SubSys use during operations. The tool did not replace the hospital's paper medical records, but pages could be printed from SubSys to be inserted into the hospital records.

The MDT made decisions relating to patient management in four different settings. First, an annual retreat day was attended by all team members and support staff. During this day, joint solutions were developed for broad clinical questions pertaining to practice, such as preferred front line chemotherapy regimes, follow up protocols, and how to obtain appropriate referrals from GPs. Protocols agreed upon at this meeting were closely followed in making subsequent specific treatment decisions. These protocols were kept in a binder, and at the time of fieldwork had not been incorporated into SubSys to flag inconsistencies in treatment decisions.

Second, the MDT held twice-weekly meetings to discuss and coordinate patient care in a forum where all relevant workers could have input into the process. Around 20 patients were discussed each meeting. Both the diagnosis and treatment plan became the formal 'output' of the meeting and were recorded in the medical record as an official account. Approximately 25–30 people were involved in the meetings. Discussions were chaired by a surgeon and generally conformed to the protocols developed at the annual meeting. Summaries and treatment decisions were entered by an administrator present at the meetings so that they would be immediately available during the subsequent clinic for use. During the final month of fieldwork SubSys was also used to support the meeting with patient information, replacing the paper notes.

A third context for collaborative decision making occurred during the multidisciplinary clinic which occurred directly after the MDT meetings. During these clinics decisions arrived at during the meetings were discussed with the patients and were refined or sometimes altered. Discussions held during the previous meeting were often continued in the large back office room of the clinic. SubSys was used to record and review patient information.

A fourth context of making decisions was during individual patient encounters. For example patients might call a nurse during the week to discuss a drug side effect or for more information regarding upcoming surgery. The nurse would potentially need to decide whether to contact the doctor, bring the patient into the next clinic or give the patient further advice. Surgeons, oncologists and radiologists held regular clinics where patients were examined, for example receiving screening mammograms or chemotherapy treatments. Surgeons and nurses also saw patients on hospital wards pre and post surgery as well as in operating theatres. In each of these circumstances team members needed to decide on the appropriate course of action in managing the patient. To support the ongoing information gathering and decision making during these encounters, portable tablets as well as the desk tops were available to clinicians.

SubSys development and implementation was jointly funded by the oncology research department, the regional cancer network and the hospital. The oncology research department was rapidly expanding and they hoped to use the system to support ongoing clinical trials by improving access to clinical information and treatments. Starting with the breast cancer team, who were pleased to implement this state of the art system, the regional cancer network planned to implement the cancer care system across all cancer groups (e.g. gynaecology, lung, urology cancer teams) in the hospital and then extend access to other cancer centres in the region to enable patient and clinician mobility.

The official purpose of SubSys was twofold. In the first instance it would provide electronic, and therefore immediate, access to patient related data, which would inform decision making. Thus all x-rays, surgical procedures and observations were available for team members to log into, either during MDT meeting, or during other points of patient consultation. Secondly, the tool was to develop a repository of patient details and outcomes which could be used to inform either practice or research in the future. They could search through the database and find all previous patients with a similar diagnosis and profile (staging, age, etc.).

> The core strategy has always been ... to help support ... patient care. First of all it's cancer patient care, because we believe that if we get that right then all [uses] fall out of it. (System admin)

Overall, the implementation of SubSys was considered a success, and it was gradually adopted in several other tumour groups in the following year, as well as being sold to other hospitals. However, the occupational groups reacted to and engaged in using the tool quite differently. Radiologists were the clinical leaders in using the system, both for entering and finding information when making decisions. Surgeons entered data into the system during initial patient consultations fairly consistently, though they returned to the paper records to retrieve information. Nurses used SubSys to check on patient history, treatment plans and diagnosis, as well as test results when counselling patients, but were reluctant to write their own notes onto the system. Pathologists had difficulty with accuracy in data entry via pull down menus, but extensively used the free formatting space for detailed narrative. Oncologists used SubSys minimally. In fact, somewhat ironically, this area of the system was the least developed, even though oncology were primary funders of the project.

CASE FINDINGS

We begin the analysis with a vignette from the fieldnotes of an MDT meeting to provide a sense of how information was 'pooled' and drawn on in one setting in deciding on the management of a particular patient.

> The team discusses the relative benefits of a mastectomy and there is marked disagreement. Mammograms and pathology are projected onto the screens. A radiologist reads the assessment summary from SubSys' print out form.

Radiologist: '[Patient] was seen in clinic . . . [and has advanced disease] . . . here is the extensive shadowing on the x-ray'. (Points it out and describes, highlighting large tumour and the minimal invasion of other areas . . . Pathologist shows a slide depicting advanced cancer cells).

Surgeon1: 'I don't think surgery [is a good option as the] patient's prognosis is poor anyway . . . and the added stress of surgery [is not helpful].'

Surgeon2: '[surgery] won't have a chance of curing her anyway . . .'

Oncologist: 'No, [but I think] that the tumour may be halted by [surgical removal] . . . and then [we should give chemotherapy . . .]' (Lengthy discussion continues between them. An oncologist cites drug trials related to case.)

Nurse reads through the patient's 'yellow card' and waits several minutes for an opportunity to join the debate: 'This woman has very large breasts and . . . she will be lopsided . . . if she has a mastectomy. [Having spoken to the patient, I know] she will want the other one off as well to maintain balance.'. . .

A clerical administrator is filling information from the meeting onto a summary form on SubSys. She selects and inputs entries for test results, diagnosis and management plan whilst listening. A nurse sitting beside her helps with the terminology. This entry is kept in the MDT meeting folder within this patient's electronic record. Individual disciplinary assessments are kept in separate folders.

(Reconstructed from the field notes)

The vignette highlights the competing views of the specialists on how to treat the patient. The surgeons focus on cure whilst the oncologists focus on the longer term survival rate. The nurse, who has difficulty joining the conversation, privileges the psychosocial perspective of the patient; here the whole discussion turns to consider the potential prophylactic removal of the nondiseased breast. We suggest the different ways of knowing-in-practice about the patient were central as to how SubSys was used to support the team's decision-making process. We examine the dynamic interplay between disciplinary practices and the manner by which patient notes were observed to be used in supporting knowledgeability and knowledge sharing. Rather than focusing on the consequences of technology in use, we highlight the ways in which members' interactions during ongoing work practice were constitutive of knowledge in quite distinctive ways.

ONCOLOGISTS

An important reason for initiating and funding the SubSys project was that it would support research and clinical trials. The professor of oncology who led the development of SubSys had realised that the system would support the growing cancer research capacity. New funding had been acquired by a national cancer collaborative to develop clinical trials whilst genomics research was also expanding.

A large group of basic science researchers were moving here to carry on cancer related research. And the carrot that they use to draw people here is that

there would be a large clinical practice very close by . . . [Oncology professor]
realized early on that if you want good clinical info that can support research
then you need a robust IT system. (Radiologist)

The radiologist explained that the carrot for attracting scientists was the promise
of close cooperation with the clinical community in the adjacent hospital. This growing research program in close association with oncology was an important basis of
their power and central to their identity in practice.

[Oncology] has a lot of research – a lot of research in drug development . . .
and genetics of course . . . that is their power basis. (Nurse)

Drug trials and participating in the wider research community is an important oncology practice. Medical oncology is a relatively new medical profession established
in the 1980s by the growing pharmaceutical technologies such as chemotherapy
and more recently moving into biotechnologies and genomics. During the annual
protocol meeting and twice-weekly MDT meetings, the oncologists frequently referred to various drug trials and explained the set up of their own trials being conducted on site. Drug trial patients were generally followed for 5–10 years in order to
determine mortality and morbidity associated with the treatments rendered. This
contributed to a relatively future orientated practice. Additionally, research, publications and the anticipated discovery of new treatments gave oncologists power,
in forms of resources and the ability to articulate their views in terms of 'evidence
based medicine'.

Though the oncology department funded the development and implementation
of SubSys, their system usage was low as highlighted by team members.

Oncologists like to have a lot of data available on the patient and their
outcomes. (pause) but it's interesting that they are not able to actually use
SubSys to input their own treatment . . . So even though it is an oncology
initiative, they are further behind radiology and surgery in many respects . . .
(Radiologist)

Ironically, one of the reasons given for the lack of use was the challenge oncologists faced in collecting high volumes of information about their patients during
assessments. Keeping track of numerous side effects and individual reactions to
chemotherapy and radiation treatments is an important part of their practice. They
articulate the patients' responses to treatment through detailed lists tracking patient responses in relation to the outcomes of published drug trials.

[Oncology has been slow to use SubSys] . . . Because it's actually quite a lot of
information gathering. The consultants, [have to document] . . . a whole raft
of problems, and they are all graded from 1 to 4. (System admin)

As there were so many pieces of information to document over a lengthy time period, they found the current tick the box paper documents simpler to quickly collate
the patients' symptoms rather than opening the numerous pull down menus. Thus

the large quantities of patient related information that was relevant to chemotherapy and radiotherapy treatments, such as hair loss, regular blood counts and weight, were held in paper-based records.

Oncologists generally met with patients for relatively lengthy consultations (comparatively to surgeons for example) where they discussed the diagnosis, the range of treatments and side effects. Patients were often affected by aggressive disease and were followed indefinitely. The practice of collecting information was to qualitatively document the patient's symptomatic experience, rather than altering treatment decisions, and the focus during consultations was to provide patient support during their period of suffering. This differed from pathology, for example, whose practice involved viewing every slide taken of tissue samples to progressively make a case for their diagnosis.

> In oncology you have to be mainly aware of the studies and the charts ... So the quality of the assessment is slightly different. (Pathologist)

The details had to be recorded, but were not immediately influencing oncologists' decisions. Decisions were being taken with longer time frames, such that outcomes were determined in years or decades. During the MDT meetings, oncology patient data was verbally summarised but seldom displayed.

However by having other disciplinary groups use SubSys, the oncology research practices were nonetheless supported. While they could hire an assistant to go through their own oncology records to collect missing data, finding and deciphering surgical data was more difficult. The system gave them important access to clinical data to support research practices that would otherwise be inaccessible to oncologists.

SURGEONS

The surgeons were the most powerful group within the MDT. This was recognised by all the other disciplines.

> These guys have all the power – the surgeons. In particular surgeon Y. I mean, he runs the show (Nurse)

As a powerful group, they could have resisted the implementation of SubSys; however they realised it had potential to support their practice and improve patient management. Thus the surgeons did use the system, but were slow and incomplete. They were most consistent in using the system for the initial surgical assessment, which was also drawn on in the MDT meeting. As surgeons (with the radiologists) were frequently the first clinical contacts, their role in creating a record of the initial assessment and early findings were critical throughout the treatment process.

> We've got [surgeonX] who [is] very slow in adopting, but you see him entering data so carefully, and his drawings are beautiful, and you just think that is a total surprise, because I thought I would have to nurse him through and

encourage him. That's the last person that I would have thought would have done direct entry doing it. It's fantastic. (System administrator)

One of the reasons the surgeons liked using the system was that it helped to clearly structure the information which could be reported concisely in tick the box format and pull down menu selection. There was a sketch diagram where they could quickly mark the location of lumps. This suited their focus on brevity in note taking and interest in pragmatic cure and immediate action. In practice, they have a clear cut focus, record few observations or comments, but consistently seek to specify decisions as quickly and tersely as possible.

The surgeons . . . have a very clear cut approach . . . They are very organised, highly efficient. They are caring, . . . but very clear on their boundaries (Nurse)
    Surgeons have a much more pragmatic problem based way of thinking . . . If I do this, your choice is X, if I do the other thing, [then] your [choice is Y]. (Surgeon)

Surgeons spent very brief periods of time seeing the patients and were highly structured in their assessments and decisions. SubSys allowed them to quickly document information and decisions and move on. One surgeon summarised this sentiment aptly, by contrasting a surgical approach with medical oncologists:

Oncologists think about possibilities, surgeons make clear decisions.

Surgeons were motivated to get the patients' details into SubSys at the initial assessment as they anticipated being able to draw information from the system concerning local outcomes for various treatments and make better decisions. Whilst oncologists primarily used results for bona fide clinical trials, surgeons placed pragmatic value in knowing more about local practice outcomes. However they did not feel they were getting sufficient feedback into their current practice decisions to more consistently use SubSys.

[The surgeons] need output from SubSys to be able to influence practice and at present there is none. (Radiologist)
    [SubSys] does not allow us to know the outcomes or survival at the moment . . . [SubSys] should do that for us . . . that is the only reason to have it . . . [initially] the oncologists wanted all this stuff about date of menarche, how many children the patient had, did you breast feed them. That is an example of trash that no one will ever use . . . so we collect all this stuff . . . and we don't even know what our local reoccurrence and survival is. [SubSys] works well for collecting data, but that is the LEAST interesting part of it. You need to know [current] outcome data. (Surgeon, his emphasis)

The surgeon in the quote emphasises the difference between the type and amount of data the oncologists would like to record and collect on SubSys compared to surgeons. Information about parity and menarche could be useful in research where the patient history could potentially be linked to certain disease outcomes in the future. However it did not have immediate relevance for patient treatment. In addition, after the initial appointments, the surgeons had already documented their decisions, and subsequent record keeping was primarily descriptive of the patient's response. The lack of perceived usefulness dissuaded the surgeons from making the extra effort to fully embrace the system.

One of the difficulties for surgeons was the number of locations where they met with the patient. Whilst oncologists saw most of their patients in clinics, the surgeons would have to remember to come and pick up the mobile tablet and bring it to patient encounters elsewhere in order to use the system.

> Getting the surgeons to use the system during theatre means that they have to come to the unit and bring up the tablets. [A key] obstacle is that they actually have yet another task to think about before they head to theatre. (Radiologist)

Surgical patients treated in the operating room and seen on the ward were thus not recorded on SubSys. Rather patient treatments (such as operation notes) were dictated immediately following the interactions later transcribed by secretaries and put in paper files. During the meeting discussion, other team members relied upon the surgeons' verbal descriptions of the surgical procedure.

RADIOLOGISTS

The director of radiology had a personal interest in computers and was the clinical champion for SubSys. On the whole radiologists are comfortable with new technology, given the explosion of new technologies within their field. Thus radiology practice has seen significant changes over the years, as they have developed new roles, and more interaction with other disciplinary groups;

> Radiologists, historically, they used to be back sitting in a dark room – sitting there with their glasses on. They didn't speak to people. But actually *now* they are rather the hub of the hospital (Radiologist)

The radiologists were active in the user group meetings and gave regular feedback on the design of SubSys. As opposed to the future orientated interest of oncologists in using SubSys to support research, radiologists, like surgeons, focused on the current decisions being made. The radiologists assessed patients at an early point in the patient's encounter with hospital medicine, and thus the design of the system was well suited to the initial phases of the patient assessment. They filled in their assessment data reporting their clinical impressions of various radiology tests, and were frequently observed to take the portable tablets into the patient assessment area to record information while interacting with the patient. When reviewing patient management they would generally log into SubSys to look up patient details as they found this easier than searching for the paper records. As the radiologists and surgeons worked side by side in the common clinical assessment area, their uses of

SubSys were frequently compared by the administrator in charge of the implementation process.

> The radiology guys have been always very good at entering their data. And the surgery guys have always been sort of slow in entering their data ... And I think there is an irksome feeling there now ... amongst the radiology guys. 'Why should we do it if you're not doing it.' (System administrator)

> Radiologists look back over the pathway and get all their information from SubSys rather than look at the notes. But then surgeons will ask their secretaries to do it, so the secretaries will pull up SubSys and ... look ... In the back office SurgeonY will come in and say 'I need to find out about so-and-so, can you get me their notes'. And [his PA] will say 'well let's look on SubSys'. She pulls the patient up, and SurgeonY will read letters and things like that. So the secretary initiates that use, rather than the surgeon. (System administrator)

The administrator highlights that the radiologists not only use the system to record patient details, but they also use it to make subsequent decisions in patient management. As radiology images could be accessed through the database, this made SubSys expedient to use in practice. They also did not have as much secretarial support as the well resourced surgeons.

As the radiologists were heavily involved in the various groups and committees giving feedback to SubSys designers, the system had a well developed interface for the initial clinic assessment where the radiologists practised. SubSys enabled them to compare archival x-rays through the system, which would be uploaded onto the screen. Having a graphical knowledge focus in the patient information they collected, they assessed potential diagnoses and responses to treatment by examining the characteristics and potential changes in films taken at standard intervals.

The lead radiologist wanted to use SubSys during MDT meetings, rather than bringing in paper records or hard copies of films, as it gave added flexibility to the range of patient information that could be viewed, should it be required. As the surgeons were firmly in control of the these meetings, they preferred to use hard copies of films and slides projected onto a large screen, and photocopies of the initial assessments which could also be projected on an overhead. This enabled the team to get through the material quicker, as there was no risk of system down time, and no time lags in between screens.

NURSES

A nurse met with all the patients during their initial assessment and they made themselves available to be contacted during the week, should a patient be in need of extra support. The patients and carers frequently wanted to discuss the treatment options further, after having had time to reflect. Thus nurses had varying levels of contact with the patients, and many of those contacts were sporadic and intense. Their knowledge focus was on patient experience rather than illness presentation. However, they did not enter their assessments onto SubSys.

We put in a few notes of our own to give us a bit of background, you know the family situation, and the person's psychological and emotional and social cycle ...which we certainly wouldn't want going out, live and public – even if it is just for the team, I don't think we would want something so confidential go out of *just our* [nurses] circulation. (Specialist nurse, her emphasis)

As explained in the above quote, the nurses felt the information that they collected was very personal and not entirely relevant to the rest of the team. They were resistant to having to put such information on a computer, which was seen to be '*live and public*'.

They sought to retain the yellow card index system that they used to keep notes on patient stories and encounters.

We haven't moved to using [SubSys]. But we still use our written information .... And I think we want to keep those (yellow cards) as long as we can. (Nurse)

The cards, as used by the nurse in the opening vignette, were seen by the nurses as not merely proving information, but actually representing the patient in question,

[The cards] are just a little nudge really, a little reminder – We almost refer to these cards as 'her'. 'Oh yes, there she is' or 'I have got that lady'. Umm – They are almost sort of personable. They sort of replace the person we met because it is an association in our minds. – we can picture the lady, or we can picture the room. It just helps us remember her, out of all the patients, and be able to say, 'oh yes I remember that lady'. It is something to do with the yellow card. (Nurse)

As the nurses had the potential to develop very close and intimate relationships with the patients, and having extended and often tearful telephone conversations with them over the weeks of waiting and treatment, the purpose of the information gathering was not primarily to make treatment decisions, but to understand the patient experience and discern how to be supportive. As such, in practice the card often became synonymous with the patient, a tangible object reifying the patient.

If we can't find a card, we look in our box, we keep boxes for each year, so look back through 2003, 2002 Mrs T for instance and I will say, 'there she is' for instance, you know. It is just like I found the person I am looking for and associate it – the card and the person come together. (Nurse)

Ideally these cards were meant to extend the patients' voice during the decision making through the nurses' input, though the nurses often found it difficult to participate.

The MDT is very useful, if we are allowed to make comments ... because we can add in at that point if there is something relevant about the patient ... like

[patient X's] biopsy came back and she has got cancer. They were talking
about wide local incisions with radiotherapy afterwards. Well, actually this
woman is 92, lives alone at home and is not going to want to come up for
radiotherapy...It might not be for her. [That is why I] bring the yellow cards.
I can't remember the patients unless I have that little blurb written down.
(Nurse)

The electronic record was perceived to alter the reified relationship that the yellow card enabled. In addition to being more structured, they would be unable to
hold and carry around electronic notes in the same way that they currently did.

[SubSyst] is very structured...We try to give a quite personable impression
and approach to the people ... and it is something to do with doing it all on
computer. [SubSys] ... is more structured and clinical.... The personal touch,
I suppose it comes together with the yellow cards. (Nurse)

Whilst the portable tablets did enable the nurses to potentially carry the 'records'
around, for them it did not represent one particular patient, and thus did not support the nurses' practice in being patient centred and mindful of the patient's very
personal experience.

Nursing data was often viewed to be marginal to medical research objectives
where quantifiable patient characteristics were uniquely relevant. Similarly nursing
information and decisions were not accessed by other disciplinary groups during
their ongoing practice in the same way that, for example, the surgical plans might.
If a doctor wanted to get more information on a patient's psychosocial experiences
they would readily discuss the details with the nurse. Thus inputting the nurses' information was fairly low on the list of priorities for both implementers and users
and there was no move to force the nurses into compliance.

PATHOLOGISTS

The pathology department was historically associated with the university rather
than the hospital, and the pathologists were on the whole less integrated with the
rest of the team. However, they were also regarded as an ivory tower, somewhat removed from the practicalities of patient management making decisions in a time
pressured and uncertain context.

We call pathology the palace of truths. (Radiologist)

A key decision made by pathologists was to specify the histology label. While they
have extensive classification systems of cell morphology, not all cells in a tissue will
look the same; thus providing the diagnostic label is not as straightforward as often
assumed by non pathologists:

Pathology is the gold standard (for diagnosing) but our [knowledge is
not] conclusive...Some things are black and white and these are easy to

> specify . . . but there are also some areas of grey . . . When you are training these often seem even more grey but as you get more experience . . . pathologists learn how they will consistently call a particular presentation . . . 'Is it yes or no doctor,' the patient asks and a shade of grey is not acceptable . . . So you have to say – cancer or not. Having to tick boxes to fill in forms and databases accentuates this tendency to erase the greyness and makes [diagnoses] more clear cut than they really are. (Pathologist)

The basis for pathology decision making did not revolve around the patient per se, but around tissue samples which were examined comparatively with standard samples seen in the past to determine where the cells would most closely be aligned. The immediate urgency of the patient's voice and the distress of their tears was not at the forefront of their thinking, but rather how does this sample compare to other previous samples of this nature.

The pathologists felt that the surgeons and oncologists didn't understand the complexity of pathology practice. Each case was unique and cells were on a continuum in all dimensions on which they were reporting. Just rhyming off the numbers seemed to miss the nuances of the particular patient.

> I went through 70 slides . . . because you have to block off the area, to make sure that there isn't an invasive tumour, and work all the margins out . . . so you might sit in a meeting and say 4 of the lymph nodes are negative, in seconds – but that might have been 2 hours of work. (Pathologist)

The pathologists' preferred method of reporting was to write narrative descriptions concerning cellular morphology. Their differing knowledge focus on descriptions became more pronounced after implementing SubSys. The pathologists preferred to use free text rather than the tick boxes and menu choices; when they filled in the appropriate records, they would frequently make mistakes and select the wrong label. However they spent considerable time making sure that the written narrative record was accurate.

> How do I put this politely? There has always been a . . . problem with pathology data . . . Pathologists have always written a free text descriptive story about what pathology is. . . . According to [network guidelines] instead of saying 'this tumour is an XXXX, it measures such and such' you just put in [the numbers in the menu] . . . [But] the pathologists are very attached to their free text so they feel that they won't give that up though they agree [to fill out the pull down menus] . . . But they don't see it as the medical record – they see the free text as the medical record. . . . So they will make sure the free text is accurate but not the [tick boxes]. But the radiologists and the surgeons and the oncologists are saying to them 'we make our decision on the [tick boxes] data, not on the free text. Therefore it is more important that the [tick box] is accurate.' (System administrator)

A system administrator recounts that one of the entries concerning the pathology diagnosis was 16 pages long, highlighting the issue. This led to a degree of tension between pathologists and others, though most particularly the surgeons, who were the most concerned with efficient use of time.

> Pathology says 'I want to give you the whole story. And that covers me completely'...And what the surgeons and oncologists are saying is 'Well if we cannot understand that, then that does not cover you legally because we cannot make the decision if we cannot understand your free text report.' And the pathologists are saying 'Well you should learn to understand it.' (System administrator)

The nurses and several radiologists acknowledged the marginalisation felt by the pathologists and highlighted the importance of the pathology role in the information pooling process. Radiologists were similarly interested in whether the histology diagnosis matched with the radiological diagnosis, and found the learning in conjunction with superimposing the two views to be very important.

> [The pathologists] should have more respect afforded them, really. I mean they are **crucial**. If they don't give us the right answer, we are making decisions based on nonsense ... there are not enough pathologists...a national shortage ... and they are working under extreme pressure ... [so] they are not integrated into the [decision making] process. (Nurse)

Pathologists did not want to rush cases in the event of making a mistake and they wanted to explain the rationale behind less clear cut conclusions. As pathologists were generally less powerful within the hospital environment (which compounded difficulties in trainee recruitment nationally), they had not yet been successful in securing the added resources to cope with an increasing workload.

DISCUSSION AND CONCLUSIONS

We examine how knowing was being co-constructed across the disciplinary groups during the ongoing flow of medical activity and decision making. The new system provided occasion for examining how different groups engaged with knowledge and practice differently. These divergent ways of knowing-in-practice posed added challenges to developing an electronic patient record that would adequately support decision making across the unique context of each disciplinary group.

The knowing-in-practice perspective highlights how technology in use differed across disciplinary groups; difference went beyond the assumptions and expectations of the technology (Orlikowski and Gash, 1994; Barrett, 1999; Davidson, 2002). Building on the cognitive concept of framing, a knowing-in-practice lens (Orlikowski, 2000; 2002) reveals how diverse situated practice captures an important social aspect to how technology interacts with concrete elements of ongoing work. Rather than focusing on the shared beliefs about the technology in a particular community group, the multidisciplinary context of our study showed the variegated capacity of the system to support the ongoing practice decisions. As the nature of practice and process of interactions varied across the occupational communities, so did the manner in which the system supported their work.

Our case provides insights as to how decisions and clinical judgements amongst the multidisciplinary team differed in knowledge focus, temporal elements and issues of power. Acting knowledgeably as part of their daily routines of practice, the focus of knowing is constituted in the communities' practices. Whilst one community (nurses) focuses on how to understand the social context of a patient, and what decisions might lead to appropriately timed support, another disciplinary community (oncologists) focuses on future survival rates. Different disciplines and types of decisions are located on a hierarchy of importance; thus the manner by which diverse practices are supported through SubSys is uneven and subject to complex relations of power. We discuss these briefly in turn below.

Influence of knowledgeability on decision making

Firstly, disciplinary groups each have a different knowledge focus in accessing and recording information. Nurse specialists view their own records as reminders of the patient, wanting to document brief cues pointing to tacitly held knowledge. The types of decisions they made frequently involved knowing how to respond appropriately to patients rather than 'doing something to them' as was more typical of the doctors' work. As highlighted by Benner *et al.* (1994) a response-based expertise relies heavily on intuition to direct decisions and thus relies minimally on recording explicit data. Information sharing between nurses and other team members was most frequently accomplished orally, either through phone calls or face to face, rather than looking up the nurse reports. Thus the nurses' knowledge in practice was not an explicit representation of patient facts, but their records underpinned a holistic understanding formed of the patients' situation (Benner, 1994).

On the other hand, pathologists recorded their information in such a way that their reasoning behind the diagnosis was understandable by others. Their work consisted mainly of graphic comparisons of the patient's cells with previous cases in diagnostic categories. Decision making was a labour intensive process of systematically lining up slides to determine the best fit. The process of reasoning behind the diagnosis given was to them as important as the conclusion drawn. This knowledge focus contrasted sharply with surgeons who primarily wanted to record succinct information that would direct the immediate patient related decisions. Descriptive statements were brief. Surgical practice entailed extreme efficiency and moving people through, even if the information at hand remained uncertain. Making decisions in uncertain circumstances also characterised their operative work, as bed closures or adverse patient reactions under anaesthesia frequently forced them to make quick decisions. Whilst they envisioned SubSys supporting their practice to a certain extent, the impracticality of entering data, when secretaries were at hand to type or search information, made the database's utility inconsistent. However, the close collaboration between surgeons and radiologists during initial assessments enabled the radiology champions to know how to support the user needs of the surgeons, rendering the system amenable to the surgical practice.

Implications of temporal differences on IT use in decision making

Secondly, we highlight how temporal differences and interactions between occupational groups' practice influenced the process of system design and use. For example, oncologists did not value the use of the system for real time decision making preferring to collect information to support future research and future practice. Oncologists generally meet their patients over many years of follow up and have lengthier consultations than do surgeons. Thus they have more information to document and an ongoing relationship with patients where they can discuss with patients. Having prolonged periods of contact with patients they are more able to develop a rapport and history of the patient. Whilst the side effects of their treatments are usually significant, they generally focus decisions on the long-term survival rates rather than current discomforts.

One surgeon explained how he and his colleague were surprised at the little long-term improvement which was predicted for common oncology treatments. The surgeons' more immediate temporal focus led them to privilege knowing about the immediate suffering caused by many of the chemotherapies as outweighing their possible future benefits;

> [Oncologists] would happen to think that a 3% [chance of benefit] is a great benefit to get where as we would think 3% is quite small and there are these side effects ... Sometimes it is difficult ... to say 'no treatment' is an option ... At the beginning we [surgeons] felt that the oncologists would exaggerate the benefits they could impart to a patient ... but we have thrashed it out and produced a guideline ... but my feeling is we still use too much chemotherapy. (Surgeon)

The ongoing collaborative decision making at the annual review day and the weekly meeting challenged the oncologists in their conventional way of knowing-in-practice. Whilst they previously would have recommended a therapy that large scientific trials suggested would give them 1–2 % chance of increased longevity, after several years of close collaboration with surgeons they questioned this perspective. One surgeon explained that he generally looked for an anticipated 5–7 % improvement in expected mortality prognosis before he recommended surgery, as he did not feel the current complications and side effects were worth it for the patient. This was one of the reasons why surgeons (and radiologists) were particularly keen to generate local outcomes for their current patients from SubSys, rather than relying solely on distant clinical trials. As a group, the team eventually decided to desist from recommending oncology treatments where less than 2 % life expectancy was predicted according to published trials. One oncologist explained his changed perspective;

> When I first came, I used to feel that surgery was very nihilistic, they just had to take the bit out and off they went. Whereas now, you know, I have listened to them, and yes, there is a lot more respect ... – I have moved – I have become much more surgical actually (Oncologist)

Another temporal aspect of disciplinary practice that affected decision making and SubSys use was the timing of patient contact. For example, surgeons and radiologists met patients at clearly defined points in time, with clinic appointments being arranged in advance and being highly structured. Nurses on the other hand did not have specific time limits on their consultations with patients, but tended to triage their available time with those patients they felt were most needy of their support. Depending on the varied needs being presented, the nurses would potentially need to contact an array of other health professionals, such as counselling, support groups or home care. They tried to fit their work around the assessments being conducted by the doctors and the scheduled clinics. The varied rhythm and uncertain structure of the encounter made the information gathering and their decision making dispersed across time. For example, if a support group failed to return a telephone call, then they would need to rearrange their plans; if the patient was ready to go home, they could plan to follow up by telephone. Needing to coordinate and communicate with numerous others meant they could not, as the surgeons did, readily document their findings and best treatment plan.

This ongoing collage of responses to patient needs and available resources was compounded by the unpredictable nature of the support they would provide during non clinic hours, when patients may telephone. Needing to quickly recall patient details when a patient telephoned unexpectedly, they could quickly reach for the holder containing the yellow cards to prompt their memory. Needing to log in to a closed computer system randomly would be disruptive of the delicate juggling characteristic of their practice.

Temporal elements of specific disciplinary practice influence how knowledge is developed and used (Nanhakumar and Jones, 2001; Yakura 2002). As recently argued by Labianca, Moon and Watt (2005) temporal issues tend to fade into the background of organisational research, such that we are often blinded to their importance. They highlight the divergence of temporal schemas which challenge the notion that time is linear, objective and uniform. Qualitative studies within organisational research have underscored how time is socially constructed out of diverse human experiences (Giddens, 1984; Gherardi and Strati, 1985; Yakura 2002) and this has been labelled as 'pluritemporalism' (Nowotny, 1992). This focuses on ways in which time is interpreted and given meaning (Hassard, 1996). As such it is not surprising that occupational subcultures construct and interpret time differently (Traweek, 1988; Barley, 1988; Zerubavel, 1981).

Research on time in teams has primarily examined how team members perceive deadlines, and how team members organise their activities around temporal agendas (Labianca *et al.*, 2005; Gersick, 1988; Waller, Conte, Gibson and Carpenter, 2001). However, as is evident in our case, different disciplinary groups have different temporal rhythms in practice which influences technology adoption and use for decision making.

Power and decision making

Thirdly, we highlight how power and hierarchy affect the use of SubSys and information sharing, whereby some disciplinary groups are privileged in the decision-making process. Knowledge is directly tied to professional specialist juris-dictions (Abbott, 1988) and legitimacy as being 'specialists' rests on maintaining a distinctive knowledge base. Sustaining control over professional jurisdiction not only requires a codified body of knowledge for which members are accredited, but also relies on members enacting the case for the special tacit knowledge they alone are seen to bring to bear upon every clinical decision. Such tacit knowledge cannot be replicated by others not socialised into the profession. Freidson (1986) argues that formal knowledge of professional disciplines shapes the way human institutions are organised (1986: 6) and suggests that this form of normalisation is a central in-strument of professional power.

Surgeons were the most powerful group within the team and had acquired signifi-cant resources such as secretarial support as well as holding administrative authority as team leaders. The final decision to adopt SubSys had been theirs. However they resisted the adoption of SubSys during the MDT meetings in presenting patient in-formation. Similarly oncologists gained significant status on the team through their participation in large research trials. This type of knowledge production, associated with 'Evidence Based Medicine' is considered within the current medical context as being the most authoritative (Sackett *et al.*, 2000). Used as a gold standard in the medical decision making (Berg and Timmerman, 1998) this enabled oncologists to promote drug treatments shown to be statistically effective in large clinical trials even if the actual impact on the patient was in fact minimal. We suggest evidence-based medicine was a discursive strategy used by medical professionals, and oncol-ogists in particular, to maintain jurisdictional authority; this served to render their disciplinary knowledge 'technical' and beyond democratic discussion.

Nurses on the other hand were the least powerful professional group in the team. There are well documented historical and gendered reasons for nurses' subjuga-tion to the medical professions (Freidson, 1972; Menzies, 1985; Abbott, 1988; Star and Bowker, 1999) that relate to their institutional development. In the context of SubSys development, our study highlights the largest discrepancy with the system's design and intended use with the nurses' knowledge and practice. However, for the duration of the study, the nurses' lack of use of the system did not create concern for the doctors or administrators, possibly because their knowledge was considered tangential to real (medical) patient care and research practice. As highlighted by Star and Strauss (1999) the relatively invisible nature of nursing work renders their knowledge and practice less relevant to the decision-making processes of doctors. Invisible work is relegated to the background and is frequently not noticed unless it ceases to be done. Overall, hierarchy privileged some perspectives, orchestrating unified decision making in 'scientific' language.

Conclusion

Our study demonstrates the value of a knowing-in-practice approach in deepening our understanding of the use of IT to support multidisciplinary decision making. The role and use of IT in supporting the team's practice highlighted temporal-ity, power, and knowledgeability as critical influences on the dynamics of decision making.

Our findings implore us to go beyond the findings of earlier research on information pooling which focused on the role of IT in enabling the pooling of more integrated and complete information for decision making. While this may be important, our practice approach focuses on the underlying reasons as to why pooling is not always easy, desirable, or possible. For example, the system design may be perceived to be inappropriate in supporting the *temporality* of the practice, which has a different rhythm (e.g. action orientation of surgeon vs. slower and methodical practice of the pathologist) or other temporal features (e.g. immediacy vs long term).

Our approach also shifts the focus away from whether information is recorded or not and why it is pooled to appreciate the *knowledgeability* inherent within the practice. The issue is not only about the challenge of making tacit knowledge explicit and recorded as information. Rather, our findings point to the perceived appropriateness of the knowledgeability of different communities, which is partly conditioned by *power* relations across members of the multidisciplinary team. Intriguingly, the level of authorial control of team members afforded by the system design reinforced these relations of power. Pathologists, for example, had limited control as to how they author their texts (i.e. free texts vs. tick the boxes) and this made it more difficult for them to share knowledge.

Further, a historical and institutional focus inherent in the practice approach aids our understanding as to why and what explicit knowledge is encoded (or not) in the system by the different disciplines. For example, the ordering, priority, and value of nurses' knowledge by other medical groups influenced the information pooling process. Nurses failed to pool information through SubSys, not only because of its sensitive, personal, and biographical nature but because their social contributions were often not valued as 'critical' to medical decision making by more technically oriented groups. In contrast, radiologists and pathologists provide information for decision making that powerful others such as surgeons depend on and coordinate their practice around. This finding also highlights that not only is the structure and design of system important as to how information is pooled but so are 'practice' dependencies. In other words, one needs to explicitly understand dependencies within and between the practices and the different forms of coordination used to manage the dependencies (Crowston and Osborn, 2003) when using IT to support multidisciplinary decision making.

Within the specific area of multidisciplinary decision making in a healthcare setting, the image of information pooling as drawing on integrated and complete information for decision making is illusory. Multidisciplinary decision making in healthcare happens not only in the formal team meeting context, but involves healthcare professionals making their decisions in individual patient interaction settings. The system enables specialists to draw on the information in the database from other disciplines during their decision-making process. However, because of different groups' attitude towards 'pooling' information, the reality is a much more fragmented information pool, which has significant implications as to the nature, type, and quality of decision making.

Our study aims to provide some preliminary insights on the role of IT and multidisciplinary decision making in a healthcare setting. We hope that it will provide a starting point for further work on digitization and multidisciplinary decision making, which is growing in significance and scope across a range of professional contexts.

NOTES

1. Rather than a patient having an appointment in a surgical clinic, then being referred with a different appointment to radiology services for imaging to be taken of suspected cancer regions, and then needing yet another reappointment with surgery to discuss the results of the imaging and then enter into treatment phase which may have needed an appointment with the oncologist, the one-stop clinic allowed the patient to see all clinicians required for diagnosis in one visit.

REFERENCES

Abbott, A. (1988) *The System of Professions: An Essay on the Division of Expert Labor.* Chicago: The University of Chicago Press.

Aram, J. (2004) Concepts of inter-disciplinarity: Configurations of knowledge and action boundaries, *Human Relations*, 57, 379–412.

Ashforth, B., and Mael, F. (1989) Social identity theory and the organization, *Academy of Management Review*, 14, 20–39.

Barley, S. (1988) Technology as an occasion for structuring: Evidence form observations of CT scanners and the social order of radiology departments, *Administrative Science Quarterly*, 31 (1), 78–108.

Barrett, M. (1999) Challenges of EDI adoption for electronic trading in the London insurance market, *European Journal of Information Systems*, 8 (1), 1–15.

Bechky, B. (2003) Sharing meaning across occupational communities: the transformation of understanding on a production floor, *Organization Science*, 14 (3), 312–330.

Beers, P.J. *et al.* (2006) Common ground, complex problems and decision making. *Group Decision and Negotiation*, 15 (6), 529–556.

Benner, P., and Nodding, G. (1994) 'Caring Practice', in S. Gordon, P. Benner, and N. Noddings (eds) *Care Giving: Readings in Knowledge, Practice, Ethics, and Politics.* Philadelphia: University of Pennsylvania Press, 40–55.

Benner, P. (1994) *Interpretive Phenomenology: Embodiment, Caring and Ethics in Health and Illness.* Thousand Oaks, CA: Sage.

Berg, M. (1997) *Rationalizing Medical Work: Decision Support Techniques and Medical Practices.* New Baskerville: Massachusetts Institute of Technology.

Berg, M. (1999) Patient care information systems and health care work: A sociotechnical approach, *International Journal of Medical Informatics*, 55, 87–101.

Berg, M. (2003) The search for synergy: Interrelating medical work and patient care information systems, *Methods of Information in Medicine*, 42 (4), 337–344.

Brodbeck, F., Kerschreiter, R., Mojzisch, A., and Schulz-Hardt, S. (2007) Group decision making under conditions of distributed knowledge; the information asymmetries model, *Academy of Management Journal*, 32 (2) 459–479.

Brodbeck, F., Kerschreiter, R., Mojzisch, A., Frey, D., and Schulz-Hardt, S. (2002) The dissention of critical, unshared information in decision-making groups: The effects of prediscussion dissent, *European Journal of Social Psychology*, 32, 35–56.

Bunderson, J., and Sutcliffe, K. (2002) Comparing alternative conceptualisations of functional diversity in management teams: Process and performance effects, *Academy of Management Journal*, 45 (5), 875–893.

Bunderson, J., and Sutcliffe, K. (2003) Management team learning orientation and business unit performance, *Journal of Applied Psychology*, 88 (3), 552–560.

Bunderson, J., and Sutcliffe, K. (2005) Information handling challenges in complex systems, *International Public Management Journal*, 8 (3), 417.

Carlile, P. (2002) A pragmatic view of knowledge and boundaries: Boundary objects in new product development, *Organization Science*, 13 (4) 442–455.

Carpenter, M., Geletkanycz, M., and Sanders, W. (2004) Upper echelons research revisited: Antecedents, elements and consequences of top management team composition, *Journal of Management*, 30 (6) 749–778.

Christensen, C., and Abbott, A. (2000) 'Team Medical Decision Making' in G. Chapman and F. Sonnenberg (eds) *Decision Making in Health Care*. Cambridge: Cambridge University Press, 267–285.

Crossan, J., Stroebel, C., Scott, J., Stello, B., and Crabtree, B. (2005) Implementing an electronic medical record in a family medicine practice: Communication, decision making, and conflict, *Annals of Family Medicine*, 3, 3007–3011.

Crowston, K., and Osborn, C.S. (2003) 'A coordination theory approach to process description and redesign', in T. Malone, K. Crowston, and G. Herman (eds) *Organising Business Knowledge*. Boston, MA: MIT Press, 335–371.

Damon, W. (1991) 'Problems of direction in socially shared cognition', in L.B. Resnick, J. Levine, and S.D. Teasley (eds) *Perspectives on Socially Shared Cognition*. Washington DC: American Psychological Association, 384–397.

Davidson, E. (2002) Technology frames and framing: A socio cognitive investigation of requirements determination, *MIS Quarterly*, 26, 329–358.

Dougherty, D. (1992) Interpretive barriers to successful product innovation in large firms, *Organization Science*, 3, 179–202.

Edmondson, A. Bohmer, R., and Pisano, G. (2001) Disrupted routines: Team learning and new technology implementation in hospitals, *Administrative Science Quarterly*, 46 (4), 685–716.

Edmondson, A., Winslow, A., Bohmer, R., and Pisano, G. (2003) Learning how and learning what: Effects of tacit and codified knowledge on performance improvement following technology adoption, *Decision Sciences*, 34 (2), 197–223.

Ellingsen, G. (2003) Coordinating work in hospitals through a global tool, *Scandinavian Journal of Information Systems*, 15, 39–54.

Fleissig, A., Jenkins, V., Catt, S., and Fallowfield, L. (2006) Multidisciplinary teams in cancer care: Are they effective in the UK? *The Lancet: Oncology*, 7, 935–943.

Ford, P, and Kubu, C. (2006) Stimulating debate: Ethics in a multidisciplinary functional nerurosurgery committee, *Journal of Medical Ethics*, 32, 106–109.

Freidson, E. (1972) *Profession of Medicine: A Study of the Sociology of Applied Knowledge*. New York: Dodd Mead and Co.

Freidson, E. (1986) *Professional Power: A Study of The Institutionalization of Formal Knowledge*. Chicago: University of Chicago Press.

Geissbuhler, A., and Miller, R. (2000) Computer-Assisted Clinical Decision Support', in G. Chapman and F. Sonnenberg (eds) *Decision Making in Health Care*. Cambridge: Cambridge University Press, 362–385.

Gersick, C. (1988) Time and transition in work teams: Toward a new model of group development, *The Academy of Management Journal*, 31 (1), 9–41.

Gherardi, S. (2000) Practice-based theorizing on learning and knowing in organizations, *Organization*, 7 (2), 211–223.

Gherardi, S., and Strati, A. (1985) The temporal dimension in organizational studies, *Organization Studies*, 9 (2), 149–164.

Giddens A. (1984) *The Constitution of Society: Introduction of the Theory of Structuration*. California: University of California Press.

Golden Biddle, K., and Locke, K. (1997) *Composing Qualitative Research*. Thousand Oaks, CA: Sage.

Goodstein, J., Gautam, K., and Boeker, W. (1994) The effects of board size and diversity on strategic change, *Strategic Management Journal*, 15, 241–250.

Hassard, J. (1996) 'Images of Time in Work and Organization', in S.R. Clegg, C. Hardy, and W. Nord (eds) *Handbook of Organization Studies*. Thousand Oaks, CA: Sage, 581–598.

Hoffman, L.R., and Maier, N.R.F. (1961) Quality and acceptance of problem solutions by members of homogeneous and heterogeneous groups, *The Journal of Abnormal and Social Psychology*, 62 (2), 401–407.

Hambrick, D., Cho, T., and Chen, M. (1996) The influence of top management teams' heterogeneity on firm's competitive scores, *Administrative Science Quarterly*, 41, 659–684.

Hunter, D. (2006) The diseases of occupations, *Occupational Medecine*, 56 (8), 520.

Jehn, K., Northcraft, G., and Neale, M. (1999) Why difference make a difference: A field study of diversity, conflict, and performance in workgroups, *Administrative Science Quarterly*, 44, 741–763.

Jones, M. (2003) Computers can land people on Mars, why can't they get them to work in a hospital? *Methods of Information in Medicine*, 42 (4), 410–415.

Jones, M. (2004) Learning the lessons of history? Electronic records in the United Kingdom acute hospitals, *Health Informatics Journal*, 10 (4), 253–263.

Labianca, G., Moon, H., and Watt, I. (2005) When is an hour not 60 minutes? Deadlines, temporal schemata, and individual and task group performance, *Academy of Management Journal*, 48, 677–694.

Lanceley, A., Savage, J., Menon, U., and Jacobs, I. (2008) Influences on multidisciplinary team decision making, *International Journal of Gynecology Cancer*, 18, 215–222.

Lave, J., and Wenger, E. (1991) *Situated Learning: Legitimate Peripheral Participation*. Cambridge: Cambridge University Press.

Levine, J.M., and Resnick, L.B. (1993), Social foundations of cognition, *Annual Review of Psychology*, 44, 585–612.

Mannix, E., and Neale, M.A. (2005) What Differences Make a Difference? *Psychological Science in the Public Interest*, 6 (2), 31–55.

Mason, J. (2002) *Qualitative Researching*. London: Sage Publications, 2nd edition.

Menzies Lyth, I. (1985) *The Dynamics of the Social*. London: Free Association Books.

Milliken, F., and Martins, L. (1996) Searching for common threads: Understanding the multiple effects of diversity in organizational groups, *Academy of Management Review*, 21, 402–433.

Nandhakumar, J., and Jones, M. (2001) Accounting for Time: Managing time in project-based teamworking, *Accounting, Organizations and Society*, 26, 193–214.

Nonaka, I. (1994). A dynamic theory of organisational knowledge creation, *Organization Science*, 5 (1), 14–37.

Nowotny, H. (1992) Time and social theory, *Time and Society*, 1, 421–454.

Oborn, E. (2008) *Processes of Knowing In Multidisciplinary Team Practice: A Study of Specialist Cancer Care in England*. Saarbrucken, Germany: Verlag.

Orlikowski, W., and Gash, D. (1994) Technological frames: Making sense of information technology in organizations. *ACM Transactions on Information Systems*, 12 (2) 174–207.

Orlikowski, W. (2000) Using technology and constituting structures: A practice lens for studying technology in organizations, *Organization Science*, 11 (4), 404–428

Orlikowski, W. (2002) Knowing in practice: Enacting a collective capability in distributed organizing, *Organization Science*, 13 (3), 249–273.

Pelled, L., Eisenhardt, K., and Xin, K. (1999) Exploring the black box: An analysis of work group diversity, conflict, and performance, *Administrative Science Quarterly*, 44.

Polanyi, M. (1958) *Personal Knowledge*. Chicago: University of Chicago Press.

Polanyi, M. (1968) *Knowing and Being*. London: Routledge & Kegan Paul.

Sackett, D., Strauss, S., Richardson, W., Rosenberg, W., and Haynes, R. (2000) *Evidence Based Medicine: How To Practice And Teach EBM*. Toronto: Churchill Livingstone

Salas, E., Stagl, K., and Burke, S. (2004) '25 Years of Team Effectiveness in Organizations: Research Themes and Emerging Needs', in C. Cooper and I. Robertson (eds) *International Review of Industrial and Organizational Psychology, Vol. 19*. Chichester, West Sussex: John Wiley & Sons, Ltd, Chapter 2, 47–91.

Schön, D. (1983) *The Reflective Practitioner*. USA: Basic Books Inc.

Schultz-Hardt, S., Brodbeck, F., Mojzisch, A., Kerschreiter, R., and Frey, D. (2006) Group decision making in hidden profile situations: Dissent as a facilitator for decision duality, *Journal of Personality and Social Psychology*, 91, 1080–1093.

Sidhom, M., and Poulsen, M. (2006) Multidisciplinary care in oncology: Medicolegal implications of group decisions, *The Lancet: Oncology*, 7, 951–954.

Smith, K., Smith, K., Olian, J., Sims, H., Obannon, D., and Scully, J. (1994) Top management team demography and process: The role of social integration and communication, *Administrative Science Quarterly*, 39, 412–438.

Star, S., and Bowker, G. (1999) *Sorting Things Out*. Cambridge, MA: MIT Press.

Star, S., and Strauss, A. (1999) Layers of silence, arenas of voice: The ecology of visible and invisible work, *Computer Supported Cooperative Work*, 8 (1-2).

Stasser, G., Steward, D., and Wittenbaum, G. (1995) Expert roles and information exchange during discussion: The importance of knowing who knows what. *Journal of Experimental Social Psychology*, 31 (3), 244–265.

Strauss, A., Fagerhaugh, S., Suczek, B., and Wiener, C. (1985) *Social Organisation of Medical Work*. New Jersey: Transaction Publishers.

Swann, W., Polzer, J., Seyle, D., and Ko, S. (2004) Finding value in diversity: verification of personal and social self-views in diverse groups, *Academy of Management Review*, 29 (1) 9–27.

Traweek, S. (1988) Feminist perspectives on science studies: Commentary, *Science, Technology, and Human Values*, 13 (3/4), 250–253.

Triandis, H.C., Hall, E.R., and Ewen, R.B. (1965) Member heterogeneity and dyadic creativity, *Human Relations*, 18 (1), 33–55.

Tsoukas, H. (2003) 'Do We Really Understand Tacit Knowledge?', in M. Easterby-Smith and M.A. Lyles (eds) *The Blackwell Handbook of Organizational Learning and Knowledge Management*. Oxford: Blackwell Publishing, 410–427

Tsui, A., Egan, T., and O'Reilly C. (1992) Being different: Relational demography and organizational attachment, *Administrative Science Quarterly*, 37, 549–579.

van Aalst, J., and van der Mast, C. (2003) Performer: An instrument for multidisciplinary courseware teams to share knowledge and experiences, *Computers and Education*, 41, 39–48.

Van Maanen, J. (1979) The fact of fiction in organizational ethnography, *Administrative Science Quarterly*, 24, 539–550.

Vikkelsø, S. (2005) Subtle redistribution of work, attention and risks: Electronic patient records and organisational consequences, *Scandinavian Journal of Information Systems*, 17 (1) 3–30.

Waller M., Conte, J.M. *et al.* (2001) The effect of individual perceptions of deadlines on team performance, *The Academy of Management Review*, 26 (4), 586–600.

Wears, R., and Berg, M. (2005) Computer technology and clinical work, *Journal of American Medical Association*, 293 (10) 1261–1263.

Wenger, E. (1998) *Communities of Practice: Learning, Meaning and Identity*. Cambridge: Cambridge University Press.

Williams, K., and O'Reilly, C. (1998) 'Demography and Diversity in Organisations', in B. Straw and R. Sutton (eds) *Research in Organizational Behaviour*. Greenwich, VT: JAI Press.

Williams, M. (2001) In whom we trust: Group membership as an affective context for trust development, *Academy of Management Review*, 26 (3), 377–396.

Yakura, E. (2002) Charting time: timelines as temporal boundary objects, *The Academy of Management Journal*, 45 (5), 956–970.

Zerubavel, E. (1981) *Hidden Rhythms*. University of Chicago Press.

Zigurs, I., and Buckland, B. (1998) A theory of task/technology fit and group support systems effectiveness, *MISQuarterly*, 313–334.

Part V

RECENT EMPIRICAL FINDINGS THAT
SUPPORT THEORIES AND VIEWS

16

The Bradford Studies: Decision Making and Implementation Processes and Performance

Susan Miller

Research and Researchers – A Brief Overview

The Bradford Studies is one of the world's longest running decision-making research programmes. Beginning in the 1970s and spanning over 30 years it continues through to the present day. Although, as its name suggests, it has been centred on the University of Bradford in the UK its researchers have come from many other universities and not all are British, and while the programme began by exploring decision making it has subsequently branched out, exploring how decisions are implemented, their success, and how decision making differs across cultures.

To tell the story of the research is also to tell the history of the research team and this itself is something of a saga, for in many ways the Bradford Studies has been a tale of personal commitment and dogged tenacity in times of insecurity and uncertainty. It is a chronicle of long-term persistence in the face of unpredictable short-term funding.

The research was spearheaded by David Hickson, working closely with Richard Butler and David Wilson, but the core projects have been shaped by other key researchers including Graham Astley, Runo Axelsson, David Cray, Geoff Mallory, and myself, and at least six others, Carlos Arruda Oliveira, Graham Kenny, Les Davies, Richard Pike, Suzana Rodrigues, and John Sharp, have developed projects stemming from the focal research.

The story begins with David Hickson, who came to Bradford as a Professor in 1970 from the University of Alberta where he had been working for two years with Bob Hinings, Hans Pennings, and others on understanding power in organizations. Prior to this David had been part of the Aston group based at the Birmingham College of Advanced Technology, later to become Aston University in the UK, working

Handbook of Decision Making. Edited by Paul C. Nutt and David C. Wilson
© 2010 John Wiley & Sons, Ltd

with Derek Pugh and colleagues on the measurement and explanation of organizational structure. Together he and Richard Butler, who returned to the UK from the US in 1973, led the first project in what was eventually to become a programme of research.

As David noted (Hickson, 1988) much of the work that was to give rise to the Bradford Studies was carried out in a climate of scarcity with insecure and often insufficient funding. While the research team did attract monies from the UK Social Science Research Council (the forerunner of the Economic and Social Research Council) and these were of course welcome, general economic straitening caused by the oil price increases of the 1970s meant that UK research had to be seen to have fairly direct and immediate pay-offs. Small grants were provided for short periods which meant that, on occasion, staff working on a contractual basis worked with an uncertain future and, occasionally, worked for nothing. In this climate the requirement to submit a stream of funding applications before ideas were sufficiently advanced to be convincing (and thus capable of attracting more long-term support) was challenging. As the researchers remarked in the book of this first study, *Top Decisions*, it was 'an uphill struggle to carry through large-scale, long-term research on small-scale, short–term grants' (1986: xi). Commitment, endurance, and dogged determination were all crucial to sustaining the research and fulfilling its promised potential.

In spite of these relatively unpropitious circumstances the work progressed, developing into a flourishing research programme, although in true incrementalist fashion the eventual direction and diversity were not planned at the outset. It began with an interest in exploring power and influence which, the team began to recognize, was manifested in decision-making processes. They noted that, while earlier theorists such as Barnard (1938), Cyert and March (1963), and Simon (1947) had provided an illuminating account of organizational decision making, there was still work to be done in conceptualizing decision-making processes, in seeing how far processes differed and finding explanations for difference. Is it the case that decisions are made in broadly similar ways or is every decision unique? If there are differences what explains these – is it, for example, the kind of organization or topic? These questions give a flavour of the kinds of debates that provided impetus for the research.

The focus of the Bradford Studies was on strategic rather than operational decisions and, while this distinction is relative – what is strategic to one organization might be operational to another – strategic here means something comparatively rare and novel, with widespread repercussions, which commits significant resources and set precedents for later decisions. In short strategic decisions are 'unusual, substantial, and all-pervading' (Hickson *et al.*, 1986: 28).

The first major study spanned approximately 10 years, from the mid 1970s to the mid 1980s and investigated 150 strategic decisions in 30 UK public and private sector organizations. Key findings were that strategic decision processes could be categorized as being either sporadic (informally spasmodic and protracted), fluid (steadily paced, formally channelled, and speedy), or constricted (narrowly channelled) (Hickson *et al.*, 1986: 117) and that the 'dual explanations' for why processes varied was due to the *complexity* of the problems and the *politicality* of the interests involved (Hickson *et al.*, 1986: 173). Following this, some work was done to examine cross-cultural differences in decision making, focusing particularly on Sweden, Brazil, and the US, while Richard Butler and colleagues (1991) pursued a study of one particular type of topic – investment decisions.

Rodrigues and Hickson (1995), using a separate data base, examined 53 decisions in eight UK organizations and identified factors that appeared to be related to the successfulness of the decisions while Miller's later work (1997) centred specifically on implementation and success. These studies, together with a generous offer of funding from the US Army Research Institute, provided the spur for another large project bringing together David Hickson, David Wilson, and myself to explore implementation. Following up 55 of the original 150 'Top Decisions' this study identified two ways of managing implementation so as to increase the chances of success. The first, labelled the Experience-based approach, is the more planned of the two; the second, labelled the Readiness-based approach, is more about prioritizing implementation and then 'learning by doing'. This research began in the mid early 1990s and continued through that decade. It should be mentioned that many of the earlier articles and chapters mentioned throughout can be found in a compilation text: *The Bradford Studies of Strategic Decision Making* (Hickson, Butler, and Wilson, 2001). Unfortunately the *Top Decisions* monograph is now out of print.

This chapter now explores this body of work in greater detail. It begins with the *Top Decisions* study and the various spin-off projects which focus on decision making. The next section covers the international comparative aspects of this work. We then turn to examine how decisions are implemented and the relationship with decision success. Understanding the trajectory of decisional processes through the deciding into the implementing allows for some interesting observations about the connections which hold these long-term activities together and this is reviewed in the section that follows. The final part of the chapter takes a more holistic overview of how this area of research relates to other contemporary issues in the field of strategy.

However, before we embark on this research journey it is necessary to take a short excursion to critically examine the concept of 'decision' as this is central to all that follows. While this text, of which this chapter is a part, is firmly about decision making it should be acknowledged that this concept is both controversial and contested, and that key debates have involved some of the protagonists mentioned above.

THE CONCEPT OF DECISION: A HELP OR A HINDRANCE?

The discussion centres on how far organizational members actually make decisions. Do they actively choose between alternative courses of action, or is the term 'decision' merely a post-hoc rationalization used to describe actions that have occurred as a response to events? Are decisions deliberated and deliberate, or are they simply a sense-making construct applied to a collection of loosely connected and sometimes serendipitous behaviours that emerge over time? Mintzberg and Waters (1990) argued in the journal *Organization Studies* (OS) that the concept of decision is unhelpful. Decisions in organizations are often hard to identify and track, actions often occur without decisions having been taken, and firms can be pushed into activity by environmental demands. They also pointed to situations where decisions are taken by organizational elites but action is either subverted or blocked by others so that decisions are stalled. From their own work in decision making and strategy they come to the view that an emphasis on decision as a commitment to action is misplaced and underplays the way in which intentions are reshaped, elaborated, and defined through complex interactive processes over time. Thus the term decision is an artificial construct which gets in the way of understanding behaviour and the ways that strategies emerge.

David Hickson was Editor-in-Chief of OS at the time and he invited other contributors to comment. Thus Richard Butler (1990) maintained that, while Mintzberg and Waters raised some concerns, these could be accommodated within existing theory. So, for example, decision research recognizes that the locus of decision making can be diffuse making it hard to pinpoint exactly where a decision is made, the link between a decision and action (or inaction) is about decision implementation, and action without a decision is a possibility which March and Simon's (1958) notion of programmed decisions explicitly recognizes. The other contributor, Andrew Pettigrew (1990), was somewhat more sympathetic to the underlying concerns of Mintzberg and Waters. In emphasizing the importance of both content and context in understanding how change occurs, Pettigrew mooted that concentration on a decision episode limits understanding of the dynamic and continuous processes that shape events and actions in organizations and urges attention to the interconnections of the past, present, and future, as history and expectations impact on current activity. Interestingly, Pettigrew's views anticipate later work by Hickson and his colleagues on the connectedness between deciding and implementing (see later in this chapter).

However there remains the troublesome question of level of analysis. Both Mintzberg and Waters and Pettigrew weave between decisions and strategies and, while the call to focus on the dynamics of process is well made, the unavoidable practicalities of research demand that ongoing temporal processes are delimited for analytical purposes. No researcher, or decision maker, can follow everything, everywhere through to an indefinable 'end'. As with historians, organizational researchers must perforce be selective. Overall, in terms of the general utility of the concept, managers used the term unproblematically, and the Bradford team took the view that a focus on processes which actors engage in when they believe they are making decisions was still a useful way of understanding some aspects of organizational behaviour. Nonetheless these concerns rumble on and will be returned to in the final section when we assess the contribution of the Bradford Studies in relation to contemporary themes and debates.

Making Top Decisions

The key contribution of the Bradford Studies is the identification of varying types of decision-making process and an explanation for this variation. Analysing something as seemingly amorphous and ephemeral as a decision-making process is something of an achievement in itself. For many writers decision making is a somewhat riotous and disordered game, played out in a chaotic arena and ruled by power-play. Hickson depicts this scenario colourfully:

> Boundaries are elastic, the field is bumpy, and the number of teams in play fluctuates. They disagree as to where the ends of the field are, but eventually 'one team or coalition of teams pushes its way through holding the ball to where it says the end is' (Hickson *et al.*, 1986). This is a game in which the heavier or better protected players have a greater chance of shaping what is going on and where it is going to. The shape of the ball itself can be changed. (Hickson, 1987: 166)

A key consideration for the Bradford team was therefore to track and analyse process. Since process is movement and movement is ongoing, one of the first issues was to select a meaningful time-span for analysis, not straightforward given the above discussion about whether a decision episode imposes artificial 'start' and 'stop' points. Fully recognizing that there are no finite beginning and end points to these long-term, winding developments the researchers studied decisions from the 'first recalled deliberate action which begins movement towards a decision' to when the approved choice is authorized (Hickson *et al.*, 1986: 100). This allowed for most of the gestational pre-decision deliberations to be encompassed as well as the major activities at the heart of the process (such as gathering and making sense of information, having discussions, and holding meetings) but gave an identifiable close to the research.

Both organizations and decisions were selected to give as wide and diverse a collection of cases as time and resources would allow. One hundred and fifty decisions covering a variety of topics (for example internal restructurings, new product and service developments, company mergers, and building of new plant and premises) were studied in 30 UK organizations (including public and private sectors firms in manufacturing and service industries); five decisions in each. Data were collected by interviews lasting several hours with managers and administrators who had been personally involved. Six of the cases were studied in particular detail and three of these were followed in real time as the decision unfolded. The informants provided information about what had happened, which departments were involved, which interests were influential, and provided a narrative account of the main events and the way the process unfolded.

Several hundred informants were interviewed during the research, not including the many that were called upon during interviews to corroborate or provide additional material. More still participated in the intensive case studies carried out in six of the organizations. Their stories, together with secondary data, provided the substantial data base from which the findings were drawn.

As analysis progressed features of decision making emerged to form the basis for case comparison. These coalesced around two factors: the complexity of the problem or issue giving rise to the decision and the political behaviour of those interests implicated in the making of it. Together these two factors, 'complexity' and 'politicality', provided a dual explanation for process variation. Each is now elaborated.

Problems and complexity

Previous theorists had already noted the challenges provided by the multifaceted nature of many decisions. Simon's (1947) notion of 'satisficing' refers to the less than optimal choices which can result when making nonprogrammed decisions due to decision makers' limited cognitive capacities and lack of time and energy. In these situations comprehensive searches and detailed evaluation of alternatives are echewed in favour of circumscribed and more cursory examinations to find a solution which is good enough and will suffice. Similarly Cyert and March (1963) observed that 'simple-minded search' was likely when facing complex organizational realities.

Data from the Bradford Studies allowed the team to develop these ideas by distinguishing the different causes of complexity and showing how they shaped deciding. The source of complexity lies in the rarity, consequentiality, precursiveness, and involvements of what is being decided. That is, the frequency with which similar decisions occur (*rarity*); the radical, serious, widespread, and long-term nature of the consequences (*consequentiality*); the degree to which the decision sets parameters which constrain decisions that follow (*precursiveness*); and the more interests that get involved (*involvements*). Together these give rise to decisions which are more or less complex in nature, as experienced by those involved in making them. Yet these involvements also prelude the second factor, politicality, since those involved may have different views and agendas.

Interests and politicality

Politicality arises from *cleavage*, the fact that organizations are structured around a division of labour that differentially allocates tasks, authority, and power to particular groups or 'interests'. Thus differences between interests are built into the fabric of the organization and while interests get drawn into the making of decisions, they do not always share the same goals, leading to conflict and *contention*. Politicality emanating from cleavage and contention emphasizes the political nature of organizational decision making, reinforcing Pettigrew's (1973) portrayal and underlining why Lindblom's (1959) cautious incrementalism is needed to build support in politically charged environments.

The Bradford researchers examined all interests, classifying them into 14 types based on their primary role in the organization, noting that while interests are relatively constant across decisions, their objectives may change from one to the next. This makes for a shifting field of action as coalitions change from one decision to another. While the degree of involvement may influence complexity, involvement does not necessarily equate with influence. So politicality is about who exerts influence during decision making; in this sense it is power in action. Prominent among the influential internal interests are production (and the equivalent service delivery functions in nonmanufacturing organizations) and marketing whereas personnel and purchasing tend to be the least influential, a point returned to in the section on Connecting Deciding and Implementing.

As an aside, it should be noted that the team found that the outcome of almost a third of these decisions was fairly well known in advance – not exactly a foregone conclusion, but it was apparent to many involved that some avenues had already been closed off. Even so, the process was still gone through, to reaffirm this, or to convince others remaining to be won over, or to check prior assumptions. This *quasi-decision making* is clearly a normal practice in organizations.

Three types of process

Varying combinations of politicality and complexity lead to variations in the course that decision making takes. As Hickson and his colleagues remark, the 'process of making a decision is a response to the problems and interests inherent in the matter for decision, a response to their complexity and politicality' (Hickson *et al.*, 1986: 96). Conceptualizing 'process' is about describing movement, as the matter for decision progresses through the organization, and through time, given impetus by activities such as holding meetings, gathering and analysing information, and engaging in informal discussions. The duration of the process varies (in this study the shortest was around a month, the longest four years, and the mean around a year), which is partly a function of impediments and delays. Hence one key element of process is its *discontinuity*. Another is its *dispersion*, that is, the degree to which decision-making is spread throughout the managerial cadre. The three types of process identified are *sporadic*, *fluid*, and *constricted* and each varies around these two dimensions of discontinuity and dispersion.

Relative to the other two, *sporadic* decisions are characterized by more interrupting delays, with information of uneven quality coming from a wider range of sources, much informal interaction with room for some negotiation, and a longer process time. Thus sporadic decisions are high on discontinuity and relatively widely dispersed. They tend to be authorized at the highest level.

Fluid processes are almost the opposite. While there is scope for negotiation and the decision is still fairly widely dispersed, the process is formally channelled through committees, working parties, and project teams. It is subject to less disruption and delaying discontinuity, so tends to be speedy, but is also authorized at the highest level.

Finally, *constricted* processes have more delays than fluid processes, but not as many as sporadic ones. Their key characteristic is that they are narrowly channelled within the organization. While they do draw on information from a wide range of sources, this information is readily to hand, does not require any special investigations outside of the organization, does not give much scope for negotiation, does not feature much on the formal committee agendas, and does not create much informal activity. Around mid-way between sporadic and fluid processes in terms of discontinuity, constricted processes are much lower than either in terms of dispersion. They are usually made below the highest level of authorization.

Revealing these three types of process is not the whole story however. The team were also able to show what kinds of matter being decided – each being a combination of complexity and politicality – led to which process. Once again, there are three types: *vortex*, *tractable*, and *familiar*.

Vortex matters are controversial and suck in many throughout the top management levels in a whirlwind of activity. They are the most complex and political of all subjects and tend to be processed in sporadic ways. *Tractable* matters are less complex and the least political and tend to lead to fluid processes. Finally, *familiar* subjects are the least complex and of middling politicality (less political than a vortex decision but more so than a tractable one) and are likely to be processed in constricted ways.

Hence the Bradford Studies are able to both describe process and posit explanations in terms of the nature of what is being decided that account for it. Managers need to be aware that when they engage in making strategic choices they will have to contend with both the complexity of the task and nature of interactions generated by the interests brought in.

Organizations and decisions

About one third of the 150 decisions was made in each of the processes identified – sporadic, fluid, and constricted; each type can occur in any one organization and was found in all types of organizations studied. So there was so such thing as an organization which made all its decisions in, say, a fluid way, neither was it the case that, say, all manufacturers made decisions in a constricted way. In summary, all three types of process can be found in public and private firms and in manufacturing and services sectors. That said, there are some general tendencies. The research established that both manufacturing and public sector firms lean towards more sporadic processes, while services and privately owned organizations tend toward fluid ones, though the relatively small number of firms in each category necessitates a cautious interpretation here. In terms of size, smaller firms display a tendency towards marginally more speedy decisions but the difference is small and the range wide. An important point to note is that speedy decisions do not necessarily equate with *successful* ones, as later research was to demonstrate.

While on the subject of organizations, it is worth mentioning the separate study carried out in the voluntary sector by David Wilson and Richard Butler (Wilson and Butler, 1986). Their examination of four leading UK voluntary organizations operating in child welfare, public transport, emergency sea rescue, and disaster relief supported a resource dependence interpretation, finding that their strategies were shaped by their organizational dependencies. Thus, while voluntary organizations need to work with a range of agents and funding providers, in many ways the shaping of decision making is not so different to other types of organizations.

In term of types of decisions, Richard Butler looked at a different set of cases with a different group of Bradford colleagues (Butler *et al.*, 1991). In their examination of capital investment decisions they also found processes that were characterized by political behaviour and uncertainty. Interestingly though, they went further by studying the effectiveness of these decisions, as perceived by those involved. This pre-empts the next stage of research using the original *Top Decisions* data base which, as further resources became available, provided a spur to following up some of the cases to find out what happened next, and is discussed later in this chapter.

In the final analysis, in answer to the fundamental question of what really accounts for process – the type of organization, sector, or topic or some other factor, the Bradford Studies researchers were clear that it was the nature of what was being decided – in terms of its complexity and politicality – that was key. In their words: 'The matter for decision matters most' (Hickson et al., 1986: 248), meaning that the way the matter was perceived and thus who it drew in and how widely views differed fashioned the kind of course that followed.

CROSS-CULTURAL DIFFERENCES IN DECISION-MAKING

While the *Top Decisions* cases were all in UK organizations, the findings fostered an interest in how far processes might vary across national cultures. One way to examine this is by contrasting local companies with comparable foreign-owned subsidiaries in the same country. The Bradford Studies contained two American-owned manufacturing subsidiaries with wholly British managements, one owned by a chemical/food producer and making chemicals and paints, the other owned by an engineering group and fabricating precision tools. These were compared with two UK subsidiaries, one owned by an engineering group and manufacturing building contractors' equipment and the other owned by an engineering/textile group and making automotive components (Mallory *et al.*, 1983). Since five decisions were studied in each organization this made a set of 20 cases for comparison. Decisions concerned products and plant, marketing, business planning, and personnel. In fact the differences were not extensive and the authors did not find that American ownership spurred British managements into the 'more risk-taking mode of proactive, short term' decision-making (Mallory *et al.*, 1983: 201) that some scenarios had conjured. What they did find was that the British owned companies utilized more formal forms of interaction such as standing committees rather than the less formal working groups favoured by the US subsidiaries (though the British companies were larger so size may also come into this), although the British companies were also more likely to follow standardized procedures (and thus authority was formally institutionalized into the process through these committees). However, perhaps the most stark finding was that the UK decisions took about twice as long to make as the American ones (a mean of around 14 months in the former and seven in the latter). Furthermore, the UK decisions were more likely to have a recognizable gestation period before the subject finally got onto the agenda as a matter for decision, indicating that British companies were more likely to contemplate things for months or years before moving on it.

Further work compared the Bradford Studies with a parallel study of 50 strategic decisions in 10 Swedish organizations by Runo Axelsson, a member of the original Bradford team (Axelsson *et al.*, 1991). The key findings were that the Swedish style of decision making was marked by 'higher levels of influence and conviction, but lower levels of contention' (Axelsson *et al.*, 1991: 365). The Swedes tend to carry out considerable searches for information and emphasize negotiation with a restricted group of participants. In contrast, British decision making involves more parties who have only a marginal interest in the outcome, monitoring what goes on but having little influence on it. Overall there is less effort expended in making the

British decisions, but this is concentrated in fewer hands. The Swedish style leads to much slower processes with gestation and decision-making processes taking around twice as long (although the differences may have been exaggerated by the number of decisions about making large investments in technology).

The final study in this area concerned decision making in Brazil. In an intriguing comparative study Carolos Alberto Arruda interviewed six English-speaking Brazilian managers working in England and six English (Portuguese-speaking) managers who had worked in Brazil and/or with Brazilian managers (Arruda and Hickson, 1996). These interviews, together with sociological, literary, and historical sources, were used to generate cultural profiles of each culture. Relative to the English, Brazilian culture is high power distance, showing a medium tendency to manage uncertainty by the use of formalized rules (Hofstede, 1991), though with an emphasis on immediacy illustrated by a stronger risk-taking capacity. Brazilian society is peaceful and nonaggressive and is based on strong interpersonal links. The broad traits of English culture were lower power distance and uncertainty avoidance, conservatism, viewing change as a more gradual rather than an abrupt process, more individualistic, and with greater personal competitiveness.

This was followed by a study of 40 cases of managerial decision making, 20 Brazilian and 20 English, using broadly the same variables as those used in the Bradford Studies, but with some variation to take account of the Brazilian setting. While Brazilian and English strategic decision-making processes have some areas in common – for example, the process circles around the top elite and there is informal negotiation and interaction about the matter in both cultures – there are some marked differences. One is that the English processes were less authority-focused and more involving, whereas in the Brazilian cases decision making orbits around the very top echelons, dominated by the chief executive – as befits a higher power distance culture.

But perhaps the most marked difference is that of time. Whereas in the English sample the mean mirrored that found in the Bradford Studies, i.e. around one year, in the Brazilian sample the mean was only eight months. What is particularly interesting in this research is how each group of managers perceived themselves and the other group. So, for example, the Brazilians viewed their style as appropriate, even innovative, whereas the English saw this as daring, even risky. In contrast the English conservatism was seen by English managers as careful while the same characteristic was perceived as over-cautious by the Brazilians. How fascinating then that the speedier Brazilian managers felt they had enough time, but the slower English managers wanted more. In other words: '... the immediatists [the Brazilians] felt their shorter time had been enough, the gradualists [the English] felt their longer time had rushed them!' (Arruda and Hickson, 1996: 194).

SUCCESSFUL DECISION MAKING – IMPLEMENTATION AND OUTCOMES

The Bradford Studies accomplished a great deal in fleshing out the characteristics of organizational decision making, but most research raises new questions as well as addressing existing ones. The compelling unanswered question raised by these studies is what happened next once decisions were arrived at. How successful were they? What about their implementation and outcomes? Another Brazilian researcher, Suzana Braga Rodrigues, using a new UK sample not a Brazilian one, provided the beginnings of an answer to the issue of decision success (Rodrigues and Hickson, 1995). The defining of success is itself not an easy task, for while commercial success can be judged in numerical ways, for example by profitability or growth in market share, this cannot be easily extrapolated to public or third sector organizations where outcomes may not have such a readily quantifiable metric. Even in business firms a new product launch may have more quantifiable outcomes than, say, a reorganization. The challenge is therefore to find indicators of success that are generic to all kinds of organizations and types of decisions.

Analysing 53 cases in five business firms and three nonbusiness organizations (two universities and a District of the National Health Service), Rodrigues' key aspects of success concerned how far the decision realized the opportunities which sparked it off and whether it gave rise to unforeseen propitious or unpropitious situations. She found that success (as gauged by those involved) in each sector was not evaluated in the same way. In business firms success depended on there being sufficient pertinent knowledge – and people, finance, and time to implement the decision – while decisions in nonbusiness firms were deemed a success when the right people got involved without too much top-level interference.

My own initial work in this area followed a similar path, setting out to discover the factors that appeared to lead to decision success (Miller, 1997). The focus was primarily on implementation and explored 11 cases in six organizations to understand what factors appeared to enhance the chances of a successful outcome. Again the dependent variable of success was conceptualized in such a way as to include the achievement of objectives in a timely and acceptable way. A number of factors emerged from intensive case analysis which appeared to separate into two groupings. The first, labelled the 'Enablers', described those factors that go some way toward helping, such as having relevant experience, making the decision a priority, and having sufficient resources. However, the second grouping, labelled the 'Realizers' seemed to be needed to achieve comprehensive success. These included having backing for what was intended, being able to assess the outcomes and specify what had to be done to achieve them, and having a receptive climate.

This was the immediate forerunner to the final (so far!) extension of the Bradford Studies. Armed with some understanding about the kinds of things that might be important during implementation and, very importantly, with a generous and unexpected offer of funding from the US Army Research Institute, it was time to add new data to the existing data base, offer an account of what happened next, and so add a new chapter to the Bradford Studies.

The team this time was David Hickson, David Wilson, and myself and together we revisited 55 of the original 150 cases of decision making in 14 organizations – just over one third of the original cases in just under half of the organizations (Miller et al., 2004; Hickson et al., 2003). Since implementation was the focus of this research the key criteria for case selection were that they had to involve the actioning of something (rather than decisions not to proceed) and there had to be accessible informants who had been centrally involved in both making and implementing.

In terms of organizations, it was important that they still existed in the same form (that is, not merged or taken over) and that the proportion of public/private, manufacturing/service companies should be similar. These conditions resulted in new research being carried out on the full number of five cases in each of three organizations, four cases in seven others, and three in each of the final four organizations. Altogether six manufacturers, five services companies (all privately owned), and three state-owned services were studied, and all topics covered in the original study were covered here.

A similar methodology was employed as in the *Top Decisions* study. Interviews lasting about two hours were carried out with informants who provided an undirected narrative account of what was done to put the decision into effect, and then responded to open-ended questions which probed those accounts further, providing information about the perceived objectives of the decision, who was involved and their influence, the resourcing, and the reasons for success, or the lack of it, and so on.

Success here is defined as 'achievement'. But in this study it was recognized that this may fluctuate over time since some decisions start well and fade while others begin poorly but improve over time. Thus the operationalization of achievement incorporates this dynamic aspect, being defined as 'the extent to which the performance over time of what was done was as expected or better'. Factors explaining this success were found to fall into two groupings, each constituting a different approach to the management of implementation which, if followed, seemed likely to enhance the chances of high achievement. The first, labelled the Experience-based approach is predicated on there being relevant experience available. This can be either already in the organization, or it can be brought in through new appointments or the use of consultants. This enables those involved to identify the objectives, specify what has to be done to achieve them, and provide appropriate resources. This is the more planned approach of the two. However this does not guarantee success; it leads to a state of acceptability which means those involved give implementation their support. This is an important point, as we emphasize:

> Planning, of itself, does not lead directly to success. It must achieve a state of accord. Only if people are comfortable with what is going on and so are generally supportive, or at least do not oppose it, will planned implementation have the most favourable chance of moving forward to success. Here, perhaps, is the reason why the voluminous planning literature has consistently led to such inconsistent conclusions about the effect of planning on performance ... (Hickson *et al.*, 2003: 1823).

The second approach is labelled the Readiness-based approach and may be thought to occur when the climate is receptive but experience relatively lacking. Thus it is predicated upon there being a conducive climate for what is being proposed so that managers can ensure that structure and authority are not obstacles and implementation is accorded priority so that it is given time and energy and stays on the managerial agenda, rather than being lost among competing demands for attention. This is less about planning implementation, and more about being predisposed to get things started, prioritizing this and learning by doing.

While both approaches used singly can lead to high levels of success, this is riskier than doing both together. Having some experience relevant to what has to be done and having a receptive climate is the surest way to success. In the study, cases which used a clear full dual approach had an over 80 % chance of achieving high levels of success.

CONNECTING DECIDING AND IMPLEMENTATION

Tracking these Top Decisions through their implementation and long-term success means that not only do we know something about how the decision is made, how is carried out, and to what extent it achieves its objectives, but it also means that the whole process can be seen in its entirety and its development analysed longitudinally.

One especially revealing area proved to be an analysis of which interests were involved throughout the process and which of these were most influential (Miller *et al.*, 2008). Detailed examination of the data across both the *Top Decisions* study and the subsequent extension of this looking at implementation highlighted those central interests who were most often involved and most influential, and a peripheral group least involved and least influential. Most importantly, it found that while there was some movement between the deciding and the doing there was remarkable consistency in the core grouping which was both highly involved and influential during the making of the decision and also during its implementation. This group comprised the CEO (refuting the usual view that while chief executives might engage with top management decisions, they rarely see things through), production (or equivalent functions in service organizations), and marketing. While finance and suppliers (the latter the only external interest of any importance) featured strongly in decision making, their influence usually waned once the decision was made. Interests such as research and development, purchasing, and shareholders were less likely to be involved in making the decision, although they could be influential when brought in, but only research and development retained influence during implementation. Interests performing a liaison function (such as those departments dealing with customer queries and complaints) and the occasional competitor were the opposite, less likely to be involved in both decision making and implementation but more influential during the latter stages when the decision is put into effect. Finally the personnel function, together with external interests such as customers, government, and unions were both least often involved and least influential throughout.

This offers a fascinating picture of who is enmeshed in these long-term organizational practices and who wields the real power. More than this it may help answer questions about how continuity is facilitated in organizational settings. While garbage can models posit a decoupling of means and ends and more recent views of strategy have emphasized the transitory and fragmentary nature of much of organizational life, this study counters this somewhat by showing that the continued

presence and active involvement of the CEO, marketing, and those involved in producing goods or services ensure some continuity over time, so that what is decided
ought to happen has some chance of actually being realized as intended.

RELOCATING THE BRADFORD STUDIES

We have already hinted at the ways in which this large body of work ties to existing
thinking in the area and to current research in the contiguous domain of strategic
management. This section situates the Bradford Studies in these discourses by examining the implications of this work for other scholars in the field. It also looks at
the lessons for practitioners.

One of the achievements of this corpus of work is to contribute towards a better
understanding of 'process' in the realm of strategic decision making. Processes are
dynamic, and often transient and ephemeral. They are hard to define and distinguish, fleeting instances of movement between an unspecified past and an indeterminate future. The Bradford Studies provides concepts to help build a language
of process – fluid, formally channelled, speedy, and so on. These concepts are the
building blocks which enable different types of process to be identified, such as sporadic, fluid, and constricted. More than this, the Bradford team found explanations
for why processes differed. Differentiation occurs due to variations in the degree of
politicality and complexity in the matter for decision. Controversial and complex
vortex matters tend to be processed in sporadic ways, less complex and least political tractable matters tend to be processed in fluid ways, while familiar matters which
are the least complex and of mid-level politicality follow constricted ways.

Following decisions through into implementation throws up two ways of enhancing the chances of a successful outcome, either by the more planned Experienced-
based or the more receptive and prioritized Readiness-based approach, though using both together improves the chances even more.

What of the implications for practitioners? If you have sufficient familiarity with
what has to be done, or recognize the knowledge gap and can fill it by bringing
in other people or using consultants, you can embark on the more planned way
of implementing. If not, you need to ensure that you create a receptive climate so
those involved are willing to learn by doing. If you can plan and prioritize, so much
the better. Managers therefore need a variety of skills. A varied repertoire, employed
flexibly, is required as each decision will be different. Thus, for example, creating a
favourable context may work in one instance but this will have to be re-thought to
match what is required in the next.

And who are these managers? The ones most likely to be involved and have influence over the deciding and the implementing are those in the marketing area and
those in producing goods or services, not forgetting the important role of the CEO
throughout. Finance is important, particularly at the deciding stage, as are suppliers, but their influence fades during implementation. These interests connect the
deciding with the doing, helping to bring some coherence to these long-term processes. They are the key makers and shapers of strategic decisions in these organizational arenas.

Recent work in the field of strategic management has placed great emphasis on the micro processes of strategizing (Johnson *et al.*, 2003) through which managers shape the structural context and the interpretations of organizational members (Jarzabkowski, 2008,). While there may be some disagreement in this field about the fundamental ontological status of 'decision' as we saw at the opening of this chapter, and the consequent methodological implications (Balogun *et al.*, 2003), the Bradford Studies too found that managers' key roles concerned attending to structural conditions and shaping how receptively organizational members viewed what was being proposed.

In the final analysis, as in much research, the Bradford Studies offer a version of strategic processes that can be corroborated, contested, or countermanded. That further work has continued to the present day demonstrates what a rich seam was revealed by the original research team.

References

Arruda, C.A., and Hickson, D.J. (1996) 'Sensitivity to societal culture in managerial decision-making: An Anglo-Brazilian comparison,' in P. Joynt and M. Warner (eds) *Managing across Cultures: Issues and Perspectives*. International Thomson Business Press: London, 179–201.

Axelsson, R., Cray, D., Mallory, G.R., and Wilson, D.C. (1991) Decision style in British and Swedish organizations: A comparative examination of strategic decision making, *British Journal of Management* 2, 67–79.

Balogun, J., Huff, A.S., and Johnson, P. (2003) Three responses to the methodological challenges of studying strategizing, *Journal of Management Studies* 40, 197–224.

Barnard, C. (1938) *The Functions of the Executive*. Cambridge, MA: Harvard University Press.

Butler, R. (1990) Studying deciding: an exchange of views, *Organization Studies*, 11 (1), 1–16.

Butler, R., Davies, L., Pike, R., and Sharp, J. (1991) Strategic investment decision-making: Complexities, politics and processes *Journal of Management Studies*, 28, 395–415.

Cyert, R., and March, J.K. (1963) *A Behavioral Theory of the Firm*. Englewood Cliffs, NJ: Prentice-Hall.

Hickson, D.J. (1987) Decision-making at the top of organizations, *Annual Review of Sociology* 13, 165–192.

Hickson, D.J. (1988) 'Ruminations on munificence and scarcity in research,' in A. Bryman (ed.) *Doing Research in Organizations*. London: Routledge, 136–150.

Hickson, D.J., Butler, R.J., Cray, D., Mallory, G.R., and Wilson, D.C. (1986) *Top decisions: Strategic Decision Making in Organizations*. Oxford: Blackwell and San Francisco: Jossey-Bass.

Hickson, D.J., Butler, R.J., and Wilson, D.C. (2001) *The Bradford Studies of Strategic Decision Making. Classic Research in Management*. England: Ashgate.

Hickson, D.J., Miller, S.J., and Wilson, D.C. (2003) Planned or prioritized? Two options in managing the implementation of strategic decisions, *Journal of Management Studies*, 40 (7), 1803–1836.

Hofstede, G. (1991) *Cultures and Organizations: Software of the Mind*. London: McGraw-Hill.

Jarzabkowski, P. (2008) Shaping strategy as a structuration process, *Academy of Management Journal*, 52 (4), 621–650.

Johnson, G., Melin L., and Whittington, R. (2003) Micro strategy and strategizing: Towards an activity-based view, *Journal of Management Studies*, 40 (1), 3–22.

Lindblom, C.E. (1959) The science of 'muddling through', *Public Administration Review*, 19 (2), 79–88.

Mallory, G.R., Butler R.J., Cray, D., Hickson, D.J., and Wilson, D.C. (1983) Implanted decision-making: American owned firms in Britain, *Journal of Management Studies,* 20 (2), 191–211.

March, J.G., and Simon, H.A. (1958) *Organizations.* New York: John Wiley and Sons, Inc.

Miller, S. (1997) Implementing strategic decisions: Four key success factors, *Organization Studies,* 18 (4), 577–602.

Miller, S., Wilson D.C., and Hickson, D.J. (2004) Beyond planning: Strategies for successfully implementing strategic decisions, *Long Range Planning,* 37 (3), 201–218.

Miller, S., Hickson, D.C., and Hickson, D.J. (2008) From strategy to action: Involvement and influence in top level decisions, *Long Range Planning,* 41, 606–628.

Mintzberg, H., and Waters, J. (1990) Studying deciding: An exchange of views, *Organization Studies,* 11 (1), 1–16.

Pettigrew, A.M. (1973) *The Politics of Organizational Decision-making.* London: Tavistock.

Pettigrew, A. (1990) Studying deciding: An exchange of views, *Organization Studies,* 11 (1), 1–16.

Rodrigues, S., and Hickson, D.J. (1995) Success in decision making: Different organizations, differing reasons for success, *Journal of Management Studies,* 32, 655–678.

Simon, H.A. (1947) *Administrative Behaviour.* New York: Free Press.

Wilson, D.C., and Butler, R.J. (1986) Voluntary organizations in action: Strategy in the voluntary sector, *Journal of Management Studies,* 23, 519–542.

17

Comparing the Merits of Decision-making Processes

PAUL C. NUTT

INTRODUCTION[1]

Decision makers (DMs) make decisions by following a process made up of a series of steps and tactics to carry out each step (Nutt, 2002; 2008). DMs work through the process steps to uncover what to do and why. Several kinds of processes can be found in the literature, bracketed by what decision makers do and what researchers believe they should do (e.g. Harrison and Phillips, 1991; Eisenhardt and Zbaracki, 1992; Nutt, 1989; Daft, 1995). This study examines how four such processes differ and their success, measured by the extent of decision adoption, value, and duration for each process type. In addition, the study examines the tactical options that DMs use to carry out process steps, reporting how the available tactics improve or diminish success prospects for each process type.

Descriptive/interpretive research finds that DMs cater to the interests of powerful stakeholders (Cyert and March, 1963; Laroche, 1995) by looking for ready-made solutions they can support (Carter, 1971; Cosier and Schwenk, 1990). A ready-made solution allows the DM to visualize a course of action and its ramifications before making commitments (Wildavsky, 1979; Mintzberg and Westley, 2001). This process is called 'idea imposition' because an idea prompts action. Prescriptions found in the literature suggest a very different process. Decision makers are called upon to gather intelligence about needs, specify desired results, uncover options, evaluate options according to their benefits, and implement by working with interest groups and their perceptions to install the most beneficial option (Eisenhardt and Zbaracki, 1992; Harrison and Phillips; 1991; Daft, 1995). This process will be called 'discovery' because learning about possibilities is stressed. Circumstances may arise that force a DM to alter a process. If the idea touted as an idea imposition proves to be ill-advised, DMs may shift to a 'redevelopment' process to find a replacement.

Handbook of Decision Making. Edited by Paul C. Nutt and David C. Wilson
© 2010 John Wiley & Sons, Ltd

A discovery process may be abandoned if an opportunity is spotted that seems beneficial (March, 1994).

My goal is to identify the frequency of use and the success of discovery, idea imposition, emergent opportunity, and redevelopment, controlling for context and content (decision type). Such a study poses formidable challenges. Process, success, content, and context must be conceptualized and measured. To do so calls for documenting organizational decisions with cases, like those offered by Snyder and Page (1958), Cyert and March (1963), Soelberg (1967), Witte (1972), Allison (1971), McKie (1973), Mintzberg *et al.* (1976), Nutt (1984), Hickson *et al.* (1986), and Numagami (1998). This has prompted simplifications that limit the number of decisions (e.g. Bower, 1970), consider select process steps (Dean and Sharfman, 1996), ignore outcomes (Mintzberg *et al.*, 1976), or use process features, such as the extent of interaction or information sources, as outcomes (Hickson *et al.*, 1986). My research set out to document *how* decisions are made, addressing some of the limitations in past efforts. A data base of 176 decisions was collected to document process steps, success, content, and context. To make such research manageable, a single process step was investigated in each published paper, as summarized in Table 17.1. In this study, the steps examined in past studies are assembled into *processes*. Two hundred and two *additional* decisions were examined to identify decisions that used a discovery, idea imposition, redevelopment, or emergent opportunity process. This was done by matching the steps and step sequences followed by DMs in making these decisions to those called for by the four process types.

The study reports on the success of the four process types, controlling for context and content, to answer key process research questions. They include: Do decision makers use the four processes of interest, and do they modify them as suggested? If so, what is the frequency of use and success of each process type? Do the successful decisions suggest one way or many ways to sequence process steps? Which process steps have the greatest influence on success? How do the best practice tactics influence process success? To deal with this question, the study will explore how tactical options to collect intelligence, establish a direction, uncover alternatives, do evaluations, and implement a favored alternative influence process success. Questions include: Can best practice tactics create a best practice process? Finally, the study will consider whether the process types are more successful under particular conditions, calling for a contingency theory. Answers offer insights into an action theory for decision making that includes best practices and crucial contingencies.

DECISION MAKING

To study decision making, researchers select a unit of analysis and then identify factors for study (Bell *et al.*, 1998). Key factors have been action-taking approach, context, content (kinds of decisions), and outcome – the benefits realized (Ragagopalan *et al.*, 1998). The more astute investigators call for studies that examine decision making within an organization in which managers, facing an important concern or difficulty, take *action* to make choices that produce outcomes with immediate and downstream effects. How a DM takes action appears to influence the

TABLE 17.1 Tactics used in the process steps

Step/Tactic	Source/Assessment (success measures*)	Key Features	Illustration
Claim interpreted by: Needs	Nutt (1998a; 2007) More successful (CA: 68 % IA: 68 % R: good/ex. T: 6.7mo.)	Performance-driven, calling for better results after examining concerns.	Concerns in warehouse operations uncovered, identifying needs for better utilization.
Opportunities	Less successful (CA: 28% IA; 47 % R: good T: 6.2mo.)	Action-driven, calling for an idea drawn from a claim.	Claims made by stakeholders in an insurance agency called for purchase of new PCs.
Directions from: Ideas	Nutt (1993a;1992) Less successful (CA: 38 % SA; 56 % R:adq T:9mo.)	Infer reason for acting from the benefits implied by the idea.	Company develops a solar heat pump suggested by another firm.
Problems	Less successful (CA: 45 % SA; 54 % R: adq. T: 12mo.)	Infer solutions from a problem analysis to guide solution search.	The Ohio Department of Claims analyzes its claims backlog to find reasons for delays.
Objectives	More successful (CA: 66 % SA; 72 % R: good T: 8mo.)	Set a target indicating the hoped-for results to guide solution search.	Hospital identified a cost reduction target and authorized departments to find ways to cut cost that could meet the target.
Solutions found by:	Nutt (1993b; 2000)		

(Continued)

TABLE 17.1 (Continued)

Step/Tactic	Source/Assessment (success measures*)	Key Features	Illustration
Ideas	Less successful (CA: 41 % SA; 58 % R: adq T: 8,5mo.)	No search. (Impose a ready-made solution.)	A new sports arena was proposed by community leaders, calling attention to the economic benefits of an arena to local businesses.
Benchmarking	More successful (CA: 51 % SA; 63 % R: adq./good T: 7.5mo.)	Ideas found in the practices of others.	Materials management system redesign based on practices of competitor.
Solicitation	More successful (CA: 51 % SA; 63 % R: good T: 11.8mo.)	Ideas found in the bids submitted by vendors/consultants.	The DIA sent a 'request for proposal' to potential vendors of a baggage handling system.
Innovation	More successful (CA: 51 % SA; 63 % R: good T: 15.3mo.)	Design a custom-made solution.	Ford Pinto gas line protection 'flack suit' designed without reference to the remedies devised by others.
Evaluation by: Analysis	Nutt (1998b) More successful (CA: 64 % SA; 75 % R: good T: 9.6mo.)	Manipulate performance data found in archives, pilots, or mockups, creating summative information to prioritize options.	Cost–benefit analysis of computer aided design systems, using advertised features.

Bargaining	More successful (CA: 65 % SA; 74 % R: good T: 5.8mo.)	Group interprets data found in records, archives, or user views to prioritize options.	Stakeholders rank inventory control proposals after debating the merits of the proposals.
Subjective	Less successful (CA: 37 % SA; 65 % R: good/adq. T: 10mo.)	DM draws facts from experts, records, and experiences to support a favored choice.	Consultant brought in to demonstrate what works and why in support of new way to solicit customers at CompuServe.
Judgment	Less successful (CA: 36 % SA; 47 % R: adq T: 7.5mo.)	No public justification offered.	Prepare a purchase order to acquire a production planning system.
Implementation by: Persuasion	Nutt (1986;1998c) Less successful (CA: 49 % IA: 58 % R: adq./good T: 26mo.)	Call for adoption by citing the benefits that support a preferred option.	Head of an MIS department presents system upgrades and demonstrates how each could benefit key users by improving EDP department capacity.

(*Continued*)

TABLE 17.1 (*Continued*)

Step/Tactic	Source/Assessment (*success measures**)	Key Features	Illustration
Edict	Less successful (CA: 38 % IA; 50 % R: adq. T: 17mo.)	Install by drawing on power, indicating what people must do to comply.	Announce a new software package by sending employees a schedule that indicates how to use the package and when it will be available.
Participation	More successful (CA: 71 % IA; 85 % R: good T: 16mo.)	Delegate to a task force, indicating expected results.	Director of a state mental health department carries out a $ 150 million downsizing by having task forces set targets and make recommendations for cuts, with the understanding that all reasonable ideas would be adopted.
Intervention	More successful (CA: 100 % IA; 90 % R: ex T: 11mo.)	Document current performance; network to demonstrate performance gap; hold back until agreement about need to act emerges.	Show the stock out levels of competitors and how the practices found in a materials management system eliminate nearly all stock outs at reasonable costs.

* CA, completed adoption rate, IA, initial adoption, SA, sustained adoption, R, rating, T, time in months.

choices made and their benefits (Dean and Sharfman, 1996; Nutt, 2002). Context and content are also believed to influence choices and benefits (Hickson *et al.*, 1986; Bell *et al.*, 1998). Each is considered in the discussion that follows.

To deal with confounding, both decisions and choice opportunities (sorting alternatives) have been suggested as the *unit of analysis* (Bell *et al.*, 1998). Decisions are preferred because such an investigation considers the full spectrum of issues that can arise during decision making. The level of analysis is also a crucial consideration, which can be confounded with the unit of analysis. Confounding arises in several ways. Some studies include decisions that span several managerial levels (Bell *et al.*, 1998) or consider decisions made by CEOs, top management teams, middle managers, and department heads (Nutt, 2001c). Confounding also results when several related decisions are examined to capture a key organizational issue, such as the management of disasters (Weick, 2001) or a large-scale project (Cameron and Lavine, 2006). Decisions and organizations are confounded when multiple decisions are drawn from several organizations (e.g. Hickson *et al.*, 1986). To deal with confounding, factors must account for who is involved, the type of DM (e.g. CEOs), the link of decisions to projects or issues, and the identity of the organization in which each decision takes place.

Benefits identify decision results, and whether the results are justified given the cost, disruptions, and distractions to make it. Determining results requires documenting outcomes and measuring their effects (Hickson *et al.*, 1986; Nutt, 1986; Bell *et al.*, 1998; Papadakis and Barwise, 1998). These effects can take many forms. Bower (1970) argues that training is important. Others call for determining changes in people's behavior and interpretations (Bryson *et al.*, 1990), measuring process outcomes (timeliness, commitment, and learning), documenting features of action-taking, such as disruption and scope of negotiations (Hickson *et al.*, 1986), or developing indicators of success (Nutt, 2002).

Context specifies the environment in which a decision is made. Both internal and external environmental factors are believed to influence what is decided and how the decision is made (e.g. Thompson, 1967; Perrow, 1967; Bell *et al.*, 1998). Internal factors include surprise, confusion, and threat (March and Simon, 1958); organizational features, such as approaches to communication and control and resistance to change (e.g. Nutt, 2002); as well as decision importance (Bell *et al.*, 1998), complexity (Nutt, 1998), and uncertainty (Thompson, 1967). Decision-maker attributes such as the propensity to take risks, tolerance for ambiguity, creativity, decision style, intelligence, need for control, power, experience, education, and values have been suggested (Bell *et al.*, 1998). External factors include organizational differences, such as public or private (Nutt, 2004b), as well as prevailing economic conditions, given by interest rates and the like (Bell *et al.*, 1998). Researchers include contextual factors to test contingency arguments, which assert that context influences the choice and its outcome, as well as how a decision is made.

Content captures the type of decision. Many claim to study 'strategic' decisions, but define strategic quite differently. Some focus on the crucial but infrequent decisions made by top managers to select a core business that offers competitive advantage (e.g. Hitt *et al.*, 2003). In their seminal work, Mintzberg *et al* (1976) call a decision strategic if it has long-term effects, demands considerable resources, and sets precedents. This opens the door to a variety of somewhat smaller scale decisions. The Bradford studies (Hickson *et al.*, 1986) adopt this view, as have many others. Decisions can be subjective or objective. Subjective choices involve agenda setting, selecting topics for future decisions (Bell *et al.* ,1998), and ethical considerations, value positions to be taken when making a decision (Nutt, 2002). Hickson *et al.* (1986) looks at decisions 'objectively' identifying eight types (products/services, financing, internal operations/controls, personnel policy, marketing, buildings, technologies, and reorganizations). Like context, content is believed to influence the choices made, the benefits realized, and the processes applied (Butler, 1998).

Action-taking identifies the procedures followed by DMs to make a decision. Researchers approach action-taking very differently. Some draw on philosophy of science (e.g. Dewey, 1910) to gain insight into how decisions *should* be made. This has led to formulating processes by specifying procedures (e.g. Simon, 1977; Perrow, 1967; Thompson, 1967; Nutt, 1989; Daft, 1995). The plethora of such efforts has prompted investigators to integrate procedural elements into hybrid processes seeking an *underlying* process as well as processes that have particular applications, such as decision making (e.g. Havelock, 1973; Nutt, 2004a). Another kind of effort explores what decision makers *do*, looking for an underling framework (e.g. Witte, 1970; Soleberg, 1970; Mintzberg *et al.*, 1976). Such studies examine DM behavior, using interviews, surveys, and the like to uncover procedures used in practice (e.g. Nutt, 1984; Fredrickson, 1985; Hickson *et al.*, 1986; Dean and Sharfman, 1996). The aim is to document 'process' – the steps followed to make a decision – to find essential steps (Bell *et al.*, 1998). Related research combines prescriptive and behavioral perspectives to uncover what DMs do and how this deviates from recommendations (Nutt, 2002). Finally, some add cognition and measure process features (Ragagopalan *et al.*, 1998). This asserts that cognition determines the kind of process selected. (Cognition is made up of factors such as uncertainty and risk tolerance, which many treat as contextual factors.) Process descriptors include comprehensiveness, involvement, and the like.

Framework captures the posited relationship between process (action-taking steps), context (importance, urgency, etc.), content (e.g. the eight Hickson types), and the costs and benefits of a decision. Several relationships have been suggested in which process is causal, mediating, or an outcome. For example, Butler (1998) identifies relationships among what he calls problem (content), solution (outcome), and choice (process) in which each can be a cause, an effect, or an interaction, linking them to computation, expertise, negotiation, and inspirational decisions. (Context is not considered.) In expertise decisions, outcomes dictate content and process with process and content interacting. Negotiation calls for process to be causal with content and outcome interacting. Bell *et al.* (1998) posit a relationship in which context is causal, first influencing process and content and then outcome. Downstream effects are acknowledged, contending that a choice influences the host of tangential interpretations (Bryson *et al.*, 1990) and that benefits can be delayed (Nutt, 2002). Rajagopalan *et al.* (1998) posit that context (made up of environmental and organizational factors) and content jointly influence decision-maker cognitions and the process that is embraced, with the outcome stemming from process as well as being influenced by context and content. Drawing on such relationships, researchers speculate about how outcomes are influenced by process, the situation, the type of decision, or by combinations of these factors.

Empirical research to study such relationships has many challenges. Investigators have coped with these challenges by examining select factors and by limiting the cases collected for study. There appears to be agreement on several points. Taking a single decision from each participating organization provides generalizability (Nutt, 2002) and avoids aggregations that can mask crucial effects by averaging (Bell *et al.*, 1998). Core business decisions are infrequent and difficult to accumulate in sufficiently large numbers for a study. To cope, many adopt the definition of 'strategic' first offered by Mintzberg *et al.* (1976). This allows a variety of decisions to be collected, facilitating comparisons. The eight objective decision types uncovered by Hickson *et al.* (1986) provide a benchmark to generalize about organization decision making (Nutt, 2001b). Most call for outcomes to be documented with effectiveness measures. Process measures offer little insight into effectiveness, so measures of decision costs and benefits are preferred.

Decision-making studies that have made these assumptions offer many insightful observations. However, an integration of the findings is limited by the differences in conceptualizations. The types of outcome, content, and context considered vary widely, as have the measures used to capture them. Perhaps more importantly, investigators conceptualize process very differently. Most research efforts identify some features of a process, or its motivation, but not *how* the decision was made. For example, Dean and Sharfman (1996) classify a process by procedural features such as rationality (systematic collection and interpretation of information), political behavior (using power), and flexibility (adaptability). Hickson *et al.* (1986) use process descriptors such as sporadic (with delays and negotiation), fluid (formalized process), or constricted (low effort). Fredrickson (1985) classifies a process by its comprehensiveness. Bell *et al.* (1998) identifies rational, comprehensive, political action, and sub-unit involvement types. Others treat process as coalition formation or social process control and focus on decision-maker attributes such as tolerance for ambiguity, uncertainty, or risk aversion (Poole and Van de Ven, 2004). Although interesting, these studies say little about *how* a decision is made. Classifications, such as comprehensive, analytical, or political, fail to explain how a decision maker acts comprehensively, conducts analysis, or engages politically. This void in the literature motivated my work.

Four process types are considered in this research. A 'discovery process' was derived from prescriptions (e.g. Daft, 1995) and composite processes, made up of steps and step sequencing believed to be useful (e.g. Mintzberg *et al.*, 1976). Such recommendations have a 'think first' approach, as noted by Mintzberg and Westley (2001), which stresses logic and analysis. Prescriptions often call for gathering intelligence about needs, followed by steps to find and manage peoples' interests, set a direction to guide a search, engage a search to uncover options, and evaluate the options uncovered.

'Idea imposition' was taken from descriptive/interpretive studies that find DMs to be idea-driven (Snyder and Page, 1958; Cyert and March, 1963; Soelberg, 1967; Witte, 1972; McKie, 1973; Mintzberg and Waters, 1982; Hall, 1984; Nutt, 2002). DMs seem not to know what they want until they see what they can get (Wildavsky,

1979) and make sense of their circumstances by exploring concrete actions (Weick, 1979; Weick and Quinn, 1999), suggesting a 'see first' approach (Mintzberg and Westley, 2001). This is demonstrated in the BART system that sought to mimic European mass transit (Hall, 1984), in Steinberg's 'wholesale Groceteria' that gave rise to the self-service grocery store (Mintzberg and Waters, 1982), and in acquisitions such as the purchase of Snapple by Quaker that mimicked a prior Gatorade acquisition (Nutt, 2002). Such decisions begin with an idea, followed by evaluation and implementation.

Idea imposition and discovery can be abandoned. When this occurs, it is logical to expect a new process to emerge with different steps. The idea triggering idea imposition may prove to be unwise, calling for 'redevelopment' to find a replacement. An 'emergent opportunity' can displace development process. Here an idea arrives *after* the decision-making process has begun that replaces a discovery process with an emergent opportunity process. The motivation to adopt an emergent opportunity can be linked to satisficing (March and Simon, 1958), substituting an available and acceptable solution for the elusive ideal solution. When either shift occurs, the steps undertaken in the now abandoned process continue to influence what is done, adding new steps to redevelop or deal with the emergent idea.

Support for a *discovery* process can be found in the prescriptive literature. Proponents offer logic and case histories to justify its use (e.g. Daft, 1995; Nutt, 1989; Perrow, 1967; Thompson, 1967), but have yet to conduct systematic tests of their recommendations in real settings. Prescriptions call for DMs to work their way through intelligence gathering, implementation, and direction setting early in the process because these steps are believed to have the greatest impact on success (Lant and Menzias, 1992; Nadler and Hibino, 1990). Support for idea imposition can be found in the descriptive/interpretive literature, which finds decision makers to be idea-driven (Mintzberg and Westley, 2001). Such studies uncover the steps applied by DMs to make decisions and imply that they merit emulation. These studies rarely link the process uncovered with the results it produced, beyond the case used to derive it (e.g. Weick, 2001; Mintzberg *et al.*, 1976). Without empirical studies of comparable cases support for these processes is largely indirect.

Indirect evidence can be found by comparing and assessing what each process advocates. In an *idea imposition* process, a ready-made plan initiates action; followed by an idea-derived direction, evaluation, ending with implementation. The implied benefits of the idea become a proxy for expected results. The ready-made idea is defensively evaluated to provide supporting arguments (Cohen *et al.* 1972; Mausch and LaPotin, 1989). There is little motivation to look for other ideas. As a result, DMs gather little intelligence, leave directions implicit, skip search, use their resources to promote the idea, and pay little attention to people's interests; although decisions fail for just these reasons (Nutt, 1999). The discovery process calls for gathering intelligence, marshalling support, establishing a direction, and conducting a search as separate activities making it more open to identifying possibilities. Searching broadly, with minimal constraints, is often advocated in the literature (e.g. MacCrimmon and Taylor, 1976). Although success has a produce–product relationship – it cannot be guaranteed – indirect evidence suggests that discovery is more *apt* to be successful, suggesting that:

H1: The prospect of success increases when DMs follow a discovery process compared to an idea imposition process.

H1 merits study for several reasons. Discovery prescriptions, despite their seeming merit, are seldom followed in practice (Nutt, 1999; 2002). Furthermore, there are many descriptive/interpretative studies that advocate an idea-driven process, implying that such a process is desirable or pragmatic or both (Mintzberg *et al.*, 1976; Langley *et al.*, 1995; Weick, 1979). But success is seldom considered in these studies, allowing researchers to conclude that what was uncovered merits emulation. There is little empirical evidence to support either decision-making prescriptions or what decision makers prefer to do, making such research a priority.

Process Shifts. Sustaining a discovery process can be difficult when there is pressure to act (Janis, 1989). Such pressure intensifies (Starbuck, 1983) should a stakeholder spot an opportunity (MacCrimmon and Taylor, 1976; Cohen *et al.*, 1972). If a discovery process is abandoned to accommodate the opportunity, search would be terminated (Mausch and LaPotin, 1989; Eisenhardt and Zbaracki, 1992). This suggests that the initial steps follow those of discovery, terminating search and adding evaluation to test the emergent idea (Table 17.2). Little is known about such a process. Adopting an *emergent opportunity* may have little effect on success because the emergent idea must measure up to the expectations set during direction setting. But search is terminated before it can provide results and search is widely recommended (e.g. MacCrimmon and Taylor, 1976; Nisbett and Ross, 1989; Kolb, 1983), suggesting that:

H2: The prospect of success declines when DMs apply an emergent opportunity process, compared to a discovery process.

Another kind of process shift occurs when the ready-made plan in an idea imposition effort proves to be ill-advised. This suggests a *redevelopment process* to find a replacement, adding search to the process steps (Table 17.2). Idea aborts are not discussed in the literature so little is known about such efforts, posing several questions. Does the prospect of success decline after an idea abort? Can a redevelopment effort approximate the success of discovery? One can surmise that the prospect of success would decline for DMs who have advocated an ill-advised idea (Kolb, 1983; Janis, 1989), which could taint a redevelopment effort. Also, redevelopment has some but not all of the steps recommended for discovery, suggesting that:

H3: The prospect of success declines when DMs use a redevelopment process, compared to a discovery process.

Situational Influences. Contingency models identify boundary conditions, which indicate conditions under which a particular kind of action is preferred. Daft (1995), Thompson (1967), and many others (e.g. Allison, 1971; Perrow, 1967; Nutt, 1989) incorporate situational factors into their decision-making models. Advocates contend that differences in environmental stability (Mintzberg and Waters, 1982), time pressure (Vroom and Yetton, 1973), novelty (Fredrickson, 1985), complexity (Perrow, 1967), resource dependency (Daft, 1995), and the like call for a different approach (e.g. Bell *et al.*, 1998). Applied to decision making, a process type is matched to high and low complexity, etc. Some of the implied relationships have

TABLE 17.2 Matching the process types to the steps and tactics

Intelligence Gathering	Proactive Implementation:	Direction Setting:	Option Development:	Evaluation:	Reactive Implementation:
Discovery processes					
Need-based	Tactics: Intervention or Participation	Tactics: Objectives or Problems	Tactics: Solicitation, Benchmarking, or Innovation	Tactics: Analysis, Bargaining, Judgment, or Subjective	
Idea imposition processes					
Opportunity-based		Opportunity (a ready-made idea)			Tactics: Persuasion or Edicts
Emergent Opportunity processes					
Need-based	Tactics: Intervention or Participation	Tactics: Objectives or Problems	Opportunity (a ready-made idea emerges)	Tactics: Analysis, Bargaining, Judgment, or Subjective	Tactics: Persuasion or Edicts
Redevelopment processes					
Opportunity-based		Opportunity (the ready-made idea fails)	Tactics: Solicitation, Benchmarking, or Innovation	Tactics: Analysis, Bargaining, Judgment, or Subjective	Tactics: Persuasion or Edicts

been subjected to empirical testing (e.g. Dean and Sharfman, 1996; Bell *et al.*, 1998; Bryson *et al.*, 1990). This has led to recommending 'rational methods' for nonurgent and nonroutine decisions to be made in stable environments (e.g. Daft, 1995).

Extending such arguments suggests that discovery should be limited to nonurgent, routine decisions. This appears to contradict the arguments offered to build discovery-like processes. Furthermore, empirical studies have been contradictory. Fredrickson (1985) found that comprehensiveness (a proxy for discovery) works best in stable environments. Other researchers find just the opposite: comprehensive methods (like discovery) work better in high velocity (unstable) environments (Eisenhardt and Bourgeois, 1989; Eisenhardt, 1989). Miller *et al* (1997) found that extensive analysis (as called for in discovery) was preferred in formalized and centralized settings. Alter and Hage (1993) found that centralization and formalization discourage a discovery-like approach. In addition, these studies typically consider a limited number of contextual factors. As a result, little can be said about the decision situation beyond the factor considered, such as complexity (Carley, 1986), urgency (Pinfield, (1986), or risk (Schilit, 1987).

Deriving a hypothesis requires generalizing to the processes being investigated. Because action-taking has been treated differently in past work, it is difficult to sum up the effects of context on process (defined as how DMs take action). Empirical research has examined how *tactics* (that make up a process) are influenced by decision type, the organization's profit status (profit or nonprofit), DM level (top, a CEO, COO, or CFO; or middle) as well as complexity, urgency, importance, staff skill, resources, and initial support (Nutt, 1992; 1993a; 1998b; 2001). These studies find that the best performing tactics provide the best result, regardless of the situation. Following the more important steps and relying on the better performing tactics, as is called for by discovery, is apt to have the same effect, suggesting that:

H4: For each of the contingencies considered, such as high and low urgency, the prospect of success will be greater when DMs follow a discovery process, compared to the three other processes.

The Influence of Best Practice. Some tactics are more successful than others, as shown in Table 17.1. Combining the more successful or best practice tactics into a process would seem likely to improve the prospect of success. This suggests that:

H5: DMs who apply best practice tactics throughout a decision making process will have more success than DMs who use any other combination of tactics.

It is tempting to call H5 tautology – selecting best practice tactics would seem to be correlated with superior performance. To do so, however, is to overlook two factors. First, best practice tactics can have synergy. Some may work better together than others. Second, decision makers seldom apply the best practice tactics (Nutt, 1999). There appears to be a strong preference for the less effective tactic (Nutt, 1984). This may stem from erroneous beliefs about what works and why or concerns and situations that merit empirical study. Both suggest that an empirical look at the success of various tactic combinations will offer useful insights for a process theory.

METHODS

The explanatory variables are made up of the process types and the context and content factors, with success indicators as the dependent variables. Comparing the success realized by discovery, idea imposition, emergent opportunity, and redevelopment as well as comparing the success of the process types under various conditions provides a way to test the hypotheses. The tactic hypothesis will be tested by comparing each process with best practice tactics, as shown in Table 17.1, to the four processes with the tactical options shown in Table 17.2. Use questions are addressed by how often the process types are found in practice. In this section, definition and measurement of the variables is presented along with the analysis approach.

Explanatory factors

Process Types. The process types are constructed from the findings of prior studies. This requires discussion of data gathered for both the prior work and the current study and how the findings of past studies are merged to form the process types. The findings identified in past studies (Table 17.1) were derived from a data base of 176 decisions. A single process step was investigated for in each study noted in Table 17.1. The current study draws on a data base of 224 decisions gathered after the first 176 decisions, following the same data collection procedures. The two data bases are similar. There are comparable numbers of profit and nonprofit organizations, both have top managers (CEOs, COOs, CFOs, etc.) and middle managers as participants, and include the eight decision types identified in the Bradford studies of products/services, financing, internal operations/controls, personnel policy, marketing, buildings, technologies, and reorganizations (Hickson *et al.*, 1986). A partial listing of the decisions and the organization in which each was made appears in Appendix I. The scope of decision makers, decision types, and decision settings suggest that the decisions considered are broadly representative of those being made in contemporary organizations.

Actions were elicited from independent interviews with the decision maker and one other person involved with the decision (see Appendix II for details). The guidelines of Lincoln and Guba (1984), Huber and Power (1985), Denzin (1989), and Patton (1990) were followed to construct the interview protocol. The uncovered actions were triangulated by reconciling the views of two informants with one another, and with existing documents. The reconciled actions were recorded in diagrams that summarized what was done (see Nutt, 1984; 1992). Tactics were uncovered from an analysis of DM *actions* in the summaries.

Decisions were classified according to the tactics applied by a DM to complete *each* of the decision-making steps in Table 17.1. Explanation building suggested by Yin (1993) was followed to make the tactic classifications. For a given step, decision summaries are placed with others in which the DM took similar actions, grouping them into tactic categories or an unknown category. To avoid making assumptions about how tactics were applied, all of the DM actions uncovered to make a decision were considered to make a classification. Colleagues reviewed the decision summaries and, applying the definitions in Table 17.1, indicated which tactic they believed was being used for each step, including an unclassified category. Agreement was 89 % or more in the first data base of 176 decisions.

The same approach was applied for the second set of decisions. Here, the lowest agreement for the tactic classifications was 90 %. Only decisions with agreement were used, *reducing* the data base from 224 to 202 decisions. The 22 discarded decisions either had too little detail to tell what was done or unresolved disagreements. Appendix II and the Table 17.1 citations offer additional detail on how decisions were solicited, documents investigated, interview procedures applied to uncover the actions taken in making a decision, the triangulation procedures used to reconcile the two informants' recall of the actions taken, procedures applied to reconcile recall with the documents, case summary creation, and the classification procedures.

DMs were found to work their way through a process by activating some steps and ignoring others, sequencing selected steps in several ways. A variety of tactics could be selected by the DMs for each activated step. The tactics show how the DMs *went about* gathering intelligence, setting directions, searching for options, evaluating alternatives, and implementing a preferred course of action. Appendix III provides additional detail on how each tactic is applied.

As DMs work their way through a process, selecting and sequencing steps, they can elect a variety of tactics for each activated step. A decision-making process is given by the tactics that are selected to carry out intelligence gathering, direction setting, option identification, evaluation, and implementation (see Table 17.1). Theoretically, there are 384 ($2 \times 3 \times 4 \times 4 \times 4$) processes that can be formed from all tactical combinations. A subset of these processes is investigated that adhere to the steps and tactics called for in idea imposition, discovery, emergent opportunity, and redevelopment. Table 17.2 provides a flow chart that shows how the steps in the four processes unfold and the available tactical options. The study will also assess the impact of best practice tactics, as shown in Table 17.1, used in each of the four process types.

Specifying the Process Types. The first row in Table 17.2 indicates the steps and step sequencing for *Discovery* as well as feasible tactics. Discovery requires considerable information gathering. Row 2 in Table 17.2 identifies the steps, step sequences, and available tactics for *idea imposition*. Here a ready-made plan prompts action. Row 3 in Table 17.2 identifies the steps, step sequences, and available tactics for *emergent opportunity*. Here a solution displaces a discovery process and its search for an elusive ideal solution. Row 4 in Table 17.2 identifies the steps, step sequences, and available tactics for *redevelopment*. Here a failed idea in an idea imposition process prompts an effort to find a replacement. The steps initially undertaken in an abandoned process continue to influence what is done.

The 202 decisions in the second data base were studied to find decisions in which the four process types were applied. The steps and tactics linked to *discovery* were found in the prescriptive literature. Prescriptions typically call for information gathering, finding and managing peoples' interests, specifying desired results, a search for alternate solutions, and an evaluation to find the preferred alternative, as shown in the first row of Table 17.2. The range of tactics recommended to carry out a process step is also shown in the first row of Table 17.2. A process was classified as discovery if the DM activated steps that identified a need, led with implementation, using intervention or participation tactics, and directed search with either a problem or an objective, using any of the search and evaluation tactics. The steps and tactics linked to *idea imposition* were also derived from the literature. Descriptive/interpretive studies of DM find that a ready-made plan initiates action, followed by an idea-derived direction, any of the evaluation tactics, with implementation located at the end the process using either persuasion or an edict (Table 17.2). In idea imposition, the idea arrives with a claim. Decisions were classified as idea imposition if the DM followed steps that began with a ready-made plan (and an idea direction), did *not* activate a search, applied any of the evaluation tactics, and implemented using either persuasion or an edict. For *emergent opportunity*, the idea arrives *after* a decision-making process has been initiated. The idea displaces a discovery process with an emergent opportunity process, whereas the idea drives the process in idea imposition. An available and acceptable solution displaces the elusive ideal solution. (Although it is also reasonable to expect that an emergent opportunity can displace the idea in an idea imposition process, this was not observed.) To be classified as an 'emergent opportunity', the process began as discovery and applied discovery steps until an emergent idea terminated search. Then steps were taken to evaluate the emergent idea (any tactics), using the information obtained in the evaluation to implement. Decision makers could alter their initial implementation stance (switching to persuasion or edicts) or maintain it (continuing to use intervention or participation). When the idea in an idea imposition process was discredited there was an effort mounted to find a replacement, to shift the process to redevelopment. A redevelopment process begins with an opportunity and an idea direction, followed by an appraisal that found the opportunity to be ill-advised. Any of the search tactics can be used to seek a replacement idea coupled with any of the evaluation tactics with implementation applying either edict or persuasion. When either shift occurs, the steps undertaken in the now abandoned process continued to influence what was done. Decisions classified as discovery, idea imposition, emergent opportunity, and redevelopment explicitly adhered to these steps, step sequences, and tactical options.

The four process types employed the sequence of steps and tactics choices shown in Table 17.2. The 202 decisions in the second data base were reviewed to find decisions with a process that matched each process type. Decisions in the data base were classified as using a discovery process if the DM followed steps that identified a need, led with implementation, using intervention or participation tactics, and directed search with either a problem or an objective, using any of the search and evaluation tactics. An idea imposition process is opportunity-driven, using evaluation and implementation to win over stakeholders in an attempt to put a ready-made solution to use. Decisions were classified as using idea imposition if a DM followed steps that began with a ready-made plan (and thereby used an idea direction), did *not* activate a search, applied any of the evaluation tactics, and implemented using either persuasion or an edict. To be classified as discovery or idea imposition required that each of the step sequences and tactical options noted above were *explicitly* followed.

Next decisions in which the DM abandoned discovery or idea imposition were identified. An 'emergent opportunity' arose as some of the DMs were working through a discovery process. In some of these decisions, the opportunity was adopted and search was terminated. Any of the evaluation tactics could be used to highlight the merit of the idea found in the opportunity. To be classified as an 'emergent opportunity', the process must begin as a discovery process and apply discovery steps until an emergent idea stopped a search. Then steps were taken to evaluate the emergent idea, using the information obtained in the evaluation to implement with persuasion or with an edict. Decision makers could alter their initial implementation stance (using intervention or participation) or maintain it (using persuasion or edicts). If these steps and tactics were applied the process was classified as an emergent opportunity.

Another shift in process occurs when the idea in an idea imposition process is discredited. If effort was mounted to find a replacement for the abandoned idea, the process became a candidate for redevelopment. The redevelopment process begins with an opportunity claim and an idea direction, followed by an appraisal that found the opportunity to be ill-advised. If this prompted the DM to add any of the search tactics to seek a replacement idea, the process was called redevelopment. Any of the evaluation tactics could be used with implementation applying either edict or persuasion. To be classified a redevelopment, this step sequence and tactical options had to be explicitly followed.

Success indicators

Indicators of effectiveness and efficiency are used to measure success. Effectiveness is measured by use and estimates of value assuming that only decisions put to use will realize hoped-for benefits (Beyer and Trice, 1982). Efficiency is measured by duration. DMs report that they prefer rapid action (e.g. Starbuck, 1983), suggesting duration as an indicator. These measures are independent. Decisions with considerable perceived value may not be put to use and vice versa, and the adopted as well as the high valued decision can be delayed. Decisions may take an extended period of time and considerable effort, but have little effect.

Instrumental use is key (Beyer and Trice, 1982; Pelz, 1978), which requires an adoption. Symbolic use, finding a desirable action but taking no action to realize it, and conceptual use, indicating aims without follow through, are not used in this study. Delays in use, proportion of use, and terminated use provide adoption qualifications. The 'sustained adoption' measure adds ultimate adoptions and deletes ultimate failures, measured two years later, to capture downstream changes in use. The 'complete adoption' measure treats a decision with partial use as a failure, indicating the extent of use.

Objective indicators of value are preferred but hard to collect. Many of my informants declined to provide data about benefits, such as utilization or turnover. In addition, utilization, turnover, and related measures must be converted to a common metric, such as cost. Such conversions are argumentative, difficult to describe, and distract from the message. Bryson and Cullen (1984), Alexander (1986), and Hughes *et al.* (1986) offer a way around these difficulties; their studies find that objective indicators are highly correlated with a well placed informant's subjective estimate of value. Many researchers who study decisions use subjective measures of value (Papadakis and Barwise, 1998).

Decision makers can make self-serving estimates. To avoid this, only the two *secondary* informants made estimates of decision value. An anchored rating scale with five anchors was used to collect decision value ratings from the informants. The scale anchors called a rating of 5 *outstanding* to be assigned to decisions that made a decisive contribution by providing exceptional perceived quality. A rating of 1, termed *poor*, was assigned to decisions that had no impact or merit. The remaining scale points for the decision value measure were termed *good* for a rating of 4, *adequate* for a rating of 3, and *disappointing* for ratings of 2. The two informants, independently and without discussion, checked along a rating scale with these anchors to indicate their views of decision value. At this point, a researcher can measure differences or take steps to enhance precision. In this study, attempts were taken to improve precision. Estimate-discuss-estimate (EDE) was used because research shows that this procedure moves a subjective estimate toward a true value, using reflection to improve rater recall (e.g. Gustafson *et al.*, 1973). First, an average of the initial ratings is computed. Then, informants discuss the result. If individual ratings are far from the average there is pressure to explain. Informants offer reasons for rating a decision as they did. In the exchange, the more compelling arguments carry the most weight. When informants consider such arguments it shifts the average rating toward a true value. The average of the informants' second rating was used in the analysis.

Efficiency is measured by elapsed time (Hickson *et al.*, 1986; Cray *et al.*, 1991) made up of the time period from recognition to finding a remedy *and* the time that follows, ending when the decision was adopted or abandoned. These indicators were also collected from the two secondary informants. First, informants estimated the time from recognition to the development of a remedy and then the elapsed time from the end of development to use or abandonment. The EDE procedure was used to improve the precision of these estimates, as described above.

Context and content factors

The survey given to the two secondary informants also contained rating scales for the contextual factors (see Appendix II). Decision urgency, importance, staff skill, resources, and initial support were collected in the survey (Nutt, 1986; 1993a; 1998a; 2001b). Informants independently and without discussion checked along anchored rating scales with indicators that ran from 1=least to 5=most for each contextual measure to rate each factor. The EDE process was used to improve precision of the estimates and to deal with common method variance (Podsakoff and Organ, 1986). DM level (top, a CEO, COO, or CFO; or middle), the organization's profit status (profit or nonprofit), and decision type (the eight Hickson types) were also coded.

Analysis

Analysis was carried out with MANOVA and ANOVA. MANOVA controls for correlations among the success measures (sustained adoption, complete adoption, decision value, and total time) that may have arisen in the data. The MANOVA analysis combines the success measures into a single outcome measure, weighting each equally, reversing the scale of the time measure so desirable outcomes move in the same direction. If the MANOVA and the ANOVA produce comparable results correlations the dependent variables had little effect upon the results, allowing the easier to interpret ANOVA findings to be used.

The ANOVA format identifies the success of the process types with their sustained adoption, complete adoption, decision value, and total time. In addition, the four processes were also examined to determine which tactics led to the best success profile. To test H5, the success for typical practice (shown in Table 17.3) was compared with the success realized when each of the feasible tactics was used in the four process types. ANOVA requires a cell size of four to compute a variance (Box *et al.*, 1978), so classifications with fewer than four decisions are not considered. A Duncan Multiple Range Test (DMRT) identifies significant differences in the mean values of a success indicator when more than two categories are compared. The results denoted by the letter 'A' indicate the best results ($p < .05$), 'B' the second best, and so on. The process type with the most 'A' designations is the most successful. The adoption measures are binary, but the F tests used to draw inferences are robust. Departures from normally distributed standard errors, which arise when binary values are used as the dependant variable, can be tolerated if the proportion of adoptions to rejections is less than one in four (Box *et al.*, 1978). The 37 % to 50 % failure rates in the data base met this test.

The study is also concerned with the interaction of the contextual factors and the content factors with the process types. Internal support, importance, urgency, resources, and staff support measures were collapsed into 'high' and 'low' signifying 4 or 5 as high and the rest as low. Decision-maker level and profit status were coded with two levels. Content was made up of the eight decision types. The interaction of the process types with these factors was considered one factor at a time to see if the conclusions about process types can be generalized to decisions classified as high and low urgency, etc.

RESULTS

Results of the analyses appear in Tables 17.3 to 17.8. The data reported in Table 17.3 provide a test of H1, H2, and H3. Look across the rows in a table to determine the success of each process type (the bold type indicates the best result). Compare row 1 with row 2 to test H1. Compare row 1 with row 3 and row 1 with row 4 to test H2 and H3. In these analyses, the MANOVA proved to be significant, so the mean values for the success measures in the ANOVAs can be interpreted. A test of H4 is provided by grouping the process types according to each contingency (see Table 17.4). A DMRT was carried out to order the four processes for each condition (e.g. high urgency) according to their success, indicating the most successful with bold type. To confirm a contingency argument, a different process will have more success for a given contingency (e.g. discovery best for high urgency, another process for low urgency).

The success realized by each process when using each feasible tactic, compared with typical practice, shown in Tables 17.5 to 17.8, is carried out to identify best practice. The analysis has two steps. The tactical choices available for each process (Table 17.2) are compared to find tactics that enhance success of each process type. This analysis is shown in the bottom half of Tables 17.5 to 17.8. The relevant tactics are compared using DMRT to find those with significantly more success. As above, the letter A signifies the best performing process, B the second best, etc. The best results are shown in bold type. Then the result realized when each process applies the best performing tactics was found in the data base. Decisions using the best performing tactics are then compared to typical practice in the top two lines of Tables 17.5 to 17.8. To test H5, compare the best practice line to the typical practice line in the tables.

Discussion is organized by decisions that continued a process and those with alterations. Decisions are drawn from the data base to illustrate how a decision is made with each process type, exploring each to uncover what led decision makers astray and how things could be improved.

DECISIONS WITH CONTINUITY

The discovery process had far more success than the idea imposition process, offering considerable support for H1 (p<.05). The discussion that follows documents and then explores this finding.

Idea Imposition. For 57, or 28 %, of the decisions, decision makers used an idea imposition process: beginning with a claim that suggested a solution and then evaluated the idea and installed it. About half (29 or 51 %) of the idea imposition efforts were completed. (The remainder shifted to a redevelopment process to replace a failed idea, discussed later in the paper.) In idea imposition, the claim contains a solution, or implies one, prompting a solution-champion to show how the idea would work. When a remedy activates a decision-making process, no target was set or search attempted. Instead, claimants argued that the organization should adopt a remedy they were touting. This puts a remedy on the table at the outset and channels subsequent actions. The remedy was evaluated to certify its value and to determine its acceptance to key people, such as users or customers. Implementation follows using the arguments marshaled from the evaluation to justify adoption. The solution may be refined but the basic idea remained unchanged in the idea imposition decisions that were studied. Overall, idea imposition had a 55 % sustained adoption rate, which fell to 41 % when partial use was accounted for (Table 17.3). The process was inefficient, averaging 20.5 months to complete, producing 'adequate to good' decision results. Decision makers were drawn to idea imposition because it seemed timely and pragmatic. The quick fix in the ready-made solution realized neither. The results indicate little timeliness and very low adoption rates.

TABLE 17.3 The success of process types

| PROCESS TYPES | USE | | | | EFFECTIVENESS | | | | EFFICIENCY | |
| | Frequency | | Sustained Adoption | | Complete Adoption | | Decision Value | | Total Time | |
	N	Freq.	Rate	DMRT[1]	Rate	DMRT	Rating[2]	DMRT	Months[3]	DMRT
Discovery	39	19%	**90%**	A	**85%**	A	**4.3**	A	**11.9**	B
Idea Imposition	29	14%	55%	C	41%	D	3.5	B	20.5	C
ANOVA/ p value (two contrasts)			.0005		.0001		.05		.01	
MANOVA / p value[4]			.01							
Abandon discovery for an emergent opportunity										
Emergent opportunity	15	7%	73%	B	66%	B	3.6	B	21.7	C
Find replacement for failed idea										
Redevelopment	28	14%	64%	B	57%	C	3.6	B	16.9	B
ANOVA/ p value (four contrasts)			.01		.005		.05		.03	
MANOVA / p value[4]			.03							
Total	111	55%								
Totals for the data base	202	100%	63%		50%		3.6		17.1	

1. Duncan Multiple Range Test: The letter codes indicate significant differences in the mean values with the equivalent of a paired t-test, p < .05, with letter A denoting the best outcome, B the second best, etc. Best performing process outcomes are shown in bold.
2. Scale: 5 = outstanding, 4 = good, 3 = adequate, 2 = disappointing, 1 = poor.
3. Time is measured in months from beginning of development to the ultimate use or abandonment of the decision.
4. The value, adoption, and efficiency measures are weighted equally in the MANOVA, reversing the scale for efficiency.

Decision makers embrace a ready-made solution in an idea imposition process, as did the CIO of Limited when calling for a 'state of the art' information system. Existing systems applications were to be inventoried and replaced with newly developed systems that contained the latest advances in information technology to position the company for the next decade (remedy). The CEO bought into the remedy. After years of effort and considerable investment by the company, the CIO was unable to move his IS vision from the drawing board to reality. Critics contended that the project would be too big and the technology untried. Costs grew to well beyond initial estimates. Surveys indicated that users failed to see how the system would help them (analytical evaluations). Users saw the proposed information system as forcing applications of questionable value, while ignoring their information needs (failed persuasion). After four years of effort and $ 30 million in expenditures, the IS idea was abandoned and the CIO was asked to resign. Note how directions were implicitly set according to what a ready-made plan can do (better information with new technology). Organizational members failed to question why we need to change (alter the current information system) or ask about the results expected (reduced costs, better service, etc.). In decisions of this type, there is seldom clarity about the direction (hoped-for benefits). And no one looks for competing ideas (other ways to garner information) because the remedy displaces a search.

Discovery Processes. Compare the results noted for idea imposition to those obtained for discovery in Table 17.3. Use rates nearly doubled. Discovery produced far better outcomes with 90 % sustained adoptions, 85 % complete adoptions, rated as good to excellent, completed in nearly half the time (11.9 months). Discovery was more efficient *and* more effective than idea imposition ($p < .05$).

Discovery was applied for 54, or 26 %, of all decisions. Discovery begins by documenting a need, followed by implementation and direction steps and then search and evaluation steps, selecting tactics to set a direction, implement, search, and evaluate. Two-thirds (39 or 72 %) of these decision-making efforts were completed. (In the others, an emergent opportunity displaced a search, discussed later in the paper.) During discovery, the decision makers infer needs from claims, set directions, and consider barriers to action before they search or evaluate. Needs indicate what was to be improved, such as utilization, revenues, or production capacity. The need clarified the results wanted so solutions that offered performance improvements were put on the table for discussion. For instance, the CEO of the Mead Paper Company found that company production costs exceeded those of their key competitors (claim). The CEO (the DM) enlisted key managers to serve on teams to look for cost cutting ideas (implementation). There was no resistance when the DM set cost reduction targets to guide the team's efforts (directions), as key players had bought into the need for change. Next the lead team hired McKinsey Consulting (search) and their Delta-p cost reduction program to address the cost reduction target (direction). The consultants conducted pilots to verify that costs would be lowered (evaluation).

This sequence of steps differs from the sequence found in idea imposition. Decision making was triggered by needs that make performance (e.g. utilization or cost) shortfalls the focus of attention. The DM marshaled support by showing that the performance needs are real. A successful demonstration helps to enlist people in a solution search and to guide their efforts with a target, which indicates improvements seen as both desirable and feasible and identifies the information to be collected for an evaluation.

Decisions that altered a process

Discovery and idea imposition are abandoned in a number of the decisions and each has a different pattern of success, although none was as successful as discovery, supporting H2 and H3 ($p<.05$).

Emergent Opportunity. In one-third of the discovery efforts an emergent opportunity stopped an ongoing search. (Emergent opportunities did not interrupt idea imposition in the decisions studied.) Search was terminated after a seemingly desirable remedy materialized – either from an outsider or from the DM. An 'emergent opportunity' process follows a need-implementation-direction-emergent opportunity/displaced search-evaluation-installation sequence of steps.

Decisions classified as an emergent opportunity had mixed results. Sustained adoptions (factoring in abandoned decisions and those that were ultimately used) were 73 %, which fell to 66 % when degree of use was accounted for (Table 17.3). These decisions were quite inefficient, taking nearly twice the time of that required for discovery (21.7 months) and rated as 3.6 (adequate to good). Emergent opportunities proved to be neither timely nor pragmatic, with lower ratings and increased failure as well as a drawn out process compared to discovery, supporting H2 ($p<.05$).

The Dunning-Lathrop Insurance Company used this process to revise a bonus system that had been inherited from a merger. The bonus system was thought to be too subjective, based solely on the discretion of the former owner, and too generous, often exceeding 20 % of an employee's annual salary. With these payments, the wages paid far exceeded other pay, when the company was looking for ways to cut labor cost (need). The CEO (the DM) wanted to half the size of the bonus (objective) and assigned the task to his COO, who set out benchmark bonus systems in local companies (search). The CEO intervened after three months and no apparent progress. He wrote a memo stating that future bonuses would be based on commissions (opportunity/judgmental evaluation/edict implementation), ending the search to uncover bonus practices.

This decision, like other emergent opportunity decisions in the data base, terminated search before options could be uncovered. The interview data show that the secondary informants believed search was terminated prematurely, contending it could have found ideas to challenge the emergent idea or be incorporated with it. The success data bear this out, as noted above. Decisions that followed an emergent opportunity process were rated below that of decisions that let a search play out ($p<.05$). Adopting an emergent opportunity failed to save time. Installation was drawn out when insiders resisted the plan and demanded more justification. In these decisions, the secondary informants saw the decision makers' motives as suspect. The time for the decisions was drawn out to reassure stakeholders with suspicions and mollify those with something to lose, making the emergent opportunity process inefficient.

Redevelopment. Decision makers abandoned an idea imposition process in nearly half of such efforts. The idea was discarded when opposition emerged or when the cost and effort to install it appeared to exceed alleged benefits. In all such instances, effort was mounted to find a replacement. A redevelopment process followed an opportunity-idea/failure-search-evaluation-installation sequence of steps.

The success rate for redevelopment was far below discovery (p<.05). Sustained adoptions fell to 64 %, complete adoptions to 57 % for decisions rated at between adequate and good (3.6), carried out in 16.9 months (see Table 17.3). But terminating an idea imposition process is better than continuing it. Success improved substantially compared to idea imposition processes followed to completion. The outcomes for redevelopment indicate that adoption rates rise and duration falls, compared with discovery efforts, supporting H3 (p<.05).

CCH Computax, with annual revenues of $ 200 million, provide computerized tax processing services to CPAs, lawyers, and others involved in tax accounting. CCH had a three-year lease of two IBM 3090 mainframes that did both tax processing and administrative tasks: such as accounting and budgeting. The executive vice president of CCH was alarmed by the rapid switch of CCH customers from mainframe-based products to PC-based products (claim). The CEO (the DM) chose to mollify customers and maintain the old system because the mainframes were too expensive for just administrative tasks (opportunity). This proved to be unwise and customers went elsewhere. To get his customers back, the CEO looked for a vendor who, in three years, could provide software for internal budgeting and accounting that would run on a standalone PC and do at least what current systems could do (search). Search was focused on finding a way to realize the implied benefits of an unworkable idea and not more broadly to find a cost-effective way to replace the mainframe with better information handling capability that could also meet the need of customers.

Redevelopment efforts engaged a search to find a replacement idea without thinking about a direction. The rejected idea's alleged benefits were substituted for setting a direction. Vendors who were asked to provide a replacement found the expected results to be ambiguous. The vendors contacted by CCH were focused on getting software in place and not on recapturing lost customers. All of the redevelopment processes initiated search with such vague expectations. This allowed the ideas being offered to serve the needs of the vendor, such as force fitting an off-the-shelf product, which reduced the prospect of success.

Situational influences

The impact of contextual factors on the four processes is shown in Table 17.4. The process-context interaction is statistically significant for urgency, importance, resources, and decision-maker level, internal support, extent of staff assistance, and profit status (p<.05) so each will be discussed. For the process-content interaction, several of the decision type-process combinations had insufficient observations

TABLE 17.4 Context and process types

PROCESS/FACTOR	USE		EFFECTIVENESS				Decision Value		EFFICIENCY	
	Frequency		Sustained Adoption		Complete Adoption				Total Time	
	N	Freq.*	Rate	DMRT	Rate	DMRT	Rating	DMRT	Months	DMRT
Process with high urgency										
Discovery	16	41%	**91%**	A	**82%**	A	**4.5**	A	**12.0**	A
Idea	8	27%	72%	B	69%	B	3.8	B	16.0	C
Redev.	6	21%	50%	C	33%	C	3.8	B	14.6	B
EO	2	13%	–		–		–		–	
Process with low urgency										
Discovery	23	59%	**95%**	A	**90%**	A	**4.4**	A	**15.0**	A
Idea	21	73%	57%	C	57%	C	3.5	B	18.0	B
Redev.	22	79%	68%	B	64%	B	3.6	B	17.7	B
EO	13	87%	69%	B	61%	B	3.5	B	19.3	B/C
Process with high importance										
Discovery	29	75%	**89%**	A	**96%**	A	**4.5**	A	**11.3**	A
Idea	10	35%	70%	C	42%	C	3.6	B	24.0	B
Redev.	19	68%	84%	B	74%	B	**4.1**	A	**10.8**	A
EO	10	66%	70%	C	70%	B	3.5	B	19.5	B
Process with low importance										
Discovery	10	25%	70%	B	70%	B	3.5	B	13.7	B
Idea	17	65%	59%	C	41%	C	3.6	B	**11.8**	A
Redev.	9	32%	22%	D	22%	D	2.6	C	17.1	C
EO	5	33%	**80%**	A	**80%**	A	**4.0**	A	24.7	D

(Continued)

TABLE 17.4 (Continued)

| PROCESS/FACTOR | USE | | EFFECTIVENESS | | | | | | EFFICIENCY | |
| | Frequency | | Sustained Adoption | | Complete Adoption | | Decision Value | | Total Time | |
	N	Freq.*	Rate	DMRT	Rate	DMRT	Rating	DMRT	Months	DMRT
Process with high resources										
Discovery	14	36%	**91%**	A	**68%**	A	**4.6**	A	**14.1**	A
Idea	12	41%	58%	B	50%	B	3.7	B	32.0	B
Redev.	10	36%	43%	B/C	50%	B	3.9	B	**14.9**	A
EO	7	46%	60%	B	28%	C	2.8	C	16.7	A/B
Process with low resources										
Discovery	25	64%	**89%**	A	**84%**	A	**4.0**	A	10.8	A/B
Idea	17	59%	53%	C	35%	.C	3.5	B	**7.9**	A
Redev.	18	64%	59%	C	61%	B	3.5	B	18.2	B
EO	8	54%	**90%**	A	67%	B	4.4	A	25.5	C
Process with top managers										
Discovery	22	56%	**91%**	A	**97%**	A	**4.4**	A	**9.7**	A
Idea	20	71%	55%	C	45%	C	3.8	B	22.7	C
Redev.	24	86%	71%	B	63%	B	3.7	B	15.5	B
EO	9	60%	67%	B	67%	B	3.3	B/C	17.2	B/C
Process with middle managers										
Discovery	15	44%	**80%**	A	**87%**	A	**4.0**	A	**14.5**	A
Idea	6	21%	67%	B	50%	C	3.8	B	16.7	A/B
Redev.	4	14%	25%	C	25%	D	3.2	B/C	22.2	C
EO	6	40%	**83%**	A	67%	B	**4.2**	A	33.0	D

* proportion of the process type

Process with internal support										
Discovery	26	45%	**88%**	A	81%	A	**4.1**	A	**13.4**	A
Idea	16	27%	50%	C	44%	C	3.6	B	18.0	C
Redev.	11	19%	**80%**	A	**80%**	A	3.3	B	14.9	B
EO	5	9%	60%	B	60%	B	3.4	B	19.5	D
Process lacking internal support										
Discovery	9	27%	**88%**	A	**89%**	A	**4.6**	A	**7.2**	A
Idea	9	27%	55%	B	33%	C	2.6	D	18.5	B
Redev.	11	33%	18%	C	18%	D	3.6	B	17.7	B
EO	4	12%	50%	B	50%	B	3.0	C	24.7	C
Process with high staff skill										
Discovery	25	48%	88%	B	**84%**	A	**4.5**	A	**10.1**	A
Idea	9	17%	**100%**	A	77%	B	**4.6**	A	28.7	D
Redev.	10	19%	80%	B	**80%**	A	**4.2**	A	21.7	C
EO	8	15%	75%	C	75%	B	3.7	B	18.7	B
Process with low staff skill										
Discovery	12	27%	**92%**	A	**92%**	A	**3.8**	A	**12.5**	B
Idea	19	34%	37%	D	26%	C	3.1	B	17.8	A
Redev.	18	32%	55%	C	44%	D	3.3	B	14.9	C
EO	7	12%	70%	B	57%	A	**3.6**	A	24.0	D

(*Continued*)

TABLE 17.4 (Continued)

PROCESS/FACTOR	USE		EFFECTIVENESS						EFFICIENCY	
	Frequency		Sustained Adoption		Complete Adoption		Decision Value		Total Time	
	N	Freq.*	Rate	DMRT	Rate	DMRT	Rating	DMRT	Months	DMRT
Process in for profit org.										
Discovery	14	47%	**100%**	A	**86%**	A	**4.2**	A	10.3	B
Idea	6	20%	33%	C	17%	D	3.0	B	**5.7**	A
Redev.	4	13%	50%	B	25%	C	3.2	B	22.8	D
EO	6	20%	50%	B	50%	B	3.1	B	17.5	C
Process in non profit org.										
Discovery	25	31%	84%	A	84%	A	**4.3**	A	**12.9**	A
Idea	23	28%	61%	B	48%	D	3.7	B	23.7	D
Redev.	24	30%	67%	B	63%	C	3.7	B	19.0	C
EO	9	11%	**89%**	A	77%	B	**4.0**	A	16.7	B

(three or less), so these results are not considered. Discussing the main effects of the contextual factors is beyond the scope of the paper.

A contingency argument requires process success to be dependent on prevailing conditions – some processes being more successful under one set of conditions, others under another. The data in Table 17.4 summarize the effects of the 14 conditions that were tested. Discovery had significantly more success than the other processes for nine of the conditions (p<.05) and comparable success for four of the conditions. To illustrate, for *high urgency decisions* discovery had 91 % sustained adoptions, 82 % complete adoptions, a rating of 4.5 (good to excellent), and was carried out in 12 months (see Table 17.4). The next best performing process, applied to decisions with high urgency, had 72 % sustained adoptions, 69 % complete adoptions, a rating of 3.8 (good), and required 16 months to complete. For only one of the conditions tested did discovery fail to have superior or equal success, and for that condition discovery was a close second (p<.05). Discovery was clearly superior when more *demanding* conditions were being confronted by a DM; as noted for urgent decisions, important decisions, decisions lacking internal organizational support, decisions lacking staff support, and decisions with limited resources (p<.05).

Emergent opportunity was *as* successful as discovery in nonprofit settings, for low importance decisions, for middle managers, and when resources were lacking. This argues against allowing an emergent opportunity to terminate discovery in *for profit* settings and when the more demanding conditions identified above are present. The data show that idea imposition was often unsuccessful. Only when there was *substantial* staff support did idea imposition produce the best results (p<.05). Discovery was more successful than idea imposition for 13 of the 14 conditions tested, with greater adoptions and higher ratings completed in a shorter time period (p<.05). These differences were often very large (see Table 17.4). When facing the more tying conditions that can arise during decision making, the data suggest that a DM should avoid emergent opportunities and let discovery play out. Also, DMs should not expect a redevelopment process to bail out a failed idea-driven process. The success of discovery was noted for nearly the entire range of decision-making conditions considered (p<.05), offering considerable support for H4.

The findings for *content* follow a pattern similar to that found for context. Discovery had comparable or better success than the other three processes (p<.05) for all decision types with sufficient observations to analyze. (Four of the eight types had three or fewer observations.)

Best practice processes

Each of the four processes was further examined to determine if a particular set of tactics improves the prospect of success. Each process was explored to see how success is influenced when each tactic was employed. To test H5, compare the success profile for typical practice (shown in Table 17.3) with the success realized when the best practice tactics were used in each process type. The empirical results are summarized in Tables 17.5 to 17.8.

Best Practice for Discovery. Tactical choices for discovery include objectives or problems as a direction, any of the search tactics, using participation or intervention to implement, and any of the evaluation tactics. Despite the already high rate of success for discovery, some of the tactical choices made a notable improvement in the success of discovery, supporting H5 (p<.05). Best practice calls for using an objective, searching with either benchmarking or innovation, using analytical or participation evaluation tactics, and implementing with participation or intervention, as shown by the data in the lower half of Table 17.5. Decisions made with a discovery process that applied these best practice tactics were sought in the data base. These decisions had sustained adoptions of 94 %, complete adoption of 88 %, and duration of 11.8 months. Comparing with typical practice finds that sustained adoptions declined to 79 %, complete adoptions to 72 %, and duration increased to 13.3 months (p<.05). The tactical choices had little influence on decision value.

Best practice for discovery calls for an objective-driven search that either benchmarks what others do or seeks innovation and evaluates either analytically or with participation. To illustrate, GE Abrasives set a production capacity target (objective) to guide a successful innovation effort that uncovered a way to revamp its production planning system. Contrast this with problem-directed search that identifies what is wrong to provide a direction. Decision makers begin with an assessment to determine what is wrong, offering a direction that calls for overcoming the problems identified. Nationwide, a large insurance company with many specialized insurance products sold to a variety of customers, had problems with its data processing system. The system was near 100 % capacity, making downtime very disruptive. The CIO deferred new ideas for computer use to study the capacity problem, concluding that many user requests were frivolous (the problem), so new capacity was not needed. A consultant was hired to find ways to set priorities and devise preemption rules to free up computer time for high priority jobs (solicitation). Note how the problem direction narrowed the scope of search, limiting what was considered to priority setting and preemption rules.

Solicitation may reduce the prospect of success because many vendors and consultants force fit their off-the-shelf products to a client's situation. Tailoring comes later to accommodate the client's needs. This tailoring was found to be both expensive and incomplete, never fully accounted for client needs.

Best Practice for Idea Imposition. Improvements in the idea imposition process are limited to evaluation tactical choices and implementation with persuasion and an edict. Best practice avoids analytical evaluations. As shown in Table 17.6, decision in the data base that adopted these best practice tactics improved sustained adoption rates from 52 % to 75 %, complete adoption from 36 % to 50 %, decision value from above adequate to good, and drastically cut duration from 22.5 to 5.5 months (p<.05). This provides a sizable improvement in success, supporting H5. However, the success realized from using best practice tactics coupled with idea imposition falls far short of the success realized with discovery, without best practice tactics, providing further support for H1 (p<.05). One quarter of the idea imposition decisions with best practice tactics continue to be failure-prone.

The CEO of Anthony Thomas, a candy manufacturing company, visited a trade show and saw a packaging machine that offered a pilfer-proof package that could be resealed (opportunity). The pilfer-proof feature seemed desirable (judgment) and

TABLE 17.5 Best practice for discovery

	USE		EFFECTIVENESS						EFFICIENCY	
			Sustained Adoption		Complete Adoption		Decision Value		Total Time	
		Frequency								
PROCESS TYPES	N	Freq.	Rate	DMRT	Rate	DMRT	Rating	DMRT	Months	DMRT
Best practice (Objectives; innovation or benchmarking)	15	38%	**94%**		**88%**		**4.3**		**11.8**	
Typical Practice	23	62%	79%		72%		3.9		13.3	
ANOVA / p value		.05			.05		.08		.09	
MANOVA / p value		.09								
Direction										
Objectives	16	41%	**94%**		**88%**		**4.2**		11.4	
Problems	10	25%	80%		70%		3.9		11.2	
ANOVA/p value			.05		.04		.08		ns	
MANOVA/ p value				.08						
Search										
Innovation	20	51%	**95%**	A	85%	A/B	**4.2**	A	12.6	B
Benchmarking	11	28%	**91%**	A	**91%**	A	**4.5**	A	**8.7**	A
Solicitation	8	20%	75%	B	75%	B	4.0	A/B	14.2	B
ANOVA/ p value			.05		.05		.07		.06	
MANOVA/ p value			.05							

(Continued)

TABLE 17.5 (Continued)

PROCESS TYPES	USE		EFFECTIVENESS				Decision Value		EFFICIENCY	
	Frequency		Sustained Adoption		Complete Adoption				Total Time	
	N	Freq.	Rate	DMRT	Rate	DMRT	Rating	DMRT	Months	DMRT
Evaluation										
Analytical	8	20%	88%		88%		4.4		13.2	
Bargaining	3	7%	95%		95%		4.5		17.1	
Subjective	15	38%	93%		87%		4.1		14.8	
Judgment	3	7%	95%		90%		4.3		9.3	
ANOVA/ p value			Ns		.ns		ns		ns	
MANOVA/ p value			Ns							
Implementation										
Intervention	14	36%	93%		86%		4.5		11.9	
Participation	25	64%	88%		84%		4.1		11.8	
Persuasion	0	–								
Edict	0	–								
ANOVA/ p value			Ns		ns		ns		ns	
MANOVA/ p value			Ns							
Totals	39	100%								

TABLE 17.6 Best practice for idea imposition

PROCESS TYPES	USE		EFFECTIVENESS						EFFICIENCY	
	Frequency		Sustained Adoption		Complete Adoption		Decision Value		Total Time	
	N	Freq.	Rate	DMRT	Rate	DMRT	Rating	DMRT	Months	DMRT
Best practice (Evaluation avoid analysis; edict implementation)	4	13%	**75%**		**50%**		**4.0**		**5.5**	
Typical practice	25	87%	52%		36%		3.5		22.5	
ANOVA / p value			.02		.01		.08		.01	
MANOVA / p value			.04							
Evaluation										
Bargaining	4	13%	**75%**	A	**75%**	A	**4.5**	A	20.3	B
Analytical	5	17%	33%	B	33%	B	3.5	A/B	18.6	B
Subjective	10	34%	**70%**	A	40%	B	3.7	A/B	30.0	C
Judgment	3	10%	**67%**	A	**67%**	A	3.6	A/B	**6.5**	A
ANOVA/ p value			.05		.05		.08		.05	
MANOVA/ p value			ns							
Implementation										
Persuasion	23	79%	52%		35%		3.5		23.4	
Edict	6	21%	**67%**		**66%**		**4.0**		**11.2**	
Participation	0									
Intervention	0									
ANOVA/ p value			.05		.01		.04		.03	
MANOVA/ p value			.05							
Totals	29	100%								

the machine and accessories were purchased and used to package some company products (edict). The candy with a reseal package did not seem to sell because the package looked generic, suggesting a bulk product, which did not conform to the company's carefully crafted image of high-quality candy. The CEO asked staff to find another use for the machine or a buyer. They failed to do either and the machine remained idle. The CEO resisted an analytic evaluation and persuasion. Both would set in motion events that could have revealed concerns about sales of candy with a generic look.

Other idea imposition decisions suggest that DMs, pushing an idea, fear such evaluations thinking that a careful evaluation may lead to criticism of their ideas. Others are propelled by a sense of urgency. When a 'good idea' is spotted they want to 'get it done' and push for action. This avoidance of objective data and evoking power to get an idea installed gets rapid results, but fails to ensure an adoption for about half of these decisions. About a quarter are ultimately withdrawn. Best practice tactics improve the prospect of success for idea imposition but success realized falls far short of that noted for discovery.

Best Practice for Emergent Opportunity. DMs who followed an emergent opportunity process selected among the evaluation and implementation tactics. The success of the tactical options is shown in Table 17.7. The data show that DMs using an emergent opportunity process typically call for an analytical evaluation and rarely use a judgment or a subjective evaluation. Analytic evaluations seem to be preferred because an emergent idea is apt to raise questions about its merit. Solid evidence showing that a problem can be overcome or an objective met is required to demonstrate merit. Success was influenced by the choices made to guide search, in the now abandoned discovery effort. If a problem, and not objective, was used to guide a search the prospect of success for an emergent opportunity declined dramatically.

The data also show that decision makers can make tactical selections that can doom the emergent opportunity. Discovery processes lead a decision effort with implementation, so either intervention or participation is in place (Table 17.3). The emergent opportunity provoked two outcomes. Decision makers using intervention rejected the emergent opportunity and maintained a discovery process. The idea was held in abeyance and added to the pool of ideas uncovered in the ongoing search. When an opportunity surfaced and participation was being used, some DMs abandoned discovery. Some of these DMs terminated participation and resorted to persuasion, drawing on the support gleaned from an evaluation to sell the 'opportunity'. The more successful decision makers maintained participation and offered the idea to the team conducting the search, seeking ratification. When decision makers maintained participation in this way, the prospect of success for an emergent opportunity improved.

This suggests that best practice for emergent opportunity continues the best practice commitments in the now discarded discovery process. When objectives and participation were in place, success approached that of discovery. Adoptions for best practice emergent opportunity are 85 to 86 % for outcomes rated as good, carried out in 12.7 months (Table 17.7). Compare this to discovery with 85 to 90 % adoptions, rating of good plus and 11.8 months' duration. If discovery is being

TABLE 17.7 Best practice for emergent opportunity

PROCESS TYPES	USE		EFFECTIVENESS						EFFICIENCY	
	Frequency		Sustained Adoption		Complete Adoption		Decision Value		Total Time	
	N	Freq.	Rate	DMRT	Rate	DMRT	Rating	DMRT	Months	DMRT
Best practice (begin discovery with participation and objectives)	5	33%	**86%**		**85%**		**4.0**		**12.7**	
Typical practice	10	66%	59%		48%		3.3		29.0	
ANOVA/ p value			.04		.03		.05		.01	
MANOVA/ p value				.04						
Direction										
Objectives	5	33%	**83%**		**82%**		**4.3**		**10.0**	
Problems	9	60%	53%		55%		3.2		24.5	
ANOVA/ p value			.03		.01		.04		.01	
MANOVA/ p value			.04							
Evaluation										
Analytical	17	**80%**	**70%**		**60%**		**3.5**		**10.1**	
Subjective	2	13%	–		–		–		–	
Judgmental	1	7%	–		–		–		–	
Bargaining	0									
ANOVA/ p value										
MANOVA/ p value										
Implementation										
Persuasion	6	40%	50%		33%		3.0		10.0	
Edit	0	–								
Participation	7	46%	**85%**		**85%**		**4.0**		**26.4**	
Intervention	1	7%	–		–		–		–	
ANOVA/ p value			.03		.01		.04		.03	
MANOVA/ p value			.04							
Totals	29	100%								

directed by problems and decision makers discard participation for persuasion success declines. Adoptions dropped to 59 to 48 %, outcome ratings fall to just above adequate, and duration swells to 29 months. Without best practice, abandoning discovery for an emergent opportunity resulted in a large drop in success (p<.05).

To see how this comes about, consider a decision to upgrade a materials requirements planning (MRP) system in the Wireless Communications (WC) division of AT&T. The decision involved several departments and various branches of the company. The WC division manager formed a team (participation) to identify problems. The team uncovered a number of problems including material shortages, customer complaints regarding service quality, late delivery, and high cost. When the team clarified the magnitude of the problems it alarmed the division manager, prompting him to take immediate action by recommending a pre-packaged MRP system (persuasion). This was justified by the seeming severity of the problems and because an apparent solution popped up at a conference that the WC division manager attended. The performance data offered at the conference suggested that an MRP system had been successful in other similar situations (evaluation). The system was installed but had many glitches, causing a three-day plant shutdown. For the next three months the MRP system was continually modified until it fit local needs and operations.

A problem-directed discovery process was twice as likely to be abandoned for an emergent opportunity as an objective-directed one. A reading of the cases suggests two explanations. The objective makes expected results clear. An emergent opportunity would not seem useful unless the expectations are met. But an emergent idea can provide relief from a threat prompted by an unresolved problem. Pressure mounts to defuse the threat. Hoping to neutralize the threat in an unresolved problem, even savvy decision makers adopted the quick fix found in the emergent idea and terminated an ongoing search. Unless best practice tactics are used, the result is a sharp decline in the prospects of success.

Redevelopment Best Practice. The solution prompting an idea imposition effort was discarded and a replacement sought in half of these decisions. Redevelopment calls for selecting tactics to search, evaluate, and install a remedy. The motivation to act continued to be focused on the implied benefits of the discarded idea. Decision makers could have reverted to direction setting to identify a problem or to set an objective, but did not choose to do so. Instead, DMs engaged a search to find a replacement solution, seeking benefits that measure up to those expected for the now abandoned idea. The analysis reported in Table 17.8 shows that none of the search or evaluation tactics improve the prospect of success for a redevelopment process. Best practice stems from using edicts to install the replacement solution. Improvement is small, but supports H5 (p<.05). Complete adoptions rose from 56 % to 67 %, outcome ratings from adequate/good to approaching excellent, and time was cut from 17.5 to 13.7 months. Best practice for redevelopment takes more time than discovery and has significantly fewer adoptions.

In redevelopment decisions, it was assumed that people had a clear picture of expected benefits. This was seldom the case. The failure to clarify expectations often made search clueless. A cardiologist in a university medical school attended a conference and saw a demonstration of a computerized EKG system. The

TABLE 17.8 Best practice for redevelopment

| | USE | | EFFECTIVENESS | | | | | | EFFICIENCY | |
| | Frequency | | Sustained Adoption | | Complete Adoption | | Decision Value | | Total Time | |
PROCESS TYPES	N	Freq.	Rate	DMRT	Rate	DMRT	Rating	DMRT	Months	DMRT
Best Practice (Innovation and Edict implementation)	3	11%	**67%**		**67%**		**4.7**		**13.7**	
Typical practice	25	89%	64%		56%		3.5		17.5	
ANOVA/ p value MANOVA/ p value			Ns	.07	.06		.05		.05	
Search										
Innovation	3	11%	**90%**	A	**67%**		**4.0**	A	19.3	A/B
Benchmarking	16	57%	63%	B	56%		**3.8**	A	17.0	A/B
Solicitation	9	33%	55%	B	50%		3.4	A/B	**15.5**	A
ANOVA/ p value MANOVA/ p value			.05	Ns	ns		.08		.09	
Evaluation										
Analytical	9	33%	67%		67%		4.0		**15.3**	A
Bargaining	0	–	–		–		–		–	
Subjective	9	33%	56%		56%		3.3		17.1	A/B
Judgmental	2	7%	0%		0%		2.5		22.5	C

(*Continued*)

TABLE 17.8 (Continued)

| | USE | | EFFECTIVENESS | | | | | | EFFICIENCY | |
| | Frequency | | Sustained Adoption | | Complete Adoption | | Decision Value | | Total Time | |
PROCESS TYPES	N	Freq.	Rate	DMRT	Rate	DMRT	Rating	DMRT	Months	DMRT
ANOVA/ p value			Ns		ns		ns		.05	
MANOVA/ p value			Ns							
Implementation.										
Participation	9	33%	**78%**	A	55%	B	3.7	B	16.1	B
Persuasion	16	57%	55%	C	47%	C	3.3	C	18.4	C
Edict	3	11%	67%	B	**67%**	A	**4.7**	A	**13.7**	A
Intervention	0	–								
ANOVA/ p value			.05		.05		.04		.05	
MANOVA/ p value		.05								
Totals	28	100%								

demonstration suggested that the system could be useful for both research and practice (opportunity). The system was rejected by his colleagues because it used a 12-lead system that was seen as out-of-date (subjective evaluation). The hospital CEO liked the idea (persuasion). He authorized the cardiologist to pursue it and offered seed money to support the effort. The cardiologist contracted with faculty in the university's industrial engineering department to develop a 3-lead EKG system (solicitation). The effort ultimately failed when continuing funding could not be found. It turned out that many 3-lead systems had been developed with federal funding and could be purchased from vendors. Note that the redevelopment effort had no objective, such as improved service or improved system reliability. Nor were there any problems to be overcome. Development just assumed that the idea was valuable. Undirected benchmarking and innovation fared no better than solicitation and analytical evaluations are unable to improve the prospect of success.

CONCLUSIONS

Previous decision-making research focused on use of analysis, comprehensiveness, leadership, personality, groups, and the like so these constructs have been drawn upon to fashion decision-making theory. This study adds action-taking to the list, offering insights into 'how' questions for decision-making theory. How questions concern process, the sequence and nature of actions that increase the chance of success.

Four processes were considered. Descriptive/interpretive studies suggest a 'solution-first' process. Prescriptive work calls for a process with learning that offers an appraisal of needs and desired results to direct a search. A solution-first process has a 'see first' motivation (e.g. Mintzberg and Westley, 2001; Langley et al., 1995) because managers examine a solution to make sense of their needs. This creates a preference for ready-made plans and the urge to adopt an emergent opportunity (e.g. Olsen, 1976; Mausch and LaPotin, 1989). Prescriptions call for deliberation that emphasizes a systematic gathering of information to learn about the decision and its prospects. In this study, a solution-first process was termed idea imposition and the learning process was called discovery. Some of the discovery and idea imposition efforts were abandoned in the decisions studied, idea imposition when the idea failed and when an emergent opportunity supplanted discovery. When an idea failed the process shifted to a redevelopment effort and an emergent opportunity process displaced some discovery efforts.

There was no empirical support for an idea imposition process and the support for a discovery process was compelling. Discovery was attempted in 26 % of the decisions studied and idea imposition attempted in 28 % of the decisions. Discovery was also far more successful than either of the modified processes of emergent opportunity and redevelopment. Discovery was more successful than the other three processes even when these processes applied best practice tactics. Furthermore, discovery was more successful than the other processes for the more demanding conditions (e.g. high urgency) and more successful than emergent opportunity for all but the low importance decision. Despite this, decision makers were as apt to use the failure-prone idea imposition process as the more successful discovery process. A third of the discovery efforts were abandoned when an emergent opportunity surfaced and half of the ideas in an idea imposition effort proved to be ill-advised, with redevelopment applied to find a replacement. Emergent opportunity replaced discovery and redevelopment replaced idea imposition as theorized. Neither process was as successful as discovery for most of the conditions considered in this study. Best practice tactics improved the success rate for all four of the processes. However, the success of discovery, without best practice tactics, was better than the success realized when best practice tactics were used in idea imposition, redevelopment, and emergent opportunity. The success realized by discovery generalizes to a number of relevant conditions that can arise during decision making and is better than decisions made using other processes that apply best practice tactics.

The findings add insights into the sequencing of process steps and the importance of each step for theory building. The steps followed during decision making matter. The more important steps investigate claims, conduct a stakeholder-sensitive implementation, and set a direction. Successful DMs carry out these steps early in their decision-making efforts. There appear to be no shortcuts. Essential steps stress logical and political rationality, calling for expectations to be set and politics to be managed early in the process. Compared to the others, evaluation is the least important step, suggesting that political and logical rationality are more important than economic rationality. If the direction is clear *and* the social and political forces are managed, success is likely. If these steps are not engaged, evaluations have little influence on success.

Idea imposition and emergent opportunity are *idea-driven*. Both are guided by a ready-made solution and mobilize action to put the solution to use, as noted in the candy wrapper and information system decisions. DMs who prefer idea imposition seem wedded to rapid action. The preference for a 'quick fix' is motivated by pragmatics and by fear. Being decisive by seizing an opportunity is seen as the hallmark of a successful executive (Brunsson, 1982), creating a preference for speed (Starbuck, 1983). When an appealing opportunity surfaces, some decision makers act quickly to document its alleged benefits (e.g. more candy sales via the new package, more information broadens managers' purview). This deflects situations that could spin out of control and harm a career. The quick fix has several important shortcomings. It creates a trap that limits search and discourages knowledgeable people from offering ideas. The 'opportunity' often appears to be a pet idea, raising questions about the DM's motives. The hoped-for rapid response is delayed as the DM lines up support for a defense. In addition, the time to tailor a ready-made plan to fit with the organization and its environment is often underestimated (Nutt, 1984). All this directs people's energy and company resources away from learning (Senge, 1990). Instead, time and energy are devoted to finding desirable attributes of the solution, promoting it, or tailoring it to fit the organization. Had replacing the failed idea been factored into the success profile of an idea imposition process, its success would fall to even more dismal levels.

Themes of opportunity, ambiguity, and paradox suggest additional avenues for theory building. Opportunities seem compelling but made decision making failure-prone. As a result, remedy-driven conceptions of decision making, such as sense making (Weick, 1979), describe what decision makers may *prefer* to do, but fail to capture what *should* be done. This occurs because imposing a remedy creates a misleading clarity of purpose. Sources of ambiguity are swept aside. Consider the fiasco produced by Limited's information system decision. Organizational members never questioned why the company needed to change its approach to information gathering and dissemination, or asked about expected results. Decisions that begin with a remedy found in an opportunity consider only that idea. Reframing questions such as 'why do we need a new system?' or 'how do we reduce costs or provide better service?' are not posed. This difficulty arose in redevelopment as well. When seeking a replacement for a failed idea, expected results remained vague. With little to guide the effort, redevelopment took many unproductive turns.

Ambiguity adds another ingredient for process theory building. As Wildavsky (1979) points out, people don't know what they want until they see what they can get. Having an answer sweeps aside ambiguity, giving temporary relief: but this derails search. Beginning with a remedy is rash when decision makers lack an understanding of their needs. Instead of contemplating needs, decision makers are drawn to documenting the virtues of an idea and stakeholders' reactions to it. The more blatant this becomes the more defensive the evaluation, seeking to turn aside a critic's objections. The ambiguity provoked by knowing what is wanted but lacking an adequate remedy is a powerful motivator to find remedies for troubling issues.

Paradoxes offer some concluding insights for process theory development. Paradoxes arise in setting of directions, in finding new ideas, and in the installation of a preferred course of action. Selecting a direction sets aside all other possible directions. A reading of the cases suggests that decision makers who failed to set a direction frequently overlook useful ideas. To avoid this DMs are admonished to avoid the 'error of the third kind' (Raiffa, 1969), solving the wrong problem. No tests are offered by Raiffa or his followers to find a 'best' direction. Consider a car dealer that links lost sales to training. The focal direction calls for better training. To enrich the search, consider a narrower direction of salesperson behavior and a broader one of profits (Nutt, 1992). By searching in all three domains, more possibilities are considered including ways to avoid turning off customers, pricing policy, buyer incentives, and the like that could increase sales and profits. Directions have a hierarchical relationship. The decision makers must deal with behavioral issues to do training and training is needed before incentives and promotions can work (Nutt, 2004). Anything that widens a search increases the chance of finding a solution with a significant advantage.

The power paradox arises when DMs overuse their position power. Pushing a preferred solution is viewed as a manager's prerogative. But the more one uses position power, the less effective it becomes. Merely asking someone for their views empowers the person and does nothing to erode the manager's prerogatives. Pushing an idea over people's objections requires a manager to ratchet his/her power until all resistance disappears. As power is used, social credit is gradually lost. Ultimately, every decision becomes a test of will. To challenge the appearance of unilateral action even disinterested stakeholders resist a decision. The less decision makers use their power the more they acquire. Delegating a decision invariably sparks requests for guidance, allowing a DM to offer a preference without creating suspicion about his/her motives (Nutt, 2002).

An innovation paradox arises when DMs endorse new ideas and then erect barriers that make innovation all but impossible. Innovation requires a safe space in which to speculate about possibilities (Ray and Meyers, 1989) and a new space that lets creative juices flow (Nutt, 2002). Administrative structures that call for immediate accountability by evaluating ideas as they are suggested make innovation difficult, if not impossible. Yet many DMs in my studies made just these demands and then called for creativity. Understanding how to deal with the paradoxes of direction, power, and innovation is essential to build a process theory. My research shows that clear directions, innovation promotion, and artful implementation are the key to success. Ways to deal with the paradoxes offer some of the essential pieces for theory development.

Several questions merit further study. Exploration of the interactions of process types with each of the contextual factors offers additional qualifications. Space has prohibited exploring the nuances offered by the interaction of decision type, urgency, importance, resources, staff support, internal organizational support, the organization's profit status, and decision-maker level with the process types. Generally, a discovery process success is unaffected by these factors. But the other three processes are influenced in very negative ways by some of the contingencies. Exploring these effects may offer additional insight into factors that limit success. Also, examining other contextual factors that could influence a discovery process seems needed. Additional testing of the 'content question' with additional decisions that add to the limited numbers of decision types would be useful. Factors such as high velocity environments, decision style, uncertainty, and risk may be important. They may identify additional conditions under which a discovery process may or may not be successful, how such conditions arise, and ways to limit or exploit them to increase the chance of success. Comparison of the relative importance of context and process was carried out but not reported. The test was made by comparing the size of the main effect of 'process' to the main effects of the 'contextual factors' to see whether process or context explain more of the variance in the success measures. Process explains significantly more variance, suggesting that process has more influence on success than do contextual factors. Space limitations prohibited discussion of this finding. About half of the decisions fit none of the process types examined in this study. Exploration of these yet to be classified decisions may be useful, revealing other kinds of processes that can be labeled in various ways, such as 'mixed mode'. Other process types, such as chance (Cohen *et al.*, 1972), may be linked to the decisions in the data and offer interesting findings. Several questions about such processes warrant attention, such as identifying the features of processes that are highly successful or very unsuccessful. Cycling and interrupts cause steps to be repeated and the process to backtrack. The measures collected for these factors proved to be unreliable so cycling and interrupts could not be included in the analysis. Thus, little is known about how each influences the four process types. Better measures of each factor could elaborate the findings in useful ways.

APPENDIX I: ILLUSTRATIONS OF ORGANIZATIONS AND DECISIONS IN THE CASE DATA BASE

Organizations*	Decisions
Quaker-Snapple	Acquisition of Snapple
Ross Laboratories	Marketing infant formula to developing countries
Florida Medicaid Division	Fraud management system
Ohio DNR	Supporting wildlife programs
U.S. Air Force	Decompression service
Veterans Administration	Restructuring
City of Columbus, Ohio	Light rail
Ohio DOT	Budget system revamping
Michigan Health Department	Dispose of contaminated cattle
Public School System	Redesign curriculum
U.S. Navy	Radar Development
McDonald's	New location and design
Korean Tire Co.	Marketing in South America
Nationwide Insurance	Computer system capacity
Allied Van Lines	Pricing Services
Marshall Fields	New product line
Bank One	Sell Visa Cards
Fifth-Third Bank	Drop Saturday service
GE	MRP system
National City Corp.	Private label credit card
Lennox	Recycle toxic waste
Mead Paper	Cost cutting system
Anthony Thomas Candy	New Product
Delco	Tariff management
CompuServe	New on-line service
Bethlehem Steel	Scheduling blast furnace maintenance
Battelle Memorial Inst.	Contract bidding
Toyota Dealership	Increase sales
Nationwide	Build hockey arena
Limited, Inc	Purchase an information system
American Electric Power	CAD/CAM system
General Motors	Robotic assemblers
Shell	Dispose of the Brent Spar oil platform
Huntington Bank	Billing and collection procedures
American Telephone and Telegraph	Marketing Plan

(Continued)

Organizations*	Decisions
400 bed acute care urban hospital	Lithotripsy service
McDonald-Douglas	TQM teams
Barings Bank	Allow unsupervised commodities trading
Dunning Lathrup Insurance	Modify bonus policy
Disney	Locate EuroDisney in Paris
1000 bed University hospital	Purchase a magnetic resonance imager
343 bed acute care hospital	Create a DeTox unit
Lane Bryant, Inc.	Intimate Apparel
For-Profit abstracting company	Reference library
A large company	Marketing program
Delco, electronics	Inventory control system
Hertz-Penske Rental	Customer Service system
NCR	Cash Flow Management

*Some organizations requested anonymity

APPENDIX II: COLLECTING THE DATA BASE OF DECISIONS

Soliciting Participation – People holding key positions in organizations were asked to participate in a long-term effort to accumulate decisions to uncover decision-making practices. A decision was defined as an episode, beginning when the organization first became aware of a motivating concern and ending with an implementation attempt. To ensure interest and first hand knowledge, the contact person was asked to select a recent decision (made within the past six months) of consequence, due to the resources required and presidents set. The contact person was asked to identify *three* people that could be interviewed, including the person who had primary responsibility for the decision. Typically, the contact person suggested a decision for which he/she was responsible and became the primary informant. The contact person was then asked to solicit two additional informants who were familiar with the decision. Cases grew in this way for 20 years.

Informants – The three informants had different roles. The primary informant, the decision maker, provided information about the steps followed to make the decision. *One* of the secondary informants, selected by the decision makers as the more knowledgeable, also provided a listing of steps as a check. The two secondary informants filled out questionnaires to rate the decision's value and most of the contextual factors (urgency, importance, etc.), and indicate duration. To separate thinking about outcomes from the recall of how the decision was made for the secondary informant who also listed decision steps, the questionnaire data was collected prior to the interview and on a separate day.

Interviews – Data collected to recall events can be biased by inaccurate information caused by self-justification, memory lapses, and logical inconsistencies. To cope with these difficulties, steps were taken to improve the prospect of full and accurate disclosure. They call for multiple informants and data sources, focusing on factual events in interviews, seeking convergence of interpretations, and a second chance review to jog memory. Recent decisions reduced memory lapses. Only informants with first-hand knowledge were consulted. Also, archival records, and documents, cross-checking the sources, were used to validate. The interviews sought to converge on an understanding of the actions taken to make each decision and not on measuring differences. Two informants were independently interviewed to uncover these actions. The interview procedure was devised to deal with the dual problems of what people remember and choose to tell. In separate interviews, the informants were asked to recall what *first* captured their attention. Questioning proceeded from this point asking 'what happened next'. For example, after an informant described what captured his/her attention, he/she was asked why this seemed important and merited action. Questioning took cues from the last response to fashion the next query. The information gleaned from the second informant was used to corroborate what the primary informant said.

Triangulating Responses – I prepared a narrative of about 20 pages to record the interview information that described the decision and the actions taken to make it, as recalled by *each* informant. The informants reviewed their narrative separately and made any changes they believed were warranted. Then, documents such as notes, proposals, or files that still existed were collected and reviewed. Documents and the actions noted by the informants were compared to find inconsistencies and gaps in their 'story'. Inconsistencies and gaps were explored in a follow-up interview with the *primary* informant, the decision maker. In this interview, attempts were made to reconcile differences and fill in gaps. Thus, method and two types of informant triangulation were used to test the accuracy of each decision description. A clear picture of the actions taken, agreeable to the primary informant, was required to include a decision in the data base. A number of decisions failed to meet the clarity or agreement tests and were abandoned. Summary case profiles were prepared for surviving decisions. The profiles listed the actions taken by tracing them through a 'transactional model' to depict how (and if) recommended decision-making steps were activated, and how each was carried out, tracing the order of actions taken through the transactional model (Nutt, 1993a).

Identifying Tactics – Tactics were uncovered by the author from the narratives and the profiles, using questionnaire data and other documents when disagreements or gaps arose. The narratives and the profiles provided the key information source used to determine actions taken to make each decision. Data from the questionnaires were used to refine some of these actions. Separate reviews of the data were carried out for each tactic. Each decision was examined to determine how intelligence was gathered, direction set, options identified, evaluations done, and implementation carried out. The cases were sorted to find distinct tactics, repeating each sort until there was classification agreement. Each sort put the decisions into expected tactic categories (e.g. participation for implementation), emergent categories (e.g. intervention for implementation), or an unknown category (no clear pattern). The sort was then repeated to see if the tactic categories could be reproduced. When previous classifications were reproduced, it was assumed that intra-rater reliability was achieved. Inter-rater reliability was determined by having colleagues sort the decisions. Using the definitions, the second rater matched cases and categories; which led to a 90 % agreement.

APPENDIX III: HOW THE TACTICS ARE USED DURING DECISION MAKING

Gather intelligence – Decisions begin with claims (Toulmin, 1979) that call into question organizational practices and suggest ways to cope (Downs, 1967; Pounds, 1969; Nutt, 1979). Decision makers respond in one of two ways. Some selected among several of the claims, according to the power and influence of the claimant (Cyert and March, 1963; Pfeffer, 1992). Because a claim suggests what to do, such as buy new computers or conduct training, this commits the DM to an action. The claimant's power and influence create pressure to buy the new computers or conduct the training. Other decision makers gather information and talk with trusted associates to uncover and investigate concerns that underlie alleged unsatisfactory conditions. Information gathering was not limited to those making claims but included others with stakes and interests. As a result, intelligence gathering took one of two forms. Some DMs acted on an opportunity found in a claim; others explored the claims being offered to uncover needs (Nutt, 1998a). DMs who acted on an opportunity were much less successful than DMs who looked for needs. Success stemmed from revealing underlying and hidden concerns, enlarging the arena of action. The broader range of concerns often pointed to issues that had little relation to those noted in a claim. A decision-making effort with a larger arena of action had access to a broader scope of potential remedies and was more successful (Nutt, 2002).

Set Directions – Needs and opportunities provided different points of departure for the decision-making process (Table 17.2). DMs who adopted a solution found in a claim looked to the solution to provide direction, as shown in the direction setting column in Table 17.2. Reasons for action were inferred from the solution's alleged benefits. Other DMs explored needs to find reasons for taking action. These DMs looked for ways to define the need by identifying a problem, such as finding why training or customer satisfaction is lagging, or by setting an objective indicating expected results, such as reducing turnover or increasing customer satisfaction (Nutt, 1992). A problem identifies what is wrong that requires fixing. An objective delineates desired results. Research shows that success increased when DMs set a direction with a statement of hoped-for results (Nutt, 1993a; Lock et al., 1988; 1990). Decision making guided by an objective was more successful than decision making guided by solutions or problems.

Uncover Options – At this point, *some* DMs were attempting to uncover ideas, as shown by the option development column in Table 17.2; others were opportunity-driven. An opportunity-driven process skips a formal search (Mintzberg et al., 1976; Eisenhardt and Zbaracki, 1992; Harrison and Phillips, 1991). The remaining processes were directed by a problem or an objective. For both a problem-driven and an objective-driven process, search is required to find solutions to overcome a problem or meet an objective. Search is more successful if multiple solutions with innovative ideas are sought (Maier, 1970; MacCrimmon and Taylor, 1976; Nutt, 1984,

Gemuden and Hauschildt, 1985). Multiple options increase the number of ideas considered, which improves the chance of finding a superior one. My studies find that benchmarking, solicitation, and innovation are used by DMs to search (Nutt, 1993b). To use benchmarking, a DM visits a respected organization or a high performing work unit to document their business practices for adaptation (Hart and Bogan, 1993). Solicitation makes the organization's needs known to vendors or consultants. Innovation requires a new idea, one that has not been previously recognized (Van de Ven *et al.*, 1999), or 'radical innovation', ideas that are new to an industry (Damanpour, 1991), seeking first-mover advantage in a marketplace. Both require a custom-made solution, calling on DMs to look for a new idea without reference to ready-made plans, the practices of others, or vendor ideas. My research finds that taking the time to learn with a search tactic pays big dividends, confirming prior work on the value of a broad search (Pettigrew, 1987; Kobe, 1983; Nutt, 2001a). Each of the search tactics can be successful if an objective is set and multiple options are sought (Nutt, 1993a; 2000).

Evaluate Alternatives – DMs evaluated alternatives by using judgment, bargaining, analysis, and subjective tactics (see Table 17.1). DMs who use judgment apply intuition to make a choice (Mintzberg *et al.*, 1976). Bargaining calls on DMs to assemble the parties to a decision, asking them to reach a consensus about the merits of alternatives (Langley *et al.*, 1995). DMs apply analysis to make a factual assessment of benefits (e.g. Soelberg, 1967; Cohen *et al.*, 1972; Simon, 1977). Subjective tactics examine information drawn from archives, experts, or stakeholders, extracting arguments to support a course of action (Nutt, 2000). Subjective evaluations draw on sponsor reflections and expert testimony to make arguments that cite data, stakeholder experience, or expert testimony about what works and why. Analytic and bargaining tactics were often successful, subjective tactics had a mixed record of success, and judgmental tactics had a poor success record (Nutt, 1998b).

Implement – Implementation can begin early or late in the process, as shown by the proactive and reactive implementation columns in Table 17.2. To be proactive, a DM sets the stage by managing the social and political forces that can block a decision (Beyer and Trice, 1982). Decision makers lead with implementation by attempting to proactively manage such forces. The remaining DMs in my studies waited for an evaluation before attempting implementation, making it reactive. The motivation was to wait until benefits were uncovered so arguments and justifications could be marshaled from the evaluation to support a preferred plan of action.

DMs who *led* with implementation applied one of two tactics (Table 17.2). The participation tactic promoted ownership by giving people with interests (Hickson *et al.*, 1986; Cray *et al.*, 1991; Rodriguez and Hickson, 1995), or their representatives, membership in a decision-making group. The group carries out many of the key steps such as inventorying concerns, documenting needs, suggesting useful actions, and offering evaluations. Early and broad participation is best, with a group involved in several process steps (Nutt, 2002). This is similar to the bonding approach suggested by Beyer and Trice (1982). Another tactic, called intervention, calls on decision makers to justify the need for change (Nutt, 1986). DMs use networking to guide key stakeholders, one at a time, through an appraisal of needs and possible actions. DMs work through the key stakeholders to evolve a picture of what is feasible and desirable, seeking remedies stakeholders can support. The rationales uncovered are used to sell a remedy to the remaining stakeholders. This approach is similar to the transformational ideas of Leavitt (1987) and the benevolent autocratic role suggested by Likert (1967). Edict and persuasion tactics are used when implementation *follows* evaluation (see Table 17.2). Persuasion amasses arguments that support a decision, calling attention to benefits (Churchman, 1975; Ginsberg and Schultz, 1987). This captures tactics found in the prescriptions of Quinn (1980) and the 'informational' approaches identified by Beyer and Trice (1982). An edict dictates the behavior required to realize a decision. Position power is the key feature. Power is applied incrementally to push the recalcitrant and the uninformed toward acceptance (Quinn, 1980). Edicts have control (Beyer and Trice, 1982) and autocratic (Likert, 1967) features.

Intervention is nearly always successful; participation is often successful; persuasion works about half of the time; and edicts are failure-prone (Nutt, 1998c). During persuasion, DMs use evaluations defensively, seeking arguments that support a preferred course of action. This reduced their chance of success. Edicts failed when countervailing power was provoked. Because the barriers to action were considered early in the process, leading decision making with intervention or participation tactics had more success.

NOTE

1. This chapter is a longer version of a paper published in 2008 by JMS.

REFERENCES

Alexander, L. (1986) 'Successfully Implementing Strategic Decisions', in Mayon-White (ed.) *Planning and Making Change*. London: Harper Row.

Allison, G.T. (1971) Conceptual models and the Cuban Missile Crisis, *American Political Science Review*, 63, 968–1718.

Alter, C., and Hage, C. (1993) *Organizations Working Together*. Sage, CA: Newbury Park.

Bell, G., Bromley, P., and Bryson, J. (1998) 'Spinning a Complex Web: Links Between Strategic Decision Making Context, Content, Process, and Outcome', in V. Papadakis and P. Barwise (eds) *Strategic Decisions*. Boston, MA: Kluwer.

Beyer, J.M., and Trice, H.M. (1982) The utilization process: A conceptual framework and synthesis of empirical findings, *Administrative Science Quarterly*, 27 (4/5), 591–622.

Bower, J.L. (1970) *Managing the Resource Allocation Process: A Study of Corporate Planning and Investment*. Homewood, IL: Irwin.

Box, G., Hunter, S, and Hunter, W. (1978) *Statistics for Experimenters*. New York: John Wiley & Sons, Inc.

Brunsson, N. (1982) The irrationality of action and action rationality: Decisions, ideologies, and organization action, *Journal of Management Studies*, 19, 29–44.

Bryson, J.M., Bromiley, P., and Jung, V.S. (1990) The influences of context and process on project planning success, *Journal of Planning Education* 9 (3), 183–195.

Bryson, J.M., and Cullen, J.W. (1984) A contingent approach to strategy and tactics in formative and summative evaluation, *Evaluation and Program Planning*, 7, 267–290.

Butler, R. (1998) 'Strategic Decision Making: A Contingency Framework and Beyond', in V. Papadakis and P. Barwise (eds) *Strategic Decisions*. Boston, MA: Kluwer.

Cameron, K., and Lavine, M. (2006) *Making the Impossible Possible: Leading Extraordinary Performance – the Rocky Flats Story*. San Francisco, CA: Barrett-Koehler.

Carley, K. (1986) 'Measuring Efficiency in a Garbage can Hierarchy', in J. March and R. Weissinger-Baylor (eds) *Ambiguity and Command*, Marshfield: Pitman, 165–194.

Carter, E. (1971) The behavioral theory of the firm and top-level corporate decisions, *Administrative Science Quarterly*, 16, 413–428.

Churchman, C.W. (1975) 'Theories of Implementation', in R.L. Schultz and D.P. Slevin, *Implementing Operations Research/Management Science*. New York: Elsevier.

Cohen, M.D., March, J.P., and Olsen, J.P. (1972) A garbage can model of organizational choice, *Administrative Science Quarterly*, 17, 1–25.

Cosier, R., and Schwenk, C. (1990) Agreement, consensus, and thinking alike: ingredients for poor decisions, *Academy of Management Executive*, 4, 69–74.

Cray, D., Mallory, G., Butler, R., Hickson, D., and Wilson, D. (1991) Explaining decision processes, *Journal of Management Science*, 28 (3), 227–251.

Cyert, R.M., and March, J.G. (1963) *A Behavioral Theory of the Firm*. Englewood Cliff, NJ: Prentice-Hall.

Daft, R. (1995) *Organization Theory and Decision*. St Paul, MN: West Publishing Co.

Damanpour, F. (1991) Organizational innovation: A meta analysis of determinants and moderators, *Academy of Management Journal*, 34 (3) 555–590.

Dean, J., and Sharfman, M. (1996) Does decision making matter? A study of strategic decision making effectiveness, *Academy of Management Journal*, 39 (2), 368–396.

Denzin, N.K. (1989) *The Research Act*. Englewood Cliffs: NJ: Prentice Hall.

Dewey, J. (1910) *How We Think*. New York: Heath

Downs, A. (1967) *Inside Bureaucracy*. Boston, MA: Little & Brown.

Eisenhardt, K. (1989) Making fast decisions in high velocity environments, *Academy of Management Journal*, 32, 543–576.

Eisenhardt, K., and Bourgeois, J. (1989) 'Charting Strategic Decisions in the Micro Computer Industry: Profile of an Industry Starr', in M. Van Glenow and S. Moyermann (eds) *Managing Complexity in High Technology Organizations, Systems, and People*. New York: Oxford University Press, 74–89.

Eisenhardt, K., and Zbaracki, M. (1992) Strategic decision making, *Strategic Management Journal*, 13, 17–37.

Fredrickson, J.W. (1985) Effects of decision motive and organizational performance on strategic decision processes, *Academy of Management Journal*, 28, 821–843.

Genmunden, H., and Hauschildt, J. (1985) Number of alternatives and efficiency in different types of management decisions, *The European Journal of Operational Research*, 22 (2), 178–190.

Ginsberg, M.J., and Schultz, R.L. (1987) Special issues in implementation, *Interfaces*, 17 (3).

Golden, B. (1992) The past is the past – or is it? The use of retrospective accounts as indicators of past strategy, *Academy of Management Journal*, 35, 848–860.

Gustafson, D., Shukla, R., Delbecq, A., and Walster, G. (1973) A comparative study in subjective likelihood estimates made by individuals, interactive groups, and nominal groups, *Organizational Behavior and Human Performance*, 9, 280–291.

Hall, P. (1984) *Great Planning Disasters*. Berkeley, University of California Press.

Harrison, M., and Phillips, B. (1991) Strategic decision making: An integrative explanation, *Research in the Sociology of Organizations, JAI Press* 9, 319–358.

Hart, C., and Bogan, A. (1993) *The Baldridge Prize*, McGraw Hill.

Havelock, R.G. (1973) *Planning for Innovation*. Ann Arbor, Michigan: CRUSK, The Center for Utilization of Scientific Knowledge, fourth printing.

Hickson, D., Butler, R., Gray, D., Mallory, G., and Wilson, D. (1986) *Top Decisions: Strategic Decision making in Organizations*. San Francisco, CA: Jossey-Bass.

Hitt, M., Ireland, D., and Hoskisson, R. (1997) *Strategic Management*. St Paul, MN: West.

Huber, G., and Power, D.J. (1985) Retrospective reports of strategic-level managers: Guidelines for increasing their accuracy, *Strategic Management Journal*, 6, 171–180.

Janis, I.J. (1989) *Crucial Decisions*. New York: Free Press.

Kolb, D.A. (1983) 'Problem Management: Learning from Experience', in S. Srivastra (ed.) *The Executive Mind*, San Francisco, CA: Jossey-Bass.

Langley, A., Mintzberg, H., Pitcher, P., Posada, E., and Macary, J. (1995) Opening up decision making: The view from the back stool, *Organization Science*, 6 (3), 260–279.

Lant, T.K., and Mezias, S.J. (1992) An organizational learning model of convergence and reorientation, *Organization Science*, 3 (1), 47–71.

Laroche, H. (1995) From decisions to action in organizations, *Organization Science*, 6 (1), 47–71.

Leavitt, H.L. (1987) *Corporate Pathfinders*. New York: Penguin.

Likert, R. (1967) *The Human Organization*. New York: McGraw-Hill.

Lincoln, Y., and Guba, E. (1984) *Naturalistic Inquiry*. Beverly Hills, CA: Sage.

Locke, E.A., and Latham, G.P. (1990) *A Theory of Goal Setting and Task Performance*. Englewood Cliff, NJ: Prentice Hall.

Locke, E.A., Latham, G.P., and Erenz, M. (1988) The determinants of goal attainment, *Academy of Management Review*, 13, 23–39.

MacCrimmon, K.R., and Taylor, R.N. (1976) 'Decision making and Problem Solving,' in M. Dunnette (ed.) *Handbook of Industrial and Organizational Psychology*. Chicago: Rand-McNally.

Maier, N.R.F. (1970) *Problem Solving and Creativity: In Individuals and Groups*. New Uork: Brooks-Cole.

March, J. (1994) *A Primer on Decision Making: How Decisions Happen*. New York: Free Press.

March, J.G., and Simon, H.A. (1958) *Organizations*. New York: McGraw-Hill.

Masuch, M., and LaPotin, P. (1989) Beyond garbage can: An AI model of organizational choice, *Administrative Science Quarterly*, 34, 38–67.

McKie, D. (1973) *A Sadly Mismanaged Affair: The Political History of the Third London Airport*. London: Croon Helm.

Miller, C., Cardinal, L., and Glick, W. (1997) Retrospective reports in organizational research: A re-examination of recent evidence, *The Academy of Management Journal*, 40 (1), 189–204.

Mintzberg, H., Raisinghani, D., and Theoret, A. (1976) The structure of unstructured decisions, *Administrative Science Quarterly*, 21 (2), 246–275.

Mintzberg, H., and Waters, J.A. (1982) Tracking strategy in an entrepreneurial firm, *Academy of Management Journal*, 25 (3), 465–499.

Mintzberg, H., and F. Westley (2001) Decision making: Its not what you think, *MIT Sloan Management Review*, 42 (3), 89–93.

Nadler, G., and Hibino S. (1990) *Breakthrough Thinking*. Rocklin, CA: Prima.

Nisbett, R., and Ross, L. (1989) *Human Inferences: Strategies and Shortcomings of Human Judgments*. New York: John Wiley & Sons, Inc. (revised edition).

Numagami, T. (1998) The infeasibility of invariant laws in management studies: A reflective dialogue in defense of case studies, *Organizational Science*, 9 (1), 1–15.

Nutt, P.C. (1979) Calling out and calling in the dogs: Managerial diagnosis in organizations, *Academy of Management Review*, 4 (2), 203–214.

Nutt, P.C. (1984) Types of organizational decision processes, *Administrative Science Quarterly*, 29 (3), 414–450.

Nutt, P.C. (1986) The tactics of implementation, *Academy of Management Journal*, 29 (2), 230–261.

Nutt, P.C. (1989) *Making Tough Decisions*. San Francisco, CA: Jossey-Bass.

Nutt, P.C. (1992) Formulation tactics and the success of organizational decision making, *Decision Sciences* 23 (5), 519–540.

Nutt, P.C. (1993a) The formulation processes and tactics used in organizational decision making, *Organization Science*, 4 (2), 226–251.

Nutt, P.C. (1993b) The identification of solution ideas during organizational decision making, *Management Science*, 39 (9), 1071–1085.

Nutt, P.C. (1998a) Framing strategic decisions, *Organizational Science*, 9 (2), 195–206.

Nutt, P.C. (1998b) Evaluating complex strategic choices, *Management Science*, 44 (8), 1148–1166.

Nutt, P.C. (1998c) Leverage resistance and the success of implementation approaches, *Journal of Management Studies*, 35 (2), 213–240.

Nutt, P.C. (1999) Surprising but true: Half of organizational decisions fail, *Academy of Management Executive*, 13 (4), 75–90.

Nutt, P.C. (2000) 'Context, tactics, and the examination of alternatives during strategic decision making, *The European Journal of Operational Research*, 124 (1), 159–186.

Nutt, P.C. (2001a) Decision debacles and how to avoid them, *Business Strategy Review*, 12 (2), 1–14.

Nutt, P.C. (2001b) A taxonomy of strategic decisions and tactics for uncovering alternatives, *The European Journal of Operational Research*, 132 (3), 505–527.

Nutt, P.C. (2001c) 'Strategic Decision-Making', in M. Hitt, R. Freeman, and J. Harrison (eds) *The Blackwell Handbook of Strategic Management*. Oxford, United Kingdom: Blackwell Publishers Limited.

Nutt, P.C. (2002) *Why Decisions Fail: Avoiding The Blunders and Traps that Lead to Debacles*. San Francisco, CA: Barrett-Koehler.

Nutt, P.C. (2004a) On doing process research, *International Journal of Management Concepts and Philosophy*, 1 (1), 3–26.

Nutt, P.C. (2004b) Expanding search during strategic decision making, *Academy of Management Executive*, 18 (4), 13–28.

Nutt, P.C. (2007) Intelligence gathering for decision making, *OMEGA: the International Journal of Management Science*, 35 (1), 604–622.

Nutt, P.C. (2008) Investigating decision making processes, *Journal of Management Studies*, 45 (2), 425–455.

Olsen, J.P. (1976) 'Choice in Organized Anarchy', in J. March and J. Olsen (eds) *Ambiguity and Choice*. Bergen: Universities for Laget.

Papadakis, V., and Barwise, P. (1998) *Strategic Decisions*. Dordrecht, Netherlands: Kluwer Academic Publishers.

Patton, M.E. (1990) *Qualitative Evaluation and Research Methods*. Los Angeles, CA: Sage.

Pelz, D.C. (1978) 'Some Expanded Perspectives on Use of Social Science in Public Policy', in M. Yinger and S.J. Cutler (eds) *Major Social Issues: A Multidisciplinary View*. New York: Free Press, 346–357.

Perrow, C. (1967) A framework for the comparative analysis of organizations, *American Sociological Review*, 32 (4), 194–208.

Pettigrew, A. (1987) Context and action in the transformation of a firm, *Journal of Management Studies*, 11 (2), 31–48.

Pfeffer, J. (1992) *Managing with Power: Politics and Influence in Organizations*. Boston, MA: Harvard University Press.

Pinfield, L. (1986) A field evaluation of perspectives an organizational decision-making, *Administrative Science Quarterly*, 31, 365–388.

Podsakoff, P., and Organ, D. (1986) Self reports in organizational research, *The Journal of Management*, 12 (4), 531–544.

Poole S., and Van de Ven, A. (2004) *Organizational Change and Innovation*. New York: Oxford University Press.

Pounds, W. (1969) The process of problem finding, *Industrial Management Review*, Fall, 1–19.

Quinn, J.B. (1980) *Strategies for Change: Logical Incrementalism*. Homewood, IL: Dow Jones-Irwin.

Raiffa, H. (1970) *Decision Analysis: Introductory Lectures on Choice Under Uncertainty*. Reading, MA: Addison-Westley.

Rajagopalan, N., Rasheed, A., Datta, D., and Spreitzer, G. (1998) 'A Multi-theoretic Model of Strategic Decision Making Processes', in V. Papadakis and P. Barwise (eds) *Strategic Decisions*. Boston, MA: Kluwer Academic Publishers.

Ray, M., and Myers, R. (1989) *Creativity in Business*. New York: Doubleday.

Rodriguez, S., and Hickson, D. (1995) Success in decision making: Different organizations, different reasons for success, *Journal of Management Studies*, 32 (5), 654–679.

Schilit, W.K. (1990) A comparative analysis of strategic decisions, *Journal of Management Studies*, 27 (5), 435–461.

Senge, P. (1990) *The Fifth Discipline: The Art of Management of the Learning Organization*. New York: Doubleday.

Simon, H.A. (1977) *The New Science of Management Decision*. Englewood Cliffs, NJ: Prentice Hall (revised edition).

Snyder, M., and Page, G. (1958) The United States decision to resist aggression in Korea: The application of an analytical scheme, *Administrative Science Quarterly*, 3, 341–378.

Soelberg, P.O. (1967) Unprogrammed decision making, *Industrial Management Review*, Spring, 19–29.

Starbuck, W.O. (1983) Organizations as action generators, *American Sociological Review*, 48, 91–102.

Stein, M.R. (1975) *Stimulating Creativity: Vol. 2, Group Procedures*. New York: Academic Press.

Thompson, J.D. (1967) *Organizations in Action*. New York: McGraw Hill.

Toulmin, S. (1979) *Knowing and Understanding: An Invitation to Philosophy*. New York: Macmillan.

Van de Ven, A., Polley, D., Grund, R., and Venkataraman, S. (1999) *The Innovation Journey*. Oxford, England: Oxford University Press.

Vroom, V., and Yetton, P. (1973) *Leadership and Decision Making*. Pittsburgh, PA: University of Pittsburgh Press.

Weick, K.E. (1979) *The Social Psychology of Organizing*. Reading, MA: Addison-Wesley, 2nd edition.

Weick, K.E. (2001) *Making Sense of the Organization*. Oxford, England: Blackwell.

Weick, K.E., and Quinn, R. (1999) 'Organizational Change and Development', in J. Spence, J. Darley, and D. Foss, *Annual Review of Psychology, vol. 50*, Palo Alto, CA: Annual Reviews, 361–386.

Wildavsky, A. (1979) *Speaking Truth to Power*. Boston, MA: Little, Brown.

Witte, E. (1972) Field research on complex decision making process – The Phase Theory, *International Studies of Management and Organization*, 56, 156–182.

Yin, R.K. (1993) *Applied Case Study Research*. Hollywood, CA: Sage.

18

Of Baseball, Medical Decision Making, and Innumeracy

LORI FERRANTI, STEVEN CHENG, AND DAVID DILTS

INTRODUCTION

Consider for a moment the following five baseball scenarios:

- *The Weekend Pitcher.* Weekend pitcher Jim, is a fastball pitcher and because fastballs have retired the previous two batters, he throws nothing but fastballs to the next batter, Marc. Although, Marc is a fastball hitter, Jim is indifferent to Marc's preferences. Practicing the 'law of small numbers' principle (Tversky and Kahneman, 1971), Jim relies on his experience with the two previous batters.

- *The Minor League Pitcher.* Sam, a minor league baseball pitcher, is preparing for his first game against the Carolina Mudcats; he consults with another pitcher on his team for advice on pitching to them. Jose, his teammate who has previously pitched the last time they played the Mudcats, advised Sam to throw curve balls down and out as, in general, Mudcats do not hit curve balls very well. Even though Sam has a better fastball than curve ball, the information provided by his teammates helps Sam to strikeout the first two batters by throwing curve balls.

- *The Major League Coach.* Preparing for today's game, Major League Baseball pitching Coach Charlie studies game statistics from the previous month and finds that most of the players have successfully hit fastballs. Coach Charlie relays this information to his pitchers. In addition, he provides today's pitcher with more detailed information about the batters from their previous games, offering detailed information on strikeouts, home runs, and walks. As the game progresses, Coach Charlie compiles additional batting statistics for his players as well as his pitching staff's performances against particular batters. This knowledge assists him when instructing the pitcher and catcher on what pitch

Handbook of Decision Making. Edited by Paul C. Nutt and David C. Wilson
© 2010 John Wiley & Sons, Ltd

to throw to which batters or suggest a pitching change during an upcoming innings.

◆ *The Broadcast Booth Announcer.* Major League Baseball commentator Joe proudly announces to the listening audience that the starting pitcher in today's game will only last one or two more innings as he has thrown 89 pitches and 40 are fastballs through four innings. Joe is basing his assertion on data indicating that the pitcher's normal pitch count has never been above 100. Unbeknownst to the pitching staff, the broadcast booth announcers observe the umpire's strike zone has become very narrow. Using technology, the broadcast booth and viewers see after each pitch the strike zone and pitch location. While this information can be relayed at the end of an inning, the announcers are privy to the information earlier, permitting them to 'suggest' the pitch location and speed for each batter even between pitches to the current batter. The broadcast booth uses current real-time data to help them relay information to the viewing public.

◆ *The Baseball Fan.* Alan has been a baseball fan all his life and his beloved Cleveland Indians are down 3 to 2 in the top of the 7th inning to the NY Yankees. Because he follows 'The Tribe' passionately, he knows that the current pitcher has had trouble in the past with the Yankee line-up. With ready access to his computer, he quickly searches the Major League Baseball web site for pitcher and batter statistics. While this information is not as up-to-date as that available to the announcer, he is certain that with these data and his years of experience he can predict what the manager should do with the pitcher.

Now let us see how these baseball analogies reflect the practice of medical decision making. Similar to the weekend pitcher, whose previous limited experience was that throwing fastballs led to strikeouts, and the minor league pitcher's informal 'consultations' with a colleague, physicians frequently rely on their previous limited successful treatment plans to treat an illness or informally consult colleagues (Coleman, Katz *et al.*, 1966; Fontanarosa and DeAngelis, 2003; Schechter and Margolis, 2005). As few physicians have time to access all the recent knowledge of the available treatments and their effectiveness, this route to information is relatively quick.

However, physicians (and baseball aficionados alike) have the ability to make decisions based on more recent data than their counterparts decades ago. Interestingly, physician medical decision making and baseball have evolved very similarly. During its initial inception, baseball teams played with much uncertainty. Not only did the team members frequently change, but also, scores were often not reported for years (Major League Baseball, 2009). This uncertainty left others, not privy to watching the game and the specific players, little information upon which to base their opinions of a team's or player's abilities in order to develop a strategy for playing against the team.

Moving forward a few decades, baseball became more organized and players and coaches became more aware of the other teams and members' abilities. In addition, teams also had the advantage of previous meetings' recollection. However, even though prior knowledge was gleaned from previous years, any real-time current season statistics were not available. Decisions were frequently based on how a player performed last season; for example, how a left-handed pitcher performed against a left-handed batter, not particular to the batter or the pitcher facing today.

Today, Major League Baseball has advanced to that state where not only are games tracked but there is the ability to track a particular player's statistics from game to game, from pitcher to pitcher, as well as from one at bat to the next, under a wide variety of circumstances. Concurrently, while tracking a particular batter, a manager can track his team's pitcher or the other team's pitcher's performance, pitch count, tendencies, and velocity (Stallings, Bennett *et al.*, 2002). Thus, not only is the manager aware of the pitcher's performance in his most recent outing but is also aware as the game progresses. This detailed real-time tracking permits the manager to instruct his batter to adjust to the pitching changes from one batter to the next; or to substitute a new pitcher.

Similar to baseball's informal beginnings, physicians (prior to the 1950s) informally consulted colleagues or had to rely on their own expertise to treat a new illness (Coleman, Katz *et al.*, 1966). Few physicians (like baseball managers) had access to recent knowledge of the available treatments or their overall effectiveness. While some physicians may have started their own collection of statistics, or 'mini-registry', most relied on implementing 'the law of small numbers' (Tversky and Kahneman, 1971), to organize their treatment plan.

In the 1960s, Spratt, an oncologist, recognized the importance of tracking information on cancer patients and developed the first paper-based registry (Spratt, 1966). While medicine has long recognized the need to track incidence and prevalence rates since 'Typhoid Mary', the availability of readily understandable and timely statistics is still a rarity. Presently, physicians have a greater ability to make decisions based on very up-to-date data than ever before, using technologies such as a medical registry (Ferranti and Dilts, 2005). A medical registry, which is a collection of medical data from multiple sources, has the ability to compile and evaluate near real-time data. Similar to the manager changing pitchers from one batter to the next, the registry permits a physician the opportunity to alter the ongoing treatment based upon the changing data available. In many instances, this access permits current patients to benefit from the most recent treatment options.

Interestingly, one fundamental assumption made when supplying the voluminous quantity of data possible from either a registry, or from a baseball statistics repository, is that the target audience has sufficient mathematical skills to understand the meaning of the data. Much like the avid baseball fan, many patients feel that they can make a more informed decision if only supplied with the same information as their healthcare provider. While registry information is presented in a way that is most familiar and useful to the healthcare provider, it may not be in a familiar setting for the patient, who thus may miss some of the nuances of the numeric data. While there are definitive concerns of the depth of understanding patients will have with complex medical issues, we are concerned with a more basic level of understanding: numeracy.

INNUMERACY

Numeracy's influence on medical decision making continues to remain problematic as it is frequently perceived to be either a non factor or only a minor limitation of a research study, particularly when compared to the perceived importance of patient or physician's age, gender, or propensity for risk (Benowitz, 2000; Institute of Medicine, 2001; Berwick, 2003; Lewis, Robinson *et al.*, 2003). Thus, the importance of literacy in numerical meanings, or numeracy, is rarely evaluated before moving forward in assessing the influences of medical decision making. Historically, most major physician–patient healthcare decisions were made by physicians, with limited patient participation (Quill and Brody, 1996). However, with direct-to-consumer advertising for pharmaceuticals (Toop and Mangin, 2007; Evans and McCormack, 2008), increase in privacy and safety issues (Institute of Medicine, 2001; Rothstein and Talbott, 2006), and a dramatic rise in availability of patient-obtained medical information (Xie, Dilts *et al.*, 2006), the current trend in medical decision making is to inform and involve patients intimately in their medical treatment plan. This is considered a top priority in the medical community to promote shared decision making (Lipkus, Samsa *et al.*, 2001). However, do patients understand numeracy issues when presented for healthcare decisions and, of importance for this paper, does the educational background of the patient impact the degree of numeracy?

Most medical decision recommendations are structured on the assumption that patients understand quantitative information (Schwartz, Fisher *et al.*, 1997). Ubel (2002) cites a 1997 Schwartz *et al.* study of the public's ability to understand probabilities in medical scenarios– where only one third of the respondents answered three quantitative questions correctly – as an obstacle to patient participation in medical decision making, particularly when decision alternatives are presented as probabilities or likelihoods. Merely presenting patients with numerical data does not guarantee that they understand the information provided or can correctly interpret the values, numbers, probabilities, or outcome likelihoods provided (Skinner, Kreuter *et al.*, 1998; Ubel, 2002; Gurmankin, Baron *et al.*, 2004). As noted in Bramwell *et al.* (2006) even those providing the statistics may not accurately interpret the results; they found an average 86 % of incorrect responses provided by obstetricians, midwifes, pregnant women, and companions accompanying the pregnant women.

Part of the problem may lie with healthcare providers in disseminating such numeracy information because, as suggested by Weinfrut *et al.* (2005) and Chao *et al.* (2003), risk and benefit quantitative information can be confusing even for medically knowledgeable participants. Yet, this has not hindered the pharmaceutical industry or the national media in inundating the public with 'health statistics' such as: 1 in 10 people develop a certain disease; that the 'western diet', i.e. fried foods, salty snacks, and meat, accounts for approximately 30 % of heart attack risk worldwide (American Heart, 2008); or that individuals should buy a home defibrillator since 'less than 1 in 20 people survive largely because a defibrillator was not available' (Philips, 2005).

While there are numerous potential decision-making issues with respect to numeracy, we focus on three primary areas: (1) informed consent, (2) patient knowledge, and (3) healthcare providers' numeracy proficiency, and communication. The following discussion encompasses influences and obstacles presented in all three areas.

Informed consent and numeracy

Informed Consent, as defined by the American Medical Association (AMA), is a process of 'communication between a patient and physician that results in the patient's authorization or agreement to undergo a specific medical intervention' (American Medical Association, 2009) evidenced by a patient signing a written consent form. It has been assumed in the past that merely signing the form was adequate proof of consent and understanding. However, broader definitions also mention the physicians' ethical obligation to ensure that the patient understands what is being presented and is 'competent' to participate in the decision-making process (Wagner and Keany, 2006). Numeracy becomes a significant issue when informed consent is required for a clinical trial, as potential risks and benefits are typically presented in numerical formats.

Need for additional patient knowledge has become more pronounced as treatment options per disease increase, as patients demand additional information to assist in their decision making (Damberg, Hiatt *et al.*, 2003), and as HIPAA requirements specify that patients make decisions about their medical records. With such growth comes an increase in informed consent protocols and a subsequent need for improvement to the informed consent process (Kaufmann, 1983; Varricchio and Jassak, 1989; Jimison, Sher *et al.*, 1998). Even though informed consent has many purposes and provides an excellent opportunity for physicians and patients to engage in an active dialog to verify comprehension, this dialog frequently does not occur due to such factors as time limitations (Braddock, Edwards *et al.*, 1999), patient anxiety (Buchanan, 1995; Faden and Beauchamp, 1996; Jimison, Sher *et al.*, 1998), or poor literacy skills (Taub, Baker *et al.*, 1986; Flory and Emanuel, 2004). To further complicate matters, research shows that only half of the individuals receiving health education information comprehend such information (Holt, Hollon *et al.*, 1990; Doak, Doak *et al.*, 1996; Jimison, Sher *et al.*, 1998). For example, one study of cancer clinical trials consent forms showed that they contained 73 % of passages written at a college level or above for populations where 20 % are considered functionally illiterate (Jimison, Sher *et al.*, 1998). So even when the physician attempts to communicate such risk and provide written explanations, comprehension remains an obstacle in many of the simplest situations (Ancker and Kaufman, 2007; Peters, Hibbard *et al.*, 2007).

Furthermore, as the lines blur between informed consent for treatment and informed consent for research, the complexity and amount of information communicated between the patient and physician become increasingly difficult. Examples of this include such obstacles as variable probabilities depending on placebo or 'drug' used in a study, or the use of Bayesian probabilities for potential outcomes. Additionally, there is the possibility that neither the patient nor the physician will understand such statistically variable side effects or outcomes.

Patient-obtained medical information and numeracy

Jimison *et al.* (1998) noted that patients had four major reasons for wanting information: (1) treatment compliance, (2) to veto the physician's decision, (3) to enhance their own decision making, and (4) respect for their wishes. Three of these reasons may be directly applicable to their medical treatment options (Lidz, Meisel *et al.*, 1983) . Thus, this list highlights the necessity that both the physician and the patient understand the information communicated and presented.

Outcomes research poses a particular need for numeracy in medical decision making. Such research addresses the nuances involved when there is no single treatment best for all patients and the physician is tasked with presenting multiple options (Damberg, Hiatt *et al.*, 2003). Wennberg *et al.* (1993) observe that 'when the outcomes of a particular treatment are multiple and when more than one treatment option exists, an optimal treatment choice for individuals depends on the evaluations they give to the risks and benefits associated with alternative treatments with the outcomes that matter to them'. While taking into account patient desire for information so that they can prioritize such issues as quality of life, many authors argue that this information is not easily accessed, organized, or understandable to patients when they are trying to make their treatment choice (Damberg, Hiatt *et al.*, 2003; Erickson, 2004; Whitney, Holmes-Rovner *et al.*, 2008) or that access to such data leads to 'rational' decision making in all cases (Ubel, 2002). Others cite financial or administrative burdens that may bias rational decision making (Sanidas, Valassiadou *et al.*, 2000; Damberg, Hiatt *et al.*, 2003).

Another issue is the increase in patient-obtained medical information (Xie and Dilts, 2006); such information, gathered from Google or PubMed (for the more knowledgeable patient), may bias the patient to an inappropriate choice. The physician is then charged with parsing, addressing, and interpreting the large volume of misinformation that the patient obtained from questionable information resources. One component of this information concerns numeracy as it often contains proportions, probabilities, or frequencies to communicate the success of the treatments.

Healthcare provider and numeracy

Such numeracy challenges do not only pertain to the patient side of the equation; deficient numeracy skills are also found in the healthcare professional (Nelson, Reyna *et al.*, 2008). Merz *et al.* (1991) noted that physicians were inconsistent in qualitatively categorizing risk; and furthermore physicians find it challenging to work with odds ratios or decimals. Gramling *et al.* (2004) found that 97 % of physicians maintained higher confidence with qualitative versus quantitative formats for risk communication. Consistent with the theory of Reasoned Action and the theory of Self-Efficacy (Gramling, Irvin *et al.*, 2004), these findings imply that the physicians are more inclined to communicate risk qualitatively as 93 % of their respondents stated that qualitative risk was important to their practice; yet 76 % also perceived quantitative risk as important; however, 84 % perceived qualitative risk as more important than quantitative; hence, while they believe that quantitative risk is important, when required to present the risk to their patients, physicians communicated risk qualitatively more often than quantitatively. Furthermore, physicians indicated that only 36 % felt they could effectively communicate numeric risk as compared to their 87 % confidence in their ability to communicate qualitative information (Gramling, Irvin *et al.*, 2004). This factor is important as literature shows that the method the physician chooses to present the information also presents inherence biases (Ancker and Kaufman, 2007).

Qualitative and quantitative dissemination methods continue to evolve as new and innovative decision aids are created. Examples span from disease-specific patient chat rooms and physician-only message boards to web sites where personal diagnosis information is entered for analysis. While some of these methods are a mixture of quantitative and qualitative, many of these decision aids are based on numeracy concepts (Lipkus, Samsa *et al.*, 2001), such as the Canadian Cancer Society's decision aid for breast surgery, which states probabilities such as 6 out of 100 (Canadian Cancer Society, 2001).

While the number of decision aids have prospered, mathematical computations and probability understanding and proficiency that were once assumed have become a question of concern, resulting in studies addressing the influence of numeracy on medical decisions both by physicians as well as in physician–patient collaboration (Paulos, 1990; Black, Nease *et al.*, 1995; Adelsward and Sachs, 1996; Schwartz, Fisher *et al.*, 1997; Lipkus, Samsa *et al.*, 2001).

As shared decision making has increasingly been identified as a goal in risk communication between doctors and patients (Lipkus, Samsa *et al.*, 2001) particularly in decisions with treatment options and medical interventions producing equitable outcomes (Charles, Gafni *et al.*, 1997; Frosch and Kaplan, 1999; Lipkus, Samsa *et al.*, 2001), lack of numeracy comprehension or at least fear of numbers remains a valid stumbling block.

Much like numeracy itself, a sparsely studied aspect of numeracy is the potential impact that educational background may have on medical decision making. The question of interest for our study is: does educational background impact numeracy skills? If this is the case, then the education background of both the healthcare provider (in our case, senior level nursing students) and the patient (senior level engineering students and graduate management students) must be taken into account when designing medical decision-making tools. In order to answer this question, we tested frequencies, probabilities, and risk levels with students from three different discipline majors: engineering, nursing, and management. Our prior expectation is that engineers, with their heavy training in mathematics, would have better numeracy skills, followed by nurses, and management students least.

METHODS

Building on postulates of innumeracy influence (Ubel 2002), we adapted three questions from Schwartz *et al.* (1997), placing them in three different hypothetical medical scenarios. Two of the questions assessed familiarity with probabilities and one question required respondents to convert a percentage to a proportion. When designing the survey questions, the numeracy definition utilized by Estrada (2004) was followed, namely: 'Numeracy is defined as the ability to handle basic probability and numerical concepts' (Estrada, Martin-Hryniewicz *et al.*, 2004). All results were evaluated using chi-square (χ^2) statistics, with alpha level of significance of 0.05.

Sample

A random sample of students from a private top 50 ranked university's School of Engineering ('engineers'), School of Nursing ('nurses'), and Graduate School of Management ('managers') were surveyed. For all three groups, questionnaires were distributed as part of their respective classes and participants were given a two-minute verbal description of the study, which included disclosure of survey anonymity and voluntary participation. A total of 486 surveys were returned, of which 153 were undergraduate engineering students, 206 were undergraduate and graduate nursing students, and 127 were graduate management students. There were 282 female respondents and 204 male respondents. Overall, 58 % of the respondents were female (n=282), with nurses comprising significantly more female respondents than the other majors (68 %, n=193; engineers 16.3 %, n=46; managers 15.2 %, n=43, p<0.001).

The mean age of all the groups was 25.5 (SE 0.27), with engineers younger at 20.5 years old (SE 0.08, P<0.001) than the other two populations – nurses 27.5 (SE 0.49), and managers 28.4 (SE 0.26).

RESULTS

Overall, 25.7 % of respondents answered all questions correctly; meaning that 74.0 % of the respondents incorrectly answered at least one question. This result does not take into account partial credit for question 3, which is discussed later.

Simple percent

The first question required calculating a number from a percent, in the scenario:

> If there is a 1% chance that a stomach ulcer will reappear after a treatment, how many cases of reappearing ulcers will occur if exactly 100 patients are treated?

Table 18.1 illustrates the results, which indicate that 7.8 % of nurses provided incorrect answers, with 5.9 % and 5.5 % of engineers and managers respectively with incorrect responses. These differences were not significant (p=0.696).

Complex percent

The second innumeracy question required respondents to evaluate three equal probable outcomes for a brain tumor operation:

> A brain tumor operation has three equally probable outcomes. 1) The tumor is completely removed, 2) the tumor is completely removed, but the patient is

TABLE 18.1 If there is a 1 % chance that a stomach ulcer will reappear after a treatment, how many cases of reappearing ulcers will occur if exactly 100 patients are treated?

Group	Incorrect		Correct	
	N	% of Total	n	% of Total
Engineers	9	5.9 %	144	94.1 %
Nurses*	16	7.8 %	189	91.7 %
Managers	7	5.5 %	120	94.5 %
Total	32	6.6 %	453	93.2 %

*1 missing response from nursing sample.
**No statistically significant differences among Group Factor not statistically significant (Pearson Chi-Squared: p=0.696).

paralyzed, or 3) the tumor is not completely removed. If 1200 operations are performed, how many patients will have no tumor remaining?

The first evaluation, a strict correct or incorrect result, showed 54.4 %, 40.5 %, and 37 % incorrect responses by nurses, engineers, and managers respectively (p<0.001) (Table 18.2a). Due to the complexity of the question, we further evaluated the answers by analyzing the answers that were correct, incorrect, or 'nearly correct', defined by the fact that the question was misinterpreted or misread and, in post-survey debriefing sessions, the respondents indicated that they overlooked or ignored the fact that option #3 included that there was no more tumor. This is an interesting result in itself as it showed that the respondents tended not to read the complete question, but rather only part of the question. Further investigation should be completed to see if this is a common phenomenon with patients and healthcare providers.

TABLE 18.2a A brain tumor operation has three equally probable outcomes. 1) The tumor is completely removed, 2) the tumor is completely removed, but the patient is paralyzed, or 3) the tumor is not completely removed. If 1200 operations are performed, how many patients will have no tumor remaining?

Group	Incorrect		Correct	
	n	% of Total	n	% of Total
Engineers	62	40.5 %	91	59.5 %
Nurses*	112	54.4 %	86	41.7 %
Managers	47	37.0 %	80	63.0 %
Total	221	45.5 %	257	52.9 %

*8 missing response from nursing sample.
**Group Factor statistically significant (Pearson Chi-Squared: p<0.001).

TABLE 18.2b Correct, Nearly Correct, and Incorrect

Group	Incorrect		'Nearly Correct'		Correct	
	n	% of Total	n	% of Total	n	% of Total
Engineers	13	8.5 %	49	32.0 %	91	59.5 %
Nurses*	18	8.7 %	94	1.0 %	86	41.7 %
Managers	12	9.4 %	35	27.6 %	80	63.0 %
Total	43	45.5 %	178	36.6 %	257	52.9 %

*8 missing response from nursing sample.
**Group Factor statistically significant (Pearson Chi-Squared: p<0.001).

The 'incorrect' responses dropped significantly in all three groups once partial credit was given for the 'semi-correct' answer. Utilizing the new scoring format, engineers had 8.5 % incorrect answers, 32 % nearly correct, and 59.5 % correct, with nurses having 8.7 %, 45.6 %, and 41.7 %, and managers 9.4 %, 27.6 %, and 63 % of incorrect, 'nearly' correct, and correct answers respectively (Table 18.2b). Overall, the percentages were: 8.8 %, 36.6 %, and 52.9 % (p<0.001).

Simple probability

The next probability question asked participants to compute:

If there is a 1 in 5 chance of prostate cancer remaining after treatment, how many patients will still have prostate cancer if 1000 undergo treatment?

Overall, Table 18.3 illustrates that 4.7 % of the respondents provided incorrect answers, with 7.3 % of nurses, 4.6 % of engineers, and 0.8 % of managers answering incorrectly (p=0.006).

TABLE 18.3 If there is a 1 in 5 chance of prostate cancer remaining after treatment, how many patients will still have prostate cancer if 1000 undergo treatment?

Group	Incorrect		Correct	
	n	% of Total	n	% of Total
Engineers	7	4.6 %	146	95.4 %
Nurses*	15	7.3 %	186	90.3 %
Managers	1	0.8 %	126	99.2 %
Total	23	4.7 %	458	94.2 %

*5 missing response from nursing sample.
**Group Factor statistically significant (Pearson Chi-Squared: p=0.006).

Discussion

The results of this study support previous research findings that poor numeracy knowledge and lack of probability knowledge may result in misappropriate use of quantitative information. Surprisingly, even though our respondents were well above the norm in educational level, as all of our respondents had some college education (most with at least a junior level status), 25.7 % experienced difficulty utilizing quantitative data.

Although few disagree that patients need to be involved in their medical decision-making treatment choice, few agree on the best way to present the information. While some advocate the use of numbers or probabilities, often citing that uncertainties communicated verbally are frequently interpreted differently among the patients with large variation as well as the propensity of vagueness that leads to higher variability (Gurmankin, Baron *et al.*, 2004), others note that numbers are more difficult for patients to understand and words are easier to comprehend (Gurmankin, Baron *et al.*, 2004). And as Huizinga *et al.* (2008) found, the framing of information presentation affects the patient's ability to understand what is presented and 'may impact health outcomes'.

Our results concur with findings that show that numbers were difficult to compute and understand. Our numeracy results were not quite as positive as Gurmankin *et al.* (2004) as their sample 'on average' answered seven out of nine questions correctly while ours 'on average' only answered about one out of four (25.7 %). These results are more similar to Lipkus *et al.*'s (2001) overall result of 'on average, 18 % and 32 %' of participants providing correct answers and slightly higher than Schwartz *et al.*'s (1997) result of 16 %.

Another finding is the difficulty that future nurses had with numeracy scenarios, where they were often statistically less likely to arrive at correct results than either future engineers or managers. As nurses are one of the major sources of medical information provided to patients, such a finding is troubling (Ernst, 2008).

One surprising result of our study is the difficulty that all participants showed in their inability to successfully answer the mixed mode questions such as 'completely removed, not completely removed, and completely removed but paralyzed', Acknowledging this deficit is especially important since many of the medical decision options are phrased in this manner, for example 'partial removal of impinging disc with some remaining limitations, or complete removal of disc with higher probability of more serious side effects' (Erstad, 2008); and because many available decision aids have scenarios phrased in this way (Canadian Cancer Society, 2001).

Conclusion

With mean office visit time ranging between 14 and 17 minutes (Braddock, Edwards *et al.*, 1999), it is no surprise that physicians do not always provide complete explanations or confirm that patients understand completely treatment options and probabilities before a patient leaves the physician's office. Yet, patients continue to request more information, frequently resorting to the Internet for more disease-specific treatment options and potential outcomes statistics (Damberg, Hiatt *et al.*, 2003). As other studies (Ancker and Kaufman, 2007; Institute of Medicine, 2007; Evans and McCormack, 2008; Nelson, Reyna *et al.*, 2008) have indicated, much of this information is at least partially presented in numeric format with percentages and probability interpretation knowledge required. Our findings confirm that even in highly educated populations, such information may be misunderstood.

Consumer-driven healthcare is based on permitting patients to consider their own values or preferences for particular treatments or outcomes, rather than having a physician only provide generalized information of the options and outcomes (Dowding, Swanson *et al.*, 2004). Although O'Connor *et al.*'s (2003) results indicate that those patients using decision aids increase their knowledge, this may not translate to increased numeracy knowledge. Their study also found that patients who utilized decision aids with detailed descriptions of probabilities as well as other detailed information were more likely to have realistic risk and benefit expectations (O'Connor, Legare *et al.*, 2003; O'Connor, Stacey *et al.* 2003). Given our results, it would be interesting to understand the background of the patients in their study.

Edwards and Elwyn's (2001) systematic review suggests 'that probability estimates can be effective for improving outcomes, particularly if tailored to the individual'. However, this assumes that the patient understands the numeracy estimates provided. Damberg *et al.*'s (2003) systematic review acknowledged the potential numeracy limitations, as it conceded that numeracy is difficult to understand. In this review, these same studies indicate that while some prefer quantitative information, many prefer qualitative risk presentation such as high or low. Our finding, supported by numerous education and psychology studies that people learn in different manners, further emphasizes the need to present the information in multiple ways, incorporating educational background, in order to best assure that the interpretations are correct.

Our results further underline the need to assess numeracy knowledge in both the patient and healthcare provider populations so that deficiencies in numeracy can be appropriately addressed. Merely eliminating numeric information from treatment explanations is not a plausible short-term or long-term option, especially given the increase in avenues for patients to obtain information.

Providing numeracy education and training for healthcare providers (nurses and physicians) as well as patients will assist in reducing the innumeracy levels. Future research in decision tools should include the addition of qualitative factors to explain the more complex scenarios involving numeracy.

While there are numerous potential decision-making issues with respect to numeracy, we focused on three primary areas: (1) informed consent, (2) patient knowledge, and (3) healthcare providers' numeracy proficiency, and communication, and this research indicates that each of these areas are not independent of one another. Although future research is needed to assess the interaction of these areas, it is a reasonable assumption that by ensuring that the informed consent adheres to the fifth grade level reading comprehension and more informed patients and improving healthcare providers' proficiencies in communication of statistics, both providers and patients will benefit.

Returning again to baseball, the degree of numeracy skills assumed to exist in the typical baseball fan is significant. While simple additive statistics for pitchers, such as innings pitched or strikeouts, are easily comprehensible, one wonders about the degree of comprehension of Win-Loss percentages, or the more complex ERAs. While it would not be surprising to discover that potential patients more easily understand complex baseball statistics than simple likelihoods in medicine, it is equally disturbing as the 'game' being 'played' in medicine is 'life'!

REFERENCES

Adelsward, V., and Sachs, L. (1996) The meaning of 6.8: Numeracy and normality in health information talks, *Soc Sci Med*, 43 (8): 1179–1187.

American Medical Association (2009) 'Informed Consent.' Retrieved March 1, 2009, from http://www.ama-assn.org/ama/pub/category/4608.html.

AmericanHeart (2008) 'Western diet increases heart attack risk globally.' Retrieved Nov 19, 2008, from http://www.americanheart.mediaroom.com/index.php.

Ancker, J.S., and Kaufman, D. (2007) Rethinking health numeracy: A multidisciplinary literature review, *J Am Med Inform Assoc*, 14 (6), 713–721.

Benowitz, S. (2000) Children's oncology group looks to increase efficiency, numbers in clinical trials, *J Natl Cancer Inst*, 92 (23), 1876–1878.

Berwick, D.M. (2003) Errors today and errors tomorrow, *N Engl J Med*, 348 (25), 2570–2572.

Black, W.C., Nease, Jr, R.F., *et al.* (1995) Perceptions of breast cancer risk and screening effectiveness in women younger than 50 years of age, *J Natl Cancer Inst*, 87 (10), 720–731.

Braddock, C.H., 3rd, Edwards, K.A. *et al.* (1999) Informed decision making in outpatient practice: time to get back to basics, *Journal of the American Medical Society*, 282 (24), 2313–2320.

Bramwell, R., West, H. *et al.* (2006) Health professionals' and service users' interpretation of screening test results: experimental study, *BMJ*, 333 (7562), 284.

Buchanan, M. (1995) Enabling patients to make informed decisions, *Nursing Times*, 91 (18), 27–29.

Canadian Cancer Society (2001) Making decisions about the removal of my breast: What do I prefer? Booklet and Cassette.

Chao, C., Studts, J.L. *et al.* (2003) Adjuvant chemotherapy for breast cancer: How presentation of recurrence risk influences decision-making, *J Clin Oncol*, 21 (23), 4299–4305.

Charles, C., Gafni, A. *et al.* (1997) Shared decision-making in the medical encounter: What does it mean? (or it takes at least two to tango), *Soc Sci Med*, 44 (5), 681–692.

Coleman, J., Katz, E. et al. (eds) (1966) *Medical Innovation: A Diffusion Study*. New York: The Bobbs-Merrill Company.

Damberg, C., L. Hiatt, *et al.* (2003) *Evaluating the Feasibility of Developing National Outcomes Data Bases to Assist Patients with Making Treatment Decisions*. RAND.

Doak, C.C., Doak, L.G. *et al.* (1996) *Teaching Patients with Low Literacy Skills*. Philadelphia, PA: Lippincott Williams & Wilkins.

Dowding, D., and Swanson, V. *et al.* (2004) The development and preliminary evaluation of a decision aid based on decision analysis for two treatment conditions: Benign prostatic hyperplasia and hypertension, *Patient Educ Couns* 52 (2), 209–215.

Edwards, A., and Elwyn, G. (2001) Understanding risk and lessons for clinical risk communication about treatment preferences, *Qual Health Care* 10 Suppl 1, i9–13.

Erickson, P. (2004) A health outcomes framework for assessing health status and quality of life: Enhanced data for decision making, *J Natl Cancer Inst Monogr* 33, 168–177.

Ernst, J. (2008) 'Oncology Nurses to Provide Information Patients Forget.' Retrieved December 4, 2008, from http://www.hcplive.com/mdnglive/webexclusives/Oncology_Nurses_Provide_Info.

Erstad, S. (2008) 'Decompression Laminectomy.' Retrieved December 4, 2008, from http://www.blueshieldca.com/hw/articles/hw_article.html.

Estrada, C.A., Martin-Hryniewicz, M., Peek, B.T., Collins, C., and Byrd, J.C. (2004) Literacy and numeracy skills and anticoagulation control, *Am J Med Sci* 328 (2), 88–93.

Evans, W.D., and McCormack, L. (2008) Applying social marketing in health care: Communicating evidence to change consumer behavior, *Med Decis Making* 28 (5), 781–792.

Faden, R., and Beauchamp, T. (1996) *A History and Theory of Informed Consent*. New York: Oxford University Press.

Ferranti, L., and Dilts, D. (2005) *A Review of Medical Registries and Outcomes: Potential Use for Real-Time Improvement in Patient Safety. The Dearth of Real-Time Science-Based Medicine*. Boston, MA: AcademyHealth.

Fontanarosa, P.B., and DeAngelis, C.D. (2003) Translational medical research, *JAMA* 289 (16), 2133.

Frosch, D.L., and Kaplan, R.M. (1999) Shared decision making in clinical medicine: past research and future directions, *Am J Prev Med* 17 (4) 285–294.

Gramling, R., Irvin, J.E. *et al.* (2004) Numeracy and medicine: Key family physician attitudes about communicating probability with patients, *J Am Board Fam Pract* 17 (6), 473.

Gurmankin, A.D., Baron, J. *et al.* (2004) The effect of numerical statements of risk on trust and comfort with hypothetical physician risk communication, *Med Decis Making* 24 (3), 265–271.

Holt, G.A., Hollon, J.D. *et al.* (1990) OTC labels: Can consumers read and understand them? *Am Pharm* NS30 (11), 51–54.

Huizinga, M.M., Elasy, T.A. *et al.* (2008). Development and validation of the Diabetes Numeracy Test (DNT), *BMC Health Serv Res* 8, 96.

Institute of Medicine (2007) Summaries for patients. Different ways to describe the benefits of risk-reducing treatments, *Ann Intern Med* 146 (12), I50.

Institute of Medicine, I. (2001) *Crossing the Quality Chasm*. Washington DC: The National Academy Press.

Jimison, H.B., Sher, P.P., Appleyard, R., and LeVernois, Y. (1998) Advances in health information technology for patients, *Journal of AHIMA/American Health Information*, Sept 69 (8), 42–46.

Kaufmann, C.L. (1983) Informed consent and patient decision making: Two decades of research, *Soc Sci Med* 17 (21) 1657–1664.

Lewis, D.K., Robinson, J. *et al.* (2003) Factors involved in deciding to start preventive treatment: Qualitative study of clinicians' and lay people's attitudes, *BMJ* 327 (7419), 841.

Lidz, C., Meisel, A. *et al.* (1983) Barriers to informed consent, *Ann Intern Med* 99 (4), 539–543.

Lipkus, I.M., Samsa, G. *et al.* (2001) General performance on a numeracy scale among highly educated samples, *Med Decis Making* 21 (1), 37–44.

Major League Baseball (2009) 'History.' from http://mlb.mlb.com/mlb/history/.

Merz, J.F., Druzdzel, M.J. *et al.* (1991) Verbal expressions of probability in informed consent litigation, *Med Decis Making* 11 (4) 273–281.

Nelson, W., Reyna, V.F. *et al.* (2008) Clinical implications of numeracy: Theory and practice, *Ann Behav Med* 35 (3), 261–274.

O'Connor, A.M., Stacey, D., Entwistle, V., Llewellyn-Thomas, H., Royner, D., Holmes-Royner, M., Tait, V., Tetroe, J., Fiset, V., Barry, M.J., and Jones, J. (2003). Decision aids for people facing health treatment or screening decisions, *Cochrane Database Syst Review*, 319 (7212), 731.

Paulos, J.A. (1990) *Innumeracy: Mathematical Illiteracy and its Consequences.* New York: Vintage Books.

Peters, E., Hibbard, J. *et al.* (2007) Numeracy skill and the communication, comprehension, and use of risk-benefit information, *Health Aff (Millwood)* 26 (3), 741–748.

Philips (2005) 'Home Defibrillator.' from http://www.heartstarthome.com/content/ heartstart_featured.asp.

Quill, T.E., and Brody, H. (1996) Physician recommendations and patient autonomy: Finding a balance between physician power and patient choice, *Ann Intern Med* 125 (9), 763–769.

Rothstein, M.A., and Talbott, M.K. (2006) Compelled disclosure of health information: Protecting against the greatest potential threat to privacy, *JAMA* 295 (24), 2882–2885.

Sanidas, E.E., Valassiadou, K.E. *et al.* (2000) Organisation of a trauma registry in a regional Greek university hospital: The first two years experience, *Eur J Surg* 166 (1), 13–17.

Schechter, M.S., and Margolis, P. (2005) Improving subspecialty healthcare: Lessons from cystic fibrosis, *J Pediatr* 147 (3), 295–301.

Schwartz, L.M., Fisher, E.S. *et al.* (1997) Treatment and health outcomes of women and men in a cohort with coronary artery disease *Arch Intern Med* 157 (14), 1545–1551.

Skinner, C.S., Kreuter, M.W. *et al.* (1998) Perceived and actual breast cancer risk: Optimistic and pessimistic biases, *Journal of Health Psychology* 3 (2), 181.

Spratt, J. (1966). *The Tumor Registry – A Definition.* American Cancer Society.

Stallings, J., Bennett, B. et al. (eds) (2002) *Baseball Strategies.* Human Kinetics.

Taub, H.A., Baker, M.T. *et al.* (1986). 'Informed Consent for research. Effects of readability, patient age, and education.' *J Am Geriatr Soc* 34 (8), 601–606.

Toop, L., and Mangin, D. (2007) Industry funded patient information and the slippery slope to New Zealand, *BMJ* 335 (7622), 694–695.

Tversky, A., and Kahneman, D. (1971) Belief in small numbers, *Psychological Bulletin* 76 (2): 105–110.

Ubel, P.A. (2002) Is information always a good thing? Helping patients make 'good' decisions, *Med Care,* 40 (9 Suppl), V39–44.

Varricchio, C.G., and Jassak, P.F. (1989) Informed consent: An overview, *Semin Oncol Nurs*, 5 (2), 95–98.

Wagner, R., and Keany, J. (2006) 'Informed Consent.' Retrieved November 19, 2008, from http://www.emedicinehealth.com/informed_consent/page13_em.htm.

Weinfurt, K.P., Depuy, V. *et al.* (2005) Understanding of an aggregate probability statement by patients who are offered participation in Phase I clinical trials. *Cancer* 103 (1), 140–147.

Wennberg, J.E., Barry, M.J. *et al.* (1993) Outcomes research, PORTs, and health care reform, *Ann N Y Acad Sci* 703, 52–62.

Whitney, S.N., Holmes-Rovner, M. *et al.* (2008) Beyond shared decision making: An expanded typology of medical decisions, *Medical Decision Making*, 28 (5), 699–705.

Xie, B., Dilts, D.M. *et al.* (2006) The physician-patient relationship: The impact of patient-obtained medical information, *Health Econ* 15 (8), 813–833.

19

The Dimensions of Decisions: A Conceptual and Empirical Investigation

Lori S. Franz and Michael W. Kramer[*]

Introduction

Effective decision making has long been seen as an essential competency for individual and organizational success. Although extensive research on decision making has occurred in a variety of fields, only a small amount of research has focused on delineating a comprehensive typology of decision characteristics that define the dimensions of decisions. The few decision categorizations that have appeared have focused on specific elements of decisions such as decision models, decision-maker limitations and styles, decision processes, decision environments, and mathematical models for decision making, without taking a comprehensive perspective on the nature of decisions. We intuitively recognize that all decisions are not alike and that different decision types may require different processes for successful outcomes. Current research provides little insight concerning the dimensions that make various decisions similar or different or how those differences influence decision-making effectiveness.

At least part of the difficulty of analyzing the decision as the variable of interest is the difficulty in conceptualizing a decision (Chia, 1994; Chapman and Niedermayer, 2001) or in identifying the moment at which a decision is made (Huisman, 2001). Mintzberg *et al.* (1976) defined a decision as a commitment to a future action. It is this construct of decision that has eluded full elaboration with respect to useful classification and labeling. Mintzberg and Waters (1990) go so far as to argue that the concept of decision may actually get in the way of understanding

[*]Acknowledgement: The authors would like to thank Dr Suraj Commuri for helpful comments in the construction of the survey.

Handbook of Decision Making. Edited by Paul C. Nutt and David C. Wilson
© 2010 John Wiley & Sons, Ltd

behavior. They point out that the unclear nature of the concept of decision can create confusion about interpreting personal or organizational actions. Namely, they observe that actions can occur without commitment to act, actions can occur without consensus or in response to environmental factors, and that there is difficulty in identifying the clear point of commitment. They concluded that studies of decisions were instead studies of actions which are the 'traces actually left behind in organizations' (Mintzberg and Waters, 1990: 1). Niedermayer and Chapman (2001) clarify that actions and inactions were perceived as decisions; however, actions were viewed more like decisions only if the action was viewed as more intentional than the inaction.

Some scholars suggest that decisions should be decoupled from actions. Chia (1994) argues that decisions are active operations which bring forth discrete events or entities and may then appear to be discrete, independent, and identifiable. Thus the specification of the concept of decision is an act of sense-making which allows humans to construct a version of reality. He points out that the desire exists to allow the concept of decision 'to stand alone' and 'appear to be what it is' (Chia, 1994: 785). Laroche (1995) views decisions as social representations which influence processes and facilitate action. He notes that 'there is a lot of talk about decisions, decisions that have been made, will be made, should be made', and 'about who makes decisions, when, how, why and with what results' in organizational life (Laroche, 1995: 67). Thus the social representation of decisions in the individual's mind can give meaning to processes and concerns.

Regardless of the difficulties incumbent in an attempt to define and describe decisions, the concept cannot be ignored. Considerable research and theory about both individual and organizational decision making has developed despite the lack of specificity with respect to the concept decision. Perhaps the unwillingness to further specify the concept can be summed up by Yates' less introspective comment: 'Everybody knows what a decision is' (1990: 3). However, even with intuitive understanding of the concept, clearly, not all decisions are the same.

The purpose of this study is to isolate the decision as a separate unit of analysis and elaborate the dimensions of a decision according to characteristics inherent in all decisions. Understanding those dimensions can lead to insights into the decision process and decision success. By elaborating and isolating the dimensions of decisions, a better understanding of decision making can result and additional enhancements to decision-making theory can be developed. Specifically, this study seeks to develop and test a model of the dimensions of a decision from which their relationship to decision processes and success can be posited.

THE STUDY OF DECISIONS IN DECISION MAKING

Most discussions of decisions are embedded in the analysis of decision making. Bazerman (2001) concisely divides the study of decision making into two parts: prescriptive models and descriptive models, recognizing naturalistic decision making as an offshoot of behavioral decision making. Prescriptive models, which are generally proposed by economists, statisticians, and management scientists, describe what should be done rather than actual courses of action. Behavioral theory, which has grown out of prescriptive theory, attempts to explain decision-maker actions, usually through carefully constructed experiments in a laboratory which isolate the behaviors of interest.

The subdisciplines of decision making are described as classical decision making, behavioral decision theory, judgment and decision making, organizational decision making, and naturalistic decision making (Lipshitz, Klein, Orasanu, and Salas, 2001). Naturalistic decision theory, the newest and least developed area of study, extends behavioral theory to focus on how people make meaningful and familiar decisions in the context of a real decision environment. Similarly, Dholakia and Bagozzi (2002) characterize the overall field of decision making by separating it into two subfields: the decision scientists' study of decision antecedents and the applied psychologists' study of post decision issues such as how decisions are maintained, protected, and implemented.

In almost all cases, the specific study of the decision itself is excluded. Of note however is the work of researchers who examined decision making via case studies involving actual organizational decisions (Nutt 1998a; Nutt, 1998b; Hickson *et al.*, 1986). In the Bradford studies, 150 decisions in 30 organizations were analyzed over a six-year period via hundreds of structured interviews with managers and other informants (Hickson *et al.*, 1986). Similarly, Nutt (1998a; 1998b; 2001) created a database of 376 organizational decisions. These studies sought to explain the differences in decision making, describing the broad process of arriving at the decision as well as the 'matter for decision' which includes the problem, its political interests, and the process in the organizational context (Hickson *et al.*, 1986). Size, importance, and the high-stakes nature of the decision have been used as variables to study decision-making characteristics in practice (Sutcliffe and McNamara, 2001)

Scope, structure, span of control, and participation

Although no comprehensive model of decisions with an encompassing categorization of decision characteristics has appeared, the literature is replete with isolated descriptions of various decision characteristics. Examination of the literature reveals decisions which can be described in scope as personal/individual, interpersonal, family, community, corporate or organizational, which recognizes the ultimate stakeholders of the decision. A preponderance of the managerial research appears to address personal (individual, consumer, or managerial) and organizational (corporate, public, or community) decisions. Very few studies were found which compare decisions across categories. A notable exception lies in the work of Wilson and Woodside (2001), who compared executive and consumer decision processes. No studies were found comparing family decisions to organizational decisions, although one might suspect that there could be some similarities. There has been considerable interest in the degree to which decisions described as organizational decisions may actually be individual decisions and how the two relate. Shapira (1997) frames a discussion of whether studies in behavioral research of individual decision making differ from studies of organizational decision making.

Within the scope of personal, family, organization, and community, decisions can also be classified as either individual or group participative, depending on whether a single person is responsible or whether a collective judgment produces the action which is taken. Interestingly, even a personal decision may incorporate group participation. Individual decision makers may act alone or base their decision on the advice of others. Thus, classification of a decision by participation type quickly evolves into a description of the decision process which elaborates on how the participation takes place. Some decision makers with sole responsibility for the decision may seek advice or input or rely on others for analysis; others may prefer to act alone, relying on their own resources. Similarly, groups may provide input and advice, or formal structures such as votes or consensus building may be used to derive the action plan. Participants, either individual or group, may have differing levels of involvement in the decision, with some decisions classified as high-involvement, based on the level of interest, activity, and interaction generated by the decision process. Others may profess to have broad participation, but would be described as low-involvement based on the actual actions of the participants. Various models of personal involvement in decision making can be found in Verplanken and Svenson (1997). In addition to involvement in the decision process by advising, lobbying, shaping via vote, or other means, stakeholders also participate in the evaluation of the decision's outcomes.

Types of outputs and actions generated

A number of early studies and scholarly works have defined salient elements of decisions based on type of output. Barnard (1948) classified decisions as either positive (including direct action, cessation of action or preventions of action) or negative (deciding not to decide). Salveson (1958) posited four kinds of decisions: (1) decisions of understanding such as legislative agreements or acceptance of common assumptions or definitions; (2) decisions of recognition in which an object is recognized as a member of a set; (3) decisions of action by which some state of nature is changed; and (4) decisions of enterprise by which policies, protocols, mores, and objectives are set. Simon (1960; 1976) used type of decision process to classify decisions as either programmed or nonprogrammed based on the approach to the process steps of intelligence, design, and choice. Gorry and Scott Morton (1971) conceptualized the same decision types as structured, semi-structured or unstructured. A structured decision exhibited known procedure for all steps of the decision process while an unstructured decision had no specified solution procedure for any step in the process. They further defined organizational decisions in response to needs for operational control (routine, repetitive task oriented), managerial control (acquiring and using resources to achieve goals), or strategic planning (addressing long-term goals and resources).

In an alternate approach, Yates (1990) defines decision type according to the form of action adopted by the decision maker. Three different decision types are noted: choices, evaluations, and constructions, although Yates notes that these are not necessarily independent of one another. In a choice decision, the decision maker considers a well-defined set of alternatives, selecting the best one or more from this set. In an evaluation decision, the decision maker determines the worth of alternatives, selecting from among those the one(s) with the greatest worth. A construction type decision entails the act of designing the best alternative given a set of limited resources. Klein (1998) studied 156 decision points involving experienced firefighters in nonroutine instances and added a fourth decision type, the recognition-primed decision (RPD) which uses mental simulation. RPD involves a simultaneous process by which decision makers size up the situation as similar to other situations they have seen to identify sensible courses of action, and evaluate them by imagining the outcome, if the action is implemented. The recognition-primed strategy was more likely to be used in cases where there was greater time pressure, higher experience level, more dynamic conditions, and ill-defined goals. A rational choice strategy appeared more likely when there was a need for justification, conflict resolution, optimization, or greater computational complexity. He points out that his model is incomplete in that it does not describe decisions made by teams or organizations.

Beach (1998) developed image theory, which is a special case of naturalistic decision theory. Image theory describes two kinds of decisions. Adoption decisions involve screening out actions incompatible with the strategic image of good solutions and choice of the best alternative from the survivors of the screening. Progress decisions attempt to forecast the compatibility of the current or adopted plan with the ideal future image. Using an alternative framework from consumer behavior provided by Weinberg (1981), Fischer and Hanley (2006) studied four different types of decisions: extensive, limited, impulsive, and habitual. Both extensive and limited decisions are considered to be cognitive processes, which are characterized by varying need for additional information and sense of personal involvement, which could be strong or limited, respectively. In contrast, impulsive and habitual decisions do not rely on cognitive processes, but rather on spontaneous reactions to stimuli. Habitual decisions are routine, with little need for information and little emotional involvement. It is not clear the degree to which these same decision types might be reflective of organizational decisions or overlap with other decision types.

Importance and difficulty

Decisions can also be classified by their relative importance gauged by their salience to the decision maker and stakeholders. Moody (1983) suggests that five factors should be evaluated to assess a decision's importance. First the magnitude or length of commitment to the decision determines whether it is major or nonmajor. Commitments of considerable capital, sizable numbers of people, or long-term impact could all signal major decisions. A second factor is the flexibility of the planning involved, including whether the course of action could be reversed or if the decision reduces other options once made. Certainty of goals and premises is a third factor, suggesting that well-established goals lead to decisions which have less impact than those invoked in an environment of fluctuating goals. Fourth, the nature of the data as quantifiable and certain leads to less important decisions than when data is more difficult to specify and interpret. Finally, the greater the human impact of the decision, either in severity of impact or numbers of people impacted, the greater the importance of the decision becomes. Although this discussion of importance appears relevant to large organizational decisions based on the examples of Moody, the relevance to other settings has not been established.

Moody also elaborates five decision characteristics which can define the decision: (1) how the decision may influence the future (futurity); (2) the difficulty by which the decision could be reversed (reversibility); (3) the extent of the impact of the decision (impact); (4) the quality of the decision with respect to various stakeholders (quality); and (5) the frequency with which the decision is made (periodicity).

Decisions are frequently described as 'hard'. The difficulty level can be created by one or more of four possible sources according to Clemon (1996). The complexity of the decision situation is a primary source of difficulty. Complexity is created when a myriad of issues, data sources and/or stakeholders must be considered, and/or when a large number of alternatives and outcomes are possible. Typically, complex decisions are associated with the higher levels of analysis needed to make meaning out of the varied inputs. A second source of difficulty is uncertainty with respect to data, future events or outcomes. The existence of multiple and often competing objectives inevitably makes decisions more difficult as tradeoffs among the objectives must be considered. Finally, decisions become more difficult if there are varying perspectives which may lead to alternative solutions, depending on the individuals or groups evaluating the outcomes. Some complex, multifaceted problems with only unattractive solutions may be referred to as 'wicked' (Churchman, 1967) thus spawning a new dimension of difficulty.

In the Bradford studies of decision making in 30 organizations, complexity of the problem was operationalized with the variables rarity (how frequently similar issues arise), radicality of consequences (magnitude of change), seriousness of consequences, diffusion of consequences, endurance of consequences, number of interests involved, diversity of interests involved, openness to alternatives, and precursiveness (Hickson et al., 1986). Precursiveness describes the degree to which a decision will establish parameters for future decisions. In a simplifying attempt, Scherpereel (2006) created a decision taxonomy which classifies decision as first order, second order or third order, depending on ascending levels of uncertainty, complexity, and dynamism.

Moody (1983) also defines five basic ingredients of the art of decision making: facts, knowledge, experience, analysis, and judgment. A dimension of any decision depends on the decision maker's perception about how these five elements are essential to the decision. Decision processes then involve the combination of these elements to determine the course of action. For instance, decisions may be described as intuitive, subjective, objective, and or rational depending upon the balance of facts and analysis as compared with judgment and experience when determining the action to take. Attributes of decision alternatives included quality and quantity of information in a study of decision effectiveness (Keller and Staelin, 1987). Knowledge and experience may be stronger factors in cases where the decision is initiated by the decision maker than cases where others initiate the decision process. Klein defines a negative extension to Moody's five ingredients, hyper-rationality, which is the 'attempt to apply deductive and statistical reasoning and analysis to situations where they do not apply'(1998: 289).

Relationship to other decisions

Frequently in the study of decisions and decision making, research methodologies are developed which isolate the decision so that the decision process can be understood or outcomes predicted. Despite attempts to focus on single and independent decisions in research analysis, most decisions arise in a context in which a given decision is related in some way to preceding, concurrent, and/or successive decisions (Langley, Mintzberg, Pitcher, Posada, and Saint-Macary, 1995). In addition to precursiveness, decisions may be clustered in sets of multiple related decisions which have similar timing and which affect one another's outcomes; or they may be dependent on receipt of information about either preceding decisions or their outcomes before being made. In other cases, decisions can be regarded as simple or stand-alone, because they either are substantially independent of other decisions or dwarf them in importance. In like manner, a decision may be unique, unlike anything the decision maker has encountered before, or similar to previous decision experiences. A decision may be classified as a single event or as an event which is repeated over time. For example, the decision to lose weight might be a single event such as the decision to undergo a gastric by-pass operation, or the repeated resolve to maintain a diet regime.

Decision type defined by organizational function

As one of only a few researchers to attempt to identify appropriate tactics for determining alternatives for specific decision types, Nutt (2001) defined eight types of strategic organizational decisions: technology, reorganization, control, marketing, product, services, personnel, and financing (inputs). These decision types were based on the work of Hickson *et al.* (1986) whereby nine similar organizational decision types were identified. Nutt identified six key features of these decision types to provide additional insight into each decision type. The key features were evaluated as being high, moderate, low or variable on (1) stakes and interests; (2) available precedents; (3) importance of new ideas; (4) need for secrecy; (5) scale of effort; and (6) time required. Employing a database of 376 strategic decisions from 47 organizations, the authors looked at decision success when different tactics to uncover alternatives were deployed. In a similar analysis, Clark and Shrode (1979) developed a typology of the general decision situations which are faced in public sector decision making, concluding from empirical analysis that program, budget, personnel, and organizational decision situations and their subgroups define the gamut of decision structures in that public sector.

Decision processes and models

Although decision-making research and theory may attempt few comprehensive classifications of decisions, a large number of studies have examined the broad decision process. Simon (1960; 1976) defined decision types as programmed and non-programmed according to characteristics of a three-step decision process related to the decision: intelligence (problem identification and data collection), design (determination of approach and search for alternatives) and choice (select best alternative). Beach (1997) characterizes decision making as the process of accomplishing a series of decision tasks. The tasks are diagnosis of the existing problem, selection of an action from a set of potential actions, and the implementation of the action. A number of sources present step by step decision process recommendations which are supported by research findings (Hammond, 1999; Russo, 2002; Welch, 2002). Most sequential decision processes generally include consideration of most, if not all, of these steps outlined by Hammond (1999): (1) problem definition; (2) decision objectives; (3) alternative generation; (4) anticipated outcomes; (5) trade-offs between alternatives and outcomes; (6) assessment of uncertainty; (7) risk tolerance; and (8) impact on related decisions. Decision analysis, which is widely taught as a managerial methodology, is another popular structured approach to decision making suggesting a specific step by step analytical approach (Keeney, 2004).

A number of decision-making models have emerged which attempt to describe decisions and organizational decision processes (Daft, 2003). From prescriptive decision theory, the classical or rational model assumes that decision makers are rational, seeking the best alternative to maximize the achievement of goals. The decision-maker attempts to optimize assuming clear goals, certain information, and good analytical skills. From behavioral decision theory we have learned more about the actual behavior of decision makers. The administrative model recognizes human limitations and the complexity of the environment. It assumes that decision makers attempt to satisfice based on a simplification of the data and the problem. The mixed-scanning model assumes that the decision maker will make incremental decisions which accomplish at least some progress toward goals or mission. The incremental model is based on a strategy of limited comparisons of actions designed to avoid negative consequences, described as 'muddling though' by Lindblom (1959). The garbage can model (Cohen *et al.*, 1972) recognizes that not all decision making is rational; rather chance occurrences may allow solutions to be identified. The political model fosters the realization that personal or group goals may supersede rationality in the selection of the action to take.

The impact of the environment and the situation on the decision and decision making is reflected in many studies of the decision process. The contingency models of decision making of Vroom and Yetton (1973) and Vroom and Jago (1988) show that the decision situation, which can include decision characteristics, tends to be more important than individual differences in determining the action of the leader.

Parallel research by group and communication scholars also focus on decision processes and have produced similar findings. In a representative study, Fisher (1970) explored how communication changes over time during the decision-making process. During the first phase of decision making, which he termed orientation, group members clarify the problem and become familiar with each other. Their communication is often tentative and ambiguous; they ask questions and avoid disagreeing with each other. During the second phase, called conflict, differences become clear as members frequently disagree with each other and are more direct in their communication. Strong opinions are frequently stated instead of asking questions. During emergence, the third phase, agreement becomes more common than disagreement as members gradually discover common ground for a decision. Finally, during reinforcement, the fourth phase, members agree on a decision, ask questions to clarify its implementation, and even congratulate themselves on their decision. Various scholars report similar phase models as descriptive of the process (e.g. Tuckman, 1965).

Critiques of these process models suggest that groups frequently do not follow such a linear progression towards a decision. Some scholars suggest that the process is more cyclical as groups fluctuate between phases and only gradually spiral toward decisions (Schiedel and Crowell, 1964). Others suggest that there is no particular pattern or phases of communication in most decision-making groups (Poole, 1981; 1983a; 1983b). Instead the difference between effective and ineffective group processes is the group's ability to conduct four activities during the decision-making process: conduct problem analysis, determine decision objectives, produce alternatives, and evaluate the positive and negative aspects of the alternatives; however, the order in which these occur is not important to the outcome (e.g. Hirokawa and Rost, 1992). Collectively, this research focuses on rational decision making in which group members analyze problems, develop criteria, and evaluate potential solutions as key aspects of communication during decision making.

In contrast to these rational approaches to decision making, research by Gersick (1988) suggests that the decision-making process is primarily influenced by time issues. She found that groups tended to start off on a particular trajectory or direction almost immediately, but then at about the midpoint of the time allowed (whether it is hours or weeks) groups make an adjustment after brief discussions, usually based on some external feedback, and then continue on that new trajectory until completing their activities. This suggests a two-phase process that is far less rational than the other models.

Decision outcomes/success

As defined by Yates (1990), a decision is successful if it brings about outcomes at least as satisfying as would have occurred by any other action which might have been pursued. Economists would describe decision success as the decision maker's maximization of his or her utility function. However, in the case of most decisions, the outcome of the other actions which could have been pursued will never be known, and thus such measurement becomes impossible in real-world settings. Likewise the outcome of any decision is also difficult to judge, because of the outside influences which may affect the outcome after the decision is made (Moody, 1983). Keeney describes good decisions as those which, on the average, have good consequences, admitting that even good decisions cannot guarantee good consequences because of the uncertainties involved (Keeney, 2004).

As a surrogate for decision success, decision quality is often discussed. Moody (1983) conceptually describes actual decision quality as a bell-shaped curve of quality outcomes which ranges from unacceptable to outstanding. He suggests that when thinking about decision outcomes, most decisions can be classified as acceptable and will fall within one standard deviation of the mean outcome (68%) on that curve. Recognizing the unlikelihood of making really great or really abysmal decisions, he categorizes those falling between one and two standard deviations above or below the mean as superior or poor, respectively (14 % each) and those lower or higher than two standard deviations as unacceptable or outstanding (2 % each). To measure the quality of decisions, Moody suggests that the decision outcome can be compared to the expectation prior to making the decision, provided that an identifiable goal for the outcome was established prior to the decision.

The satisfaction of the decision maker and/or stakeholder is often used as a surrogate for measures of decision quality. Perceptions of the results are an important component in measuring the ultimate quality or success of a decision, thus are often used to evaluate the decision (Nutt, 1998a). Perceptions, however, have numerous limitations. The popularity of the decision and/or the memory of the decision process could color the perception of the quality of decision. For instance, lack of controversy and ease or difficulty of agreement may mask the quality of the decision. Timeliness of the decision and the perceived speed of decision maker's response can also be part of the perception of quality of the decision.

Hough and Ogilivie (2005) looked at outcomes of decision quality, decisiveness, and perceived effectiveness associated with individual decision makers' cognitive styles as measured by the Myers-Briggs Type Indicator (MBTI) instrument. They found that cognitive styles had an influence on both decision outcomes and on how others perceived the performance of decision makers.

In experimental studies, quality of decision is sometimes operationalized by predefining an optimal decision for the exercise such as the 'crashed on the moon' or 'crashed in the desert' exercises in which participants rank order the importance of various objects and compare responses to expert rankings. For example, Williams *et al.* (2005) measured decision quality with a 0-1 variable which equaled one if the participant of their experiment selected a predetermined correct alternative, thus inferring a correct decision had been made. In these experimental settings, the quality decision making can be attributed to the actions which bring about optimal results. Because of the measurement difficulties, however, few measures exist for personal or group decision success for real world decisions other than those who rely on perception and satisfaction measures.

Organizational research does provide insight into strategic decision effectiveness as defined by attainment of the objectives which brought forth the decision (Harrison and Pelletier, 1998). Trull (1966) developed one of the early models of organizational decision success by identifying two clusters of variables which had causal impact on decision success in observations of 100 case examples. From this, he operationalized decision success as the function of decision quality and implementation. A quality decision was compatible with operating constraints, completed near the optimal time for the decision, used appropriate but not excessive information, and exhibited congruence between decision-maker effort and authority level. Successful decisions avoided conflict of interest with organizational goals, had an acceptable reward–risk tradeoff and the implementation was understood by those with the task of implementation who also had the means to follow through.

Dean and Sharfman (1996) defined the effectiveness of a strategic decision as 'the extent to which a decision achieves the objectives established by management at the time it is made', concluding that decision processes do influence the effectiveness of strategic decisions (p 372). Degree of goal realization was found to be a result of decision process characteristics (Dholakia and Bagozzi, 2002). Nutt (1998a) observed that objective measures of decision success in organizations still remain difficult as the information about its value is extremely difficult to collect. He points out that financial competitive positioning information that might be associated with decision outcomes is typically not shared and, if available, would be difficult to compare among firms or projects. Metrics, other than dollar measures, which are difficult to compare, are not available. He used a combined measure of success in evaluation of 352 strategic decisions which included: (1) whether the decision was adopted and the adoption sustained; (2) the time to decision; and (3) the subjective success decision value rating provided by two secondary informants. The subjective ratings were ranked from 1 = poor to 5 = outstanding. This subjective ranking was based on the high correlation between managers' subjective and objective measures (Alexander, 1979).

The Study

The previous literature provides a long and varied list of possible dimensions for defining the concept of decision as the focal point of decision making that have not previously been gathered in one place. Table 19.1 provides a fairly comprehensive compilation of these dimensions along with the characteristics or typologies that have been suggested for each dimension. The purpose of this study was to explore these dimensions empirically to determine if the conceptual distinctions made by researchers were perceived as discrete characteristics by individuals involved in decision making.

Methods

Procedure and respondents.   Students from a Midwestern university enrolled in an introductory business class and in sections of an introductory public speaking classes were recruited to participate in this study in exchange for extra credit. Those who were interested went to an online web address where they agreed to an informed consent statement prior to beginning the survey. Participation was voluntary and an alternative assignment was offered to students who chose not to take the survey but wanted the extra credit. As part of the 20-minute survey, respondents were instructed to recall their decision to attend the university as the context for the decision discussed in the survey. In terms of type, this example was a choice decision.

Respondents consisted of 439 undergraduate students. Of these 255 (58 %) were female and 183 (42 %) were male. Nearly all were full-time students (434 or 99 %). In addition the majority (262 or 60 %) held jobs involving weekly work of some type while attending college.

Survey development.   Because no available survey addressed the multiple dimensions of decision making, a new survey was developed. Based on the information in Figure 19.1, a series of 21 potential characteristics were considered, including concepts such as the uniqueness and timeliness of the decision. For each concept, a series of

TABLE 19.1 Dimensions of decision making

Dimension	Characteristics					
Scope	Personal	Interpersonal	Family	Organizational	Community	Societal
Type	Choice	Evaluation	Construction	Recognition primed	Adoption	Progress
Structure	Structured	Mostly structured	Semi-structured	Mostly unstructured	Unstructured	Amorphous
Span of Control	Impulsive	Habitual	Operational	Managerial	Strategic	Momentous
Importance	Negligible	Low	Moderate	High	Very High	Preemptive
Difficulty	Very Little	Little	Moderate	High	Very High	Wicked
Relationship to Other Decisions	Independent	Similar	Connected	Concurrent	Antecedent to	Related in multiple ways Interdependent
Participation	Individual Low involvement	Individual High involvement	Group Advisory Low involvement	Group Advisory High involvement	Group Directive Low involvement	Group Directive High involvement
Outcomes	Abysmal Very unsatisfactory	Unacceptable unsatisfactory	Slightly unacceptable Slightly unsatisfactory	Acceptable Slightly satisfactory	Positive Satisfactory	Outstanding Very satisfactory

3–8 semantic differential-type items were generated. For example, for the concept of uniqueness, the ends of the scale were 'Routine' and 'Non-routine', or 'it was similar to a previous decision' and 'it was not like any other decision I made'. After the initial generation of items, a third individual examined the items for thoroughness and clarity. Based on this feedback, several items were reworded and additional items added. In all, a total of 103 items were generated.

In addition to the 103 items, the survey directly measured the respondent's perception about the scope of the decision (individual, family, community). It also asked a number of demographic questions and questions about the decision (e.g. how long ago was it made). For the dimension scope, a single item was created asking the respondents to indicate the major stakeholder(s). Since selecting a college is a choice, there were no items assessing this dimension.

Results

In order to empirically test these potential dimensions, exploratory factor analysis (principal components, varimax rotations, eigenvalues >1) was used to identify underlying factors and to reduce the number of items.[1] To be retained, items needed to load at >.50 on one factor and at <.40 on all other factors. After eliminating items that failed to meet these criteria, a 21-factor solution emerged consisting of 84 items and accounting for 71 % of the variance (see Table 19.2). Additional analyses confirmed that all but the final two factors had acceptable reliabilities of α >.70.

Of these, six of the broader dimensions indicated in Table 19.1 were represented by 20 factors while one factor represented the outcomes dimension. Table 19.3 provides a listing of each of the 21 factors as dimensions under the broader characteristics previously identified.

Seven of the factors seemed to suggest dimensions of the broader construct of the structure of the decision. *Limited knowledge* (5 items, $\alpha = .81$) indicated the degree to which individuals felt that the decision could be structured around facts, analysis, and knowledge. A second factor, *slow or delayed* decision (4 items, $\alpha = .89$), represented whether the decision was structured so that it could be delayed until the last minute or made later. *Incomplete information* (4 items, $\alpha = .76$) focused on whether the decision was structured so that it was difficult to find trustworthy information in a timely manner. The fourth factor, *uncertain about results* (5 items, $\alpha = .81$), indicated that the nature of the decision made it difficult to determine desired goals and results for the participants. By contrast, the next factor, *uncertain setting* (5 items, $\alpha = .75$) represented the degree to which the results of the decision were predictable, changing, and uncertain. *Inconsistent effort* (3 items, $\alpha = .75$) focused on whether the decision was structured so that it could be worked on periodically or randomly rather than constantly. The seventh factor, *rational decision* (2 items, $\alpha = .48$), indicated whether the decision was intuitive or common sense rather than based on information and reasoning. Its low reliability suggests the need for further conceptual development.

The construct span of control was represented by only one factor. *Short term impact* (3 items, $\alpha = .74$) represented the degree to which the decision had limited impact rather than long-term consequences for the decision maker.

TABLE 19.2 Factor analysis results

Simple, easy decision (11 items; $\alpha = .93$):

Very stressful—not very stressful	.758
Frustrating—not frustrating	.747
Lots of effort—not much effort	.735
Hard—easy	.729
Rational—emotional	.713
Complex—simple	.703
Worried a lot—not worried	.698
Lots of analysis—no-brainer	.696
Anxious—not anxious	.630
Lots to consider—one thing to consider	.606
Required persistence—no persistence	.587

Satisfaction with decision (4 items; $\alpha = .93$):

Satisfied—dissatisfied	.850
Happy/proud—regretful	.849
Good—bad	.836
Comfortable—uneasy	.718

Limited knowledge based decision (5 items; $\alpha = .81$):

Knowledge—not depend on knowledge	.771
Facts—facts not considered	.722
Experience—not depend on experience	.694
Input from others—little input from others	.677
Common sense—common sense no help	.675
Analysis—not depend on analysis	.649

Unimportant decision (4 items; $\alpha = .88$):

Mattered a lot—didn't matter much	.866
Highly significant—not very significant	.840
Highly engaged—not very engaged	.712
Effects my future—won't effect future	.701

Slow/delayed decision (4 items; $\alpha = .89$):

Timely—late	.820
On time/early—last minute	.802
Did not delay—delayed as long as possible	.750
Speedy—slow	.646

Easy to implement decision (4 items; $\alpha = .83$):

Lots of work/energy—little work/energy	.825
Lost of resources/funds—few resources	.824
Big commitment—little or no commitment	.805

TABLE 19.2 (*Continued*)

Long commitment—no commitment	.598

Few options considered (4 items; $\alpha = .82$):

Screened many options—didn't screen	.796
Choose from good alternatives—few alternatives	.773
Evaluated many alternatives—evaluated few	.747
Creativity needed—creativity not involved	.596

Uncommon decision (3 items; $\alpha = .85$):

Frequently make decision like this—not frequent	.889
Similar to previous decision—not like other	.848
Routine—non-routine	.802

Web of decisions (4 items; $\alpha = .80$):

Unrelated decision—group of decisions	.756
Stand alone decision—dependent on other decisions	.746
One thing to consider—lots of things to consider	.650
Single stage decision—multiple stage decision	.610

Incomplete information (4 items; $\alpha = .76$):

Trustworthy information—lacked trustworthy information	.769
Enough information—lacked information	.736
Had time to consider—lacked time to consider	.593
Didn't need expertise—needed more expertise	.572

Low pressure situation (4 items; $\alpha = .76$):

Decision had to be made—no consequence to delay	.737
Under time pressure—no time pressure	.672
Pressure on myself—no pressure on myself	.555
Pressure from others—no pressure from others	.505

Uncertain about results (5 items; $\alpha = .81$):

Clear goals—fuzzy goals	.744
Helped my plan/goals—not thought of plan or goal	.633
Knew result I wanted—Wanted result was unclear	.591
Knew what results would be—uncertain about results	.515
Confident—unsure	.502

Unpopular decision (3 items; $\alpha = .87$):

Popular with others—unpopular with some	.854
Everyone agrees—lots of opinions	.843
Easily agreed upon—controversial	.694

Unchangeable decision (3 items; $\alpha = .83$):

Can be undone—never can be undone	.860
Easy to reverse—hard to reverse	.858

TABLE 19.2 (*Continued*)

Can be modified—cannot be modified	.786

Highly uncertain setting (5 items; $\alpha = .75$):

Future predictable—future unpredictable	.645
Things about the same—things were changing	.631
No chance of mess up—things could mess up decision	.599
Low risk—high risk	.592
Certain environment—uncertain environment	.545

Serve individual interest (3 items; $\alpha = .70$):

People lobbied me—no one lobbied me	.750
Did what someone else wanted—what I thought best	.708
Others sought selfish gains—no one tried to gain	.656

Inconsistent effort (3 items; $\alpha = .75$):

Worked on constantly—work on it on and off	.817
At it all the time—a stop and go process	.780
Constantly on my mind—seldom thought about it	.658

Individual decision (3 items; $\alpha = .70$):

Relied on others—relied on myself	.779
Deferred to others—use my own judgment	.724
Sought input from others—acted alone	.658

Short term impact (3 items; $\alpha = .74$):

May change the future—not much future impact	.698
Long term impact—short term impact	.633
High impact on me—not much impact on me	.513

Self-initiated (3 items; $\alpha = .63$):

Initiated by others—initiated by me	.719
Dictated by circumstances—dictated by me	.660
Someone else could have decided—it was up to me	.536

Rational decision (2 items; $\alpha = .48$):

Intuitive—based on information	.710
Required good sense—required logic and reasoning	.698

Three factors suggested dimensions of the broader construct importance. The factor *unimportant* (4 items, $\alpha = .88$) indicated the degree to which individuals perceived the decision as not mattering much, not very significant, and unlikely to affect the future. A second factor, *low pressure* (4 items, $\alpha = .76$), suggested the decision was of little importance because it could be delayed and there was no pressure

TABLE 19.3 Exploratory factor analysis results as dimensions of decision making

Dimensions	*Characteristics*					
Scope	Personal	Interpersonal	Family	Organizational	Community	Societal
Type	Choice	Evaluation	Construction	Recognition primed	Adoption	Progress
Structure	Structured	Mostly structured	Semi-structured	Mostly unstructured	unstructured	Amorphous
Limited knowledge						
Slow/Delayed						
Incomplete information						
Uncertain about results						
Uncertain setting						
Inconsistent effort						
Rational decision						
Span of Control	Impulsive	Habitual	Operational	Managerial	Strategic	Momentous
Short term impact						
Importance	Negligible	Low	Moderate	High	Very high	Preemptive
Unimportant						
Low pressure						
Unchangeable						

(*Continued*)

TABLE 19.3 (*Continued*)

Dimensions	Characteristics					
Difficulty Simple/Easy Easy to implement Few options	Very little	Little	Moderate	High	Very high	Wicked
Relationship to Other Decisions Uncommon decision Web of decisions	Independent	Similar	Connected	Concurrent	Antecedent to	Related in Multiple ways Interdependent
Participation Serve individual interest Individual decision Self initiated Unpopular decision	Individual Low involvement	Individual High involvement	Group advisory Low involvement	Group advisory High involvement	Group directive Low involvement	Group Directive High involvement
Outcomes Satisfaction	Abysmal Very unsatisfactory	Unacceptable Unsatisfactory	Slightly unacceptable Slightly unsatisfactory	Acceptable Slightly satisfactory	Positive Satisfactory	Outstanding Very satisfactory

to make a decision. The third factor, *unchangeable* (3 items, $\alpha = .70$) represented the importance of the decision by indicating whether it was possible to reverse or modify the decision at a later time.

Three factors represented the broader construct difficulty. One factor, *simple/easy* (11 items, $\alpha = .93$), focused on whether the decision required much effort and produced much stress or anxiety. The second factor, *easy to implement* (4 items, $\alpha = .83$), focused not on the ease of making the decision, but rather on whether implementing the decision involved a lot of effort, resources, and commitment. The third factor, *few options* (4 items, $\alpha = .82$), related more to the ease of making decisions based on the number of options and how carefully they were evaluated.

The broader construct of relationship to other decisions was represented by two factors. One factor, *uncommon decision* (3 items, $\alpha = .85$), represented whether the decision was like other decisions or routine although not necessarily directly related to those decisions. A second factor, *web of decisions* (4 items, $\alpha = .80$), focused more on whether the decision was interrelated to other decisions or part of a sequence of decisions.

Four factors represented dimensions of participation. The first factor, *unpopular decision* (3 items, $\alpha = .87$) represented the degree to which others were involved in evaluating the decision and agreed with it. *Served individual interests* (3 items, $\alpha = .70$) indicated that the participants were able to act without others attempting to influence the decision. *Individual decision* (3 items, $\alpha = .70$) represented the degree to which the individuals felt they could make the decision on their own. A third factor, *self-initiated* (3 items; $\alpha = .63$) also focused on participation by indicating whether the individual initiated the decision or someone else did.

The other factor, *satisfaction* (4 items, $\alpha = .93$), represented the affective outcome of the decision, that is, the degree to which individuals were happy, comfortable, and satisfied with their decision. For this study, there was no attempt to measure the effectiveness of the outcome given the difficulty of providing any objective measure of this for choosing a college.

Taken together, the results of the factor analysis indicate that a decision is a complex, multi-dimensional concept. The presence of these different dimensions in the one type of decision studied here suggests that these dimensions likely vary significantly from decision to decision.

DISCUSSION

Most previous decision-making research has focused on variables related to the decision-making process without examining the central concept in the process, the nature of the decision itself. This lack of focus on defining decisions is likely due to the difficulty in conceptualizing a decision (Chia, 1994; Niedermayer and Chapman (2001) and an intuitive sense that '[e]verybody knows what a decision is' (Yates, 1990: 3). In an effort to address this omission in previous research, this preliminary study explored previous research for the conceptual development of the dimensions of decisions and then created a series of scales to measure those dimensions.

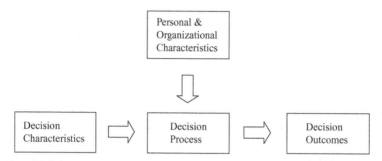

FIGURE 19.1 Model of decision making.

The dimensions identified can lead to a richer understanding of the concept of decisions and decision-making processes. Future extensions of this study will allow researchers to enhance knowledge of decision making and decision processes.

The decision model

Three theoretical orientations to the research regarding decisions typically have been suggested: prescriptive, descriptive, and naturalistic (Beach, 1997). Each of these approaches is compatible with the overall conceptual model of decision making found in Figure 19.1. The model suggests the following relationships: (1) Characteristics of the decision should predict the decision process used. (2) Proper pairing of the correct decision process with the type of decision at hand leads to positive decision outcomes. (3) Contextual factors such as personal and organizational characteristics may act as intervening variables which affect the decision process, and hence also impact the decision outcomes.

Whereas, previous research has frequently examined the relationship of the decision process to decision outcomes and how contextual factors like personal or organizational characteristics influence decision outcomes, the role of the nature of the decision has been under-studied and under-developed. The development of the scales in the current study will allow for a more nuanced examination of how the nature of the decision itself interacts with the process and the contextual environment. By analyzing the type of decision in conjunction with studies of decision-making processes, researchers may eventually be able to prescribe appropriate and/or efficient processes for certain types of decisions. Likewise, study of the prevalence of certain types of decisions in organizations and in personal settings may focus attention on decision types which have received very little attention and analysis by scholars, yet comprise an important subset of decisions.

In addition, the decision maker's perception of the decision may also prove to be a valuable predictor of that decision maker's actions during the process. Very little is known about how the decision maker's perception of the decision may influence his or her actions. This more nuanced examination of the nature of decisions may also allow for improved decision-making processes and outcomes. It seems apparent that the processes that lead to effective and satisfying decision outcomes for major strategic decisions are most likely not the same processes that are effective and satisfying for decisions which have little future impact and involve only one person. However, in cases where the decision maker perceives the decision to be simpler or more complex than others might judge it to be, or to construe the decision in some other atypical way, the processes used may be found to be misaligned with the decision type. Consider for example, the manager who may choose to use an information intense group consultative process which delays action on a decision which most group members would classify as an unimportant operational decision. Only with the development of ways to classify and measure the dimensions of decisions can these distinctions be made. The scales developed here allow for the development of a more specific contingency model of decision making.

The ability to identify and measure the dimensions of decisions will also allow for a more complete understanding of how individuals and organizational groups make decisions. For example, when faced with an uncommon decision that is of high importance, decision makers more likely respond by considering different options than when faced with a low importance, routine decision. The ability to conceptualize decisions along these dimensions allows for an examination of when and how individuals consider some factors as important and others unimportant. The understanding of the process activities for addressing certain decision types would be a positive extension of this study.

Future research studies which examine the similarities and differences between personal, consumer, interpersonal, and organizational decisions are also suggested by this study. Whether a single typology of decisions can cover all types of decisions, as posited by this paper, remains to be seen. Additional studies with varied respondents, including practicing managers, will add to the robustness of the research.

Finally, in addition to advances in research, the findings will allow development of ways to effectively communicate knowledge of the effective strategies associated with specific decision types to prospective decision makers. Although a number of books oriented to managerial and personal decision making are on the market, much of the content is descriptive rather than prescriptive. Many business courses and executive seminars have focused on the quantitative models of decision making or other subsets of decision making such as negotiation. By approaching decision making from a typology of decisions, attention can be directed toward specific situations and appropriate responses.

Limitations

This preliminary study identified dimensions of decisions based on one type of decision, a choice. It will be important to test these dimensions for other types of decisions, as well. It may be that the dimensions identified here are not common across decisions or that there are additional decision dimensions that were not relevant or distinct in the choosing of a college. In addition, using college students recalling a decision made anywhere from a year to four years earlier may have led to certain biases. However, if such biases exist in the results, the biases are probably indicative of the conceptual frameworks that are used to make sense of decision making by an array of individuals. Further research can address these concerns by having organizational decision makers focus on a variety of current or recent decisions.

Conclusion

Whereas most previous research has focused on decision making, this study examined the central construct in decision making, the decision itself. In so doing, this research contributed to the research on decision making by delineating the dimensions of decisions, an area of research that has generally been neglected. Future research which applies this conceptualization of the decision in connection with the decision context and decision process should lead to a deeper understanding of ways to improve individual and organizational decision making.

NOTES

1. Although conventional practice used to be that researchers needed large samples, such as 10 subjects per item in order to use exploratory factor analysis, researchers have demonstrated that small samples are sufficient especially when factor loadings are >.60 (Meyer, Bates, and Gacono, 1999). Over 82 % of the 84 items met this criterion. To further assess the factors identified, various combinations of factors were run. In these analyses, the factors generally maintained their structures. These results, in addition to the high internal reliabilities (>.70) of 19 of the 21 factors provided evidence that the factors were appropriately identified.

REFERENCES

Alexander, E.R. (1979) The design of alternatives in organizational contexts: A pilot study, *Administrative Science Quarterly*, 24 (3), 382–404.

Barnard, C.I. (1948) *The Functions of an Executive*. Cambridge, MA: Harvard University Press.

Bazerman, M.H. (2001) The study of 'real' decision making, *Journal of Behavioral Decision Making*, 14, 353–384.

Bazerman, M.H. (2006) *Judgement in Managerial Decision Making*. Hoboken, NJ: John Wiley & Sons, Inc.

Beach, L.R. (1998) *The Psychology of Decision Making*. Thousand Oaks, CA: Sage.

Chapman, G.B., and Niedermayer, L.Y. (2001) What counts as a decision? Predictors of perceived decision making, *Psychonomic Bulletin and Review*, 8 (3), 615–619.

Chia, R. (1994) The concept of a decision: A deconstructive analysis, *Journal of Management Studies*, 31 (6), 781–806.

Churchman, C.W. (1967) Wicked problems, *Management Science*, 14 (4), 141–142.

Clark, T.D., and Shrode, W.A. (1979) Public-sector decision structures: An empirically-based description, *Public Administration Review*, 39, 343–354.

Clemen, R.T. (1996) *Making Hard Decisions*. Belmont, CA: Duxbury Press, 2nd edition.

Cohen, M.D., March, J.G., and Olsen, J.P. (1972) A garbage can model of organizational choice, *Administrative Science Quarterly*, 17, 1–25.

Daft, R.L. (2003) *Organizational Theory and Design*. Cincinnatii, OH: Southwestern.

Dean, J.W., and Sharfman, M.P. (1996) Does decision process matter? A study of strategic decision-making effectiveness, *The Academy of Management Journal*, 39, 368–396.

Dholakia, U.M., and Bagozzi, R.P. (2002) Mustering motivation to enact decisions, *Journal of Behavioral Decision Making*, 15, 167–188.

Fischer, A., and Hanley, N. (2007) Analyzing decision behaviour in stated preference surveys: A consumer psychological approach, *Ecological Economics*, 61 (2–3), 303–314.

Fisher, B.A. (1970) Decision emergence: Phases in group decision making, *Speech Monographs*, 37, 53–66.

Gersick, C.J.G. (1988) Time and transition in work teams: Toward a new model of group development, *Academy of Management Journal*, 31, 9–41.

Gorry, G.M., and Morton, M.S. (1971) A framework for management information systems, *Sloan Management Review*, 13 (1), 55–70.

Hammond, J.S. (1999) *Smart Choices*. New York: Broadway Books.

Harrison, E.F., and Pelletier, M.A. (1998) Foundations of strategic decision effectiveness, *Management Decision*, 36 (3), 147–159.

Hickson, D. Butler, R. Gray, D., Mallory, G., and Wilson, D. (1986) *Top Decisions: Strategic Decision-making in Organizations*. San Francisco, CA: Jossey-Bass.

Hirokawa, R.Y., and Rost, K.M. (1992) Effective group decision making in organizations: Field test of the vigilant interaction theory, *Management Communication Quarterly*, 5, 267–288.

Hough, J.R. and D.T. Ogilvie (2005) An empirical test of cognitive style and strategic decision outcomes, *Journal of Management Studies*, 42 (2), 417–448.

Huisman, M. (2001) Decision-making in meetings as talk-in-interaction, *International Studies of Management and Organization*, 31 (3), 69–90.

Keeney, R.L. (2004) Making better decision makers, *Decision Analysis*, 1 (4), 193–204.

Keller, K.L., and Staelin, R. (1987) Effects of quality and quantity of information on decision effectiveness, *Journal of Consumer Research*, 14, 200–213.

Klein, G. (1998) *Sources of Power*. Cambridge, MA: MIT Press.

Langley, A., Mintzberg, H., Pitcher, P., Posada, E., and Saint-Macary, J. (1995) Opening up decision making: The view from the black stool, *Organization Science*, 6 (3), 260–279.

Laroche, H. (1995) From decision to action in organizations: Decision-making as a social representation, *Organization Science*, 6 (1), 62–75.

Lindblom, C.E. (1959) The science of muddling through, *Public Administration Review*, 19, 79–88.

Lipshitz, R., Klein, G., Orasanu, J., and Salas, E. (2001) Taking stock of naturalistic decision making, *Journal of Behavioral Decision Making*, 14, 331–352.

Meyer, G.J., Bates, M., and Gacono, C. (1999) To Rorschach rating scale: Item adequacy, scale development, and relations with the big five model of personality, *Journal of Personality Assessment*, 73, 199–244.

Mintzberg, H., Raisinghani, D., and Theoret, A. (1976) The structure of 'unstructured' decision process, *Administrative Science Quarterly*, 25, 465–499.

Mintzberg, H., and Waters, J. (1990) Does decision get in the way? *Organizational Studies*, 11 (1), 1–16.

Moody, P.E. (1983) *Decision Making: Proven Methods for Better Decisions*. New York: McGraw-Hill Book Company.

Niedermayer, L.Y., and Chapman, G.B. (2001) Action, inaction, and factors influencing perceived decision making, *Journal of Behavioral Decision Making*, 14, 295–308.

Nutt, P.C. (1998a) Framing strategic decisions, *Organizational Science*, 9 (2), 195–216.

Nutt, P.C. (1998b) How decision makers evaluate alternatives and the influence of complexity, *Management Science*, 44 (8), 1148–1166.

Nutt, P.C. (2001) A taxonomy of strategic decisions and tactics for uncovering alternatives, *European Journal of Operational Research*, 132 (3), 505–527.

Poole, M.S. (1981) Decision development in small groups I: A comparison of two models, *Communication Monographs*, 48, 1–24.

Poole, M.S. (1983a) Decision development in small groups II: A study of multiple sequences in decision making, *Communication Monographs*, 50, 206–232.

Poole, M.S. (1983b) Decision development in small groups, III: A multiple sequence model of group decision development, *Communication Monographs*, 50, 321–341.

Russo, J.E. (2002) *Winning decisions*. New York: Currancy Doubleday.

Salveson, M.E. (1958) An analysis of decisions, *Management Science*, 4 (3), 203–217.

Scheidel, T.M., and Crowell, L. (1964) Idea development in small decision groups, *Quarterly Journal of Speech*, 50, 140–145.

Scherpereel, C.M. (2006) Decision orders: A decision taxonomy, *Management Decision*, 44 (1), 123–136.

Shapira, Z. (ed.) (1997) *Organizational Decision Making*. New York: Cambridge University Press.

Simon, H.A. (1960) *The New Science of Management Decision*. New York: Harper and Row.

Simon, H.A. (1976) *Administrative Behavior*. New York: Free Press, 3rd edition.

Sutcliffe, K.M., and McNamara, G. (2001) Controlling decision-making practice in organizations, *Organization Science*, 12 (4), 484–501.

Trull, S.G. (1966) Some factors involved in determining total decision success, *Management Science*, B270–B280.

Tuckman, B.W. (1965) Developmental sequence in small groups, *Psychological Bulletin*, 63, 384–399.

Verplanken, B., and Svenson, O. (1997) 'Personal Involvement in Human Decision Making: Conceptualizations and Effects on Decision Processes', in R. Ranyard, W.R. Crozier, and O. Svenson (eds) *Decision Making: Cognitive Models and Explanations*. London: Routledge, 40–57.

Vroom, V.H., and Jago, A.G. (1988) *The New Leadership: Managing Participation in Organizations*. Englewood Cliffs, NJ: Prentice Hall.

Vroom, V.H., and Yetton, P.W. (1973) *Leadership and Decision Making*. Pittsburgh PA: University of Pittsburgh Press.

Weinberg, P. (1981) *Das Entscheidungsverhalten der Konsumenten*. Schoningh: Paderboren.

Welch, D.A. (2002) *Decisions, decisions: The art of effective decision making*. Amherst, MA: Prometheus Books.

Williams, M.L., Dennis, A.R., Stam, A., and Aronson, A.J. (2005) The impact of DSS use and information load on errors and decision quality, *European Journal of Operational Research*, 176 (1), 468–481.

Wilson, E.E., and Woodside, A.G. (2001) Executive and consumer decision processes: Increasing useful sensemaking by identifying similarities and departures, *The Journal of Business & Industrial Marketing*, 16 (5), 401–414.

Yates, F.J. (1990) *Judgement and Decision Making*. Englewood Cliffs, NJ: Prentice Hall.

Part VI

Methodology For The Study of Decision Making

20

Empirical Methods for Research on Organizational Decision-Making Processes[1]

Marshall Scott Poole and Andrew H. Van de Ven

Introduction

The study of decision-making processes is premised on the assumption that to understand decision making we must explore how decisions come about, how they develop over time. This requires us to move beyond input (such as leadership structure), surrogates for process (such as conflict management style), and decision outcomes, such as decision quality or member satisfaction with the decision to the actual observation or reconstruction of how the decision comes about.

Research on decision processes requires an approach more like those of the historian and evolutionary biologist than the traditional psychologist or economist. The investigator must follow the decision along its winding and often surprising path through time, reconstructing its significant features and looking for temporal patterns and complex relationships among multiple interdependent variables. Processes are shaped by the continuous well-behaved causality emphasized in psychology and economics, but also by contingencies, complex conjunctions, historical and social context, intermittent causal factors that impinge on the process at only a single point in time, and path dependence.

Processes are best depicted and explained in narratives (Polkinghorne, 1988). Narrative explanation involves fundamentally different assumptions about the relationships among constructs and the nature of explanation than do the causal explanations traditionally favored in empirical psychology, sociology, and economics. Moreover, the methodologies used in most social science – quantitative and qualitative alike – are not well suited to the study of processes. The strategies traditionally

Handbook of Decision Making. Edited by Paul C. Nutt and David C. Wilson
© 2010 John Wiley & Sons, Ltd

trained social scientists use to frame research questions and plan research handicap those trying to think in terms of processes. To a great extent we have to start afresh when devising ways to study processes like decision making.

In this chapter we attempt to delineate some guidelines for the empirical study of decision-making processes. We will first discuss the nature of the process approach to research on decision making, emphasizing key elements of process theory and research. The next section introduces a typology of process theories, basic explanatory schemes for processes, each of which has its own particular characteristics and temporal pattern. These theories are meant to provide a 'vocabulary' for describing and understanding processes. The third section discusses empirical methods for studying and characterizing decision-making processes. This section focuses on how to test for or to recognize the process theories in the appropriate types of data. The fourth and final section outlines four distinct approaches to the study of process. Our goal is to give readers some templates for thinking about decision-making processes and for designing studies of decision processes.

Two characteristics of organizational decision making set the parameters for this chapter. First, decision making is a complex process. In the narrow sense decision making refers to the process of evaluating and choosing among alternatives. For the purposes of this chapter, however, we will take a more comprehensive view and refer to the entire process, from problem identification to implementation planning, as decision making. All of the following activities may fall within the scope of the term *decision making* as it will be used in this chapter: problem formulation, problem analysis, criteria development, solution development, solution evaluation and selection, and implementation planning.

Decision making is also a multilevel process, with smaller decisions typically nested within larger decisions, which may themselves be part of larger group projects (McGrath and Tschan, 2004). 'Every decision involves a series of activities and choices nested in choices of broader scope, rather than a single simple choice' (Poole and Hirokawa, 1996: 9). Moreover, it is often difficult to understand a single decision without considering larger issues and prior decisions and without grappling with relatively fuzzy boundaries of the larger issues (Tracy and Standerfer, 2003).

With these constraints in mind we turn to approaches to the study of decision-making processes.

VARIANCE AND PROCESS RESEARCH APPROACHES

Mohr (1982) originally differentiated variance and process approaches in social scientific research, and Poole, Van de Ven, Dooley, and Holmes (2000) extended his distinction to incorporate multiple developmental models. In general terms, a *variance theory* explains change in terms of relationships among independent variables and dependent variables, while a *process theory* explains how a sequence of events leads to some outcome. Figure 20.1 shows a pictorial comparison of the two approaches, and Table 20.1 provides a comparison in terms of basic assumptions and

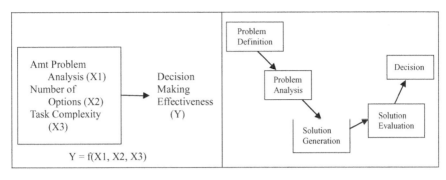

Variance Theory   **Process Theory**

FIGURE 20.1 Variance and process theories.

characteristics, which we will briefly discuss drawing on a more extended discussion in Poole *et al.* (2000) and Poole (2004).

The primary components of a variance theory are (1) variables that capture the important aspects or attributes of the subject under study and (2) relationships among those variables. Explanations in variance theories take the form of causal

TABLE 20.1 Variance and process approaches contrasted

The Variance Approach: Key Assumptions

- Focus on fixed entities with variable attributes (variabilization of phenomena)
- Satisfactory explanations are based on necessary and sufficient causality
- Satisfactory explanation is based on efficient causality
- The generality of an explanation depends on its ability to apply uniformly across a broad range of cases and contexts
- Monotonic, 'well-behaved' causal flow through hierarchical levels

The Process Approach: Key Assumptions

- The world is composed of entities which participate in events and which may change as a result
- Satisfactory explanations are based on necessary causality
- Satisfactory explanations are based on final and/or formal causality combined with efficient causality
- Generality of explanations depends on their *versatility*
- Temporal ordering is critical to the outcome
- Explanations include layers of causation operating at different levels and temporal scales
- Causes are often not 'well-behaved'

statements or models that incorporate these variables (e.g. X causes Y which causes Z), and an implicit goal of variance research is to establish the conditions necessary and sufficient to bring about an outcome. Causation is literally the driving force of variance theories in that causes are assumed to produce the effects in a regular manner, and knowing the values of the causal variables is sufficient to know what effects will occur. Causes are assumed to act in the manner of Aristotle's efficient cause, as the immediate forces which bring something about or change something. Due to its focus on variables, variance research is concerned with developing reliable and valid measures of those variables and is grounded in the general linear model that underlies most common linear statistical methods. A key criterion for assessing variance theories is their generality, which refers to the range of cases, phenomena, or situations the causal explanation applies to.

A variance theory of group decision making might explain decision-making effectiveness in terms of variables such as amount of problem analysis, number of options considered, group cohesion, and task complexity (Gouran and Hirokawa, 1996; Hollingshead *et al.*, 2005). In general the amount of problem analysis and number of options should positively affect decision-making effectiveness. Group cohesion should have a curvilinear effect on decision-making effectiveness: effectiveness should increase as cohesion increases up to a point, but very cohesive groups are less effective, because members are more interested in socializing than working. Task complexity should have a negative relationship with effectiveness and should interact with problem analysis so that more problem analysis for complex problems will enhance effectiveness (Hirokawa, 1990). To test the theory, an experiment or survey might be conducted and these variables could be entered severally into a regression equation predicting effectiveness.

In this theory, the variables are assumed to capture the aspects of decision-making activity that are relevant to explaining effectiveness, and hence variables abstracted from the phenomenon are the central focus. Note also that two of the variables, amount of problem analysis and number of options, are surrogate measures of group process that summarize the nature of the interaction in synoptic constructs. The third variable, group cohesiveness, is an outcome of group processes that subsequently influences decision making. These variables are treated as though they are immediate, efficient causes of effectiveness in this theory; just as a blow with a hammer drives in a nail, so increases in number of options enhances decision-making effectiveness.

Philosophers have debated the meanings of cause, effect, and causation for centuries (see a review in Shadish *et al.*, 2002: 3–7). Briefly, the debate contrasts essentialist versus probabilistic meanings of causation. *Essentialists* focus on the *causes of effects* by arguing that causation requires showing that the independent variables are necessary and sufficient conditions for the effect to occur in the dependent variable (i.e. X is a full cause of Y). In contrast, *probabilists* focus on the *effect of causes* by taking a manipulative account of causation where X causes Y when the experimenter manipulates X, and observes outcomes in Y. (Here there is no presumption that X is the full cause of Y.)

In organization studies an essentialist account of causation is illustrated in Mohr's (1982) discussion of necessary and sufficient conditions in causal relationships. He stated that 'in a variance theory *the precursor (X) is a necessary and sufficient condition for the outcome (Y)*' (Mohr, 1982: 38; italics in the original). He argued that if X only serves as a sufficient condition then the causal theory is unsatisfactory, for a change in Y might occur without a change in X (since X is not necessary). What makes Y occur when X does not? We might theorize that X is a cause of Y and may have found important cases where X sometimes causes Y, but this falls somewhat short of providing a necessary and sufficient explanation for Y.

Most social scientists adopt a probabilistic or manipulative view of causation, and reject an essentialist view of causation (Cook and Campbell, 1979: 15). This is so for several reasons. First, most social phenomena cannot be isolated in closed systems as is necessary to evaluate essentialist views of causality (Bhaskar, 1975). Second, given the reflexive nature of human behavior, outside variables typically impinge on a dependent variable, and effects are inevitably influenced by factors or events other than those hypothesized. Hence, observed causal relationships between independent and dependent variables will be probabilistic. Probabilistic relationships are viewed as weak to essentialists who seek explicit functional laws that express inevitable relationships among a set of observables, and in this sense provide a complete causal understanding of a particular event (Cook and Campbell, 1979: 15). However, such an essentialist view of causation is an unrealistic and misleading aspiration. All social science can do is *probe but not prove a causal hypothesis* (Campbell and Stanley, 1963).

Charles Sanders Peirce and David Hume (among others) argued that causality is not a property of the world; instead it serves as a way for humans to make sense of the world. It is something inferred from an observed association between events. Variance researchers typically regard causal relationships as the heart of scientific explanation.

Even if such relationships cannot be 'proven' empirically (just as no generalization can be proven by scientific evidence), [variance] researchers have found it useful to think causally (Blalock, 1969: 6) and have found working with causal hypotheses to be a very productive way of doing science. (Cook and Campbell, 1979).

A process theory, in contrast, conceptualizes the decision-making process as a series of events that bring about or lead to some outcome. The unit of analysis is not the variable, but an evolving central subject which makes events happen and to which events occur (Abbott, 1988), and the unit of observation is the event. Explanations in process theories take the form of theoretical narratives that account for how one event led to another and that one to another, and so on to the final outcome. These theoretical narratives tend to be more complex than the causal chains advanced in variance explanations due to the complexity of events, the need to account for temporal connections among events, different time scales in the same process, and the dynamic nature of processes. It is difficult to separate independent from dependent variables in processes, because events are interrelated in a complex fashion.

Process explanations may include (1) an account of how one event leads to and influences subsequent events (e.g. events of type A have a .7 probability of being succeeded by events of type B and a .3 probability of being succeeded by events of type C); (2) an explication of an overall pattern that generates the series (e.g. the process develops in three stages, A, B, and C); (3) an explication of the generative mechanism that drives the process (e.g. emergence of norms in interaction is a function of evolutionary processes whereby random variations in current norms are tested and selected in group interaction and preserved through repetition); or (4) preferably, two or more of the above (in which case the connections among them should be articulated).

Process theories may incorporate several different types of explanatory factors, including critical events and turning points, contextual influence at various points in the process, formative patterns that give overall direction to the change, and causal factors that influence the sequencing of events. Process explanations may incorporate as many as three of Aristotle's four causes, adding formal and final causation to the efficient causation that is the basis of causal explanation in variance research (Poole *et al.*, 2000). Efficient causation exerts itself through the factors that operate immediately within events and also sometimes through 'pushes' that move the central subject from one event to the next. The essence of a process theory, however, is accounting for change over time, and this is primarily done through articulating larger patterns in the events that account for or bring about change. Such accounts cannot be framed in terms of efficient causality, which operates only in the immediate moment.

While efficient causality plays a role in process explanations, its role is secondary to the explanations of temporal patterns provided by final and formal causes. Final causality posits an end or goal that guides the unfolding of development and change. We most often think of goals in terms of human agency, but final causality also includes natural ends and outcomes of natural processes. In its broadest sense, final causality is any end-state that attracts a developmental or change process to itself. As such, the final cause draws the central subject along the path it follows to its end, within the constraints of particular events and conjunctures that occur along the way. Some of these events and conjunctures function to advance the final cause; while others are 'accidents' in that they either do not serve or detract from attainment of the final cause. For example, the decision can serve as a final cause of the decision-making process. Since decisions typically are actions that respond to problems or exigencies, the nature of the end shapes what happens in the discussion, encouraging the group to analyze the problem and consider options that address it.

Formal causation is grounded in a template that patterns change. The form must be applied to the developing entity somehow, either through plan or through some other governing mechanism. In the group arena, for example, one important type of form is a procedural agenda, such as a list of requirements that a quality team must fulfill in carrying out its projects. In the case of decision making, one or more organizational members are likely to have learned the decision-making procedure that mandates analysis of problems before solutions, carefully evaluating whether solutions actually solve problems, etc. Members use the procedure to steer the discussion so that it follows the sequence. Both final and formal causes provide patterns that shape the unfolding of the process over time. In Mohr's (1982: 59) terminology, process theories incorporate a '*pull-type causality*: X [the precursor] does not imply Y [the outcome], but rather Y implies X'. The purpose or form that is to be realized is what drives the process.

A process theory of group decision making might posit that groups make a decision by working through several phases: orientation, problem definition, problem analysis, solution generation, solution analysis, choice, and implementation planning. The degree to which the group carried out the activities in each phase completely and effectively would determine the ultimate effectiveness of the decision. The sequence of phases is defined in terms of a logic of decision making that follows John Dewey's discussion of reflective thinking as a description of how effective decision making proceeds from doubt to certainty, and thus embodies formal causality driven by the form of a good decision process. To the extent that the group does not adequately and fully carry out each phase, the group is likely to run into problems and either need to double back to 'redo' previous phases or simply finish out the sequence with an inferior decision.

In this process theory of decision making the decision is represented as a sequence of micro-level events – actions – that are organized into macro-level events – phases – which are the means of getting from the beginning of the discussion to the decision. The decision is explained in terms of the theoretical narrative of the progression through a sequence of phases that is necessary to make a good decision, and effectiveness is explained in terms of adherence to this sequence. In this model variables are not the primary focus; instead events, in this case actions and phases, are primary. To test the adequacy of the theory, the investigator must (1) determine the degree of correspondence between the actual temporal pattern of events, and that expected based on the theory and (2) also test for additional indicators that the generative mechanism is in operation (Poole *et al.*, 2000: 84–86 and 98–99). One such additional indicator might be evidence that group members are actively trying to manage their discussion so that it follows the steps of reflective thinking.

Several other aspects of process research are noteworthy in the example. First, temporal ordering is critical to process explanations. A group which follows the normative sequence closely is fundamentally different from a group that goes to consider solutions first, without defining or characterizing its problem. From this it follows that the significance and impact of later events is critically dependent on the specific events that precede them (i.e. the process is path dependent). Third, process theories can provide necessary though not sufficient explanations. Each event in a sequence of events is a necessary condition for those that follow, but no single event is sufficient to bring about a particular sequence of subsequent events. The complex influences in operation in processes guarantee that until the final event in the sequence has occurred, there is no sufficiency. Fourth, explanations in process research are always after the fact in the sense that until the process is complete, there is no way to determine if a given pattern applies. These characteristics make process explanations fundamentally different from variance explanations. Finally, efficient causes operate at several levels in this explanation as well. They may operate at the micro-level to influence moves from act to act (e.g. a directive leader may move the group to a new stage in the process) or external events such as a rejection of the group's decision by an upper-level manager may cause a reorientation of the decision process at a single point in time.

Process research employs eclectic designs that identify or reconstruct the process through direct observation, archival analysis, or multiple case studies. Analysis of process data requires methods (1) that can identify and test temporal linkages between events and also overall temporal patterns (Poole *et al.*, 2000) and (2) that can cope with the multiple time scales that often occur in processes (where some events extend for years, other events embedded in them run for shorter periods, and others embedded within these even shorter periods) (Langley, 1999). Process studies often derive theory from observation, but in some cases they test hypothesized models of the change process, and in others they use retroduction whereby theories are used to guide observation that further specifies the theories (Poole *et al.*, 2000: 115–117). As a result both quantitative and qualitative approaches may be used in process research (Langley, 1999).

Types of Processes

Having discussed the general contours of the process approach to the study of decision making, we now turn to the question of what types of process explanations there are. As the next section shows, the basic template for explaining processes is to identify generative mechanisms that produce patterns over time. These generative mechanisms give a general pattern to the process, and supplemented by critical events, external shocks, and historical and social context, allow a full account of the process to be written.

Figure 20.2 illustrates the four ideal type theories of processes that were defined by Van de Ven and Poole (1995) and extended in Poole and Van de Ven (2000). As Figure 20.2 shows, each theory views the process of development as unfolding in a fundamentally different progression of change events, and to be governed by a different generating mechanism or motor. Variations of each of the basic theories will also be discussed.

Life cycle theory

A *life cycle* theory depicts the decision process in terms of a necessary sequence of stages or phases. The specific content of these stages or phases is prescribed and regulated by an institutional, natural, or logical program prefigured at the beginning of the cycle. Life cycle theories assume that all decisions progress through the same unitary sequence of stages or phases.

The form or pattern in a *life cycle* motor is either immanent in the developing entity or imposed on it by external institutions. Examples of life cycle theories include Bales's (Bales and Strodtbeck, 1951) model of group problem solving and March and Simon's (1993) theory of organizational decision making. The goal and end point of the change process is defined from the start for a life cycle through a natural or logical developmental progression or through institutionally prescribed rules or regulations. In Bales and Strodtbeck's and March and Simon's models, the stages of problem solving are logically required. However, a life cycle may also be imposed

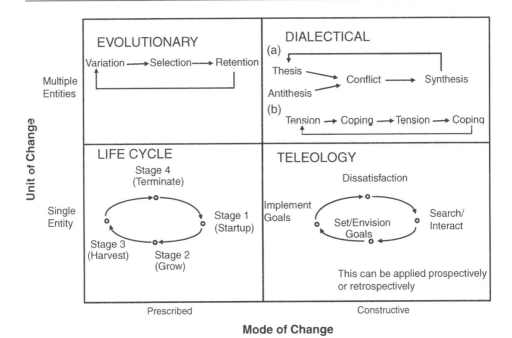

FIGURE 20.2 Typology of Process Theories

by an external institution, as when government regulations require a set sequence of stages in the approval of a new drug or medical procedure.

Transitions from stage to stage involve a qualitative change in the decision process. Moving from problem analysis to solution generation, for instance, involves a qualitative shift in the content of the decision and in how the decision-making unit is operating. As the name implies, time for a life cycle theory is cyclic: life cycle models are comprised of repeating milestones that take the unit from inception to demise or fulfillment. Once the end the cycle has been attained, the process is set to commence anew, with either the same or a different entity.

Teleological theory

A *teleological* process views decision making as a cycle of goal formulation, implementation, evaluation, and modification of actions or goals based on what was learned or intended by the entity. This sequence emerges through the purposeful enactment or social construction of an envisioned end state among decision makers.

Examples of teleological theories of decision making include most models of strategic planning and decision making (Chakravarthy and Lorange, 1991; Mintzberg, Raisinghani, and Theoret, 1976; Nutt, 1984; Shrivastava and Grant, 1985). In a teleological theory setting a goal in response to a perceived problem or opportunity puts the process in motion. The unit is assumed to be purposeful and adaptive; by itself or in interaction with others, it constructs an envisioned end state, takes action to reach it, and monitors its progress. Thus, teleological theories view development as a repetitive sequence of goal formulation, implementation, evaluation, and modification of goals based on what was learned or intended by the unit.

Teleological processes are goal driven, and hence the developmental path followed by the decision-making unit is not predetermined, but is generated by activities necessary to get to a decision. Since there are many ways to get to a decision, multiple paths are possible and there is no present sequence of stages or steps. While a number of teleological theories define steps or stages, there are multiple paths through these steps and the path is determined by exigencies that arise during the process as problems to be solved by the developing unit.

For example, Mintzberg et al.'s (1976) model of strategic decision making posits that management must recognize problems or opportunities, develop a diagnosis of the situation, come up with solution, satisfy stakeholders, and gain authorization for the decision. Ten distinct activities contribute to producing the five prerequisites, and decision makers can engage in many different sequences and combinations of these activities, depending on internal and external exigencies. There is no particular order in which the prerequisites must be addressed. In one instance a diagnosis will guide solution generation and choice, while in another a solution option may prove so persuasive that the decision makers redefine the problem and diagnosis to fit it. The process is oriented toward achieving the prerequisites of a good decision 'by hook or by crook' and without a necessary sequence of activities.

In the family of teleological models, processes based on intentional planning and on post hoc rationalization can be distinguished. A number of decision models assume that it is *intentional* and driven by rationality (if only bounded rationality). However, as March (1994) observed, sometimes reason operates after the fact. In such cases, agents rearrange the process as they make sense of what is happening (Weick, 1995). As the process unfolds, their understanding of it changes and they act according to their emerging sense of the situation and their actions form the basis for future interpretations that in turn re-establishes the grounds for action. In the case of such *sensemaking* processes, the 'decision' emerges post hoc, refashioned according to formal patterns or intentions. For example, Scottish knitwear manufacturers who employed labor intensive handwork rather than highly capitalized factories gradually articulated a strategy that focused on 'selling premium quality expensive garments through specialist distribution channels to a limited number of high income consumers' (Porac, Thomas, and Baden-Fuller, 1989: 409). The strategy was not consciously planned, but emerged as they struggled to find a market niche in the face of fierce competition. However, it has the hallmarks of intention and purpose once it emerges and shapes subsequent activity as though it were carefully set out from the beginning.

Dialectical theory

In *dialectical* theories of decision making, conflicts emerge between people or positions that represent an opposing thesis and antithesis. These collide to produce a synthesis, which in time becomes the thesis for the next cycle of a dialectical progression. The decision process driven by a dialectical motor is shaped by decision makers' efforts to deal with contradictions, conflicts, or tensions. An exemplary dialectical theory of decision making is Churchman's (1971) dialectical inquiry, as articulated by Mason and Mitroff and Mason (1981) and De Wit and Meyer's (2004) dialectical theory of strategy formation.

In dialectical theories, unlike life cycle and teleological theories, the goal or endpoint of the decision process is not clear at the beginning, but emerges from the dialectical process. In some cases decision making is driven by the conflict or contradiction itself. For example, in Churchman's dialectical inquiry, a situation is diagnosed and a decision emerges through confrontation of conflicting positions and debate between them. In other cases, the decision is shaped by attempts to resolve the conflict or tension and mitigate its negative effects. Smith and Berg (1987) posit that groups sometime deal with the tension between individual identity and the desire to be part of a collective by emphasizing one pole over the other. One group might overemphasize loyalty and conformity during its decision process, while another might put up with less cohesiveness and focus on letting members express their individualism. How the group deals with the tension gives the decision process a distinctive character.

The developmental path of dialectically driven decisions is not predetermined. Units react to and cope with conflicts, contradictions, and tensions in many different ways, and the resulting path will vary greatly from case to case. While basic moments of the dialectical process can be distinguished at a conceptual level – for example, thesis, antithesis, synthesis – often they are intertwined and overlapping. A group confronting the individualism-collectivism tension may immediately converge on a coping strategy (e.g. emphasize one pole over the other) or it may shuttle from one strategy to another in an attempt to deal with the inevitable negative consequences of any specific coping mechanism. The resulting decision paths will differ considerably for the two groups and there is literally no way to project ahead of time the shape or form of the developmental path.

Two variants of dialectical theories can be distinguished: (1) a Hegelian process of thesis, antithesis, and synthesis, and (2) a Bakhtinian process of tension-based dialectics. Hegelian dialectics operate through the emergence of an antithesis in response to a thesis and the resolution of the ensuing conflict in a synthesis. While a new cycle may begin within the achieved synthesis, the synthesis represents a temporary resolution of the conflict or contradiction. For example, the conflict between the interests of workers and those of management in a corporation facing a major strategic reorientation such as the US automakers faced at the beginning of 2009 could be expressed as follows: the worker's position emerges as an antithesis to the typical managerially controlled firm (thesis) and one common resolution would be for the workers to decide to buy out management, hence becoming their own management (synthesis). The synthesis is comprised of elements from both thesis and antithesis and represents a stable point in the change process (at least temporarily). Organizations may attempt to short circuit Hegelian dialectics, because they believe the attendant conflict will be divisive and destructive. This resistance may be effective in preventing the resolution of the dialectic, in which case the decision will be dominated by the parties in control of the organization. However, the conflict will likely continue to simmer and influence the dialectical process during the next decision cycle.

A second type of dialectical process is the tension-based dialectic (Bakhtin, 1981; Werner and Baxter, 1994), which proposes that rather than developing through a thesis-antithesis-synthesis pattern, the dialectic plays itself out in a never-ending series of tensions between dualisms such as integration-differentiation. Each side of the dualism requires the other to exist, and there is a constant interplay between the two. Rather than being resolvable, the tension is always operating and the decision is shaped by how the decision-makers deal with the dialectic. Denying one pole and emphasizing the other will lead change in one direction, while trying to acknowledge both poles and alternate between them over time will lead change in a different direction. Thus, in contrast to the Hegelian dialectic, in the *tension dialectic* oppositions, conflicts, and contradictions are never resolved. Opposing terms mutually imply each other, exist through their opposition, and always remain at work as potential sources of influence on the decision process.

In tension-based dialectical models, the decision is shaped by how the unit deals with the dialectic and the problems, challenges, and conflicts it spawns. Baxter and Montgomery (Werner and Baxter, 1994) define seven possible responses to tensions and contradictions, including: (a) denial – ignoring the tension; (b) spiraling inversion – attending to one side of the tension, then to the other, then to the first again, and so on; (c) segmentation – using different parts or aspects of the unit to relate to the two poles of the tension; (d) balance, which attempts to engage both poles, but reduce the pressure from each; (e) integration – which actively engages with both poles; (f) recalibration – reframing the situation so that the poles are no longer in opposition; and (g) reaffirmation – acknowledging both poles and actively incorporating both into the unit.

Evolutionary theory

An *evolutionary* model of decision making assumes that the ideas and premises in the decision emerge from repetitive sequences of variation, selection, and retention events. Multiple ideas exist in competitive or cooperative relationships and vie for attention and acceptance by the group. The evolutionary motor drives change through the core process of variation-selection-retention (VSR). In this familiar explanation, variations in existing ideas occur, and those that are able to withstand scrutiny and to win approval are selected for survival.

Evolutionary theory assumes that multiple variations occur and that many are fortuitous, even though the decision makers are trying to generate ideas. These variations may be entirely new ideas, but it is also possible that new ideas are the hybrid products of diverse ancestral ideas. New generations of ideas and decision premises are often (but not always) produced by events that couple or recombine pre-existing ideas or premises. The actions undertaken to create variation and to sustain it and to correct problems during competitive selection and retention cannot be projected ahead of time, because of shifting competitive pressures for scarce resources in the environment. Hence, the decision path for an evolutionary motor is weakly predetermined: one or more cycles of variation-selection-retention will occur, but how many cycles and the specific activity paths through these cycles are not determinate.

We have not been able to find an evolutionary theory of organizational decision making per se, but Campbell's (1974) socio-cultural evolutionary perspective advances an evolutionary theory of idea development that could be applied in the study of decisions, which are, after all, constituted by ideas. Campbell proposed that ideas, including symbols, texts, and the relationships among them, developed through variation-selection-retention processes. This evolutionary epistemology envisioned a social ecology of ideas that accounted for the growth of knowledge through competitive and cooperative processes. If we think in terms of decision making as the appropriation, development, and validation of ideas to guide action, then the organization becomes a social ecology of decision premises that compete for attention and adherence until they are compiled into a final decision and plan of action. This final decision and action plan then serves as a source of ideas and premises for future decisions, where it may be 'crossbred' with other ideas or premises into a novel configuration that enters into the ideational ecosystem.

Multiple motor processes

Theories of decision making are not always built around just one motor. Van de Ven and Poole (1995) argued that many theories of change exhibit combinations of two or more motors. If we consider that one, two, three, or four motors might operate in a given theory, it is evident that 15 explanations of organizational decision making are logically possible: four single-motor explanations, six dual-motor explanations, four tri-motor explanations, and one four-motor explanation.

For example, Shrivastava and Grant (1985) found that a life cycle model of two major stages – problem familiarization and solution development (with several sub stages for solution development) – characterized the overall form of strategic decision processes in the purchase of computer systems by Indian firms. However, within this general model they found four variants based on differences in the specific nature of problem familiarization and solution development activity, the types of analyses of the systems conducted prior to purchase, the role of organizational learning systems, and the way the decision makers interacted with the organizational environment: (1) the Managerial Autocracy Model; (2) the Systemic Bureaucracy Model; (3) the Adaptive Planning Model; and (4) the Political Expediency Model. The differences in how the two basic stages are enacted suggest that a teleological motor informed by the culture and standard operating procedures of each organization is generating the specific patterns of behavior that constitute the decision. Hence, Shrivastava and Grant's strategic decision processes combine a life cycle model that sets the macro-level form of the process with a teleological model that generates micro-level activities that constitute the larger stages, resulting in four distinctive sequences of activities.

If more than a single motor is found to characterize a decision process, it is important to spell out how the motors relate to each other. As in the previous example, they may operate simultaneously and on different levels. Poole and Van de Ven (2000) lay out several different dimensions of inter-motor relationships:

1. *Nature of interlevel relationships*: Motors may be nested in a *hierarchy*, such that they are interdependent, and the process in a unit at a given level is dependent on changes in units at higher and lower levels within this nested hierarchy. In other cases different levels are *entangled*, they operate somewhat independently, but still influence each other. In this case lower and higher-order motors influence each other, but are not tightly linked into a single, coherent process. In contrast to nested motors, which have tight coupling, entangled motors are moderately or loosely coupled. *Aggregated* motors, the third type, represent the case where a process on a higher level emerges from or is constituted by an aggregation of lower level processes. In this case, a higher level process is constituted by a collective of interdependent lower level processes.

2. *Type of relationship*: Motors can be related both directly and indirectly. *Direct* relationships are well-known and include *reinforcing* (positive), *dampening* (negative), and *complex* (nonlinear). There are two types of *indirect relationships*. *Entrainment* occurs when motors at the same or different levels operate independently but come into coordination due to an external pacing factor. In one common example, teleological motors of individual group members become entrained in terms of their pace of work and orientation to time by deliberating together at a characteristic pace. In this case, the decision task is the external pacing factor; other common pacing factors for individuals are diurnal cycles and pheromones, while for organizations, the calendar and government mandates are examples of pacing factors. A *cyclical* relationship among motors occurs when two or more motors alternate in their impact on the change process. This alternation is choreographed by a factor or process that determines the relative weight given to the motors as a function of time. For example, in the sociological theory of morphogenesis (Buckley, 1967) action and structure alternately dominate social processes in a cycle whereby active processes undermine current social structures and then commence to build up new ones, but at a certain point the new structures become constraints on action and a period of structural inertia ensues until new actions can undermine structures and start the cycle anew. In this case, the cycle between the predominance of action and structure respectively is governed by an evolutionary process that determines the rate at which possible changes are introduced and accepted by the system (a VSR motor).

3. *Temporal relationships*: First, decision processes may vary in terms of their *temporal velocity*, how quickly they progress. Decisions governed by a life cycle, for example, can be completed in two months or two years. The first case clearly speeds the development process much more than the second. Decision processes may also vary in terms of *duration*, how long a process takes, controlling for velocity. Two life cycles with the same velocity of moving through their phases differ in duration if one is composed of three phases and the other of eight. Third, decision processes may vary in terms of their *acceleration*, and

the degree to which their velocity changes. Some processes may accelerate as they progress, while others maintain a constant pace. Finally, processes may differ in their *temporal orientation*, the degree to which past, present, and/or future influence the process. Some decisions are greatly influenced by past debacles or successes, while others exhibit primary emphasis on the present, and still others are forward looking, as when an organization is trying to decide what it wants to be five years down the road. When motors with different temporal properties interact, the intersection of these properties should be taken into account in specifying relationships among them. However, these relationships are often complex, and we can conceive of no reliable rules for inducing them *a priori*. For instance, it is often the case that higher level processes have longer duration and slower velocity than lower level processes.

Working out any specific explanation of decision making in terms of composite theories means working out the relationships among motors across levels and time scales. And it is not just at the level of theory that relationships should be specified. Empirical research, too, should be aimed at identifying relationships among models and at testing hypothesized relationships. We now turn to consider the doing of process research on decision making.

CONDUCTING PROCESS RESEARCH: THE BASICS

In order to conduct process research it is necessary: (1) to identify events; (2) to develop a representation of the event sequence; (3) to characterize event sequences and their properties; (4) to test for temporal dependencies in event sequences; (5) to test for the presence of one or more of the developmental models discussed in the previous section; and (6) to write an account of the process. Achieving these tasks is in part a function of how researchers gather and record their data and in part a function of analytical methods. After considering some preliminary choices in research design, we will briefly discuss each of these in turn. For more detail on methodology for process research, we would refer the reader to Van de Ven and Poole (1990), Van de Ven and Poole (2002), and Poole *et al.* (2000).

Design choices

There is no single best design for a process study. In determining the nature of the sample to be drawn, researchers must consider the balance among four factors: sample size, sample diversity, intensity of data gathering, and cost. The cost of a study in terms of time and effort increases as sample size, sample diversity, and intensity increase. To keep costs in check, compromises must be made on one or two of the three factors.

Consider sample size. Generally the larger and more representative the sample, the more valid the study and the more generalizable the results. More extensive samples also allow comparative analysis and derivation of more valid typologies. However, large samples create problems of analysis and interpretation (Miller and

Freisen, 1982). These problems stem from the time required to gather data from a large sample and from the volume of data researchers must handle. When the data are event descriptions, as process research requires, rather than quantitative responses, the cost of data gathering increases still further. Holding cost constant, there is an inherent tradeoff between the intensity of data gathering – the richness and amount of data that can be acquired for each case – and sample size.

Next consider sample diversity. Should the researcher try to attain a homogeneous uniform sample or a broad, heterogeneous sample? For example, if a researcher sets out to study the process of decision making during innovation, should the sample be composed of units that are all pursuing the same type of innovation, such as a biomedical device, or of a wide variety of units pursuing different kinds of technical and administrative innovations in different industries and sectors?

A homogeneous sample has the advantage of minimizing the multitude of alternative explanations for developmental processes. This is especially advantageous in the case of lengthy sequences of events, because they are particularly vulnerable to accidental or adventitious occurrences that shift the course of development. Comparing cases that are similar in as many respects as possible facilitates identifying whether change processes are due to such transient events or to more basic developmental models. A homogeneous sample also facilitates the development and investigation of very precise, focused questions or hypotheses. Hence homogeneous sampling is useful when a well-specified theory of change or development is available. On the other hand, a case can also be made for a broad, heterogeneous sample, because it provides a better opportunity to detect whether sources of change are due to temporal development, cohort, or transient factors.

The comparative method is perhaps the most general and basic strategy for generating and evaluating valid scientific knowledge. Kaplan (1964: 52) argued that scientific knowledge is greatly enhanced when we divide the subject matter into concepts and cases that 'carve at the joints' over the widest possible ranges, types, conditions, and consequences. In this way researchers can develop and evaluate the limits of many important propositions about the subject matter.

Intensity of data gathering is another consideration. As we will see, it is important for process researchers to gather extensive, rich data. However, doing so increases costs and reduces the number of cases that can be handled adequately. If a large number of cases are desired, then it is likely at the expense of the amount of data that can be acquired for each case.

In longitudinal research, another indicator of intensity of data gathering is the number of temporal intervals or events on which data are obtained from beginning to end on each case. The number of temporal intervals or events observed depends on what constitutes the 'natural' flow of experience in the decisions being studied. Organizational decision processes vary in temporal duration and granularity. In terms of temporal duration, some organizational decisions processes, such as group decision making, may occur in committee meetings lasting no more than a few hours. Other decision processes, such as the decision to undertake development of technological and administrative innovations, may span several years. Granularity refers to the preciseness or discreteness of events that are recorded throughout the temporal duration of a case being studied.

The granularity of events may vary greatly, ranging from events of such large scope that only five to 20 might be observed to exhaust the period of study to events of such small scope that several thousand occur during the period under study. Event granularity typically increases with the micro-analytic detail of the change process being investigated. Studies of discourse associated with decision making tend to sample fine-grained events, such as speech acts and arguments, but it is also possible to focus on more coarse-grained events, such as entire meetings that occur during the course of a decision process.

Another consideration is the cost of coding events. Events that require a great amount of time and effort to observe and code are likely to be observed in shorter sequences than less costly ones. For example, it might require a great deal of time and effort to compile the complete record of all the arguments in a decision; however, to get a shorter record of some transactions by coding which decision makers attended the same meetings would be less costly. Due to the inherent tradeoffs between the temporal duration and granularity of events that can be sampled, studies of relatively brief decision processes can afford to utilize categories that code fine-grained events, while studies of lengthy decision processes are more likely to adopt categories that tap course-grained events.

In view of the tradeoffs between homogeneous and heterogeneous samples, Pettigrew (1990: 275–277) suggests four useful guidelines for selecting cases to study:

1. 'Go for extreme situations, critical incidents and social dramas.' By choosing cases that are unusual, critically important, or highly visible, researchers select cases in which the process is 'transparently observable'.
2. 'Go for polar types.' Choose cases that seem very different in terms of the processes under study. For example, researchers might compare successful and unsuccessful decision processes.
3. 'Go for high experience levels of the phenomena under study.' Choose cases that have a long track record of experience with a process.
4. 'Go for more informed choice of sites and increase the probabilities of negotiating access.' Selecting a case for one's sample is fruitless if one cannot obtain cooperation.

While process studies, with their rich data requirements, are costly, Paul Nutt's (1984; 2002) strategy of persistent data collection and gradual expansion of sample size seems to be one way of handling resource requirements. Nutt has developed a standard data collection format that he has employed over a period of 20 years to gather narratives of strategic decisions. The result is a large database of decisions. While resource limitations may reduce the number of cases we can acquire at first, if we continue our pursuit, our confidence in our results can increase over the years.

Event identification

To study decision-making processes we must be able to 'follow the action', that is, the sequence of actions or events that lead to the decision from the beginning to end. From the stream of activities, incidents, and occurrences that are observable during the decision, the investigator must identify what is significant and what patterns characterize the unfolding process. The starting point for this may be found in Abbott's (1984) distinction between an *incident* (a raw datum) and an *event* (a theoretical construct). Whereas an incident is an empirical observation, an event is not directly observed; it is a construct in a model that makes sense of or captures the import of incidents. For each event one can choose any number of incidents as indicators that that event has occurred.

This definition implies a particular kind of relationship between incidents and events. Incidents are descriptions of happenings, documentary records of occurrences. Events are meaningful parsings of the stream of incidents. They are constructions based on more or less systematic interpretation by the researcher of what is relevant to the process. The stream of incidents, a first-order construction, is translated into a sequence of events, a second-order construction. For example, Nutt (1984) might determine that a certain portion of interview data from an executive's account of a strategic decision (first order) represents an instance of concept development (second order), while another constitutes detailing. Of course, the same incidents may be interpreted in different ways, utilized as constituents of different events. The same interviews might be used to derive the arguments that constituted the decision over time in a study of the ebb and flow of influence during decision making.

Derivation of events requires that researchers have a clear definition of the central subject of the narrative (i.e. who or what the events are relevant to) and a sense of what is relevant to the decision-making process under study. Event identification often occurs through iterative analysis, moving from raw data to a set of incidents (meaningful occurrences) which serve as indicators for events, and then back again in circular fashion. In some cases systematic coding rules can be developed to make the process transparent to other researchers; systematic procedures also enable an assessment of reliability and validity of classifications. However, an investigator writing a history of a process, for example, Allison's (1970) classic in-depth analysis of decision making during the Cuban Missile Crisis, would not want to code events, instead opting to preserve their richness and multifaceted nature.

The nature of the data from which the incidents are drawn influences the derivation of events. Sources of data include direct observation of the decision process, video and audio recordings, interviews, archives, media reports, and quantitative data (if such data are gathered regularly over a long period of time – consumer confidence indices, for instance). Each data source has its own affordances and limitations for the investigator. In addition, sources vary in detail and completeness (see Poole *et al.*, 2000 for a discussion of the strengths and problems of direct observation, recordings, and archival data for process research). The corpus of data places an upper bound on the richness and complexity of events that can be derived.

The form that descriptions of events take varies considerably. Some events are described in layered, qualitative, rich terms in terms of multiple features, such as those in the Minnesota Innovation Research Project and those recorded in ethnographic studies. Other events are sparser, such as the coding of arguments into various types, yielding a sequence of arguments. Still others are very sparse, consisting only of numerical values or binary codes. And, as we mentioned previously, there is no single event that corresponds 'best' to a pattern of incidents. As historian John

Lewis Gaddis (2004) notes, which events are identified depends on the investigator's purposes. An investigation of how arguments constitute strategic decisions will draw an entirely different set of events out of the same incident stream than would an investigation of the phases of strategic decision making.

In some cases events are layered. Events in the same process may have different duration and differ in the range of actors and contexts they span. In such cases, higher-order (more macro) events can be identified from lower-order (more micro) events. For instance, an investigation of the role of argument in strategic decision processes may identify particular argument types at the micro-level and then divide the stream of arguments into more macro-level periods or phases where particular types of argument prevailed.

Representing event sequences

The representation of event sequences is an important step in process analysis. Processes extend over time and space and comprehending them requires the investigator to derive a temporal and often spatial representation of the process, a 'landscape' of its history as Gaddis (2004) puts it. Process research is all about finding temporal patterns, and the form of the representation contributes significantly to pattern recognition. Mode of representation is thus much more important for process research than it is for variance research, which finds patterns in statistical relationships among variables and hence leans heavily on numerical datasets. Several forms of representation of event sequences can be distinguished.

The most common is a *chronicle* that depicts the story line of the decision process. This takes the form of first this happened, and then this happened, and then … etc. As noted in the previous section, chronicles themselves cannot capture every detail of a decision process. They represent a selection of significant events by the investigator. As Pentland observes, narrative theory suggests that an adequate story must contain more than just a simple description of events. It must have (Pentland 1999: 712–713):

1. *Sequence in time*. Narrative should include a clear beginning, middle, and end. … Chronology is a central organizing device. The events or actions referred to in a narrative are understood to happen in a sequence …
2. *Focal actor or actors*. Narratives are always about someone or something … There is a protagonist and, frequently, an antagonist as well. The characters may not be developed or even identified by name, but, along with sequence, they provide a thread that ties the events in a narrative together …
3. *Identifiable narrative voice*. A narrative is something that someone tells (Bal, 1985), so there should always be an identifiable voice doing the narrating. That voice reflects a specific point of view (Rimmon-Kenan, 1983) …
4. *'Canonical' or evaluative frame of reference*. Narratives carry meaning and cultural value because they encode, implicitly or explicitly, standards against which actions of the characters can be judged. … But even without any explicit moral, narratives embody a sense of what is right and wrong, appropriate or inappropriate, and so on …

5. *Other indicators of content or context.* Narrative texts typically contain more than just the bare events. In particular, they contain a variety of textual devices that are used to indicate time, place, attributes of the characters, attributes of the context, and so on. These indicators do not advance the plot, but they provide information that may be essential to the interpretation of the events (e.g. knowing that the scene is a wedding changes the significance of the utterance 'I do').

In the case of complex or lengthy narratives, it is possible to simplify them for purposes of analysis by preparing summaries or digests of the narrative. The narrative can also be transformed into standardized narrative formats, such as Greimas's (1983) narratology, which is one way to distill several of the features listed by Pentland into story lines that are easily comparable across narratives. Both digests and standard narrative formats facilitate comparison of multiple narratives.

Another useful representation is a *visual map* of the process. Langley (1999) comments on the advantages of visual maps in process research:

> They allow the presentation of large quantities of information in relatively little space, and they can be useful tools for the development and verification of theoretical ideas. Visual graphical representations are particularly attractive for the analysis of process data because they allow the simultaneous representation of a large number of dimensions and they can be easily used to show precedence, parallels, and the passage of time. (p. 700)

A range of visual representations are available (Miles and Huberman, 1994), and some of the maps used to study group decision making are shown in Figure 20.3.

Poole and Roth (1989a) mapped group decision processes on a timeline that recorded the order and relative length of the phases of the decision process along a single dimension. They 'stacked' timelines for group decision phases, phases of conflict management, topical phases. Nutt (1984) defined six basic phases of decision making: signals, intentions, concept development, detailing, evaluation, and installation. He arrayed his decision-making phases in two dimensions and plotted the transitions between phases over the course of a decision on the diagram. This map showed the order in which the decision process engaged in the phases and how often it recycled among them. In both these cases events were transformed by recoding them into the phases of the decision process that they indicated prior to the mapping.

Langley and Truax (1994) created a very elaborate graphical representation of the decisions and other events involved in the adoption of new technologies by organizations. The diagram includes symbols for several different types of events, places events into different bands depending on which domain of activity they are in, and relationships among events and the effects they have on one another. This diagram depicts more complex relationships among events and is too complex to reproduce here, so we will refer you to the original article.

A third way to represent event sequences is to transform the event data into *numerical* form. While this is a drastic reduction in the information in the event

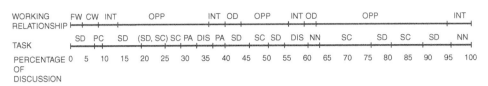

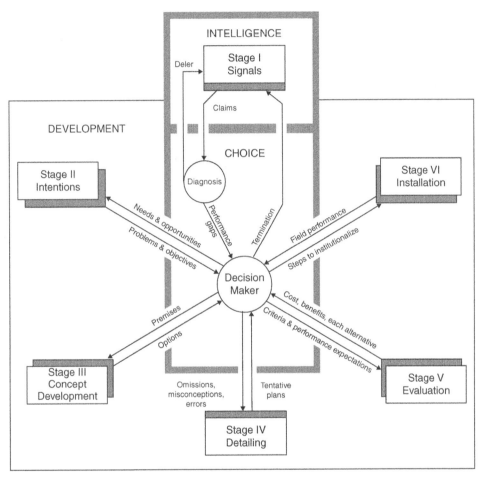

FIGURE 20.3 Two pictorial representations of processes: (a) A phasic timeline (Poole); (b) A transactional map of decision stepts (Nutt).

sequences, simplifying the events into a form that can be graphically displayed along a timeline facilitates pattern recognition and interpretation.

The type of representation that can be derived for an event sequence depends on the form of data that is available. If the event data consists of rich descriptions, then chronologies, visual representations, and numerical representations are all possible. However, if we have 'leaner' data, then some representations may not be feasible. When rich data are available it also may be useful to prepare several types of representations, as different representations are likely to reveal different aspects of the process.

Analysis of event sequence data enables researchers to evaluate process theories on their own terms or, alternatively, to derive narrative models inductively. This data can also be transformed into formats suitable for variance analyses, as we will discuss in more detail subsequently. Variance methods can be used to test hypotheses regarding characteristics of the sequence and process-outcome relationships that are suggested by one or more plausible narrative models.

Characterizing event sequences

When we have distilled and represented one or more event sequences, the next step is to describe their properties. Several different kinds of properties may be captured, either of the entire sequence or of segments of the sequence:

- *Type of sequence*: Often event sequences exhibit particular developmental paths that can be classified using typologies. One common type of developmental path is characterized by particular sequences of phases. For example, Nutt (1984) identified five decision-making sequences that occurred during strategic decision making: historical, off-the-shelf, appraisal, search, and nova, with variation in each type. Deriving typologies requires multiple event sequences (the more the better). However, investigators with only a single (hard-won) event sequence can use established typologies such as Nutt's to characterize the single sequence.
- The most straightforward way to derive typologies is to prepare standard narrative, visual, or numerical representations and group them according to similarity of appearance. Poole *et al.* (2000: ch. 5) describe a quantitative method for flexibly mapping phases in an event sequence, deriving quantitative measures of similarity between phase sequences, and deriving typologies of phase sequences using cluster analysis. This methodology is implemented in the WinPhaser program (Holmes, 2000).
- Events may also function as indicators of *event variables*, such as the level of idea development in an event or the degree to which an event indicates interventions in the innovation process by outside resource controllers. Coding procedures and analysis of visual representations may be used to generate values of the variable for each event, such as whether the event indicates resource controller intervention (a nominal variable), or the degree to which the event contributes to positive morale on the innovation team (an interval variable). Once individual events have been coded for the variable, researchers may also calculate the value of the variable for longer segments or subsequences (e.g. the total number of resource controller intervention events in a one-month period; the average level of morale across all events in a segment). These can then be utilized to derive overall developmental patterns. Coding events for variables also transforms the events into a time series of values that can be analyzed with various statistical methods (see Poole *et al.*, 2000).
- *Summary properties of a sequence*: Properties of an event sequence such as how long it is, the degree to which it matches a particular ideal type sequence, or the amount of idea development in the sequence represent variables in which

the sequence itself is the unit of analysis. This can be used to characterize the process and it also enables distinct event sequences to be compared.

- Another option is to identify the occurrence of *specific subsequences of events*, such as periods of interaction with outsiders to gather information about the decision or repetitive loops of plan-do-check activities. These can be used to characterize a sequence (e.g. in terms of when outside interaction occurred, or for comparison of different cases), or they can be extracted and studied in their own right, as independent sequences. Poole *et al.* (2000: ch. 7) describe methods of stochastic analysis that can be used to identify and to test for subsequences of events that occur repeatedly in a decision process, such as plan-do-check. For more unique subsequences, such as interactions with outsiders, qualitative approaches are more appropriate.

- It is also possible to identify *critical events* in a sequence, such as key turning points, conflicts, or when an external shock impinges on the process. For example, Poole and Roth (1989a) coded three types of critical events (breakpoints) in group decision processes: attempts to finalize decisions by groups (both successful ones and abortive ones), conflicts, and temporary adjournments of the meeting.

Identifying temporal dependencies

An important part of process research is colligation, the procedure of explaining an event by tracing its intrinsic relations to other events (Abbott, 1988) and thereby locating it in its temporal and historical context. Three types of temporal dependencies deserve attention. The first is a *critical conjunction* of events that represents a key point in a decision process. For example, the recent failure of Lehman Brothers during an economic crisis, which provoked a panicked reaction by the finance sector, created a juncture which sparked the decision that led to the implementation of a previously unimaginable $ 700 billion rescue of the financial industry. Establishing critical conjunctions requires showing a discontinuity in the process in the period before the conjuncture and the period after and showing how the conjuncture shaped subsequent events in some detail. Critical conjunctions are generally established through qualitative, historical analysis (Gaddis, 2004).

A second type of dependency is a *precursor relationship*, whereby one or more events are necessary for some later event to occur. For example, the softening of financial regulation that occurred during the late 1990s and early 2000s set up conditions for the risky decisions during the 2000s that led to the 2008 financial crisis. A precursor may happen well before its consequent event(s). For this reason historical detective work is required to establish that some event(s) was (were) indeed precursor to other(s).

A third type of dependency is the *sequential dependency* of events, such that one or more events increase the probability of the occurrence of a succeeding event. For example, engaging in discussion of the problem that a decision-making group is addressing is likely to trigger disagreements about the problem, especially when the group has a history of prior conflicts. Sequential dependencies generally occur between events that occur close to one another in time. In a first-order dependency, an event is influenced by the immediately preceding one; in a second-order dependency, an event is influenced by the two preceding ones. It is also possible for there to be a lagged dependency such that an event is influenced by the one three events back. Testing for sequential dependencies requires multiple cases of the dependency in the event sequence, since it relies on statistical analysis or on stochastic modeling techniques such as Markov analysis that were mentioned in the previous section (Poole *et al.*, 2004: ch. 7).

If sequential dependencies are found in a series of successive events, it could indicate that this particular sequence occurs regularly, suggesting a developmental type. Contingencies may also indicate causal linkages, such that event 1 leads to event 2 (efficient causality) or, alternatively that event 2 is the purpose for which event 1 occurs (final causality).

Distinguishing among alternative generative mechanisms

In the previous section we described four basic models of the decision process which incorporated different generative mechanisms. As we noted, any particular decision-making process may be explained in terms of a single model or in terms of a combination of interrelated models. How could we empirically assess whether one or more of these models operate in a given process? Several methods are available to test the plausibility of process theories and to determine which motor(s) are operating.

Table 20.2 lists the conditions for distinguishing among models. These conditions imply that the following tests might be performed to determine which of the

TABLE 20.2 Diagnostic questions to identify models

Question	Life Cycle	Teleological	Evolutionary	Dialectical
Unitary sequence invariant across cases?	Yes	No	May Be	May Be
Is there a pattern – program, routine, or code – that determines the nature of the sequence?	Yes	No	Yes	No
Is there a goal-setting process?	May Be	Yes	No	No
Is the central subject(s) an individual entity or a set of entities?	Individual	Individual	Set	Set
Are individual cases unpredictable, so that population or group of cases is the proper unit of analysis?	No	No	Yes	No
Is conflict or contradiction critical to the process?	May Be	No	Yes	Yes

generative mechanisms operate for a given case or sample:

1. *Does the process exhibit a unitary sequence of phases which is the same across cases?*
   Life cycle models posit a definite sequence of stages. Teleological models may
   exhibit stages, but the stages do not have to occur in a particular order; stages
   must occur and cumulate to satisfy the final goal or form of the process, but
   the order in which they are satisfied is not particularly important. Dialectical
   models should exhibit alternating phases of conflict/tension and resolution.
   Evolutionary motors will not necessarily exhibit stages, though they may exhibit punctuated equilibrium, where the system undergoes an upheaval and
   rapid reorientation, as Gersick (1989; 1991) observed in her studies of project
   teams.

   The methods for phase analysis mentioned in the previous section can be
   used to identify phases which may correspond to developmental stages, if any
   exist. As discussed in Poole *et al.* (2000: ch. 6), phase methods can also be
   adapted to enable researchers to evaluate sequences to determine whether
   they display a single unitary ordering (which would be consistent with a life cycle model), to identify whether there are multiple sequences of phases (which
   would be consistent with a teleological model), or whether there are alternating phases of conflict and resolution (which would be consistent with a dialectical model). Stochastic modeling of temporal dependencies among phases
   (rather than events), described in the previous section, can also be used to test
   whether phases occur in a certain order.

   Is there a patterning device, such as a program, routine, code, or rule system that determines the nature of the decision-making sequence? As noted
   above, life cycle models of organizational processes require a program or code
   either immanent within the developing entity or enforced by some external
   agency. Teleological models do not require such governing patterns; though
   the central subject may be oriented to such patterns, its activity is a result of
   willful choices and is not forced to follow a set sequence by internal or external patterns. Dialectical models, by definition, do not adhere to patterns,
   because they rely on emergence for resolution of conflicts and for coping with
   tensions. Evolutionary models are governed by patterns that drive enactment,
   selection, and retention.

   Evidence for programs, routines, codes, or rule systems must be garnered
   from sources outside the event sequence. The event sequence may contain evidence of these patterning forces, but the patterns themselves will be found
   in factors influencing the sequence. For example, a strategic decision process may be governed by procedures such as open space or future search,
   each of which guides the process through a set of norms (Seo, Putnam, and
   Bartunek, 2004; Mirvis, 2005). Organizations may also purposely promote conflict to spark ingenuity in problem solving and decision making.

   The same is true for patterning forces internal to the decision makers. Some
   evidence of the existence of a 'blueprint' that the central subject is following
   (with or without conscious choice) is required. It may be a logical scheme that
   defines why stages must logically unfold in a particular way. For example, it is

necessary to generate an idea before it can be debated and modified. Alternatively the process may be organized by an explicit patterning device, such as a strategic plan organized along the lines of the rational process. Evidence of this plan and its use can be garnered from event data.

2. *Is there a goal-setting process?* A teleological model of group decision making requires a goal setting process through which the person, group, or organization implicitly or explicitly, defines what the goal state – an acceptable decision – would be and the process through which an acceptable decision will be made. It then uses this to give form to the decision process, to guide how the process unfolds. For example, an organization might implicitly take as its goal to avoid divisive conflict during decision making and act in ways that suppress conflict and seek tradeoffs, even when conflict might be useful to rational decision process. A life cycle model of decision making may include goal setting as one stage, but there will be other clearly distinguishable stages that have nothing to do with goal setting. Dialectical models of decision making should not exhibit goal setting, because they are driven by conflicts between different positions or tensions within the organization. Finally, goals can serve the evolutionary process by defining conditions of fitness for decision premises.

Goal setting can usually be identified as part of the event sequence, but some adjunct evidence may be utilized as well. For example, evidence drawn from meeting notes or outsiders' reportage of goals may also be useful to establish goal setting.

3. *Is (are) the central subject(s) an individual entity or a set of interacting entities?* One of the critical steps in process analysis is defining who the central subject(s) is (are), that is who (or what) is driving events, or, to put it another way, who the events are happening to. In the case of decision making the central subject may be a key person, a group, an organization, or even a nonanimate entity such as the content of the decision. The body of arguments that have spun out during the process must be documented in order to define events that are relevant to the process. The model and general theoretical assumptions favored by the investigator usually imply a certain type of central subject and a choice of one versus several subjects. In addition, the process data itself conveys important information on which reading of the situation is most plausible. A researcher expecting to find two interacting central subjects in a dialectical process may find that his or her data clearly indicate the presence of only a single significant agent. When such is the case it is better to abandon the dialectical model in favor of either the life cycle or teleological models.

Interpreting raw data to derive events and larger narrative patterns is a cyclical process which follows the hermeneutic circle, tacking between particular facts and larger interpretive constructs and patterns. Cycling between raw data and narrative models provides the researcher with numerous opportunities to identify candidate subjects and to evaluate her or his choice.

4. *Are individual cases to some extent unpredictable, so that the best level of analysis is the total population of cases?* For some decisions, it is not possible to predict accurately the behavior of individual cases. This may be because each case is influenced by 'internal' factors or dynamics which are difficult to measure or

access, such as individual decision-making processes based on private prefer-ence distributions. There may also be a truly unique, unpredictable element in the case. While individuals may be difficult to explain or predict, the be-havior of a population of individuals may exhibit more regularity and allow the construction of theories of the population. In such cases, the evolutionary model is most appropriate. It explicitly deals with population-level dynamics, providing a theory of how the population of cases will evolve over time.

This test requires multiple cases in order to assess regularity at the individual case level. Both stochastic modeling and time series diagnostics provide tests for the predictability of individual cases based on the event sequence data, pro-vided the data is transformed so that it meets the assumptions of the methods. In the case of stochastic modeling a small number of states (e.g. Nutt's phases of the decision process) is needed. For time series analysis, events will have to be transformed into continuous numerical data. For example, Dooley and Van de Ven (1999) calculated the number of changes in an innovation during each month of the innovation process and fit time series to show that the first part of the process was essentially random in terms of innovation development, while the second part was predicable (see Poole *et al.*, 2000: ch. 9).

5. *Do conflicts or contradictions influence the decision process?* Conflict or tension is an important component of the dialectical and evolutionary models. The teleo-logical model, on the other hand, assumes that the consensus which underpins concerted action is necessary for concerted action; while there may be some conflict, it should be short-lived in a decision process that moves forward. Life cycle models may allow for conflict in one or more stages. Evidence external to the event sequence may also be utilized to establish the degree to which conflict is important in the process.

Table 20.2 summarizes the tests that can be used to establish the plausibility of the four models. Each row exhibits a different pattern of answers to the questions, thus ensuring that if all questions are validly addressed a unique model can be established.

A decision process shaped by one model is relatively simple. However, more than one motor may operate, especially in complex or prolonged decision processes. In such cases, tests must be 'localized' to eliminate as much interference as possible in the evaluation of each individual model. It also helps to work out the relationship between multiple motors. For example, a dialectical process may drive deliberation at the micro-level of debate and discussion while the larger decision process follows a stage model. The dialectic provides the impetus to advance through the phases, while the overarching stage model provides context for the dialectics such that the nature of the conflict changes over time, from debate and conflict over the prob-lem, then over solution options, then over the choice of an option, and finally over its implementation.

For each specific version of the four models, there will be additional assump-tions that must be tested, such as the particular number and types of stages in a life cycle model, how consensus is reached in teleological motor, how entities clash in a dialectical motor and how resolution occurs, and how retention occurs in an evolutionary model. In some instances, these tests can be conducted from the event sequence data, while in other instances special supplementary data will be required.

Establishing the nature and form of the model that governs the decision process involves specifying which types of final or formal causality are operating. It also involves spelling out the narrative explanation underlying the process. The narrative of the decision itself is, of course, more detailed than the model that underlies it.

Writing up the results

The writing of process research, which involves describing as well as explaining the course of the process, is an important part of the analytical process. There are several different formats that process studies can follow to present their results.

Some of the most influential process studies take the form of *narrative histories* that tell the story of a process in detail (e.g. Allison, 1970). These rich accounts have multiple interwoven themes and, as Langley (1999) notes, their very density may make deriving parsimonious theories something of a challenge.

A more focused approach is the *multiple case study* (e.g. Langley and Truax, 1994). These studies are designed to compare and contrast a limited number of cases that 'either (a) predict similar results (a literal replication) or (b) produce contrary results but for predictable reasons (a theoretical replication)' (Yin, 1984: 48–49) through intensive qualitative analysis. These studies often use various methods of summarization and display to draw meaning from their cases, such as visual mapping (Langley and Truax, 1994; Mintzberg, Raisinghani, and Theoret, 1976), matrix displays (Kuhn and Poole, 2000; Miles and Huberman, 1994), and comparison of extracts and digests of events (Leonard-Barton, 1990). The accounts in multiple case studies are typically quite rich, though not as detailed as narrative histories, and they often have a more compact and explicit theoretical focus than do narrative histories.

A third approach investigates processes through *quantitative analysis* of event series and presents results in a format similar to traditional quantitative social scientific articles. One study of this type (1) specifies indicators or variables that characterize attributes of events, (2) codes events to assign values to these variables, and (3) analyzes the resulting time series to test hypotheses about the sequence or identify patterns in the process. Quantitative process analyses utilize a range of techniques, including Markov analysis, multivariate time series techniques, event history analysis, and nonlinear systems analysis, to uncover and test for properties of series of events and the mechanisms that drive the process. In some cases these studies draw substantial samples (e.g. Nutt, 1984; Poole and Roth, 1989a; Shrivastava and Grant, 1985). Another approach to quantitative analysis involves developing a model of the process and analyzing its quantitative and qualitative characteristics for degree of fit to expected characteristics of the process (this will be discussed in more detail in the next section).

These methods must be applied through larger process research strategies. In the next section we delineate four distinctive strategies for research on decision processes.

STRATEGIES FOR PROCESS RESEARCH

To this point we have built a foundation by discussing the nature of process research, types of process explanations, and basic methods for conducting process studies. In this final section we will lay out four different types of process studies, each of which embodies a different strategy of inquiry.

A fundamental issue that influences our strategy for investigating processes is our ontological beliefs, in particular whether we view organizations as consisting of things or processes (Tsoukas and Chia, 2002). The basic distinction can be seen in the contrast between the views of Democritus and those of Heraclitus. Democritus believed nature was composed of stable material substance or things that changed only in their positioning in space and time. In contrast, Heraclitus, viewed reality, not as a constellation of *things*, but one of *processes*. Heraclitus argued that 'Process is fundamental: The river is not an object but an ever-changing flow; the sun is not a thing, but a flaming fire. Everything in nature is a matter of process, of activity, of change' (cited in Rescher, 1996: 10).

These contrasting views can be traced down through the years to the present. While many philosophers of the nineteenth and twentieth centuries emphasized the stabilities and fixities characteristic of the world's structure of lawful order, philosophizers such as Hegel, Marx, Peirce, James, Bergson, Dewey, and Whitehead viewed reality as a process and regarded time, change, and creativity as representing the most fundamental facts for understanding the world.

On the one hand the substantial perspective regards an organization as a social entity or structure (a thing or a noun) which retains its identity while changing from one state to another over time. For example, an organization recognizing the need for a strategic decision starts in the identification phase and once it has diagnosed its situation and the problems it faces, it then moves into a development phase in which it searches for solutions and adapts them to its situation, following which it moves into a selection phase in which it screens options, selects its best course of action, and authorizes the organization to proceed (Mintzberg *et al.*, 1976). On this view, an organization is always something in some particular state or phase of a process; there is always something there.

On the other hand the processual perspective posits that organizations are composed only of organizing processes. On this view an organization is simply a reification of a set of processes which maintain the organization by continuously structuring it and maintaining its boundaries in a field of other processes that are continuously breaking down the organization and its boundaries. In this view stability and change are explained in the same terms: stability is due to processes that maintain the organization so that it can be reified as the same thing by some observer(s), while change occurs when the processes operate in a manner that is reified by observer(s) as changing the organization. In either instance, stability or change are judgments, not real things, because the organization is a process that is continuously being constituted and reconstituted (Rescher, 1996). For example, a strategic decision would be viewed as a set of fluid processes by which issues and the objects of decision are continuously enacted, constituted, and reconstituted

Ontology
The social world is represented as being:

<table>
<tr>
<th></th>
<th></th>
<th>Substantial</th>
<th>Processual</th>
</tr>
<tr>
<td rowspan="2" style="writing-mode: vertical">Epistemology</td>
<td>Variance Approach</td>
<td>Variance studies of synoptic variables representing processes

Causal analysis of independent variables explaining dependent variable   I</td>
<td>Variance studies via modeling of decision processes

Dynamic models of complex adaptive systems   IV</td>
</tr>
<tr>
<td>Process Approach</td>
<td>Process study narrating sequence of change events in organization   II

Progressions of change (stages, cycles, etc) in the development of decision</td>
<td>Process study narrating social construction   III

Qualitative process studies of emergence of decision</td>
</tr>
</table>

FIGURE 20.4 Four Strategies for the study of Decision Proesses

throughout the process. Thinking of decision making in terms of sensemaking (Weick, 1995) is an example of this approach.

We can combine the earlier distinction between variance and process approaches (which represent epistemologies of process) with the two ontologies to derive a typology of four strategies for studying organizational decision-making processes, illustrated in Figure 20.4. Strategies I and II adopt variance and process epistemologies, respectively, to study decision making in a substantial organization. Approaches III and IV adopt variance and process methods, respectively, to study processes of decision making.

Strategy I: Substantial ontology and variance methodology: Variance studies of synoptic variables that represent processes

Strategy I applies a variance approach to the study of decision-making processes that are assumed to unfold in a substantial context. This strategy hinges on defining variables that provide a synoptic picture of the process. In some cases this involves treating decision making as a dependent variable and explaining it as a function of independent variables. This strategy is exemplified by studies of the influence on the composition of top management teams on strategic decisions and by studies which explain the decision to adopt an innovation as a function of innovation characteristics such as trialability, comparative advantage, and observability (Rogers, 2004). A second way in which this strategy can be applied is to derive variables describing the decision process, such as comprehensiveness (Fredericksen and Mitchell, 1984), and either explain them using independent variables or relate them to decision effectiveness.

While this might seem to be a 'nonprocessual' strategy, it is useful in two respects for process research. First it can be used to test for contingencies that might favor, trigger, or set into motion different types of processes. For example, Poole and Roth (1989a) found that difficult and complex decision tasks elicited simpler decision-making sequences than did simpler tasks. This strategy is also useful for evaluating the effectiveness of various types of processes. For example, Frederickson and Mitchell (1984) found that for very complex decisions, comprehensive decision processes were less effective than simpler decision processes. Since it employs standard, well-known statistical techniques Strategy I can provide powerful tests of hypotheses about processes, factors that give rise to them, and their effects.

Strategy I also has limitations. Due to its use of variance methods it can only detect regular, 'well-behaved' causality. It cannot detect the influence of factors such as critical events, multiple causes operating unevenly in different parts of the organization and at different points in time, causes operating across greatly different time scales, and sequences of events that chain together to lead up to some outcome. Such are the subject of history or biography, not structural equation models. Because it requires the abstracting of variables from the process, Strategy I also studies the process once removed (at least).

Strategy II: Process methodology, substantial ontology: Process study of events in an organizational entity

Strategy II analyzes change as a succession of events, stages, cycles, or states of decision making. In Nutt's (1993) transactional model of strategic decision, for example, the decision maker takes various actions to enact each stage, such as stating needs and opportunities in order to define intentions or taking a set of options to evaluation. Nutt derived a typology of strategic decision processes which represented different patterns of movement through the six phases, and these types were used as independent variables to explain effectiveness of strategic decision making. Some qualitative studies of organizational processes have also taken Approach II. Mintzberg et al.'s (1976) famous study of strategic decision making is firmly in this camp, as is Leonard-Barton's (1988) multiple case study of innovation. Both subdivide their subject into meaningful states and track process in terms of a succession of states. In Leonard-Barton's study, effectiveness rankings were also made for each case and related back to the description of the process.

As noted above, the most common process explanation that posits phases is the life cycle model, but evolutionary and teleological models can be conceptualized in terms of stages as well. The previous section discussed tests of phase representations that can be used to distinguish the models.

One advantage of Strategy II is that phase or stage conceptualizations are among the most popular and intuitive ways of thinking about decision making. Phase sequences provide understandable and useful maps of the decision process. There is also a liability in this approach because it tends to lead us to think about decisions as composed of 'blocks' of successive activity that are coherent in themselves. This may turn our attention away from the fact that more than one thing may be happening at a given time in a decision or that decisions emerge from more fluid processes. Phases or stages are themselves synopses of more complex processes.

Strategy III: Process methodology, processional ontology: Focus on the social construction of decisions

Strategy III presumes the world is composed of processes and applies the process research approach and hence is the most internally consistent way to pursue process research. Research employing this strategy uses qualitative approaches such as the grounded and historical narrative approaches discussed by Langley (1999). Examples include Mintzberg *et al.*'s (1995) studies of strategic decision making, Allison's (1970) lengthy study of decision making during the Cuban Missile Crisis, and Tracy and Standerfer's (2003) study of school board decision making. These studies employ inductive approaches that emphasize capturing the unique features of the case. Often this involves accounting for the ways in which decisions are constructed over the course of the process or constituted by discourse and actions. This strategy would emphasize the role of agency in decision making. It tends to produce idiographic explanations that illuminate the case(s) studied.

Strategy III is the most ideologically consistent approach to process research and Langley, among others, argues that it is the preferred approach. Strategy III is also advantageous in that it invites investigators to shed the 'blinders' imposed by substantial viewpoints and the general linear model and rethink concepts and methodological approaches. As Tsoukas and Chia (2002) argue, accommodating ourselves to Approach III means that we must truly learn to think in different terms than our largely substance-based educations have prepared us to. Weick (1995) provides a good starting point for developing a processual understanding of organizing, sensemaking, and related processes. Useful insights can also be gained from ethnomethodologists such as Garfinkel (1968) who create a vocabulary and grammar for expressing things in processional terms (which, among other things, led them to excessive use of present participle and gerundive phrases, and to awkward expressions such as 'doing social life'). On the negative side, Strategy III must confront the irony in that its representation, interpretation, and explanation of processes must always reify the processes in words and diagrams fixed statically to the page. In some sense, writing up a study of processes that is necessarily synoptic seems in tension with the processional ontology.

Strategy IV: Variance methodology, processional ontology: Process modeling

Strategy IV studies investigate processes through *quantitative modeling* of an event series. One common method of doing this involves constructing mathematical or simulation models that represent generative mechanisms thought to underlie the process. The course of the process is then simulated and the results of the simulation compared to known features of the process. Often qualitative features of the results of the simulation rather than exact quantitative fit are more important in determining whether the model is accurate. So, for example, if the time plot of results has two inflections in its curve, and it is known that the actual phenomenon has two inflections, this would be evidence for the fit of the model.

Cohen, March, and Olson (1972; see also O'Connor, 1999) advanced one of the most famous models of organizational decision making in their 'garbage can model'. This model argued that organizational decision premises are made up of problems looking for solutions, solutions looking for problems, goals, and decision opportunities (e.g. annual strategic planning sessions, where decisions must be made). The organization is a rich soup of these premises and a decision is made when all four components – problem, solution, goal, and decision opportunity – link up. They developed a simulation model based on these components.

A second means of enacting Strategy IV involves quantitative analysis of event series using longitudinal methods. Dooley and Van de Ven (1997), for example, segmented a multiyear product development process composed of numerous small decisions into months and counted the number of changes in the innovation idea, interventions by external resource controls, and feedback events per month in rich descriptions of events. They used multiple tests to ascertain the nature of the systems model that generated the observed patterns. An observed event time series may reflect one of four different dynamic patterns: periodic (or stable equilibria), chaotic (strange attractors), colored noise (that can be plotted as a negative power law characteristic of a punctuated equilibrium process), and truly random (white noise) dynamic patterns. The four patterns require different explanatory models that vary in the number of causal factors (dimensionality) and the nature of interaction between these causal factors. Low dimensional causal systems yield periodic and chaotic dynamics, while high dimensional causal systems yield pink and white noise random dynamics. Periodic and white noise dynamics stem from systems where causal factors act independently or in a linear fashion, while chaotic and pink noise systems reflect configurations where causal factors act interdependently in a nonlinear fashion.

While it is generally known that linear deterministic models (such as regression analysis) are appropriate for explaining periodic cycles or stable equilibria, and stochastic or probability models should be used to explain white noise random processes, relatively few organizational scholars have explored nonlinear dynamic models that are needed to explain chaotic and colored noise patterns. If one concludes that the event time series of an observed change process exhibits a nonlinear dynamic pattern (e.g. either chaotic or pink noise patterns), then currently the most appropriate model is based on Kaufmann's (1993) theory of complex adaptive systems (CAS). CAS theory explains systems in terms of self-organization and local action in producing aggregate system outcomes in contrast to traditional theories of central design and control (Dooley, 2004).

Models derived within Strategy IV such as these have the potential to help us derive implications of processes that cannot adequately be described verbally. The calculus lets us represent physical motion and change in ways that transcend verbal expression, and in the same way models may be able to capture processes more thoroughly and robustly than we can in verbal theories. Some may object that representation of processes in empirical time series and mathematical models overly 'variabilizes' them (Tsoukas and Hatch, 2001). However, these models have the advantage of being able to generate insights into processes that are so complex that it is impossible for the theorists to qualitatively think through how constructs interact. Moreover, simulation often enables visualization of process or analysis of how it unfolds under different conditions – these often go beyond what we could think through qualitatively.

These models have downsides as well. They represent a type of reductionism and may lose important detail due to synopticizing the variables. There is also a need for new model forms, because most current models (e.g. time series) were derived under variance assumptions. Agent-based models and models of complex adaptive systems show promise (Dooley, 2004). At the end of the day, this approach still does not capture the multifarious nature of processes, because it defines variables to depict the process, and once variables are defined, things are fixed, and 'accidental' discovery is more difficult.

CONCLUSION

Historian Arnold Toynbee wrote, 'A study of human affairs in movement is certainly more fruitful, because more realistic, than any attempt to study them in an imaginary condition of rest.' Process research requires a shift in approach to explanation and its own unique set of methods. Among the distinguishing features of the process approach are:

- The goal of process research is to use systematic observational and analytical methods to describe and explain underlying narratives.
- Data in process research reflect qualitative understandings of events and event sequences, rather than variables. When variables are used in process research, they serve as indicators of patterns or dynamics in an event sequence, not as the primary objects of interest. Process theories are not about variables; they are about the course of the decision.
- Narrative explanations feature final and formal causation as well as efficient causation. They presume that development and change are shaped primarily by final causes and formal patterns. Efficient causal forces, the focus of variance approaches, serve a secondary role in that they 'move' the entity from point to point in the sequence and introduce unique variations into the process.
- Narrative explanations take path dependence into account: they assume that events later in a sequence are conditioned by earlier ones.
- The generalizability of narrative explanations hinges on their versatility, which refers to their ability to help researchers discern a common narrative in a broad range of cases, despite the appearance of differences in event sequences. Versatile narratives can be applied across cases which differ in pace of change, variations in event duration, and particular 'local' causal factors that introduce unique turns into each sequence. Hence, the measure of generalizability of a process theory is not its ability to apply uniformly across cases, but its sensitivity to the pattern that shapes the decision.

These attributes of process theories present unique challenges for researchers. The process approach emphasizes that satisfactory explanations of decision processes are based in narratives, and investigating and establishing narrative models requires different patterns of reasoning and evidence than variable-based research. Despite its challenges, the process approach promises dividends, because it is uniquely suited to explain the course of decision making with all its twists and turns.

We do not want to claim that process theories are superior to variance theories. The two theories deal with different domains of knowledge, apply to different types of problems, and hence are complementary. Any decision process will leave 'traces' that can be studied with variance methods, such as the shape of a developmental curve. Such analyses do not get at the process directly, but they may be used to test particular assumptions of process theories. In the same vein, process approaches can be used to explore and evaluate the stories that underlie variance theories.

NOTES

1. Adapted from Poole, M. S., Van de Ven, A. H., Dooley, K., and Holmes, M. E. (2000). *Organizational change and innovation processes: Theory and methods for research*. New York: Oxford University Press; Poole, M. S. (2004). Central issues in the study of change and innovation. In M. S. Poole and A. H. Van de Ven (eds) *Handbook of organizational change and innovation* (pp. 3–31). New York: Oxford University Press; Poole, M. S. and Van de Ven, A. H. (2004). Theories of organizational change and innovation processes. In M. S. Poole and A. H. Van de Ven (eds) *Handbook of organizational change and innovation* (pp. 374–397). New York: Oxford University Press; . Van de Ven, A. H. and Poole, M.S. (1990). Methods for studying innovation development in the Minnesota innovation research program. *Organization Science, 1*, 313–335; Van de Ven, A. H., and Poole, M. S. (1995). Explaining development and change in organizations. *Academy of Management Review, 20*, 510–540; and Van de Ven, A. H. and Poole, M. S. (2002). Field research methods. In J. Baum (ed.) *Blackwell companion to organizations* (pp. 867–888). London: Blackwell.

REFERENCES

Abbott, A. (1984) Event sequence and event duration: Colligation and measurement, *Historical Methods*, 14, 192–204.

Abbot, A. (1988) Transcending general linear reality, *Sociological Theory*, 6, 169–186.

Allison, G. (1970) *The Essence of Decision*. Boston, MA: Little, Brown.

Bakhtin, M.M. (1981) *The Dialogic Imagination: Four essays by M. M. Bakhtin* (C. Emerson and M. Holquist, Trans.) Austin, TX: University of Texas Press.

Bal, M. (1985) *Narratology: Introduction to the theory of narrative*. Toronto: University of Toronto Press.

Bales, R.F., and Strodtbeck, F.L. (1951) Phases in group problem-solving, *Journal of Abnormal and Social Psychology* 46, 485–495.

Bhaskar, R.A. (1975) *A Realist Theory of Science.* Leeds, England: Leeds Books.

Blalock, H.M. (1969) *Theory construction: From verbal to mathematical formulations.* Englewood Cliffs, NJ: Prentice Hall.

Buckley, W. (1967) *Sociology and modern systems theory.* Englewood Cliffs, NJ: Prentice Hall.

Campbell, D. (1974) 'Evolutionary Epistemology', in P.A. Schilpp (ed.) *The Philosophy of Karl Popper.* Lasalle, IL: Open Court Press, 413–463.

Campbell, D.T., and Stanley, J.C. (1963) *Experimental and Quasi-experimental Designs for Research.* Chicago: Rand McNally.

Chakravarthy, B.S., and Lorange, P. (1991) *Managing the Strategy Process.* Englewood Cliffs, NJ: Prentice Hall.

Churchman, C.W. *The Design of Inquiring Systems: Basic Concepts of Systems and Organizations.* New York: Basic Books.

Cohen, M.J., March, J., and Olson, J. (1972) A garbage can model of organizational choice, *Administrative Science Quarterly,* 17, 1–25.

Cook, T., and Campbell, T. (1979) *Quasi-Experimentation: Design and Analysis Issues for Field Settings.* Chicago: Rand McNally.

De Wit, B., and Meyer, R. (2004) *Strategy: Process, Content, Context: An International Perspective.* London: Thomson, 3rd edition.

Dooley, K. (2004) 'Complexity Science Models of Organizational Change and Innovation' in M.S. Poole and A.H. Van de Ven (eds) *Handbook of Organizational Change and Innovation.* New York: Oxford University Press, 354–373.

Dooley, K., and Van de Ven, A.H. (1999) Explaining complex organizational dynamics, *Organization Science,* 10, 358–372.

Frederickson, J.W., and Mitchell, T.R. (1984) Strategic decision processes: Comprehensiveness and performance in an industry with an unstable environment, *Academy of Management Journal,* 27, 299–324.

Gaddis, J.L. (2004) *The Landscape of History: How Historians Map the Past.* Oxford, UK: Oxford University Press.

Garfinkel, H. (1968) *Studies in Ethnomethodology.* Englewood Cliffs, NJ: Prentice Hall.

Gersick, C.J.G. (1989) Marking time: Predictable transitions in task groups, *Academy of Management Journal,* 32, 274–309.

Gersick, C.J.G. (1991) Revolutionary change theories: A multilevel exploration of the punctuated equilibrium paradigm, *Academy of Management Review* 16, 10–36.

Gouran, D.S., and Hirokawa, R.Y. (1996) 'Functional Theory and Communication in Decision-making and Problem-solving Groups: An Expanded View', in R.Y. Hirokawa and M.S. Poole (eds) *Communication and Group Decision-Making.* Thousand Oaks, CA: Sage, 2nd edition, 55–80.

Greimas, A. (1983) *Structural Semantics: An Attempt at a Method.* Lincoln and London: University of Nebraska Press.

Hirokawa, R.Y. (1990) The role of communication in group decision-making efficacy: A task contingent perspective, *Small Group Research,* 21, 190–204.

Hollingshead, A.B., Wittenbaum, G.M., Paulus, P.B., Hirokawa, R.Y., Ancona, D.G., Peterson, R.S., Jehn, K.A., and Yoon, K. (2005) 'A Look at Groups from the Functional Perspective', in M.S. Poole and A. Hollingshead (eds) *Theories of Small Groups: Interdisciplinary Perspectives.* Thousand Oaks, CA: Sage, 21–63.

Holmes, M.E. (2000) *WinPhaser.* Software available from mholmes@bsu.edu.

Kaplan, A. (1964) *The Conduct of Inquiry: Methodology for Behavioral Science.* New York: Chandler.

Kaufmann, S. (1993) *The Origins of Order: Self-organization and Selection in Evolution.* New York: Oxford University Press.

Kuhn, T., and Poole, M.S. (2000) Do conflict management styles affect group decision-making? Evidence from a longitudinal field study, *Human Communication Research*, 26, 558–590.

Langley, A. (1999) Strategies for theorizing from process data, *Academy of Management Review*, 24, 691–710.

Langley, A., and Truax, J. (1994) A process study of new technology adoption in smaller manufacturing firms, *Journal of Management Studies*, 31, 619–652.

Leonard Barton, D. (1988) Implementation as mutual adaptation of technology and organization, *Research Policy*, 17, 251–267.

Leonard-Barton, D. (1990) A dual methodology for case studies: Synergistic use of a longitudinal single site with replicated multiple sites, *Organization Science*, 1, 248–266.

March, J.G. (1994) *A Primer on Decision Making*. New York: Free Press.

March, J.G., and Simon, H. (1993) *Organizations*. New York: Blackwell, 2nd edition.

Mason, R.O., and Mitroff, I.I. (1981) *Challenging Strategic Planning Assumptions*. New York: John Wiley & Sons, Inc.

McGrath, J.E., and Tschan, F. (2004) 'Dynamics in Groups and Teams: Groups as Complex Action Systems', in M.S. Poole and A.H. Van de Ven (eds) *Handbook of Organizational Change and Innovation*. New York: Oxford University Press, 50–72.

Miles, M., and Huberman, A.M. (1994) *Qualitative Data Analysis*. Newbury Park, CA: Sage.

Miller D., and Friesen, P.H. (1982) The longitudinal analysis of organizations: A methodological perspective, *Management Science*, 28, 1013–1034.

Mintzberg, H., Raisinghani, D., and Theoret, A. (1976) The structure of 'unstructured' decision processes, *Administrative Science Quarterly*, 21, 246–275.

Mirvis, P.H. (2005) Large group interventions: Change as theater, *Journal of Applied Behavioral Science*, 41, 122–138.

Mohr, L. (1982) *Explaining Organizational Behavior*. San Francisco, CA: Jossey-Bass.

Nutt, P.C. (1984) Types of organizational decision processes, *Administrative Science Quarterly*, 29, 414–450.

Nutt, P.C. (1993) The formulation processes and tactics used in organizational decision making, *Organization Science*, 4 (2), 226–251.

Nutt, P.C. (2002) *Why Decisions Fail: Avoiding the blunders and traps that lead to debacles*. San Francisco, CA: Berrett-Koehler.

O'Connor, E.S. (1997) Discourse at our disposal: Stories in and around the garbage can, *Management Communication Quarterly*, 10, 395–497.

Pentland, B.T. (1999) Building process theory with narrative: From description to explanation, *Academy of Management Review*, 24, 711–724.

Pettigrew, A.M. (1990) Longitudinal field research on change: Theory and practice, *Organization Science*, 1, 267–292.

Polkinghorne, D.E. (1988) *Narrative Knowing and the Human Sciences*. Albany, NY: SUNY Press.

Poole, M.S. (2004) 'Central Issues in the Study of Change and Innovation', in M.S. Poole and A.H. Van de Ven (eds) *Handbook of Organizational Change and Innovation*. New York: Oxford University Press, 3–31.

Poole, M.S., and Hirokawa, R.Y. (1996) 'Introduction: Communication and Group Decision Making', in R.Y. Hirokawa and M.S. Poole (eds), *Communication and group decision-making*. Thousand Oaks, CA: Sage, 2nd edition, 3–18.

Poole, M.S., and Roth, J. (1989a) Decision development in small groups IV: A typology of decision paths, *Human Communication Research*, 15, 323–356.

Poole, M.S., Van de Ven, A.H., Dooley, K., and Holmes, M.E. (2000) *Organizational Change and Innovation Processes: Theory and Methods for Research*. New York: Oxford University Press.

Poole, M.S. and Van de Ven, A.H. (2000) 'Theories of Organizational Change and Innovation Processes', in M.S. Poole and A.H. Van de Ven (eds) *Handbook of Organizational Change and Innovation*. New York: Oxford University Press, 374–397.

Porac, J.F., Thomas, H., and Baden-Fuller, C. (1989) Competitive groups as cognitive communities: The case of Scottish knitwear manufacturers, *Journal of Management Studies*, 26, 397–416.

Rescher, N. (1996) *Process Metaphysics: An Introduction to Process Philosophy*. Albany, NY: State University of New York Press.

Rimmon-Kenan, S. (1983) *Narrative Fiction: Contemporary Poetics*. London: Routledge.

Rogers, E.M. (2004) *Diffusion of innovations* (5th ed.). New York: Free Press.

Seo, M.-G., Putnam, L.L., and Bartunek, J.M. (2004) 'Dualities and Tensions of Planned Organizational Change', in M.S. Poole and A. Van de Ven (eds) *Handbook of Organizational Change and Innovation*. New York: Oxford University Press, 73–107.

Shadish, W.R., Cook, T.D., and Campbell, D.T. (2002) *Experimental and Quasi-experimental Designs for Generalized Causal Inference*. Boston, MA: Houghton Mifflin.

Shrivastava, P., and Grant, J.H. (1985) Empirically derived models of strategic planning processes. *Strategic Management Journal*, 6, 97–113.

Smith, K.K., and Berg, D.N. (1987) *Paradoxes of Group Life*. San Francisco, CA: Jossey-Bass.

Tracy, K. and Standerfer, C. (2003) 'Selecting a School Superintendent: Sensitivities in Group Deliberation', in L.R. Frey (ed.) *Group Communication in Context: Studies of bona fide groups*. Thousand Oaks, CA: Sage, 2nd edition, 109–134.

Tsoukas, H., and Chia, R. (2002) On organizational becoming: rethinking organizational change, *Organization Science*, 13, 567–582.

Tsoukas, H., and Hatch, M.J. (2001) Complex thinking, complex practice: The case for a narrative approach to organizational complexity, *Human Relations*, 54, 979–1013.

Van de Ven, A.V., and Poole, M.S. (1990) Methods for studying innovation development in the Minnesota innovation research program, *Organization Science*, 1, 313–335.

Van de Ven, A.H., and Poole, M.S. (1995) Explaining development and change in organizations, *Academy of Management Review*, 20, 510–540.

Van de Ven, A.H., and Poole, M.S. (2002) 'Field research methods', in J. Baum (ed.) *Blackwell Companion to Organizations*. London: Blackwell, 867–888.

Weick, K. (1995) *Sensemaking in Organizations*. Thousand Oaks, CA: Sage.

Werner, C.M., and Baxter, L.A. (1994) 'Temporal Qualities of Relationships: Organismic, Transactional, and Dialectical Views', in M. Knapp and G.R. Miller (eds) *Handbook of Interpersonal Communication*. Thousand Oaks, CA: Sage, 2nd edition, 323–379.

Yin, R. (1984) *Case study research: Design and methods*. Beverly Hills: Sage.

21

On the Study of Process: Merging Qualitative and Quantitative Approaches

PAUL C. NUTT

INTRODUCTION[1]

Process, suggesting how to make a decision, is an essential ingredient in the formulation of any comprehensive theory of decision making. Despite this, attention in most research efforts is directed toward structure, indicating what was decided, ignoring the actions taken to realize the decision. Such an approach is also widely applied to the study of change-related topics such as transformation, strategy, and innovation (Van de Ven and Poole, 1995; Weick and Quinn, 1999). Structure describes the features of a transformation, strategy, or innovation (Barley, 1986: Miller and Friesen, 1978; Pettigrew *et al.*, 2001). Process indicates *how* to transform, develop a strategy, or produce innovation. This chapter suggests some process questions to guide future decision-making research and offers some guidelines to carry out such studies.

Process research has many challenges. Such research seeks to uncover empirically grounded recommendations that lay out steps to follow to make a successful decision. Historically, such steps have been based upon propositions derived from consulting engagements offering idiosyncratic observations of practitioners (e.g. Covey, 1989). Process studies identify the steps followed that have empirical grounding. One way to do empirical process research is to collect multiple cases that document the actions of decision makers along with outcomes and consequences of the decision (Van de Ven, 1992; Weick and Quinn, 1999; Mackenzie, 2000). To do so, the researcher must confront a long-standing tradition in the social sciences that ignores time and thereby process (Pettigrew *et al.*, 2001). Process is treated as slices in a cross-section, overlooking the sequence of actions that are followed. A longitudinal view is needed to capture the unfolding of time as actual events occur, or

Handbook of Decision Making. Edited by Paul C. Nutt and David C. Wilson
© 2010 John Wiley & Sons, Ltd

are reconstructed (Van de Ven *et al.*, 2000). This calls upon researchers to confront the very real difficulties of doing longitudinal research. The chapter takes up this challenge, showing how decision-making theory can benefit from a specification of process and how to frame such studies to bridge the prescriptive-descriptive gap found in much of today's management research (Nutt, 2003).

Several process-related issues are considered in the chapter. The consequences of leaving process implicit in decision making are discussed, showing how process is a plausible explanation for many of the decision-making findings found in the literature. Overlooking process, or treating it as an afterthought, ignores the more important questions about decision making. Some of these questions are identified and the process-related issues that each raises are considered. To do this, an examination of decision-related processes found in the literature is carried out. Several of the processes, within and among various schools of thought, are compared to identify decision-making research questions. These questions include the need for a formal process, the value of coherent process steps, the merits of step sequences, the benefits of multiple lines of inquiry, the effects of content and situation, and the influence of scope. The research paradigm required to address such questions is then considered. Several change-related theories are applied to decision making, showing how each makes process the key to understanding what produces a decision and the success realized. Standards for such studies are presented, showing how longitudinal viewing is required to reveal the unfolding of action in a decision-making process. This calls for an action theory of decision making with prescriptive qualities, like that found in engineering and medicine (Harmon, 1980).

Prescription and Description in Process Research

The double hourglass in Figure 21.1 provides a way to visualize decision-making research. In the figure, 'Mode of explanation' identifies descriptive and prescriptive as the purposes of such research and 'level' as indicating whether these efforts are directed toward micro or macro phenomena. The vertical hourglass in Figure 21.1 provides a picture of the emphasis found in much of the existing decision-making research. The horizontal hourglass indicates the opportunities found in process research questions.

Descriptive research identifies a result – the features of a decision. Examples include the building to be constructed or the pay-for-performance scheme to be set in place. Prescriptive research suggests means, such as guidelines that identify steps required to realize the building or the pay system. Such examinations can be macro or micro, to distinguish between organizational and individual behavior. At the micro level, human behavior is considered as managers act as decision makers, considering topics such as perception, cognition, style, and the like. At the macro level collectives are considered (Wilber, 2000), dealing with topics such as the collective's leadership, its structure, and its intent, such as innovation (Van de Ven *et al.*, 1999) or downsizing (Cameron, 1995; Nutt, 2007). Units of analysis can include work groups, organizations, or power elites.

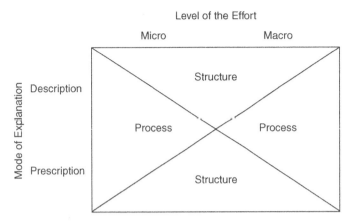

FIGURE 21.1 Classifying decision making research.

The Descriptive Tradition

Micro-descriptive research identifies what a decision maker produces. Such an approach has dominated the bulk of management-related research under the rubric 'organizational behavior', or more precisely, individual behavior. Examples include documenting the information collected by a decision maker (Tversky and Kahneman, 1974), his/her risk propensity (Slovic *et al.*, 1977), escalation of commitments (Staw *et al.*, 1981), attitude toward and response to ambiguity (Nutt, 2002), and the influence of rewards (Kouzes and Posner, 1987; 1993). Study has been directed toward attitude change, employee voice and retention, personnel selection, cognitive complexity and cue recognition, risk taking, job evaluation effects, administrative succession, whistle-blowing, parting ceremonies, and the like. In each, a descriptive orientation leads to documenting *what* was done, overlooking process, *how* 'the what' came into being. For example, personnel selection studies typically document the criteria applied, who was selected, or characteristics of candidates on the short list, but say little about how the selection process worked. Small group research has been conducted in much the same way (Hackman, 1990), skipping over *how* the group decided. Only recently has this documentation been extended to the actions taken by decision makers as they act purposely (Pettigrew *et al.*, 2001; Poole and Roth, 1989).

Schon's (1983) landmark study of practitioners illustrates micro-process research. This type of study is rare. As a result, we know comparatively little about how decision makers interact with subordinates as they design interventions, carry out performance appraisals, select team members, and undertake many other decision-making activities required in the day-to-day management of organizations. This void makes it difficult to assess decision-making practices to find those meriting wider use as well as those that should be discouraged. Schon's (1987) efforts in practitioner education illustrate one type of goal for micro-process research.

Description has dominated 'macro-descriptive' research as well. The approach resembles that of micro-descriptive efforts: variables are postulated, measures proposed, and experiments conducted (more likely data is collected from a survey) to relate the variables in a date cross-section, drawn at a particular point in time. Lawrence and Lorsch (1967), for example, explore differentiation and integration by measuring the magnitude of change in variables, saying little about processes that produced these changes. The typical study codifies a description (e.g. Burns and Stalker, 1961; Mintzberg *et al.*, 1976) with an analysis of factors (Lawrence and Lorsch, 1967). This approach fails to show how the phenomena in the description came into being. Similarly, strategic management studies take great care to describe a strategy (as a noun), depicting what an organization is doing: its market and customers, products, means of manufacture, stakeholders, and sources of support (e.g. Mintzberg and Waters, 1982; Hamel and Prahalad, 1994). Thompson (1967) labels these decisions as domain choice, defining a structure. Domain navigation suggests process. Many who characterize strategy overlook domain navigation (e.g. Thompson and Strickland, 1996; Digman, 1997; Hitt *et al.*, 1997) and thereby skip over how the strategy came into existence. An emphasis on process would study how the strategy came into being and what may alter it in the future. As Weick (1979) noted long ago – 'stamp out nouns, stamp in verbs'.

Prescriptive initiatives

Prescription can be suggestive of process, but the prescriptions offered often take shape as a structure. Scott and Cummings (1973), for example, building on the work of Skinner (1969), extend the notions of contingency reinforcement to behavioral change in subordinates. A random contingency schedule is applied to administer aversive stimuli, designed to extinguish undesirable behavior, or to offer rewards that reinforce desired behavior. A classic SOR (stimulus-organism-response) model is assumed. A random reinforcement pattern (R) is applied when particular behaviors are observed (S). In this model, the subordinate (O) does not exist suggesting that creativity and the many other potentials of people have no bearing on the outcome. The individual emerges when the *process* of applying or responding to reinforcements is considered. How a subordinate reacts, cognitively and emotionally, to rewards and punishments reveals process considerations, or how the subordinate responds to R; in the example of the random reinforcement schedule. As this process is revealed, a manager may find new opportunities to coax desirable behavior from subordinates as well as how to act ethically in their management.

Expectancy theory (e.g. Vroom, 1964) also has prescriptive goals with a structural orientation. Performance is treated as a product of motivation and ability, where motivation stems from the product of reward availability and its valiance (importance) to the performer. Using a product in the relationship stresses the importance of ability, rewards, *and* perceived reward importance. Performance plummets if any of the three factors is missing. This formulation treats the human organism (the performer) as an intervening variable. Such an approach overlooks matters of considerable importance in interpersonal dealings, such as goal formation in the performer and the way communication is delivered. Expectancy theory is silent about the formation of an individual's needs, attitudes, dispositions; memory of past dealings, and information processing limitations in the accurate recall of these incidents, and the development of norms about equity. Such models often have considerable complexity in the number of factors and factor relationships considered, such as the Porter and Lawler (1960) reward model. Here both intrinsic and extrinsic rewards are used and the linkage among these and other factors is specified – showing how factors linked to performance can be manipulated by a manager. Still, a closed loop is produced. The Porter-Lawler reward model is not open to learning, by either a decision maker or a subordinate, in which both move to higher levels of understanding. However, learning is always present when a decision maker attempts to influence others. These considerations could be revealed by process. Process shows how a performer and the decision maker learn and how both co-evolve toward understanding or toward conflict. The process of learning would reveal opportunities to intervene that move toward mutual understanding (Nutt and Backoff, 1986).

Contingency models, for all their virtues, also ignore process. For instance, Vroom (1973; Vroom and Yetton, 1974) offers a diagnostic procedure to select among group decision-making approaches. An SOR model is applied here as well. The stimulus (a problem) is assessed by the decision maker using preset rules to produce R, the consequences found at the end of the decision tree. All contingency models use this type of cascaded if-then conditions to provide the structuration of a process, but do not offer steps to carry out the recommendations. Other examples include leadership (e.g. Fiedler, 1967), selection of a group process (Strumpf *et al.*, 1979), matching decision implementation tactics to climates (Nutt, 1992), and Daft's (1995) decision rules derived from Thompson (1967) and Perrow (1967).

Process as a study factor

Macro-descriptive efforts, in which organizations become the unit of analysis, can inadvertently reveal process. The broader view makes process considerations harder to ignore. Responses tend to fall into two categories. In the first, process is assumed away. Examples include Hall's (1963) studies of organizations that concentrate on size, Woodward's (1964) implicit treatment of technology, and Hage's (1965) axiomatic theory of organizations. Each failed to see how process is buried in the factors that they were studying, such as how process must be embedded in technology.

A second response is to stumble over process. In searching for an explanation, process crops up as an afterthought. In these studies, the factors included in the research effort failed to account for what was observed making process a plausible causal agent. For example, Hage and Aiken's (1970) famous study of change in social work agencies attempted to use structural factors, such as formalization and centralization, to explain changes. Process was added when the structural factors could not explain all of what was observed. Research into innovation (Eveland *et al.*, 1977) and organizational regeneration (Cameron, 1995; Zand and Sorensen, 1975) discovered process in this manner. In other studies, longitudinal approach uncovers process by extending viewing time. Cyert and March (1963) tracked decision processes and found that conspicuous alternatives, supported by key power figures, tend to be adopted. The Ingram *et al.* (2002) study of governments found that leadership (a process proxy) was present in highly rated governmental agencies at the city, state, and federal levels, and absent in low-rated ones, after looking at the data over a period of several years. Nevertheless, process continues to be ignored in the discussions of factors that influence an outcome (Pettigrew *et al.*, 2001; Nutt, 2004).

Macro-prescriptive efforts also stumbled over process, as illustrated by the classic work of March and Simon (1958) and Thompson (1967). Rationality for March and Simon had a structural quality until nonprogrammed decisions were considered in their final chapter. The arguments offered were unable to deal with considerations found to be important by walking through the logic used to construct propositions in this famous and often quoted book. It is interesting to note that 'nonprogrammed decisions' is the least quoted part of their book. Co-alignment and adaptation appear at the end of Thompson's (1967) seminal work, again suggesting that process considerations were an afterthought, articulated to explain what structure failed to reveal. Thompson's (1967) notions of co-alignment and moving targets call for process but do not indicate what should make up such a process; such as the steps needed to produce co-aligned streams of organized action. Macro-level contingency tables (e.g. Lawrence and Dyer, 1983; Miles and Snow, 1978; Daft and Weick, 1984; Daft, 1995: Butler, 1998) share this problem. Process is implicit in finding cases of fit and misfit. In this way, much contemporary decision-making research either overlooks the process or treats it as an afterthought (Nutt, 2003).

THE POWER OF A PROCESS EXPLANATION

Connections that create patterns of unity and change lie behind many groundbreaking scientific explanations (Morgan, 1986). In these patterns, there is an enfolded order that explains past state changes and predicts future ones. By focusing attention on structure – what is – a researcher loses sight of process – what produced the structure and maintains its existence. The reverse is also true. Process cannot exist without structure and structure cannot exist without process. Only by considering both structure and process can each be fully appreciated. To do so calls for simultaneous viewing because there is *structure in process* and *process in structure*. For example, Iacocca's '56 for 56' financing program (a decision) rescued the 1956 Fords that were not selling (Iacocca and Novak, 1984). An internal attribution based on reading the environment – our cars are not liked but may sell if we make them financially attractive – led to the creation of a new organizational unit, a financing division. The '56 for 56' program can be viewed as structure (elements of the program, such as financing terms) or as process (the decision-making steps Iacocca took to develop and install the '56 for 56' program). In the study of the decision both structure and process must be understood.

Simon (1977) argues that decision making is made up of intelligence, design, and choice steps. Some additional insights can be gleaned from an examination of the 'process in his structure' and the 'structure of his process'. Considering intelligence, design, and choice as a duality, which is shown by the intersection of structure and process questions in Figure 21.2, offers some additional insights. For instance, cell

Process

	Intelligence	Design	Choice
Intelligence	CELL 1	CELL 4	CELL 5
Design	CELL 4	CELL 2	CELL 6
Choice	CELL 5	CELL 6	CELL 3

Structure

FIGURE 21.2 The structure-process duality applied to decision making.

one in Figure 21.2 captures the intelligence derived from an intelligence seeking process. The duality identifies both the structure (what was the intelligence) and the process (how was the intelligence obtained). The duality poses questions about how the intelligence influenced intelligence gathering as well as how gathering intelligence influenced the intelligence that was obtained. In cell two, design can be described as structure (a new product) as well as process (the ideation and developmental steps used to create the product prototype). The duality asks how the prototype influences the design process as well as how the design process influences the prototype. In cell 3, choice can be depicted as the product selected to be manufactured (structure) or as steps taken by the organizations to reach a decision about whether to offer the product. The duality calls for study of how the choice influences design and how a design influences the choice.

The off diagonal cells in Figure 21.2 are equally revealing. Cell 4 captures the intelligence-design duality in which each is treated as a structure and as a process. The duality questions how bits of intelligence (e.g. information) used in a design process influence the process and how a design (a prototype or a competitor's product) influences the process of intelligence gathering. Cell 5 depicts the choice-intelligence duality. Here the duality considers how a choice process gathers intelligence and how the process of intelligence gathering influences the choice. Cell 6 connects choice and design. The impact of a design on a choice process and the impact of a choice on the design process would be the focus of study. Each cell in Figure 21.2 poses a question – asking how structure and process presuppose one another. A decision maker should ponder each to take action. Process can be represented in these actions as either a temporal ordering of events or an explicit procedure to be followed.

The notion of a duality is found in both co-production and in producer-product relationships (Ackoff and Emery, 1972). Co-production depicts state transformations that arise when moving from time one to time two. We see a structure (product decision) by the actions of decision makers that reproduce the structure. This is a radical departure from the static views characterizing decision-making research, summarized by Eisenhardt and Zbaracki (1992). For instance, using process theory as the producer in a producer-product relationship a researcher questions how to carry out a decision-making process to produce a desired result, such as innovation (Van de Ven et al., 1999). A static view would describe the structure (product decision) by viewing the innovation and measuring various aspects of it. This eliminates insight into what produced the structure (the process) and how to reproduce its innovative results.

The structure-process duality has several uses. First, one can theorize about the extent to which decision makers, facing certain situations, are free to act. To find real and perceived constraints, and their separation, imagine where flux and resistance will occur. Second, decisions can evolve. A decision's structure (a prototype) at time one is often different from what appears at time two. A researcher understands such shift by uncovering the processes producing the shift. Thus, producer-product rather than cause and effect logic should be the focus of study (Ackoff and Emery, 1972). The reverse may also be true. Structure may explain process shifts, using the producer-product formulation. Third, a decision maker influences a structure but the structure also influences the decision maker. Decision makers react to conditions of their own making and in doing so alter implicit and explicit conditions imposed on taking action. How this is done is rooted in the structure-process duality.

Management research rarely considers both process and structure. This may stem from the complexity and confusion in inferring a producer-product relationship (Mohr, 1982). Complexity stems from the blizzard of factors that are associated with a process. To study a decision-making process, decision maker-related factors (cognitive make up, leadership style, etc.), the context (environmental hostility or stability), the history of the firm (profitability), and many other influences must be included. One can acknowledge this complexity and not dismiss it. Merging process with structure has the advantage of including outcome, situational factors, and process types, considering the likelihood that certain types of processes produce favorable outcomes under certain conditions. Both the qualification and the outcome have stochastic properties. The circumstances that led to using a particular kind of process can be linked to likely results. This permits an exploration of how the context can be changed, the process modified, or both altered together (an interaction) if results are not favorable.

Complexity has led to process studies that confuse events with outcomes. Consider the study by Eveland et al. (1977) in which the notion of 'reinvention', in a process of innovation, was used to describe both an event (an end state) and a variant (the degree to which it occurred). In addition, Zand and Sorenson (1975) treat stages of a process as both an event and a variable. These problems seem too idiosyncratic to cite as a reason not to merge the study of process and structure. Correct interpretation overcomes the problem. If stages (unfreeze, move, refreeze in the Zand and Sorenson study) can be mapped to an outcome the problem is solvent. Caution in process construction is also needed. Process stages must be viewed as states that occur in various sequences under certain conditions. To ignore factors that depict context ignores conditions that may explain much of what is interesting about the process, such as when and why it occurs. The desirability of the occurrence can be examined to determine whether process can serve as a prescription.

Analysis of the duality overcomes concerns noted by Mohr (1982) and Poole and Van de Ven (2004) about variance models and process models. This is done by recognizing that one is implicate in the other. Recognizing and dealing with this duality reconciles seemingly contradictory findings by uncovering complementariness. For instance, the Cohen *et al.* (1972) garbage can model does not account for the unfolding of process. Solutions are described without an appreciation for how these solutions would change had a different process been applied. Nutt (2002) qualified these findings by showing how the unfolding of a process accounts for some of this behavior, but not other instances. This latter study was done with a macroscope and the Cohen *et al.* study with a microscope. Together they offer a better prescription than either can individually. In the Cohen study, process is implicate and structure (the solution) explicate. In the other, the reverse is true. Each provides a complementary part of the bigger picture. Note how time is meaningless in variance explaining studies but central to process. Mohr's 'meta analysis' will accomplish little more than Collins and Guetzkow's (1964) sorts unless this distinction is considered.

Next, attention is directed to some key process research issues.

SOME PROCESS RESEARCH QUESTIONS

Empirically grounded process prescriptions are rare in decision-making research (Van de Ven, *et al.*, 1999). Typically, prescriptions offer action-taking propositions based on experience, organizational practices, personal reflections, or consulting engagements – coupled with observations about what seems to work and why. This makes much of the prescriptive decision-making literature practice-based. Such process descriptions lack repeatability and tests of comparative value so the means to select among prescriptions is missing. Each proponent invents process labels, names stages to suggest critical actions, and proposes action sequences. As the list increases the difficulty of sorting out what works and what does not grows as well. To illustrate, Table 21.1 summarizes processes drawn from several such sources. Comparisons identify process similarities and differences.

Many investigators require stages of activity that include a search to uncover ideas and an evaluation of the options identified. Researchers also call for intelligence, need identification, solution development, implementation, and outcome monitoring. The stimulus to act is explored with devices such as tensions (Nutt and Backoff, 1993), interests (Hickson *et al.*, 1986), sensing (Ansoff, 1984), interpretations (Hudson, 1968), and still other forms of *intelligence*. *Needs* are identified by framing activities that establish values (Hampden-Turner, 1990), missions (Hurst, 1986), aims (Beyer and Trice, 1978), purposes (Nadler, 1981), issues (Nutt and

TABLE 21.1 A comparison of processes

Process type	Implementation Beyer and Trice (1978)	Social Change Hage & Aiken (1970)	Organizational Development Lewin (1951)
Process Summary	– Sensing unsatisfied need – Search for response invent or search for alternatives – Evaluation of alternatives – Decision to adopt – Initiation of action within the system – Implementation of changes – Institutionalization of changes	Events: – Evaluation Study & assess need for a new program – Initiation Try off-the-shelf idea – Implementation Deal with problems – Routinization Fine tune plan	Phases: – Unfreeze – Change – Refreeze Steps for each Phase: – Objectives from general to specific – Break old social ties & establish new ones – Heighten self-esteem – Move from external to internal motives

(Continued)

Process type	Program Planning Delbecq and Van de Ven (1971)	Corporate Planning Ackoff (1981)	Systems Engineering Churchman (1968; 1979)
Process Summary	Problem Exploration – Nominal group (NGT) – Competent clients – Identify critical problems Knowledge Exploration – NGT – Diverse experts – Identify solution requirements & resources (new, old) Priority Development – Presentation – Identify acceptable solutions & needed compromises Program Development – (Delegated) Control & Evaluation – Recheck solution validity – Test acceptability with clients	Formulating the Mess – Systems analysis – Obstruction analysis – Reference projections (Threats & opportunities considered) Ends Planning (desirable future specified) Means Planning (inventing ways to approximate the desired future) Resources Planning (identification of ways to obtain resources) Design of Implementation and Control (control of plans and planning)	Justification Plan System I/O Components Identification of the Decision Maker – Criteria – Rules of Thumb Organizational Design Group Planning – 1st stage goal – 2nd stage goal – Ultimate objective criterion – Estimate optimum Test – Stimulate – Control

(Continued)

TABLE 21.1 (*Continued*)

Process type	Systems Analysis USAF Systems command manuals	Ideals Nadler (1970; 1981)

Process
Summary
	Mission statement
	  – Problem recognition
	  – Initiation of planning
	  – Approval
	Concept
	  – <u>Basic</u>: goals, criteria
	  – <u>Feasible</u>: constraint components, system description
	  – Preliminary developmental plan
	  – Feasible system (gross requirement, resources, plan
	    management approval)
	Definition Phase
	(each subsystem)
	  – <u>Analyze alternative solutions</u>
	  – Operation requirement, interfaces
	  – Measure of effectiveness
	  – Select objectives
	  – Integrate
	  – Specify.system
	Integrate subsystems –
	Test Acquisition Phase
	  – Procure
	  – Detail design
	  – Monitor, test, start, train
	  – Procedures
	  – Installation plan
	  – Operational plan
	Operation
	  – Aid in operation
	  – User evaluation (modifications by site management)
		Process Steps:
		–Function determination
		  (establish hierarchy of objectives)
		– Definition of ideal system (use system matrix
		  to define system & iterate through process
		  elaborating the matrix as necessary)
		– Information
		– Alternatives
		– Select workable from ultimate
		– Formulate details
		– Review
		– Test
		– Install
		– Performance (generate norms & controls for
		  management strategy)

Process type	*Problem Solving* Havelock (1973)	*Engineering Design* Hall (1962)	*Cultural Revitalization* Wallace (1956)
Process Summary	– Promotion & awareness – Information & interest – Demonstration & evaluation – Training & trial – Assisting & installing – Serving & adoption – Nurturing & institutionalizing	– Problem definition – Objectives setting – Synthesis – Analysis – Optimization – Selection – Implementation	– Steady state – Cultural distortion – Revitalization and reformulation – Transformation – Routinization

Process type	*Creativity* Gordon (1971)	*Strategic Management* Ansoff (1984)	*Problem Solving* Lippitt et al. (1958)
Process Summary	– Preparation – Incubation – Illumination – Verification	Sub processes: Planning – Establish purposes, guidelines & strategy Implementation – Cause of organization to behave according to purpose, guidelines, & strategy Control – Evaluate performance	– Need – Development of relationships – Diagnosis – Intentions – Translation – Generalization & stabilization – Termination

(Continued)

TABLE 21.1 (*Continued*)

Process type	Innovation Zaltman et al. (1973)	Second Order Change Levy (1983)	Social Change Rodgers (1962)
Process Summary	Stages: Initiation – Knowledge awareness – Formation of attitude toward innovation – Decision Implementation – Initial – Continued – Sustained	– Decline – Transformation – Transition – Stabilization and development	– Awareness – Interest – Evaluation – Trial – Adoption

(*Continued*)

Process type	Decision Making Mintzberg et al. (1976)	Creative Design Archer (1982)	Artificial Science Simon (1969)
Process Summary	Phases & Routines: Identification	Given objectives and resources, design process:	Problem Milieu
	– Recognition	Analytic Phase	– Environment (fixed variable goals & arena)
	– Diagnosis	– Programming	– Sanctions
	Development	– Data collection	Search
	– Search and screen	– Observation	– Search resources
	– Design	– Measurement	– Partition solution space into acceptable states
	Selection	– Inductive reasoning	– Aspiration criteria
	– Judgment: evaluation and choice	Creative Phase	– Stopping rules
	– Analysis evaluation	– Analysis & synthesis	Problem Representation
	– Bargaining	– Identify	– Factoring & decomposition
	Authorization	performance laws, i.e. ways	rules (Partition where
	Supporting Routines	performance laws affect	interdependences
	– Control	goals	expected to be minimal).
	– Communication	– Identify constraints on design variables	– 'Laws of hierarchies'
	– Politics	– Establish prevailing environmental states	– Design of components
	Dynamic Factors	– Postulate states for each design variable	Evaluation
	– Interrupts	– Determine solutions satisfactory with client	– Satisfying, optimizing, level of aspiration
	– Delays	– Calculate index of merit	– Utility & criteria
	(scheduling, FB, timing, comprehension, failure)	– Select best alternative	– Resolution of conflict procedures
			Implementation (no discussion)

(*Continued*)

TABLE 21.1 (*Continued*)

Process type	Scientific Revolution Kuhn (1970)	Dissipating Structures Prigogine and Stengers (1984)	Historical Determinism Marx

Process
Summary
	– Normal Science
	– Growth of abnormalities
	– Crisis
	– Revolution
	– New Science within new paradigm
		– Fluctuations within defined
		  boundaries
		– Fluctuations that exceed
		  threshold
		– Crisis
		– Jump to higher order
			– Steady State
			– Growing dissatisfaction
			– Conflict
			– Revolution
			– New order

Backoff, 1992), or directions (Nutt, 2002). *Ideation* requires either adaptation or invention, via creativity and innovation enhancing techniques, to identify alternative courses of action (Van de Ven *et al.*, 1999: Van de Ven *et al.*, 2000). *Development* applies planning, systems approaches and the like, to detail the alternatives (Tsoukas and Chia, 2002: Nutt, 1992; Hamel and Prahalad, 1994; Miles and Snow, 1978). Alternatives are *evaluated* using tools that measure or simulate expected results to identify outcome consequences (Keeney and Raiffa, 1976; Nutt, 1989). *Choice* selects among alternatives by drawing on evaluations, using tactics that range from formal cost–benefit comparisons to impressionistic observations (Schendel and Hofer, 1979). *Implementation* considers how the organization's social fabric will be altered by a decision and provides ways to cope using position-power, cooptation, and unfreezing to secure an adoption (Nutt, 1986). *Control* monitors outcomes to ensure that institutionalization and routinization have occurred and to verify whether good results were realized (Beyer and Trice, 1978).

There are also notable differences. None of the processes in Table 21.1 requires stages that span intelligence, framing, option search, solution development, evaluation, implementation, *and* control (Nutt, 2003; 2004). Often, a subset is prescribed. This suggests that these processes are either incomplete or apply to the situation examined to derive them. Such short cuts seem efficient but may overlook actions essential for successful decision making. For example, systems processes stress development and ignore implementation, and social change processes do just the reverse. Proponents construct a new process by engaging in a new round of stage naming, or attempt to build a composite process with incomplete knowledge of relevant processes. These repeated attempts at process construction violate one of the cannons of science: building on the best work of others.

Steps within a process stage also differ. This is surprising because a given stage, such as framing, has clear-cut requirements. However, tactics recommended to carry out a process stage seem more diverse with each new process conception, with little evidence of an empirically based synthesis. This has left questions about the comparative value of approaches such as objectives, missions, visions, aims, ideals, and identity to carry out framing. Other key questions include the merits of identifying problems versus issues during intelligence gathering and whether adaptation and innovation resolve into similar procedures for solution finding.

Process differences also arise from the scope of an effort. Some decisions deal with 'translation' – a repair. The intent is to fix something that has malfunctioned or broken down, such as an automotive company that redesigns its line of cars hoping to arrest slumping profits. Broader scope efforts call for a 'transformation' – going beyond the boundaries found in current strategic arrangements (Nutt and Backoff, 1997). The automotive company could engage in vertical or horizontal integration, make its workers owners, or create an alliance with its suppliers to improve its profit position. Translational processes stay within the bounds set by a current strategy – cars as the source of revenue – to find what has broken down or is performing poorly, and fix it. Ignoring the boundaries set by its current strategy allows the automotive company to break away from old patterns and let new ones emerge, producing a transformation. Transformations create a new order and translations modify an existing order and each may require a different process.

A key research question deals with the comparative value of the decision-making processes suggested to date. Is there an ideal approach or will any map do? Others include the value of order or coherence in process activities, the merits of using multiple processes, and the influence of content, context, and situation on process results. Next, we will consider each of these process questions.

Ideal process

The process followed by a decision maker may be less important than content knowledge acquired from years of work experience, intellectual resources, or interpersonal skills (Weick, 1979). Master decision makers may have devised a variety of practices and each may work equally well. If so, the personal characteristics of a decision maker would be more important than process, making process a less important aspect of decision-making theory, and skill a more important one. Advocates of the processes in Table 21.1 implicitly argue *against* such a view, but offer little evidence to support this position. Few, other than Schon (1983; 1987), have watched expert practitioners to identify the processes they use and outcome consequences they realize. Comparisons of the procedures used by master decision makers with the procedures used by less skilled decision makers, doing the same task, suggests an important research topic.

Step coherence and sequencing

The staging of activity, found in Table 21.1, suggests that many process theorists advocate a coherent, orderly unfolding of activity. An alternate hypothesis would argue for trial and error or heuristics that stimulate the creativity of people, hoping for eureka-like solutions. The problem-solving literature (e.g. MacCrimmon and Taylor, 1976) favors heuristics and the planning and design literature (e.g. Simon, 1969; Nadler, 1981) systematic procedure. However, there is little agreement about the recommended staging of activity in either the planning literature or the problem-solving literature (Table 21.1). Research into the merit of using a systematic compared to heuristic procedure is rare, with inconclusive findings. There are also questions about the ordering of activity. The sequence question arises for both systematic and heuristic processes. Is it best to begin with implementation concerns or with intelligence and framing? The originators of the processes in Table 21.1 take various positions on this question, but do not offer empirical tests of the merits of particular sequences.

Multiple processes and content

The master decision maker may have invented several processes that can be applied interchangeably – suggesting that there are several equally acceptable ways to make a decision, and some to avoid. A 'hierarchy' hypothesis contends that one process is best and the 'heterarchy' hypothesis argues that several can be used with equally good results. Multiple ways of acting could be desirable but process developers in

Table 21.1 offer just one approach, suggesting that they reject such a claim. Some studies of experts imply that multiple routes can be taken to reach a goal (Kiesler and Sproull, 1982) and others advocate a single process (Pettigrew *et al.*, 2001), posing yet another important process research question.

A universal process has two implications. First, causality arguments contend that a single, best, outcome will be found for a given application of a master process and its recipe for action. Process research, however, seeks to uncover a producer-product relationship (Ackoff and Emery, 1972). Following a master process would increase the *likelihood* of a good outcome and allow for a range of outcomes with good features to result from a particular process, but does not guarantee success. An 'equifinality hypothesis' contends that a good outcome is equally likely if one of several preferred processes is followed. Any of these preferred processes would produce outcomes with desirable features. Second, a universal process that sweeps in decision making, strategy, learning, and many other related topics may be so general that that it is too removed from the content of a decision. However, a universal process may offer a framework to pose useful questions. This suggests a double-tier approach in which content-dictated considerations enter in the second phase. On the other hand, a three-tiered approach may be required with the type of decision (translation or transformation), followed by heuristics or formal process selections, and then decision topic, such as acquiring financial inputs or personnel selection, to suggest what steps to follow.

Content bounding

Differences in process stages within a school of thought, such as problem solving and system analysis, seem just as great as differences among the schools (Table 21.1). This suggests that different phenomena may have been observed under special conditions to uncover these processes. By sorting out the conditions, a coherent pattern may emerge. If so, the phenomenon addressed may influence process by altering the staging of activity and steps within a stage. A content-bounded hypothesis calls for special purpose processes. If process is content-free, a generic process is feasible and may be desirable.

Content-bounding poses several questions. For instance, should process be treated as special or general purpose? Are there process groupings around themes that should be maintained? Can decision makers transport a general process to other applications; can a decision-making process be used to carry out change? Similarly, the interchangeability of processes, such as social change and systems engineering, and special processes designed for a specific application, such as morale building, merits study. Prescriptions are often made by generalizing from one use to another without considering likely results. For instance, the stages of a decision model have been used to suggest steps for performance appraisal (e.g. identify the problem, suggest alternatives, and obtain compliance). These generalizations seem reasonable but have such importance that the adaptation merits formal study.

Situational influences

Contingency theory calls for a decision-making process to be selected according to situational features, such as urgency (Vroom, 1973; Daft, 1995). This kind of contingency argument has developed considerable following in the management literature, being applied to leadership (Fiedler, 1971), implementation (Lippitt *et al.*1958), and strategic management (Nutt and Backoff, 1992), among others. Given how long and how forcefully contingency arguments have been advocated one would expect ample empirical support for situational dependence. Surprisingly, such support is rare. Before contingency arguments become institutionalized, research must show that master decision makers using a process matched to a particular task realize better results than using a generic process. Research that has approached this question finds little evidence that the typical manager has a repertoire, let alone uses it contingently (Nutt, 2002). Considering master decision makers may yield a different conclusion.

Scope

The process stages recommended for translation and those offered to make a transformation appear to differ (Table 21.1). This poses a key question: should a radical decision be carried out differently than a translational one? There are some striking similarities in processes called for to produce a radical change. Transformation is said to occur in stages that are similar to scientific revolutions, evolutionary change in biology, human growth and development, and changes in organizational culture (Giddens, 1979; Pribram, 1983; Kuhn, 1970). Do similarities among processes with a transformational purpose signify a 'deep structure' to a transformational process? This question is fundamental to developing decision-making theory. To understand transformational decision making we may need to understand and see the parallels in many kinds of radical change, such as those found in cultures or scientific communities as their world view shifts. These analogies may offer powerful metaphors to build and test process theories that contrast the transformational with the translational process.

THEORETICAL SUPPORT FOR PROCESS

Many recent theoretical developments point to the importance of process. Emerging ideas in sociology, biology, physics, cosmology, psychology, and systems argue that failing to deal with process will lead to incomplete and misleading understandings (Table 21.2). Each uses process to explain the underlying action taking and suggests ways to approach process research. Structuration, morphogenesis, autopoiesis, dialectics, and implicate order are considered to uncover the insights each offers into process.

Structuration contends that structure is reproduced through action (Giddens, 1979). Managers who accept authority limits in their decisions reproduce and validate these limits. If slavishly followed, authority limits become reified, evolving into

TABLE 21.2 Applications that call for process.

Theory	Field	Premise
Structuration (Giddens, 1979)	Sociology	Structuration (process) occurs whenever action is taken (or not taken) which continuously alters a structure
Morphogenesis (Buckley, 1968)	Biology	Instructions for change are encoded in an organism that produce favorable or unfavorable adaptations
Autopoiesis (Varela, 1979)	Biology	Organisms are self-referencing and produce change by interacting with the environment
Cybernetics two (Maruyama, 1983)	Systems	Negative feedback as well as positive feedback (difference enhancing processes) create transformations
Dialectics (Mason and Mitroff, 1981)	Planning	Change stems from a tension between opposites
Change Logistics (Morgan, 1986; 1998; 1993)	Organization theory	Flux in action taking causes a network of reactions and contradictions
Trialectics (Ichazo, 1982)	Logic	Transformations follow mutation, circulation, and attraction loops embodied as tensions between contradictions or opposites

rigid rules for decision making. When authority limits are ignored, the authority structure decays. Action creates events that shape future action forcing all structures, such as formal authority, to evolve. Because both rule adherence and rule avoidance create patterns, process becomes the key to understanding these patterns. Structure (a decision) tends to be dynamic and evolving. This argues for decision-making research to concentrate on the temporal aspects that capture the flow of action in a sea of constraints. The interplay of action with constraints, such as moral frameworks that legitimize tradition and rules, would be studied over time (Schwartz, 1991). Kairos (peak experience) time seems to be crucially important; documenting what was being done as insight emerges (Nutt, 2004).

Morphogenesis (Buckley, 1968) is used by biologists to explain the development of organisms. There may be similarities between the learning required for decision making and biological evolution. A change in physical structure and change in symbolic codes as the manager makes a decision may have useful analogies into the evolution of a higher order of understanding and devolution with a loss of understanding. Instructions encoded in an organism are altered by random processes that yield better or poorer adapted species. The better adapted organisms (master decision makers) survive, making time the means to understand this process. Time seems crucial to understanding decision making as well. By denoting when evolution is active, key features of the process may be traceable. Action, practice, and time are key elements in documenting a process (Archer, 1976).

Action would document how decision makers cope with limits in their freedom to act. To deal with action taking, process documentation would show how decision makers recognize and deal with limits in their role, resources, etc. Process captures sets of activities carried out by decision makers to take action (Mintzberg, 1975). Time must be considered to see this ordering. Morphogenesis suggests that evolution is inherent in all human activity. So people in a decision-making role must learn, grow, and adapt to new circumstances. The adaptation changes both decision maker and the practice of decision making, calling for researchers to uncover the steps undertaken as a decision maker learns.

Autopoietic systems are autonomous and closed. Attempts to introduce external factors stem from a researcher who explains what is observed from his/her external perspective, not from the viewpoint of the observed (Varela, 1976; 1979). An image of self is the dominate frame of reference making in an autopoietic system's self-referencing. For example, a decision maker is seen as autonomous and closed, striving to maintain his/her identity as challenges are encountered. The acts of a decision maker result from interactions with the environment in which the decision maker attempts to maintain his/her identity. Looking at an artificial boundary, such as the environment of a firm, would hide how the maintenance of self is bound up in the maintenance of co-evolving relationships with many important stakeholders. Decisions alter a decision maker's identity modifying his/her norms to account for the new circumstances (Quinn, 1996). The potential for change resides inside the system (decision maker) not outside. Perceived needs or opportunities suggest a need to shift one's norms. The prospect of success depends on whether the decision maker dampens these signals or amplifies them, allowing a new configuration to emerge. For example, a decision maker may fail to take into account shifts in technology or taste that can render a product decision obsolete. Other decision makers may act on their environment by changing their identity to account for recognized environment shifts. Some identities are enduring, others not. To uncover process, researchers study decision makers and interpret what they do. Self-referencing calls for an understanding of a decision maker's cognitions as well as their behavior (Simon, 1982). To locate the emergence of a decision, search for the point where a new identity emerged. Studies of what decision makers do and how they interpret their actions during an identity shift offer insights into the process of decision making. A decision is made when a decision maker either rejects or opens up to new experiences and ideas. Because the change is organism-specific, the decision maker becomes the focus of inquiry.

Dialectics contends that an emerging decision will create opposition. One defines and may even give rise to the other. To illustrate, control gives a decision meaning and the decision gives meaning to control. The tension enriches both definitions. Hegel and Marx apply these notions to societal change, contending that tension between opposites is the precursor to change. For instance, organizations impose control to preserve a decision, such as a strategic alliance, until that control becomes untenable and the decision structure (the alliance) gives way, being replaced by another, often derived in part from the old alliance. The act of control (attempting to maintain the alliance) provokes forces opposing control (new alliance opportunities), giving rise to negation that tries to reject the old alliance.

Challenges to decisions that have granted huge CEO salaries and perquisites (which continue long after the CEO has been ousted) in the face of plant closings and people being laid off contain the seeds of a new approach to CEO compensation. Executives and pay policies enter and exit, slowly altering the social fabric that makes up the underpinnings of an organization. Process describes how these decision structures give way one to the other. Successive stages of tensions, challenges, and change occur repeatedly and give rise to processes, such as control and resistance, in the organization. Process is the key to understanding how such tensions form and grow as action and counter-action take place. Break points, at which a new decision structure emerges, capture our attention but the new decision structure stems from a series of time-ordered antecedent events that must be understood to see how the decision came about.

Tensions are found in all organizations. Dialectics argues that a decision results when tensions reach a critical level (Watzlawick *et al.*, 1974). Because a tension has mutually causal elements, it cannot be understood as push causality (Mohr, 1982). A decision structure describing a pay policy has in it the seeds of its own modification. The more rigid the pay policy, the stronger the opposing forces it evokes. The resolution of these forces creates a new decision structure, producing new forms of opposition. This process reveals the forces at work to realize a decision. An analysis of tensions, both historic and current, provide a way to capture these forces, seeking to understand how and under what conditions the decision was made (Nutt *et al.*, 2000). For example, the way a master decision maker reframes tensions to pose a win-win structure that deals with the contradictions inherent in the tensions may be a key ingredient in successful decision making (Johnson, 1992). Unmanaged tensions lead to entropy in which diminished effort and loss of focus often lead to failure (Quinn, 1996).

Several applications of dialectics have been suggested. Peters and Waterman (1982) identified the paradox of simultaneous delegation and centralization in well-run companies. The tension between loose and tight control is managed by delegating job execution deep into the ranks while insisting that core values, such as service or quality, are present in all of the actions of managers. Kolb (1983) calls on leaders to engage in a form of tension management as a precursor to transformation. The vitality and success of organizations, in Kolb's view, depend on 'doing the right thing', issue surfacing, as well as doing things right – applying a best-practice process. Issue identification is characterized by a tension between rational and intuitive modes of understanding that has wave-like expansions and contractions to integrate competing ideas. Nutt and Backoff (1993) find that core values of transition, control, productivity, and equity combine to create six generic tensions (transition-control, transition-productivity, transition-equity, control-productivity, control-equity, and productivity-equity) that arise as organizational leaders make decisions. A decision maker who looks for each type of tension and then manages them realizes better results (Nutt, 2002). Pascale (1990),

Hampden-Turner (1990), and Johnson (1992) also find the recognition and successful management of tensions to be the key to success.

Ichazo (1982) offers trialectics as a way to visualize how a transformational decision flows from successive mutations, circulations, and attractions. A mutation (the transformational decision) occurs when a system moves from one state to another. Circulation holds that opposing forces will always be at work in a system. Each force will seed an opposing force and form a dialectic. Attraction leads to state changes as the system moves to a higher or a lower level. Process facilitates this motion. Transition states provide labels that capture our attention, similar to a decision structure. Mutations depict the history of a transformational decision. The process behind a decision is inferred from past states of a system, such as an individual that is learning or an organization that is evolving. In ideation, relevant states are puzzlement and knowing. The attractive and active elements of the ideation process give insight into flow. In the issue surfacing example, the attractive element is the need to know or understand and the active element is the human mind. Mutation (a decision) occurs when the mind jumps from not knowing to knowing – a eureka solution.

Circulation processes capture tensions as opposing forces, views, and explanations that contain seeds of the other, but exist independently. The process observer is urged to look for what prompts a balancing that leads to equilibrium. Searches are mounted for cycles that connect apparent opposites. In trialectics, effective decision making calls for the systematic examination of tensions to produce win-win solutions, responses that manage the tension. This view is similar to learning to learn (Argyris and Schon, 1978). Tension is produced by the results of an assessment that can be used to learn and to reflect on how insights were obtained, which leads to new ways to learn. Similar ideas can be found in Osborn's (1953) green light-red light in brainstorming, the divergence-convergence steps of Guilford (Guilford and Hoepfner, 1971), separating ideation and evaluation (Delbecq and Van de Ven, 1971), and Levy's first and second-order planned change (Levy and Merry, 1986). Each attempts to grasp reality by noting concrete experiences and then transform this reality by extending it to new circumstances. Tension between the rational and intuitive ways of knowing is consistent with the work of many recognized philosophers, such as Dewey (1910). Kolb's (1983) learning styles and Quinn's (1996) competing values framework also use tension to facilitate understanding.

In trialectics, transformational decisions offering radical change result from attractions that provide the force needed to ascend to a higher level. Quinn's (1995) cycles of excellence argument, in which organizations move to higher levels of understanding, is similar to the attraction process in trialectics. In both, a loss in energy and a descent to lower levels of understanding is also possible. The emergent state becomes attractive compared to the old state, causing an attempted transition. State changes in a focal system have a hierarchical ordering, with the higher level state possessing fewer constraints. The insightful transformational decision maker has more options than operating by tradition and imitation. A decision maker can have an ordered set of responses to particular situations that are in a continuous state of flux. These responses can degrade or evolve to higher levels of understanding. In the same way, an organization has its complexity increased or decreased by the networking activities of its executives, which leads to increased or diminished awareness (Nutt, 2001; 2004). An ascent to a higher level implies that decision makers had greater vision enabling them to see further with fewer preconceptions. As decision makers' understanding grows they have fewer illusions, beliefs, and SOPs. In this way, process becomes the modeling of attractions for ascent or descent among states of a system. To capture such a process, system states must be specified as well as the likelihood of entering each state. The state transitions are time dependent and may depend on contextual factors triggered by environmental conditions.

Trialectics offer a way to visualize a transformational decision-making process with circulation, attraction, and mutation (Voorhees, 1983). Circulation captures the equilibrium that precedes action in which the forces favoring the decision are balanced with those calling for maintenance of existing arrangements. Elements of, for instance, a transformational strategy would be examined to extract the contradictions produced by the current strategy of the organization. The apparent opposite of a firm's current markets suggests new ones. Cycles in which opposites are connected suggest key internal and contextual factors that maintain stability. Attractions identify potentials to act arranged according to the energy that each contains. Higher levels have fewer restrictions, such as greater decision-maker discretion, and lower levels greater restrictions, such as programmed decision making with SOPs. Transitions occur at the limits of a control system's power to maintain a practice, such as a current strategy. The transition recreates new order (a new strategy) which is built on the old. A mutation (a transformational decision) occurs when the attractive factors, such as perceptions of opportunity, are seen as manageable, allowing new states, a new strategy, to be visualized. When the attractive forces and the potential to act are both seen favorably, a transformational decision can occur, which is described in likelihood terms. Skillful decision makers may take steps to frame attractive forces in a favorable light, making the decision seem doable and desirable, providing the impetus for its adoption.

Bohm (1978) provides a way to uncover the process prompting circulation, attraction, and mutation. A decision stems from a process that is hidden but can be decoded by uncovering the implicate order imbedded in an observed explicate order. Consider an example (Bohm, 1980). Oil is dropped into a round container of glucose. The container is then rotated a one-quarter turn, repeating until oil has been placed at each of the four compass points. Viewing the container at any point in time shows one droplet, two smudges, and one clear compass point in the container. By rotating the container (process) the nature of the structure (location) of the oil droplets becomes understandable. Rotation reveals the oil droplets changing into smudges, disappearing, emerging again as a smudge, before reappearing. Viewing this structure at a point in time, the explicate order, reveals little about the process that created it. The process remains implicate until time-based viewing is applied, which proves a means to decode how it was generated. To apply this idea, note how key decisions of CEOs have been depicted in the literature (Land and Jarman, 1992; Tichy and Devanna, 1986). The decision is described, such as Carlzon's (1987) 'moments of truth', but not the means used to devise the 'moments of truth' idea, or how to apply it. As with the structure of oil droplets, describing Carlzon's decision reveals little about how he devised it or applied it effectively. An implicate order must be decoded to see how the observed action was discovered and carried out.

Implicate order produces the explicate order seen in organizations. An example can be found in decisions to select leaders, such as superintendents of a school system, that alternate back and forth from styles of 'stroking' to 'standing and shaking.' What underlying dynamic or implicate order produces leader decisions that select people who alternate between pacifier and dictator? Would not the leadership selection literature benefit from an investigation of the implicate order in which leader decision criteria are periodically dropped and then restored? The explicate order – who was selected and what were his/her characteristics – says little about this, but dominates much of what is offered in this literature. As this example points out, observing a decision structure or explicate order identifies an idiosyncratic instance. Codifying this instance reveals little about how the observed decision structure got that way or how it will change. Process is lost in the codification. To understand the decision, the implicit processes at work must be decoded. This calls for unfolding the implicate order embedded in decisions that produce a transformation, strategy, or leader selection to see how transformation, strategy, or leader evolves. The explicate order is made up of objects and events that occupy specific locations in space and time. To concentrate on this misses the deeper reality in which there is a potential yet to be realized. Explicate phenomena appearing in the foreground may be disappearing in the background.

An understanding of the movement between implicate and explicate orders is required to do decision-making process research. Flow can be thought of as the generative mechanism that gives rise to the explicate – the observed decision structure (Quinn, 1996). Time must be considered to capture flow, alternatively viewing with a microscope and then a macroscope to catch the implicate order. A hologram suggests how skilled action may be encoded for purposeful use (Pribram, 1983). Such coding stores a pattern that is unfolded as skill is drawn upon to take action. As skill is applied, there is an unfolding – the way that a movie of ripples in a lake, run in reverse, can identify a pebble as the cause of the ripple pattern (Ravn, 1986). The structure, surface features of the lake, says little about what caused the ripples. The origin of the structure becomes clear when it can be linked to the enfolded order, the process. For example, consider a master decision maker with many successes. To isolate the process used by such a decision maker the researcher would attempt to identify key events and link them in a sequence so they can be run forward or backward like a movie to look for what produced each success.

To uncover such decision-making practice necessitates a focus on flux, the flow of events, looking for what was crucial to success. Dive into this flow in a high performing organization to see who does what. Look for creep, slippage, and drift that prompt adaptations and variations that hold back a decision and then for a breakpoint that signals an opportunity and a possible conquest. Master decision makers are predicted to weave and then re-weave their beliefs and habits into a proposed decision, as predicted by autopoiesis in which a decision maker is driven to maintain his/her identity. This makes the decision maker the unit of analysis when looking for process. Determining the decision maker's identity in the before and after states reveals process triggers and brackets things. Structuration suggests that the decision maker's actions will either erode or reify current practices. Erosion facilitates a decision and reification restrains it. In morphogenesis, erosion actions would play out over time to evolve a new decision structure. The stream of actions in this evolution captures key events in a decision-making process. Dialectics and trialectics suggest how new identities emerge. Tensions that circulate in an organization challenge the old identity and open up a decision maker to new possibilities. When the equilibrium is upset, a balance point shifts to signal an important event. Such events can be hard to spot because of their implicate properties. To capture implicate order, and reveal its generative mechanism, requires a time-based viewing of unfolding events at an optimum distance.

DOING PROCESS RESEARCH

According to James (1998), the best way to study a religious experience is to observe a pious man during an inspirational moment. This argues for a focus on master practitioners (decision makers) during a period of peak performance. The focus on peak experience calls for Kairos time. Capturing a peak experience poses many challenges and calls for new ways to think about doing process research. Two thoughts are offered – one concerning perspective and the other process research standards.

Perspective

The master decision maker, like a storyteller, may construct action and cognition landscapes. The action specifies agents, intentionality, situation, and instrument. Knowing or thinking about a decision occurs through cognition. This link between the narrative (process) and rationale (decision structure) is enfolded in the story. Bruner (1986) points out that a master storyteller unfolds state disturbances, crises, and redress to produce a new state open to possibilities. A great tale has closure and engages the reader or listener to pursue 'what if' speculations about the next series of events.

The analogy to storytelling suggests that both action and cognition landscapes merit study in decision-making process research. A telescoping of time, or Kairos time, is needed to capture salient events. Plot is the ordering of events, from which we become aware of what has happened. The reader is transformed by the presentation, the way a master decision maker unfolds events to entice subordinates to take action. The order is captured by meaning producing anecdotes.

Having several people read a book is similar to conducting a longitudinal study. Each captures initial conditions or background, showing how a situation is rendered, resulting in multiple viewing. The observer/reader looks for triggering events that define a prepositional background and motives for action. These events set the stage and identify stimuli. Examples include perceived errors, extent errors that are recognized, failed attempts to resolve or remove a problem, and conclusions about these acts. To illustrate: a decision maker may perceive an inequity in a bonus system – high performers seem to be rewarded much like low performers. This discrepancy may not be widely recognized, calling for factual presentations. Past attempts to change the bonus system suggest what is and is not feasible.

Like the master storyteller, the skilled decision maker uses 'subjectification' to engage an engine of action. The decision maker imagines what an alternative, plausible, future might be. This future attends to value obligations, how to achieve desire ends, depicting when one must act or demur, time markings that specify the pace of change, and circumstances under which claims hold. The skillful rendering of these factors using a series of anecdotes creates a story. If the story is gripping and believable it offers the listener a way to fill in knowledge gaps to infer consequences and intentions. This construction may differentiate the master decision maker from others. The story or process seems to be the key to recognizing the plight – unequal distribution – and how plight and distribution interact to produce new policies for change, such as decisions leading to tax reform legislation.

Finally, great stories illuminate events from several perspectives, suggesting that a master decision maker takes in multiple views of the world with a multifaceted prism to refract various interpretations. Supportive views are reinforced and opposing views are dampened by the story which makes certain conclusions obvious, but not too obvious, from the context. The master decision maker when confronted with an issue may offer a parable that implicitly indicates what is good, valued, acceptable, and desirable.

To study this calls for the process researcher to adopt the approach of a historian. Historians use the barest of facts to construct the intentions of key actors and speculate on their world views. Constructions can be flawed by fact omissions and mistaken motivations, much the way reconstructive studies rely on memory traces and recall. A study of decisions may have to embrace the historians' approach, with all of the attendant problems of repeatability, to identify the generative mechanism in a peak experience. Some distinctions in the study of process and structure appear in Table 21.3.

Standards

A specialized version of logical positivism, based on contradiction and falsification, has evolved widely accepted standards, first offered by Campbell and Stanley (1966) and expanded upon by Cook and Campbell (1979) and others (Nutt, 1982). Imposing traditional standards of reliability and validity is misleading and insufficient in process studies. Other ways to determine the trustworthiness of findings are required.

Lincoln and Guba (1985) and Denzin and Lincoln (1994) replace internal validity with credibility. To demonstrate credibility, data is collected in field settings where a process of interest unfolds. Observers are positioned to observe how the process operates and take steps to check what they think they have observed. This calls for contact with natural settings and testing by comparing what has been observed by an investigator with the observations of other informants. Attempts are made to observe a process at the best distance, using several frames of reference. Observing at an optimum distance calls for the researcher to find a window with a 'resolution' that allows beginnings, endings, and key intervening events to be seen. To observe, several frames of reference are employed that use multiple and different sources, methods, investigators, and theories to represent the process.

TABLE 21.3 Distinctions in the study of structure and process

Key Features	Structure	Process
Components	The nature of an object	Means of producing the object
Theory Development	Precepts: 1. Efficient causation 2. Push causality 3. Understanding the past 4. Cause and effect	Precepts: 1. Probabilistic outcome 2. Pull causality 3. Prediction of future 4. Producer and product
Modes of Study	Statistical cross-sections	Longitudinal case study
Treatment of Time	Time invariant	Time dependent (use Chronos time to discover Kairos time)
Nature of Phenomena	Hierarchical Mechanical Linearly causal Assembly	Heterarchical Holographic Mutually causal Evolutionary
Standards	Internal validity External validity Reliability Objectivity	Credibility Transferability Dependability Confirmability
Interpretation	Nomothetic	Ideographic

Distance and frame of reference dictums provide ideals. Like the standards for internal validity, these requirements are seldom fully met (Morgan, 1986). Each is explored to determine its relevance to a given process and the insights that it provides in how to view. Then a search is mounted to find clever ways to observe and frame the process under study. Unmet standards become weaknesses that identify limitations when interpreting findings.

Triangulation improves credibility. To triangulate, agreement is sought among the representations of multiple observers, respondents, data sources (e.g. interview and archive documents), modes of measurement, and theories. Whenever possible, unobtrusive or trace measurers (Webb *et al.*, 1981) are used in conjunction with the interview, questionnaire, etc. Convergence among several theories, views, sources, critiques, and measures improve the prospect that the process has been captured, making the process observations credible.

External validity is replaced by transferability to denote the time and context in which results hold. This asks if the process description and a new context of application are sufficiently similar to export the findings. 'Sufficiently' entails a judgment. Transferability is applied in the same way as external validity. Both rely on judgment to determine if findings appear to extend to a new context. The dictum that validity follows reliability is paralleled by dependability leads to credibility. To establish dependability case splitting and audits can be used. Case splitting, for example, would divide a set of decision cases into two groups. One set of decision cases is analyzed to develop a process description and the other set of cases is fit to the process uncovered, identifying misfits and missing features. The process description is altered to account for discrepancies in the second set of decision cases. Audits examine how the process description was created to uncover the equivalent of 'creative accounting' – forcing the data to fit a preconceived pattern in the description. The audit determines if the process offers a credible representation of the data and whether the description can be supported by corroborating evidence. The audit verifies the dependability of the steps taken to describe a master decision-making process and its product.

Data and their interpretation link dependability to confirmability. Process studies focus on the quality of observations or testimony instead of quantitative indices. A standard of confirmability is applied (Lincoln and Guba, 1985; Denzin and Lincoln, 1994). Perspective rather than objectivity is sought. Perspective viewing takes place at a distance, with a particular focus, and uses multiple means, such as several disciplinary foci. If these perspectives converge, a powerful statement supporting confirmability can be made.

Confirmability is based on reproducing observations and inferences. Audits and triangulation are used. The audit (Halpren, 1983) examines the veracity of a process description, following the data trail used by an investigator. The trace begins with raw data, such as notes, moves to data reduction (e.g. qualitative summaries of stages and steps), then to salient categories, and finally to a process description (the inference). Triangulation applies multiple sources of information and interpretation (independent observers) in an attempt to reproduce the process description. Triangulation is strengthened when these observations stem from unique disciplines or different points of view. The audit verifies the confirmability of the data and triangulation the confirmability of the results.

The interpretation of master decision-making process research tends to be idiographic (case particular) unless a substantial number of decision cases can be collected, with the attendant cost and time demands. An inference is drawn from the particulars of the case or cases from which a process description is drawn. A process inference finds connections among components to identify a pattern.

IMPLICATIONS

Process is a missing ingredient in the construction of decision-making theory. Excluding process has left this theory incomplete. For example, contending that decisions accrete over time (Weick, 1979) merely poses new questions. Do events unfold by accident, habit, personal preference, or expediency as Cohen *et al.* (1972) contend or is there an enfolded order in the actions of master decision makers? And, is accretion a good thing or a bad thing? To answer such questions calls for researchers to study master decision makers during moments of peak performance. This kind of process understanding will move decision-making theory from a descriptive to a prescriptive science, aligning it with engineering and medicine.

The process gives practitioners maps from which to pick, given circumstances and needs.

Structuration, morphogenesis, autopoiesis, dialectics, trialectics, and implicate order suggest ways to look for peak experience in time-ordered activities that unfold as a decision is made. The flow of action is captured by applying a morphogenic view of adaptation and survival, an autopoietic and a structuration interpretation of a master decision maker's actions, a dialectical view of tensions and their management, adding trialectics to capture the mutation and implicate order to uncover how process is enfolded in the observed decision structure. Each offers a piece of the puzzle that shows how master decision makers take action. A synthesis of these ideas suggests several exciting new avenues for decision-making process research.

Consider how leaders replace egocentric interpretations of what they see in the environment with decisions that offer visions of paths to achieve new ends. The ability to image an opportunity, rather than a threat, may be a hallmark of the master decision maker. Master decision makers may be able to see networks of relations at key nodes in a structure that must be altered if change is to occur. To make an important decision, the master decision maker may conceptualize win-win solutions that manage contradictions expressed as tensions between opposing camps or points of view (Nutt *et al.*, 2000). This can be visualized as imaging and then exploiting a web of relationships that form alliances based on deference and dominance. Master decision makers must work in a constant state of distracted tension, as if they were caught in an elastic web of attractions and repulsions. This network of relations is in perpetual motion, reacting to disturbances by dampening or expanding them. A master decision maker may be able to visualize this web, and where it can be stretched, better than others do. Decisions may be found in the re-weaving of a master decision maker's beliefs and approaches to action taking to accommodate an emergent identity. There may be an incremental response to slippage, creep, and drift, dampening them until a moment of action emerges in which a new identity can be imaged and acted upon. To facilitate such a breakout, one must see these tensions. This goes beyond ends arguments to deeper issues that lead to appreciation (Vickers, 1965).

Finding the enfolded order in the mind of the master decision maker is the key to documenting process. For example, does the master decision maker create scenarios of possibilities and then trace pathways to pick one to pursue? Are master decision makers continuously modifying what they do, with several theories-in-action (Argyris and Schon, 1978)? Do they adjust their vision by its apparent acceptance to stakeholders (Lindblom, 1965)? Do they use multiple routines in a flexible manner, gaming situations like a chess master (Simon and Newell, 1970)? All these explanations may hold to one degree or another. A synthesis may provide an even more accurate picture of the decision-making process. Furthermore, these approaches may be idiosyncratic or they may work for anyone once codified. Decision makers may be able to learn from others or decision makers may have to evolve approaches that fit their skills, beliefs, and needs. Finding that skill is idiosyncratic would suggest that decision making is an art and should be taught through creativity techniques.

Notes

1. This chapter is adapted from: Nutt, P.C., (2004) On doing process research, *International Journal of Management Concepts and Philosophy*, 1 (1), 3–26; from Nutt, P.C. (2003) Implications for organizational change in the structure process duality, *Research in Organizational Change and Development*, JAI Press, 14, 147–194; and from a presentation made at the strategic management symposium of the Academy of Management's national conference in Denver, Colorado, August 2001.

References

Ackoff, R. (1981) *Creating the Corporate Future.* New York: John Wiley & Sons, Inc.

Ackoff, R., and Emery, F. (1972) *On Purposeful Systems.* New York: Aldine-Atherton.

Ansoff, H.I. (1984) *Implanting Strategic Management.* Englewood Cliffs, NJ: Prentice Hall International.

Archer, L.B. (1976) Systematic methods for designers, *Design*, 173–176.

Archer, M. (1982) Morphogenesis versus structuration, *British Journal of Sociology*, XXXIII, 455–483.

Argyris, C., and Schon, D.A. (1978) *Organizational Learning: A Theory of Action Perspective*, Reading, MA: Addison-Wesley.

Armstrong, J.S. (1982) The value of strategic planning for formal decisions: Review of empirical evidence, *Strategic Journal*, 3, 197–212.

Barley, S. (1986) Technology as an occasion for structuring: Evidence from observations of CT scanners and the social order of radiology departments, *Administrative Science Quarterly*, 31, 78–108.

Beyer, J.M., and Trice, H.M. (1978) *Implementing Changes: Alcoholism policies in Work organizations.* New York: The Free Press.

Bohm, D. (1978) The implicate order: A new order for physics, *Process Studies*, 8 (2), 73–102.

Bohm, D. (1980) *Wholeness and Implicate Order*, London: UK: Rutledge and Kegan-Paul.

Bruner, J. (1986) 'Two Modes of Thought', Chapter 2, in *Actual Minds, Possible Worlds.* Cambridge, MA: Harvard University Press.

Buckley, W. (1968) *Modern Systems Research for the Behavioral Scientist.* Chicago: Aldine.

Burns, T. and Stalker, G.M. (1961) *The Management of Innovation.* London: Tavistock.

Butler, R. (1998) 'Strategic Decision-Making: A Contingency Framework and Beyond', in V. Papadakis and P. Barwise (eds) *Strategic Decisions.* Boston, MA: Kluwer.

Cameron, K. (1995) 'Quality, Downsizing, and Performance', in R. Cole (ed.) *The Death and Life of the American Quality Movement.* New York: Oxford University Press, 93–114.

Campbell, D.T., and Stanley, J.C. (1966) *Experimental and Quasi-Experimental Designs for Research.* Chicago: Rand McNally.

Carlzon, J. (1987) *Moments of Truth.* New York: Ballinger.

Churchman, C.W. (1968) *The Systems Approach.* New York: Basic Books.

Churchman, C.W. (1979) *The Systems Approach and Its Enemies.* New York: Basic Books.

Cohen, M.D., March, J.P., and Olsen, J.P. (1972) A garbage can model of organizational choice, *Administrative Science Quarterly*, 17, 1–25.

Collins, B., and Guetzkow, H.A. (1964) *A Social Psychology of Group Process for Decision Making.* New York: John Wiley & Sons, Inc.

Cook, T.D., and Campbell, D.T. (1979) *Quasi-Experimentation: Design and Analysis Issues for Field Settings.* Chicago: Rand McNally.

Covey, S.R. (1989) *The Seven Habits of Highly Effective Leaders.* New York: Simon and Schuster.

Cyert, R.M., and March, J.G. (1964) *A Behavioral Theory of the Firm.* Englewood Cliffs, NJ: Prentice Hall: .

Daft, R. (1995) *Organization Theory and Decision,* St Paul, MN: West Publishing Co.

Daft, R., and Weick, K. (1984) Toward a model of organizations as interpretation systems, *Academy of Management Review,* 9 (2), 284–295.

Delbecq, A., and Van de Ven, A. (1971) A group process model for problem identification and program planning, *Journal of Applied Behavioral Science,* 7 (4), 466–492.

Denzin, N., and Lincoln, Y. (1994) *Handbook of Qualitative Research.* Thousand Oaks, CA: Sage.

Dewey, J. (1910) *How We Think.* Lexington, MA: Heath.

Digman, L. (1997) *Strategic Management Cases,* Houston, TX: Dame.

Eisenhardt, K. and Zbaracki, M. (1992) Strategic decision making, *Strategic Management,* 13, 217–237.

Eveland, J., Rogers, E., and Klepper, A. (1977) *The Diffusion of Innovation Project.* Ann Arbor, MI: CRUSK, The Center for Research Utilization of Scientific Knowledge.

Fiedler, F.E. (1967) *A Theory of Leader Effectiveness.* New York: McGraw Hill.

Fiedler, F.E. (1971) Validation and extension of the contingency model of leader effectiveness, *Psychological Bulletin,* 26, 128–148.

Giddens, A. (1979) *Central Problems in Social Theory: Action, Structure and Contradiction in Social Analysis.* London: Macmillan.

Gordon, W.J.J. (1971) *Synetics.* New York: Harper and Row.

Guilford, J.P., and Hoepfner, R. (1971) *The Analysis of Intelligence.* Toronto: McGraw-Hill.

Habermas, J. (1971) *Towards a Rational Society.* London: Heinemann.

Hackman, J.R. (1990) *Groups that Work (and Those that Don't): Creating Conditions for Effective Teamwork.* San Francisco, CA: Jossey-Bass.

Hage, J. (1965) An axiomatic theory of organizations, *Administrative Science Quarterly,* 10, 289–320.

Hage, J., and Aiken, M. (1970) *Social Change in Complex Organizations.* New York: Random House.

Hall, A.D. (1962) *A Methodology for Systems Engineering,* New York: Nostrand.

Hall, R.H. (1963) The concept of bureaucracy; An empirical assessment, *American Journal of Sociology,* 69, 32–40.

Halpren, E.S. (1983) Auditing Naturalistic Inquiries. Unpublished Doctoral Dissertation, Indiana University.

Hamel, G., and Prahalad, C.K. (1994) Competing for the future, *Harvard Business Review,* July–August, 122–128.

Hampden-Turner, C.M. (1990) *Charting the Corporate Mind.* New York: The Free Press.

Harmon, M.M. (1980) *Action Theory for Public Administration.* New York, Longmont.

Havelock, R.G. (1973) *Planning for Innovation.* Ann Arbor, Michigan: CRUSK, The Center for Utilization of Scientific Knowledge (fourth printing).

Hickson, D., Butler, R., Gray, D., Mallory, G., and Wilson, D. (1986) *Top Decisions: Strategic Decision Making in Organizations.* San Francisco, CA: Jossey-Bass.

Hitt, M., Ireland, D., and Hoskisson, R. (1997) *Strategic Management.* St Paul, MN: West.

Hudson, L. (1968) *Frames of Mind.* New York: Norton.

Hurst, D.K. (1986) Why strategic management is bankrupt, *Organizational Dynamics,* 5–27.

Iacocca, L., and Novak, W. (1984) *Iacocca: A Autobiography.* New York: Bantam Books.

Ichazo, O. (1982) *Between Meta Physics and Proto-Analysis.* New York: Arica Institute Press.

Ingram, P. (2002) The National Inter-governmental Management Evaluation Project, Talk given to the OSU-SPPM seminar series, May 2002.

James, W. (1998) 'The Varieties of Religious Experience,' Gifford Lectures, 1998.

Johnson, B. (1992) *Polarity Management*. Amherst, MA: HRD Press.

Kahneman, D., and Tversky, A. (1979) Prospect theory: An analysis of decisions under risk, *Econometrica*, 47, 263–291.

Kaplan, T.J. (1986) The narrative structure of policy analysis, *Journal of Policy Analysis and Management*, 5 (4), 761–778.

Keeney, R., and Raiffa, H. (1976) *Decisions with Multiple Objectives: Preferences and Value Trade-offs*. New York: John Wiley & Sons, Inc.

Kiesler, S., and Sproull, L. (1982) Managerial responses to changing environments: perspectives on problem sensing from social cognition, *Administrative Science Quarterly*, 27, 548–570.

Kolb, D.A. (1983) 'Problem Management: Learning From Experience', in S. Srivastra (ed.) *The Executive Mind*, San Francisco, CA: Jossey-Bass, 109–143.

Kouzes, J.M., and Posner, B.Z. (1987) *The Leadership Challenge*. San Francisco, CA: Jossey-Bass.

Kouzes, J.M., and Posner, B.Z. (1993) *Credibility*. San Francisco, CA: Jossey-Bass.

Kuhn, T. (1970) *The Structure of Scientific Revolutions*, Chicago: University of Chicago Press, 2nd edition.

Land, G., and Jarman, B. (1992) *Breakpoint and Beyond: Mastering the Future Today*. New York: Harper Collins Publishing.

Lawler, E.E. (1968) A correlational-causational analysis of the relationship between expectancy attitude and job performance, *Journal of Applied Psychology*, 52, 462–468.

Lawrence, P.R., and Dyer, D. (1983) 'Toward a theory of adaptation and readaptation, *Renewing American Industry*, New York: Free Press.

Lawrence, P.R., and Lorsch, J.W. (1967) Differentiation and integration in complex organizations, *Administrative Science Quarterly*, 12, 1–47.

Levy, A. (1983) Second order planned change: Definition and conceptualization, *Organizational Dynamics*, Spring, 5–23.

Levy, A., and Merry, U. (1986) *Organizational Transformation: Approaches, Strategies and Theories*. New York: Prager.

Lewin, K. (1951) *Field Theory in Social Science*. New York: Harper and Row.

Lincoln, Y.S., and Cuba, E.G. (1985) *Naturalistic Inquiry*. Beverly Hills, CA, Sage.

Lindblom, C.E. (1965) *The Intelligence of Democracy: Decision Process Through Adjustment*. New York: Free Press.

Lippitt, R., Watson, J., and Westley, B. (1958) *The Dynamics of Planned Change*. New York: Harcourt.

Mackenzie, K. (2000) Processes and their frameworks, *Management Science*, 46, 110–125.

March, J.G., and Simon, H.A. (1958) *Organization*. New York: McGraw-Hill.

Maruyama, M. (1983) Second order cybernetics: Deviation amplification mutual causal processes, *American Scientist*, 51, 1–24.

Mason, R.O., and Mitroff, I.I. (1981) *Challenging Strategic Planning Assumptions*. New York: Wiley-Interscience.

Miles, R.E., and Snow, C.C. (1978) *Organizational Strategy, Structure, and Process*. New York: McGraw-Hill.

Miles, R.E., Snow, C.C., Meyer, A.D., and Coleman, Jr, H.S. (1978) Organization strategy, structure, and process, *Academy of Management Review*, 2 (3), 546–562.

Miller, D., and Friesen, P. (1978) *Organizations: A Quantum View*. Englewood Cliffs, NJ: Prentice Hall.

Mintzberg, H. (1975) The manager's job: Folklore and fact, *Harvard Business Review*, 53 (4), 49–61.

Mintzberg, H. (1978) Patterns in strategy formation, *Management Science*, 24 (9), 934–948.

Mintzberg, H., and Waters, J.A. (1982) Tracking strategy in an entrepreneurial firm, *Academy of Management Journal*, 25 (3), 465–499.

Mintzberg, H., Raisinghani, D., and Theoret, A. (1976) The structure of unstructured decision processes, *Administrative Science Quarterly*, 21, 246–276.

Mohr, L. (1982) Approaches to explanation: Variance theory and process theory', in *Explaining Organization Behavior*, San Francisco, CA: Jossey-Bass, 35–71.

Morgan, G. (1986) 'The Unfolding Logics of Change', in *Images of Organization*. Beverly Hills, CA: Sage.

Morgan, G. (1993) *Imaginization*. Newbury Park, CA: Sage.

Morgan, G. (1998) *Riding the Waves of Change*. San Francisco, CA: Jossey-Bass.

Nadler, G. (1970) *Work Design; A Systems Concept*. Georgetown, Ontario: Irwin.

Nadler, G. (1981) *The Planning and Design Approach*. New York: John Wiley & Sons, Inc.

Nutt, P.C. (1982) *Evaluation Concepts and Methods*. New York: Spectrum Publishing Co.

Nutt, P.C. (1986) The tactics of implementation, *Academy of Management Journal*, 29 (2), 230–261.

Nutt, P.C. (1989) Selecting tactics to implement strategic plans, *Strategic Management Journal*, 10 (1), 145–161.

Nutt, P.C. (1989) *Making Tough Decisions*. San Francisco, CA: Jossey-Bass.

Nutt, P.C. (1992) *Managing Planned Change*. New York: Macmillan.

Nutt, P.C. (1999) Surprising but true: Half of organizational decisions fail, *Academy of Management Executive*, 13 (4), 75–90.

Nutt, P.C. (2001) Decision debacles and how to avoid them, *Business Strategy Review*, 12 (2), 1–14.

Nutt, P.C. (2001b) Organizational de-development as a way to change contemporary organizations, *Research in Organizational Development and Change*, JAI Press, 13.

Nutt, P.C. (2002) *Why Decisions Fail: Avoiding the blunders and traps that lead to debacles*. San Francisco, CA: Barrett-Koehler.

Nutt, P.C. (2003) Implications for organizational change in the structure process duality, *Research in Organizational Change and Development*, JAI Press, 14, 147–194.

Nutt, P.C. (2004) On doing process research, *International Journal of Management Concepts and Philosophy*, 1 (1), 3–26.

Nutt, P.C. (2007) Assessing downsizing guidelines with an exemplar: The Ohio Department of Mental Health success story, *Journal of Applied Behavioral Science*, 43 (3), 373–395.

Nutt, P.C., and Backoff, R.W. (1986) Mutual understanding and its impact on formulation during planning, *Technological Forecasting and Social Change*, 29, 13–31.

Nutt, P.C., and Backoff, R.W. (1992) *The Strategic Management of Public Organizations*. San Francisco, CA: Jossey-Bass.

Nutt, P.C., and Backoff, R.W. (1993) Strategic issues as tensions, *The Journal of Management Inquiry*, 2 (1), 28–43.

Nutt, P.C., and Backoff, R.W. (1997) Organizational transformation, *Journal of Management Inquiry* 6 (3), 235–254.

Nutt, P.C., Backoff, R.W., and Hogan, M.E. (2000) Managing the paradoxes of strategic change: A case study, *Journal of Applied Management Studies*, 9 (1), 5–31.

Osborn, A.F. (1953) *Applied Imagination*. New York: Scribner's.

Pascale, T.T. (1990) *Managing on the Edge*. New York: Simon-Schuster.

Perrow, C. (1967) A framework for the comparative analysis of organizations, *American Sociology Review*, 32, 194–208.

Peters, T.J., and Waterman, R.H., Jr (1982) *In Search of Excellence.* New York: Warner Books.

Pettigrew, A., Woodman, R., and Cameron, K. (2001) Studying organizational change and development: Challenges for future research, *Academy of Management Journal,* 44 (4), 697–713.

Poole, S., and Roth, J. (1989) Decision development in small groups: A test of a contingency model, *Human Communication Research,* 15, 549–589.

Poole, S., and Van de Ven, A. (2004) *Handbook of Organizational Change and Innovation,* Oxford, UK: Oxford University Press.

Porter, L.W., and Lawler, E.E. (1960) *Managerial Attitudes and Performance.* Homewood, IL: Dorsey-Irwin.

Pribram, K.H. (1983) 'The Brain, Cognitive Commodities, and the Enfolded Order', in K. Boulding and L. Senesh (eds) *The Optimum Utilization of Knowledge: Making knowledge serve human betterment.* Boulder CO: Westview Press, 29–40.

Prigogine, I., and Stengers, I. (1984) *Order Out of Chaos.* Bantam Books.

Quinn, R.A. (1995) 'Transformational Thinking; The Cycle of Excellence,' Rockefeller College of Public Affairs and Policy, SUNY, Albany NY, March 11, 1995.

Quinn, R.A. (1996) *Becoming a Master Manager.* San Francisco, CA: Jossey-Bass.

Ravn, I. (1986) 'Creating Futures and Constructing Realities', *General Systems Yearbook.*

Rodgers, E.M. (1962) *The Diffusion of Innovation.* New York: Free Press.

Schendel, D., and Hofer, C. (1979) *Strategic Management.* Boston, MA: Little, Brown.

Schon, D.A. (1983) *The Reflective Practitioner: How Professionals Think in Action.* New York: Basic Books.

Schon, D.A. (1987) *Educating The Reflective Practitioner.* New York: Basic Books.

Schwartz, P. (1991) *The Art of the Long View.* New York: Doubleday.

Scott, W.E., and Cummings, L.L. (1973) *Reading in Organizational Behavior.* Homewood, IL: Irwin (revised edition).

Simon, H.A. (1969) *Sciences of the Artificial.* Cambridge, MA: MIT Press.

Simon, H.A. (1977) *The New Science of Management Decision.* Englewood Cliffs, NJ: Prentice Hall, 2nd edition.

Simon, H.A., and Newell, A. (1970) Human problem solving – The state of the art in 1970, *American Psychologist,* February.

Simon, M.A. (1982) *Understanding Human Action.* Albany, NY; State of New York Press.

Skinner, B.F. (1969) *Contingencies of Reinforcement.* New York: Appleton Century Crafts.

Slovic, P., Fishoff, B., and Lichtenstein, S. (1977) Behavioral decision theory, *Annual Review of Psychology,* 28, 1–39.

Staw, B., Sandelands, L., and Dutton, J. (1981) Threat-rigidity effects on organization behavior, *Administrative Science Quarterly,* 26, 501–524.

Strumpf, S.A., Zand, D.E., and Freeman, R.D. (1979) Designing groups for judgmental decisions, *Academy of Management Review,* 4 (4), 589–600.

Thompson, A., and Strickland, A. (1996) *Crafting and Implementing Strategy.* Chicago, IL, Irwin, 6th edition.

Thompson, J. (1967) *Organizations in Action.* New York: McGraw-Hill.

Tichy, N., and Devanna, M. (1986) *The Transformational Leader.* New York: John Wiley & Sons Inc.

Tsoukas, H., and Chia, R. (2002) On organizational becoming: Re-thinking organizational change, *Organizational Science,* 13 (5), 567–582.

Tversky, A., and Kahneman, D. (1974) Judgment under uncertainty: Heuristics and biases, *Science,* 185, 1124–1131.

Van de Ven, A. (1992) Suggestions for studying strategy process: A research note', *Strategic Management Journal,* 13, 169–188.

Van de Ven, A., Angle, V., and Poole, M.S. (2000) *Research on the Management of Innovation.* Oxford: Oxford University Press.

Van de Ven, A., Polley, D.E., Garud, R., and Venkataraman, S. (1999) *The Innovation Journey.* New York: Oxford University Press.

Van de Ven, A., and Poole, M.S. (1995) Explaining development and change in organizations, *Academy of Management Review,* 20, 510–540.

Varela, F. (1976) On observing natural systems, *Co-Evaluation Quarterly,* Summer, 26–31.

Varela, F. (1979) *Principles of Biological Autonomy.* New York. North Holland.

Vickers, G. (1965) *The Art of Judgment,* New York: Basic Books.

Voorhees, B.H. (1983) 'Trialectics and Rational Theory Construction: A Theory of Theory', in R.E. Horn (ed.) *Trialectics.* Lexington, MA: Information Resources, 47–76.

Vroom, V.H. (1964) *Work and Motivation.* New York: John Wiley & Sons, Inc.

Vroom, V.H. (1973) A new look at managerial decision making, *Organizational Dynamics,* Spring, 66–80.

Vroom, V., and Yetton, P. (1974) *Leadership and Decision Making.* Pittsburgh: The University of Pittsburgh Press.

Wallace, A.F. (1956) Revitalization movements, *American Anthropologist,* 58 (2), 264–281.

Watzawick, P., Weakland, J., and Frisch, R. (1974) *Change.* New York: Norton.

Webb, E., Campbell, D., Schwartz, R., and Securest, L. (1966) *Unobtrusive Measures.* Chicago: Rand McNally.

Webb, E., Campbell, D., Schwartz, R., and Securest, L. (1981) *Non-Reactive Measures in the Social Sciences.* Boston, MA: Houghton Mifflin.

Weick, K.E. (1979) *The Social Psychology of Organizing.* Reading, MA: Addison-Wesley, 2nd edition.

Weick, K.E., and Quinn, R. (1999) Organizational Change and Development', in J. Spence, J. Darley, and D. Foss, *Annual Review of Psychology, vol. 50,* Palo Alto, CA: Annual Reviews, 361–386.

Wilber, K. (2000) *A Theory of Everything.* Boston, MA: Shambhala.

Woodward, J. (1965) *Industrial Organization: Theory and Practice,* Oxford: Oxford University Press.

Zaltman, G., Duncan, R., and Holbeck, J. (1973) *Innovations in Organizations,* New York: Wiley-Interscience.

Zand, D.E., and Sorensen, R.E. (1975) Theory of change and the effective use of management science, *Administrative Science Quarterly,* 20, 532–545.

22

The Bradford Studies: Issues Raised by These and Other Studies for the Understanding of Decision Making

David C. Wilson

Introduction

Although this chapter falls in a section mainly about methodology, I wanted to write about more than something strictly on methods. I wanted to reflect on the Bradford Studies (of which I was a founder member; see also Chapter 16 by Sue Miller in this Handbook). In particular, I wanted to reflect on what undertaking these extensive theoretical and empirical studies had taught me and what questions remained (in my view) to be answered. Hence, this chapter is in part a reflection and in part raises challenges for the future study of decision making. Nevertheless, in the spirit of a Handbook being something of a reference source for its readers, I have listed the main publications from the Bradford Studies in Appendix 1.

I also wanted to write a slightly more personal view (readers who think this inappropriate should skip this chapter) and, hence, the chapter will not be the usual repository of key reviews, references, and quotes (apart from Appendix 1), but mainly is a result of my own reflections on work that is still continuing after over 30 years and outlines the challenges to come in the study of decision making. The following chapter is therefore divided into sections each of which contains questions and issues I have come to see as important in decision making, drawing upon the Bradford Studies both in terms of data as well as experientially. The sections are not intended to be in any order of significance or magnitude and they are certainly not exhaustive, but I hope they resonate with current (and, hopefully, future) scholars of decision making.

Handbook of Decision Making.   Edited by Paul C. Nutt and David C. Wilson
© 2010 John Wiley & Sons, Ltd

CAPTURING THE ESSENCE OF A DECISION

To those who have never tried to capture all of what happens during decision making, it will seem on the surface of things quite an easy task. Decisions are discrete activities, they involve individuals over a period of time, they involve selection and implementation processes, and they have an end point when, for example, the new building is erected or the new product is on the market. They should be easy to study and observe. Yet adopting what social scientists would agree to be appropriate methods for studying decision-making activities represents a huge challenge to researchers. This is not to re-visit the old chestnut arguments of quantitative versus qualitative methods (that can be read in many hundreds of articles and books), but is to reflect on the difficulties of observing and capturing decisions.

The Bradford Studies began by attempting to carry out a large-scale study into the exercise of power in a range of organizations. Given that one of the founding members of the team was David Hickson, fresh from his studies in Alberta of intra and inter-organizational contingencies of power, this was perhaps not surprising. However, in the quest for seeing power in action in organizations, the research team soon found that managers continually made reference to strategic decisions to explain the exercise of power and the project slowly turned toward a study of decision making with the exercise of power being one of many factors contributing to the explanation of why decision processes were as they turned out to be.

Immediately, the problem of recording data presented itself. Some of the team favoured semi-structured interviews with key informants. I favoured case studies, staying with the company, observing the decision as it unfolded and recording what happened in the form of copious notes and records. In the end, the team used both methods, triangulating the one with the other where in-depth cases had been conducted. Of course, the question of whether or not in-depth cases really capture the essence of decision making has been contested for decades. Amongst other criticisms, case research has been accused of being overly subjective, reflecting the interests and perhaps values of the researcher more than the subject researched and certainly not open to replication or to the study of the same phenomena (the case events) by other researchers. Analysis and characterisation of the cases were largely on trust of some forms of validation being applied (and still are to some degree despite advances in validation and reliability in case study design since these early cases were researched).

During 1976, when we had just begun the first phases of fieldwork, a method of capturing decision-making action on film emerged. Spearheaded by Roger Graef, Granada Television in the UK screened a series of decisions filmed as they were being made in a number of organizations ranging from the National Health Service to a UK Steel Company. I remember at the time thinking that this represented a huge step forward in decision process analysis. For the first time, other viewers and researchers could see the actions and vocabulary of managers again and again (see Chapter 5 by Child, Elbanna, and Rodrigues in this Handbook for more detail on the film entitled the 'Korf Contract'). There was a permanent record of the case, the main actors and what they said and did; the sequences of events over time was clear, as was the outcome of each decision. Roger Graef was Director and Producer of the series called 'Decision' which was screened by Granada Television. The most 'popular' of these programmes (there were six in total) was the 'Korf Contract', shown on January 27, 1976. This depicted the decision makers of the then publicly owned British Steel Corporation deciding whether or not to invest in new technology (provided by the German firm, Korf). This has become a popular teaching case across the world, since it brings to life (quite literally) many of the decision characteristics depicted by authors such as Cyert and March, Herbert Simon, and Henry Mintzberg. Power, groupthink, uncertainty, problemistic search, sequential attention to goals, and bounded rationality are all readily visible. Nothing was staged for the camera. Roger had installed fixed cameras in British Steel's headquarters building some time before the Korf decision came into view. By this time, the cameras had become part of the fabric of the organization and were generally not noticed by British Steel managers (much as surveillance cameras in cities tend to become unnoticed parts of the street furniture today).

However, Roger Graef also used mobile cameramen who followed key actors around the building and who captured formal and informal conversations between senior managers as the decision progressed. Certainly, by 1976, sound and camera technology had progressed to a stage where cinema verite was possible enabling, at least in theory, researchers to capture something very close to 'what really happened' by bridging the gaps between representation and reality. Graef was providing for the first time (with perhaps the exceptions of the Milgram experiments on obedience to authority which were also filmed) a form of 'reality' previously unavailable to the decision theorist or researcher. Although I thought at the time that cinema verite would certainly make traditional case studies and semi-structured interview-based methods of capturing data largely redundant, this has not happened and decision researchers rely as much on these 'traditional' data capturing methods as they always have done. It is interesting to reflect on why this is the case. To do so means stepping outside mainstream debates in organization theory and reflecting on the debates in the humanities over cinema verite (there is a strong resonance with similar debates in the social sciences).

First, many commentators on the film industry argued that cinema verite was at best a form of journalism (rather than research) where who is making the film has a profound and often unknown influence on what is recorded. Bruzzi (2000: 6) notes the intense debates in the film industry over how much objective truth there really is in cinema verite. For example, she argues that many authors have queried the 'ethos of transparency and unbiased observation' claimed by the genre. Bruzzi goes on to note that documentary film makers have largely accepted their inability to capture an undistorted purely reflective picture of reality (despite the protests of some theorists). Even though technologies have advanced significantly in both sound recording and cameras (DVD and hidden for example), the problem remains that what the viewer sees is essentially a compromise reached between the subject and the recording. Even here, it seems, we cannot be free from subjectivity, bias (intended or otherwise), and selective capturing of events, actors, and processes.

Secondly, securing access to film decision makers is obviously a significant challenge, particularly when those involved will have no idea at the time what is going to happen during the process, or what the outcome will be (successful or unsuccessful). It is perhaps no surprise that after Roger Graef's 'Decision' series there has been, to my knowledge, no equivalent in-depth attempt at capturing decision making through film techniques such as cinema verite. For the foreseeable future we seem anchored to the qualitative and quantitative data gathering techniques which have become somewhat traditional in decision-making research as well as in social science more generally. Yet these are replete with problems which are explored in the following sections.

How Can We Recognise Decision-making Activity?

The debates over whether or not specific decisions are an appropriate level of analysis or not have been well rehearsed elsewhere (see for example the debates in *Organization Studies*, 1990, 11, 6: Special Issue). More pertinent from my perspective as a researcher of decision making is to be able to articulate when decision-making activities start or stop and to what extent they are separable from what might be called everyday organizational activities. How can we know when we are observing or documenting decision-making activities in an organization that we are really looking at decision-making activities? Of course, any attempts to address these questions take the debate into a fundamental modernist versus postmodernist arena. Such questions also take the debate a few steps on from the planned versus emergent perspectives popularized by Henry Mintzberg and other scholars of decision making. Mintzberg and his colleagues argued that decision making was something that emerged and that, post hoc, was made sense of in the form of a 'strategy' or a direction (often, in the process, implying a degree of planning had actually taken place but that this was either not directly observable by researchers or not undertaken by decision makers).

Yet, the emergent perspective holds fast to a modernist conception of time. That is, time can be conceived of as regular units of separable activities which are linear in form and unidirectional, from a period of lesser understanding toward a period of greater understanding. Whether a decision process is planned or emerges, the conception of time remains constant. In terms of decision making, this implies that decision makers will always know more (greater certainty) at the end of a decision process (whether emergent or planned) than they did at its beginning. The planned and emergent debates operate on the same conceptual view of time and knowledge as being cumulative (Georg Hegel and Charles Darwin were great exponents of this view). The assumptions here are of decision activities adding to or accumulating new knowledge over time and reducing uncertainties for future decisions (again, adhering to a linear conception of time). Many scholars have commented on the huge impact that modernism has had on organization theory in general and this can equally be seen as a strong legacy in decision-making research. For example, leading thinkers such as Isaac Newton and Immanuel Kant espoused what we would today know as scientific method, in particular emphasizing the benefits of identifying invariate laws (Kant) and general principles (Newton) of all activities. Kant even went as far as saying that natural science was (as he wrote) heading toward a path of certain progress now it had espoused such scientific method after groping around for too long in the realms of accidental explanations and investigations with no preconceived plans.

In terms of decision making, we can see the evolution and identification of linear (and identifiable) phases of activity springing from this thinking. The classic (or so-called rational) model of decision-making processes stemmed directly from this perspective with its neat sequences of problem identification, alternative generation, selection of best alternative, and implementation, with each subsequent decision building on (and gaining from) knowledge generated in the previous phases (in a Hegelian-like quest for knowledge build leading ultimately to some form of absolute knowledge). This theoretical perspective had dramatic implications for methodology. This was because the bulk of modernist thinkers assumed that not only do phenomena follow general patterns or laws, but that these patterns can be observed and recorded. In turn, associations between patterns can be identified and this 'knowledge' can help predict with greater accuracy the trajectories (and performance) of future decision making. Such thinking did not stop with Newton and his colleagues. There are plenty of decision consultants who claim to be able to increase the efficacy of individual and organizational decision making using just such methods.

There are at least two problems that the rise of modernism presents to the research of decision making. First, is decision-making activity really like the linear sequential model depicted above and, secondly, is it ever possible to observe and document such activities confident that these are activities which are dedicated to, or associated with, decision making and nothing else?

Whilst postmodern thinking has its critics, it nevertheless poses some challenges to the above modernist conception of decision making. To my knowledge, there has been very little postmodern work which focuses directly on decision making. I have written with Stephen Cummings on postmodern approaches to 'strategy' (see Cummings and Wilson, 2003) and Stephen also wrote about recreating strategy in a postmodern context (Cummings 2002). But there are relatively few publications in this area. There are some parallels between this work in the field of strategic management and decision making. For example, essentially, the postmodern critique is that the search for regularities (such as phases or sequences) in decision making is misguided. It asks the wrong questions. The apparent solid stability that sequences, phases, or even processes themselves underpin decision activities, is misinformed. Decision making is no more than a continual unfolding of activities and is erroneously viewed as an object which can be studied in its own right with its own set of regular characteristics Decision making, therefore, has no 'being' from the postmodern perspective. It has no right to be seen as an independent activity. To do so would impose a structure on a process which does not exist apart from the language which is commonly used to depict it. But as Wittgenstein reminds us, just as the word beauty has no absolute meaning beyond its social construction, then the vocabulary of decision making such as search, formulation, implementation, point of decision, and so on equally are not absolute. From this perspective, it makes no sense to try and compare decision-making processes either, since this would be attempting to impose a regularity and solidity of meaning to any of these characteristics which did not exist other than in the minds of individuals. As Cummings (2002: 60) argues, we would be misguided in looking for any common ground (or arguing the 'appearance' of ground) which underlies decision making.

So what is to stop such a view concluding that ultimately, decision making is simply chaotic? Deleuze and Guattari (1977; 1988) and Cummings and Wilson (2003) offer some clues. First, people act as though there were some solid ground which underpins their actions. There is a degree of common understanding of vocabulary. We may never know the extent of that commonality, but there may be sufficient to enable researchers to characterize decision processes for example. Secondly, there are arguably connections within and between decision processes, but these may not be explicit, sequential, or regular and, hence, not observable by researchers and, perhaps, also partially or wholly unknown to decision participants themselves. This is the, by now, well-known 'rhizome' perspective in which connections between actions and events are tangled, multi-directional, often underground, and indefinite (just like the root system of rhizomes themselves). Nevertheless, connections exist. All is not chaotic. Codifying and observing such connections is, however, a significant challenge for the researcher of decision making since, from the rhizome perspective, each decision process is an interconnected game played between different individuals in different ways (both explicit and implicit).

One problem with the above postmodern perspectives is that empirical evidence (in any form) is mostly absent. It is quite plausible that decision-making activities are as theorized, but we have very little evidence that this is the case. Even Roger Graef's films of decisions being made in real time reveal only the surface of individual actions, although they do provide evidence of a relatively common vocabulary with a commensurate shared understanding between actors being articulated as the decision progresses. There is some emerging empirical evidence (Miller *et al.*, 2009) that managers act as if there were some solid ground underpinning their actions. It is, as yet, slight but nevertheless gives some support to the view that managers view structure in the process and the data also show evidence of connections between aspects of decision processes, even though these are only observable connections and clearly miss most of Deleuze and Guattari's tangled underground web of connections.

CONNECTIONS IN DECISION PROCESSES

Wensley (2003: 106) argues that decision makers anticipate what they think will happen and link current actions to this future vision. Gavetti and Levinthal (2000) provide empirical evidence, derived from computer simulations, to support this proposition showing that looking forward and looking backward in decision making are closely interrelated. Decision making can thus be seen as both intentional and anticipatory in that decision participants act currently in ways they perceive the future to be. Therefore, choice and implementation are likely to be coupled in some respects since implementation is assumed to follow in temporal process and to be linked to deciding. From this perspective a strategic decision to build a new manufacturing plant, for example, will not only anticipate the kind of plant to be built (in terms of design and size) but also these choices will precede the plant being built (a tangible and chronologically later outcome of implementation). There are likely to be relational patterns between these different parts of the decision process.

Miller *et al.*'s (2009) approach relies on a conventional assumption of linear sequences from deciding to implementing. Empirical justification for this can be found in Perlow *et al.*, (2002) who reveal distinct phases in the decision process (which they call periods) showing that decisions seem to follow chronological time and follow a sequence which moves from deciding to acting. Secondly, a great deal of research concerning participation in decision making (who is involved and when) reinforces the episodic nature of the process and also its sequential flow from deciding to implementing (see Ashmos *et al.*, 2002; Wagner, 1994; Bourgeois and Brodwin, 1984; Nutt, 1986).

The first evidence of connections between phases of decisions is that high levels of political conflict during decision making (formulation) seem to fragment the focus of implementation. In other words political activities continue throughout the decision, including implementation, making it difficult for decision makers to concentrate on putting the decision into practice. Political activity does this in a number of ways. First, it reduces backing amongst the various interests for implementation. Unresolved prior contention results in a lack of support later for what has to be done. Even though a formal high-level decision may have been taken to go ahead, this does not carry everyone with it; the memory of past conflicts lingers on. From a connectedness perspective, the role of memory amongst decision participants (and the more institutionalized memories which are embedded in organizations) appears important. They are not only carriers of value-laden messages to individuals, but are also an important way of connecting various parts of decision making together.

Emphasizing the importance of memory, Miller *et al.* (2009) show that contention during decision making, which may question embedded norms and values, results in a lack of later receptivity for the decision. The most evident way in which individuals and groups resisted the decision (were unreceptive to it) was by not giving it precedence over other competing demands once the decision was to be put into practice. They did not give the decision the priority it needed to secure implementation. Disagreement over objectives tends to reduce support for what has to be done later in implementation) and diverts attention from exploiting knowledge about how to do it. Disagreement also contributes to unfavourable conditions by making a receptive organizational climate less likely (Dean and Sharfman, 1996; Sharfman and Dean, 1997; Nutt, 1998; Eisenhardt and Bourgeois, 1989).

There are two points worth emphasizing from these findings. The first is that memory appears to play an important role in decision making. It seems that such memories can be decision-specific or can be more deeply embedded in organizations so that decisions become framed or 'bounded' by the institutionalized context of organization (Wilson *et al.*, 1986). Either way, there is evidence that decision processes are connected to a greater or lesser extent by the memories of participants. Neurophysiologists have argued for many years about the importance of individual memory and the importance of various areas of the brain in retaining memory. However, the Miller *et al.* (2009) research indicates that, beyond neurophysiological explanations of individual memory, decision processes (and phases of that process over time) can be connected. The second point is that political contention can be viewed as a thread which weaves throughout the decision process, itself providing another form of connectedness.

Further connections appear to be rooted in decision makers' perception of the gravity of the problem if things were to go wrong (as they look ahead). Would failure mean a catastrophic loss in market share, a disastrous impact on reputation? If there is a chance of potentially very damaging serious outcomes, more care seems likely to be spent in thinking through the detail of implementation tasks (which, arguably, makes success more likely). More serious matters get higher priority at senior levels. Prioritizing keeps implementation at the top of the agenda. The more serious the likely impact of the decision, the more it demands such priority so that it is given a head-start, and this is crucial for chances of success (Miller *et al.*, 2004).

The above findings indicate that there are connections in decision making (at least as perceived by and acted upon by senior managers). Two important theoretical implications can be drawn. First, the role of prior contention appears to have an important influence on the subsequent characteristics of implementation. In this respect findings would defend a linear *consequential* chronology between deciding and implementing. The former precedes the latter in time. But, secondly, managers make sense of deciding by not only taking into account the process of deciding itself, but also trying to predict the consequences of deciding. Therefore, they think about and consider implementation and its *consequences* whilst deciding, thus looking forward (whilst deciding) to implementation. In this respect, deciding and implementing are intermingled in time and in sequence. As Wensley (2003: 106) notes, how one chooses to decide 'depends upon future projections, future purpose and future aspirations'.

The above data provide strong support for a path dependent, rather than deterministic, view of coupling between deciding and doing. There appear to be strong and multi-faceted couplings (connections) between deciding and implementing in strategic decision making. It is this multi-faceted coupling that mitigates any tendencies for decisions to slip into the anarchy of the 'garbage can'. The persisting involvement of key functional interests (Miller *et al.*, 2008) ensures that 'though every entrance is an exit somewhere else' (Cohen *et al.*, 1972: 3), a nucleus of principal participants remains throughout, even if others exit the stage early or make a late entrance. It has been suggested that these interests more than any others store the organizational memory of particular decisions, the recollections about the context, and events which shape the management of implementation. This is memory not only of the routines followed (Brown and Eisenhardt, 1995; Moorman and Miner, 1998), but more significantly about the process of deciding. How much disagreement was there over objectives, how long was it thought repercussions might endure?

DECISION MAKING OR NOT?

The Bradford Studies began by trying to research power in organizations and ended up studying decision making. This raises the question of what decision making *is not*, rather than what it is. Certainly, authors (including myself) present and analyse their work as if it were a focused study of decision making, collecting data and interviewing those centrally involved. Yet, it is extremely difficult to distinguish when individuals are engaged in what we might term decision-making activities and when they are not. For example, many psychologists argue that decision making is a process carried out to a large extent unconsciously. At the individual level of analysis, therefore, it can be arguably a false quest to try and observe when individuals make decisions. Recently, Soon *et al.* (2008) revealed that individuals make decisions some seconds before any observable act of decision making. It is, they argue, an unconscious act carried out up to seven seconds before observable decision time (at the same time calling into question the extent to which individuals exercise free will in decision making – it is the sub-conscious brain which decides).

Other researchers focusing on the individual level of analysis cluster under the current title of strategy as practice. This perspective takes a micro-lens to managerial activity to pick up signs of decision-making activity. Specifically, these researchers are looking for signs of what happens when managers 'strategize'. Typically, events or processes such as meetings are analysed to pick up signals of strategizing activities. Yet even in meetings which are ostensibly taking place to take decisions, it is extremely difficult for a researcher to isolate actions, behaviours, speech acts, and other activities as pertaining wholly to decision-making activity. The microsociology of how people act and behave reveals a myriad of observable and analytically possible variables but are they all focused on decision making?

In an amusing, but theoretically serious book, Mangham (1986) explores this microsociology by observing an executive group as they go about making a series of decisions aimed at developing and sustaining such things as increased market share, increased profitability, innovation, and product development. Through a variety of 'readings' of executive behaviours, Mangham argues that what we see in this microsociology of an executive group are aspects of power, status, passion, leadership, and performance. He does not focus at all on decision-making characteristics or processes (as we would perhaps traditionally understand them) but, instead, presents a picture of executive *performance*. Mangham's perspective offers an interesting answer to the question of whether we can really reveal and identify decision-making activities and behaviours as distinct from other social and interactive processes in groups and organizations. Mangham concludes that we cannot make such a distinction. His dramaturgical perspective emphasizes ritual and performance. When we research a Board meeting or the processes of any decision-making team we are more likely to observe the expressions of ritual rather than decision. Each member of the team expresses their perspectives for 'no other purpose than to confirm their reality' (Mangham, 1986: 63). We see performance and ritual rather than decision making. Such an analysis is not confined to one meeting. Performances are enacted (note the similarity here with Karl Weick's notion of enactment) in anticipation of future meetings where further performances will take place. Therefore, even a longitudinal study of decision making may turn out to be a longitudinal study of ritual and performance and little else.

From this dramaturgical perspective, decision-making research uncovers both scripted and apparently improvised performances. Yet, Mangham argues that even any apparent improvisation is likely to be a form of Commedia dell'Arte where a fixed group of characters (decision makers) act and perform the same irrespective of plot (topic) and the situations they find themselves in (context). A researcher observing a group decision involving these actors may assume all action and discourse is spontaneous and focused on the decision. Yet the alternative view is that almost nothing is spontaneous and is less decision-focused than it is performance-focused. From a methodological perspective, such arguments are challenging. Even if captured by means of cinema verite (or similar recording activities), we still cannot be certain whether or not we are observing decision-making activity or some form of ritual and performance. A key to understanding such ritualized behaviours, however, lies in Mangham's explanation of why his strategic decision-making actors engage in them. They do so, he argues, in order to exercise power; to be able to establish and maintain status from such interactions and performances and to control the outcomes and processes of decisions. Here Mangham throws us a lifeline. Perhaps the study of decision making is really the study of power (bringing this chapter neatly back to where it started). Power delimits choice activities and the performances we see are, in effect, the exercise of power. The next section looks at this aspect of choice limitation a little more closely.

Limits to the idea of choice

To talk of decision making is to talk of choice. How do people decide? Such a question is immediately simplistic and complex. Of course people make choices (what meal to have in a restaurant; what kind of car to purchase). But do they have a free choice? Who decides the menu from which people choose? How is the choice of cars made available to customers? These are, in one respect, 'small' questions – seemingly trivial and often overlooked as unimportant, but digging a little deeper reveals bigger and more important questions for decision theorists because the context of power (who decides the scope of choice) is revealed as a limitation on choice and decision theory (Flyvbjerg, 1998; 2001).

From this perspective, simply looking at the decision process over extant issues (or topics) misses the point that prior choices have already been made and these limit the scope, content, and process of what decision researchers are trying to examine and explain. Indeed, observers of a decision are very likely to be unaware of what prior choices have been made and the actions and processes the researcher observes may be more a product of earlier choices and, perhaps, power struggles. The political context of decisions can be seen in a number of specific instances. At its simplest, the concept of 'strategic choice' (Child, 1972) captures the extent to which the operating environment of the organization places limits around what managers can decide and how much autonomy they have in making those decisions. In the extreme, an organization can be 'paralyzed' in the decision actions it can take by the power of a tightly coupled network of organizations and interests (stakeholders in modern jargon). Both the content and scope of decision making are defined by these interests and managers have no autonomy over choice at all (Butler et al., 1977).

More complex are the perspectives of 'non decision making' (Bachrach and Baratz, 1970). The scope of what can be decided can be reduced through limited opportunities to participate in decision making. Only those who participate in the decision arena have true decision-making power according to Bachrach and Baratz (1970) and the rest of the organization (no matter how senior) inherit decisions which are already framed. Researchers studying decisions must know whether they are studying those who make decisions or those who inherit the decisions of others. As Mangham revealed above, this is not an easy (or obvious) choice for the researcher. How can a researcher know whether or not he or she is studying processes and actions which are already framed and constrained? Or does the researcher make the assumption that all observed processes will be framed by prior actions and then the key research question becomes one of trying to reveal the degree of such constraints. Answering that question presents a substantial challenge since it suggests that only longitudinal (and, very likely historical) methods of data collection stand a chance of capturing prior actions which frame current processes. A further problem even with these approaches is that such actions and framing may have become relatively unobservable since they have become assimilated into organizational structures and processes rather than remaining observable as over actions.

This process (which can include deliberate acts of a controlling group to limit the scope of decisional choice for others as well as unintentional acts) is the institutionalization of processes and practices in organizations. These occur over time as customs and practices develop and become sedimented acting as control mechanisms over decision makers and the scope of their actions (Meyer and Rowan, 1977). Clegg, Courpasson, and Phillips (2006: 229) remind us that choice activities are always bounded by 'a whole world of normalcy: hierarchy, rigid rationalities; domination experienced as authority ... yet we do not constantly question the normal nor do we acknowledge its power over us'. Decisions are shaped and influenced less by decision makers and more by these institutionalized and taken for granted factors. To study decision making from this perspective would involve a much greater emphasis on understanding this context and its power and much less on studying those who seemingly 'make' decisions in the Boardroom or in meetings. Although, as Mangham argues, studying at this latter level of analysis will reveal a great deal about performance and ritual rather than about decision making.

Order versus disorder

Decision-making research presents a substantial paradox. From a common-sense perspective (and from the view of practice) making decisions is about creating some sort of order where there was previously disorder (Brunsson, 1995). By choosing among many alternatives and creating order amongst them (listing which are the most attractive, for example); by debating the merits of alternative actions; by explicitly addressing trade-offs and opportunity costs; and by putting the decision into practice (launching the new product, for example) there is an explicit (and implicit) assumption that a decision process is creating order where disorder previously existed and that this is achieved over time in something called a decision process.

In many texts which are critical of the 'order' perspective, the usual targets of their critiques are focused on 'unrealistic' assumptions made by decision theorists, such as economic man, perfect knowledge, and rational-economic choice processes. Such critiques usually point to the dominance of behavioural aspects of decision making, famously depicted by Cyert and March (1963) and use these to counteract overly rational views of decision theory.

Yet, closer inspection of Cyert and March's (1963) seminal text reveals that a key assumption in this 'Carnegie' behavioural tradition is that decision-making processes are sequential in character. Sequential means that alternatives are examined one after the other, or goals are attended to one after another and that information search is serial (Warglien and Masuch, 1995). The whole behavioural process is considered to be serial (but limited because of bounded rationality). This view pervades much more recent decision theory, especially that which takes a single identifiable decision as the unit of analysis (for example, Hickson *et al.*, 1986; Nutt, 1984; Dean and Sharfman, 1993).

A contrasting view is that decision making is an activity which is parallel rather than serial. Parallel means that decision making consists of a number of processes which can be totally independent of one another, which do not necessarily follow a linear or logical path over time, and which do not necessarily follow intended plans (as laid out by standard operating procedures for example). To understand decision theory from this parallel perspective is to adopt what Cohen *et al.* (1972) termed a 'garbage can' view. There is no specified standard programme of action. Decision making is about reciprocity and adjustment which occur between often unrelated processes. Preferences are unclear and sometimes impossible to express. People do not know precisely what they want and are likely to reinterpret any preferences they may have. In this way, knowing preferences has to be learned along the way. Ends and means are confused with little idea of how cause and effect might be related. Different actors are involved in different decision arenas and can enter or leave the arena for a variety of reasons depending upon their interests or upon conflicting demands on their attention or time. These erratic characteristics lead to a view of decision making as disorder rather than order.

More precisely, the Cohen *et al.* (1972) view reveals that when we research decision-making activities, we are likely to find aspects of confusion, irrationality, and disorder. The researcher is immediately faced with a challenge. On the one hand he or she could take the view that in this confusion, complexity, and noise there was an underlying order – it is just that no-one has identified the order yet. The research challenge becomes one of revealing this previously unknown order. Such a view can be found echoed in the work of scholars such as Weick (1979; 1995) who emphasized that order and disorder are not organizational or decisional properties, but are essentially constructs of the onlooker's eyes and ways of seeing the world. On the other hand, the researcher could take the view that disorder was indeed the key feature of decision making and that the key research task was to describe and account for this disorder without attempting to package processes and actions into neatly parcelled activities. This view echoes the views of scholars such as Brunsson (1995) who view both organization and decision making as inherently ambiguous, inconsistent, and disordered.

Accepting that decision making is an inconsistent activity (and process) presents a large challenge to the researcher. Such research is likely to reveal that notions such as preferences, morals, effectiveness, efficiency, and good and bad performance are subject both to individual interpretation and to changes in fashion over time. The ways in which an organization is expected to prioritize preferences and how it should be seen to act are strongly influenced by social norms which are subject to change over time. For example, it is only relatively recently that organizations have been expected to make choices which reflect preferences for being 'green' and sustainable. Furthermore, some organizations provide services which are inherently difficult to evaluate without recourse to values and norms. These include management consultancies, marketing firms, and educational organizations. Who is to define what is good or effective consultancy? And, even if this were arguably possible (such as by the current attempts at quality rankings of educational organizations), such definitions are liable to significant changes over even quite short timescales (certainly one decade or less). This implies that research on decision making which was carried out 20 or 30 years ago will reveal arguably more about prevailing values and norms which provided the context for those decisions than the decisions themselves. In addition, it implies that research findings from decades past will likely have limited relevance and application to current contexts.

STRATEGIC DECISION MAKING AND ORGANIZATIONAL STRATEGY

My experience of teaching strategic decision making to various groups (ranging from undergraduates to senior executives) is that it is usually a rewarding task. People are interested in the topic and recognize that key factors such as politics and power, complexity and process characteristics reveal important insights into decision making. For many, examples of non decision making, order and disorder, or putting on a performance resonate with their experiences in their own organizations.

However, nearly all classes and discussions lead eventually to a thorny problem as soon as questions of performance are addressed. Accepting that, as researchers, we all suffer from relatively poor measures of performance we can, nevertheless, show how decision process characteristics and the performance of a specific decision are related. But the thorny question lies in taking the next step – trying to relate performance in strategic decision making to performance in organizational strategy. The Bradford Studies indicated quite strongly that there were few organizational effects. In other words nearly all the organizations we studied had a range of strategic decisions, each with varying levels of performance (Hickson *et al.*, 2003). Not one organization had all of its decisions in the high performance category (or vice versa), yet the organizations studied varied considerably in terms of their 'strategic' performance overall and corporate performance seemed largely unrelated to decision performance. From my perspective (based on the Bradford Studies' data), Henry Mintzberg's assertion that strategy is a 'pattern in a stream of decisions' seems not to hold when we examine performance either at the level of a decision or the level of the organization. Decision performance seems largely unconnected to organizational performance. We had organizations which were performing well, yet our research revealed that as many as four out of five strategic decisions had under-performed (at the decision level of analysis).

One reason might be, of course, that the decisions we researched were not all 'strategic' (see Chapter 1 for a broader discussion of this point). Hence, the Bradford research (and indeed other research into strategic decision making) was not really identifying the key strategic decisions but was, instead, capturing what we might term important or resource hungry decisions which informants thought were strategic (but which were not). This would be a strong criticism to level at most research on strategic decision making as Paul Nutt and I have already discussed in Chapter 1. But it certainly seems to be a feature of the Bradford Studies and other empirical research in the field. Perhaps, as researchers, we are not identifying truly strategic decisions (and possibly neither are senior managers when they are asked to identify them by researchers) so they never become part of the sample of decisions studied. This is plausible on many fronts. For example, the 'real' strategic decisions may have been taken prior to the ones we studied and may not have been openly observable (non decision style). We therefore ended up studying observable rituals associated with strategic decision making, (and we called these strategic decisions) but which were not the real thing. Possibly. But we were at pains in our empirical research to explore to what extent decisions had already been made or had been shaped by one or more previous decisions. And managers understood such concepts, yet rarely were they able to identify such shaping and effects. There is clearly a need to explore these issues in future decision-making research. I am sure that I and many other researchers will address these questions.

Another influence on decision-making research which largely emanates from the strategy literature is the emphasis on performance as the vital dependent variable. Strategy research can be characterized by having a mass of independent variables all in the search to associate some of them with performance of the organization. The effect on decision-making research has been also to emphasize not only performance, but also positive performance. What variables and factors are associated with positive decision performance? This question is one which not only characterizes a lot of decision-making research, but is also one which has been addressed widely by consultancy firms eager to point out the pitfalls of decision making (and how to avoid them). For example, the 'McKinsey Global Survey into Strategic Decision Making' conducted in 2008 identifies the key factors which lead to more successful decision making and those which detract from performance (and hence should be avoided). The latter include bias, a lack of discussion, poor execution, poor fore-casting of competitors' actions and reactions, and a failure to align incentives with objectives. Interestingly, this survey (and many others like it) spans levels of analysis in the McKinsey case conflating decision performance and corporate performance as completely aligned. As we have seen above, evidence for this is scarce, despite a strong intuitive argument which assumes high performing decisions will always be positively associated with high performing organizations.

Looking back on the Bradford Studies, however, some of the more interest-ing corners of the sample include decisions not to go ahead and decisions which went badly wrong. Although both of these factors are not as fashionable as high performance, they do (for me) highlight a relatively neglected area of decision-making research which is briefly explored in the next section.

Aborted decisions and decision failure

That we can learn as much from failures as successes is a truism. But, in strategic decision-making research, decisions which fail (and decisions not to proceed) remain relatively under-researched areas which, in my view, deserve equal attention to those decisions which are the shining stars of performance and success stories.

Decisions not to proceed are not the obvious focus of the decision-making researcher, yet they can reveal much about the process. There are two obvious points to make here. A Board (for example) making a decision not to proceed may take this decision in the light of informed investigation, a careful weighing up of the alternatives, and some careful forecasting. On the other hand, a Board may decide not to proceed because of institutionalized biases in the form of low risk preferences, political lobbying, stakeholder pressure, and organizational history amongst many other possible influences. Decisions not to do something can reveal as much about decision making and organizations as decisions to go ahead and do something. These are not the unseen decisions of non decision making. They are observable decisions on which decision makers decide not to proceed. The topic will likely have been already defined (do we launch a new service or product for example?) and yet authorization is not given to proceed and the decision is aborted in favour of others.

The above polar extreme explanations range from effective and rational risk analysis on the one hand and political suppression or screening out on the other. Both have been well-documented in the decision and power literatures, but research evidence would suggest that decisions do not proceed for many other reasons (including groupthink, hunches, gut feel, me-too strategies, partial or inaccurate data, as well as fads and fashions). A research agenda to study these areas would not necessarily suit business consultants, but the understanding of decision making can never be complete without an understanding of why certain topics are screened out and abandoned, whilst others remain on the agenda and are invested in and pursued. Medical sociology has made some progress to understand decisions not to proceed by clinicians and groups of medical practitioners. These may help in a broader understanding of organizational decisions.

For example, omission bias is 'a tendency to choose not to do something when doing something might cause harm' (Schulkin, 2000). A doctor would not prescribe HRT (for example) because of the fear of breast cancer. As Schulkin (2000: 816) notes, 'proportionality bias, on the other hand, is a tendency to overvalue or undervalue risk, and because of it physicians may not choose to prescribe HRT for fear of breast cancer, despite the low probability of occurrence'. A strong underpinning for these biases is uncertainty avoidance (well documented in the organizational literatures) although avoiding ambiguity can also characterize decision making in the light of apparently robust data.

For instance, evidence-based medicine (EBM) presents research findings derived from the application of scientific rigour in research studies. It is an information-based tool for decision making designed (amongst other uses) to minimize the effects of the various biases outlined above. Teams of experts evaluate information to decide how well studies are designed and how strong the evidence is. 'The founders of medical epidemiology and EBM sought to find rigorous scientific grounding for medical decision making by having the decision strictly follow the science. The key issue was to tie the practicing physician to research findings, and the primary validity measure was to be the randomized control trial' (Schulkin, 2000: 817). Of course, the slavish following of research findings (never complete or without ambiguity themselves) is also a form of bias and decisions can easily be aborted in the face of seemingly strong evidence that this will not work, or will not lead to expected outcomes.

Decision failure is largely treated as a separate field of study and research from the main body of decision process research. In contrast to the abortion of decision making, failure characterizes decisions which are progressed, but are ones in which the process, the outcome, (or both) goes badly wrong. Failure means not just decisions which under-perform (however measured) but includes decisions where often severely detrimental effects result from the decision such as loss of life, catastrophe, or other disaster. It is easy to see how a separate branch of organizational research developed in the area of disaster studies, but it is arguable that these fit within the purview of decision-making studies and that the study of decisions which go badly wrong is an integral part of our understanding of decision processes overall.

From one perspective, decision failures can be seen as the result of externally and internally generated shocks which organizations face. These include changes in the natural environment or macro-economic stability. Natural disasters such as hurricanes, earthquakes, or tornadoes would fall into the exogenous shock category as would disruptive technological changes which force decision makers to make choices not of their own making (technologies may be invented outside the organization, forcing decision makers in the organization to respond reactively). Few theorists however maintain that uncertainties due solely to external shocks are responsible for decision failures. Both Turner and Beck would see decision failures as either 'man-made' (Turner, 1978) or manufactured (Beck, 1992). Both these authors argue that risks which make decision failure more likely are organizationally created and these, in turn, influence the social and natural environments of organizations and decision makers. They may also influence national and global economic systems.

Events which seem to be 'natural' are argued to have an organizational origin. For example, the risks posed by earthquakes have been argued to have an organizational component, namely poor or disregarded building regulations. However, the occurrence of the earthquake itself is undeniably an exogenous risk. Technological failures, such as the Bhopal disaster, or the Challenger space shuttle, are argued to be rooted deeply in organizational processes. Perrow (1984) argued that one common factor in disasters which place people at risk is the mismatch between organizational structure and its technology in use. The explosion in the Union Carbide plant in Bhopal, India, was argued to be a result of the firm growing in size but not adapting to new technologies. When a fault occurred in the plant, it was not immediately noticed since the specialization of roles together with the remoteness of the manufacturing process (relying on arm's-length safety checks) did not accommodate inter-role communication which would have been needed to avert disaster. When a switch was thrown (accidentally) giving a false 'all systems OK' message, role specialization meant there was no possibility of checking this, despite it being obvious that something was wrong. By the time the problem was recognized it was too late. No individual had the capacity to stop the inevitable explosion which caused long-term damage to human and plant life.

Alexander (1996) accounts for the bursting of a gas pipeline in New Jersey in March 1994 as being attributable to the decision-making processes of the Texas Eastern Transmission Company, which were traditional, centralized, and inflexible, unable to cope with the demands of gas transmission. Greening and Johnson (1996) argue that highly interactive, tightly coupled, and high-risk technologies can spell high decision risk (and likely failure) in an organizational structure which is bureaucratic and inflexible. They argued that one of the problems of such organizations is the inability of top-level managers to cope with (or to prevent) disasters. This was seemingly prophetic, given the economic disasters which were to follow as a result of top-level failures (such as Enron). The events of September 11, 2001 and the subsequent invasion of Iraq have also been blamed on decision failures, in this case the paucity of information exchange between security agencies worldwide.

Looking at decision making from the perspective of these extreme failures reveals that levels of uncertainty and risk matter (as do the combination of endogenous and exogenous shocks to the organizational system). For example, new technologies and scientific developments (such as genetic engineering or gene therapy) have been described as the 'new' risks by a number of commentators (Jorian, 2000). Mostly, these are seen as exogenous risks to organizations (and to individuals in society). Nuclear power and biotechnology are developed 'out there' and provide sources of cheap energy or improved crop production for organizations. But they are considered risky since the 'downsides' of each are well-known. Decision makers inside organizations can actually increase (or multiply) these risks. For example, decision makers in Monsanto ignored public anxieties about the testing of gene technologies and it incurred heavy financial losses as a result. What began as an external risk was arguably badly managed internally and decisions made resulted in Monsanto facing even greater levels of risk (McGee, Thomas, and Wilson, 2005).

History is filled with organizational stupidity as well as organizational brilliance (according to March, 1999) and the study of stupidity (as March terms it) in decision making would seem just as important as the study of success. The sources of failure (and stupidity) through decision making are not, however, always clear and many debates surround them. For example, organizational growth, decline, and death can be argued to be a natural part of the organizational life cycle (Whetten, 1980; 1987). Decision making has little part to play in this deterministic context. Failure happens as a result of an inevitable life cycle. On the other hand, organizations and decision makers operate in societies which are themselves conglomerates of conflict and support relations, positive and negative affects, and (sometimes) indifference (Simmel, 1968). The effect of such contexts is to influence decision making sometimes towards success and sometimes towards failure, but decision makers have little 'strategic choice' in this process. From a completely opposite perspective, the values, dispositions of behaviours, and actions amongst decision makers have been argued to make decision failure more likely than any of the previous explanations (according to Kets de Vries and Miller, 1984).

Decision failure may also be organizational in origin. The term 'permanently failing organizations' (PFOs) was coined by Marshall Meyer and Lynne Zucker (1989). They observed that many organizations persist despite unsatisfactory performance. They argued that the key reason for PFOs was people's motivation to maintain organizations independently of their performance. For example, owners and shareholders may try to exit from under-performing organizations. But employees, customers, and suppliers who are dependent on these organizations generally stay loyal making exit difficult (Hirschmann, 1970). Therefore, decision making becomes frozen in patterns of behaviour when owners seeking to exit are frustrated by dependent actors seeking to delay or block exit. Secondly, managers (agents) may not tell the truth about performance. Principals (e.g. shareholders) will then have no sound basis for judgements on organizational performance. Or, those who purchase services may not be the end user (e.g. care services) and, hence, they cannot effectively evaluate performance. These are known as information asymmetries and can lead to persisting decision failure.

Organizational size (and identity) also matter. Large (and/or highly symbolic) organizations are often not permitted to go out of existence as easily as smaller ones independently of decision-making performance. For example, Lockheed went bankrupt through a series of poor decisions, but received governmental support because organizational failure would have had dire consequences of unemployment in California and Georgia where the manufacturing bases were located. Politicians lobbied strongly and got the support to ensure organizational survival. Eurotunnel, by many accounts bankrupt, is kept from failing by the UK and French governments. Many individuals (especially in France) thought this was a government project in any case

Very visible Failures such as the Columbia Space Shuttle disaster have been squarely blamed on decision-making failures. Foam insulation 'strikes' (NASA terminology) caused damage to the shuttle causing it to break up on re-entry killing all on board (February 1, 2003). Although there was plenty of previous analysis of the relationships between disasters and organizational/human behaviours (e.g. Perrow, 1984), in the case of the space shuttle, this was ignored. Why was this? According to Woods (2005), there were five classic decision-making patterns which led to failure:

1. The (unreasonable) requirement to be efficient (under time pressure) and thorough at the same time.
2. Taking past successes as indications of future performance.
3. Fragmented decision making clouds the big picture. Lots of decisions are taken but no-one has a full picture of the overall project and all the decisions made.
4. A failure to revise estimates/actions as new evidence accumulates.
5. Poor communication between organizational sub-units and their decision makers.

Whatever the causes of decision failure, it would seem too important a topic to be left off the decision-making research agenda. Although most research is understandably concerned with success and high performance in decision making, understanding the abandonment of decisions and understanding reasons for their failure would seem central to our fuller analysis of decision processes and outcomes.

FINAL THOUGHTS

Being a researcher in the Bradford Studies from start to finish taught me a great deal about the difficulties of researching decision making, both in terms of appropriate methods for data collection and in terms of theoretical approach. Research in decision making is certainly contested on nearly every front, empirically and conceptually. Yet it remains a central tenet (I would argue *the* central tenet) of understanding organizations. Decision making is too important to be left to the 'traditional' strategists who view decision making as a building block of something else (e.g. corporate strategy) or to the practice researchers in strategy where the focus is rarely on decision making as a practice. Ontological questions of what is a decision and epistemological questions of how we approach decision making conceptually remain, as do what we might term 'appropriate methods' for collecting rich and quality data to inform our understanding of decision making. There is certainly a full research agenda here for the future.

Two final thoughts remain. The first is a practical issue. I have recently supervised four PhD students all of whom wanted to study strategic decision-making processes from various perspectives. Of course, I encourage them and I am deeply flattered (and continue to be surprised) that some actually want to work with me. But they all face the problem of securing research access to organizations. Each researcher in turn has suffered from a significant lack of access to carry out research. Organizations either refuse to let research be carried out at all, or students find they cannot get access to senior management who they need to observe or interview and archival material is deemed too confidential for researchers to see. And this is in response to requests to research decisions which by and large are seen as successful by those organizations. One student who wanted to study decisions which fail ended up not getting access at all despite persistent attempts by many of us. In a tough economic climate it becomes even harder to gain the quality access needed for research (when, paradoxically, the study of decision making is arguably of greater importance than in times of resource munificence). This is a challenge which faces both researchers and practitioners alike. We have to find ways of convincing senior managers that the study of decision making is something which will be of benefit to them and is not something they should resist or try to keep hidden. I would see this operational challenge to be as great as the theoretical and empirical challenges outlined in this (and other) chapters in this Handbook.

The second thought is that the bulk of decision-making theory and evidence comes from Western, mostly highly developed Anglo-Saxon economies. A study of decision making in less developed economies or in countries where different values, norms, and expectations prevail would benefit the field enormously. Many authors in this book have made this point, so I will not labour it here. But just to take an obvious example, in countries where the Islamic faith pervades all organizational activities fundamental assumptions are subject to significant change. Personal relationships matter more than role relationships for example. Key concepts such as local rationality are likely to apply in fundamentally different ways in such contexts. Equally, in less developed nations and states, internal organizational processes such as decision making will be heavily influenced by the external macro-economic, legal, and social contexts. Africa is an obvious example. Weak and arguably ineffective governmental contexts coupled with a generally stagnant economy with negative trade balances and low levels of investment cannot do other than influence decision making at the level of every organization. And emerging economies such as China will also present contextual challenges to both researchers and to concepts developed largely in Western Anglo-Saxon nations. It goes without saying that the operational problems of access are likely to worsen in less developed and emerging economies, so I would doubt we will see a large number of international studies informing the field in the near future. Yet even the most cursory glance at books such as Hickson and Pugh's *Management Worldwide* (2001) will reveal how historically and culturally our knowledge of decision making is rooted in predominantly Western perspectives and transmitted in one dominant language – English. The view of a globalized (or international) perspective toward decision making needs substantial theoretical and empirical support (and evidence) from contexts other than English speaking and writing Anglo-Saxon economies.

Appendix 1: Major Publications from the Bradford Studies of Decision Making (in date order)

R.J. Butler, D.J. Hickson, D.C. Wilson, and R. Axelsson (1977) 'Organizational Power, Politicking and Paralysis', in M. Warner (ed.) *Organizational Choice and Constraint*. London: Sage.

David J. Hickson, W. Graham Astley, Richard J. Butler, and David C. Wilson (1981) 'Organization as Power', in L. Cummings and B. Staw (eds), *Research in Organizational Behavior, Volume 3*. Stanford, CT: JAI Press Inc., pp. 151–196.

David C. Wilson, Richard J. Butler, David Cray, David J. Hickson, and Geoffrey R. Mallory (1982) The limits of trade union power in organisational decision making, *British Journal of Industrial Relations*, 20, 322–341.

David C. Wilson (1982) Electricity and Resistance: A case study of innovation and politics, *Organization Studies*, 3, 119–140.

W. Graham Astley, Runo Axelsson, Richard J. Butler, David J. Hickson, and David C. Wilson (1982) Complexity and cleavage: Dual explanations of strategic decision-making, *Journal of Management Studies*, 19, 357–375.

Geoffrey R. Mallory, Richard J. Butler, David Cray, David J. Hickson, and David C. Wilson (1983) Implanted decision-making: American owned firms in Britain, *Journal of Management Studies*, 20, 191–211.

Graham K. Kenny and David C. Wilson (1984) The interdepartmental influence of managers: individual and sub-unit perspectives, *Journal of Management Studies*, 21, 409–427.

D. Hickson, R. Butler, D. Gray, G. Mallory, and D. Wilson (1986) *Top Decisions: Strategic Decision Making in Organizations.* San Francisco, CA: Jossey-Bass.

David C. Wilson, Richard J. Butler, David Cray, David J. Hickson, and Geoffrey R. Mallory (1986) Breaking the bounds of organization in strategic decision making, *Human Relations*, 39, 309–331.

David C. Wilson and Richard J. Butler (1986) Voluntary organizations in action: strategy in the voluntary sector, *Journal of Management Studies*, 23, 519–542.

David J. Hickson in association with Richard J. Butler, David Cray, Geoffrey R. Mallory, and David C. Wilson (1986) 'Governmental Influence Upon Decision Making in Organizations in the Private and Public Sectors in Britain', in Rolf Wolff (ed.), *Organizing Industrial Development.* Berlin/New York: de Gruyter, pp. 107–116.

Graham K. Kenny, Richard J. Butler and David J. Hickson, David Cray, Geoffrey R. Mallory and David C. Wilson (1987) Strategic decision making: influence patterns in public and private sector organizations, *Human Relations*, 40, 613–631.

David J. Hickson (1987) Decision-making at the top of organizations, *Annual Review of Sociology*, 13, 165–192.

David Cray, Geoffrey R. Mallory, Richard J. Butler, David J. Hickson, and David C. Wilson (1988) Sporadic, fluid and constricted processes: three types of strategic decision making in organizations, *Journal of Management Studies*, 25, 13–39.

David J. Hickson (1988) 'Ruminations on Munificence and Scarcity in Research', in Alan Bryman (ed.), *Doing Research in Organizations*, London: Routledge, pp. 136–150.

Henry Mintzberg and Jim Waters, A .M. Pettigrew and R. Butler (1990) Studying deciding: an exchange of views between Mintzberg and Waters, Pettigrew, and Butler, *Organization Studies*, 11, 1–16.

David Cray, Geoffrey R. Mallory, Richard J. Butler, David J. Hickson, and David C. Wilson (1991) Explaining decision processes, *Journal of Management Studies*, 28, 227–251.

Richard Butler, Les Davies, Richard Pike, and John Sharp (1991) Strategic investment decision-making: complexities, politics and processes, *Journal of Management Studies* 28, 395–415.

Runo Axelsson, David Cray, Geoffrey R. Mallory, and David C. Wilson (1991) Decision style in British and Swedish organizations: a comparative examination of strategic decision making, *British Journal of Management*, 2, 67–79.

Suzana Braga Rodrigues and David J. Hickson (1995) Success in decision making: different organizations, differing reasons for success, *Journal of Management Studies*, 32, 655–678.

Carlos Alberto Arruda and David J. Hickson (1996) 'Sensitivity to Societal Culture in Managerial Decision-Making: An Anglo-Brazilian Comparison', in Pat Joynt and Malcolm Warner (eds), *Managing Across Cultures: Issues and Perspectives.* London: International Thomson Business Press, pp. 179–201.

David C. Wilson, David J. Hickson, and Susan Miller (1996) How organizations can overbalance: decision overreach as a reason for failure, *American Behavioral Scientist*, 39, 995–1010.

Susan Miller (1997) Implementing strategic decisions: four key success factors, *Organization Studies*, 18, 577–602.

D. Hickson, R. Butler, and D. Wilson (2001) *The Bradford Studies of Decision Making: Classic Research in Management*, London: Ashgate.

D.J. Hickson, S. Miller, and D.C. Wilson (2003) Planned or prioritized? *Journal of Management Studies*, 40 (7), 1803–1836.

S. Miller, D.C. Wilson, and D.J. Hickson (2004) Beyond planning: strategies for successfully implementing strategic decisions, *Long Range Planning*, 37 (3), 201–218.

S.J. Miller and D.C. Wilson (2006) 'Perspectives on Organizational Decision-making', in S.R. Clegg, C. Hardy, T.B. Lawrence, and W.R. Nord (eds), *The SAGE Handbook of Organization Studies*, London: Sage, 2nd edition, pp. 469–484,

D.C. Wilson (2007) 'Strategic Decision Making', in G. Ritzer (ed.) *The Blackwell Encyclopedia of Sociology*. Oxford: Blackwell.

S. Miller, D.J. Hickson, and D.C. Wilson (2008) From strategy to action: involvement and influence in top level decisions, *Long Range Planning*, 41, 606–628.

REFERENCES

Alexander, C.B. (1996) Planning for disaster, *American Gas*, 78 (2), 24–27.

Ashmos, D.P., Duchon, D., McDaniel, Jr, and Huonker, J.W. (2002) What a mess! Participation as a simple managerial rule to 'complexify' organizations *Journal of Management Studies*, 39 (2), 189–206.

Bachrach, P.M., and M.S., Baratz (1970) *Power and Poverty: Theory and Practice*. Oxford: Oxford University Press.

Beck, U. (1992) *Risk Society: Towards a New Modernity*. London: Sage.

Bourgeois, III, L.J., and Brodwin, D.R. (1984) Strategic implementation: Five approaches to an elusive phenomenon, *Strategic Management Journal*, 5, 241–264.

Brown, S.L., and Eisenhardt, K.M. (1995) Product development: Past research, present findings, and future directions, *Academy of Management Review*, 20, 343–378.

Brunsson, N. (1995) 'Managing Organizational Disorder', in M. Warglien and M. Masuch (eds) *The Logic of Organizational Disorder*. Berlin: De Gruyter.

Bruzzi, S. (2000) *New Documentary: A Critical Introduction*. London: Performing Arts.

Butler, R.J., Hickson, D.J., Wilson, D.C., and Axelsson, R. (1977) 'Organizational Power, Politicking and Paralysis', in M. Warner (ed) *Organizational Choice and Constraint*. London: Sage.

Child, J. (1972) Organizational structure, environment and performance: The role of strategic choice, *Sociology*, 6 (1), 1–22.

Clegg, S., Courpasson, D., and Phillips, N. (2006) *Power and Organizations*. London: Sage.

Cohen, M.D., March, J.P., and Olsen, J.P. (1972) A garbage can model of organizational choice, *Administrative Science Quarterly*, 17, 1–25.

Cummings S., and Wilson, D.C. (2003) *Images of Strategy*. London: Blackwell.

Cummings, S. (2002) *Recreating Strategy*. London: Sage.

Cyert, R.M., and March, J.G. (1963) *A Behavioral Theory of the Firm*. Englewood Cliff, NJ: Prentice Hall.

Dean, J., and Sharfman M. (1993) Procedural rationality in the strategic decision making process, *Journal of Management Studies*, 30, 607–630.

Dean, J., and Sharfman, M. (1996) Does decision making matter? A study of strategic decision making effectiveness, *Academy of Management Journal*, 39 (2), 368–396.

Deleuze, G., and Guattari, F. (1977) *Anti-Oedipus*. New York: Viking.

Deleuze, G., and Guattari, F. (1988) *Mille Plateaux: Capitalism and Schizophrenia*. London: Athlone.

Eisenhardt, K., and Bourgeois, J. (1989) 'Charting strategic decisions in the micro computer industry: profile of an industry starr', in M. Van Glenow and S. Moherman (eds) *Managing Complexity in High Technology Organizations, Systems, and People*, New York: Oxford University Press, 74–89.

Flyvbjerg B. (1998) *Rationality and Power: Democracy in Practice*. Chicago: University of Chicago Press.

Flyvbjerg B. (2001) *Making Social Science Matter*. Cambridge: University of Cambridge Press.

Gavetti G., and Levinthal, D. (2000) Looking forward and looking backward: Cognitive and experiential search, *Administrative Science Quarterly*, 45 (1), 113–137.

Greening D.W., and Johnson, R.A. (1996) Do managers and strategies matter? A study in crisis, *Journal of Management Studies*, 33 (1), 25–51.

Hickson, D., Butler, R., Cray, D., Mallory, G., and Wilson, D. (1986) *Top Decisions: Strategic Decision Making in Organizations*. San Francisco, CA: Jossey-Bass.

Hickson, D.J., and Pugh, D. (2001) *Management Worldwide: Distinctive Styles Amid Globalization*. Harmondsworth: Penguin, 2nd edition.

Hickson, D.J., Miller, S., and Wilson, D.C. (2003) Planned or prioritised: Two options in managing the implementation of decisions, *Journal of Management Studies*, 40 (7), 1803–1836.

Hirschmann, A.O. (1970) *Exit, Voice and Loyalty: Responses to decline in firms, organisations and states*. Cambridge, MA: Harvard University Press.

Jorian, P. (2000) 'Value, risk and control: The call for integration', *Financial Times*, May 16.

Kets de Vries, M., and D. Miller, D. (1984) *The Neurotic Organisation*. San Francisco, CA: Jossey-Bass.

Mangham, I. (1986) *Power and Performance in Organizations: An Exploration of Executive Process*. Oxford: Blackwell.

March, J.G. (1999) *Organizational Intelligence*. London: Sage.

McGee, J., Thomas, H., and Wilson, D.C. (2005) *Strategy: Analysis and Practice*. Maidenhead: McGraw-Hill.

Meyer, J.M., and Rowan, B. (1977) Institutionalised organization: Formal structure as myth and ceremony, *American Journal of Sociology*, 83 (2), 340–363.

Meyer, M.W., and Zucker, L. (1989) *Permanently Failing Organisations*. Newbury Park, CA: Sage.

Miller, S., Wilson, D.C., and Hickson, D.J. (2004) Beyond planning: Strategies for successfully implementing strategic decisions, *Long Range Planning*, 37 (3), 201–218.

Miller S., Hickson, D.J., and Wilson, D.C. (2008) From strategy to action: Involvement and influence in top level decisions, *Long Range Planning*, 41(6), 606–628.

Miller, S., Hickson, D.J., and Wilson, D.C. (2009) Actioning strategic decisions: Connecting deciding and implementing, *Working paper*, Warwick Business School.

Moorman, C., and Miner, A.S. (1998) Organizational improvisation and organizational memory, *Academy of Management Review*, 23 (4), 698–724.

Nutt, P.C. (1984) Types of organizational decision processes, *Administrative Science Quarterly*, 29 (3), 414–450.

Nutt, P. C. (1986) Tactics of implementation, *Academy of Management Journal*, 29 (2), 230–261.

Nutt, P.C. (1998) Framing strategic decisions, *Organizational Science*, 9(2), 195–206.

Perlow, L.A., Okhuysen, G.A., and Repenning, N.P. (2002) The speed trap: Exploring the relationship between decision-making and temporal context, *Academy of Management Journal*, 45 (5), 931–955.

Perrow, C. (1984) *Normal Accidents: Living with High-risk Technologies*. New York: Basic Books.

Sharfman, M.P., and Dean Jr, J.W. (1997) 'The effects of context on strategic decision-making processes and outcomes', in V. Papadakis and P. Barwise (eds) *Strategic Decisions*. Dordrecht, Boston, London: Kluwer.

Schulkin, J. (2000) Decision sciences and evidence-based medicine: Two intellectual movements to support clinical decision making, *Academic Medicine*, 75 (8), 816–818.

Simmel, G. (1968) *Soziologie*. Berlin: Humbolt.

Soon, C.S., Brass, M., Heinze, H.-J., and Haynes, J.-D. (2008) Unconscious determinants of free decisions in the human brain, *Nature Neuroscience* April 13.

Turner, B. (1978) *Man-Made Disasters*. London: Wykeham.

Wagner, J.A. (1994) Participation's effects on performance and satisfaction: A reconsideration of research evidence, *Academy of Management Review*, 19, 312–330.

Warglien, M., and Masuch, M. (eds) (1995) *The Logic of Organizational Disorder*. Berlin: De Gruyter.

Weick, K.E. (1979) *The Social Psychology of Organizing*. Reading, MA: Addison-Wesley, 2nd edition.

Weick, K. (1995) *Sensemaking in Organizations*. London: Sage.

Wensley, J.R.C. (2003) 'Strategy as intention and anticipation', in S. Cummings and D.C. Wilson (eds) *Images of Strategy*. Oxford: Basil Blackwell.

Whetten, D. (1980) 'Sources, responses and effects of organizational decline', in J. Kimberley and R. Miles (eds) *The Organizational Life Cycle*. San Francisco, CA: Jossey-Bass.

Whetten, D. (1987) Organisational growth and decline processes, *Annual Review of Sociology*, 13, 355–358.

Wilson, D.C., Butler, R.J., Cray, D., Hickson, D.J., and Mallory, G.R. (1986) Breaking the bounds of organization in strategic decision making, *Human Relations*, 9, 309–331.

Woods, D.D. (2005) 'Creating foresight: Lessons for Enhancing Resilience from Columbia', in W. Starbuck and M. Farjoun (eds) *Organisation at the Limit*. Oxford: Blackwell.

Part VII

DIRECTIONS AND PERSPECTIVES

23

Discussion and Implications: Toward Creating a Unified Theory of Decision Making

PAUL C. NUTT AND DAVID C. WILSON

INTRODUCTION

Summing up presents a challenge, especially when the subject matter deals with many divergent views and conflicting opinions. Decision making is one such subject, as the forgoing chapters aptly attest. This is understandable. We approached our contributors with an offer to address what they believed to be important issues facing decision-making research. Not surprisingly, our contributor's chapters reflect their interests as investigators who do research in this area. While insightful and relevant to decision making, few address 'process questions'. This reflects the literature. Here and elsewhere the literature emphasizes factors that impinge on process (information, risk, and errors), process components (innovation and groups), and contextual issues (setting, professionalism, and knowledge). Process as action taking is largely ignored. While insightful and important, the diversity of our chapters poses difficulties. Like past effort to sum up, we are confronted with differences in content and approach that resist integration.

Many view diversity as a positive. The field is diffuse and the chapters, like the literature, reflect this reality. Many different conceptions of decision making provide many different kinds of insights to be pondered for a field that has yet to mature. Limiting development may well restrict search and thus breakthroughs. Diversity also produces some negatives. Decision-making research has yet to offer either a coherent description or prescription. Each new effort produces a new set of ideas that further complicates the task of integration. With this in mind, we will draw conclusions about the status of the field and make recommendations for future work. Our goal is to move toward integration with a prescriptive intent. We call for a focus on research that informs practice, offering managers a way to increase their prospect of

Handbook of Decision Making.   Edited by Paul C. Nutt and David C. Wilson
© 2010 John Wiley & Sons, Ltd

being successful when making a decision. We believe this will help decision-making researchers be clearer about the concepts and empirics of their research and how it fits within the broader terrain of organization theory.

Our contributors treat decision making in a number of ways. Some consider a single issue such as the chapters on innovation, groups, risk, professionalism, errors, knowledge, IT, and the like. Others offer conceptual models that suggest the beginnings of a decision-making theory such as the chapters by Mintzberg, Weick, Goia, Child, Elbanna, Rodrigues, Nutt, and Wilson. We also presented research that considers decision making as a process, incorporating action steps that range from recognition to implementation. The situation noted by Papadakis and Barwise (1998) seems to persist – research continues to be focused on adding one more piece to the puzzle. However, integration attempts are confronted with a troubling incompatibility among many of these ideas, as well as missing pieces. It appears that incremental efforts, which has characterized past research, have not provided a gradual accumulation of knowledge indicating how decisions *should* be made. As a result, we have few empirically tested prescriptions that offer practitioners anything resembling an action plan for decision making.

Several other concerns are highlighted by this volume. We find that the efforts noted here, and elsewhere, treat decision making as a structure or as a process, but seldom as both. Furthermore, we find a reluctance to deal with process. Much of the research reported here and elsewhere deals with generalizations about process (its political nature or its rationality), but not action steps. Earlier in the volume (see Chapter 21), it was shown how structure informs process and provides a basis to develop a richer process representation, potentially of value to practitioners.

Theories abound in the literature. However, we find that theory is either missing or treated implicitly in much decision-making research. Rarely is there an explicit attempt to identify and test competing theories or to use them to model action steps in a process. In this chapter, we identify a number of decision-making theories and discuss how such theories can be used to aid future research by offering process models.

Many research efforts had a vague purpose. In many of the studies we examined, it was difficult to tell if the purpose was description or prescription. Other research efforts embrace aims, such as promoting or converting. Many other purposes can be identified, providing an additional barrier to integration. Considering the insights offered by description and prescription, we show how a merger offers additional insights. We also argue that advocacy is fine but hope that other, more important, aims become priorities.

How can the rampant confusion about 'strategic decision making' that entangles strategic management with decision making be resolved? In the strategy literature, (see for example, Bower, 1997), the needs for decision-making research become lost in arguments about formulating strategy. This has led Bower to argue that decision making is resource allocation, with a little problem solving. This may capture part of needed action but ignores a number of key issues. We argue that making assessments about research needs for decision making from an appraisal of strategic management leads to a limited conception of decision making. To cope, we suggest using the content of a decision, strategic and non-strategic choices, as a factor in research efforts. Distinguishing the two and uncovering whether a different process is required to deal with each decision type will help to disentangle this issue.

We offer a series of positions on how to focus this research. Perhaps the most important of these positions is our emphasis on process. Many past efforts either ignore process, apply vague descriptors with little empirical backing to characterize process, or use a few select factors as proxies for process, such as number of participants or group involvement. We define process as action steps, either taken or inferred, and call for research that uncovers an empirically defensible documentation of the action steps. Secondly, we take an action theory perspective. Our interest is to fashion an empirically grounded set of prescriptions that indicate how to make decisions that have a better chance of success, compared to competing notions and ideas. We embrace descriptive efforts *if* such efforts include a comparison of benefits that accrue when the actions uncovered in the description are followed. Even so, we believe that behavior is but one element of an action theory. Behavioral representations added to prescriptive ideas form a more complete representation of process in an action theory. Finally, we stress the importance of codifying decision outcomes and outside influences. It is crucial to identify benefits that result when the processes of various types are followed and the influence of situational factors.

There is also a need to codify what is meant by decision outcomes. Various researchers have studied outcomes, but seldom agree about what is meant by a decision outcome. To illustrate, some see an outcome as a new building that was built as intended. Others see the outcomes as what happens in the new building and the new behaviors provoked in people working in it. On the other hand, it may be, as some have suggested, that trying to link a particular outcome to a specific decision process is misguided. According to this view, decisions yield multiple outcomes that become the basis for future decision activities rather than a discrete and perhaps directly observable outcome in its own right.

Taking Stock

The chapters in the book offer a window into the world of decision-making research. The window sheds light on a number of issues derived from the contemporary research efforts offered in our chapters. Combined with past review efforts, they profile the status of the field. Using this profile, we will infer needs and opportunities.

In Chapter 1, we identified several issues that, according to our reading of the literature, needed attention. These issues stimulated our interest and motivated the book. They included purpose, unit of analysis, defining and measuring process, the influence of contingency, produce-produce models of key factors, as well as select observations about methodology. The research presented in this volume suggests that much more work needs to be done to deal with these issues. *Purpose* clarifies the intent of decision-making research, such as offering prescription or providing descriptions. Our volume reflects the literature – in which purpose is often implicit. Our contributors (like the extant literature), examined decision making with many purposes in mind. Purposes ranged from tool development (e.g. Chapter 8), to prescription (Chapters 7 and 21) through descriptions of what decision makers do (e.g. Chapters 3 and 4), to factors impinging on the process (e.g. Chapters 10–15). Our volume also continues traditions found in the literature in which most research efforts embrace a particular facet of decision making (such as groups, risk, errors, content, or context), with only a few addressing the entire decision episode.

Integration is also hindered by framing dilemmas, the difficulties in reconciling descriptive with prescriptive findings, and missing or limited process insights. We called for a more inclusive *unit of analysis* than found in past work. Instead of focusing on choice activities, we argue for a unit of analysis that includes all of the actions required to render a decision, from recognition to implementation. Chapter 23 spells out some of the difficulties researchers will confront to follow this recommendation. Most of our contributors do not address a decision episode in this way. This reflects the literature. *Process* has been defined and measured vary differently in the literature. This persists in our volume as well. Many research efforts fail to specify action elements or do so in a way that makes integration difficult. Some researchers focus on process features, such as rationality or politics, and say little about how decisions were made. Rational and political classifications fail to address how decision makers act rationally or engage politically. This limitation continues. *Contingency theory* contends that boundary conditions stipulate when to use a given type of process. Some processes are believed to work better under some conditions, and not others. Surprisingly, little research has been carried to test this pervasive contention. Research efforts that have been conducted consider just one element of a process, such as implementation-related issues, identifying several qualifications (Vroom and Jago, 1978; Nutt, 1987). Few do so using a process. We report a study that incorporates a number of situational factors and tests the influence of these factors on process (see Chapter 17). This study finds that situational factors do not influence process results, suggesting that contingency thinking may be an unnecessary complication in theory development. Another chapter (23) concludes that in some circumstances, contingency factors seem to play an important role in shaping and influencing strategic decisions. More work is needed to validate these seemingly contradictory positions. To do so, we suggested *producer-product models* of key factors in which process (action-taking steps), context (importance, urgency, etc.), and content (strategic, nonstrategic) are linked to outcomes that produce costs and benefits. There have been many relationships suggested in which process is causal, mediating, or an outcome of some contextual factor. We find no empirical justification to posit such relationships and suggest that statistical models of main effects and interaction effects should guide future work. The observations about *methodology* remain – the debate about rigor and relevance has not been resolved. We believe that a shift toward relevance is essential. We will discuss methodology later in this chapter.

Papadakis, Thanos, and Barwise provide a review of decision-making research in Chapter 2 that adds to our findings. Chapter 2 picks up where their previous work left off, extending conclusions and offering a new appraisal. Several questions were addressed. What has the last decade or so provided? Have the problems been transcended? What remains to be done? We link their conclusions with some of our own, which were offered in Chapter 1. Several studies since 1997 have explored links between process characteristics and outcomes, at both the decision and the organizational level. Three major opportunities were identified. First, Papadakis *et al.* find that studies which linked process to outcome used process measures that were wanting. These studies measure process with simplistic generalizations, such as rational or intuitive. To overcome this they call for a multi-dimensional indicator of process. We believe that this criticism is valid, but does not go nearly far enough. Rational or intuitive says little about the nature of the actions undertaken – how did the decision maker act rationally or intuitively? A multi-dimensional factor would not help to overcome this defect found in many research efforts. Instead, we call for research that documents the actions taken by decision makers as well as the action outcomes.

Second, the Papadakis, Thanos, and Barwise review finds that the moderating effects of context have not been adequately explored. Factors such as external market environment, munificence, instability, dynamism, and uncertainty have been recently studied but internal organizational environment and the characteristics of top management have been overlooked. They also note that recent studies use data from both developed and developing countries and call for more cross-cultural research to explore how cultural differences influence decision making. We see this as a call for a more inclusive list of contextual factors to be included in a research effort. We agree. Focusing on a single factor does not allow the findings to appreciate the joint influence of these factors. A multi-factor approach is desirable. We believe, however, that an action-driven characterization of process, and its interaction with such factors, has precedence over measuring process as one would a contextual factor.

Papadakis *et al.* call for determining the relationship between decision outcomes and organizational performance. This theme was noted in their original work as well, asking researchers to do more to document the linkage. We find such efforts of questionable value. Linking firm performance, such as ROI, to an organizational decision lacks propositional validity. Many factors influence firm performance. Capturing these factors and controlling for their effects is a formidable task, seldom addressed. Similarly, attempting to trace the consequences of a decision to firm performance indicators calls for a blizzard of confounding factors in the study design, which are difficult if not impossible to identify or control. Such a trace also seems a distraction to needed research efforts.

We agree with Papadakis *et al.* that more emphasis on intuitive decision making is needed. As noted in prospect theory (Hammond *et al.*, 1980) and the information processing literature (Nisbett and Ross, 1989), many decisions are made in this way. Much of quantitative research efforts overlook this, in part because the frame employed points the researcher away from actions that suggest intuition and how intuition works in practice. Such a research effort would be vastly different from those discussed this far. Still, further work addressing intuition could be fruitful and provide an interesting complement to current views of decision making. Papadakis *et al.* argue that the effect of contextual variables on intuition should be included in these studies. We concur.

A theme in this volume (and our other writings) is the confusion inherent in calling an important decision 'strategic' (see Chapter 1). Papadakis *et al.* do not address this issue. Instead, they appear to call *all* decisions strategic. They then confuse the matter further by discussing how strategy content and process literatures have been developed independently, when they should inform one another. It is fine to argue that strategy work would benefit from merging case studies that treat strategy as a noun (content) and those that treat it as a verb (process). We agree that process and content distinctions in the literature have said little about organizational performance. This, however, does little to untangle the distinction between strategic decisions from other decisions. The key question is whether the same process is used. Disentangling the strategy literature from the decision literature seems a needed step in which investigators in both areas are free to undertake needed studies.

CREATING AN INTEGRATION: SOME SUGGESTIONS FOR FUTURE WORK

To move the field forward, a number of issues must be confronted. We identified several that merit special attention. To review, they were: purpose, unit of analysis, defining and measuring process, documenting and measuring outcome consequences, context and content factors that made up contingency relationships, and produce-produce models suggesting the relationship among key factors. Ancillary issues call attention to theory development, methodology, and the involvement of top management teams and top managers. Under each, we shall discuss what framed our quest and led to this book.

To deal with these issues, we address the 'what' and the 'how' of a proposed decision making research program. The 'what' identifies the focus of inquiry. This focus has taken many forms, as indicated by the variety of research questions considered in the work presented here, and elsewhere. We recommend a research focus that embraces action research. We acknowledge that there are many other foci but believe that an action one serves the interests of managers and researchers better than other options. This treats decision making as an applied field, like engineering and medicine, and calls for research to uncover decision-making practices (proposed and used) and testing them to find practices apt to improve results. In a sense, this is a call for evidence-based research in decision making.

Such a focus also calls for a balance between rigor and relevance. In much of the current work in decision making, and indeed, management, rigor is implicitly, if not explicitly, emphasized. This has moved researchers away from the study of decisions to research questions that allow investigators to focus on factors that can be operationalized and deftly measured in a single study. Researchers are coaxed by journal editors, and their rigor-agendas, to study tangential aspects of decision making, such as the number of participants, instead of larger questions that, by their very nature, resist precise measurements. The measure of a factor is *not* given by its measurability. To illustrate, a key factor in decision making is process. One way to measure process is to codify the actions taken by a decision maker. Documenting these actions and determining their consequences pose many methodological challenges. We believe that embracing these challenges should be the thrust of future work.

These challenges pose questions about how this can be accomplished. Thus, the 'how' involves methodology, which will be discussed in a following section. The key issue is documenting process with sufficient precision that unique types of action steps (process types) can be linked to the results produced by each process type. Subsidiary concerns involve measuring the value of the results and determining whether qualifications, which stem from content and context, influence them.

THE 'WHAT' OF DECISION-MAKING RESEARCH

Formulating an action theory research program for decision making presents many challenges. Action theory requires a focus on practice, either an evaluation of existing practice or an assessment of practice recommendations. Both call for a researcher to be clear about how decisions are and should be made. One informs the other. The researcher can ask what decision makers do in an attempt to ferret out and appreciate exemplary practice (see, for example, Schon, 1983). The researcher can document decision-maker actions and compare them to what the literature contends *should* be done. With outcomes determined and their merit assessed, the researcher can verify the merits of an 'exemplary practice', and determine what creates this value.

In this section, we will consider several key considerations that lead us to recommending this kind of research. They include the role of decision-making theory and ways to frame an action theory investigation. In the following section, we address ways to codify process, the key factor in an action theory for decision making. To do so we suggest several kinds of studies. Finally, we identify some ways to measure outcomes and suggest situational factors, and pose relationships that merit testing.

Decision-making theory

Contributors to this volume identify, directly or indirectly, several competing decision-making theories. For example, Wilson and his colleagues identify relevant theory as embedded institutionalism, politics, complexity, and knowledge. In Chapter 17, Nutt summarizes competing theories as stage-based, politics/negotiation, and chance. In Chapter 20, Poole and Van de Ven identify life cycle, teleological, dialectics, and evolution as key theories and suggest a number of ways to elaborate each. Creating some coherence among these competing ideas seems a first order of business.

An integration of competing views of theory offers a platform for others to critique and elaborate upon as they formulate their action theory investigation. Life cycle and teleological are both stage-based but have an important distinction. In life cycle, the stages have logic behind them but a fixed relationship; the stages require a particular sequence. In the teleological theory, some stages may not be activated and activated stages can have a variety of sequences. Both offer a useful elaboration of a stage-based decision-making theory. Dialectics presumes that decision making is driven by conflict; so thesis and antithesis take shape as differences between positions held by key players on important issues. This makes position taking, conflict, and synthesis the key stages. Like the life cycle decision-making theory, these stages are expected to arise in all decisions. Evolution has less staging and a more amorphous clash among emergent ideas. Ideas become the process engine in which stages of new or hybrid ideas (variation), selection, and retention repeat until an idea is recognized that seems viable. The number of idea cycles can vary along a path to retention, with some being drawn out and others occurring rapidly.

Chance theory can be incorporated with the evolutionary theory and politics and negotiation theories can fit into either teleological or dialectical theory. Chance asserts that problems, solutions, and decision opportunities mill about in an organization until they have an accidental meeting. The solution finds a home in this way, often irrespective of its merit. However, change provides but one of many idea sources in a bundle of emergent ideas. Many are unrelated to chance (Nutt, 2008). Politics and negotiation theories call for ways to resolve competing ideas. The framing event is a clash between parties to a decision, with different notions about what to do. Negotiation tactics are evoked to resolve the clash. Negotiation can also be seen as one stage of a more inclusive teleological process that also recognizes stages of issue recognition and solution implementation. Negotiation can also be seen as a dialectic in which tension is resolved with a synthesis. In either case, politics/negotiation represents what seems a choice-related set of activities that are part of a larger process.

Decision-making theories can be embellished by a host of additional features, as noted by Poole and Van de Ven in Chapter 20. Nesting in stages and sub-stages can be identified. Nesting can arise as a hierarchy or as a loosely coupled system. The relationship can be explicated, specifying whether there is a reinforcing or a dampening relationship among stages and sub-stages. Additionally, these stage linkages can be independent, cyclical, or intermittent in nature. Temporal relationships can be specified such as the speed and duration of action, as well as how urgency influences the activated process stages. The means of carrying out key stages can be explicated. For example, the conflict between a plan and a counter-plan creates a tension. Various ways to frame and manage tensions can be added to the mix to see which explains decision-maker behavior. Werner and Baxter (1994), Nutt and Backoff (1993), and Johnson (1992) offer frameworks to identify and classify tensions. Hampden-Turner (1990) and Nutt *et al.* (2000) provide ways to resolve tension types with solutions. Together they offer plausible ways to model how tensions are identified and managed in a dialectical process in a framework.

Mintzberg and Westley, in Chapter 3, identify three additional theory types applicable to decision making – see first, think first, and do first. 'Think first' has a define, diagnose, design, and decide sequence, which parallels what many call the rational process and is similar to the teleological stage-based framework, discussed above. 'See first' suggests that action should be governed by holistic conceptions or visions of what might be. Sudden insights are believed to be at the root of many successful decisions. 'Do first' draws on Weick *et al.* (see Chapter 4) and is derived from Weick's notions of sensemaking. Here insight stems from trying something out so the process is thought to involve enactment, selection, and retention. Improvisation, experimenting with what might work, is believed to be the key to success.

'Think first' draws on science, 'see first' on imagination, and 'do first' on craft. To facilitate thinking, decision makers move through the process to collect facts and then apply problem-solution and pro-con analysis, and the like. To see first, the decision maker draws a picture of possibilities. Alternatively, the decision maker can apply one of the many creativity techniques found in the literature (Stein, 1975). Improvisation is facilitated by role-play in which participants take action and adjust to others with competing ideas. Mintzberg and Westley claim that each approach should be supplemented by the other approaches and that healthy organizations use all three approaches. Somewhat in conflict with this, they offer a contingency model that matches approaches to decision tasks. The 'think first' approach is proposed for decision situations in which the motivating concerns are known, facts available, and conflict manageable. A 'see first' is suggested for decision makers facing a novel situation and/or a situation in which innovation is required. 'Do first' is preferred for confusing situations in which players have complex and potentially conflicting views. The Mintzberg and Westley model allows researchers to include intuitive decision making into their studies, comparing how well creativity as well as the teleological stage-based model (think first) work for novel and analytical decision tasks. To include a 'do first' approach in such a study will require additional clarity about its action steps.

In Chapter 4 Weick, Sutcliff, and Obstfeld discuss 'sensemaking', providing some additional rationale that supports a 'do first' approach. Sensemaking involves a retrospective construction that explains what people were doing. It involves the old adage that decision makers are unable to see what they want until they see what they can get (Wildavsky, 1979). When people understand (see possibilities), this understanding becomes a springboard for action. Thus, insight into possibilities is crucial. Two questions arise. Where do the solution ideas come from? Additionally, how is 'do first' distinct from 'see first'? In the chapter, Weick *et al.* consider some of the conundra inherent in retrospective sensemaking by suggesting a prospective version. In brief, they contend that decision makers wishing to improvise should 'make do' with steps of being resilient, relaxing constraints, imposing plausibility tests, and being persistent. This continues to overlook the source of tangible solutions. Where do these solutions come from? Until the source of solution ideas can be specified, 'do first' appears to be a subset (or an elaboration) of 'see first', which begins by finding ideas for testing. Translating 'do first' into a testable action theory will be a challenge for researchers. If the challenge is met, a 'do first' approach can be added to the mix, allowing 'think first', 'see first', and 'do first' to be applied to decision tasks with seeming matches and mismatches.

Goia and Hamilton, in Chapter 6, argue that values, ideals, principles, core beliefs, and the like constitute an organization's *identity*. They call for aligning 'who we are' with 'what we do' so organizational identity governs the choices made and the actions taken. This calls on decision makers to ask who we are before making a decision. This seems to make the quest for identity a framing key feature of a decision-making process. To understand what was done one must uncover and codify identity. This can be operationalized in several ways. Researchers can use identity to suggest what environmental features will be viewed as salient by decision makers, potentially uncovering cognitive biases, and predicting attention. Among other things, this may suggest preferred search approaches and decision rules. This makes identity an important adjunct to many decision-making theories. It has some obvious applications to Mintzberg's 'see first' theory, suggesting another way possibilities can be visualized.

Wilson picks up a similar theme in Chapter 22. While agreeing that identity reveals some of the less well researched aspects of decision making, such as core beliefs, operationalizing such concepts is difficult. The problems lie in the nonrepresentational nature of who we are and what we believe. Some aspects of 'who we are' are not only deeply embedded but also extremely difficult for the researcher to 'see' until they are made explicit both to the researcher (his or her own values and beliefs) and to decision makers. Many of these nonrepresentational aspects remain implicit. There is evidence to show that individual researchers from different cultural backgrounds look for different aspects of decision making in their research. This discards some key questions, such as the ability of decision-making researchers to include comparative international research questions. A simple example may help shed some light on this concern. Chinese opera is not to everyone's taste and many Chinese people, who are regular attendees, agree that the music and singing can be discordant and quite strange. An English person would almost certainly make the same point. However, a Chinese person will have been socialized and trained over time to look also at many different things that are happening during the opera. What is happening visually, how the set is structured, what other bit players are doing, how scenery is depicted are just some of the important factors (beyond the music) appreciated by a Chinese audience. Many of these are more important than the music. A Western audience is much more likely to concentrate solely on the music and the singing of the main actors, ignoring the other contextual factors because this is how Westerners have been socialized to watch opera. The conclusion that the music may be discordant will be the same in the case of the Westerner and the person from China, yet the Chinese person will arguably have experienced a completely different event and experienced a completely different set of actions and structures to the Westerner.

Other relevant literatures. There are a number of other literatures relevant to decision making. An important one is information processing (e.g. Nisbett and Ross, 1989). This literature reports many well-controlled experiments, conducted by psychologists, which offer insights into how humans process information (e.g. MacCrimmon and Taylor, 1976). Although these insights are useful in both the information gathering and selection steps of a decision-making process, few have put them to use in the organizational decision-making literature discussed above. Findings in the information processing literature identify framing biases such as availability, sampling errors, selective perception, vividness, concreteness, and proximity. Biases in processing information are also noted including hindsight, anchoring, and presentation effects (Kahneman and Tversky, 1973). Related literatures, such as prospect theory, are also relevant (Hammond *et al.*, 1980). Together, they identify biases that are encountered as humans collect and process information, and how to avoid them. Much of this literature was developed with naïve subjects, causing many organizational decision theorists to be leery of generalizing the findings to practicing managers. Incorporating insights about information collection and processing biases into frameworks that capture the steps required to make a decision and testing them with *real* decisions would be a welcome addition to the organizational decision-making literature.

A second literature, related to information processing, explores how *professionals* use information to make decisions. This literature has focused on a number of topics. Many involve medical decision making. These studies use real data to create simulations to determine the accuracy of diagnoses and related predictions, criteria used or emphasized, and whether protocols are followed (e.g. Goldberg, 1968). To illustrate, cancer specialists have developed protocols in which seven signs on an X-ray are used to distinguish between stomach cancer and ulcers. To test the protocol and the protocol user, X-rays are collected from post-operative patients (so a diagnosis can be confirmed). These X-rays are then given to experts who are asked to look for the seven signs and make a diagnosis, which is evaluated as to accuracy. Results show that experts are over confident of their ability to make an accurate diagnosis, with error rates that range from 30 % to 50 %. The best performing clinician has difficulty getting beyond 70 % accuracy. Residents in these studies often out-performed the Chief Radiologist. This prompted a series of 'man vs. model of man' studies in which models were constructed to process the information, as called for in protocols, noted by experts, and/or inferred by model builders.

Another key finding is how experts use information. To illustrate, physicians invariably call for 'differential diagnosis' in which information is used contingently. The values of two or more diagnostic factors must go beyond norms before an action is recommended. To confirm this, studies of physician recommendations made using hypothetical cases were carried out. In their simplest form, these cases were constructed as follows: The factor's values are mixed so they are both beyond the norm, one at or below and the other beyond the norm, and both at or below the norm. To confirm that a differential diagnosis was made, the cases with factors beyond the norm must be localized in that quadrant (both beyond the norm) of a 2×2 matrix collecting the expert's decisions. Analysis finds that diagnoses are seldom made in this way. Experts use indicators independently, not in concert as called for by a differential diagnosis. Related studies find that criteria are crimped, with experts using only a subset of those they deemed to be essential, and weighted in ways not called for in the protocol. This stream of research concludes that experts forget their protocols over time and fail to use them consistently. Models of man use data consistently, with performance accuracy (correct diagnosis in the study noted above) that matches the best performing expert. A host of related medical studies involving EKG interpretation, suicide prevention, and the like has produced similar findings.

These findings prompted a movement to augment physician decision making with information systems that aid them by providing the information processing humans find hard to do. Many repetitive and highly complex decision tasks, such as medical diagnosis, were thought to benefit from such systems. Sadly, few such have been adopted. This is due in part to the implied threat posed by the creation of the system and incorporating it into medical information systems.

This difficulty is not limited to medical applications. Recall the Willie Horton fiasco (Nutt, 1989). Horton, a convicted killer, was furloughed by state policy and killed again. The uproar that followed helped to defeat the presidential candidate from that state in the 1984 election. Using this as an example, one can suggest a 'parole board model' that follows the model building approach used for medical decision making. Experts are debriefed by an investigator to identify information (such as inmate characteristics) believed to predict criminal tendencies. A protocol is created that makes explicit what parole board members *say* they do to reach a parole decision. Alternatively, the researcher can collect data on released inmates and group them by whether or not a crime was subsequently committed. Correlate the predictors with the result (crime or no crime) using discriminate analysis. A model is built using this information, indicating criteria that predict individuals apt to commit a crime if freed. (For more detail, see Nutt, 1989; ch. 19.) Test the decision makers. Records of released inmates (who did and did not commit a crime) are reviewed to extract information called for by the protocol. Disguise the names, provide the required information about each inmate, and ask parole board members to indicate who should and who should not be released. Group the released and not released inmates and find the error rate – those recommended for release who committed a crime and those not released who did not commit a crime. This can be used to find the best (and worst) decision makers. Explorations of the best decision maker's skills, experiences, etc. suggest criteria for a superior selection process.

Similar models have been constructed for graduate admission, bond ratings, and a host of other repetitive decisions of consequence. In many of these applications, the implied threat to experts has made implementing the approach a difficult sell. Nevertheless, the methods employed can be used to gain insights into repetitive decisions, identifying error rates and ways to improve matters. Because their information processing is different and may benefit from additional investments, the crucial and repetitive decisions appear to merit study as a separate topic.

Using decision-making theory. There is considerable sentiment to make management research theory-driven (Colquitt and Zapata-Phelan, 2007). According to this view, research begins by identifying theories and demonstrating which of the extant theories merit testing. Research is carried out to make the test, reporting whether the theory can be supported. Research is confined to asking whether a theory was or was not confirmed by the data collected. Extending this research approach to decision making, researchers would be called upon to determine whether a given theory, such as those noted above, accounts for what is observed in practice. Researchers gather and record data that allow them to determine which theory best explains how a decision was made. There are several pitfalls in such an approach, which will be addressed as the theory-driven research trap.

The trap arises from the kind of inquiry often prompted by a theory-driven effort (Hambrick, 2008). The researcher is led to a description of what decision makers do, and away from what they should do. The description becomes an implicit prescription. Because the focus is on behavior, there is an implicit assumption that what is observed is useful, valuable, and desirable. Even with an estimate of outcome benefits, which is rare in this work, merit can be contentious. There is no way to know if there was a better way to act that would have yielded better results. The focus is on whether the theory fits the data, not whether the theory offers a useful set of tactics for a manager to employ. Thus, theory-driven efforts have limited value in an action theory world.

Why do theory-driven efforts ignore results? Although difficult to understand, some insight can be gleaned from theory definition offered in the literature. These definitions seldom, if ever, call for outcomes of interest to managers and management, such as cost or benefit. Look at how theoreticians dance around this issue. For example, Campbell (1990), contends that a theory identifies what variables are important and why, their interrelationship, and conditions that influence the relationship. Here a relationship of interest can be designated a theory, even if the relationship lacks any connection to cost or benefit. Such an approach has led to countless studies labeled as decision making in which a factor, such as a group, is correlated with a related factor, such a number of participants. What results are findings that have little or no interest to managers? Following a qualitative perspective, DiMaggio (1995) contends that theory accounts for the social process captured in a narrative, paying careful attention to the scope of conditions accounted for. The theory is evaluated according to the richness of the account and its insights. Neither has an explicit link to value that result. The intent is to describe or explain, not to determine value. Coming a bit closer to recognizing value, Kerlinger and Lee (2000) call on a theory to understand and predict outcomes of interest. It is interesting that so many theory definitions seem disinterested in results. We believe that a management theory in general and a decision-making theory in particular should be vitally concerned with results.

Additionally, theoretical works that appear descriptive to some are viewed as prescriptive by others. Consider the classic work of Thompson (1967), who frames his book as explicating and applying norms of rationality. Subsequently, propositions become somewhat ambiguous. For example, what seems a normative framework is offered in which assessment standards are matched to decision situations. The prescriptions implied by the framework are never fully explained. Subsequent propositions make a number of predictions, such as who will join a dominant coalition when certain conditions arise. Notice how this leaves the prescription implicit. Are better results predicted when an assessment approach is matched to the situation? Does the predicted joining behavior produce desirable results? Much of the behavioral literature follows this pattern. The boundaries between description and prescription are blurred and desirable practices have become obscured. We hope to clear away some of this confusion in future decision-making research. However, it will be no easy task to do so. The behavioral literature gained considerable ground in the 1980s and 1990s and seems to have hijacked decision-making research along the way. This literature, which was widely read in this period, contains easily understood behavioral nostrums such as re-engineering and total quality management. Unfortunately, we have little evidence that such nostrums make decision making more effective, despite strong claims by some authors to the contrary.

Of equal concern is the content of theory. Colquitt and Zapata-Phelan (2007) investigated several years of academy of management articles finding what they termed micro and macro theories. A close look at these theories finds the scope of the macro types (such as resource dependency and upper echelon) to be much like the micro types (goal setting and information processing). In many cases, what are called theories offer little beyond factors for a contingency relationship. The reach of such theories seems quite limited as well and, interestingly, excludes what many would see as a key managerial responsibility: decision making. The same finding holds true for European journals. What can we make of this? Does the exclusion of decision-making theory suggest that it lacks value or importance in the larger scheme of management interests? Whatever the answers, researchers should be aware that decision-making theory might have little interest outside academic circles.

A competing explanation for this lack of attention of the top journals may be that management research turned away from decisions and decision making that emphasized 'practice'. This relegated articles on decision making to mathematically inclined journals that stressed computations and choice (i.e. the decision sciences). The burgeoning world of 'strategy as practice' (see Chapter 1) appears to have subsumed decision making under the banner of practice.

Finally, we note that a movement away from theory-driven research is gaining support. Investigators who take stock of theories being used or promulgated are finding them lacking. Others suggest that the bank of theories still to be mined is limited. Suggestions for radical change are emerging (Suddaby, 2009). Some scholars are calling for a movement toward problem-centered research in which a key issue is identified and addressed. Others suggest model development, a perspective, or a puzzle as topics meriting research. We see action theory as an even more useful focus for future work.

The Action Theory Alternative. We offer action theory as an alternative to theory-driven research (Harmon, 1981). We propose that action theory, like that found in engineering and medicine, replace the strict adherence to theory-driven investigations.

Action theory treats description and prescription as two sides of the same coin. On the one hand, there is prescriptive science. On the other, there is a behavioral/explanatory explanation of what a researcher observes. Prescription calls for the investigator to identify relevant processes, tactics, and techniques and test them to see if they produce something of value in real world applications. Description deals with use. How many people act in a certain way, how many subordinates get involved, what is the skill level of key players? One informs the other. Theory that denies or invalidates one or the other is incomplete. Linking the actions taken to success provides a key piece of the action theory puzzle. Noting whether a prescription is followed, and how, also informs practice. One of the intents of this volume is to call for a balanced approach to decision-making research. To provide this balance, we call for integrating the prescriptive with the descriptive in research efforts.

Theory continues to be intellectual fodder to construct frameworks. Decision-making theory offers models that suggest action components, both for studies of what decision makers do and synopses of what theorists believe they should do. For example, Nutt (2002) used a teleological stage-based theory to address research questions for an action theory framework. Here the research questions took shape as selecting tactics to carry out a given process stage shown to produce the best results. In addition, this research approach asks which sequence of stages is more effective. Together such efforts identified tactics and processes with superior prospects, and others that are apt to fail. This gives managers information about what works and forms a basis to build an action theory of decision making.

Frames for action theory investigations. A framework is often developed to guide the search for decision-making actions and to portray the actions uncovered in the research effort. Linguists use 'emics' and 'etics' to bracket two vastly different ways to develop such a framework (Pike, 1967). An emic calls for capturing actions as they unfold and imposes little in the way of structure. The emic provides a minimal set of conceptual markers to capture the object. A limited number of conceptual components are used to classify the object being observed (actions revealed during decision making). This permits a rich description of the object (the decision). The investigator then studies the description to extract important identifying features and elements. The descriptions are object- (decision) specific, so each is apt to offer a somewhat different narrative description. The researcher then looks for similarities and differences among the objects (decisions), which can be done in several ways. In Chapter 20, Poole and Van de Ven call for 'following the action' in the object (decision) being profiled. A sequence of actions is tracked, from beginning to end. To do this the researcher must be clear about what constitute initiating events, beginnings, and terminating events, endings. The flow of actions is documented by identifying events and activities that occurred, finding the more significant, and determining how these events and activities unfold – their pattern. Both incidents, which are observable, and events, which are inferred, are included in the description. Events are constructions that make sense of the observed incidents by showing their importance and their flow. Each event is made up of several incidents and captures what an observer finds is needed to document a process. This can be done retrospectively, drawing on interviews and the like, or prospectively. To view prospectively, the researcher positions to observe. This requires longitudinal observation to follow a process as is unfolds, seeking to identify key features (actions) as they emerge. We will discuss both approaches in the methodology section.

The etic approach, in contrast, creates a framework that has concrete conceptual markers, which are used to profile an object (a decision) for study. Here the object, the decision, is organized according to the framework's conceptual markers, such as recommended steps. McKelvey (1978) calls this a 'phyletic' classification as it attempts to explain of the origin of types. An etic framework can be derived in several ways. For example, Nutt (1984; 1993) derived etic frameworks for decision-making research from a synopsis of the recommendations for stages and stage sequencing found in the literature, providing a structure to summarize the actions taken when making a decision. A related attempt to derive such frameworks can be found in Chapter 22. To apply an etic framework, researchers make an after-the-fact reconstruction of the decision-making process, matching what is uncovered to the framework's stages and the stage sequencing. Analysis uncovers process types that activate various features called for by the framework.

Etic and emic frameworks can be constructed by drawing on decision-making theories, such as those noted above. For example, dialectic or evolutionary theory can be used to provide conceptual markers for an emic. For dialectics, plan (proposal), counter plan (counter proposal), and synthesis provide the key markers. The researcher can search the data to find instances in which each occur, attempting to tie each to key events that explain how and why the plan, counter plan, and synthesis arise. Evolution provides another kind of conceptual marker, pointing the researcher toward fluid clashes of emergent ideas. The investigator looks for indications of repeating cycles in which the emergence of new or hybrid ideas, variation, and then selection and retention occurs. Denzin (1989) and others find following an emic frame with such a theory a distraction, keeping the observer from seeing an underlying process and the insights it contains. Such a view calls for the researcher to track what happens with a minimum of presumptions in a longitudinal data collection. This is discussed in some detail in Chapters 20. Features of life cycle and teleological theories are often found in etic frameworks. Examples can be found in Chapters 7 and 17.

Instead of choosing between etic and emic approaches, researchers are encouraged to select a frame according to their skills and interests. Both the etic and the emic approaches are valuable, but neither can provide definitive results. This occurs because frameworks introduce a 'frame bias'. We derive this from the work of Harrison and Phillips (1991) who find that a researcher with a frame tends to find what the frame calls for. For example, researchers who set out to find chance explanations in their data tend to find chance. Others looking for rationality in the same data will tend to find rationality. Thus, the organizing structure points a researcher toward what is believed to be salient, resulting in certain events being highlighted and others being overlooked. Frame bias limits the kind of data (action-taking events) that are recognized, coded, and classified. Data (action-taking events in this type of work) that fail to fit the frame are apt to be lost. Data that fit the frame are codified. In both cases, the veracity of the framework is reinforced. As a result, we call for studies that employ *both* emic and etic frameworks. Collectively, studies of both types are likely to produce insightful findings. An amalgamation of these findings is more apt to be revealing than studies that rely on one type of frame or the other.

THE 'HOW' OF ACTION RESEARCH – SOME METHODOLOGY SUGGESTIONS

The 'how' of decision-making research suggests methodological issues. The nature of the work itself – relevant study approaches – is a key consideration. We call for two distinctly different kinds of studies. They appear to contribute complimentary insights for the development of an action theory of decision making. Each approaches theory development in a similar way, seeking empirically grounded propositions in which action steps are identified that increase the prospect of success. A related issue involves doing the research – the methods to be employed. Several methodological considerations arise. Perhaps the most important addresses the uncovering of action-taking steps that make up an action theory for decision making. We call the action-taking steps 'process.' We suggest ways to use emic and etic frameworks to capture processes, and their component steps, to uncover process types that merit empirical testing. The operationalization of constructs in past work has been rife with definitional and measurement problems. Better conceptualization and measurement of process is crucial.

Several methodological considerations are identified. First, processes that are uncovered must be connected to their outcomes to document the results produced by each process. Documenting outcomes and their consequences, such as benefits and costs, poses another substantive methodological challenge. The difficulties found in documenting outcomes and the measurement of outcome consequences merit discussion. We also call attention to purpose and unit and level of analysis, elaborating on the issues noted in Chapter 1. Both merit careful thought when doing this kind of research. The influence of contingency and the development of producer-product relationships will require attention as well. Research must document the qualifications that flow from situational factors to test contingency relationships. Content, the type of decision, and context factors must be conceptualized and measured to test contingency notions. We offer some thoughts on dealing with content and context in formulating producer-product relationships for an empirical study. We believe that the validation of such models is essential to formulate an action theory of decision making.

We also argue for large databases that allow rigorous testing of the relationship between process and outcome and the influence of situational effects. Past work often employs cross-sectional designs. To establish valid causal relationships between process, context, content, and outcomes, we may need to turn to longitudinal research with an exploratory thrust. Other kinds of research such as laboratory and quasi-field work – such as experiments with working managers in training programs – are suggested to explore a key relationship for a larger research effort and for studies of techniques that can supplement a decision-making process.

Study types

Previously we identified two types of frameworks that can be used to capture the action taking that takes place during decision making. Here we will apply them to devise emergent and prescriptive process models for empirical testing. The two kinds of process models provide distinctly different ways to uncover action-taking steps. The results each produces can be compared. The findings from such studies are expected to be complementary; the insights from practitioners found to be exemplary are apt to differ from decision support steps found to have beneficial results.

Emergent process. This calls for descriptive work, with an important twist. The research is called upon to document what decision makers do, *and* the results produced by these actions. Too often past research into decision making has focused descriptions that become implicit prescriptions, without documenting value. In addition, such work often lacks a control group – there is no way to tell if another set of actions would have been better. Thus, it is incumbent on the researcher to follow a process until results can be realized and to build contrasts into the research design, so different sets of actions (process types) can be compared.

An 'emergent process' research effort faces several challenges. First, the researcher must find a way to document the process (action-taking steps) used with sufficient clarity that its distinctive features are apparent. We discuss how an emic frame can help capture the information required for such documentation. To do this the researcher uses a process theory, or better yet several theories, to summarize the action steps of practitioners. The summary identifies fits and misfits to the framework – expected actions that can be classified as well as actions that cannot be classified with the conceptual markers. For example, structuration, morphogenesis, autopoiesis, dialectics, trialectics, and implicit order offer process theories that suggest steps taken during *peak performance*. The theories suggest how to summarize an exemplary set of time-ordered activities used by a master decision maker. The action flow is captured by applying a morphogenic view of adaptation and survival, an autopoietic and a structuration interpretation of a master decision maker's actions, a dialectical view of tensions and their management, adding trialectics to capture the mutation and implicate order to document enfolded steps. Each provides a piece of the puzzle that indicates how master decision makers take action (see Chapter 7). A synthesis of these ideas may identify new avenues for decision-making process research. A requirement for such research is the identification and participation of master decision makers, to find what makes them exemplary (Cameron and Lavine, 2006; Schon, 1983). In this stream of research, best practice is believed to emerge from documenting what exemplary decision makers do and comparing the results achieved to uncover core process types.

Although theory-driven to capture the process steps observed, this type of study is less interested in testing theory and its fit to the data than finding actions that make up best practice. This makes the research more exploratory than theory-driven. The researcher follows a process to its conclusion, documenting the results produced and their consequences. In addition, data are collected that allow comparisons of what exemplary decision makers do (specifying action steps and how they differ) and the merits of each. From such studies, investigators can amass a database that identifies similarities and differences among decision makers. Tying what each decision maker does to the results produced offers an emic-based insight into what works best. This calls for such an approach to be applied to a set of master decision makers, those with a demonstrable record of accomplishment, to see if dissimilar or similar actions are equally meritorious. Other studies compare the master decision maker with others that have a mixed or a poor record, contrasting them to the actions of practitioners shown to be masters. Contrasting actions by these types of decision maker and the results realized could be enlightening.

Others prefer to use little in the way of formal theory to organize what is observed, as noted by Poole and Van de Ven in Chapter 20. Their 'Strategy III' presumes that process dominates action and uses qualitative documentation, such as the grounded and historical narrative approaches, to characterize process features. The unique features of a case history are sought along with idiographic explanations. Avoiding preconceived notions found in the traditional thinking about process and process models, which can blind investigators to important insights, is important. This kind of blinder keeps the investigator from learning how to think in terms of what is being observed. It also argues for creating a vocabulary that can express observations in processional terms.

Such an approach often requires longitudinal data collection in which the researcher follows the sequence of events to a conclusion, documenting actions and consequences. Such a research approach places less emphasis on the systematic interpretation of incidents and events, which make up action steps. Instead, a stream of incidents (first-order interpretations) is translated into second-order interpretations using inductive reasoning. The classifications are interactive, moving from core data to constructions and back to reinterpret and thereby refine the researcher's understanding of what occurred and its meaning.

Some write process history in this way. The flow of events receives minimal interpretation, such as Allison's (1970) description of decision making during the Cuban Missile Crisis. This kind of work, like many other descriptive efforts, offers little in the way of empirical findings for an action theory because such studies lack comparative insights and fail to document benefits. Without comparisons, there is no way to tell which of the action steps were exemplary. What is alleged to have made a difference in Allison's study (expanding the pool of alternatives) could have been facilitated in other ways. The documented emergent process and its features, in such a study, pose several dilemmas to theory development. It is not clear if there was a difference (results improved), what made a difference (which action was exemplary), and why another process would not be equally effective. Still, the emergent study approach offers several advantages. A key benefit is minimizing biases in the reconstruction of a process. The difficulties with this approach stem from data that resists taking shape as a process, finding action steps that can be documented and understood, and tying the process to its outcome.

Poole and Van de Ven suggest 'Strategy IV' to deal with complex studies (Chapter 20). They identify multi-faceted multiyear product development efforts made up of many small decisions as a unique type. Each decision results in changes that are provoked by external sources and by feedback events. Comparisons are limited by the set of small decisions required, different external interventions, particularistic feedbacks, and the many possible connections of feedbacks and interventions with the decisions. According to Poole and Van de Ven, capturing such a case is a challenge that requires matching to patterns such as cyclical, punctuated equilibrium, and white noise. Each pattern may require a different model or framework to classify key events. Poole and Van de Ven offer some guidance in how to conduct such a study in their chapter. Another example can be found in the Yucca flats case reported by Cameron and Levine (2006). Hitt *et al.* (2007) show that such cases have multiple levels of analysis and that the levels must be explicitly captured in empirical studies to avoid confounding the findings to the point they will be impossible to untangle. Consequently, conducting a study with this kind of case presents both level and unit of analysis complications. To cope, researchers must denote how environments, interorganizational networks, as well as the organization and its subunits, groups, and individuals were involved in the action taking, accounting for which level was activated. Although complex, such linkages will be required before multi-level cases can be subjected to comparative analysis. In some studies, this has resulted in reporting the case as a history, which limits its value in building an action theory.

An etic can also be used to capture processes for quasi-emergent studies. Such an approach is an intermediate step between emergent and prescriptive approaches, incorporating elements of description and prescription. It offers benefits of clarity about process features, documenting action steps and their sequence with greater precision. Its key failing is the tendency to be self-fulfilling. The investigator uses a framework, which indicates what is expected, which is likely to be observed (Harrison and Phillips, 1991). The researcher looks for frame-specific events and may skip over event types not found in the frame. Even if noted, a non-conforming event is apt to be lost during coding.

The etic is used to fashion a model of decision making by uncovering stages and action steps that are used by decision makers and/or recommended by the literature. Decisions are then examined with the model finding instances of fit and misfit. The misfits suggest ways to modify the model to incorporate emergent insights into the framework. Instances of fit are analyzed to uncover process types. A study that used this approach can be found in Chapter 17. Here stages of intelligence gathering, formulation, concept development, evaluation, and implementation emerged as crucial. Decision-maker actions were then fit to the framework. For each decision, investigators look for *activated* stages, how the activated stages are *carried out*, and the stage's *sequence*. The information is further analyzed to find unique process types, defined as a particular set of stages and stage sequence. This allows a variety of reliability tests to be used to refine the match of observed processes to the types to give credence to the unique nature of each observed type. The validated types are compared using success indicators, derived from decision outcomes. Such models can be used to test some aspects of prescriptions as well. If decision makers ignore a stage thought to be crucial in the prescriptive literature, such as formulation, rates of success for decisions that activated the stage can be compared to the success of decisions made without this stage. Other benefits include: documenting the behavior of decision makers (preferred process types), identifying when actions are taken or avoided (overlooked stages), and the consequences of each.

Poole and Van de Ven (Chapter 20) call this approach 'Strategy II'. They find that stage conceptualizations offer an intuitively satisfying way to think about decision making, concluding that stage sequences have provided understandable maps of decision processes in many studies. They also note some disadvantages. This approach can impose an artificial sense of coherence on process representations. This coherence keeps investigators from uncovering other, more important, events taking place at the same time. These events are more likely to emerge in a more fluid process representation. A focus on activated stages is also potentially misleading. These stages may be a condensation of more complex processes. The more complex process can be overlooked when summaries are limited to stage mapping.

Such studies have daunting demands. These demands can be made somewhat more manageable if the scope of a research project is reduced. For example, investigators can examine the decision process stage by stage, amalgamating the results into process types (see Chapter 17). Such studies would determine how each stage was carried out, and its impact on results. Interference with other stages can be handled by correlating stage activities, such as tactical options found in the literature, with success indicators holding the tactics used to carry out the other stages constant. Another dilemma arises from the time demands. Informants have limited time to participate in such studies, making interviews and other data collection needs difficult to arrange and complete. One way around this is to merge classroom experiences with student internships. Students, in conjunction with a class project, can be trained to follow a protocol and collect data during their internship experience or retrospectively by interviewing their internship mentor. If checks to ensure that the protocol was followed can be made and if the academic program encourages such real life project experiences, both research and educational goals can be satisfied.

Prescriptive process. The etic also provides ways to fashion a process model for prescriptive studies. The etic enumerates decision-making requirements, incorporating stages and action steps recommended in the literature. As a result, the same stages (e.g. intelligence, formulation, concept development, evaluation, and implementation) uncovered for emergent studies are apt to be relevant for prescriptive studies. Instead of fitting decision-maker actions to the framework, the framework is used to inventory what can be useful to carry out each process stage. Options can be identified for empirical testing by inventorying tools, tactics, and techniques that meet each stage's requirements.

An example of this kind of development can be found in Chapter 17. Here a number of options were uncovered for the stages of intelligence gathering, formulation, generating alternatives, evaluation, and implementation. The stimulus to act can be explored with devices such as tensions, interests, sensing, and interpretations to structure intelligence gathering. Formulation can be carried out by framing activities that establish values, identify missions, articulate aims, form purposes, uncover issues, or denote identities (see Chapter 7). Alternative courses of action can be identified in a decision-making process by adaptation or invention, via creativity and innovation enhancing techniques. Another example of an innovation creation process that can be subjected to this kind of testing was offered by Delbecq *et al.* in Chapter 8. Alternatives can be evaluated using a host of tools that measure or simulate expected results to identify outcome consequences. There is a substantial literature that could be inventoried to uncover techniques particularly well suited to decision making. This search could also consider the dilemma of this literature – its focus on quantitative measurement. Things that can be counted may not count for many decisions, calling for an additional search to find qualitative techniques to compare options. Implementation considers how an organization's social fabric can be altered by a decision and provides ways to cope such as using position-power, cooptation, and unfreezing to secure an adoption. Comparison of these tactics would be useful.

A prescriptive stream of research mounts studies that compare the value of tactics, tools, and techniques used to carry out a particular process stage. This can be done in a setting that approximates practice by involving experienced learners, such as those found in executive MBA programs. In class, application of the tactic, tool, or technique can be carried out, evaluating the results. Cases must be developed that offer a real world situation to apply them. This research requires the development of a role play situation (cases), experienced participants in an academic study program, learning needs that parallel the needs of the research (applying the tool satisfies learning objectives), and opportunities for data collection (compiling the results for further study). This is often possible in executive training sessions that call for skill building. Structuring the skill building project to meet the needs of both education and research is often feasible. Imagine a series of such studies that move through the tools cited in Chapter 7, stage by stage. An investigator could begin, perhaps by comparing the results produced by framing with values, missions, aims, purposes, issues, directions, and identity for the formulation stage. Many other studies of this type could be imagined in which approximations to practice are provided by experienced participants and clear protocols to carry out the techniques to be compared. The validity of such studies is enhanced by research designs with control groups, allowing assignment of learners to various groups to control for individual differences. Such studies are feasible in a learning environment in which investigators can control the terms of the learning experience and archive the results for outcome assessments. This is often feasible at some point in an academic offering.

Process could be studied this way, as well. Consider research suggested by the contingency relationships posited by Mintzberg and Westley, previously discussed in this chapter. A two-by-two design could be created in which a 'think first' model and 'see first' model are applied to cases in which there is a hypothesized fit (think first-analytical; see first-novel) and a misfit (think first-novel; see first-analytical). Experienced learners in an academic setting are randomly assigned to the four conditions as teams and asked to apply the 'think first' or the 'see first' protocols (taught as part of the class) and come up with solutions. Solutions could be assessed by experts. Alternatively, the teams could apply both process types to both cases. This would block for any residual competence effects in the participants and for their interest in the task.

Such studies move decision-making research toward its applied roots, offering empirical evidence that supports using each technique or process as well as how they can be used to best advantage. As with the etic used for emergent studies, the demands on researchers can be made more manageable by doing research one stage at a time. Such studies would select a stage, such as formulation, and compare the techniques and tactics by applying them and documenting the results realized. Studies seeking to investigate processes can be made doable by developing cases that can be managed in the time available.

The results of such studies can be amalgamated into an etic framework. The empirically validated tools and techniques in this framework can be applied to databases of decisions. The investigator would look for insights that could have been provided had the tools or tactics been applied, offering depth to the recommendations for the use of each. In addition, findings from prescriptive studies can be contrasted with findings from emergent studies to find areas of agreement and disagreement. These comparisons provide a part of the foundation required to construct the hoped-for action theory.

Documenting process

Two types of process studies have been identified: emergent and prescriptive. Emergent process requires a process description in which the investigator either positions to observe or reconstructs events. Both require qualitative methods. Prescriptive studies require the development of protocols that capture how a tool or technique can be used in practice to meet the needs of decision making. Without a defensible operationalization in these protocols, research has little value. This calls for in-depth knowledge of the tool or technique as well as how to apply in a variety of situations. In addition, cases posited to be amenable to each decision approach being tested must be developed or identified. Alternatively, several cases with generalizable features are uncovered, to which decision approaches can be applied.

Measuring process

Qualitative methods are required to capture a process, the key factor in decision-making research. Poole and Van de Ven in Chapter 20 identify key steps: identify events, represent the event, characterize event sequences, find temporal ordering and dependencies among events, and fit the findings to a framework or to a theory. To do this, the researcher must position to observe. This positioning can be retrospective or longitudinal. A retrospective approach calls on the researcher to reconstruct events. This is typically carried out by interviewing key participants and locating pertinent archive documents. There are several crucial steps: soliciting participation, identifying informants, doing interviews, triangulating responses to document key events and event sequencing, and classifying the results. (For additional information, see Nutt (2002); Appendix I.)

To get close to the phenomena of interest, a decision, one must involve people holding key positions in organizations. Getting busy executives to participate can be difficult. We recommend going to people with whom the researcher has connections, such as alumni, former associates, friends, and the like. In addition, student projects can be used to gather information, as discussed above. From this base, a participant can be asked to solicit others who may have an interest in participating. A database of cases can grow in this way, gradually adding cases. A number of years will be required to amass sufficient cases for analysis.

When soliciting participants, researchers must make the purpose of the research effort clear. For example, a potential participant can be told that the project's purpose is to 'study decision making to find what works and why'. It is also important to be clear what is meant by a decision, such as the actions taken beginning when the organization first became aware of a motivating concern and ending with implementation attempts. To ensure interest, first hand knowledge, and recall of what was done limit study to recent decisions of consequence, that require considerable resources and/or set important precedents. The contact person is asked to identify people that could be interviewed, including the person who had primary responsibility for the decision. Often, a contact person will suggest a decision for which he/she was responsible and became the primary informant. The contact person is asked to solicit the participation of additional informants who are apt to be familiar with the decision and its outcome.

Informants have several roles in such a study. The primary informant must be the decision maker, the individual who was responsible for taking action. It is also useful to have a second informant who is knowledgeable about what was done, and why. Both are interviewed to identify their recall of the actions undertaken to make the decision. Secondary informants fill out surveys to quantify a variety of situational factors, such as urgency, novelty, resources, etc., and some outcome types, such as value and impact. It is desirable to solicit one set of informants to be interviewed to uncover action steps and another set of informants fill out the surveys. This is done to divorce assessments of the situation and outcome from recalling how a decision was made.

Interview protocols must be carefully constructed. This is essential because informant recall can be influenced by self-justification, memory lapses, and logical inconsistencies (Miller *et al.*, 1997). Such recall biases will introduce errors. An interview that focuses on factual events limits recall failures. The selection of recent decisions reduces memory lapses, as will the use of informants with first-hand knowledge. The purpose of the interviews is to converge on an understanding of events (actions taken to make each decision), *not* to measure and report differences. The interview procedures must deal with the dual problems of what people remember and choose to tell (Yin, 1993). To do this, ask the informant to recall what *first* captured attention. Questioning can proceed from this point asking: 'What happened next.' After informants describe what captured attention, ask them why this seemed important and merited action. In this way, questioning can take cues from the last response to fashion the next question. To improve the prospect of full and accurate disclosure, multiple informants and data sources are recommended (Huber and Power, 1985). The interviews can be compared, seeking a convergence of interpretations. A final interview with the primary informant with this information is often useful. This 'second chance' interview jogs memory and allows the primary informant to fill in gaps and add detail. Archival records and documents as well as cross-checking sources are also useful validation tools.

To triangulate responses, information is summarized to capture key features. There are many ways to do this, as noted in the discussion on framing (for another example, see Chapter 17). Triangulation among informants is also recommended. Show the primary informant the summary of his/her listing of key events and ask for corrections and additions. Then compare events summaries of different informants. This allows the researcher to find the version of events that is the most defensible and plausible. In addition, archival documents such as notes, proposals, or files can be collected. The actions noted by the informants can be tested against these sources to find additional inconsistencies and gaps in the 'story' depicting a decision. Inconsistencies and gaps can be explored in a follow-up interview with a primary informant to reconcile differences. This allows researchers to apply several triangulations of the data, which will increase the prospect that the information collected approximates what a longitudinal study would reveal.

Process types are identified from the validated summaries. The summaries offer a reconstruction of actions taken to make a decision. If an etic is used, each reconstructed decision is analyzed to find the steps in the framework that were carried out and omitted, and the action sequence. A more intuitive sort is required if an emic is being used. (See Poole and Van de Ven, Chapter 20 for details). To find similar patterns the researcher sorts and classifies the case summaries according to process types. To improve reliability, the summaries can be sorted and resorted until classification agreement is realized. When previous classifications are reproduced, it can be assumed that intra-rater reliability has been achieved. Inter-rater reliability can be determined by having colleagues repeat the classification sorting, comparing the extent to which the second rater made the same classifications for each decision.

Other approaches can be used to uncover qualitative data and profile the data for analysis. See Denzin (1989), Lincoln and Guba (1984), and Patton (1990) for details. In addition, Poole and Van de Ven (Chapter 20) discuss some additional considerations including database size, data diversity, range of decisions considered, intensity (depth or richness) of the profiling, and homogeneity vs. heterogeneity of the cases. They also offer insights into creating process summaries.

Protocol development follows a somewhat different procedure. Here the key issue is capturing how to carry out required steps to provide a faithful representation of the procedures called for by the tools or techniques under study. This often poses difficulties, as we noted for the 'see first' and 'do first' approaches discussed previously. To do this research, an *assumption* was made that connected the visualization required in 'see first' to creativity. This can be operationalized by linking creativity techniques to visualization in ways that the originators may or may not approve. It does, however, offer a definitive way to explore intuitive decision making. When doing this kind of research, similar compromises often arise. The operationalization of the construct being studied can oppose questions that challenge the connection of the protocol to the construct to be tested. It is wise to field test these protocols before investing in research. Have both potential participants and originators comment on the operationalization and offer suggestions.

Cases that can be used to apply the tools or processes being examined can be mined from the cases collected in emergent type studies. Such cases are often reported in the literature (e.g. Hickson *et al.*, 1986; Nutt, 2002). Chapter 7 provides four additional case examples.

Outcomes

Different kinds of outcomes are called for in the proposed studies, creating different measurement demands. In prescriptive studies, the result takes shape as an outcome requiring external assessment to judge its merits, such as using experts. For example, framing tools that establish values, missions, aims, purposes, issues, directions, and identity for the formulation stage can be assessed using proxy indicators. The insightfulness or novelty of the framing result (e.g. the aim or the identity suggested) could be assessed by people who use this information, by tool developers, or by both. An additional step can be taken that generates solutions using each result (aim, identity, etc.), assessing the merits of the solutions. In both cases, proxies are used that draw upon subjective measures of value. Methods to do this have been widely reported. (See the appendices in Hickson *et al.*, 1986 and Nutt, 2002.)

For descriptive studies, we have argued that the value of the research is dependent on the linkage of actions taken to an outcome. This takes advantage of the key benefit of doing this kind of research – the availability of a real result with consequences to assess. The actions (the description) get their validation from the results they produce. Ignoring the outcome makes the action lack a rationale. The action may seem reasonable, or even insightful, but it has no utility in an action theory world without documentation of its value. We further argue that a process description must continue until its outcomes can be documented. Documenting the results produced poses a number of challenges.

We contend that all decisions must produce outcomes that have consequences, which create costs and benefits for an organization. Capturing these results, the costs and benefits, poses a number of conceptual and measurement difficulties. Cost may seem straightforward, but should include the cost to make a decision, such as meeting times and the demands placed on top managers, with the cost of the decision. Decision-making costs are rarely, if ever, recorded. In addition to the difficulties of accounting for decision-making costs, investigators must identify building costs for a building decision and operating costs for a control system. Fearing loss of competitive advantage and/or disclosure of errors and mistakes, managers are often reluctant to divulge this information. Consequently, subjective measures are often required to capture cost, such as anchored rating scales that identify cost as above or below that of the typical decision. Fortunately, research shows that such subjective measures approximate actual values as long as knowledgeable informants are used (Alexander, 1986).

Selecting outcome measures can be controversial. Some argue for linking a decision to firm-wide performance measures, such as ROI. Even if we limit our inquiry to the strategic decisions involving competitive advantage, this practice seems fraught with problems due to endless confounds that have a plausible link to, for example revenues. Identifying and controlling for such factors is rarely feasible. For the non-strategic decisions, as we identify them, the propositional validity of contending that a decision involving personnel policy or a control system will have firm-wide effects is implausible. Instead, we argue for measuring decision results directly by codifying its costs and benefits.

This also poses challenges. One large-scale effort found that two-thirds of the participants were unwilling to disclose cost and benefit data (Nutt, 2002). When such data were made available, the indicators were difficult to map to a common metric. For example, occupancy improvement can be an outcome for decisions made in hospitals and hotels. Converting occupancy to revenue gains requires many assumptions. Similar problems arise when measuring the benefits of personnel decisions, control systems, marketing plans, etc. Two choices emerge. The researcher can limit study to decisions in which the decision makers disclose costs and benefits and convert them to a common metric. Alternatively, proxy measures, such as adoption rates and subjective assessments of value, can be used (see Hickson *et al.* 2003; Miller *et al.*, 2004 and Chapter 17). Both approaches have limitations. Limiting study to decisions with disclosed outcomes may bias the results toward decisions that are more apt to be successful. Using proxy measures poses difficulties as well. The arguments derived from such studies lack the authority that a cost- or a benefit-based result would have. One way around this is to use both kinds of outcome and interpolate between them. For instance, compare the results using proxies with actual cost and benefits and see if failed decisions are excluded.

Also, consider using outcome indicators that can be reconstructed from an interview. Often such indicators provide a definitive indication of results realized. One such indicator is success, defined as whether or not a decision was adopted (Nutt, 2002; 2008). Degrees of adoption can also be inferred from interviews such as immediate adoption, delayed adoption, and partial adoptions. All can be contrasted with nonadopted decisions. This allows a variety of success/failure studies in which decisions are grouped according to these categories. Discriminate analysis can be used to find process differences.

In addition, subjective measures can be effectively used. Several large-scale studies have collected these indicators to sort decisions according to their benefits (Hickson *et al.*, 1986; Nutt, 1984; 2008). As noted above, subjective measures such as impact and value correlate well with actual benefits.

Contingencies

Contingency thinking has dominated management research for decades. As we point out in Chapter 1, empirical research that supports contingency theory applied to decision making is surprisingly sparse. Nevertheless, the compelling nature of the arguments that have been made by theorists and the demands of most journals will make it mandatory to include such factors in decision-making studies.

Contingency models identify boundary conditions that link to particular kinds of actions. Boundary conditions define the situation being confronted, typically with contextual factors and content factors, and occasionally with process-related factors. Contextual factors can be internal to the organization or external. Internal factors include time pressure (Lippitt and Mackenzie, 1976), importance (Nutt, 2001; 2002), resource dependency (Daft, 1995), organizational centralization and formalization (Alter and Hage, 1993), as well as past performance, related decisions, power, and the like. External factors include environmental stability (Mintzberg and Waters, 1982; Eisenhardt and Bourgeois, 1989), munificence (March and Simon, 1958), public or private settings (Rainey *et al.*, Chapter 13), as well as economic and competitive forces. Process factors include comprehensiveness (Fredrickson, 1985), decision-maker style (Nutt, 1990), cognitive skills (Ragapolian *et al.*, 1998), tolerance for ambiguity and uncertainty, information collection and processing biases (Nisbett and Ross, 1989), errors (see Boal *et al.*, Chapter 12), risk (see Bromiley *et al.*, Chapter 11), professionalism (Morris and Greenwood, Chapter 10), knowledge (Tsoukas, Chapter 14), and information technology support (Barrett and Oborn, Chapter 15). Content factors include novelty (Fredrickson, 1985), complexity (Perrow, 1967), objective types as identified in the Bradford studies (Hickson *et al.*, 1986), subjective types (Bell *et al.*, 1998), repetitive and nonrepetitive decisions, and the strategic/nonstrategic distinctions discussed in Chapter 1. Applying the logic of a boundary condition argues that a decision-making process (e.g. 'see first') matched to an appropriate application (i.e. novelty) will yield optimal results.

Many of such relationships have been identified but few have been subjected to empirical testing involving process types. One such test is reported in Chapter 17. This research examined how the success of four process types were influenced by Hickson's decision types, the organization's profit status (profit or nonprofit), DM level (top or middle) as well as complexity, urgency, importance, staff skill, resources, and initial support. In this study, the best-performing process was found to work best, regardless of the situation (i.e. high or low importance) identified by these factors. A number of the factors identified here and elsewhere have yet to be studied. As a result, assertions that limit 'think first' to non-urgent, routine decisions, and 'see first' to novel ones, as is often reported in the literature, have little empirical support.

Several such studies are recommended. First, studies that explore whether strategic and nonstrategic decisions are more amenable to a particular kind of process are needed. This was discussed in some detail in Chapters 1 and 22. Other decision content issues also merit investigation. Franz *et al.* in Chapter 19 offer a new way to differentiate between decision types. This, coupled with the Hickson classification scheme, could reveal much about the generality of process types and the scope of their application.

Process factors involve how the cogitative make up of decision makers influences their choices. Several such studies have been reported, showing, for example, how decision style influences the choices of practicing managers in simulations (Nutt, 1990). Extending the recommended studies by including measurement of the psychological make up of decision makers participating in actual decisions would be a valuable extension of this work. The challenges here will be formidable. Asking for this information, in addition to the extensive time required to collect case data, is apt to test the patience of volunteer participants. Nevertheless, identifying the impacts of these factors in real decisions provides an important extension to current understandings.

Many contextual factors have yet to be adequately explored in process-like studies. The sheer number of such factors, and their potential to offer important qualifications in prescriptions found in an action theory, suggest a number of important process-related studies. At stake here is whether contingency theory need be applied to decision making. The researcher is called upon to carry out studies that determine if the practice of incorporating situational factors that include context, content, and process into decision-making prescriptions is warranted. If not the models suggested by Daft (1995), Thompson (1967), and many others (e.g. Allison, 1971; Perrow, 1967; Nutt, 1989) must be revised.

Modeling relationships

The proposed studies have two distinctively different kinds of factors. The first involves process. After extensive process work, in which the *action features are carefully specified*, the result can be classified by type, such as 'see first' or 'teleological stage-based'. Next, factors measured by more traditional methods, such as context (e.g. urgency), content (e.g. strategic or nonstrategic), and cognition (e.g. tolerance for ambiguity or MBTI), would be considered.

The relationship posited among these factor types can take several forms. Some argue for a particular causal sequence between the factors, contending that context (environmental and organizational factors) influences cognitions and the selection of a process which, ultimately, influences outcome (Rajapolian *et al.*, 1998). Others assert that a variety of relationships may exist such as outcome or content dictating process (Butler, 1998). We find these relationships to be interesting but lacking in any empirical justification. Instead of a complex relationship, in which factors are cascaded as mediating or moderating and the like, we recommend that statistical interaction models be used. In this approach, a factor can act alone or with others as an interaction. Statistically significant interactions have factors acting jointly. When this is noted a process, for example, will produce significantly better outcomes for one condition and not another, such as high and low urgency. (See Chapter 17 for details on how to do this.) The relationship to be explored takes on a producer-product form in which process alone or together with another factor is explored to see if main effects and interactions alter the prospect of success.

This approach combines elements of Poole and Van de Ven's Strategies I and III (see Chapter 20). The approach suggested here overcomes many of the Strategy I limitations that they note. Variance methods are applied to situational factors and how they influence process types, asking if there is a joint effect (process and situation) on outcomes. Factors such as critical events, time periods, and sequences of events that chain together are captured by the process type and explicated during process type discussions.

CONCLUSIONS

This chapter pulled together the offerings of our contributors, and similar contributions made by others, to appraise the status of decision-making research and suggest future directions for investigators. We found the field to be diffuse but interesting, challenged but with interesting possibilities. To create some focus for further work we called for a move from theory-driven efforts toward action theory in which the researcher searches for productive behavior and useful tools that improve the prospect of success. This moves decision-making research from explanatory to exploratory efforts that seek to inform practice by offering a list of what works, what does not, and why. We include in the mix studies of master decision makers hoping to find what makes them masterful.

Our journey finds that many past efforts fail to consider action. What decision makers do or should do is seldom considered. Processes made up of action-taking steps, used or recommended, tend to be overlooked. Instead, research efforts explore process caricatures at the expense of documenting the *actions* taken. In such research, process was classified by the actions implied such as whether there was a systematic collection and interpretation of information, whether power was used, coalitions were formed, flexibility or adaptability observed, comprehensiveness was noted, subunits were involved, and the like. We discourage such efforts because they measure process caricatures, which say little about how effective action was taken. Classifications such as whether analysis was used, coalitions were formed, or flexibility and adaptability were observed fail to explain how decision makers conduct analysis, form coalitions, engage flexibly, or promote adaptability. Studies with process proxies such as the extent of subunit involvement and number of participants say little about the process used. Even when outcomes are considered, which is rare, factors such as involvement are little more than a side show to the action taking in a process. The key step in improving decision-making research is to concentrate on measuring process to determine process elements apt to improve success.

We suggested two kinds of studies that together offer the potential to build a process-based action theory of decision making. Both call for careful process measurement, as noted above. The first explores what decision makers do, seeking to uncover best practice action taking. This research was labeled 'emergent'. Its goal was to uncover the practices of master decision makers and distinguish them from others with a less distinguished record of accomplishment. This calls for a variety of research efforts. Researchers must determine whether master decision makers deserve such a designation. A series of research projects was envisioned that would test the results produced by those designated as 'masters' and verify their superiority. If superiority can be verified, research can identify differences in their practices and convert these differences into action-taking steps that others can emulate. Another stream of studies explores a cross-section of decisions makers to find practices that produce superior results and those that can be linked with failure. A list of practices that produce good results would be gleaned from this stream of research. In both types, researchers were called upon to measure the effects of situational factors and determine the extent to which situation or action taking, by a decision maker, explains decision effectiveness. If action taking explains more of the variance in factors measuring effectiveness, as it has in several contemporary studies (Nutt, 2002; 2008), the effects of contingency would be discounted. The joint effects of the action-taking practices uncovered and a situational factor can be explored, one factor at a time, to test whether a contingency relationship exists.

A second research stream was labeled prescriptive. Here the researcher was called upon to model decision making in some way to identify a series of action types that stage action taking, fitting tools and techniques identified in the literature to the stages. Research efforts were called for that coppered the merits of the results produced when each was applied to a cross-section of cases in a role-play environment. The cases can be systematically altered to capture important situational effects. This allows research design principles to be used that increase the prospect that the findings about tools and techniques will be free of situational influences or that situational effects can be measured and quantified. This allows the researcher to explore systematically the merits of tools and techniques and to identity whether these benefits are dependent on the situation being confronted.

The action theory called for provides managers with a tool set with a demonstrable success record, which include the effects of situational factors. If contingency relationships can be verified, the action theory would explicitly include these factors and denote their effects. Such a research effort is apt to demand many separated projects, each calling for an extended time period to collect, analyze, and interpret the required data. The benefits from such an effort appear to outweigh these difficulties. First, and perhaps most important, such a set of projects would allow an integration of findings that has eluded integration attempts to date. Second, the work is focused on providing something of value to practice. This addresses the oft-cited criticisms of management research, which claim the projects undertaken have little relevance to managers and management because the topics addressed have increasingly become a cascaded set of differentiations of differentiations, which resist integration. Such research steams are unlikely to add up to anything of value, now or in the future. In contrast, the proposed research steam moves decision-making research from emphasizing rigor to the point that relevance has been dismissed to a more healthy balance between rigor and relevance.

REFERENCES

Alexander, L. (1986) 'Successfully Implementing Strategic Decisions', in B. Mayon-White (ed.) *Planning and Managing Change.* London: Harper Row.

Allison, G.T. (1971) Conceptual models and the Cuban Missile Crisis, *American Political Science Review*, 63, 968–718.

Alter, C., and Hage, C. (1993) *Organizations Working Together.* Newbury Park, CA: Sage.

Astley, W., Axlesson, R., Butler, R., Hickson, D., and Wilson, D. (1982) Complexity and cleavage: Dual explanations of strategic decision making, *Journal of Management Studies*, 16 (4), 357–375.

Bell, G., Bromley, P., and Bryson, J. (1998) 'Spinning a Complex Web: Links Between Strategic Decision Making Context, Content, Process, and Outcome', in V. Papadakis and P. Barwise (eds) *Strategic Decisions.* Boston, MA: Kluwer.

Bower, J. (1997) 'Process Research on Strategic Decisions: A Personal Perspective', in V. Papadakis and P. Barwise (eds) *Strategic Decisions.* Boston, MA: Kluwer.

Bryson, J.M., Bromiley, P., and Jung, V.S. (1990) The influences of context and process on project planning success, *Journal of Planning Education*, 9 (3), 183–195.

Bryson, J.M., and Cullen, J.W. (1984) A contingent approach to strategy and tactics in formative and summative evaluation, *Evaluation and Program Planning*, 7, 267–290.

Butler, R. (1998) 'Strategic Decision Making: A Contingency Framework and Beyond', in V. Papadakis and P. Barwise (eds) *Strategic Decisions.* Boston, MA: Kluwer.

Cameron, K., and Lavine, M. (2006) *Making the Impossible Possible: Leading Extraordinary Performance – the Rocky Flats Story.* San Francisco, CA: Barrett-Koehler.

Campbell, D. (1990) 'The Role of Theory in Industrial and Organizational Psychology', in M. Dunnette and L. Hough (eds) *Handbook of Industrial and Organizational Psychology*, Vol. 1, Palo Alto, CA: Consulting Psychologists Press, 39–74.

Colquitt, J., and Zapata-Phelan, C. (2007) Trends in theory building and theory testing: A five decade study of AMJ, *Academy of Management Journal*, 50 (6), 1281–1303.

Daft, R. (1995) *Organization Theory and Decision.* St Paul, MN: West Publishing Co.

Denzin, N.K. (1989) *The Research Act.* Englewood Cliffs, NJ: Prentice Hall.

DiMaggio, P. (1995) Comments on 'What Theory is Not', *Administrative Science Quarterly*, 40, 391–397.

Eisenhardt, K., and Bourgeois, J. (1989) 'Charting Strategic Decisions in the Micro Computer Industry: Profile of an Industry Starr', in M. Van Glenow and S. Moyermann (eds) *Managing Complexity in High Technology Organizations, Systems, and People.* New York: Oxford University Press, 74–89.

Eisenhardt, K. and Zbaracki, M. (1992) Strategic decision making, *Strategic Management Journal*, 13, 17–37.

Fredrickson, J.W. (1985) Effects of decision motive and organizational performance on strategic decision processes, *Academy of Management Journal*, 28, 821–843.

Goldberg, L. (1968) Simple models or simple processes – some research on clinical judgments, *American Psychologist*, 23 (7), 483–496.

Hambrick, D. (2008) The field of management's devotion to theory: Too much of a good thing?, *Academy of Management Journal*, 50 (6), 1346–1352.

Hammond, K., McClelland, G., and Mumpower, J. (1980) *Human Judgment and Decision Masking*. New York: Praeger.

Hampden-Turner, C. (1990) *Charting the Corporate Mind*. New York: Free Press.

Harmon, M. (1981) *Action-Theory for Public Administration.* New York: Longman.

Harrison, M., and Phillips, B. (1991) Strategic decision making: An integrative explanation, *Research in the Sociology of Organizations*. JAI Press 9, 319–358.

Hickson, D., Butler, R., Cray, D., Mallory, G., and Wilson, D. (1986) *Top Decisions: Strategic Decision making in Organizations*. San Francisco, CA: Jossey-Bass.

Hickson, D.J., Miller, S., and Wilson, D.C. (2003) Planned or prioritized? *Journal of Management Studies*, 40 (7), 1803–1836.

Hitt, M., Beamish, P., Jackson, S., and Mathieu., J., Building theoretical and empirical bridges across levels: Multilevel research in management, *Academy of Management Journal*, 50 (6), 1385–1400.

Johnson, B. (1992) *Polarity Management*. New York: HRD Press.

Kahneman, D., and Tversky, A. (1973) Subjective probability: A judgment of representativeness, *Psychology Review*, 80, 237–251.

Kerlinger, F., and Lee, H. (2000) *Foundations of Behavioral Research*. Fort Worth, TX: Harcourt.

Lincoln, Y., and Guba, E. (1984) *Naturalistic Inquiry*. Beverly Hills, CA: Sage.

Lippitt, M., and Mackenzie, K. (1976) Authority task problems, *Administrative Science Quarterly*, 21 (4), 643–660.

MacCrimmon, K.R., and Taylor, R.N. (1976) 'Decision Making and Problem Solving', in M. Dunnette (ed.) *Handbook of Industrial and Organizational Psychology*. Chicago: Rand-McNally.

McKelvey, B. (1978) Organizational systematics; Taxonomic lessons from biology, *Management Science*, 24, 1428–1440.

March, J.G., and Simon, H.A. (1958) *Organizations.* McGraw-Hill: New York.

Miller, C., Cardinal, L., and Glick, W. (1997) Retrospective reports in organizational research: A re-examination of recent evidence, *The Academy of Management Journal*, 40 (1), 189–204.

Miller, S., Wilson, D.C., and Hickson, D.J. (2004) Beyond planning: Strategies for successfully implementing strategic decisions, *Long Range Planning*, 37 (3), 201–218.

Mintzberg, H., and Waters, J.A. (1982) Tracking strategy in an entrepreneurial firm, *Academy of Management Journal*, 25 (3), 465–499.

Nisbett, R., and Ross, L. (1989) *Human Inferences: Strategies and Shortcomings of Human Judgments*. New York: John Wiley & Sons, Inc. (revised edition).

Nutt, P.C. (1984) Types of organizational decision processes, *Administrative Science Quarterly*, 29 (3), 414–450.

Nutt, P.C. (1987) Selecting tactics to implement strategic plans, *Strategic Management Journal*, 10 (1), 145–161.

Nutt, P.C. (1989) *Making Tough Decisions*. San Francisco, CA: Jossey-Bass.

Nutt, P.C. (1990) Strategic decisions made by top managers with data and process dominant styles, *Journal of Management Studies*, 27 (2), 173–194.

Nutt, P.C., and Backoff, R.W. (1993) Strategic issues as tensions. *Journal of Management Inquiry*, 2 (1), 28–43.

Nutt, P.C. (2001) A taxonomy of strategic decisions and tactics for uncovering alternatives, *The European Journal of Operational Research*, 132 (3), 505–527.

Nutt, P.C. (2002) *Why Decisions Fail: Avoiding the Blunders and Traps that Lead to Debacles*. San Francisco, CA: Barrett-Koehler.

Nutt, P.C. (2008) Investigating decision making processes, *Journal of Management Studies*, 45 (2), 425–455.

Papadakis, V., and Barwise, P. (1998) *Strategic Decisions*. Boston, MA: Kluwer Academic Publishers.

Patton, M.E. (1990) *Qualitative Evaluation and Research Methods*. Los Angeles, CA: Sage.

Perrow, C. (1967) A framework for the comparative analysis of organizations, *American Sociological Review*, 32 (4), 194–208.

Pike, R.L. (1967) *Language in Relation to a Unified Theory of the Structure of Human Behavior*. The Hague: Mouton.

Rajagopalan, N., Rasheed, A., Datta, D., and Spreitzer, G. (1998) 'A Multi-theoretic Model of Strategic Decision Making Processes', in V. Papadakis and P. Barwise (eds) *Strategic Decisions*. Boston, MA: Kluwer Academic Publishers.

Schon, D. (1983) *The Reflective Practitioner: How Professionals Think in Action*. New York: Basic Books.

Stein, M. (1975) *Stimulating Creativity, Vol. 2: Group Procedures*. New York: Free Press.

Suddaby, R., Hardy, C., and Huy, Q. (2009) Theory development: Where are the new theories of organization?, *Academy of Management Review*, 34 (2), 361–362.

Thompson, J.D. (1967) *Organizations in Action*. New York: McGraw Hill.

Vroom, V., and Jago, A. (1978) On the validity of the Vroom-Yetton model, *Journal of Applied Psychology*, 63, 151–162.

Werner, C.M. and Baxter, L.A. (1994) 'Temporal Qualities of Relationships: Organismic, Transactional, and Dialectical Views', in M. Knapp and G. Miller (eds) *Handbook of Interpersonal Communication*. Thousand Oaks, CA: Sage, 323–379.

Wildavsky, A. (1979) *Speaking Truth to Power: The Art and Craft of Policy Analysis*. Boston, MA: Little, Brown.

Yin, R.K. (1993) *Applied Case Study Research*, Hollywood, CA: Sage.

Index